THE HISTORY OF THE YORUBAS

Dr. O. Johnson.

THE HISTORY OF THE YORUBAS

From the Earliest Times to the Beginning of the British Protectorate

BY

The REV. SAMUEL JOHNSON,

Pastor of Ọyọ

EDITED BY

DR. O. JOHNSON, Lagos

C.M.S. (NIGERIA) BOOKSHOPS
LAGOS

First published 1921
Reprinted 1937
Reprinted 1956
Reprinted 1957

PRINTED IN GREAT BRITAIN BY
LOWE AND BRYDONE (PRINTERS) LIMITED, LONDON, N.W.10

Dedication

To the revered memory of

THE REV. DAVID HINDERER,

THE PIONEER MISSIONARY OF THE C.M.S. IN YORUBA
PROPER—WHOSE UNTIRING ENERGY, SELF-DENYING
DEVOTION, AND DETERMINATION OF PURPOSE (IN
SPITE OF PRIVATIONS AND BODILY INFIRMITIES) WILL
EVER REMAIN A MODEL OF TRUE MISSIONARY ENTER-
PRISE, AND WHO HAS LEFT AN IMPERISHABLE NAME,
AND A RECORD OF LABOUR HITHERTO UNSURPASSED
IN THIS COUNTRY—THESE LINES ARE INSCRIBED BY
A FORMER PUPIL.

AUTHOR'S PREFACE

WHAT led to this production was not a burning desire of the author to appear in print—as all who are well acquainted with him will readily admit—but a purely patriotic motive, that the history of our fatherland might not be lost in oblivion, especially as our old sires are fast dying out.

Educated natives of Yoruba are well acquainted with the history of England and with that of Rome and Greece, but of the history of their own country they know nothing whatever ! This reproach it is one of the author's objects to remove.

Whilst the author could claim to be a pioneer in an untrodden field, he can by no means pretend to have exhausted the subject ; but he hopes by this to stimulate among his more favoured brethren the spirit of patriotism and enquiry into the histories of the less known parts of the country. It may be that oral records are preserved in them which are handed down from father to son, as in the case of the better known Royal bards in the Metropolis, such records though imperfect should surely not be under-rated.

In the perusal of this feeble attempt, the author craves the forbearance of his readers ; he deprecates the spirit of tribal feelings and petty jealousies now rife among us. In recording events of what transpired, good or bad, failures and successes, among the various tribes, he has endeavoured to avoid whatever would cause needless offence to anyone, or irritate the feelings of those specially interested in the narratives, provided only that the cause of truth, and of public benefit be faithfully served.

With respect to the ancient and mythological period he has stated the facts as they are given by the bards, and with respect to the History of comparatively recent dates, viz., from the time of King Abiọdun downwards, from eye-witnesses of the events which they narrate, or from those who have actually taken part in them. He has thus endeavoured to present a reliable record of events.

He is greatly indebted especially to the honoured David Kukomi, the patriarch of the Ibadan Church, (the now sainted father of the Rev. R. S. Oyebọde). Kukomi was a young man in the days of King Abiọdun, and it was his fortune (or misfortune) to take part in the wars and other national movements of the period as a common soldier, and was thus able to give a clear and reliable account of the sayings, persons, and events of those stirring times, being a cool man of judgment, observant, and remarkably intelligent.

vii

Also to Josiah Oni, an intrepid trader in those days, an active and intelligent observer who was well acquainted with almost every part of the country, and took part in some of the most stirring events of a later period.

And last though not least to his highness the venerable Lagunju, the renowned Timi of Ẹdẹ, so well known all over the country as a gifted and trusty historian of the Yoruba Country.

And to others also who are not here mentioned by name.

The histories of all nations present many phases and divers features, which are brought out by various writers in the lines in which each is interested ; the same method we hope will be pursued by writers in this country until we become possessed of a fuller History of the Yorubas.

S. JOHNSON,

Ọyọ, 1897. *Añla Ogun.*

EDITOR'S PREFACE

A SINGULAR misfortune, which happily is not of everyday occurrence, befel the original manuscripts of this history, in consequence of which the author never lived to see in print his more than 20 years of labour.

The manuscripts were forwarded to a well-known English publisher through one of the great Missionary Societies in 1899 and —*mirabile dictu*—nothing more was heard of them !

The editor who was all along in collaboration with the author had occasion to visit England in 1900, and called on the publisher, but could get nothing more from him than that the manuscripts had been misplaced, that they could not be found, and that he was prepared to pay for them ! This seemed to the editor and all his friends who heard of it so strange that one could not help thinking that there was more in it than appeared on the surface, especially because of other circumstances connected with the so-called loss of the manuscripts. However, we let the subject rest there. The author himself died in the following year (1901), and it has now fallen to the lot of the editor to rewrite the whole history anew, from the copious notes and rough copies left behind by the author.

But for many years after his death, partly from discouragements by the events, and partly from being appalled by the magnitude of the task, the editor shrank from the undertaking, but circumstances now and again cropped up showing the need of the work, and the necessity for undertaking it ; besides the almost criminal disgrace of allowing the outcome of his brother's many years of labour to be altogether lost. No one, who has never made the attempt, can have the faintest idea of the great difficulties that attend the efforts to elicit facts and accuracy of statements from an illiterate people : they are bewildering with repetitions, prolix in matters irrelevant, while facts germane to the subject in hand are more often than not passed over : they have to be drawn out by degrees patiently, and the chaff has to be constantly sifted from the wheat. In no sphere of labour is patience and perseverance more required than in this. It shows strongly the magnitude of the labours of the original author, labours undertaken along with the unremitting performance of his substantive duties.

When all this had to be done with the daily exactions of a busy profession, and other demands on his time, friends will judge the editor leniently for having taken such a long time to repair the loss sustained many years ago. Some chapters had to be rewritten, some curtailed, others amplified, and new ones added where necessary.

But this history has a history of its own, for apart from the mishap that befel the original manuscripts as above detailed, its vicissitudes were not yet over. When at last the task of re-writing it was completed, it was forwarded to England by the " Appam," which left Lagos on the 2nd of January, 1916. The Appam was at first supposed to be lost, but was afterwards found in America, having been captured by the raider Moewe. Nothing was heard of the manuscripts again for nearly two years, when they were at last delivered to the printers ! By that time, paper had become so dear in England that it was deemed advisable to wait till after the War before printing. The manuscripts were next sent back by request to the editor, who in order to obviate a future loss, undertook to have it typewritten, but in the meantime even typewriting paper became difficult to obtain. All these drawbacks were successfully overcome in the end, as well as the difficulties in passing the work through the press.

He now lets the book go forth to the public, in the hope that it will fulfil the earnest desire of the original author.

O. JOHNSON,

Ajagbe Ogun.

CONTENTS

PART I

THE PEOPLE, COUNTRY, AND THE LANGUAGE.

PART II

FIRST PERIOD

MYTHOLOGICAL KINGS AND DEIFIED HEROES

CHAPTER I.—THE FOUNDERS OF THE YORUBA NATION

SECOND PERIOD

GROWTH, PROSPERITY AND OPPRESSION

CHAPTER II.—HISTORICAL KINGS

CHAPTER III.—THE KINGS OF OYO IGBOHO

CHAPTER IV.—A SUCCESSION OF DESPOTIC KINGS

CHAPTER V.—BASORUN GAHÁ AND HIS ATROCITIES AND
ABIODUN'S PEACEFUL REIGN

THIRD PERIOD

REVOLUTIONARY WARS AND DISRUPTION

CHAPTER VI.—THE REVOLUTION

CHAPTER VII.—THE RISE OF THE FULANIS TO POWER

CHAPTER VIII.—CONSEQUENCES OF THE REVOLUTION

CHAPTER IX.—FURTHER DEVELOPMENT OF THE ANARCHY

CHAPTER X.—SPREAD OF THE ANARCHY

CHAPTER XI.—THE REVOLUTION IN THE EPO DISTRICTS

CHAPTER XII.—WARS FOR THE CONSOLIDATION AND BALANCE OF POWER

CHAPTER XII.—(continued)

CHAPTER XIII.—THE LAST OF KATUNGA

CHAPTER XIV.—THE INTERREGNUM

FOURTH PERIOD

ARREST OF DISINTEGRATION. INTER-TRIBAL WARS

BRITISH PROTECTORATE

CHAPTER XV.—THE NEW CITY, NEW GOVERNMENT, ILỌRIN CHECKED

CHAPTER XVI.—FRATRICIDAL WARS

CHAPTER XVII.—SUBJUGATION OF THE IJẸṢAS AND EKITI'S SOCIAL REFORMS

CHAPTER XXV.—Ibadan at its Extremity

CHAPTER XXVI.—Failures at Reconciliation

CHAPTER XXVII.—A Rift in the Cloud

CHAPTER XXVIII.—The Rev. J. B. Wood and the A.O.K.

CHAPTER XXIX.—The Intervention of the British Government

CHAPTER XXX.—Dispersal of the Combatants by Special Commissioners

CHAPTER XXXI.—Disturbance in every part of the Country

APPENDIX A—(*continued*)

APPENDIX B

§ 1. INTRODUCTION

THE Yoruba country lies to the immediate West of the River Niger (below the confluence) and South of the Quorra (*i.e.*, the Western branch of the same River above the confluence), having Dahomey on the West, and the Bight of Benin to the South. It is roughly speaking between latitude 6° and 9° North, and longitude 2° 30′ and 6° 30′ East.

The country was probably first known to Europe from the North, through the explorers of Northern and Central Africa, for in old records the Hausa and Fulani names are used for the country and its capital ; thus we see in Webster's Gazetteer " YARRIBA," West Africa, East of Dahomey, area 70,000 sq. miles, population two millions, capital KATUNGA. These are the Hausa terms for YORUBA and for OYO.

The entire south of the country is a network of lagoons connecting the deltas of the great River Niger with that of the Volta, and into this lagoon which is belted with a more or less dense mangrove swamp, most of the rivers which flow through the country North to South pour their waters.

It will thus be seen that the country is for the most part a tableland : it has been compared to half of a pie dish turned upside down. Rising from the coast in the South gradually to a height of some 5-600 ft. in more or less dense forest, into a plain diversified by a few mountain ranges, continuing its gentle rise in some parts to about 1,000 ft. above sea level, it then slopes down again to the banks of the Niger, which encloses it in the North and East.

In a valuable letter by the Rev. S. A. Crowther (afterwards Bishop) to Thomas J. Hutchinson, Esq., Her Britannic Majesty's consul for the Bight of Biafra and the Island of Fernando Po, published as Appendix A to the book entitled " Impressions of Western Africa,"[1] we find the following graphic description of the country :—

. . . " This part of the country of which Lagos in the Bight of Benin is the seaport, is generally known as the Yoruba country, extending from the Bight to within two or three days' journey to the banks of the Niger.[2] This country comprises many tribes governed by their own chiefs and having their own laws. At one time they were all tributaries to one Sovereign, the King of Yoruba, including Benin on the East, and Dahomey on the West, but are now independent.

---

[1] Longmans, Green & Co., 1858.
[2] *i.e.* At the time of writing.—Ed.

The principal tribes into which this kingdom is divided are as follows :—

The Egbados : This division includes Otta and Lagos near the sea coast, forming a belt of country on the banks of the lagoon in the forest, to Ketu on the border of Dahomey on the West ; then the Jebu on the East on the border of Benin ; then the Egbas of the forest now known as the Egbas of Abeokuta.

Then comes Yoruba proper northwards in the plain ; Ife, Ijesha, Ijamo, Efon, Ondo, Idoko, Igbomina, and Ado near the banks of the Niger, from which a creek or stream a little below Iddah is called Do or Iddo River."

. . . " The chief produce of this country is the red palm oil, oil made from the kernel, shea butter from nuts of the shea trees, ground nuts, beniseed, and cotton in abundance, and ivory—all these are readily procured for European markets.

. . . The present seat of the King of Yoruba is Ago other-wise called Oyo after the name of the old capital visited by Clapperton and Lander.

A King is acknowledged and his person is held sacred, his wives and children are highly respected. Any attempt of violence against a King's person or of the Royal family, or any act of wantonness with the wives of the King, is punished with death. There are no written laws, but such laws and customs that have been handed down from their ancestors, especially those respecting *relative* duties, have become established laws.

The right to the throne is hereditary, but exclusively in the male line or the male issue of the King's daughters.

The Government is absolute, but it has been much modified since the kingdom has been divided into many independent states by slave wars, into what may be called a limited monarchy . . . "

Physical features.—The country presents generally two distinct features, the forest and the plain ; the former comprising the southern and eastern portions, the latter the northern, central and western. Yoruba Proper lies chiefly in the plain, and has a small portion of forest land. The country is fairly well watered, but the rivers and streams are dependent upon the annual rains ; an impassable river in the rains may become but a dry water-course in the dry season.

There are a few high mountains in the north and west, but in the east the prevailing aspect is high ranges of mountains from which that part of the country derives its name, EKITI—a mound —being covered as it were with Nature's Mound.

The soil is particularly rich, and most suitable for agriculture, in which every man is more or less engaged. The plain is almost entirely pasture land. Minerals apparently do not exist to any appreciable extent, expect iron ores which the people work them-selves, and from which they formerly manufactured all their implements of husbandry and war and articles for domestic use.

Flora.—The forests teem with economic and medicinal plants of tropical varieties, as well as timber, of which mahogany, cedar, brimstone, counter, and *iroko* are the principal.

There are also to be found the *Abura*, useful for carving purposes, ebony, *Ata* a hard wood used for facing carpenters' tools, the *Iki*, a hard wood which when dry is very difficult to work, as it speedily blunts edged tools. The *Ori*, another hard wood useful for making piers on the coast, and the *Ahayan*, a very hard wood, unaffected by ordinary fires, dry rot, or termites.

All these are indigenous, but recently " Indian teak " has been introduced, and it flourishes widely, as well as the beef wood tree on the coast.

Although a large variety of fruits can be grown, yet the people do not take to horticulture ; what there are grow almost wild, very little attention being paid to them. Papaw, bananas of several varieties, plantain, oranges, pineapples, the *Oro*, plums (yellow and black), the rough skin plum, the butt lime, are to be found everywhere. Some fruit trees have been introduced, which have become indigenous, e.g., the sweet and sour sop, the avocado (or alligator) pear, guavas of two kinds, pink apples, rose apple, mangoes, the bread fruit and bread nut trees, the golden plum, etc. All these are cultivated, but not widely.

Vegetables, of which there are several kinds, are largely cultivated. Yam, koko, cassada, sweet potatoes, are the principal " roots " used as diet, also beans (white and brown), small and large, and the ground nut are largely grown for food. The guinea corn grows in the north, and maize in the south. The calabash gourd and the Egusi from the seeds of which Egusi oil is pressed, grow everywhere.

Fauna.—Big game abound, especially in the north, where the lion is not far to seek, also the elephant, buffalo, leopard, wolf, foxes, jackals, monkeys of various species, deer, porcupine, etc. The hippopotamus is found in large rivers, and alligators in the swamps and lagoons in the south.

The usual domestic animals and poultry are carefully reared.

Of birds, we have the wild and tame parrots, green pigeons, stork, crown birds, and others of the tropical feathered tribe.

The country was at one time very prosperous, and powerful, but there is probably no other country on this earth more torn and wasted by internal dissensions, tribal jealousies, and fratricidal feuds, a state of things which unhappily continues up to the present time.

When the central authority which was once all-powerful and far too despotic grew weak by driving the powerful chiefs into rebellion and internecine wars, the entire kingdom became broken up into petty states and independent factions as we now know them.

As far as it is possible for one race to be characteristically like another, from which it differs in every physical aspect, the Yorubas

—it has been noted—are not unlike the English in many of their traits and characteristics. It would appear that what the one is among the whites the other is among the blacks. Love of independence, a feeling of superiority over all others, a keen commercial spirit, and of indefatigable enterprise, that quality of being never able to admit or consent to a defeat as finally settling a question upon which their mind is bent, are some of those qualities peculiar to them, and no matter under what circumstances they are placed, Yorubas will display them. We have even learnt that those of them who had the misfortune of being carried away to foreign climes so displayed these characteristics there, and assumed such airs of superiority and leadership over the men of their race they met there, in such a matter of fact way that the attention of their masters was perforce drawn to this type of new arrivals ! And from them they selected overseers. These traits will be clearly discerned in the narratives given in this history. But apart from the general, each of the leading tribes has special characteristics of its own ; thus dogged perseverance and determination characterise the Ijẹbus, love of ease and a quickness to adapt new ideas the Egbas, the Ijẹsas and Ekitis are possessed of a marvellous amount of physical strength, remarkable docility and simplicity of manners, and love of home.

Among the various families of Yorubas Proper, the Ibarapas are laborious farmers, the Ibọlọs are rather docile and weak in comparison with others, but the Epos are hardy, brave, and rather turbulent ; whilst the Ọyọs of the Metropolitan province are remarkably shrewd, intelligent, very diplomatic, cautious almost to timidity, provokingly conservative, and withal very masterful.

The whole people are imbued with a deep religious spirit, reverential in manners, showing deference to superiors and respect to age, where they have not been corrupted by foreign intercourse ; ingrained politeness is part and parcel of their nature.

The early history of the Yoruba country is almost exclusively that of the Ọyọ division, the others being then too small and too insignificant to be of any import ; but in later years this state of things has been somewhat reversed, the centre of interest and sphere of importance having moved southwards, especially since the arrival of Europeans on the coast.

Such is the country, and such are the people whose history, religion, social polity, manners and customs, etc., are briefly given in the following pages.

THE YORUBA LANGUAGE

THE Yoruba language has been classed among the unwritten African languages. The earliest attempt to reduce this language into writing was in the early forties of the last century, when the Church Missionary Society, with the immortal Rev. Henry Venn as Secretary, organized a mission to the Yoruba country under the leadership of one of their agents, the Rev. Henry Townsend, an English Clergyman then at work at Sierra Leone, and the Rev. Samuel Ajayi Crowther, the first African Clergyman of the C.M.S., also at work in the same place.

After several fruitless efforts had been made either to invent new characters, or adapt the Arabic, which was already known to Moslem Yorubas, the Roman character was naturally adopted, not only because it is the one best acquainted with, but also because it would obviate the difficulties that must necessarily arise if missionaries were first to learn strange characters before they could undertake scholastic and evangelistic work. With this as basis, special adaptation had to be made for pronouncing some words not to be found in the English or any other European language.

The system, or rather want of system, existing among various missionary bodies in Africa and elsewhere emphasized the need of a fixed system of orthography. It was evidently essential for the various bodies to agree upon certain rules for reducing illiterate languages into writing in Roman characters, not only because this would facilitate co-operation, but also because it would render books much cheaper than when separate founts of type must needs be cast for every separate system (scientific or otherwise) that each body may choose to adapt for one and the same purpose.

In this effort, the Committee of the C.M.S. were ably assisted by certain philological doctors, as Professor Lee of Cambridge, Mr. Norris of London, and notably by Professor Lepsius of Berlin, to whom was entrusted the task of establishing a complete form of alphabetic system to which all hitherto unwritten languages could be adapted.

The following remarks are largely derived from the second edition of Prof. Lepsius' work.

The Professor consulted earlier efforts that had been made in India and elsewhere to transliterate foreign (Eastern) characters into the Roman, and out of the chaos then existing he established

on a firm scientific basis the STANDARD ALPHABET in which the
Yoruba language is now written. This was adopted by the
C.M.S. in 1856. By this system therefore former translations had
to be transliterated under certain fixed rules.

The number of letters in the Standard Alphabet is necessarily
very large, as it was designed to meet the requirements of all
nations ; but with diacritic marks on cognate sounds and accents,
and the introduction of three characters from the Greek, the
Roman characters furnish all that is necessary from which every
unwritten language can draw.

It is very unfortunate indeed that the system has not been
faithfully followed by all, for reasons we regard as inadequate and
inconclusive. This has provoked the caustic remark of the distinguished philologist, Dr. R. N. Cust, that . . . " no class of mankind is so narrowminded and opinionated as the missionary except
the linguist." For even in the Yoruba which professed to have
adopted Lepsius' Standard, certain particulars (as we shall see)
have been departed from, by no means for the better. Keen was
the controversy on these points between the English and German
missionaries of the Yoruba Mission in its early days. In the
following pages the style commonly used in the familiar Yoruba
translations is departed from in some important particulars, as
they present some peculiar defects which ought to be rectified.
We shall endeavour to follow Professor Lepsius' Standard Alphabet
as closely as possible.

The Professor himself has conceded that shades of sound can
be adapted therefrom to meet special requirements without departing from the principles laid down. Says he in his second edition:
" The exposition of the scientific and practical principles
according to which a suitable alphabet for universal adoption in
foreign languages might be constructed has (with few exceptions
above mentioned) remained unaltered. These rules are founded
in the nature of the subject, and therefore though they may admit
of certain carefully limited exceptions, they can undergo no change
in themselves : they serve as a defence against arbitrary proposals
which do not depend upon universal laws ; they will explain and
recommend the application which has been made of them already
to a series of languages and will serve as a guide in their application
to new ones.

" But we have not concealed from the very beginning that it
is not in every person's power to apprehend with physiological
and linguistic accuracy the sounds in a foreign language or even
those of his own, so as to apply with some degree of certainty the
principles of our alphabet to a new system of sounds containing

its own peculiarities. A few only of our most distinguished grammarians are possessed of a penetrating insight into the living organisms of sounds in those very languages they have discussed ; much less can it be expected of missionaries, who are often obliged without previous preparation to address themselves to the reduction and representation of a foreign language, that everything which belongs to a correct adjudication of particular sounds (frequently apprehended only with great difficulty even by the ear) or to their connection with one another and with other systems of sounds, should present itself spontaneously to their minds."

Certain rules of transcription are imperative for a correct scientific method of procedure. Whatever may have been the difficulties encountered in the ancient written languages, so far as the Yoruba and other unwritten languages are concerned, the field lies clear.

The English mode of pronouncing the vowels had to be rejected in favour of the Italian or continental mode.

The following rules or principles have been laid down :—

1. The power of each letter as representing certain sounds as handed down from antiquity should be retained.

2. The orthography of any language should never use (a) the same letter for different sounds, nor (b) different letters for the same sound.

In violation of (a) note the force of the letter *g* in the English words give, gin ; of *a* in man, name, what ; of *ea* in treat, tread ; of *ei* in weight, height ; of the consonants *ch* in archbishop, archangel ; of *augh* in slaughter, laughter ; also the sound of *ch* in chamber, champagne, chameleon where the same letters are used for different sounds.

In violation of (b) note the last syllables in the words atten*tion*, omis*sion*, fa*shion*, where different letters are used for the same sound.

3. Every simple sound is to be represented by a single sign. This is violated by writing *sh* to represent the " rushing sound " of *s*. This, as we shall see below, is quite unnecessary in the Yoruba language. Here we find an application of the principle that where a new sound is not found in the Roman alphabetic system a diacritical mark on the nearest graphic sign should be used. A diacritical mark therefore over *s* will more fitly represent the English sound of *sh*.[1] This is also in accordance with the *sin* and *shin* in the Hebrew and Arabic, where the difference

---

[1] Publishers' Note. It must be noted, however, that in printing this work ṣ has been used throughout to represent the sh sound.

between the soft and the rushing sound is indicated by diacritical points, *e.g.*,

Heb. שׁ שׂ   Arab. ﺵ ﺱ

Again the letter *h* is a sign of aspiration (as the *spiritus asper* in the Greek) as in it, hit ; at, hat ; owl, howl, etc. It would therefore be unscientific to accord it a new meaning altogether by such a use of it in violation of rule 1.

Apart from this is the fact that the letter *s* with a diacritical mark over it has been employed about twenty years previously by oriental scholars transcribing Indian letters into the Roman.

4. Explosive letters are not to be used to express fricative sounds and *vice versa*, *e.g.*, the use of *ph* as *f* where *p* is clearly an explosive letter.

5. The last rule is that a long vowel should never be represented by doubling the short. This method seems to have found favour with some transcribers, there being no fixed system of transcription.

THE ALPHABET

In a purely scientific alphabetic system, it would seem more correct that the alphabets be arranged according to the organ most concerned in the pronunciation of the letters, *e.g.*, all sounds proceed from the fauces, and are modified either at the throat, by the teeth, or by the lips ; hence they may be classified as guttural, dental, or labial. But nothing is gained by altering the order which came down to us from remote antiquity as the Romans received it from the Greek, and these from the Phœnicians, etc.

THE VOWELS.

The vowels in Yoruba may be built upon the three fundamental vowels, a, i, u, with the two subsidiary ones, e formed by the coalescence of the first two a and i, and o by the coalescence of a and u from which

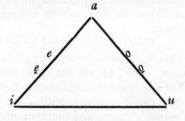

we have a, e, i, o and u. These are the recognised principal vowels and are pronounced after the Italian method (ah, aye, ee, o, oo), but whereas in the English language the short sound of e is written *eh* and that of o as *aw*, these sounds, according to the standard system in accordance with rule 3, are represented by a dot or dash under the cognate sounds, hence we have ẹ and ọ. A complete representation of the vowels in Yoruba therefore is as follows :—a, e, ẹ, i, o, ọ, u (pronounced ah, aye, eh, ee, oh, aw, oo), the original taking precedence of the diacritic. Note that *u* is not to be pronounced as " you " but as oo in food.

Nasalization.—The clear vowels are capable of a peculiar alteration which is produced by uttering the vowel through the nasal canal. There is no consonantal element brought into play, but it is an alteration entirely within the vowel. Nasalization is very largely used in the Yoruba, and consequently its orthography should be free from any ambiguity. In the Standard Alphabet the circumflex (˜) is placed over the nasalized vowel to indicate such a sound. Unfortunately the Yoruba as written by missionaries substitute the letter *n* for this sign, a cause of some ambiguity in writing certain words as Akano, Akinọla, Morinatu, Obuneko, where the letter *n* stands between two vowels, and is liable to be pronounced with the latter, *e.g.*, A-ka-no, A-ki-nọ-la, Mọ-ri-na-tu, Ọ-bu-ne-ko ; but following the Standard Alphabet, the words should be written Akão, Ọbũeko, just as the Portuguese names are written Semão, Adão, João, etc. Indeed certain sections of the Yoruba tribes that use nasalization very sparingly do pronounce these words as written without any sign of nasalization. The *n* therefore is not only unnecessary but it is also misleading.

In the following pages, the Standard System will be adhered to, where such ambiguities are liable to occur : but for the sake of simplicity and to avoid the unnecessary use of diacritical marks, *n* as a nasal sign may be used where it cannot cause any ambiguity, *e.g.*,

1. When it precedes a consonant as njẹ, ndao, nkò.
2. When it closes a word, as Awọn, Basọrun, Ibadan, Iseyin.

As nasalization is said to be caused by the dropping of a nasal consonant, such a limited use of *n* as a nasal sound may be justified. No pure, uneducated Yoruba man can pronounce a word ending in a consonant, he will instinctively add an *i* or *u* to it. There is therefore no closed syllable in Yoruba, *n* at the end of a word is purely nasal.

THE SYSTEM OF CONSONANTS

There are sixteen distinct consonantal sounds in the Yoruba language, each having the same force and power as in the English alphabet ; they are : b, d, f, g, h, j, k, l, m, n, p, r, s, t, w, y. No consonants are used to represent a vowel by perverting them from their legitimate consonantal sounds as h, w, and y are sometimes used in English.

Besides the above, there are two other sounds not represented in the Roman or in any other European system ; they are explosive sounds peculiar to the Yoruba and allied tribes formed by the lip and jaw, *viz.*, gb and kp.   They are regarded as guttural modifications of b and p, and as they appear to result from a combination of two organs concerned in speech, but the component parts of which are so intimately connected they are rightly represented by two letters, though not contravening rule 3.

As to kp, since usage makes it evident that the Yorubas never pronounce the letter p but as kp, it is therefore not considered necessary to include kp in the Yoruba alphabet as is done in the Ibo ; the simple *p* does perform its duty satisfactorily.

Here we find a fit application of Professor Lepsius' remarks that " The general alphabet, when applied to particular languages, must be capable of simplification as well as of enlargement.   All particular diacritical marks are unnecessary in those languages where none of the bases have a double value ; we then write the simple base without a diacritical mark.   Where two sounds belong to the same base, one only of the signs will be wanted. . . ." This is well exemplified here.   We therefore write p and not kp in Yoruba.

The same may be said of the letter s and the sound sh, referred to above.   The difference is indicated in the Standard Alphabet by a diacritical mark, *e.g.*, s, ṣ (for sh).   The Yorubas can safely dispense with the latter, and for the sake of simplicity this ought to have been done, as no difference as to the meaning of a word is suggested by the same word being pronounced soft or harsh. And more also because in some parts of the country, notably the Ẹkun Osi district (the most northerly), the harsh sound is unpronounceable, whatever may be written ; *e.g.*, *shall, shop*, will be pronounced *sall, sop*.   In the Epo district, on the other hand, it is just the reverse ; the harsh sound will be pronounced instead of the soft, thus *same, son* will be pronounced *shame, shon*.

But all over the country women and children invariably use the softer sound for the same word, which, if thus used by men is considered affectatious, except in the Ẹkun Osi district, where the purest and most elegant Yoruba is spoken.

Ṣ (for sh) therefore might have been dropped from the Yoruba alphabet with no harm resulting ; it is, however, retained because over a great part of the country a distinction is made between the two sounds ; apart from the fact that it would often be required in representing the sounds of some words of foreign origin.

From the above modifications therefore we have the Yoruba alphabet as now used :—

a b d e ẹ f g gb h i j k l m n o ọ p r s ṣ t u w y .

Accents or Tones

An accent in the accepted sense of the term denotes the stress laid upon a particular syllable, be it the ultimate, penultimate or antepenultimate syllable of a word. In Yoruba it is used differently. What are called accents, and for which the usual symbols are used are really tones, of which there are three : the elevated, the middle and the depressed ; for the first and the last the acute and the grave accents are used respectively, the middle tone in its simplest form requires no accent sign.

In Yoruba, vowels are of greater importance than consonants, and tones than vowels ; hence the peculiarity of this language, that musical sounds can be employed to convey a correct idea of words in speech.

Another error into which those responsible for the present mode of writing Yoruba have fallen, by departing from the Standard System, is the introduction of the circumflex (˜) and its indiscriminate use as a sign of a so-called long vowel.

There are really no long or short vowels in Yoruba as understood in the English language ; what appears to be long is the coalescence of two or more vowels with an elision of the intervening consonants, e.g., Bāle is a contraction of Baba-ile, i.e. father (or master) of the house. Here the second b is dropped, the two a's coalesce, and the i is absorbed in them, being represented by a prolongation of the tone. The vowels are therefore simple and compound.

The meaning of a word varies as the tone, e.g., we may say :—bá ba, bà, the voice being raised, even or depressed respectively. The first bá means to meet, the second ba to lie in ambush, and the third bà to alight upon.

So we may have bẹ́, bẹ, bẹ̀ : bẹ́ means to split open, bẹ to be officious, and bẹ̀ to beg.

Also bú, bu, bù : bú means to abuse, bu to be mouldy, and bù to cut open.

In this way each vowel with each tone accent may be combined with each of the consonants to form words of different meanings ; or in other words, thus may every consonant be used with each of the vowels in turn, forming different words by varying the tone.

The Use of the Accents

To this method of using the accents over the vowels Professor Lepsius made the strongest objections, as by such a use the accents have been diverted from their proper uses to serve another purpose.

He therefore proposed to place the *tone accents* to the right-hand side of the vowel instead of over it, so as to distinguish a *word accent* from a *tone accent*, as is done in the Chinese and other cognate languages : *e.g.*, word accent would be written bá, bà ; tone accent, ba´, ba`.

In this proposal the professor agrees with the Rev. T. J. Bowen an American Baptist Missionary in his Yoruba Grammar and Dictionary published in 1858 by the Smithsonian Institution. But Crowther—a Yoruba man—did not in his grammar make any such distinction. He thinks the existing accents will do well enough, and for the best of reasons, there is no *word accent* in Yoruba, the tone governs everything, and Europeans cannot speak without a *word accent*.

The language moreover abounds in contractions and elisions, a whole syllable may be dropped but the tone remains. This is the crux of difficulty with foreigners trying to speak the language, and to what extent they are able to overcome this, to that extent their Yoruba is said to be perfect.

COMBINATION OF THE ACCENTS

As remarked above, there are no closed syllables in the Yoruba language, every syllable must end in a vowel and every vowel must be one of the three tones represented by the accents. Words of three or four syllables are often contracted into two, the coalescence of the tones forming the compound vowels.

The entire scheme of the accents or tones may be thus represented :—

I. Simple vowels with the varied tones.

á, in which the tone is raised : as ká, to pick ; bá, to meet ; lá, to lick.

a, in which the tone is even : as pa, to kill ; ba, to ambush ; ta, to kick.

à, in which the tone is depressed : as rà, to buy ; kà, to count ; fà, to draw.

II. Compound vowels in which a single vowel bears more
than one tone :—

A. Compounds of the raised tone.

á´, in which the raised tone is doubled, *e.g.*, Á´yan, contracted from Áríyan, *i.e.*, cares, worries.

á-, in which the raised tone is combined with the middle, *e.g.*, Kí-nla from Kínila—a form of exclamation.

á` in which the raised tone is combined with the depressed, *e.g.*, bêni from bẹ́hẹ̀ni, so it is.

B. Compounds of the middle tone.

ā′ in which the middle tone is combined with the raised ; *e.g.*
    À′yán from a-háyan, a cockroach ; Ọ′ri from Oriri, a tomb.

ā‾ in which the middle tone is combined with itself, *e.g.*, Tā‾ni
    from Ta-ha-ni—who is it ?

ā‛ in which the middle tone is combined with the depressed,
    e.g., Ẹ‛rù from ẹrìrù, spice ; kẹrẹ́ from kẹhẹ̀rẹ́, a screen.

C Compounds of the depressed tone.

à′ in which the depressed tone is combined with the raised,
    e.g., à′nu from àni-inú, mercy ; ò′tọ from òtitọ̀, truth.

à- in which the depressed tone is combined with the middle,
    e.g., kò⁻ᵏᵒ̀ from kòrikò, a wolf.

à‛ in which the depressed tone is combined with itself, *e.g.*,
    Ò′rì contracted from Òrìrì, black plum.

In this way words of four or five syllables may, by elision and absorption, be contracted into two or three ; *e.g.*, àfin from àwọ̀fin, the palace ; hence Alâfin from Aní-à-wọ̀-fin, Lord of the royal palace.

Ọ-ọ̀ni fromỌwọ̀ni, which is itself a contraction of Ọmọ olùwọ̀ni, son of a sacrificial victim.

The consonants may be dropped, the vowels absorbed, but the tones are always preserved ; the first and last syllables only are essential, the voice can glide over all the intervening tones for the sake of shortness.

This is at once the chief characteristic and—to foreigners—the main difficulty of the Yoruba language. In order to avoid such complicated tone accents it would be preferable to write out the words in full, although the contracted form may be used in speaking or reading, *e.g.*, otitọ for ò′tọ ; korikò for kò⁻ᵏᵒ̀.

Words similar in form, distinguished only by their tones.

Words of two syllables :—

Apá	..	the arm	Iná	..	fire, louse
Àpà	..	a prodigal	Ìnà	..	flogging
Àpá	..	a scar	Ìná	..	a tattoo mark
Àlọ́	..	a riddle	Idì	..	the eagle
Àlọ̀	..	something ground	Ìdí	..	the seat
Àlọ	..	going	Ìdi	..	bunch of fruit
Àwo	..	a dish	Ìlú	..	a town
Àwó	..	a crash	Ìlù	..	a drum
Awò	..	a fishing net	Ìlu	..	a gimlet
Awó	..	a guinea-fowl			
Awo	..	a secret			

Agba	..	a rope	Ìyá	.. a mother
Àgbà	..	an elder	Ìyà	.. punishment
Àgbá	..	a cannon	Ìya	.. a separation
A'yan	..	anxiety, care	Ikọ́	.. a cough
À'yan	..	a cockroach	Ikọ̀	.. a state messenger
A'yán	..	a hardwood	Ìkọ́	.. a hook or hanging
Baba	..	father	Orí	.. the head
Bábá (adv.)		quite full	Òri	.. shea butter
Bàbà	..	guinea corn	Òrì	.. black plum
Epo	..	palm oil	Òpó	.. a post
Epo	..	bark	Opó	.. a widow
Epò	..	weeds	Òpò	.. to be busy
E'ri	..	corn chaff	Ọkọ	.. a husband
E'ri	..	dirt	Ọkọ́	.. a hoe
Eri (for Ori)		the head	Ọ̀kọ̀	.. a spear

Words of three syllables similarly distinguished:—

Àpáta	..	a rock	koríko	.. grass
Apata	..	a shield	kòrikò	.. wolf
Àpatà	..	a butcher		

Words of four syllables.

Kọ́lọ́kọ́lọ́	..	stealthily
Kọ́lọkọ̀lọ	..	circuitously
Kọ̀lọ̀kọ́lọ́	..	muddy, miry
Kọ̀lọ̀kọ̀lọ̀	..	the fox

A SKETCH OF YORUBA GRAMMAR

THE efforts we have seen made to produce a Yoruba Grammar on the exact lines of an English or Latin Grammar represent in our opinion an honest labour, highly commendable indeed it may be, but totally in the wrong direction, and little calculated to elucidate the genius of the language. On the contrary, they go a long way to obscure it.

The Yoruba belongs to the agglutinated order of speech, not to the inflectional. When therefore particles are used to form cases, etc., it is mere pedantry to talk of declensions.

It is a notorious fact that educated Yorubas find it much easier to read an English book than a Yoruba production—which until recently are mostly translations. With an effort they may plod through it, but they do not enjoy reading it, and sometimes do not even understand it. The main reasons for this are :—

1. The orthography of the language is still very defective.

2. The style in which the books are written. This may simply be described as English ideas in Yoruba words : the result is often obscurity and confusion of thought.

In the " Church Missionary Intelligencer " for March, 1880, a missionary to Japan, who had experienced a similar difficulty, wrote thus :—

" There is great danger, in all use of this language, of thinking that when we have rendered various English words into Japanese we have of necessity expressed the thoughts which the English words convey. Language may correspond to language, but the thoughts to which the language is the vehicle may be as distant as the poles. Our language must be idiomatic or the natives will fail to see the points on which we are endeavouring to lay so much stress."

The writer has on several occasions read portions of Yoruba translations to intelligent but purely uneducated Yoruba men. They would show that they comprehended (not without an effort) what was read to them by putting pertinent questions, but then they would add, " We can understand what you mean to say, but what you read there is not Yoruba ; it may be *book language* (Èdè Iwe)." The rock of stumbling is the desire of translators to reproduce every word and particle of the English in its exact equivalent in Yoruba, regardless of idiom, and thereby obscuring the sense of the latter.

In taking up a Yoruba book one is forcibly struck by the difference in style between quotations of pure Yoruba stories, phrases, or proverbs, and the notes and observations of the writer. The former runs smooth and clear, the latter appears stiff and obscure, because the writer, with his knowledge of the English grammar and language, wrote English ideas and idioms in Yoruba words, illustrating what is said above.

When such systems are employed in writing a Yoruba Grammar, such a grammar may be useful in teaching English to Yoruba boys, but that is not a Yoruba grammar.

We deem these observations necessary because in the following pages we shall have occasion to render Yoruba words into English and *vice versa* ; a very literal translation will not be adhered to when, by so doing, the sense and force of the language will be obscured and weakened.

THE FORMATION OF WORDS

The formation of words in Yoruba appears to be a very simple process ; any consonant with a vowel attached will form a word (or three words, according to the variation of the tone or accent). That word will probably be a verb ; it will certainly possess the form of one, either current or obsolete. This word will, moreover, be the root of a whole class of words. By prefixing a vowel to it a noun may be formed ; with other prefixes also some other words may be formed from the same root, *e.g.*, dá to make, ẹda, a creature ; from which we have ẹlẹda, creator. Là, to split ; ilà, a cut ; ẹlà, halves of a whole ; àlà, a boundary. Rù, to carry ; ẹrù, a load ; alarù, a carrier ; ẹlẹrù, owner of a load. Fẹ, to love ; Ifẹ, love ; Ifẹni, brotherly love, charity.

Thus verbs are mostly monosyllables, formed by one consonant and a vowel, and nouns disyllables in which the first syllable is a vowel, and the second a verbal root. The penultimate vowel is sometimes strengthened by a consonant.

Adjectives are mostly formed from nouns (or as nouns) by prefixing the consonant of the verbal root ; *e.g.*, dida, made or created ; lilà, fissured ; so also from mọ, to know ; imọ, knowledge, mimọ, known.

Adverbs are generally duplication of the adjective, *e.g.*, didun, sweet ; didun-didun, very sweet ; dara, good ; dara-dara, very good.

What is here called a verbal root may be an obsolete word or one not generally in use, but other words can be formed from it all the same.

There are some primitive words the origin of whose roots has been lost, *e.g.*, omi, water ; ina, fire ; igi, wood ; aṣọ, clothes ; etc.

With rare exceptions, nouns not beginning with a vowel are either of foreign origin, or onomatopoetic : this latter being very common.

There are, of course, exceptions to the above rules, but these will be found to be the fundamental methods of forming Yoruba words.

We cannot within the compass of an introduction, give a complete sketch of a Yoruba Grammar, but we may state that the lines laid down in Crowther's Vocabulary of the Yoruba language and in Notes on the Formation of Words by the Rt. Rev. O. E. Vidal, the first Bishop of Sierra Leone, if properly developed and fully worked out, will prove both very useful and instructive.

The Parts of Speech

There are eight parts of speech. They are as in the English Grammar, the " Article " being excepted.

The Yoruba language has no article, but when definiteness is required the numeral *kan* (contracted from *Ọkan*, one) is used for *a* or *an*, and the demonstrative nâ or nì (that, the said one) is used for the definite article *the*.

The use of the numeral one in place of the article is not unknown even in English. " The numeral one is an indefinite demonstrative when used as the article *an* "—Mason.

The word *kan* therefore cannot be correctly called an article simply because it is made to do duty for it.

In Yoruba books translated from the English, where the translator endeavours to render every word and particle into its Yoruba equivalent, we often find these particles used where a pure Yoruba, speaking, would not use an article. Hence the Yoruba of translations often sounds rather quaint.

Literal translations regardless of differences of idiom, often result in ambiguity or nonsense.

In the British colonies of Sierra Leone and Lagos, where the Yoruba element predominates, and where the English language is often heard spoken with local accents and local idioms, the articles are frequently left out where an Englishman would use them, *e.g.*, I see snake, for I saw *a* snake.   Water full, for *the* river is full. Here the local English sounds rather quaint, because the speaker simply expresses his Yoruba ideas in English words without the article.   Again, we may say in Yoruba, O joko lori aga " (He is sitting on a chair)   " O ñmu kòkò taba " (he is smoking a pipe) No one would ever think of adding the particle *kan* after *aga* or

kòkò taba by way of expressing the article *a.* So also we may say
" Mo pade Yesufu ni Odo Ọṣun " (I met Joseph at the River
Ọsun), or " Mo ñlọ sí ọja " (I am going to the market). No one
would use the particle *nâ* after Ọsun or ọja to indicate the article
the as its English equivalent. But we can say " Ọkọnrin nâ ti de "
(the man is ҫome). " Mo pade Ọkọnrin nâ " (I met the man).
" Ọmọde kan ñduro dè ọ " (a child is waiting for you). " Mo pa
ejò kan " (I have killed a snake). In which cases definiteness is
required and consequently the particles representing the articles
a, an and *the* are used.

These examples are sufficient to show that the articles do not
exist in the Yoruba language, but where definiteness is required,
equivalents can be found.

We deem these illustrations necessary as in books on Yoruba
Grammar the " article " forms one of the Parts of Speech.

NOUN

Nouns generally in their simplest form are formed by prefixing
a vowel to a verbal root ; as bẹ, to shear ; abẹ, razor ; dé, to cover
(the head) ; adé, crown ; dá, to cease ; òda, drought ; ṣè, to
offend ; ẹṣẹ, sin. So also the verbals àlọ, going ; abọ̀, coming from,
lọ, to go ; and bọ̀, to come.

But the prefixes have certain peculiarities of their own. Thus :
a prefixed indicates an agent, one who does a thing, *e.g.,* ke, to cut ;
aké, an axe—an agent for cutting wood. Da to break ; àda,
a cutlass ; yùn, to file, ayùn, a file or a saw.

o or ọ, the same as *a* but restricted in their use, *e.g.,* lu, to bore ;
olu, a gimlet ; lò, to grind ; olò, a grinder ; wẹ̀, to swim ; owẹ̀,
a swimmer ; dẹ, to hunt ; ọdẹ, a hunter.

ẹ prefixed indicates a noun in the concrete, *e.g.,* rù, to carry ;
ẹrù, a load ; mi; to breathe ; ẹmi, the breath, spirit.

i prefixed denotes a noun in the abstract, *e.g.,* mọ̀, to know ;
imọ̀, knowledge ; ri, to see ; iriri, experience.

The vowels *e* and *u* are rarely used.

Gender.—The Yoruba language being non-inflective, genders
cannot be distinguished by their terminal syllables, but by prefixing the words *akọ,* male, and *abo,* female, to the common term ;
and sometimes *ọkọnrin,* a man and *obirin,* a woman ; *e.g.,* akọ-
ẹṣin, a horse, stallion   abo-ẹṣin, a mare ; akọ-malû, a bull ; abo-
malû, a cow. Ọmọ· ọkọnrin, a boy, *i.e.,* a man child ; ọmọ-birin,
a girl.

In one case the masculine seems to be formed from the feminine,
e.g., Iyawo, a bride, ọkọ-iyawo, a bridegroom.

There are a few words in the Yoruba language in which different terms are used for the male and female of the objects, e.g. :—

Baba	..	father	Igbekun	..	a male captive
Iya	..	mother	Igbęsin	..	a female captive
Ǫkǫnrin	..	man	Ǫso	..	a wizard
Obirin	..	woman	Aję	..	a witch
Ǫkǫ	..	husband	Agbo	..	a ram
Aya	..	wife	Agutan	..	a sheep, a ewe
Apǫn	..	a bachelor	Obukǫ	..	a he-goat
Wundia	..	a spinster	Ewurę	..	a goat
Apǫn	..	a widower	Akukǫ	..	a cock
Opo	..	a widow	Agbebǫ	..	a hen

No other distinction of genders is known.

The words arakǫnrin and arabirin, used in translations for brother and sister, are purely coined words, not known to the illiterate Yoruba man not in touch with missionaries. To him they are " book-language " and must be explained.

The English words brother and sister show the relations as to sex only without indicating the relative age ; but the Yorubas, with whom distinction in age and seniority of birth are of primary importance, generally use the words egbǫn and aburo, i.e., the elder and the younger relative, words which show the relative age only, without indicating the sex and are equally applicable to uncles, aunts, nephews, nieces and cousins however far removed, as well as to brothers and sisters.

Our translators, in their desire to find a word expressing the English idea of sex rather than of age, coined the above words " arakǫnrin," i.e., the male relative ; " arabirin," the female relative ; these words have always to be explained to the pure but illiterate Yoruba man.

But the words egbǫn ǫkǫnrin or obirin and aburo ǫkǫnrin or obirin would be more intelligible to them and should be preferred, especially as it is always easy enough to find out the relative ages of the said brother or sister.

We would recommend this to our translators.

Proper names rarely show any distinction of sex, the great majority of them apply equally well to males as to females. See under " Yoruba Names," page 79.

Number.—The plural of nouns cannot be formed from the singular, either by addition or by a change of form ; only from the context can it be known whether we are speaking of one or more than one : but when specification is desired the demonstrative pronoun awǫn (they) or won (them) is used with the words, e.g.,

B

Awǫn ǫkǫnrin nâ ti lǫ (the men have gone away). The bells are ringing—Awǫn agogo nâ nlù. Awǫn, however, is rarely used with things without life. When the plural nouns are indefinite, that is to say, without the definite article, the demonstrative awon is omitted, e.g., Walaha okuta meji—two tables of stone.

Case.—There are three cases, the nominative, objective and possessive, as in the English language ; but in none of them is there a change of form. The nominative precedes and the objective follows after the transitive verb and preposition as usual, but in the case of the possessive, the thing possessed stands before the possessor with the particle *ti* expressed or understood between them, e.g., Moses' book, Iwe ti Musa, in which the particle *ti* is expressed. Iru ęsin, the horse's tail, in which the particle *ti* is understood. But although the particle *ti* is not expressed, yet its middle tone is preserved by lengthening the tone of the final vowel of the thing possessed. Thus we may say : Iwe (e) Musa, the book of Moses. Iru(u) ęsin, the tail of the horse. Ǫrǫ(ǫ) Ǫlǫrun, the word of God. Agbala(a) Ǫba, the court of the King. Oko Ǫrę(ę) mi, My friend's farm.

The sound of the added tone is sometimes so slight as to be almost imperceptible, but it is always there, and is one of those fine points which are so difficult for the ear of foreigners to catch, and the absence of which marks out their defective accents.

But when the noun in the possessive case stands alone, the particle *ti* must be expressed, e.g., David's, *Ti Dauda.* Moses's, *Ti Musa.* It is Joseph's, *Ti Yesufu ni.*

ADJECTIVES

Adjectives are generally placed after the nouns they qualify, as Ęsin dudu, a black horse ; ǫmǫ rere, a good child. They are placed before the nouns when some special attribute of that noun is to be emphasized, e.g., agidi ǫmǫ, a stubborn child ; apà ǫmǫ, a slovenly child ; alagbara ǫkǫnrin, a brave fellow ; akǫ okuta, a very hard stone.

These are really substantives used attributively. They may more correctly be regarded as nouns in the construct state, and not pure adjectives, e.g., " a brute of a man " is a more emphatic expression than " a brutish man." This view of showing the identity of a substantive with an adjective is clearly shown by Mason :—

" The adjective was originally identical with the noun which, in the infancy of language, named objects by naming some attributes by which they were known.

" In course of time the adjective was developed into a separate part of speech, the function of which was to attach itself to the noun ; even now it is sometimes difficult to draw the line between them, as nouns are sometimes used attributively and adjectives pass by various stages into nouns."

COMPARISON OF ADJECTIVES

Degrees of comparison cannot be formed from Yoruba adjectives. The words *ju* and *julǫ* which are generally used in Yoruba books and translations, and even stated in some grammars as forming the comparative and superlative degrees, are really adverbs signifying a *greater* or *less degree than* and as such may give *a comparative sense only* to the adjectives to which they are attached. The superlative is really non-existing ; it can only be gathered from the context. The word *ju* is only used in an elliptical sense for *julǫ* when a comparison is being made, and it often appears in the form of tmesis ; *e.g.*, Ile re tobi *ju* ti emi *lǫ*—Your house is larger than mine ; where *lǫ* is separated from *ju* by the words *ti emi*, and may be omitted without affecting the sense. When used otherwise, *i.e.*, without any idea of comparison, *ju* is purely an adverb signifying *too, too much* or *too little, e.g.*, O ga ju, it is too high ; O kere ju, it is too small. But a comparative idea can be gathered only from the context, and also whether the comparison is between two or many, and it is in that way alone a comparative and a superlative degree can be made out. " If we say, ' John is *taller* than all the other boys in the class,' we express the same relation as to height between John and the rest as if we should say, ' John is *the tallest* boy in the class.' But in the former case John is considered *apart from* the other boys of the class, so that the *two* objects which we have in mind are *John* and *the other boys in the class*. When the superlative degree is used John is considered as *one of the group* of boys compared with each other."—*Mason.*

This latter sense is what cannot be expressed in Yoruba and therefore the language cannot be said to possess a superlative degree. The superlative idea can only be gathered from the context.

It would be absurd to thus compare the adjective tall :— Positive, *ga* (tall) comparative, *ga ju* (too tall) ; superlative, *ga ju lǫ* (more tall than) which are not adjectives in the comparative and superlative sense at all.

To use words like these : Oga ogo julǫ, for the Most High ; or, Owù mi behe pupò julǫ for I am most pleased at it, is to speak vile Yoruba. No pure Yoruba man uncontaminated with English ideas would speak in that way at all.

As the genius of the Yoruba language, the working of the

Yoruba mind, its ideas and idiosyncracies do not run in an Anglo-Saxon channel, it is not to be expected that the mode of expression will agree in every particular. Some teachers of the Yoruba language often fall into this error in their endeavours to find the exact equivalent in both languages.

THE FORMS AND USES OF ADJECTIVES

Every adjective has two forms, the attributive and the predicative, each depending upon the use thereof, *e.g.* :—

A high mountain (attributive), Oke giga.

The mountain is high (predicative), Oke nâ ga.

In Yoruba, the attributive is formed from the predicative by reduplicating the initial consonant with the vowel *i*, *e.g.*, strong *pred.*, le, *attrib.*, lile ; sweet, *pred.*, dùn, *attrib.*, didùn ; hot *pred*, gbona, *attrib.*, gbigbona ; good, *pred.*, dara ; *attrib.*, didara, etc. Disyllables with the vowel *u* as a rule undergo no change, *e.g.*, tutu, cold ; dudu, black ; funfun, white, etc. (the *n* being purely nasal). Although not in use, the same rule even here may also be applied.

PRONOUNS.

Pronouns are used in the same sense as in English. They are: I Personal, II Relative, and III Adjective ; there is no distinction in genders in any of the forms.

The Personal includes the Reflexive.

I. Personal Pronouns.

(a) Nominative Case.

		Singular		Plural
1st Pers. :	I	Emi, mo (mọ, mi) ñ	We	Awa, a
2nd ,,	thou	Iwọ, o, (ọ)	you	ẹyin, ẹ
3rd ,,	he, she it	Oñ, ó, (ọ́)	they	Awọn, wọ́n

The full forms (sing.) emi, iwọ, oñ, (plural) awa, ẹyin, awọn, are used when emphasis is to be laid on the person, but ordinarily the second forms (sing.) mo, o, ó, (plural) a, ẹ, wọn, are used. Those in brackets (mọ, mi, ọ, ọ́) are mere provincialisms for the former.

Ñ in the 1st person is used only with the incomplete and future tenses, *e.g.*, ñlọ for emi yio lọ, or Mo ñlọ, I am going, Ño lọ for Emi yio lọ, I shall go.

He, when used in an indefinite sense, is *ẹni*, as : Ẹni ti o ba ṣe e, He that doeth it. Ẹni ti o ba wa si ihin, He who comes here.

(b) Possessive Case.

		Singular	Plural
1st Pers. :	Mine	Ti emi	Ours ti àwa
2nd ,,	Thine	Ti iwọ *or* ti irẹ	yours ti ẹyin
3rd ,,	his, hers, its	Ti oñ *or* ti irẹ̀	theirs ti àwọn

It will be observed that the possessive forms are simply the nominatives with the particle *ti* (meaning of) prefixed ; so that literally they are *of me, of you, of him*, etc. In ordinary speech, however, the vowel of the particle always suffers elision in the singular number, but in the plural it is the initial vowel of the pronoun that is elided. Thus we have :—

Sing. : t'emi, t'iwọ *or* t'irẹ, t'oñ *or* t'irẹ̀.
Plural : ti'wa, ti'yin, ti'wọn.

The apostrophe mark of elision is generally dispensed with in writing, *e.g.*, we write temi, tiwa, tiwọn, etc.

Special notice should be taken of the forms tìrẹ and tirẹ̀ ; in the 2nd and 3rd pers. singular the difference lies only in the tone (or accent) ; in the 2nd pers. the tone of the first syllable is depressed, the second is middle, it is *vice versa* in the 3rd person.

(c) Objective Case.

		Singular		Plural
1st Pers. :	me	mi	us	wa
2nd ,,	thee	ọ	you	yin
3rd ,,	him, her, it	a, e, ẹ, i, o, ọ, u	them	wọn

The objective case as may be seen, consists of fragments of the nominative. It is really the terminal syllables of the first second and third persons, singular and plural. The third person singular calls for special remarks :—

It consists of the whole of the vowels, but the particular vowel made use of in each case is that of the transitive verb which precedes the pronoun and governs the case, *e.g.*, O pá a (he killed it), Mo pè é (I called him), Wọn tẹ̀ ẹ (they bent it), A bò o (we covered it), etc. Where the verb ends in a nasal sound the vowel is also nasal, *e.g.*, O kàn ã (he nailed it), A fun ũ (we gave him), etc.

The tone of the pronoun in the objective case is influenced by that of the verb which governs it ; when that of the verb is raised the objective maintains the middle tone, *e.g.*, O lọ́ ọ (he twisted it), Mo ká a (I picked it) ; and *vice versa* when that of the verb is middle, that of the objective is raised, *e.g.*, O ṣe é (he did it), O pa á (he killed it), O kan mí (it aches me). Again, when the tone of the verb is depressed, that of the pronoun is raised, *e.g.*, O kàn mi (it touched me), Mo kà a (I counted it), A pè wọn (we called them).

THE REFLEXIVE

The word tìkára, incorporated wih the personal forms, is used to indicate the Reflexive. It is placed between the nominative and possessive cases, *e.g.*,

	Singular	Plural
1st Pers.:	Emi tikara mi	Awa tikara wa
2nd ,,	Iwọ tikara rẹ	Ẹyin tikara yin
3rd ,,	Oñ tikara rẹ̀	Awọn tikara wọn

The harsh *r* is generally softened into *l* so that instead of tikara we say tikala ; but in a flowing speech the *l* is dropped off altogether and the two *a*'s blended and lengthened ; so we often hear Emi tikā mi, Oñ tikā rẹ̀, Awa tikā wa.

II Relative Pronouns

The Relative pronoun who, whose, whom, which, what, or that in Yoruba, is the simplest in any language. It consists solely of the particle *ti* and is used for every number, gender, person or case, *e.g.*, I *who* çalled thee, Emi *ti* o pè ọ. The man *whom* I saw, Ọkọnrin *ti* mo ri. The birds *which* flew, Awọn ẹiyẹ *ti* wọn fò.

III. Adjective Pronouns

These are :—(a) Possessive ; (b) Demonstrative ; (c) Distributive ; (d) Indefinite ; and (e) Interrogative.

(a) Possessive :—

	Singular		Plural	
My	mi		Our	wa
thy	rẹ		your	yin
his, her, its	rẹ̀		their	wọn

Note.—Like adjectives, they come *after* the nouns they qualify, *e.g.*, My king, ọba mi ; your children, awọn ọmọ yin ; their cattle, awọn ẹran-osìn wọn.

(b) Demonstratives :—

	Singular	Plural
this	yì, eyi, eyiyi	these wọnyi, iwọnyi
that	nì, eyini, nâ	those wọnnì, iwọnnì

Note.—The simple forms yi, nì, wọnyi, wọnnì, are used with the nouns they qualify, *e.g.*, This man, ọkọnrin yi ; that book, iwe nì ; these children, awọn ọmọde wọnyi ; those houses, ile wọnnì. But when the nouns are not expressed, the forms with a vowel prefixed are used, *e.g.*, This is not good, eyi kò dara ; this very one, eyiyi ; these are not ripe, iwọnyi kò pọn ; those are very good, iwọnni dara jọjọ. Nâ refers to something spoken of or understood.

(c) Distributive :—

each	olukuluku, ęnikankan
every	ęnikan, or gbogbo
either	ęnikan
neither	ko si ęnikan

Note.—The Yoruba use of the distributives is rather idiomatic. " Each " is *olukuluku*, but when used in the sense of " one by one " it is *ęnikankan.* For " every one " the Yoruba is *gbogbo, i.e.,* all, *e.g.,* it touches every one of us. (In Yoruba) It touches all of us, Gbogbo wa li o kàn. " Either of them," is " one of them." Either of us may go, Ǫkan ninu wa le lǫ.

(d) Indefinite :—

All	..	Gbogbo	One	.. kan, ęnikan
Any	..	eyikeyi	Other	.. ekeji
Both	..	mejeji	Another	.. ęlomiran
Certain	..	(ęni) kan	One another ⎱ Each other ⎰	ara wǫn
Few	..	dię	Several	.. pupǫ
Many	..	ǫpǫlǫpǫ, pupǫ̀	Some	.. dię (a few)
Much	..	pupǫ̀, ǫ̀pǫ̀	Such	.. bayi
None	..	ko si ęnikain	Whole	.. ǫtǫtǫ, gbogbo

The Yoruba language s very defective in distinctive terms expressive of the indefinite pronouns. One word must do service for different terms in which there is a shade of difference of meaning, *e.g.,*

Gbogbo is used for all, whole.

Pupǫ or *ǫ̀pǫ̀* for many, much, several.

Ęnikan for certain, one.

None is expressed by " there is no one."

(e) Interrogative :—

Who ?	Tahani ? contracted to tāni ?
Whose ?	Titahani ? contracted to titāni ?
Which ?	Ewo ? wo ?
Whom ?	Tāni ? ęniti ?
What ?	Kini ?

Note.—The *n* in kini is often converted or rather softened into *l* in speech. What shall we do ? Kini awa yio sę ? is softened into Ki l' a o sę ?

VERBS

Verbs are transitives and intransitives. There are no auxiliary verbs as known in the English and other languages ; certain particles are used to mark out the moods, tenses and other forms, for which auxiliary verbs are used, consequently the verb " to be " as an auxiliary is wanting.

In the English language there are six auxiliary verbs, *viz.*, be, have, shall, will, may, do ; each of them may be used as the principal verb, and also as an auxiliary to other verbs when they help to form the moods and tenses ; but the particles that are used in Yoruba for such purposes are not verbs, and cannot be used as such, and therefore cannot be correctly termed auxiliary verbs as some compilers of Yoruba grammars have tried to make out.   For example, the particle *ti* placed before a verb denotes a completed action, *e.g.*, Ajayi ti lo, Ajayi *has* or had gone.   The particle *yio* in the same way points out a future tense, *e.g.*, Ajayi yio lo, Ajayi will go.   The nasal *ñ* prefixed to any verb shows an incomplete action as Ajayi ñlo, Ajayi is going.

There being no auxiliary verbs as such, the Passive Voice cannot be formed in the usual way, the first or third person plural of the verb transitive is used for the passive voice, *e.g.*, " A snake is killed " will be A pa ejo kan, or Won pa ejo kan.   Or if we say " The snake was killed by Joseph " the Yoruba will be " A ti owo Yesufu pa ejo nâ, which is literally, " We by the hand of Joseph killed the snake," but usually the active transitive is preferred, *viz.*, Yesufu li o pa ejo nâ, " It is Joseph that killed the snake." As was observed above, the majority of Yoruba verbs in their simplest form consist of monosyllables—a consonant and a vowel, *e.g.*, *ka*, to pick, *kà* to count, *rà* to buy, *lo* to go, *wa* to come, *sun* to sleep, etc.   They are non-inflective and do not show any distinction in number or person.

Disyllabic verbs are almost invariably compound words resolvable into their component parts ; they may be a verbal root compounded with a preposition, a noun or an adverb (some roots, however, have become obsolete), *e.g.*, Bawi, to scold, from *ba*, with, and *wi*, talk. Dahun, to answer, from *da*, to utter, *ohun*, a voice. Dapo, to mingle, from *dà*, to pour or mix, and *po*, together. Sunkun, to weep, from *sun*, to spring, and *ekun*, tears.

Some are transitives, others intransitives.

The noun or pronoun governed by the transitive verb is invariably placed between the component parts, *e.g.*, Bawi, to scold. O ba mi wi, He scolded me.

Pade, to close.   O pa ilekun de, He closed the door.

Here the *mi* is placed between the *ba* and the *wi*.   It is not O bawi mi for He scolded me, but *O ba mi wi*.

So also ilekun is placed between *pa* and *de*, not O pade ilekun, but *O pa ilekun de* for He closed the door.

Verbs compounded with a Preposition :—

Bawi, to scold. O ba mi wi, He scolded me.

Pade, to shut. Pa ilękun de, Close the door.

Dimu, to take hold of. Di mi mu, Take hold of me.

Dasi, to spare. Da wǫn si, Spare them.

Verbs compounded with an Adverb :—

Baję, to spoil. Ba inu ję, Grieve, "Spoil the mind."

Dapǫ, to mingle. Da wǫn pǫ, Mix them together.

Tuka, to scatter. Tu wǫn ka, Scatter them.

Daru, to confound. Da wǫn ru, Confound them.

Pamǫ, to keep. Pa mi mǫ, Keep or preserve me.

In verbs compounded with a noun, the noun always has the preposition *ni* (softened into *li*) before it, *e.g.*,

Daju, evident, from *da*, clear, and *oju*, the eyes—clear to the eyes. *O da mi l'oju*, It is evident to me

Tìju, to be ashamed, from *tì* to cover, *oju*, the eyes—covering the eyes. *O ti mi l'oju*. It shames me.

Dahun, to answer, from *da*, to utter, *ohun*, a voice. *Da mi l'ohun*, Answer me.

Jiya, to suffer, from *je*, to eat, iyà, punishment. *O ję mi ni iyà*, He punished me.

Gbǫwǫ, shake hands, from *gba*, take, *ǫwǫ*, hand. *O gbà mi l'ǫwǫ*, He shook hands with me.

Ranșę, to send a message, from *ran*, send, *ișę*, a message. *Mo ran a ni ișę*, I have sent him.

The Intransitive verbs of this class are usually neuter verbs compounded with nouns of similar import and therefore do not admit of any nouns or pronouns being inserted into their component parts, *e.g.*,

Sunkun, to cry, from *sun*, to spring, shed, *ękun*, tears.

Sǫrǫ, to talk, from *sǫ*, to utter, *ǫrǫ*, a word.

Kunlę, to kneel, from *kun*, to fill, *ilę*, the ground.

Pàde, to meet, from *pa*, to keep, *àde*, a coming.

Duro, to stand, from *dá*, to keep, *iro*, upright.

MOODS AND TENSES

In the formation of Moods and Tenses certain particles are made use of. They may have been the roots of obsolete verbs, but they cannot now be used as verbs but as particles ; we therefore refrain from applying the terms " defective " or " auxiliary verbs " to them. Such are the following :—

Bi, ba or *iba*, implying if, should, or would, *e.g.* Bi o ba lǫ, if he should go. Oñ iba lǫ, should he go

Jẹ or *ki*, or *jẹki*, implying permission, *e.g.*, Jẹ ki o lọ *or* kî o lọ, let him go.

Lè, implying permission. O le lọ, he may go.

Má or *Maṣe*, implying prohibition (authoritative).

Maha, implying permission (authoritative), *e.g.*, Maha lọ, be going

Yio, often contracted to *o*, sign of the future, *e.g.*, Yio lọ, he will go. Emi o lọ, I will go.

Ati or *ni ati*, softened into *lati*, implying an intention, *e.g.*, Ati lọ, to go. Lati jẹun, to eat (intending to).

N or *ng*, sign of incomplete action, *e.g.*, Emi ñlọ, I am going. Ojò ñrọ̀, it is raining.

Ti, a sign of the past tense, *e.g.*, O ti lọ, he has gone.

From these particles the Moods and Tenses are formed.

MOODS

The Indicative, Subjunctive, Potential, Imperative, Infinitive and the Participal Moods can be well expressed in Yoruba, and all but the first can be formed by the use of one or other of the above particles.

The Indicative is the verb in its simplest form, *e.g.* lọ, to go. Emi lọ, I went. Ojo sare, Ojo ran.

The Subjunctive is formed by prefixing the conjunction *bi* (if) before the subject of the verb, with or without the particle *ba*, *e.g.*, Bi emi lọ *or* Bi emi ba lọ, If I were to go. Bi emi ba fẹ lọ, If I wish to go.

The Potential is formed by adding the particle lè befóre the verb, *e.g.*, Emi lè lọ, I may go (lit. I am able to go).

The Imperative is formed by the permissive sign Jẹ ki, *e.g.*, Jẹ ki emi lọ, Let me go. [Besides the direct forms lọ (go thou) ; ẹ lọ (go ye).]

The Infinitive is formed by adding the particles *ati* or *lati* before the verb, *e.g.*, Ati lọ, to go. Lati mọ, to know.

The Participle is formed by prefixing the particle ñ (or ng) to the verb, *e.g.* ñlọ, going.; ñbọ, coming.

TENSES

There are only three tenses in Yoruba, properly speaking, the preterite, the incomplete, and the future.

An action just done is a completed action and is therefore past ; one doing is incomplete, consequently what may be considered present may be merged in the completed action, and is therefore taken as preterite, or in the incomplete, as the sense may require.

The simple verb is always expressed in the past indefinite or preterite tense, *e.g.*, Mo lọ, I went ; Mo wẹ, I washed. O rẹrin, he laughed or laughs ; O joko, he sat or sits.

The complete tenses, past or present, are expressed by prefixing the particle *ti* before the preterite, *e.g.*, Mo ti wẹ, I have, or had washed. O ti lọ, he has or had gone.

The incomplete tense is formed by prefixing the particle ñ (or ng) to the verb, *e.g.*, Emi ñwẹ, I am washing. Emi ñrẹrin, I am laughing.

The future tense is formed by placing the particle *yio* (contracted to o) before the verb, *e.g.*, Emi yio wẹ, I shall wash. Emi o lọ, I shall go. Awa o maha yọ̀, We shall be rejoicing.

The future complete (or second future) tense is formed by adding the particles indicating the future and the complete tenses to the verb *e.g.*, Emi *yio ti* wẹ, I shall have washed. Emi *o ti* lọ, I shall have gone.

ADVERBS

Adverbs are used in the same way as in the English, to modify or limit the meaning of a verb, an adjective, or another adverb, and are generally placed after the words they qualify, *e.g.*, O sọrọ daradara, He spoke well. O sọro jọjọ, It is very difficult. After an intransitive verb, they come directly after the verb, as O sùn fanfan, He slept soundly. O sure tete, He ran swiftly. But after a transitive verb they come after the noun or pronoun in the objective case, *e.g.*, Mo mọ Yesufu daju-daju, I know Joseph well. O le wọn sẹhin-sẹhin, He drove them far back.

Adverbs of manner, quality and degree are mostly formed by a reduplication of the word (especially an adverb or a verb), *e.g.*, O sọrọ daradara, He spoke very well, O duro ṣinṣin, He stood firmly. Dajudaju, evidently. Mo fẹran rẹ̀ gidigidi, I love him well.

Adverbs of time, place and quantity are used in the same way as in the English, and call for no special remarks. We may note, however, that in these, words of more than one syllable not onomatopoetic in origin are capable of being resolved into their elementary parts—usually into a particle (a preposition) and a noun, *e.g.*,

Nigbagbogbo, *always*, can be resolved into ni (at), igba (time), gbogbo (all), *i.e.*, at all times.

Nigboṣe, *when*, can be resolved into *ni* (at or in), *igba* (time), *ti* (which), *o se* (it happened), *i.e.*, at the time when it happened, *i.e.*, when.

Nihiyi, *here*, ni (at), *ihin* (here), *yi* (this), at this place.

Loke, *upwards*, ni or li (at), *oke* (the top).

Nibomiran, *elsewhere*, ni (at), *ibi* (place), *omiran* (another), at another place.

But there is also a use of adverbs peculiar to the Yoruba language, an onomatopoetic idea is often connected with it, and consequently it is always formed to suit the word it qualifies, and thus intensify the idea conveyed by the word. A form that is applicable to one verb or adjective may not be applicable to another, and therefore adverbs of degree or quality cannot be enumerated. For instance:

The adverb gògòrò can only apply to height, as o ga gògòrò, It is very high. A reduplication of the word can further intensify the idea, O ga gògòrò gogoro, It is very, very high. In the same way the word gbàgàdà can only apply to something of a huge size, and a reduplication of it, gbàgàdà gbagada, intensifies the idea. Also the word repete or ràpàtà-rapata implies not only a large size, but also a massive one, one in which the space covered is much more than the height.

Apart from intensifying the ideas, other qualities can also be expressed by the character of the adverb made use of; in other words, the adverbs often suggest some other ideas inherent in the qualities they describe although they cannot be so expressed in English, e.g., we may say, O pón fò ò, It is bright red. Here the adverb fò ò, besides being aptly applying to what is red, also suggests the *warmth* of the colouring. So also O pón roro, It is deep red; O pón rokiroki, i.e., It is bright red, almost yellow. In the last two examples *róró* and *rokiroki* refer simply to the depth of the colouring.[1]

One or two more illustrations will develop the above ideas fully. In the matter of length, we may say O gun tùnu tunu, It is very long. This can only apply to a long road, the idea of distance being implied. O gun gbòrò-gboro, It is very long. This conveys an idea of a long pole, or a rope, or a serpent or the like. So also with respect to height, we may say, O ga *fio fio*, It is very high. This can only apply to something on the top of a great height, or the top of a high object—as a tree, standing on the ground. O ga *tian-tian*, It is very high. This can only apply to an object at a great height, not connected with the ground, as a bird flying at a great height.

In all these examples, the adverb *very* is used to qualify the adjectives in English, no other ideas being conveyed; in this respect the Yoruba is more expressive.

PREPOSITIONS

Prepositions are particles placed before nouns or pronouns to show their relation to other words in the sentence.

---

[1] See Vidal's Notes to Crowther's Yoruba Grammar.

In Yoruba they are mostly monosyllables, *e.g.*, si, ni, fun, de, etc., as : O lọ *si* ile, He goes into the house. O wa *ni* oko, He is in the farm. O kọ́ ile *fun* Baba, He has built a house for the father. Duro *dè* mi, Wait for me.

Words of more than one syllable when used as prepositions are capable of being resolved into their component parts, *e.g.*, O nbọ̀ *lẹhin* mi, He is coming behind me. Here, the preposition lẹhin is resolvable into *li* (at) and *ẹhin* (the back). O wa *leti* ile, He is near the house ; *leti* is resolvable into *li* (at) and *eti*, the ear, or the edge that is within the hearing or at the edge of the house.

Under Verbs we have already considered those peculiar forms compounded with prepositions.

CONJUNCTIONS

Conjunctions are particles which serve to connect words or sentences ; they are copulative and disjunctive.

Copulative.

Ati, and or both. *Ati* Baba *ati* ọmọ, Both father and son. The initial *a* may be omitted, *e.g.*, Tiwọ tirẹ̀ *for* ati iwọ ati irẹ̀ (you and he).

Oñ, and or both. O lọ t'oñ ti ọmọ, He left both himself and child. It may be noted that *oñ* is never used to copulate pronouns of the 1st and 2nd persons.

Bi, if. Bi o jẹ ṣe ọmọ. If he would be a child. (This is used for *an obedient child*).

Nitori, because. Nitori t'emi, Because of me.

Njẹ, then. Njẹ o yio lọ ? Then will you go ?

Disjunctive.

Ṣugbọn, but. O de ile *sugbon* ko ba mi, He called but did not meet me at home.

Tabi, or. Emi tabi iwọ, I or you.

Bikoṣe, unless. Bikose pe o juba rẹ̀, Unless he pays regard to him.

Adi, although. Adi o ngbọ gbogbo rẹ̀, Although he hears it all.

Amọpe, idiomatic for *be it* known.

INTERJECTIONS

Interjections are any form of exclamation or ejaculation expressing some emotions of the mind. Any words may be used for the purpose, but very few convey any meaning apart from the tone in which they are expressed.

Exclamations of surprise : Yê ! O ! pâ ! emọ̀ ! hepà !

Exclamations of disgust : Ṣọ̀ ! Ṣiyọ !

It is rather curious that tribal peculiarities are marked in some forms of exclamations.

Favourite expressions of Ọyọs : Hâ ! Kinla ! Emọdẹ ! Gbaga-dari !

Favourite expressions of Egbas and Ijebus : Hẹre or herekẹ̀ ! heparipà ! payẹntiwà !

The usual exclamation in law courts for " silence " is : Atoto ! *lit,* enough of your noise !

Kagbohun ! *lit,* let us hear the sound of a (single) voice.

The tone of voice thrown into the exclamation in particular marks the expressions of grief, surprise, admiration or contempt.

We close this portion with the exclamation usually addressed to kings—Kabiyesi ! May long life be added !

NUMERALS

Numerals in Yoruba, although formed on a definite plan, yet are more or less complicated ; the tone (or accent) plays an important part in them.

All numerals refer to some noun (person or thing) expressed or understood. They are Cardinal and Ordinal or Serial.

The Cardinal has three forms, *viz. :* (1) simple enumeration ; (2) numeral adjectives ; and (3) numismatics. To these may be added adverbs of number and of time.

1. SIMPLE ENUMERATION

1 ... ... Enì		22 ... ... Èjilelogun
2 ... ... Èji		23 ... ... Ètalelogun
3 ... ... Ẹ̀ta		24 ... ... Ẹ̀rinlelogun
4 ... ... Èrin		25 ... ... Ẹdọgbọn
5 ... ... Àrun		26 ... ... Ẹ̀rindilogbọn
6 ... ... Ẹfa		27 ... ... Ẹ̀tadilogbọn
7 ... ... Èje		28 ... ... Èjidilogbọn
8 ... ... Ẹjọ		29 ... ... Ọ̀kandilogbọn
9 ... ... Ẹsan		30 ... ... Ọgbọn
10 ... ... Èwa		35 ... ... Àrundilogoji
11 ... ... Ọ̀kanla		40 ... ... Ọ̀jì
12 ... ... Èjila		45 ... ... Arundiladọta
13 ... ... Ẹ̀tala		50 ... ... Àdọta
14 ... ... Èrinla		55 ... ... Arundilọgọta
15 ... ... Ẹ̀dogun		60 ... ... Ọgọta
16 ... ... Ẹ̀rindilogun		65 ... ... Àrundiladọrin
17 ... ... Ẹ̀tadilogun		70 ... ... Àdọrin
18 ... ... Èjidilogun		75 ... ... Àrundilọgọrin
19 ... ... Ọ̀kandilogun		80 ... ... Ọgọrin
20 ... ... Ogun		85 ... ... Àrundiladọrun
21 ... ... Ọ̀kanlelogun		90 ... ... Àdọrun

SIMPLE ENUMERATION—*Continued.*

95 ...	... Àrundilǫgǫrun	4,000 ...	... Ẹgbaji
100 ...	... Ǫgǫrun	5,000 ...	... Ẹdẹgbata
200 ...	... Igba	6,000 ...	... Ẹgbata
300 ...	... Ǫdunrun	7,000 ...	... Ẹdẹgbarin
400 ...	... Irinwo	8,000 ...	... Ẹgbarin
500 ...	... Ẹdẹgbẹta	9,000 ...	... Ẹdẹgbarun
600 ...	... Ẹgbẹta	10,000 ...	... Ẹgbarun
700 ...	... Ẹdẹgbẹrin	20,000 ...	... Ẹgbawa or
800 ...	... Ẹgbẹrin		Ǫkẹ kan *i.e.* one bag (of
900 ...	... Ẹdẹgbẹrun		cowries).
1,000 ...	... Ẹgbẹrun		Higher numbers as 40,000,
2,000 ...	... Ẹgbàwá		60,000, etc. being so many bags.
3,000 ...	... Ẹgbẹdogun		

2. QUANTITATIVE OR NUMERAL ADJECTIVES

One ... ... Ǫkan	Twenty-nine ... Mǫkandilogbǫn
Two ... ... Méji	Thirty ... ... Ogbǫn
Three ... ... Mẹ́ta	Thirty-five ... Marundilogoji
Four ... ... Mẹ́rin	Forty ... ... Ojì
Five ... ... Márun	Forty-five ... Marundiladǫta
Six ... ... Mẹ́fa	Fifty ... ... Adǫta
Seven ... ... Méje	Fifty-five ... Marundilǫgǫta
Eight ... ... Méjǫ	Sixty ... ... Ǫta
Nine ... ... Mẹ́san	Sixty-five ... Marundiladǫrin
Ten ... ... Mẹ́wa	Seventy... ... ... Adǫrin
Eleven ... ... ∴ Mǫ́kanla	Seventy-five ... Marundilǫgǫrin
Twelve ... ... Méjila	Eighty ... ... Ogǫrin
Thirteen ... ... Mẹ́tala	Eighty-five ...Marundiladǫrun
Fourteen ... ... Mẹrinla	Ninety ... ... Adǫrun
Fifteen ... ... Mẹdogun	Ninety-five ...Marundilǫgǫrun
Sixteen ... ... Merindilogun	One hundred ... ... Ǫrún
Seventeen ... Mẹtadilogun	One hundred and ten ... Adǫfà
Eighteen ... Mejidilogun	,, ,, ,, twenty Ogǫfa
Nineteen ... Mǫkandilogun	,, ,, ,, thirty Adoje
Twenty ... ... Ogun	,, ,, ,, forty Ogoje
Twenty-one ... Mẹkanlelogun	,, ,, ,, fifty Adojǫ
Twenty-two ... Mejilelogun	,, ,, ,, sixty Ogojǫ
Twenty-three ... Mẹtalelogun	,, ,, ,, seventy Adǫsan
Twenty-four ... Mẹrinlelogun	,, ,, ,, eighty Ogǫsan
Twenty-five ... Mẹdogbǫn	,, ,, ,, ninety
Twenty-six ... Merindilogbǫn		Mewadinigba
Twenty-seven ... Mẹtadilogbǫn	Two hundred ... ... Igba
Twenty-eight ... Mejidilogbǫn	etc., etc.

3. NUMISMATICS

One cowry ... ... O ókan[1]	Three cowries ... ... Ẹ́ta
Two cowries ... ... E éji[1]	Four ,, ... Ẹ́ érin

---

[1] *Lit.*, one money, two monies ; cowry shells being used for money.

Numismatics—*Continued*

Five cowries	...	... A árun	500 cowries	...	E-edegbeta
Six	,, ...	... E éfà	600	,, ...	... Egbeta
Seven	,, ...	... E éje	700	,, ...	E-edegberin
Eight	,, ...	... E ejo	800	,, ...	... Egbèrin
Nine	,, ...	... E ésan	900	,, ...	E-edegberun
Ten	,, ...	... E éwa	1,000	,, ...	Egbèrun
Eleven	,, ...	...O-ókanla	1,200	,, ...	... Egbèfa
Twelve	,, ...	... E-éjila	1,300	,, ...	E-edegbèje
Thirteen	,, ...	Eetala	1,400	,, ...	... Egbèje
Fourteen	,, ...	... Eerinla	1,500	,, ...	E-edegbèjo
Fifteen	,, ...	... Eedogun	1,600	,, ...	... Egbèjo
Sixteen	,, ...	Eerindilogun	1,700	,, ...	E-edegbèsan
Seventeen cowries		Eétadilogun	1,800	,, ...	... Egbesan
Eighteen	,,	Eejidilogun	1,900	,,	Egbadin-ogorun
Nineteen	,,	Oókandilogun	2,000	,, ...	... Egbàwá
Twenty	,,	... Okòwo	2,200	,, ...	Egbokanla
Twenty-five	,,	E edogbon	2,400	,, ...	... Egbèjila
Thirty	,,	Ogbonwo	2,500	,,	Egbètaladin-ogorun
Forty	,,	... Ogoji	2,600	,, ...	Egbetala
Fifty	,,	... À-adota	2,800	,, ...	Egbèrinla
Sixty	,,	... Ogota	3,000	,, ...	Egbèédogun
Seventy	,,	À-adorin	3,500	,, ...	Egbejidilogun-
Eighty	,,	... Ogorin			din-ogorun
Ninety	,,	À-adorun	3,600	,, ...	Egbejidinlogun
One hundred	,,	... Ogorun	4,000	,, ...	... Egbaji
110 cowries	...	... À-adofa	4,500	,, ...	Egbetalelogun-
120	,, ...	... Ogofa			din-ogorun
130	,, ...	... À-adoje	5,000	,, ...	Egbedogbon
140	,, ...	... Ogoje	5,500	,,	...Egbetalelogbon-
150	,, ...	... À-adojo			din-ogorun
160	,, ...	... Ogójo	6,000	,, ...	... Egbata
170	,, ...	À-adosan	7,000	,, ...	Edegbarin
180	,, ...	... Ogosan	8,000	,, ...	... Egbarin
190	,, ...	Ewadinigba	9,000	,, ...	Edegbarun
200	,, ...	... Igbiwo	10,000	,, ...	... Egbarun
210	,, ...	Ewalerugba	15,000	,, ...	Edegbajo
220	,, ...	Ogunlugba	16,000	,, ...	... Egbajo
230	,,	Ogbonwolerugba	18,000	,, ...	... Egbasan
240	,, ...	- Ojulugba	20,000	,,	Egbawa (Oke kan)
250	,,	A-adotalerugba	30,000	,, ...	E-edogun
260	,, ...	Otàlugba	32,000	,, ...	Erindilogun
270	,,	A-adorinlerugba	34,000	,, ...	Etàdilogun
280	,, ...	Orinlugba	36,000	,, ...	Ejì-dilogun
290	,,	A-adorunlerugba	38,000	,, ...	Òkàndilogun
300	,, ...	Odunrun	40,000	,,	Egbagun (Oke meji)
400	,, ...	... Irinwo			

THE ORDINAL

The first	...	...	Ekini	
,, second	...	...	Ekeji	
,, third	...	...	Eketa	
,, fourth	...	...	Ekerin	
,, fifth	...	...	Ekarun	
,, sixth	...	...	Ekefa	
,, seventh	...	...	Ekeje	
,, eighth	...	...	Ekejo	
,, ninth	...	...	Ekesan	
,, tenth	...	...	Ekewa	
,, eleventh	...		Ikokanla	
,, twelfth	...	...	Ikejila	
,, thirteenth		...	Iketala	
,, fourteenth		...	Ikerinla	
,, fifteenth	...		Ikedogun	
,, sixteenth	...		Ikerindilogun	
,, seventeenth			Iketadilogun	
,, eighteenth			Ikejidilogun	
,, nineteenth			Ikokandilogun	
,, twentieth	...	...	Ogun	
,, twenty-first			Ikokanlelogun	
,, twenty-fifth			Ikedogbon	

The thirtieth	...	...	Ogbon
,, thirty-fifth	Ikarundilogoji
,, fortieth	...	...	Oji
,, forty-fifth	...	Ikarundiladota
,, fiftieth	...	...	Adota
,, fifty-fifth	...	Ikarundilogota
,, sixtieth	...	...	Ogota
,, sixty-fifth	Ikarundiladorin
,, seventieth	...	Adorin
,, seventy-fifth	Ikarundilogorin
,, eightieth	...	...	Ogorin
,, eighty-fifth	Ikarundiladorun
,, ninetieth	...	...	Adorun
,, ninety-fifth	Ikarundilogorun
,, hundredth	...	...	Ogorun
,, hundred and first	...	Ikokan-lelogorun

From the first to the ninth— Ikokanle to Ikokandin—the tenths merge into those of simple enumeration.

ADVERBS OF NUMBER

One by one	...	...	Okankan
Two by two	...	...	Meji-meji
Three by three		Meta-meta
Four by four		Merin-merin
Five by five	...	Marun-marun
Six by six	...	...	Mefa-mefa
Seven by seven		...	Meje-meje
Eight by eight		...	Mejo-mejo
Nine by nine		Mesan-mesan
Ten by ten	...	Mewa-mewa

Continue to reduplicate the numerals up to nineteen by nineteen then—

Twenty by twenty	...	Ogo-gun
Thirty by thirty	...	Ogbogbon
Forty by forty	...	Ogogoji
Fifty by fifty	...	Aradota

Sixty by sixty	...	Ogogota
Seventy by seventy	...	Aradorin
Eighty by eighty	...	Ogogorin
Ninety by ninety	...	Aradorun
Hundred by hundred	Ogogorun

Thus from one to nineteen the numbers are reduplicated, also from 21-29 ; 31-39 ; 41-49 ; and so on, but for 20, 30, 40, 60, 80, 100 only the reduplication of the first two letters takes place, e.g., Ogogun, Ogbogbon ; for 50, 70, 90, the same occurs only the euphonic " r " takes the place of " d " e.g., Aradota for Adodota ; Aradorun for Adodorun.

ADVERBS OF TIME

Once	...	...	Erinkan	Four times	...	... Erin-merin
Twice	...	...	Erin-meji	Five ,,	...	Erin-marun
Thrice	...	...	Erin-meta	Six ,,	...	... Erin-mefa

ADVERBS OF TIME—*Continued*

Seven times ...	Ẹrin-meje	Seventy times	Igba-adọrin
Eight ,, ...	Ẹrin-mẹjọ	Eighty ,,	Igba-ọgọrin
Nine ,, ...	Ẹrin-mẹsan	Ninety ,,	Igba-adọrun
Ten ,, ...	Ẹrin-mẹwa	Hundred ,,	Igba-ọgọrun

The same to nineteen times.

Twenty times	Igba-ogun
Thirty ,,	Igba-ogbon
Forty ,,	Igba-ogoji
Fifty ,,	Igba-adọta
Sixty ,,	Igba-ọgọta

Thus " Ẹrin " is prefixed to all the numerals, but the multiples of ten take " Igba " before them. *Note.*—' Ẹrin " is usually softened to ẹẹ, *e.g.*, ẹ̀ẹ̀kan, ẹ̀ẹ̀meji and so forth.

ANALYSIS OF THE NUMERALS

FROM one to ten, different terms are used, then for 20, 30, 200 and 400 ; the rest are multiples and compounds. Thus 11, 12, 13 and 14 are reckoned as ten plus one, plus two, plus three and plus four ; 15 to 20 are reckoned as 20 less five, less four, less three, less two, less one, and then 20.

In the same way we continue 20 and one, to 20 and four, and then 30 less five (25), less four, and so on to 30, and so for all figures reckoned by tens.

There is no doubt that the digits form the basis of enumeration to a large extent, if not entirely so. Five, ten, twenty, *i.e.*, the digits of one hand, of two, and the toes included, and their multiples form the different stages of enumeration.

Beginning from the first multiple of 20 we have ogoji, a contraction of ogun meji, *i.e.,* two twenties (40), Ọgọta, three twenties (60), Ọgọrin, four twenties (80), Ọgọrun, five twenties (100), and so on to ten twenties (200), when the new word *Igba* is used.

The intermediate numbers (30 having a distinct terminology), 50, 70, 90, 110, 130 to 190 are reckoned as : 60 less ten (50), 80 less ten (70), a hundred less ten (90), and so on to 200.

The figures from 200 to 2,000 are reckoned as multiples of 200 (400, however, which is 20 × 20, the square of all the digits, has a distinct terminology, Irinwo or Erinwo, *i.e.*, the elephant of figures—meaning the highest coined word in calculation, the rest being multiples).

Thus we have Ẹgbẹta, a contraction of Igba-mẹta, *i.e.*, three two-hundreds (600), Ẹgbẹrin, from Igba-merin, four two-hundreds (800), Ẹgbẹrin, five two-hundreds (1,000), and so on to Ẹgbàwá, ten two-hundreds (2,000), which in its turn forms the basis of still higher calculations.

The intermediate figures of 300, 500, 700, 900, 1,100 to 1,900 are reckoned as 100 less the multiple above them, *viz.*, Ọdunrun, contracted from Orún-din-ni-irinwo, *i.e.*, 100 less than 400 (300), Orún-din-ni-egbeta, 100 less than 600 (500), Orún-din-ni-egberin, 100 less than 800 (700) ; and so on to 2,000.

By a system of contraction, elision, and euphonic assimilation, for which the Yoruba language is characteristic, the long term Orún-din-ni (Egbeta or Egberin and so on) is contracted to Edé or Odé, *e.g.*, Edegbeta (500), Edegberin (700), Edegberun (900) and so on.

But the multiples of 200 do not end with ten times, although that figure is the basis of the higher calculations, it goes on to the perfection (or multiple) of the digits, *viz.* : twenty times (two hundred) ; thus we have Egbokànla, that is, Igba mokànla, 11 two-hundreds (2,200) ; Egbejila, twelve two-hundreds (2,400), and so on to twenty two-hundreds or Egbaji, that is, twice two thousand (4,000).

With this ends the multiples of 200. The intermediate figures of 2,300, 2,500, 2,700, 2,900 are reckoned the same way as before, *viz.* : 100 less than the next higher multiple.

As already mentioned, Egbàwá (or Egba), 2,000, forms the basis of still higher calculations ; the multiples of Egba are Egbaji, two two-thousands (4,000) ; Egbata, three two-thousands (6,000) ; Egbarin, four two-thousands (8,000) on to Egbawa, ten two-thousands (20,000), which in its turn forms the basis of the highest calculations.

The intermediate figures of 3,000, 5,000, 7,000, 9,000, 11,000 onwards are reckoned as 1,000 less than the multiple above them. The more familiar terms for 3,000 and 5,000, however, are Egbe dogun, or fifteen two-hundreds, and Egbedogbon, 25 two-hundreds.

For those figures beyond 20,000 the contracted forms which are generally used are : Òkànla (for Egbamokanla) 11 two-thousands ; Èjila, Etàla on to Egbagun, *i.e.*, 20 two-thousands, *i.e.*, forty thousand.

Summary.—Thus we see that with numbers that go by tens five is used as the intermediate figure—five less than the next higher stage. In those by 20, ten is used as the intermediate. In those by 200, 100 is used, and in those of 2,000, 1,000 is used.

The figure that is made use of for calculating indefinite numbers is 20,000 Egbawa, and in money calculation especially it is termed Oke kan, *i.e.*, one bag (of cowries). Large numbers to an indefinite amount are so many " bags " or rather " bags " in so many places.

THE HISTORY OF THE YORUBAS

PART I

CHAPTER I

ORIGIN AND EARLY HISTORY

The origin of the Yoruba nation is involved in obscurity. Like the early history of most nations the commonly received accounts are for the most part purely legendary. The people being unlettered, and the language unwritten all that is known is from traditions carefully handed down.

The National Historians are certain families retained by the King at Ọyọ whose office is hereditary, they also act as the King's bards, drummers, and cymbalists ; it is on them we depend as far as possible for any reliable information we now possess ; but, as may be expected their accounts often vary in several important particulars. We can do no more than relate the traditions which have been universally accepted.

The Yorubas are said to have sprung from Lamurudu one of the kings of Mecca whose offspring were :—Oduduwa, the ancestor of the Yorubas, the Kings of Gogobiri and of the Kukawa, two tribes in the Hausa country. It is worthy of remark that these two nations, notwithstanding the lapse of time since their separation and in spite of the distance from each other of their respective localities, still have the same distinctive tribal marks on their faces, and Yoruba travellers are free amongst them and *vice versa* each recognising each other as of one blood.

At what period of time Lamurudu reigned is unknown but from the accounts given of the revolution among his descendants and their dispersion, it appears to have been a considerable time after Mahomet.

We give the accounts as they are related :—

The Crown Prince Oduduwa relapsed into idolatry during his father's reign, and as he was possessed of great influence, he drew many after him. His purpose was to transform the state religion into paganism, and hence he converted the great mosque of the city into an idol temple, and this Asara, his priest, who was himself an image maker, studded with idols.

3

Asara had a son called Braima who was brought up a Moham-medan.   During his minority he was a seller of his father's idols, an occupation which he thoroughly abhorred, but which he was obliged to engage in.   But in offering for sale his father's handi-work, he usually invited buyers by calling out :   " Who would purchase falsehood ? "   A premonition this of what the boy will afterwards become.

By the influence of the Crown Prince a royal mandate was issued ordering all the men to go out hunting for three days before the annual celebration of the festivals held in honour of these gods.

When Braima was old enough he seized the opportunity of one of such absences from the town of those who might have opposed him to destroy the gods whose presence had caused the sacred mosque to become desecrated.   The axe with which the idols were hewed in pieces was left hanging on the neck of the chief idol, a huge thing in human shape.   Enquiry being made, it was soon discovered who the iconoclast was, and when accosted, he gave replies which were not unlike those which Joash gave to the Abiezrites who had accused his son Gideon of having performed a similar act (see *Judges* vi, 28–33).   Said Braima, " Ask that huge idol who did it."   The men replied, " Can he speak ? "   " Then," said Braima " Why do you worship things which cannot speak ? " He was immediately ordered to be burnt alive for this act of gross impiety.   A thousand loads of wood were collected for a stake, and several pots of oil were brought for the purpose of firing the pile. This was signal for a civil war.   Each of the two parties had powerful followers, but the Mohammedan party which was hitherto suppressed had the upper hand, and vanquished their opponents. Lamurudu the King was slain, and all his children with those who sympathized with them were expelled from the town.   The Princes who became Kings of Gogobiri and of the Kukawa went westwards and Oduduwa eastwards.   The latter travelled 90 days from Mecca, and after wandering about finally settled down at Ile Ifẹ where he met with Agbọ-niregun (or Sẹtilu) the founder of the Ifa worship.

Oduduwa and his children had escaped with two idols to Ile Ifẹ.   Sahibu being sent with an army to destroy or reduce them to submission was defeated, and amongst the booty secured by the victors was a copy of the Koran.   This was afterwards pre-served in a temple and was not only venerated by succeeding generations as a sacred relic, but is even worshipped to this day under the name of *Idi*, signifying Something tied up.

Such is the commonly received account among this intelligent although unlettered people.   But traces of error are very apparent

on the face of this tradition.   The Yorubas are certainly not of the
Arabian family, and could not have come from Mecca—that is
to say the Mecca universally known in history, and no such
accounts as the above are to be found in the records of Arabian
writers of any kings of Mecca ; an event of such importance
could hardly have passed unnoticed by their historians. But
then it may be taken for granted that all such accounts and
traditions have in them some basis in actual facts, nor is the subject
under review exempted from the general rule, and this will become
apparent on a closer study of the accounts.

That the Yorubas came originally from the East there cannot
be the slightest doubt, as their habits, manners and customs, etc.,
all go to prove.   With them the East is Mecca and Mecca is the
East.   Having strong affinities with the East, and Mecca in the
East looming so largely in their imagination, everything that comes
from the East, with them, comes from Mecca, and hence it is
natural to represent themselves as having hailed originally from
that city.

The only written record we have on this subject is that of the
Sultan Belo of Sokoto, the founder of that city, the most learned
if not the most powerful of the Fulani sovereigns that ever bore
rule in the Soudan.

Capt. Clapperton (*Travels and Discoveries in Northern and Central
Africa*, 1822—1824) made the acquaintance of this monarch.
From a large geographical and historical work by him, Capt.
Clapperton made a copious extract, from which the following is
taken :—" Yarba is an extensive province containing rivers,
forests, sands and mountains, as also a great many wonderful
and extraordinary things.   In it, the talking green bird called
babaga (parrot) is found."

" By the side of this province there is an anchorage or harbour
for the ships of the Christians, who used to go there and purchase
slaves.   These slaves were exported from our country and sold
to the people of Yarba, who resold them to the Christians."

" The inhabitants of this province (Yarba) it is supposed
originated from the remnant of the children of Canaan, who were
of the tribe of Nimrod.   The cause of their establishment in the
West of Africa was, as it is stated, in consequence of their being
driven by Yar-rooba, son of Kahtan, out of Arabia to the Western
Coast between Egypt and Abyssinia.   From that spot they
advanced into the interior of Africa, till they reach Yarba where
they fixed their residence.   On their way they left in every place
they stopped at, a tribe of their own people.   Thus it is supposed
that all the tribes of the Soudan who inhabit the mountains are

originated from them as also are the inhabitants of Ya-ory.   Upon
the whole, the people of Yarba are nearly of the same description
as those of Noofee (Nupe)[1] "

In the name Lamurudu (or Namurudu) we can easily recognize
a dialectic modification of the name Nimrod.   Who this Nimrod
was, whether Nimrod surnamed " the strong," the son of Hasoûl,
or Nimrod the " mighty hunter " of the Bible, or whether both
descriptions belong to one and the same person, we cannot tell,
but this extract not only confirms the tradition of their origin but
also casts a side light on the legend.   Arabia is probably the
" Mecca " of our tradition.   It is known that the descendants of
Nimrod (Phoenicians) were led in war to Arabia, that they settled
there, and from thence they were driven by a religious persecution
to Africa.   We have here also the origin of the term Yoruba,
from Yarba, their first permanent settlement in Africa.   Yarba
is the same as the Hausa term Yarriba for Yoruba.

It is very curious that in the history of Mahomet we read of
a similar flight of his first converts from Mecca to the East Coast
of Africa (the first Hegira), due also to a religious persecution;
this fact will serve to show that there is nothing improbable in
the accounts as received by tradition.   Again, that they emigrated
from Upper Egypt to Ile Ifẹ may also be proved by those sculptures
commonly known as the " Ifẹ Marbles," several of which may be
seen at Ile Ifẹ to this day, said to be the handiwork of the early
ancestor of the race.   They are altogether Egyptian in form.
The most notable of them is what is known as the " Ọpa Ọrañyan,"
(Ọrañyan's staff) an obelisk standing on the site of Ọrañyan's
supposed grave, having characters cut in it which suggest a Phoenician origin.   Three or four of these sculptures may now be seen
in the Egyptian Court of the British Museum, showing at a glance
that they are among kindred works of art.

From these statements and traditions, whether authentic or
mythologic, the only safe deductions we can make as to the most
probable origin of the Yorubas are :—

1. That they sprang from Upper Egypt, or Nubia.

2. That they were subjects of the Egyptian conqueror Nimrod,
who was of Phoenician origin, and that they followed him in his
wars of conquest as far as Arabia, where they settled for a time.
How subjects term themselves " children " or offspring of their

---

[1] Vide *Narratives of Travels and Discoveries*, by Major Denham
and Capt. Clapperton, 1826.   Appendix XII., Sec. IV.
A Tropical Dependency, by Flora L. Shaw (Lady Lugard), 1905,
pp. 227—228.

sovereigns is too well-known in this country, as we shall see in the course of this history.

3. That from Arabia they were driven, on account of their practising there their own form of worship, which was either paganism or more likely a corrupt form of Eastern Christianity (which allowed of image worship—so distasteful to Moslems).

Again, the name of the priest " Asara " is also a peculiar one ; it is so much like " Anasara " a term which Moslems generally applied to Christians (which signifies ' followers of the Nazarene ') as to make it probable that the revolution spoken of was in connection rather with Mohammedanism, and the corrupt form of Christianity of those days.

Lastly, the sacred relic called IDI from its being bound up and preserved, and which is supposed to have been a copy of the _Koran_, is probably another error. Copies of the _Koran_ abound in this country, and they are not venerated thus, and why should this have become an object of worship ? The sacred book of the party opposed to them ! One can hardly resist coming to the conclusion that the book was not the _Koran_ at all, but a copy of the Holy Scriptures in _rolls_, the form in which ancient manuscripts were preserved. The _Koran_ being the only sacred book known to later generations which have lost all contact with Christianity for centuries after the great emigration into the heart of Africa, it is natural that their historians should at once jump to the conclusion that _the thing bound up_ was the _Koran_. It might probably then be shown that the ancestors of the Yorubas, hailing from Upper Egypt, were either Coptic Christians, or at any rate that they had some knowledge of Christianity. If so, it might offer a solution of the problem of how it came about that traditional stories of the creation, the deluge, of Elijah, and other scriptural characters are current amongst them, and indirect stories of our Lord, termed " son of Moremi."

But let us continue the story as given by tradition. Oduduwa and his sons swore a mortal hatred of the Moslems of their country, and were determined to avenge themselves of them ; but the former died at Ile Ife before he was powerful enough to march against them. His eldest son Okànbi, commonly called Idekoseroake, also died there, leaving behind him seven princes and princesses who afterwards became renowned. From them sprang the various tribes of the Yoruba nation. His first-born was a princess who was married to a priest, and became the mother of the famous Olowu, the ancestor of the Owus. The second child was also a princess who became the mother of the Alaketu, the progenitor of the Ketu people. The third, a prince, became king of the

Benin people.   The fourth, the Qrangun, became king of Ila ; the
fifth, the Onisabẹ, or king of the Ṣabẹs ; the sixth, Olupòpo, or king
of the Popos ; the seventh and last born, Qrañyan, who was the progenitor of the Yorubas proper, or as they are better distinguished
Qyọs.

All these princes became kings who wore crowns as distinguished
from those who were vassals who did not dare to wear crowns,
but coronets called *Akoro*, a high-crowned head-gear, embroidered
with silver.

But it may be remarked that the Olowu's father was a commoner,
and not a prince of the blood, and yet he became one of the crowned
heads.   The following anecdote will explain how this came about.

The Yoruba princesses had (and still have) the liberty of
choosing husbands according to their fancy from any rank in life ;
the King's eldest daughter chose to marry her father's priest, for
whom she had the Olowu.

This young prince was one day playing on his grandfather's
knees, and he pulled at the crown on his head ; the indulgent
parent thereupon placed it on the child's head, but like some spoiled
children, he refused to give it up when required, and so it was left
with him, the grandfather putting on another.   The child had the
crown on his head until he fell asleep in his mother's arms, when
she took it off and returned it to her father, but the latter told her
to keep it for her son, as he seemed so anxious to have it.   Hence the
right of the Olowu to wear the crown like his uncles.   The same
right was subsequently accorded to the Alaketu, i.e., the progenitor
of the Ketu people.

It was stated above that Qrañyan was the youngest of Oduduwa's
grandchildren, but eventually he became the richest and   most
renowned of them all.   How this came about is thus told by
tradition :—

On the death of the King, their grandfather, his property was
unequally divided among his children as follows :—

The King of Beniñ inherited his money (consisting of cowry
shells), the Qrangun of Ila his wives, the King of Ṣabẹ his cattle,
the Olupòpo the beads the Olowu the garments, and the Alaketu
the crowns, and nothing was left for Qrañyan but the land.   Some
assert that he was absent on a warlike expedition when the partition
was made, and so he was shut out of all movable properties.
Qranyan was, however, satisfied with his portion, which he proceeded forthwith to turn to good account with the utmost skill.
He held his brothers as tenants living on the land which was his ;
for rents he received money, women, cattle, beads, garments, and
crowns, which were his brothers' portions, as all these were more

or less dependent on the soil, and were deriving sustenance from it. And he was the one selected to succeed the father as King in the direct line of succession.[1] To his brothers were assigned the various provinces over which they ruled more or less independently, Orañyan himself being placed on the throne as the ALÂFIN or Lord of the Royal Palace at Ile Ifẹ.

According to another account, Orañyan had only a bit of rag left him, containing earth, 21 pieces of iron, and a cock. The whole surface of the earth was then covered with water. Orañyan laid his portion on the surface of the water, and placed on it the cock, which scattered the earth with his feet ; the wide expanse of water became filled up, and the dry land appeared everywhere. His brothers preferring to live on dry land rather than on the surface of the water were permitted to do so on their paying an annual tribute for sharing with their younger brother his own portion.

It will be noticed that both traditions attribute the land to Orañyan ; hence the common saying " Alâfin l'oni ilẹ " (the Alâfin is the lord of the land) : the pieces of iron representing underground treasures, and the cock such as subsist on the land.

The former account seems more probable, the latter being little else but a travesty of the story of the creation or the flood. But it is fair to mention that the more generally received opinion is, that Orañyan became more prosperous than his brothers owing to the fact of his living virtuously, they being given up to a life of unrestrained licentiousness ; and being also by far the bravest of them all, he was preferred above them and was seated on the ancestral throne at Ile Ifẹ which was then the capital of the Yoruba country.

The Alake and the Ọwa of Ilesa are said to be nearly related to the ALÂFIN ; the former was said to be of the same mother with one of the earliest Alâfins. This woman was called Ẹjọ who afterwards took up her abode with her youngest son until her death : hence the common saying " Ẹjọ ku Ake " Ẹjọ[2] died at Ake.

The Ọwa of the Ijẹsas claimed to be one of the younger brothers, but his pedigree cannot now be traced ; the term " brother " being a very elastic one in Yoruba and may be applied to any relative far or near, and even to a trusty servant or to one adopted

---

[1] The reason assigned for this was that he was "born in the purple," that is to say born after the father had become King. This was at one time the prevailing custom for the "Aremo Oyè," i.e., the first born from the throne, to succeed the father.

[2] Ẹjọ means a palaver. The phrase then means a case decided at Ake is final.

into the family.[1] In olden times when there was universal peace throughout the country, before the commencement of the destructive intertribal wars which broke up the unity of the kingdom and created the tribal independence, this relationship was acknowledged by the Qwa paying a yearly tribute of a few heads of cowries, mats and some products of his forests to the ALÂFIN, while the latter sent him presents of tobes and vests, and other superior articles well worthy of him as an elder brother.

That the ALÂFIN, the Alake, and the Qwa were children or grandchildren of Qrañyan seems probable from the fact that to this day none of them is considered properly installed until the sword of state brought from Ile Ife where Qrañyan was buried is placed in his hands.

Qrañyan was a nickname of the prince his proper name being Qdede. He was a man of great physical powers. He first obtained renown as a mighty hunter ; and in process of time he also became, like Nimrod, a mighty conqueror.

The expedition against Mecca.—When Qrañyan was sufficiently strong, he set off for an expedition against " Mecca " to which he summoned his brothers, to avenge the death of their great-grandfather, and the expulsion of his party from that city. He left Adimu one of his father's trusty servants in charge of the royal treasures and the charms, with a strict injunction to observe the customary worship of the national gods IDI and ORISA OSI.

This is an office of the greatest importance pertaining to the King himself ` but how slaves or high servants are often entrusted with the duties of the master himself is well-known in this country as we shall see in the course of this history.

It is said that the route by which they came from " Mecca " and which occupied 90 days, was by this time rendered impassable owing to an army of black ants blocking up the path, and hence, Qrañyan was obliged to take another route which led through the Nupe or Tapa Country. All his brothers but the eldest joined him, but at Igangan they quarrelled over a pot of beer and dispersed refusing to follow his lead. The eldest brother calculating the distance through the Tapa country lost courage and went eastward promising to make his attack from that quarter should his brother Qrañyan be successful in the West.[2] Qrañyan pushed on until he found himself on the banks of the River Niger.

The Tapas are said to have opposed his crossing the river, and as he could not force his way through, he was obliged to remain for a while near the banks, and afterwards resolved to retrace his

---

[1] A fuller account will be found under "The origin of the Ijesas."
[2] The geography of our historians may be excused.—ED.

steps. To return, however, to Ile Ifẹ was too humiliating to be
thought of, and hence he consulted the King of Ibariba near whose
terrıtory he was then encamping as to where he should make his
residence. Tradition has it, that the King of Ibariba made a
charm and fixed it on a boa constrictor and advised Ọrañyan to
follow the track of the boa and wherever it remained for 7 days
and then disappeared, there he was to build a town. Ọrañyan
and his army followed his directions and went after the boa up to
the foot of a hill called AJAKA where the reptile remained 7 days,
and then disappeared. According to instructions Ọrañyan halted
there, and built a town called ỌYỌ AJAKA. This was the
ancient city of Ọyọ marked in ancient maps as Eyeo or Katunga
(the latter being the Hausa term for Ọyọ) capital of Yarriba (see
Webster's pronouncing Gazetteer). This was the Eyeo visited
by the English explorers Clapperton and the Landers.

Ọrañyan remained and prospered in the new home, his decendants
spread East, West, and South-west ; they had a free communication with Ile Ifẹ, and the King often sent to Adimu for whatever
was required by him out of the royal treasures for the new city.

In process of time Adimu made himself great because he was
not only the worshipper of the national deities, but also the
custodian and dispenser of the King's treasures, and he was
commonly designated " Adimu Ọlà " i.e. Adimu of the treasures,
or Adimu là i.e. Adimu is become wealthy.

But this Adimu who became of so much consequence from his
performing royal functions was originally the son of a woman
condemned to death, but being found at the time of execution
to be in the way of becoming a mother she was temporarily
reprieved, until the child was born. This child at its birth was
dedicated to the perpetual service of the gods, especially the
god Ọbatala, to which his mother was to have been sacrificed.
He was said to be honest, faithful and devoted to the King as to
his own father, and therefore he was loved and trusted.

When Adimu was announced to the Kings and Princes all
around as the person appointed by the King to take charge of
the treasures, and to worship the national deities during his
absence, it was generally asked " And who is this Adimu ? The
answer comes " Ọmọ Oluwọ̀ ni " the son of a sacrificial victim :
this is contracted to Ọwọ̀ni (Oluwọ being the term for a sacrificial
victim). So in subsequent years when the seat of government
was removed permanently to Ọyọ but not the National Deities,
Adimu became supreme at Ile Ifẹ and his successors to this day
have been termed the Oloriṣas i.e. high priests or fetish worshippers
to the King, and people of the whole Yoruba nation. The name

Adimu has since been adopted as the agnomen, and the term Ọwọni as the title of the " Kings " or more properly the high priests of Ifẹ to this day, the duties of the office being not local or tribal, but national.

According to another account, after the death of Ọkànbi, Ọrañyan having succeeded and assumed the command emigrated to Okò where he reigned and where he died, and the seat of government was removed thence in the reign of Sango to Ọyọkoro, i.e., the aforesaid ancient City of Ọyọ.

Ọrañyan may have actually died at Okò, but his grave with an obelisk over it is certainly shown at Ile Ifẹ to this day. It is a custom among the Yorubas—a custom observed to this day—to pare the nails and shave the head of any one who dies at a considerable distance from the place where they would have him buried. These relics are taken to the place of interment, and there decently buried, the funeral obsequies being scrupulously observed as if the corpse itself were buried there. Hence although (as we have on probable grounds assumed) Ọrañyan may have died at Oko, and the art of embalming lost or unknown, his relics could thus have been taken to Ile Ifẹ where to this day he is supposed to have been buried. A more romantic account of his death, however, will be given in Part II of this history.

As the Yorubas worship the dead, and have the belief that prayers offered at the grave of deceased ancestors are potent to procure temporal blessings, all succeeding Yoruba Kings on their accession and before coronation are expected to send to perform acts of worship at the grave of Oduduwa and to receive the benediction of the priest. The sword of justice known as IDA ỌRANYAN (Ọranyan's sword) is to be brought from Ile Ifẹ and ceremoniously placed in their hands ; without this being done, the King has no authority whatever to order an execution. Ọrañyan's descendants in process of time were divided into four distinct families, known by their distinctive dialects, and forming the four provinces of Yoruba proper viz. the Ẹkun Ọtun, Ẹkun Osì, Ibọlọ and Epo provinces. The Ẹkun Ọtun and Ẹkun Osì or right and left, i.e., Eastern and Western provinces are the towns lying to the East and West of the City of Ọyọ.

1. The Ẹkun Ọtun or Western province included all the towns along the right bank of the River Ogùn down to Ibẹrẹ kodo, Igana being the chief town. The other important towns are :—Ṣàki, Oke'ho, Isẹyin, Iwawun, Eruwa, Iberekòdo, etc. In this province two distinct dialects are spoken ; the people inhabiting the outermost borders are known as Ibarapas and are distinguished by a nasal twang in their speech.

2. The Ẹkun Osì or Metropolitan province comprised all the towns east of Ọyọ, including Kihisi and Igboho in the north, Ikoyi being the chief town. Other important towns are, Ilọrin Irawọ, Iwere, Ogbomọsọ etc. including the Igbônas in the utmost limit eastwards, and the Igbọn-nas as far as Ọrọ̀.

The Igbônas are distinguished by a peculiar dialect of their own. The Ẹkun Osi Ọyọs are regarded as speaking the purest Yoruba. The ancient city of Ọyọ also lies in this province.

3. The Ibọlọ province lies to the south-east of the Ẹkun Osì towns as far down as Ẹde, Irẹsa being the chief town. The other important towns are Ọfa (?) Ọyan, Okuku, Ikirun, Osogbo, Ido, Ilobu, Ejigbo, Ẹde.

4. The Epos are the towns lying to the South and South-west of Ọyọ the chief town of which is Idodẹ. Other important towns in this division are: Masifa, Ifẹ odan, Arà. Iwo, Ilọra, Akinmọirin Fiditi, Awẹ, Ago Ọja.

They are called Epos (i.e. weeds) because they were then in the remotest part of the kingdom, rude and uncouth in manners, very deceitful, and far from being as loyal as the other tribes. The Owus were usually reckoned amongst them, but they are rather a distinct tribe of Yoruba although now domiciled amongst the Ẹgbas.

Great changes have been effected in these divisions by means of the revolutionary wars that altered the face of the country about the early part of the XIXth century.

In the Ẹkun Ọtun district Igana has lost its importance and its place taken by Iseyin.

In the Ẹkun Osi, Ikoyi the chief town has been destroyed by Ilọrin, and Ilọrin itself brought under foreign allegiance by the Fulanis. The city of Ọyọ now lies in ruins, its name and position being transferred to Ago Ọja in the Epo district. In the Ibọlọ district Irẹsa has ceased to exist being absorbed by Ilọrin and its place taken by Ọfa, which in its turn was partially destroyed by the Ilọrins in 1887 with several other towns in this district. Modakẹkẹ a large and growing town, peopled by Ọyọs of the Ẹkun Osi, has sprung up in the Ifẹ district just beyond the borders of the Ibọlọs.

Owu has been destroyed never more to be rebuilt.

The Epo district now includes Ibadan, Ijaye and other towns formerly belonging to the Gbaguras. Idodẹ has ceased to be the chief town, that position now properly belongs to Iwo, being a royal city. But Ibadan which was originally an Ẹgba village then the military station of the confederate army which destroyed the city of Owu and the Ẹgba villages, and afterwards a settled Ọyọ town, has by means of its military force assumed the lead not only

C

over the Epo district, but also over a large area of the country as well. It has a mixed population including every tribe of the Yorubas.

Ijaye formerly an Ẹgba town became peopled by Ọyọs chiefly from the Ẹkun Osi (Ikoyi) districts.

All these including hundreds of important towns within the area are peopled by Yorubas proper or Ọyọs as they are generally called, and constitute the more important portion of Yoruba proper.

The Ẹgbas, who were for the most part off-shoots of these, and formerly living in hamlets and villages independently of one another have through the exigencies of these wars collected themselves from 153 hamlets or " townships " to form one town, Abẹokuta. A further account of this will be given in its place. All these are reckoned as descendants of Ọrañyan.

By the advent also of the white men from the coast, the centre of light and civilization has removed to the south, so that the Epos may soon cease to be the " weeds " of the country, as they may receive the inspiration of civilization from the south instead of from the north as hitherto.

CHAPTER II

THE ORIGIN OF THE TRIBES

ALL the various tribes of the Yoruba nation trace their origin from Oduduwa and the city Ile Ife. In fact Ile Ife is fabled as the spot where God created man, white and black, and from whence they dispersed all over the earth. We have seen in the previous chapter which are the principal tribes that sprang from Oduduwa's seven grandchildren, viz. : The Yorubas proper from Oranyan, the Benins, Ilas, Owus, Ketus, Sabes, and the Popos. Some of the other tribes were offshoots of one or other of these, as we shall see further on. Some authentic tradition will be given relative to the formation of some of them.

An important fact which must also be borne in mind is, that the country was not altogether unpeopled when Oduduwa and his party entered it from the East ; the probability is, that the aboriginal inhabitants were conquered and absorbed, at least at the central if not at the remote provinces of the Yoruba kingdom.

In ancient patriarchal times, the king of a country was regarded as the father or progenitor of his people. This view will to some extent explain what would otherwise appear to be a marvellous (if not impossible) instance of fecundity in any one king, e.g., Oranyan peopling so vast a region as that attributed to him, in so short a time—the more warlike the king, the more extensive his dominion, and the more numerous, it would seem, his progeny.

In fact we may almost take it as proved that as Oranyan and his army, as well as his brothers', pushed on their conquests in every direction, the princes and the war-lords were stationed in various parts to hold the country, and from them sprang the many provincial kings of various ranks and grades now existing.

This also accounts for the tradition that the Yoruba sway once extended as far as Ashanti and included the Gâs of Accra, for the Gâs say that their ancestors came from Ile Ife; and the constitution of the Gâ language is said to be more like Yoruba than like Fanti, the language of the Gold Coast, and the area in which that language is spoken is strictly limited. And, certainly, until comparatively recent times the Popos and Dahomians paid tribute regularly to Oyo as their feudal head ; it is certain, therefore, that the generals and war-lords of Oranyan pushed on far beyond the limits of the Yoruba country as now known, and although in places remote from

15

the centre, as the Benins and Sekiris in the east and the Popos, Dahomians and Gâs in the west, the Yoruba language is not spoken, yet the knowledge of it exists among the ruling chiefs and the priestly caste who still maintain their connection with Ile Ifẹ, the place of their common origin. This view will also to some extent explain the mutual understanding and bond of sympathy existing between the Ifẹs, Ekitis, and allied families as remnants of the largely diluted aboriginal elements still having many things in common, and their natural antipathy—more or less—to the Ọyọs or Yorubas Proper.

It is also worthy of remark that all the *principal* rulers of the country, to show the validity of their claims, must trace their relationship by one way or another to the ALÂFIN OF ỌYỌ, who is the direct descendant of Ọrañyan, son and successor of Oduduwa, the founder ; which simply implies that the children and offspring of the conqueror are the chief rulers over the different parts of the conquered territories.

YORUBA PROPER

Ọrañyan was already distinguished as a brave and war-like prince during his father's lifetime, and he probably owed his succession to this fact, as was usual in those stormy times. On his accession to the throne, when he set out from Ile Ifẹ on his famous expedition to " Mecca " to avenge the death of his great grandfather, he was certainly accompanied ·by his conquering hordes ; and if we trace his route from Ile Ifẹ northwards to the banks of the Niger, whence he turned westward to the borders of the Baribas, and then to the ancient Ọyọ (Eyeo) which he founded, and where he settled, and from whence he spread southwards towards the coast, we shall see that the people embraced in this vast region, viz., with the Ifẹs in the east, the Niger on the north, the Baribas on the west as well as the Dahomians, and the Egbados on the south, are those known as the Yorubas Proper, or as they are generally termed by the other tribes the Ọyọs, and are the so-called descendants of Ọrañyan, and the cream of his conquering army. These then constitute Yorubas Proper.

We have stated in a previous chapter how they are divided into four distinct provinces, but there has always been among them a bond of sympathy and union, apart from what they have in common with the other tribes. They have always retained their loyalty—more or less—to the successors of Ọrañyan, their common father, even when the revolutionary wars left the country no longer united under one head as in the days of Sango down to those of Abiọdun

THE EGBAS

The Egbas are a small offshoot of the Yorubas Proper, who occupy the south-eastern districts of that province. They originally occupied the area bounded by certain imaginary lines drawn, say, from Ijaye to meet the Ogun River at Olokemeji, and along it to its mouth, and another from the same point via Ibadan to the west of Jẹbu Rẹmọ down to the coast. They lived in hamlets and villages for the most part independently of one another, and never under one rule. All the principal families of the Egbas trace their origin from Ọyọ, hence the common saying " Egbas who have not their root in Ọyọ are slaves," i.e., belong to the conquered aboriginal population. Most of the chiefs sprang from the Esọs of Ọyọ. It would seem then that during the wars of conquest, a number of these warlike Esọs, under the leadership of the King's half-brother, was detached from the main army, carrying their arms to those regions where they subsequently settled, in the immediate neighbourhood of the Owus. Abẹokuta, as we now know it, of course had no existence then. Each of what is now called the " townships " was a separate village or hamlet with its own chief ; they were loosely grouped into three divisions, but rather independent of one another, but all acknowledging the King's brother (the Alake) as their PRIMUS. They were :

1. Egba Agbẹyin. These were the Egbas proper, and nearest the Ijẹbu Rẹmọs. The principal towns were : Ake, the chief town, Ijeun, Kemta, Iporo, Igbore, etc.

2. Egba Oke Ọna, i.e., those situated near the banks of the River Odo Ọnà. Ọkò the chief town, Ikereku, Ikija, Idomapa, Odo, Podo, etc. Their chief is called the Ọsilẹ.

3. Egba Agura or Gbagura : these were situated near the Ọyọ districts, and indeed they contain genuine Ọyọs in large numbers, and generally they partake of their characteristics largely, hence they are nick-named " Ọyọs among Egbas." The principal towns were : Agura the chief, Ilugun, Ibadan, Ifaye, Ika, Ọjọ, Ilawọ, etc.

The Egbas were on the whole few in number, and occupied a limited territory ; this can very well be proved by the fact, that after a period of more than half a century, they have been compelled by stress of circumstances to live together within one wall, and in spite of large accessions from other tribes, they still form but a single large town. Situated, as they were then, far from the centre of life and activity, they were little thought of. They had no separate king because all the principal chiefs and distinguished personages were office bearers of the ALÀFIN, hence

the common saying, " Ẹgba kò l'olu, gbogbo nwọn ni nṣe bi Ọba ":
(Ẹgbas have no King, they are all of them like masters) " Olu wà'
l'Ọyọ " (The King is at Ọyọ). It may be noted, that every child
born to a reigning Alake must have an Ọyọ facial mark ; and that
is so to this day. In early times the Alake ranks among the
junior members of the Royal Family ; for that reason there has
never been a distinct royal family among the Ẹgbas. The chief
rulers in each division were usually elected (by divination) from
any one of the 153 townships ; an Ikija man for instance has been
" king " of Itẹsi, an Ijeun man an Alake, etc., as we shall see in the
Appendix. In this respect also the Gbaguras differ from the
others.

In later times, at Abẹokuta, one Jibọdẹ, a wealthy trader and
traveller, who vainly endeavoured to obtain the Primacy of Ake,
left children and grandchildren who eventually attained the
coveted position, which was a singular instance of more than one
member of a family becoming an Alake,[1] but then they were
all born in different townships.

The Ọsilẹ is said to be an unfortunate title because, more than
any of the other divisions, the Oke Ọna people were more prone to
slaughter human victims ; everytime the Ọsilẹ entered the Ogboni
house, he must walk on the blood of a male victim, and when he
comes out on that of a female ! Also that Ọsilẹs never die a natural
death ; when their excesses became unbearable they were usually
stoned to death ; hence the appellation of their chief town, " Ọkò "
—i.e., a pelting stone. For that reason the Ẹgbas were reluctant
to resuscitate the title at Abẹokuta until Governor McCallum
of Lagos in 1897 on the occasion of the Queen's Diamond Jubilee
ordered the Ẹgbas and others to reorganise their government, and
fill up vacant titles.

Since the destruction of the City of Owu (as we shall see below)
and the unification of the Egba villages, the Owus have domiciled
amongst them. Hence the so-called FOUR UNITED KINGS OF THE
ẸGBAS : although Owu is not Ẹgba.

THE IJẸBUS

The origin of the Ijẹbus has been variously given ; one account
makes them spring from the victims offered in sacrifice by the
King of Benin to the god of the ocean, hence the term Ijẹbu
from Ijẹ-ibu, i.e., the food of the deep. The Ijẹbus themselves

---

[1]The case of Gbadebo, son of Okukenu, occurred subsequently to
the establishment of the British Protectorate.

claim to have descended from Ọba-nita, as they say of themselves, "Ogetiele, ẹru Ọbanita," i.e., Ogetiele,[1] servants of Ọbanita.

But who was this Ọba-nita ? Tradition says he also was a victim of sacrifice by the Olowu or King of Owu. It was said that the Olowu offered in sacrifice a human being where two roads cross ; this was termed " Ẹbọ-ni-ita," a sacrifice on the highway, the victim being mangled and left for dead ; he, however, revived at night, and crawled away into the forest, where he subsequently recovered and survived. He lived on fruits, on the chase, and then did a bit of farming, With an access of population, being the oldest man met in those parts, he was regarded as the father, and subsequent generations call him their ancestor, and so the Ijẹbu tribe was formed, and the term " Ẹbọnita " (a sacrifice on the highway) was converted to " Ọbanita " (a king on the high-way). There was really nobody of that name. A forest is still shown near the village of Ahà where he is annually worshipped, from whence he was supposed to have ascended into heaven.

It is rather curious that both accounts should have made them descended from victims of human sacrifices. This latter account is reconcilable with the former, which says they are " the food of the deep," for the population of which Ẹbọnita was the head may have been largely augmented by the victims of the ocean so as to give the name Ijẹ-ibu to the whole of them.

There are also other important facts and curious coincidences connected with the Ijẹbus which have strong bearings on this tradition of their origin.

1. Of all the Yoruba tribes, with the exception of the Ifẹs they were the most addicted to human sacrifices, which they practised up to 1892 when the country was conquered by the English. The victim also usually offered to " Ọbanita " annually was always a human being, but this was never killed ; he was, however, always acted upon in some way or other unknown (by magic arts) that he always became demented, and left to wander about sheepishly in the Aha Forest, until he perished there. This is, no doubt, due to the fact that the ancestor " Ẹbọnita " himself, when a victim, was not killed outright.

2. They were, before the conquest, the most exclusive and inhospitable of the whole of the tribes. Very few, if any, outsiders were ever known to have walked through the country with impunity under any circumstance whatever ; not a few of those who attempted to do so were never seen nor heard of any more !

---

[1] An untranslatable word, an onomatopœic expression for whatever is immense and magnificent.

Commercial transactions with outsiders were carried on in the frontier or in the borders of neighbouring towns.

3. And if the latter account of their origin from the Owu victim be the correct one, it is very singular indeed that it was mainly due to the Ijẹbus with their firearms that the Owus owed their fall and complete annihilation as an independent state to this day. A full account of this will be given in due course.

The King of the Ijẹbus is known as the Awujalẹ. His origin was thus given by authentic tradition, the event with which it is connected having occurred within authentic history :

There were formerly two important towns called Owu Ipole and Isẹyin Odò in a district between the Owus and Ifẹs ; they were settlements from the city of Owu and Isẹyin respectively. A quarrel once arose between them on the matter of boundaries, and the dispute having been carried on for many years, developed into an open fight, and both the Olowu and the Ọwọni of Ifẹ (both being interested parties) were unable to put an end to the strife. Messengers were now sent to the King at Ọyọ who sent out a special Ilari and a large number of attendants to put an end to the strife. The person of an Ilari being inviolable, he cáme and settled down between the two contending parties, in the midst of the disputed plot, and thus compelled them to keep the peace. The Ilari was named " Agbejailẹ or Alajâilẹ " (an arbiter of landed dispute). This term was subsequently softened down to Awùjale.[1] This event occurred during the reign of King JAYIN.

As it was customary to pay royal honours to the King's messengers out of courtesy, this Ilari was accorded royal honours in due form, and he remained there permanently and became the King of that region over the Ijẹbus who up to that time had no tribal " king " of their own and rather held themselves aloof from their neighbours. Subsequently he removed to Ode. The Awujalẹ ranks after the Ọyọ provincial kings such as the Onikoyi, Ọlafa, Arẹsa, Asẹyin.

ORIGIN OF THE IJẸSAS AND EKITIS

Two accounts are given of the origin of the Ijẹsas ; both may practically be regarded as in the main correct, so far as they are not really contradictory ; for it would appear that the Ijẹsas of the present day are not the same people or, rather, not the descendants of the aboriginal inhabitants of that province.

The first account relates to the earliest period when the Yorubas have just entered into, and subdued, the country, and the ALÂFINS

[1]An Ilari title at Ọyọ to this day.

then resided at Ile Ifẹ, i.e., prior to the reign of Sango. Human
sacrifices were common in those days, and in order to have victims
ready to hand, it is said that a number of slaves were purchased
and located in the district of Ibokun ; there they were tended as
cattle, under the care of Ọwajù, and from them selections were
made from time to time for sacrificial purposes ; hence the term
Ijẹsa from Ijẹ Orisa (the food of the gods). They are described as
stumpy, muscular, and sheepish-looking, with a marked want
of intelligence : they never offered any resistance to this system,
hence the saying "Ijẹsa Ọmọ Owajù ti ifẹ ọpọ iyà " (Ijẹsas children
of Ọwaju, subject to much sufferings). There is also a legend
that when the nations began to disperse from Ile Ifẹ and members of
the Royal Family were appointed kings and rulers in divers places,
a young and brave scion of the house was appointed the first
Ọwa or king over the Ijẹsas, but that he returned to the ALÂFIN
and complained that his territory was too small, and his subjects
few, the sire thereupon ordered a large bundle of sticks to be
brought to him, and these sticks he converted into human beings
for the Ọwa, in order to increase the number of his subjects. Hence
to this day the Ijẹsas are often termed by their neighbours " Ọmọ
igi " (offspring of sticks !)

This, of course, is a pure myth invented by their more wily
neighbours to account for the notorious characteristics of the Ijẹsas
generally, who are as proverbially deficient in wit as they are
remarkably distinguished for brute strength.

But one fact holds good down even to our days, viz., that up
to the recent total abolition of human sacrifice by the British
Government (1893) the Ifẹs, who, far more than any other, were
addicted to the practice, always preferred for the purpose to have
an Ijẹsa victim to any other ; such sacrifices were considered more
acceptable, the victims being the " food of the gods."

This preference was the cause of more than one threatened rupture
between the Ifẹs and their Ijẹsa allies during the recent 16 years'
war, and would certainly have developed into open fights, but
for the Ibadan army vis-à-vis threatening them both.

The other account relates chiefly to the present day Ijẹsas of
Ilẹsa (the home of the gods) the chief town. According to this
account, they hailed from the Ekitis ; or as some would more
correctly have it, they were the Ijẹsas from the neighbourhood of
Ibokun who first migrated to Ipọle near Ondo, and thence back
to Ilẹsa. It appears that a custom then prevailed of going out
hunting for their king three months in the year, and on one such
occasion they found game so plentiful in the neighbourhood of
Ilẹsa, the climate very agreeable, the country well-watered, and

the Ijẹṣas there extremely simple, peaceful, and unwarlike (probably the remnants and descendants of the old sacrificial victims) whilst at home they endured much oppression from their Ọwa, that they there and then conceived and carried out the idea of settling on the spot at once, making it their home, and of reducing into subjection the aboriginal inhabitants.

These objects were easily enough accomplished ; but they spared the principal chief, a kindly old gentleman who had an extensive garden plantation. He was called " Ọba Ila," i.e., Okra king, from his Okra plantation, and he was placed next in rank to the chief of the marauders. That nickname is continued to the present time as a title Ọba'la[1] and is conferred on the most distinguished chief after the Ọwa of Ileṣa. It would appear then that although the term Ijẹṣa is retained by the people of that district, and those who are ignorant of the origin of the term take some pride in it, yet it is evident that the present inhabitants are not all of them the descendants of the aboriginal settlers, the " food of the gods," but are largely from the Ekitis by admixture ; the pure type Ijẹṣas are now and again met with at Ileṣa and neighbourhood.

This fact is further shown by the want of homogeneity amongst the principal chiefs of Ileṣa at the present day, for when the town was growing, the settlers did cast about for help ; they sought for wiser heads to assist them in the building up and the management of their country, e.g., from the Ọyọs or Yorubas Proper they had the Ọdọle from Irèhé, the Esawẹ from Ọra, the Saloro from Ọyọ (the ancient city), and the Sorundi also from the same city—all these came with a large number of followers ; from the Ondos, the 'Loro, and the Salosi from Ijama in the Ondo district ; from the Ekitis, the Arapatẹ from Ara, the Lejọka from Itaje ; and lastly, the Ogboni from the white cap chiefs of Lagos, the only one privileged to have on his headgear in the presence of the Ọwa. The Ọwa himself is as we have seen, a junior member of the royal house of Ọyọ.

It is also said that when the town of Ileṣa was to be laid out a special messenger was sent to the ALÂFIN to ask for the help of one of the princes to lay out the town on the same plan as the ancient city of Ọyọ. That prince ruled for some years at Ileṣa.

THE EKITIS

The Ekitis are among the aboriginal elements of the country absorbed by the invaders from the East. The term Ekiti denotes a Mound, and is derived from the rugged mountainous feature of

---

[1]Often miscalled Ọbanla by young Ijẹṣas outside Ileṣa.

the country. It is an extensive province and well watered, including several tribes and families right on to the border of the Niger, eastward. They hold themselves quite distinct from the Ijesas, especially in political affairs. The Ekiti country is divided into 16 districts, each with its own Owa or King (Owa being a generic term amongst them) of which four are supreme, viz. :—

1.	The Òwòre of Òtun	3.	The Elewi of Adó
2.	The Ajero of Ijero	4.	The Elekòle of Ikole

The following are the minor Ekiti kings :—

5.	Alara of Ara	11.	Oloja Oke of Igbo Odo
6.	Alâye of Efon Ahaye	12.	Oloye of Oye
7.	Ajanpanda of Akure	13.	Olomuwo of Omuwo
8.	Alagotun of Ogotun	14.	Onirè of Irè
9.	Olojudo of Ido	15.	Arinjale of Isè
10.	Ata of Aiyede	16.	Onitaji of Itaji

The Orangun of Ila is sometimes classed among them, but he is only Ekíti in sympathy, being of a different family.

An Ijesa account of the Owa ot Ilesa and some of the principal Ekiti kings :

The Olofin (? Alâfin) king of Ife had several children, grandchildren, and great grandchildren ; amongst them were, the king of Ado or Benin, the King of Oyo, the Osomowe of Ondo (from a daughter), the Alara of Ará, the Ajèro of Ijero, the Alaye of Efon, the Owore of Òtun, the Orangun of Ila, the Aregbajo of Igbajo, the Owa Ajaka of Ilesa. When the Olofin became blind from old age he was much depressed in mind from this cause ; efforts were put forth to effect his cure, all of which proved fruitless, when a certain man came forward and prescribed for him a sure remedy which among other ingredients contained salt water. He put the case before his children, but none made any effort to procure some for him save his youngest grandson. This was a very brave and warlike prince who bore the title of *Esinkin* amongst the King's household warriors, a title much allied to that of the *Kakanfo*, He was surnamed *Ajaka*, i.e., one who fights everywhere, (on account of his proclivities) being fond of adventures. He volunteered to go and fetch some wherever procurable.

Having been away for many years and not heard of, the aged sire and every one else despaired of his ever coming back ; so the King divided his property amongst the remaining grown-up children. Although the Alado (king of Benin) was the eldest yet the Oloyo was the most beloved, and to him he gave the land, and told him to scour it all over, and settle nowhere till he came to a slippery place, and there make his abode ; hence the term Ọyọ (slippery) and hence Ọyọs are such slippery customers !

After they had all gone and settled in their respective localities, all unexpectedly, the young adventurer turned up with water from the sea ! The monarch made use of it as *per* prescription and regained his sight ! Hence the Ijẹsas who subsequently became his subjects are sometimes termed " Ọmọ Obokun," children of the brine procurer.

Having distributed all his property he had nothing left for Ajaka he therefore gave him a sword lying by his side with leave to attack any of his brothers, especially the Alará or Aladó, and possess himself of their wealth, but should he fail, to retire back to him ; hence the appellation " Ọwa Ajaka Onida ráharàha " (Ọwa the ubiquitous fighter, a man with a devastating sword).

The Ọwa Ajaka settled a little way from his grandfather, and on one occasion he paid him a visit, and found him sitting alone with his crown on his head and—out of-sheer wantonness—he cut off some of the fringes with his sword. The old man was enraged by this act, and swore that he would never wear a crown with fringes on.[1]

The Aregbajọ was one of those who had a crown given to him, but the Ọwa Ajaka, paying him a visit on one occasion, saw it, and took it away, and never returned it : hence the kings of Igbajọ never wear a crown to this day.

The Ọwa also attacked the Olojudo and defeated him, and took possession of his crown ; but he never put it on. On every public occasion however, it used to be carried before him. This continued to be the case until all the tribes became independent.

The Ọwa's mother, when married as a young bride, was placed under the care of the mother of the Ọlọyọ, hence the ALÂFIN of Ọyọ often regarded the Ọwa as his own son.

The Ọrangun of Ila, and the Alará of Ará were his brothers of the same mother.

The Ọwọ̀ni of Ifẹ was not a son of the Ọlọfin, but the son of a female slave of his whom he offered in sacrifice. The Ọlọfin kept the boy always by him, and when he sent away his sons, this little boy took great care of him and managed his household affairs well until his death : hence the Ọlọyọ on succeeding the father authorised the boy to have charge of the palace and the city, and he sent to notify his brothers of this appointment. So whenever it was asked who was in charge of the house the answer invariably was

---

[1] Only those with fringes on are really crowns.

" Ọmọ Oluwọ̀ ni " (It is the son of the sacrificial victim). This has been contracted to the term Ọwọ̀ni.

The Ọwa and his brothers used to pay the ALÂFIN annual visits, with presents of firewood, fine locally-made mats, kola nuts and bitter kolas ; the Owòrè of Ọtun with sweet water from a cool spring at Ọtun—this water the ALÂFIN first spills on the ground as a libation before performing any ceremonies. The other Ekiti Kings used also to take with them suitable presents as each could afford, and bring away lavish presents from their elder brother.

This Ajaka subsequently became the Ọwa of the Ijẹsas.

THE ONDOS

The custom of killing twins prevailed all over the country in early times ; it has died out all over the greater part of it so long ago, that no one can say precisely when or by whom a stop was put to it. But it happened once upon a time when the practice still prevailed that one of the wives of the ALÂFIN (King Ajaka) gave birth to twins, and the King was loth to destroy them, he thereupon gave orders that they should be removed—with the mother—to a remote part of the kingdom and there to remain and be regarded as dead.

So she left with a large number of friends and retinue to the site of the present Ode Ondo, then sparsely peopled by a tribe named Idoko, and there settled, hence the term " Ondo," signifying the " Settlers." The people of the district knowing who the strangers were, yielded them ready obedience, and the strangers became rulers of the district.

Probably it was from this time infanticide received its death blow—in Yoruba Proper at least. It is said to linger still at Akụre and the adjacent regions, but as a rule, in ancient times, whatever the custom set or discountenanced at the Metropolis, the effect thereof was rapidly felt all over the country.

The Ondos are sometimes classed among the Ekitis but that is hardly correct ; although lying at the border of the Ekitis, they are really a mixture of Ọyọs and Idokos, and their sympathy is with all.

CHAPTER III

RELIGION

THE Yorubas originally were entirely pagans. Mohammedanism which many now profess was introduced only since the close of the eighteenth century. They, however, believe in the existence of an ALMIGHTY GOD, him they term QLQRUN, i.e., LORD of HEAVEN.

They acknowledge Him, Maker of heaven and earth, but too exalted to concern Himself directly with men and their affairs, hence they admit the existence of many gods as intermediaries, and these they term Orisas.

We may note here that the term Qlorun is applied to GOD alone and is never used in the plural to denote Orisas. Kings and the great ones on earth may sometimes be termed Orisas (gods) by way of eulogy, we are also familiar with the common expression, " Oyinbo ekeji Orisa " i.e., white men are next to the gods (i.e in their powers); but the term Qlorun is reserved for the GREAT GOD alone.

They also believe in a future state, hence the worship of the dead, and invocation of spirits as observed in the Egũgun festival, a festival in which masked individuals personate dead relatives.

They have a belief also in a future judgment as may be inferred from the following adage, " Ohungbogbo ti a se l'aiye, li a o de idena Qrun ka " (Whatever we do on earth we shall give an account thereof at the portals of heaven).

They also believe in the doctrine of metempsychosis, or transmigration of souls, hence they affirm that after a period of time, deceased parents are born again into the family of their surviving children. It is from this notion that some children are named " Babatunde," i.e., father comes again. " Yetunde," i.e., mother comes again.

OBJECTS OF WORSHIP

1. *The Kori.*—Originally, the Kori was the only object of worship. It consists of the hard shells of the palm nut strung into beads, and made to hang from the neck to the knees. In modern times it is no longer regarded as an object of worship by adults, but little children go about with it to the market places begging for alms. The object of worship is then worn by one of their number, who goes before, his companions following behind him, shouting the

praises of the ancient god Kori.   In this way they parade the
market places, and sellers before whom they halt to sing, make
them presents of money (cowries) or whatever they may happen to
be selling, usually articles of food.   Thus the little children
perpetuate the memory and worship of this deity, hence the ditty :

> " Iba ma si ewe, Kori a ku o."
> (But for little children Kori had perished).

In later times heroes are venerated and deified, of these Sango,
Oya, Orisa Oko, may be mentioned as the chief.   The origin of
their worship will be noted hereafter.

2. *Orisala.*—To Orisala are ascribed creative powers.   He is
regarded as a co-worker with Olorun.   Man is supposed to have
been made by God in a lump, and shaped as he is by Orisala.   Its
votaries are distinguished by white beads worn round the neck,
and by their using only white dresses.   They are forbidden the
use of palm wine.   Sacrifices offered by them are not to be salted.
Albinoes, dwarfs, the lame, hunchbacks, and all deformed persons
generally are regarded as sacred to this god ; hence they are
designated " Eni Orisa " (belonging to the god), being regarded as
specially made so by him.

Orisala is the common name of the god known and worshipped
by different townships under different appellations, e.g., it is
called Orisa Oluofin at Iwòfin ; Orisàkò at Okò ; Orisakirè at Ikire ;
Orisagiyan at Ejigbo ; Orisaeguin at Eguin ; Orisarowu at Owu
Orisajaye at Ijaye ; and Obatala at Obà.

3. *Ori.*—The Ori (head) is the universal household deity
worshipped by both sexes as the god of fate.   It is believed that
good or ill fortune attends one, according to the will or decree of
this god ; and hence it is propitiated in order that good luck might
be the share of its votary.   The representing image is 41 cowries
strung together in the shape of a crown.   This is secreted in a
large coffer, the lid of which is of the same form and material.
It is called " Ile Ori " (Ori's house), and in size is as large as the owner
can afford to make it.   Some usually contain as much as 6 heads
(12,000) of cowries, and the manufacturer who is generally a worker
in leather receives as his pay the same amount of cowries as is
used in the article manufactured.

As the Kori is the children's god so the Ori is exclusively
worshipped by the adults.   After the death of its owner, the image
of Ori with the coffer is destroyed, and the cowries spent.

4. *Ogun.*—This is the god of war, and all instruments made of
iron are consecrated to it, hence Ogun is the blacksmiths' god.
The representing image is the silk cotton tree specially planted,

beneath which is placed a piece of granite on which palm oil is poured and the blood of slain animals—generally a dog.

5. *Esu* or *Elegbara*.—Satan, the Evil One, the author of all evil is often and specially propitiated. Offerings are made to it. The representing image is a rough lateritic stone upon which libations of palm oil are poured. It is superstitiously believed that the vengeance of this god could be successfully invoked upon an offender by the name of the person being called before the image while nut oil is being poured on it. The image of a man, with a horn on its head curving backwards, carved in wood and ornamented with cowries, is often carried by its devotees to beg with on public highways. Passers-by who are so disposed may give each a cowry or two, or handfuls of corn, beans, or any product of the field at hand, as he or she may choose. This curved headed figure is called " Ǫgǫ Elegbara "—the devil's club.

6. *Sǫpǫna* or the small pox is generally believed to be one of the demons by which this lower world is infested, and has its special devotees. The representing image is a broom· made from the branches of the bamboo palm, stripped of its leaves, and besmeared with camwood. To invoke its vengeance parched corn or beniseed is usually thrown hot upon the image, and then it is believed the epidemic will spread,. But they certainly have a more direct means of spreading the disease.

Persons dying of this plague are buried only by the devotees of this god, who account it as their special right to bury such corpses, being victims of the vengeance of their god. For a propitiation, they often demand from the relatives of the victims 5 head (*i.e.*, 10,000) of cowries, a tortoise, a snail, a fowl, a pigeon, a goat, an armadillo, a ground pig, camwood, shea butter, a quantity of palm oil, two kinds of beads, green and yellow, called respectively *Otutu* and *Opon*, together with all the effects of the deceased, which are regarded as theirs by legitimate right. The corpse is buried either in the bush, or by the side of a river.

The following anecdote was related by a devotee. He was confirmed—said he—in his belief in the existence of the gods and as helpers in the government of the world from the following incident. Said he, " A young man once fell into a swoon, and having revived, he related the vision which he had seen. He said he saw the GREAT GOD sitting on a throne, covered with a flowing garment, attended on His right and left by Orisala and Ifa his counsellors : behind him was a pit into which the condemned were cast. Ogun and Sǫpǫna were ministers of his vengeance to execute justice upon offenders. Ogun armed with 4,000 swords (or daggers) went out daily to slay victims, his food being the blood of the slain. Sǫpǫna

also had 4,000 viols hung about his body.   His also was the work
of destruction as he disappeared immediately for another victim
after presenting one.   Sango also appeared, a mighty destroyer
who, when about to set forth on his journey to earth, used to be
cautioned by both Oriṣala and Ifa to deal gently with their
respective worshippers."

It is with such stories as this that the credulity of the simple folk
is usually wrought upon with a view to strengthen their belief in
the so-called gods.

7. *Egugun.*   The period when the worship of spirits or the
souls of departed relatives was introduced into the Yoruba country
will be noted in a future chapter.   The representing forms are
human beings of the exact height and figure of the deceased, covered
from head to foot with cloths similar to those in which the said
deceased was known to have been buried, completely masked and
speaking with an unnatural tone of voice.   This feigned voice is
said to be in imitation of that of a species of monkey called *Ijimere.*
That animal is regarded with superstitious reverence, the power
of walking erect and talking being ascribed to it and is esteemed
a clever physician.   Some professed " medicine men " usually
tame and keep one of these creatures, and pretend to receive
instructions and inspirations from it.

In these later times, the Egũgun worship has become a national
religious institution, and its anniversaries are celebrated with
grand festivities.   The mysteries connected with it are held
sacred and inviolable, and although little boys of 5 or 6 years of
age are often initiated, yet no woman may know these mysteries
on pain of death.

The dress of the Egũgun consists of cloths of various colours
or the feathers of different kinds of birds, or the skins of different
animals.   The whole body from head to foot is concealed from view ;
the Egũgun seeing only from the meshes of a species of network
covering the face, and speaking in a sepulchral tone of voice.   The
women believe (or rather feign to believe) that the Egũguns came
from the spirit world.   An Egũgun (the Agan) is the executor of
women accused of witchcraft, and of those who are proved guilty
of such crimes as murder, incendiarism, etc.

The high priest of the Egũgun is called the Alagbâ, and next
to him is the Aláran, and after this the Eṣọrun, and then the
Akẹrẹ whose insignia of office are a bundle of *Atori* whips.   These
officials are higher in rank than all the Egũguns under the mask,
and hence the common saying :—" Egũgun baba Alagbâ, Alagbâ
baba Egũgun " (The Egũgun is the father of the Alagbâ, the
Alagbâ the father of the Egũgun).

It is considered a crime to touch an Egūgun dress in public, and disrespectful to pass him by with the head uncovered. Even a boy Egūgun is considered worthy of being honoured by his (supposed) surviving parents, he salutes them as elderly people would do, and promises the bestowal of gifts on the family.

In every town there are several Alagbâs or head priests of Egūgun out of them a president is elected, at whose house all the others meet on special occasions.

The individual who fills the highest rank in the Egūgun worship is the Alapīni, one of the seven great noble men of Ọyọ (the Ọyọ Mesi). He resides always in the royal city of Ọyọ. There can be but one Alapīni at a time, and by virtue of his office he must be a *monorchis*. Thus qualified, he shares with the eunuchs in all their privileges, and at the same time enjoys the lion's share in the Egūgun department.

In a large town, every quarter has its own Alagbâ in whose house a special apartment is dedicated to the Egūgun worship, where all the Egūgun dress in that part of the town are kept until required for use on special occasions or at the annual festivals.

Egūguns are generally worshipped with a kind of cake made of beans and palm oil (Ọlẹlẹ) in the month of February, after the beans harvest in January ; and the Egūgun anniversary is usually held in the month of May or June. These festivals are lucky times for the men, for on these occasions, the women are made to spend largely to feast " deceased relatives," while the food is consumed by the men in the Alagbâ's department. The number of fowls and goats killed and devoured at such times is simply prodigious. Such is the force of habit engendered by blind superstition, that although in reality the women are no longer deceived, as regards these alleged visits of their dear departed, yet they make their offerings with cheerfulness, and with a sure expectation of blessings.

It has already been noted above that the Yorubas believe in a future state. It cannot be considered too far fetched to say that this periodical re-appearance of the dead as symbolized in the Egūgun " mystery " is an embodiment of the idea of the Resurrection, although that doctrine as taught by Christianity cannot be said to be identical with what they hold and practise ; but this festival is usually observed with all the zeal and fervour with which Christians celebrate the Christmas and Paschal festivals.

This anniversary is the time of reunion among absent friends and relatives. The town then puts on its best appearance, the streets are everywhere cleaned and put under repairs, and the citizens appear abroad in their holiday dress.

The celebration is usually preceded on the eve of the festival by a vigil termed in Yoruba " Ikunlẹ " or the *kneeling*, because the whole night is spent in kneeling and praying in the grove set apart for Egũgun worship, invoking the blessings and the aid of the departed parent. The blood of fowls and animals offered in sacrifice is also poured on the graves of the ancestors.

On the morning of the festival the whole of the Egũguns, including all the principal forms accompanied by the Alagbâs and minor priests form a procession to the residence of the chief ruler of the town ; they there receive the homage of the chief, and in turn give him and the other chiefs and the whole town their blessings ; they then spend about three hours doing honours to the chief, playing and dancing to their peculiar music ; and after receiving presents they disperse to continue the play all over the town, each confining himself more or less to his own quarter of the town.

The festival is continued for seven days, and on the eighth day, there is another gathering at the Chief Alagbâ's and the festivities are brought to a close with games, sports, and a display of magic tricks.

For three weeks to a month, lesser Egũguns may still be seen making their appearance ; these as a rule, belong to poorer districts which were backward in their preparations for the annual feast. Everyone, however, still keeps to the same rule of seven days' appearance and disappearing likewise on the eighth day after a grand display.

The Adamuoriṣa and the Gẹlẹdẹ.

In imitation of the Egũguns, some littoral tribes adopt similar forms of representation of their departed dead ; such are the Adamuoriṣa among the Aworis, and the Gẹlẹdẹ among the Ẹgbado tribes.

The Adamuoriṣa is sometimes called Ẹyọ ; the former term signifies the god with the nasal twang—on account of the artificial voice they affect, and the latter, Ẹyọ, simply means Ọyọ being an imitation or parody of the Ọyọ system of Egũgun worship.

But whereas the Egũguns appear annually, at a fixed period of the year, viz. at the feast of the first fruits in June, these are used as a part of the funeral obsequies of a chieftain, or well-to-do citizen who can afford a carnival in connection with his funeral rites. The effigy of the departed is set up in state in the house, the immediate relatives are dressed in their very best, and all hold horse-tails in their hands to dance with. The play lasts for one day only and generally ends with a big feast.

The Gẹlẹdẹ is also a human being in a mask the head of which is exquisitely carved in wood, and made to represent that of a man or woman with all their tribal marks and sometimes any of the lower animals such as the alligator.   They are more generally of a female form, with carvings of plaited hair, and .magnificent busts ;   they are elaborately or fantastically dressed, bedecked with a wealth of female ornaments of native manufacture, such as ear-rings, bangles, beads, etc., with jingles on their ankles ;   they dance and move majestically, treading heavily to the rhythmic sound of drums and other musical instruments.

They are much besmired with chalk and camwood, presenting rather a frightful (if harmless) appearance.

8. *Orò*.   The Orò system is also said by some to have been borrowed from the red monkey called *Íjimerè*.   It consists of a flat piece of iron or stick, with a long string, attached to a pole. This when whirled swiftly in the air produces a shrill sound which is called " Aja Orò " (Orò's dog).   A larger kind whirled with the hand gives a deep bass tone.   This is the voice of the Orò himself.   Amongst the Ijẹbus and the Ẹgbas, Orò is much more sacred and important than the Egūgun, and is the executor of criminals.   The Ẹgbas pay homage also to another god called Ologboijeun, who is personated by a man under a mask with a drawn sword in his hand.

Other gods of the same class are the Igis (trees) also personified by human beings, masked and carrying an image on the head. Some of these are male figures with branching horns, on which are carved figures of monkeys, snakes and other animals.   Others are female figures which are called Ẹfun-gbà-rokù.

Amongst the Ọyọs (Yorubas Proper) the people of Isẹyin and Jabata are the principal Orò worshippers.   Seven days are set apart annually for its worship.   Except for a few hours during which they are permitted to procure provisions, women are kept indoors throughout the day.   On the seventh day even this small indulgence is not allowed, but they are rigidly shut up the entire day.   It is certain death for any one of them to be found without and this penalty is exacted whatever may be the title, or wealth, or position of respectability of any woman who ventures to have a peep at the Orò.

9. *Ífa*.—This is the great consulting oracle in the Yoruba country and was introduced at a late period by King ONIGBOGI, who was said to have been dethroned for having done so.

Another tradition says it was introduced into the Yoruba country by one Sẹtilu, native of the Nupe country, who was born blind. This was about the period of the Mohammedan invasion.

Ṣẹtilu's parents regretting their misfortune in having a blind son, were at first of doubtful mind as to what course they should pursue, whether to kill the child, or spare its life to become a burden on the family. Parental feelings decided them to spare the child. It grew up a peculiar child, and the parents were astonished at his extraordinary powers of divination. At the early age of 5, he began to excite their wonder and curiosity by foretelling who would pay them a visit in the course of the day and with what object. As he advanced in age, he began to practise sorcery and medicine. At the commencement of his practice, he used 16 small pebbles and imposed successfully upon the credulity of those who flocked to him in their distress and anguish for consultation. From this source, he earned a comfortable livelihood. Finding that the adherents were fast becoming Ṣẹtilu's followers, and that even respectable priests did not escape the general contagion, the Mohammedans resolved to expel Ṣẹtilu out of the country. This being effected, Ṣẹtilu crossed the river Niger and went to Benin, staying for a while at a place called Ọwọ̀, thence to Ado. Subsequently he migrated to Ile Ifẹ, and finding that place more suitable for practising his art, he resolved to make it his permanent residence. He soon became famous there also, and his performances so impressed the people, and the reliance placed in him was so absolute, that he had little difficulty in persuading them to abolish the tribal marks on their faces, such marks of distinction not being practised in Nupe, Ṣẹtilu's own country.

In process of time palm nuts, pieces of iron and ivory balls were successively used instead of pebbles. At the present day, palm nuts only are used as they are considered more easily propitiated, the others requiring costly sacrifices and even human blood.

Ṣẹtilu initiated several of his followers in the mysteries of Ifa worship, and it has gradually become the consulting oracle of the whole Yoruba nation. In order to become an Ifa priest, a long course of serious study is necessary. To consult Ifa, in the more common and ordinary way, 16 palm nuts are to be shaken together in the hollow of both hands, whilst certain marks are traced with the index finger on a flat bowl dusted with yam flour, or powdered camwood. Each mark suggests to the consulting priest the heroic deeds of some fabulous heroes, which he duly recounts, and so he goes on with the marks in order, until he hits upon certain words or phrases which appear to bear upon the matter of the applicant before him. Very often answers are given much after the manner of the ancient oracle at Delphi.

Ifa was really met in this country by the Yorubas, for ODUDUWA met Ṣẹtilu at Ile Ifẹ, but the worship of it was officially recognized by KING OFIRAN son of ONIGBOGI.

10. *Sango.*—Sango was the fourth King of the YORUBAS, and was deified by his friends after his death. Sango ruled over all the Yorubas including Benin, the Popos and Dahomey, for the worship of him has continued in all these countries to this, day.

It is related of him, that being a tyrant he was dethroned by his people, and expelled the country. Finding himself deserted not only by his friends, but also by his beloved wife OYA, he committed suicide at a place called Koso. His tragic end became a proverb and a by-word, and his faithless friends were ashamed on account of the taunts cast upon the name and fame of the unfortunate King. To atone for their base action in deserting him, as well as to avenge the insults on his memory they went to the Bariba country to study the art of charm-making, and also the process of attracting lightning upon their enemies' houses.

On their return home they put to practice with a vengeance the lessons they had learnt. From the too frequent conflagrations which were taking place, as well as deaths from lightning strokes, suspicions were aroused, and enquiries were set on foot. Then Sango's friends said that the catastrophe was attributable to the late King taking vengeance on his enemies on account of the indignities they had heaped upon his memory. Being appealed to, to propitiate the offended King in order that he may stay his vengeance upon the land, his friends offered sacrifices to him as god, and hence these intercessors became the " Mọgba " (advocate) and priests of Sango ; and to this day their descendants hold the same office.

The emblems of worship representing Sango are certain smooth stones shaped like an axe head commonly taken for thunder bolts.

They are supposed to be hurled down from the heavens when the god would kill any one who has incurred his displeasure.

The following is the process to be gone through at the initiation of any one into the mysteries of Sango worship :—The priests demand a ram, a water bird called Ọsìn, a tortoise, a snail, an armadillo, a large rat called Okete, a toad, a tadpole, the *Otutu* and *Ọpọn* beads, the red tail of a parrot, a guinea fowl, shea butter, salt, palm oil, the flesh of an elephant, venison, the tẹ̀tẹ̀ (greens) the leaves of the evergreens called Etipoñọla, Ọdŭdun, and iperegun tree ; a small knife called " abẹ-eṣu " (the devil's razor) a white country cloth of 10 breadths, a mat called fãfã (mats made of the pith of bamboo palm branches) together with 7 heads of cowries (14,000 cowry shells) as carriage fee.

The leaves are bruised in a bowl of water, and with the infusion the candidate is to purify himself. He is then seated on a mortar and shaved. The birds and tortoise are killed and their hearts taken out, and these with slices of the flesh of all the animals above-mentioned are pounded together with the evergreens, and a ball is made of the compound. The candidate now submits to incisions on his shaven head and the ball of pounded articles is rubbed into the wounds. The neophyte now becomes a recognised devotee of Sango.

Important ceremonies are performed when a house is struck by lightning. The inmates are not allowed to sleep in any house, but in booths or blacksmith's shops, until the so-called thunderbolt is dug up and removed from the premises. A garland of palm leaves is generally hung up at the entrance of the devoted house to forbid any but Sango priests to enter. A watchman is kept on the premises at the expense of the sufferers from the divine visitation, and it is the duty of this man to ward off trespassers from what is now regarded as sacred ground, till the ceremonies shall have been performed, and the offended god appeased. With the sole exception of the great King, the ALÁFIN of Ọyọ, all the provincial kings and ruling chiefs in whose town the catastrophe happens to take place, are bound to repair to the spot to do homage to Sango, who is said to pay a visit to earth.

Such occasions are greatly prized by the worshippers who swarm to the place in numbers with their Bāyāni, a sort of crown made of cowries, and they are all to be entertained at the expense of the sufferers and also by the neighbours.

The king or chief coming to pay his respects to Sango is to receive 11 heads of cowries, a goat, and a slave in three payments.

In the case of a poor house, a member of the family is seized if not quietly given up, and has to be ransomed at a considerable sum, which must be paid and the above mentioned articles procured, before the ceremony can be performed. Then all being ready the priests having now assembled, the tẹtẹ (greens) etipọñọla, together with the evergreens Ọdūdun and peregun are bruised in a bowl of water, and with this they purify themselves before entering the house. They are preceded by one holding an iron instrument (the divining rod) with which a search is made for the spot where the bolt is believed to have entered the ground. After some pretence they arrive at a spot in which one of their number had previously buried one of these sharp stones. Here the ground is ordered to be dug, with a show of solemnity, and, of course, the thunder-bolt is found and exhumed with well-sustained marks of piety and reverence.

Thus the common people are deceived and imposed upon, and

very few besides the priests are aware of the tricks systematically played upon their credulity.

The concluding ceremony still bears hardly on the poor sufferers. They are required to give over a son to the priests to be initiated in the mysteries of the cult, and further they are to pay something in order to obtain permission to rebuild their houses. Hence an accident of this kind means great calamity to any one, and heavy debts are incurred. The unfortunate sufferers already deprived of their all (much or little) by this sudden stroke of ill-fortune are often obliged to put their children to service in order to raise money sufficient to meet the demands of the greedy worshippers of this heartless god. The fines obtained are shared between the king or head chief, and the town authorities ; but the articles purchased for the performance of the ceremonies are perquisites which are appropriated by the priests alone.

This " descent of Sango " on earth is never done but with a view to show his displeasure on persons who are guilty of perjury and lies. The town for a while is as it were placed under an interdict, and during that brief period the worshippers of the god are allowed to seize with impunity whatever they can come at in the public streets in the vicinity of the catastrophe, such as sheep, goats, poultry and things of greater or less value.

Sango worshippers are forbidden to touch the large white beans called Sèse, because it is used for counteracting the evil effects of the agencies employed in attracting lightning on people's houses.

11. *Qya.* This was the name of Sango's faithful and beloved wife. She alone of all his wives accompanied him in his flight towards the Tapa (Nupe) country his maternal home. But courage failed her at a place called Ira, her native town which she was never to see any more should love for her husband prevail to make her resolve to share with him in his destiny. But the prospect of making her home among entire strangers in a strange land among a people speaking a strange tongue, and of leaving parents and home for ever, so overpowered her that she hesitated to proceed.

As she could not for very shame return to Qyọ she remained at Ira ; and hearing that her husband had committed suicide, she summed up sufficient courage to follow his example.

She also was deified. The river Niger is sacred to her, and hence that river is called all over Yoruba land ODO QYA after her name. As thunder and lightning are attributed to Sango so tornado and violent thunderstorms, rending trees and levelling high towers and houses are attributed to Qya. They signify her displeasure.

Deified heroes and heroines are never spoken of as dead, but as having disappeared. Thus the saying :—

> " Oya wọlẹ̀ ni ile Irá
> Sango wọlẹ̀ ni Koso."
> (Oya disappeared in the town of Ira
> Sango disappeared at Koso).

Two naked swords and the horns of a buffalo are the representative image of Oya. Her followers are forbidden to touch mutton, they are distinguished by a particular kind of red beads which are always tied round their necks.

12. *Ẹrinlẹ*. Erinlẹ was originally a hunter, native of Ajagbusi. He was poor and unmarried. Having no home, he dwelt in a booth erected under a large *gbingbin* tree by the river side, whence he made his expeditions to shoot monkeys for sale by which he earned his livelihood. He is said to have been accidentally swept down the river by a strong current and was drowned. A river flowing by the present town of Ilobu, which empties itself into the Osun river was named after him. The representing image consists of black smooth stones from that river, and an image of iron surmounted by the figure of a bird. The followers are distinguished by wearing a chain of iron or brass round their necks, and bracelets of the same material.

13. *Orisa Oko*. Orisa Oko was also a hunter, a native of Iràwọ. He used to entrap guinea fowls in nets set in the farm of one Ogunjẹñsọwẹ̀, a wealthy farmer, and by this means he gained his livelihood. He kept a dog and a fife, and on several occasions when lost in the bush his whereabouts were discovered by his dog at the sound of the fife. He lived to a good old age, and when infirm and unable to pursue his calling as a hunter, he practised soothsaying and numbers flocked to him.

It may be observed that in countries where letters are not known and the language not reduced to writing the aged are the repositories of wisdom and knowledge, hence the younger generation regard their seniors as guides and prophets, and their vast stores of experience serve as keys to unlock many a doubtful point in the affairs of the young. The latter used to regard the foresight displayed by the elders as a marvel ; it is easy, therefore to understand how it came about that extraordinary powers are attributed to them. It is only thus that one can account in a way for the success of those who are often styled " medicine men " " sorcerers " " soothsayers," etc.

As witchcraft was punished with death, persons accused of it were taken to Orisa Oko for trial. He was accustomed to lead the accused to a cave supposed to be inhabited by a demon called Polo. In this cave Orisa Oko practised his sorcery. In cases where an accused was innocent, he would return with him ; if otherwise, then his head is thrown out to those awaiting a decision. Polo the demon executed the guilty. The fame of Orisa Oko spread and numbers resorted to him in taking oaths. His oracle was regarded as infallible, and appeals to him were final.

After his death, his followers practised his methods taking the precaution to secrete a strong man in the cave to act the part of the supposed Polo.

But a striking exposure soon brought the practice into disrepute, and it was abolished. It happened thus. A man was accused and as usual, was taken to the cave ; but he proved to be a far stronger man than the supposed Polo, and the result was that he killed the counterfeit demon, and threw his head out of the cave to those who were eagerly waiting for the decision of the god.

The representing image is a fife made of ivory or a flat piece of iron 5 or 6ft. in length similar to what is given as a sign of acquittal to those in whose favour the god had decided.

The ẸRÙGÙN mystery is of a kind similar to that of the Orisa Oko worship. It also was practised in a cave by the side of a mount called the Ẹrùgùn mount.

The above are the principal gods worshipped by the Yorubas. There are besides many inferior divinities to whom offerings are made. In fact the whole number of gods and goddesses acknowledged is reckoned at 401. Propitiatory sacrifices are also offered to whatever in nature is awe-inspiring or magnificent such as the Ocean, huge rocks, tall trees, and high mountains. To the last named especially offerings are made for the procreation of children.

MOHAMMEDANISM as was observed above, was introduced towards the close of the eighteenth century ; it numbered very few adherents up to the time when the Fulanis by stratagem, seized Ilorin and overran the northern provinces, as we shall find related in the second part of this history. The towns in the plain were swept with fire and the sword, with the alternative of the acceptance of the Koran, and submission to the Fulanis ; the southward progress of the conquerors, however, was stopped at Osogbo, where the Ibadans met and crushed them, and in the direction of the Ijesa and Ekiti provinces, the forests and mountain fastnesses offered insurmountable obstacles to these intrepid horsemen, who could neither fight on foot nor engage in a bush warfare ; hence Mohammedanism prevailed chiefly in the north, but latterly it spread southwards by peaceful means, chiefly by traders and itinerant mendicant preachers. It is now embraced by thousands, as it appears to be a superior form of religion to the paganism of their ancestors.

CHRISTIANITY. Christianity was introduced by the Church Missionary Society in 1843, first into Abẹokuta via Badagry, and from thence to Ibadan in May 1851, and also to Ijaye. On January 10, 1852, the C.M.S. removed their base from Badagry to Lagos. From Abẹokuta, mission stations were planted at the Oke Ogun and Ẹgbado districts, from Ibadan missions were planted at Iwo, Modakẹkẹ, Ifẹ, Osọgbo and Ilẹsa. Missions were established also at Ọyọ and Ogbomọsọ before the Ijaye war broke out in 1860, which put a stop to the progress of missions all over the country. The intertribal wars which followed and which convulsed the greater part of the country, and devastated large areas, prevented its growth northwards, but at Abẹokuta where it was first planted, it grew so rapidly that at the time of the British occupation, Christian adherents could be numbered by thousands ; schools had been established, and evangelistic work among the surrounding kindred tribes systematically undertaken and was being vigorously carried on.

The Bible in the vernacular was the most potent factor in the spread of the religion. The sincerity of the converts, and the firm hold the religion has attained, have been fully tested by several bloody persecutions endured for the faith, through which they came out triumphant.

The forces organized for home defence chiefly against the Dahomian attacks contained a compact body of Christians under their own captain, the *esprit de corps* existing among them, and the invariable success which always attended their arms, won for them the respect and admiration, of their pagan rulers and countrymen. This contributed not a little to the cessation of persecutions and the increase of their number.

The establishment of the British protectorate saw the mission, established at Ijẹbu, where it has since been spreading phenomenally and also in the Ijẹsa and Ekiti provinces. It is self-propagating by means of the people learning to read the Bible in their own tongue. To God be the praise.

Chapter IV

GOVERNMENT

The entire Yoruba country has never been thoroughly organized into one complete government in a modern sense. The system that prevails is that known as the Feudal, the remoter portions have always lived more or less in a state of semi-independence, whilst loosely acknowledging an over-lord. The king of Benin was one of the first to be independent of the central government, and was even better known to foreigners who frequented his ports in early times, and who knew nothing of his over-lord in the then unexplored and unknown interior.

Yoruba Proper, however, was completely organized, and the descriptions here given refer chiefly to it. With some variations most of the smaller governments were generally modelled after it, but in a much simpler form, and solely in their domestic affairs; foreign relations so far as then obtained, before the period of the revolution were entirely in the hands of the central government at Ọyọ (Eyeo or Katunga). It should be remembered that the coast tribes were of much less importance then than now, both in population and in intelligence; light and civilization with the Yorubas came from the north with which they have always retained connection through the Arabs and Fulanis. The centre of life and activity, of large populations and industry was therefore in the interior, whilst the coast tribes were scanty in number, ignorant and degraded not only from their distance from the centre of light, but also through their demoralizing intercourse with Europeans, and the transactions connected with the oversea slave trade.

This state of things has been somewhat reversed since the latter half of the XIXth century, by the suppression of the slave-trade, and the substitution therefor of legitimate trade and commerce: and more especially through the labours of the missionaries who entered the country about the same time as the springing up into being of the modern towns of Lagos, Abẹokuta, and Ibadan, through which western light and civilization beam into the interior.

The government of Yoruba Proper is an absolute monarchy; the King is more dreaded than even the gods. The office is hereditary in the same family, but not necessarily from father to son. The King is usually elected by a body of noblemen known as Ọyọ Mesi, the seven principal councillors of state.

40

The vassal or provincial kings and ruling princes were 1060 at the time of the greatest prosperity of the empire which then included the Popos, Dahomey, and parts of Ashanti, with portions of the Tapás and Baribas.

The word " king " as generally used in this country includes all more or less distinguished chiefs, who stand at the head of a clan, or one who is the ruler of an important district or province, especially those who can trace their descent from the founder, or from one of the great leaders or heroes who settled with him in this country. They are of different grades, corresponding some-what to the different orders of the English peerage (dukes, marquises, earls, viscounts and barons), and their order of rank is well-known among themselves. The Onikoyi as head of the *Ekùn Osi* or metropolitan province was the first of these " kings " and he it was who used to head them all to Ọyọ once a year to pay homage to the ALÂFIN or King of the Yorubas.

THE ALÂFIN

The ALÂFIN is the supreme head of all the kings and princes of the Yoruba nation, as he is the direct lineal descendant and successor of the reputed founder of the nation. The succession as above said is by election from amongst the members of the royal family, of the one considered as the most worthy, age and nearness to the throne being taken into consideration. It might be mentioned also in passing that the feelings and acceptance of the denizens of the harem towards the king-elect are often privately ascertained and assured of previously.

In the earliest days, the eldest son naturally succeeded the father, and in order to be educated in all the duties of the kingship which must one day devolve upon him, he was often associated more or less with the father in performing important duties and thereby he often performed royal functions, and thus gradually he practically reigned with his father under the title of AREMỌ (the heir apparent) having his own official residence near the palace ; but as the age grew corrupt, the AREMỌ often exercised sway quite as much as or more than the King himself, especially in the course of a long reign, when age has rendered the monarch feeble. They had equal powers of life and death over the King's subjects, and there are some cases on record of the AREMỌ being strongly suspected of termin-ating the father's life, in order to attain full powers at once. It was therefore made a law and part of the constitution that as the AREMỌ reigned with his father, he must also die with him. This law had the effect at any rate of checking parricide. It continued to take effect up to the last century when (in 1858)

it was repealed by ATIBA one of the later Kings in favour of his
AREMO ADELU. The AREMO may now succeed if found worthy,
but he must be elected in the usual way ; but if passed over or
rejected by the king-makers he must leave the city and resort
to a private retirement in the provinces. This however, is not
really obligatory, but as he must be superseded in his office,
such a course is inevitable, unless he chooses of his own accord
to die with the father.

The choice may sometimes fall upon one of the poorer princes,
in the quiet pursuit of his trade, with no aspiration after the
throne ; such a one is sent for, and unnecessarily ill-used for the
last time to his own surprise ; this was done probably for the
purpose of testing his temper and spirit. He may not be aware
of the intentions of the OYO MESI until he is being admonished
by them as to the duties and responsibilities of the exalted position
he is soon to fill.

The nominators are three titled members of the royal family,
viz., the ONA-ISOKUN, the ONA-AKA, and the OMO-OLA, uncles
or cousins of the King, but generally entitled the " King's fathers."
These have to submit or suggest the names to the noblemen for
election, but the Basorun's voice is paramount to accept or to
reject.

Curious and elaborate ceremonies precede the actual accession
to the throne. After all arrangements have been made, the
ceremonies begin by a sacrifice brought from the house of the
ONA-ISOKUN by a body of men called OMO-ninari ; these belong
to a family specially concerned in carrying out all menial duties
connected with the offering of sacrifices and in waiting upon the
King and the priests. As soon as they enter the house where
the King-elect is, he is called out, and he has to stand up with an
attendant by his side. He is touched on the chest, and on the
right and left shoulders with the bowl of sacrifice, the attendant
in the mean time uttering some form of words. This is the signal
that he has been called to the throne. On the evening of the same
day, he is conducted quietly into the house of the ONA-ISOKUN
where he spends the first night. In order to avoid the crowd, the
attention of the populace is usually diverted by a procession of the
Kings' slaves and others with much noise and ado, as if escorting
him, whilst the king-elect accompanied by the Aregbe'di, a titled
eunuch, and a few of the Omo-ni-nari come up quietly a long way
behind.

At the ONA-ISOKUN'S house, he is attended solely by the Omo-
ni-nari. He is admonished and advised by those who stand to
him in place of a father. Some ceremonies of purification are gone

through, propitiatory sacrifices are again offered which are carried to various quarters of the city by the *Ọmọ-ni-nari*.

The next night he passes at the house[1] of the Ọtun-Iwẹfa (the next in rank to the chief of the eunuchs). This official being a priest of Sango, it is probable that the king-elect spends the night with him in order to be initiated into the sacerdotal part of his office, the ALÂFIN having as much spiritual as well as secular work to perform, being at once King and Priest to his people; and probably he learns there also the usages and doings of the huge population in the inner precincts of the palace with which the eunuchs are quite conversant. After this, he is conducted into one of the chambers in the Outer Court of the palace (Ọmọ ile) where he resides for three months, the period of mourning, until his coronation.

The main gateway to the palace being closed at the demise of the King, a private opening is made for him in the outer wall through which he goes in and out of his temporary residence. During this time he remains strictly in private, learning and practising the style and deportment of a King, and the details of the important duties and functions of his office. During this period he is dressed in black, and is entitled to use a " cap of state " called " Ori-kò-gbe-ofo." (The head may not remain uncovered).

The affairs of state are at this time conducted by the Basọrun.

THE CORONATION

The coronation takes place at the end of three months, really at the third appearance of the new moon after the late King's death. The date is generally so fixed as to have it if possible before the next great festival. It is attended with a great public demonstration. It is a gala day in which the whole city appears in holiday dress. Visitors from the provinces and representatives of neighbouring states also flock into the city in numbers.

This day is generally known as " The King's visit to the BARÀ." It is the first but most important act of the ceremonies.

The BARÀ or royal mausoleum is a consecrated building in the outskirts of the city, under the care of a high-priestess named IYAMọDẸ; there the Kings were formally crowned, and there buried. The King enters it but once in his lifetime, and that is

---

[1] Tradition says that in the early times while the King -elect is in the Ọtun'ẹfa's house among other dishes brought to him to partake of is one prepared from the heart of the late King which has been extracted and preserved. After partaking of this he is told he has " eaten the King." Hence the origin of the word Jẹ Ọba, to become a King (lit. to eat a King).

at the coronation with marked pomp and ceremony. The actual crowning does not now take place in the BARÀ as it seems to have been, but at Koso the shrine of Sango, but the visit to the BARÀ is so important and indispensable a preliminary that it has become more closely identified with the coronation than that to the other shrines visited on that occasion.

Leaving the IPADI—his temporary chambers—there are two stations at which the King elect has to halt before reaching the sacred building ; the first is the *Abátá* or area in front of the palace where a tent of beautiful cloths has been erected for him. Here he has to change his mourning dress for a princely robe. He then proceeds to the second station at the Alapini's midway on his route where a large tent and an enclosure have been erected for his reception. Here he is awaited by a vast concourse of people and welcomed with ringing cheers. Here he receives the congratulations and homage of the princes, the nobles, the chiefs and the people and is hailed as the King. Some ceremonies are here gone through also which include distribution of kola nuts, etc., to the princes and chiefs without.

After this he proceeds to the BARÀ accompanied by the whole concourse of people who have to remain outside. He enters the sacred precincts attended by the Magaji Iyajin (his official elder brother) the princesses, the Ọna-Onṣẹ-awo (an official), the Ọtun-wẹfa (the next to the chief of the eunuchs) who is a priest and the Ọmọ-ni-nari, a set of servants. These last are to slaughter and skin the animals to be offered in sacrifice.

At the BARÀ he worships at the tombs of his fathers, a horse, a cow, and a ram being offered at each tomb ; portions are sent out to each of the noblemen, princes, and chiefs waiting outside, the Baṣọrun receiving the first and the lion's share or the whole. He invokes the blessings of his deceased fathers and is hereby said to receive authority to wear the crown. The visit to the BARÀ then is for the purpose of receiving authority or permission from his deceased ancestors to wear the crown, hence it is spoken of as the coronation. It is a fixed rule that the whole of the meat is to be totally consumed at the BARÀ ; under no circumstance should any be taken home.

This over, the King returns hence with great pomp and show to his temporary chambers, amid the firing of *feu de joie*, the bleating of the Kakaki trumpet, drumming, etc.

On the fifth day after this he proceeds to Koso, the shrine of Sango, for the actual crowning. Here he is attended by the Ọtun-wẹfa who has the charge of the shrine, the Bale (mayor) of Koso a suburban village, the Ọmọ-ni-naris, and the Iṣọnas.

[The Iṣọnas are a body of men whose sole employment is to do all needle and embroidered work for royalty. They are also the umbrella-makers. The crown, staff, robes, and all ornamental beadworks, and workings in cotton, silk, or leather are executed by them].

Surrounded by the principal eunuchs and princes the great crown is placed on his head with much ceremony by the Iyàkere. Who the Iyàkere is, for whom is reserved this most important function will be seen below. The royal robes are put on him, the Ejigba[1] round his neck, the staff and the SWORD OF MERCY are placed in his hands.

On the fifth day after this, he proceeds to the shrine of Ọrañyan, here the GREAT SWORD OR SWORD OF JUSTICE brought from ILE IFẸ is placed in his hands, without which he can have no authority to order an execution.

After another interval of five days, he proceeds to the shrine of Ogun the god of war, and there offers a propitiatory sacrifice for a peaceful reign. The offerings consist of a cow, a ram, and a dog ; this last being indispensable in any sacrifice to the god of war.

From the shrine of Ogun, the procession goes straight on to the palace, entering now for the first time by the main gate opened for him, the former opening through the outer wall to the temporary chambers being quickly walled up. Thus he enters the palace proper as THE KING.

But a new opening is made for him at the Kọbi Aganju through which he enters the inner precincts of the palace. This entrance is for his exclusive use in and out of the Kọbi during his reign : at his death it is closed up. At this entrance they offer in sacrifice a snail, a tortoise, an armadillo, a field mouse (ẹmọ́) a large rat (okete) a toad, a tadpole, a pigeon, a fowl, a ram, a cow, a horse, a man and a woman, the last two being buried at the threshhold of the opening ; on the blood of the victims and over the grave of the two last, he has to walk to the inner court.

Human sacrifices however (now totally abolished) were not commonly practised amongst the Ọyọs, but such immolation was always performed at the coronation and at the burial of the sovereign. By these sacrifices he is not only crowned King with

---

[1] The Ejigba is a string of costly beads reaching down to the knees. Beads are used for precious stones. This represents the chain of office. Chains—they say—are for captives, hence they use beads instead.

D

power over all, man and beast, but he is also consecrated a priest to the nation. His person, therefore, becomes sacred.

All this having been performed, it is now formally announced to the assembled public, that King " A " is dead (or rather has entered into the vault of the skies—O wọ Àja) and King " B " now reigns in his stead.

During the interval of the late King's illness, up to the time of his death, the business of state is carried on normally by the palace officers, the Osi-'wẹfa personating the King, even to the extent of putting on his robes and crown, and sitting on the throne when such is required ; but as soon as it is known that he is dead the Baṣọrun at once assumes the chief authority, and nothing can be done without him.

The King having been crowned, he is henceforth forbidden to appear in public streets by day, except on very special and extra-ordinary occasions ; he is, however, allowed evening strolls on moonlight nights when he may walk about *incognito*.

This seclusion not only enhances the awe and majesty due to a sovereign, but also lends power and authority to his commands, and is the best safe-guard for public order at their present stage of civilization. Besides, it would be very inconvenient to the citizens if the King were always coming out, for according to the universal custom of the country, whenever a chief is out, all his subordinates must go out with him. It is an inviolable law and custom of the country, and is applicable to all, whatever their rank : thus, if the Baṣọrun is out, all the Ọyọ Mesi must be out also. If the Balẹ of any town is out, all the chiefs of the town must be out also, and if the King is out, the whole city must be astir and on the move, all business suspended, until he returns into the palace.

Igba Iwà

At the commencement of every reign, the Igba Iwà or Calabashes of divination are brought from Ile Ifẹ to the new King to divine what sort of reign his will be.

Two covered calabashes, of similar shape and size but with quite different contents are brought, one containing money, small pieces of cloth and other articles of merchandize, denoting peace and prosperity ; the other containing miniature swords and spears, arrows, powder, bullet, razor, knives, etc., denoting wars and trouble for the country. The King is to choose one of them before seeing the contents, and according as he chooses so will be the fate of the Yoruba country during his reign.

THE ARẸMỌ

The very first official act of the new King after his coronation is to create an Arẹmọ, and a Princess Royal or an equivalent. The Arẹmọ is the Crown Prince. The term simply denotes an heir, but it is used as the title of the Crown Prince of Ọyọ.

The title is conferred upon the eldest son of the sovereign in a formal manner, the ceremony being termed the " christening " as of a newly born child, hence he is often termed " Ọmọ " (child) by way of distinction   The title of Princess Royal is at the same time and in the same manner conferred upon the eldest daughter of the sovereign as well ; this, however, is of much less importance than the other.   When the King is too young to have a son, or his son is a minor, the title is temporarily conferred upon a younger brother, or next of kin that stands to him in place of a son, but as soon as the son is of age, he must assume his title and begin to act under the guardianship of the eunuchs who are his guardians.

The method is as follows :—Both of them must have a Sponsor, or " father " as he is called, chosen by divination from among the titled eunuchs ; this done, the Arẹmọ repairs to the house of the Ọna-Iṣokùn to worship at the graves of the deceased Arẹmọs, who were all buried there, and the princess to that of her deceased predecessor in her mother's house ; the King supplying them with a bullock each. The whole day is thus spent in festivities. On their return in the evening they both proceed direct to their sponsor's house where they must reside four days, each day being marked with festivities, the king supplying two bullocks every day, and this is further supplemented by the Arẹmọ himself. The feasts are open to the general public, whoever likes to repair to the house is a welcome guest, portions are also sent out to the princes, the noblemen, and other distinguished personages. At the end of the fourth day the Arẹmọ, invested with the robes of his office and with a coronet, is conducted to his official residence where he takes up his permanent abode, and the princess suitably clad likewise repairs to her own home.

PUBLIC APPEARANCES OF THE KING

The King generally appears in public on the three great annual festivals of Ifa, Ọrun, and the Bẹrẹ. In two at least of these festivals (that of the Ọrun and the Bẹrẹ), the Baṣọrun is equally concerned with him.

These festivals have certain features in common, although each has its own marked characteristics. They are all preceded by the worship of Ogun (the god of war) and on the third day after, the firing of a royal salute, and the sound of the ivory trumpet announce to the public, that the King may now be seen in state, sitting on his throne, and all loyal subjects who wish to have a glimpse of his majesty now may repair to the palace.

The festival of IFA or MOLẸ takes place in the month of July, nine days after the festival of Sango. The Ifa is the god of divination. One day in the week is generally given to the consultation or the service of Ifa, but an annual festival is celebrated in its honour at Ọyọ.

The ỌRUN festival takes place in September. At this festival the King and the Baṣọrun worship together the ORI or god of fate. The Ọrun from which it appears the Baṣọrun derives his name and title is a curious if not rather a mystical rite. The word " Ọrun " signifies heaven. The title in full is Iba Oṣọrun i.e. the lord who performs the Ọrun or heavenly mysteries.

The King and his Oṣọrun are often spoken of as " Ọba aiye " and " Ọba Ọrun " i.e., King terrestrial and King celestial. In what way His Supernal Highness performs the Ọrun, or what position he assumes towards the sovereign in this ceremony, is not generally known, because it is always done in private. But the rite seems to deal with affairs connected with the King's life. It is to him a periodic reminder of his coming apotheosis, and the emblem of worship is said to be a coffin made of or paved with clay in which he is to be buried. It is kept in charge of the " Iya Ọba " (the King's official mother) in a room in her apartments, visited by no one, and the ceremonies are performed in private once a year by the King himself, his " mother " and his Oṣọrun, the latter taking the chief part ; consequently very little is actually known of the doings of these three august personages. But this much is allowed to be known, that the Baṣọrun is to divine with kola nuts, to see whether the King's sacrifices are acceptable to the celestials or not, if the omen be favourable the ALAFIN is to give the Baṣọrun presents of a horse and other valuables ; if unfavourable, he is to die, he has forfeited his right to further existence. But there can be no doubt that under such circumstances, it can always be managed between them that the omens be always favourable.

From this and other circumstances, it would appear that the King on this occasion occupies a humiliating position as one whose conduct is under review, hence the great privacy observed, for it is a cardinal principle with Yorubas that the ALAFIN, as the representative of the founder of the race, is to humble himself before no mortal ; if such a contingency were to occur, he is to die.

Hence, no doubt, that his natural mother (if then living) is to make way for her son ascending the throne, so there will be no occasion to violate any filial duty imperative on a son who is at the same time the King. His majesty must be supreme. Even in performing reverential duties before the priests of Sango, when such are required, some privacy must be observed.

The Bẹrẹ festival takes place in January, towards the end of the year, the new year commencing in March. It is the most important and the grandest of the three. It is primarily the harvest home festival, symbolized by ceremoniously setting the fields on fire to indicate that it has been cleared of the fruits of the earth.

It is an important one at Ọyọ, not only because it closes the civil year, but also because by it the King numbers the years of his reign.

The Bẹrẹ itself which seems to be the symbol of so many ceremonies, is a common grass which grows only in the plain country and is used mainly for thatching houses. It is considered the most sumptuous of all other materials used for covering houses : it is the coolest, the neatest, the most durable, and lends itself best for ornamental purposes ; consequently it is highly thought of.

The festival proper is always preceded by two important ceremonies, the *Pakudirin* indicating the beginning, and the *Jẹlẹpa* the end of the ingatherings.

The *Pakudirin* is performed by the Ọna-'wẹfa or chief of the eunuchs, by the Basọrun or his representative and the Ab'ọbaku or master of the horse.

The King in semi-state appears in the Kọbi Aganju to witness the same, with several of the ladies of the palace around him, and at the entrance of the Aganju, the musicians making the occasion very lively.

The King is supposed not to have seen the new Bẹrẹ grass of the year, the Ọna-'wẹfa first steps forwards before him with a scythe made of brass or copper, performing in the air a mimic act of mowing the grass, and one of the ladies of the palace deputed for the purpose, extending her wrap as it were to receive the same, hugging it as something precious. This is done two or three times, the Basọrun then follows and goes through the same forms, and then the master of the horse. Each of these chiefs now makes a short speech congratulating the King on the advent of a new year, wishing him a long life and prosperous reign.

After this, about half-a-dozen men with small bundles of the Bẹrẹ grass, neatly done up, enter the palace, with measured steps to the sound of music, and come dancing before the King in front of the Aganju. His Majesty is supposed to see the grass now for the first time that year. This ceremony is brought to a close by presents given to the men, and then all spectators disperse. From nine to seventeen days are now allowed for harvesting before the fields are set on fire.

The *Jelepa* is the ceremony of setting the fields on fire. This is performed by the Basọrun outside the city walls. Booths and enclosures of palm leaves having been erected for the purpose, the Basọrun with a princely train repairs thither on the day appointed. He is met there by a number of women from the palace bringing a large calabash draped with a white cloth and containing Ọlẹ̀lẹ̀ (a sort of pudding made of white beans and palm oil) and Ẹko (a kind of blanc-mange made of soaked corn flour), corn and beans being taken as the staples of life, the principal products of the field.

His Supernal Highness first offers a morsel of these in sacrifice as a harvest thank-offering for the Yoruba nation, after which both himself and those with him partake of the rest accompanied with palm wine or beer made from guinea corn, thanking God for the blessings of the field. This over he orders the fields to be set on fire : but if by an accident the fields have already been fired, a bundle of dry grass brought from home is used instead, for the purpose of the ceremony.

The firing of a *feu de joie* now serves to show that the ceremony is over and the parties are returning to the city. This is done in state. The Basọrun robes in one of the enclosures : he is attended by hundreds of horsemen and footmen, horsemen galloping backwards and forwards before him, the firing and the fifing and drumming are quite deafening. With such a right royal procession His Supernal Highness re-enters the city. On the evening of the same day, the King worships the Ogun which is a preliminary to every annual festival.

The following day is a very busy one at Ọyọ. It is a day of paying tributes of Berẹ grass. The whole of the Ọyọ MESI first send theirs to the King, the Basọrun alone would send about 200 bundles, the subordinate chiefs send to the senior chiefs, every one to his feudal lord or chief, each man according to his rank and position and so on to the lowest grades, the young men to the heads of compounds, so that it is usual to see loads of Berẹ passing to and fro all over the town the whole day. From the provinces also tributes of Berẹ come to Ọyọ later on ; e.g. from the Asẹyin of Isẹyin, the Oluiwo of Iwo, the Balẹ of Ogbomọsọ and other cities of the plain where the Berẹ grows.

This being the recognized principal festival of the ALÂFIN other towns in lieu of Berẹ send congratulatory messages with presents, or tributes ; the Ibadans in their marauding days used to send slaves ; from the Ijẹṣas and Ekiti countries come kola nuts, alligator pepper, firewood and other forest products. Towns nearer the coast send articles of European manufacture, and so on during this season.

The day after, being the third day of the ceremony of *Jẹlẹpa* and the worship of Ogun, the public festival takes place.

THE KING IN STATE

The King generally appears in state on these three festive occasions.

Facing the large quadrangle of the outer court are the six principal Kọbis, that in the centre is what is known as the KỌBI AGANJU or throne room where the ALÂFIN always appears on state occasions. It is always kept closed, and never used for any other purpose but this.

On such occasions, the floor is spread all over with mats, and the front of the throne overspread with scarlet cloths ; the posts all around are decorated with velvet cloths, and the walls with various hangings.

The *throne* or chair of state was made of wood at a time when the knowledge of carpentry was not common in this country ; it cannot boast of any artistic merit, but it is highly valued for its solidity, hoary age, and tradition. It is of a large size and covered over with velvet.

The *crown* is made of costly beads such as coral, agra, and the like, which in this poor country stand to the people instead of precious stones. It is artistically done up by experts, with fringes of small multi-coloured beads depending from the rim, which serve to veil the face.

The *robes* are usually silks or velvets, of European manufacture, which were of much greater value in earlier days when intercourse with the coast was not so common or easy as it now is.

The *Ejigba* is the " chain of office." This is made of a string of costly beads going round the neck and reaching as far down as the knees.

The *Ọpa Ilẹkè* is the staff or sceptre artistically covered all over with small multi-coloured beads.

The Irù kẹrẹ is a specially prepared cow's tail of spotless white which the King generally holds in front of his mouth when speaking for it is considered bad form to see him open his mouth in public. He makes his speech *sotto voce*, and it is repeated to the assembly in a loud voice by the chief of the Eunuchs. The white tail is moreover an emblem of peace and grace.

The State Umbrellas. Umbrellas in this country are part and parcel of state paraphernalia. In fact there was a time when private individuals dared not use an umbrella ; that was in the days before cheap foreign ones were obtainable. The prohibition was first done away with at Ibadan, where the war boys were allowed to enjoy themselves in any way they liked, and use any materials of clothing and ornament they could afford, as it might be for only a few days before they laid down their lives on a battlefield.

However, those of a chief are easily distinguished now by their size and quality. They are almost always of bright colouring usually of damasks. The size and number are in proportion to the rank of the chief, usually of European manufacture now, though there is a distinct family of royal umbrella makers kept at Ọyọ who make those of the largest size. Most of the umbrellas foreign or locally made are decorated with certain emblems indicative of rank. About two dozen or more are used on these festive occasions.

Music. The Kọbi, third or fourth to the Agaṅju is occupied by the musicians. The musical instruments consist of almost every description of fifes, trumpets and drums, of which the ivory and Kakaki trumpets and Ogidigbo drum are peculiar to the sovereign.

The King enthroned is surrounded by his favourite wives, one of whom, the Arẹ-ori-itẹ, holds a small silk parasol over his head from behind as a canopy.

About 30 or 40 female *Ilaris* with costly dress and velvet caps on, are seated on the scarlet cloth on the right and on the left in front of the throne, but in the open air, under two large umbrellas, one on either side, a wide space being left between them.

Then there is a row of about ten large umbrellas each on the right and the left, both rows facing each other, leaving a wide avenue between from the throne to the main entrance gate ; under those on the right are seated the Crown Prince supported by all the princes and the principal eunuchs : under those on the left are the younger eunuchs, the Ilaris, the Tẹtus, and other palace officials. Behind these on either side are the crowds of spectators.

At a considerable distance in front of the throne, in the avenue left between the two groups, stand the Baṣọrun and the rest of the Ọyọ Mẹsi to do homage. This is done by taking off their robes, wrapping their cloths round their waists, leaving the body bare ; three times they have to run to the main entrance gate, sprinkle earth on their heads and on their naked bodies, and run back half way towards the throne, prostrating themselves on the bare ground, on the stomach and on the back!

Then follows the customary oration from the throne, the King speaking in an undertone with the *iru kere* in front of his mouth, and the chief of the eunuchs, who with his lieutenants the Otun and the Osi'wefa is standing midway between the throne and the noblemen in the avenue between the spectators, acts as his spokesman, repeating his message in a loud voice to the Basorun and his colleagues. The Basorun replies first, congratulating His Majesty, wishing him long life and prosperity, the other noblemen follow in regular order, the Asipa being the last. The chief of the eunuchs in like manner repeats the congratulatory address to their lord.

That over, the sacrificial feast is now brought forward for distribution. About 40 dishes of stewed meat, 40 baskets of eko, 15 pots of beer, a bowl or two of boiled yam, a large quantity of boiled corn (maize) to these is added in later years a demijohn of rum.

The Adà-há or king's taster now steps forward with a rod in his right hand, and a shield on his left, accompanied by his drummer. He first dances before the King and then retreats taking with him his own portion, a basket of eko, a plate of meat, a pot of beer, one yam, a head of corn; he is to have a taste of each of these in the presence of the king, and the concourse of spectators present, after which his followers make away with the rest of his portion.

Next comes the Olosa or king's robber, playing the clown. He is dressed in a flowing garment, creeps about on all fours, performing mimic acts of robbery for the amusement of the spectators. After a few more amusements, the curtain drops. The rest of the dishes are cleared away into the dining hall where the Asipa by virtue of his office subsequently distributes them among the noblemen and their followers according to their rank, that of the Basorun being one half of the whole. When the curtain rises again, the King appears in a more gorgeous robe, with another crown on his head. His Majesty now steps out of the Kobi with his staff in hand, and walks towards the Ogidigbo drum, stately and majestic, and the Basorun comes dancing to meet him; all at once the drums, fifes, and trumpets strike up in concert, the two rows of umbrellas move forward meeting in the centre to form a shady avenue for the two august personages, the King stepping forward with measured treads to the sound of the music, and the Basorun, dancing, and meeting him, receives from him one head of stringed cowries. This however is expected to be returned the next day, the apparent gift being merely a part of the ceremony.

This usually ends the show, but on the Bẹrẹ festival the King continues his walk right on to the great entrance gate, then half round the quadrangle giving the spectators a full view of himself, then by a side door disappears into the inner precincts of the palace. The spectators thereupon disperse.

These three festivals are concluded by a few male Ilaris carrying sacrifices to certain quarters in the outskirts of the city in a state of perfect nudity, which is rather a trying time for them ; there is always a rush of the women clearing out of their way, on the approach of them ; the performance being symbolic of some religious rite. If it is violated by any show of natural excitement, it must be atoned for, and there is but one penalty, viz., decapitation ! But there is no record of any such case occurring within living memory. Their reward for this trying ordeal is, that after their return, being properly dressed, they are admitted into the King's presence, who, sitting in state, receives them with marks of honour.

This ends the ceremonies of the festivals.

But at the *Bẹrẹ* season, one more ceremony remains, that known as the ceremony of " *Touching the grass.*" About 5.30 p.m. on a day appointed, the King issuing from the palace is accompanied by his slaves who have been engaged in piling into two or three heaps the bundles of bẹrẹ grass scattered about in the area in front of the palace, including those brought from the provinces. The piles are done up in an artistic manner, 8 or 10ft. high in an open space away from any risk of fire. His Majesty now steps forward, and lays both hands upon each of the heaps, making a short speech, invoking blessings on the Yoruba nation, congratulating himself for being spared to see another year. This brings the *Bẹrẹ* festival to a close.

THE FUNERAL OF THE KING

Although the funeral of the King cannot properly he said to be one of his public appearances, yet it is considered more convenient to describe it in this place along with other public ceremonies of which he is the centre.

The Kings are buried in the *Barà*. The funeral usually takes place at night. It is notified to the public by the sounding of the Ọkinkin (a musical instrument like the bugle), the ivory trumpet, and the Koso drum, a drum which is usually beaten every morning at 4 a.m. as a signal for him to rise from his bed ; to beat it at night therefore, is to indicate that he is retiring to his final resting place.

The body is removed to the *Barà* on the back of those whose office it is to bury the Kings the chief of whom is a titled personage known as the Ọna-onṣẹ-awo, and his lieutenants. At certain stations on the route between the palace and the *Barà*, eleven in all, they halt and immolate a man and a ram, and also at the *Barà* itself, four women each at the head and at the feet, two boys on the right and on the left, were usually buried in the same grave with the dead monarch to be his attendants in the other world, and last of all the lamp-bearer in whose presence all the ceremonies are performed.

All these practices, however, have long been abolished, a horse and a bullock being used instead of human beings.

The King is buried in black and white dress ; but the crown on his head, the gorgeous robe with which he was laid out in state, and with which his corpse was decked to the *Barà*, and the bracelets on his wrists and ankles are never buried with him, these become the perquisites of the Ọna-oñṣẹ-awo and his lieutenants.

The *Barà* in which the Kings are buried is distinguished by its aloof situation from public thoroughfares in the outskirts of the city, and having to it as many *kọbis* as there are Kings lying there, one being erected over each. The present *Barà* enshrines the bones of King OLUEWU the last of ancient ỌYỌ with those of the late Kings of the present city. It is not open to the public ; several of the late King's wives are secluded here (as in a convent) and charged with the sole duty of taking care of the graves of their departed husbands.

Their mother superintendent is the Iyamọdẹ generally styled " Baba " (father). She is thus styled because being entirely devoted to the worship of Sango, one of the earliest deified Kings, she is often "inspired" or " possessed " by the god, and thus came to be regarded as the embodiment of that famous King.

Additions are made to their number at every fresh burial, usually from among the favourites of the deceased husband. These women must all be celibates for life, unfortunately among the number are usually found some who are virgins and must remain so for life : any misbehaviour is punished with the death of both culprits, the man on the day the crime is detected, and the woman after her confinement.

Besides those who are immolated at the death of the sovereign there used to be some " honourable suicides " consisting of certain members of the royal family, and some of the King's wives, and others whose title implies that they are to die with the King whenever that event occurs. With the title they received as a badge a cloth known as the " death cloth," a beautiful silk damask wrapper, which they usually arrayed themselves with on special occasions

during the King's lifetime. Although the significance of this was
well-understood both by themselves and by their relatives, yet it
is surprising to see how eager some of them used to be to obtain the
office with the title and the cloth. They enjoyed great privileges
during the King's lifetime. They can commit any crime with
impunity. Criminals condemned to death and escaping to their
houses become free. These are never immolated, they are to die
honourably and voluntarily.

Of the members of the royal family and others to die were :—

1. The Arẹmọ or Crown Prince who practically reigned with his
father, enjoyed royal honours, and had equal power of life and death.

2. Three princes with hereditary titles viz., the Magaji Iyajin,
the Agunpopo, and the Olusami.

3. Two titled personages not of royal blood viz., the Osi'wẹfa
and the Olokun-ẹsin (master of the horse) who is generally styled
" Ab'ọbaku," i.e. one who is to die with the King.

4. The female victims were :—

ıya Ọba, the king's official mother ; Iya Naso, Iyalagbọn
(the Crown Prince's mother) ; Iyale Mọlè (the Ifa priestess), the
Ọlọrun-ku-mẹfun, the Iyamọnari, the Iya'-le-ori (these are all
priestesses) and the Arẹ-ori-itẹ the chief favourite.

It will be observed that all the above-mentioned are those who
by virtue of their office are nearest to the King at all times, and
have the easiest access to his person ; to make their life dependent
on his, therefore, is to ensure safety for him against the risk of
poisoning, or the dagger of the assassin.

The custom is that each should go and die in his (or her) own
home, and among his family. The spectacle is very affecting.
Dressed in their " death cloth," they issue from the palace to their
homes surrounded by their friends, and their drummers beating
funeral dirges, eager crowds of friends and acquaintances flocking
around them, pressing near to have a last look at them or to say
the final farewell as they march homewards. The house is full
of visitors, mourners and others, some in profuse tears ; mournful
wailings and funeral odes are heard on all sides enough to break
the stoutest heart. While the grave is digging, the coffin making,
a parting feast is made for all the friends and acquaintances ; and
as they must die before sunset, they enjoy themselves as best they
can for that day by partaking of the choicest and favourite dishes,
appearing several times in changes of apparel, distributing presents
with a lavish hand around, and making their last will disposing
of their effects. When everything is ready, the grave and the
coffin approved of, they then take poison, and pass off quietly.
But if it fails or is too slow to take effect, and the sun is about to

set, the last office is performed by the nearest relatives (by strangling or otherwise) to save themselves and the memory of their kin from indelible disgrace. The body is then decently buried by the relatives and the funeral obsequies performed.

In many cases voluntary suicides take place. Some of the King's favourite slaves who are not required to die often commit suicide in order to attend their master in the other world expecting to enjoy equally the emoluments of royalty in the other world as in this.

But these customs are now dying out with the age especially since King ATIBA in 1858 abolished that of the Crown Prince dying; the loss of experienced princes like the Iyajin around the throne is also felt irreparable. With the exception of the women, all the men now refuse to die and they are never forced to do so, but are superseded in their office if the next King wills it; they must then retire quietly from the city to reside in any town in the country in order to prevent the confusion of two individuals bearing the same title. As for the Crown Prince, he expects to succeed his father on the throne but if he is rejected by the king-makers, he also has to retire from the city.

COURTIERS AND HOUSEHOLD OFFICERS OF THE CROWN

The palace officials consist of :—
I. Titled officers. II. The Eunuchs. III. The Ilaris.
Some reside in the palace, others attend at regular hours every day for duty.
I. The principal officers having duties in the palace are :—

1. *The Ọna-Olokun-ẹsin* or *Ab'Ọba-ku* i.e. the master of the horse, i.e. one who is to die with the King. This officer resides in his own house but repairs to the palace daily on duty. He has free access equally with the Eunuchs to all the apartments. The title is hereditary. As his name implies he is to die with the King to be his attendant in the other world, and consequently he is granted unrestricted liberty to live as he likes, and to do whatever he likes, and, like all other officials who must die with the King, his house is a sanctuary of safety and reprieve for all criminals condemned to death, if they can escape thither.

2. *The Ọna-ile-mọlẹ* is the Ifa priest or chief diviner, a kind of domestic chaplain. He has for his assistants the Arẹ-awo and others. They are to consult the Ifa oracle for the King every fifth day called Ọjọ-Awo i.e. the day of the mysteries.

3. *The Ọna-Oñsẹ Awo.* The daily duties of this officer are not so well-defined, but he has to attend daily at the palace. He has

his lieutenants to the sixth grade. But their chief duty is to carry the remains of the deceased monarch from the palace to the *Barà* for interment.

4. *The Ọna-mọdekè.* This is the civil counterpart of the military title of Seriki. This officer is the head, or leader of all the youths in the city and country, capable of bearing arms, whoever may be their father or master. He forms a band of them all, and is supposed to train them in manly sports and civic duties. It is his prerogative to shield members of his band from the penalties of the law whenever they have become liable to such, by any rash act.

5. *The Iṣugbins.* These are members of the palace orchestra. They number about 210 persons, playing on fifes, the Ọkinkin and the Ivory trumpets, and the special drums Koso and Gbẹdu, etc.

    (a) *The Alukoso* or Koso drummer's chief duty is to wake up the King every morning at 4 a.m. with his drum.

    (b) *The Aludundun* or the Dundun drummer. He has to attend at the palace every day within certain hours, including the visiting or business hours. He has one of the front Kọbis assigned to him, where he sits discoursing events with his drum, all during his office hours. With it, he pre-announces the presence of any visitor in the palace, so that in whatever part of the palace the King may be, he can tell by the sound of the drum who has entered the court yard before the personage is actually announced. This is one of the peculiarities of the Yoruba language, and the art of the drummers. The names, praises and attributes of every family of note are known to all drummers, and musicians, and they are experts in eulogizing and enlarging on the praises of any one they wish to honour, *speaking* it with their drums. If for instance a white man enters the palace, the drummer would strike up : " Oyinbo, Oyinbo, afi okun ṣe ọnà " (the white man, the white man who makes of the ocean a high way). In strains like this he would continue for a while enlarging upon his praises.

6. *The Arọkins.* These are the rhapsodists or national historians, an hereditary title ; they have an apartment to themselves where they repeat daily in songs the genealogy of the Kings, the principal events of their lives and other notable events in the history of the Yoruba country.

7. *The Ile màle* is the palace surveyor. He has charge of all

the buildings within that vast compound, especially of the Kọbis.
He is to see that every part is kept in good repair. He is also
to attend to the drains and the grounds, especially after a heavy
fall of rain. He is said to be the principal officer who is to wash
the corpse of the King and dress it before it is placed in the coffin.

8. *The Tètus.* These are the sheriffs or King's executioners.
They are about 19 in number, each one of them with his
subordinates has specified duties to perform e.g., it is the duty
of the 15th with his subordinates to clear the grounds and dishes
after the King has entertained the ỌYọ MESI. They number
about 150 in all.

II. *The Eunuchs.* The Eunuchs are called Iwẹfa or Iba-āfin
(contracted to Baāfin) i.e. lordlings of the palace. The principal
are :—The Ọna'ẹfa or chief of the Eunuchs, the Ọtun'ẹfa and the
Osi'ẹfa his principal lieutenants, and others to the sixth grade.
Besides these are the untitled ones, and boys.

The Ọna'ẹfa is a high legal personage ; he hears and decides
suits and appeals brought to the King whenever His Majesty
cannot sit in person, and his decision is as good as the King's
whose legal adviser he is. We have seen above the principal part
he plays in public festivals and state ceremonies.

The Ọtun'ẹfa has the charge of the suburban town of Koso,
built in honour of the national god Sango. It is his duty to worship
at the shrine at stated periods on behalf of the Yoruba people.
He sometimes helps to decide cases. He is also one of the chief
guardians of the King's children.

The Osi'ẹfa or *Olosi* although the least of the three yet is the
most honoured. He represents the King on all occasions and in
all matters civil as well as military. He sometimes acts as
commander-in-chief in military expeditions, he is allowed to use
the crown, the state umbrellas, and the Kakaki trumpet, and to
have royal honours paid to him. On such occasions he is privileged
also to dispense the King's prerogatives. His ordinary duties
are : to be near the King's person at all times, having free access
to every part of the palace including the harem ; to see that the
King's bed is properly made, before he retires every night ; to
visit him at midnight and at cock-crow to see if he has had a
restful night, and to call him up at 4 a.m. before the Koso drum
begins to sound. He is to head those of the King's wives who
are to dance at the Akẹsan market once a year, after the deity
presiding over markets has been propitiated. With Ẹni-ọjà one
of the titled ladies of the palace, he has charge of the King's market
and enjoys in part the emoluments accruing therefrom.

Why these exceptional honours are bestowed upon the third

in rank among the Eunuchs, will be told hereafter in the history of one of the early kings.

The Eunuchs are a grade higher than the Ilaris and must be respected by them ; however young a Eunuch may be, he must be addressed as " Baba " (father) by any Ilari even the oldest.

The custom of castrating a man is said to have originated from the punishment inflicted for the crime of incest or of beastiality.

The Eunuchs are distinguished by the manner they wear their gowns gathered on the shoulders, leaving their arms bare. They are now generally chosen from boys bought with money, and employed first as pages to the King, or attendants on one of his wives. The custom of choosing boys was introduced by one of the later Kings ; his reason for it was, that before the age of puberty, boys will hardly be cognizant of their loss, and he would thus spare himself the remorse of conscience which would follow the mutilation of an adult, and also save his victim from a life-long mortification.

Emasculation of an adult is now only resorted to instead of capital punishment in cases of adultery with the wife of a king ; but in order that the system may not be abused, provincial kings are not allowed to resort to this mode of punishment, nor even to keep Eunuchs ; any one really guilty must be sent to the capital where a special surgeon is kept for the purpose who is skilful in the art.

The Eunuchs are the guardians of the King's children, the princes and princesses as a rule are born in the house of one of the principal Eunuchs for as soon as any of the King's wives becomes a mother, she is separated from the other women, and placed under the guardianship of one of them, and she is not to return to the palace until the child is weaned.

The titled ones among them are masters of large compounds, and they also keep their own harems as well ; their wives are called " Awewo," i.e. one with hands tied ; because they are doomed to be for ever childless. In cases of adultery disclosed by pregnancy both the defaulters in early days were to suffer capital punishment ; the man on the day the crime was proved against him, and the woman with the issue on the day she is delivered. These extreme measures, however, have been allowed to die out, in favour of fines or other less severe punishments.

The Eunuchs have the exclusive right of seizing anything in the market with impunity. They have also the unenviable privilege of mingling with the King's wives either in the harem or whenever they appear in public on any festive occasion.

III. *The Ilaris.* The term Ilari denotes parting of the head, from the peculiar way the hair of the head is done. They are of both sexes, they number some hundreds, even as many as the King desires to create.

The individual to be created an Ilari is first shaved completely, then small incisions, are made on the occiput (if a male) and on the left arm, into both of which a specially prepared ingredient is rubbed, supposed to be a charm capable of giving effect to whatever the name given to the individual at the same time signifies. Their names generally signify some attributes of the King, or are significant of his purpose, intention or will, or else the preservation of his life, e.g. Ọba l'olu, the King is supreme ; Ọba-kò-ṣe-tan, the King is not ready ; S'aiye ro, the upholder of the world (i.e. the kingdom) ; Ọba gb'ori, the King the overcomer ; Madarikàn, do not oppose him. The following are the names of some of the principal Ilaris, all of which will be seen to be significant.

1 Kafiaiye f' Ọba	30 Ọtẹ d'afo
2 Madarikàn	31 Aiye-gbemi
3 Ikudẹfùn	32 Magb'orimipete
4 Ilugbeñka	33 Kutiyà
5 Ọbajuwọnlọ	34 Kapẹ laiye
6 Ọpayàkàtà	35 Agbasa
7 S'aiyero	36 Ilugbohun
8 Mob'oludigbaro	37 Ọba gb'aiye
9 Ọbagbeñle	38 Agbelegbiji
10 Ọbagbori	39 Ọba diji
11 Ayunbọ	40 Kosiku
12 Ọtẹ ọ lọwọ	41 Olu orin-kàn
13 Kotito	42 Kosijà
14 Ọbakoṣetan	43 Ẹnu f'ọba
15 Oriṣa fẹtu	44 Ọba l'agba
16 Ọba d'origi	45 Makọ'hun
17 Sunmọ-Ọba	46 Ọsan
18 Olukòbinu	47 Ọba gbede
19 Kafilegbọin	48 Ọba fẹmi
20 Ọbadirere	49 Ọba gba-iyò
21 Makòbalapẹ	50 Ikufò
22 Mab'ọbadù u	51 Orikunkun
23 Temilekè	52 Makọ'hun
24 Ọba-ni yio jilọ	53 Olufọwọti
25 Ori-ehin	54 Imọ kojọ
26 Ọba-tun-wa-ṣe	55 Ilusinmi
27 Agbàlà	56 Ọdọdun
28 Agbàrò	57 Ẹni-iran
29 Kutenlọ	58 Agbe dẹfun

59 Ọba-li-a-isin   64 Madawọ t'ọba-lori
60 Emi-mọ l'Ọba-mi   65 Ma-ni-Ọba lara
61 Igba-abẹrẹ   66 Marọ-Ọba-lohun
62 Ọba l'olu   67 Oridagogo
63 Akegbe   68 Apeka

Every male Ilari has a female counterpart who is called his companion. The Ilaris themselves by courtesy call them their "mother." They are both created at one and the same time and they are supposed to seek each other's interest, although there must be no intimacy between them; the female Ilaris being denizens of the King's harem; the only attention they are allowed to pay each other is to make exchange of presents at the yearly festivals.

Each Ilari has a representative image made of clay called "Sugudu," having incisions on its head and arm similar to his own, with the same ingredient rubbed into them.

The Ilaris are to keep the head shaved, one half being done from the middle line downwards alternately every fifth day except the circular patch on the occiput where the incisions were made; there the hair is left to grow as long as possible being always plaited and sometimes dyed black with indigo.

The male Ilaris are the King's body guard or "The keepers of his head." They are of different grades including high-placed servants, messengers, and menials. Some of the favoured ones are made masters of large compounds, the King supplying them with horses and grooms, and assigning to them certain gates where they collect tolls, the proceeds being divided between their master and themselves for their maintenance; they are also feudal lords of some masters of large compounds in different parts of the city who serve them in various capacities in war or in time of peace.

All the inmates of their houses are for the most part the King's slaves, and every newly made Ilari is handed over to the charge of one or other of these highly-placed ones.

These favoured ones ride upon the tallest horses whenever the King goes out in public, forming his body guards; others are servants to these; but their chief work one and all is that of house repair year by year.

On any festive occasion when the King appears in state, as many of the male Ilaris as are required to be present must each one take his "sugudu" with him to his seat. They are on such occasions to be without a headgear or breeches with only a cloth over the body, passed under the right arm, and knotted on the left shoulder, the arms being left bare.

It is the especial privilege of the Ilaris, male or female, to carry nothing on the head save their hats or caps.

LADIES OF THE PALACE

The ladies of the palace consist of eight titled ladies of the highest rank, eight priestesses, other ladies of rank, besides Ilaris and the Ayabas or King's wives.

The whole of them are often spoken of loosely as " the King's wives," because they reside in the palace, but strictly speaking the titled ladies and the priestesses at least should not be included in the category. Again, all the ladies of rank are often spoken of as Ilaris, but there is a marked difference between them.

The following are the ladies of the highest rank in their due order :—

1 Iya Oba	5 Iya-fin-Ikù
2 Iya kere	6 Iyalagbon
3 Iya-Naso	7 Orun-kumefun
4 Iya-monari	8 Are-orite

1. *The Iya Oba* is the King's (official) mother. For reasons stated above (vide p. 48) the King is not to have a natural mother. If his mother happens to be living when he is called to the throne, she is asked to " go to sleep," and is decently buried in the house of a relative in the city. All the inmates of that house are accorded special privileges and enjoy marked deference as " members of the household of the King's mother."

The King sends to worship at her grave once a year. One of the ladies of the palace is then created *Iya-Oba*, and she is supposed to act the part of a mother to him. It is her privilege to be the third person in the room where the King and the Basorun worship the Orun in the month of September every year.

She is the feudal head of the Basorun.

2 *The Iya kere*. Next to the King's mother, the Iya kere holds the highest rank. Greater deference is paid to the *Iya Oba* indeed, but the Iya kere wields the greatest power in the palace. She has the charge of the King's treasures. The royal insignia are in her keeping, and all the paraphernalia used on state occasions, she has the power of withholding them, and thus preventing the holding of any state reception to mark her displeasure with the King when she is offended. We have seen above that she is the person entitled to place the crown on the King's head at the coronation.

She is the " mother " of all the Ilaris male and female, for it is in her apartment they are usually created ; she keeps in her custody

all the " sugudus " bearing the marks of each Ilari in order to
ensure the safety of the King's life.

Great and honourable as is the Olosi, she exercises full power
over even him, and can have him arrested and put in irons if he
offends. She is the feudal head of the Aseyin, Oluiwo, and the
Bale of Ogbomoso. With the assumption of this office, she is, of
course, to be a celibate for life.

3. *The Iya-Naso* has to do with the worship of Sango generally
and is responsible for everything connected with it.

The King's private chapel for Sango worship is in her apartment,
and all the emoluments and perquisites arising therefrom are
hers. She has also to do with the same at Koso.

4. *The Iya-monari* is the first lieutenant and assistant to the
Iya-Naso. It is her office to execute by strangling any Sango
worshipper condemned to capital punishment, as they are not to
die by the sword, and hence cannot be executed by the Tètus.

5. *The Iya-fin-Ikù* is the second lieutenant and assistant
to the Iya-Naso. She is the King's " Adosu Sango," i.e. the King's
devotee to the Sango mysteries. As all Sango worshippers are
to devote one of their children to the worship of the god, she stands
in place of that to the King. She has the charge of the sacred
ram which is allowed to go everywhere and about the market
unmolested, and may eat with impunity anything from the
sellers.

6. *The Iyalagbon.*—The mother of the Crown Prince is always
promoted to the rank of *Iyalagbon.* In case she is not living
whoever is promoted to that office acts like a mother to him. She
enjoys great influence, and controls a portion of the city.

7. *The Orun-kumefun* is also connected with the Aremo.

8. *The Are-oritè.* This official is the King's personal attendant.
She is to see that his meals are properly prepared, and his bed
properly made, and also to see him comfortably in bed before
retiring to her own apartment. She is to hold the silken parasol
over his head as a canopy when enthroned, and is constantly
by his side to perform small services for him on state and other
occasions.

These eight ladies holding responsible positions are each of
them the head of a small compound within the palace walls.

THE PRIESTESSES

1. Iya'le Ori	5. Iya Olosun
2. Iyale Molè	6. Iyafin Osun
3. Iya Orisanla	7. Iyafin Eri
4. Iya Yemaja	8. Iyafin-Orunfũmi

(1) *Íya' le Ori* is the priestess of the god *Ori* or god of fate. In her apartment is the King's *Ori* and she is the one to propitiate it for him.

(2) Iya'le-molę has in her keeping the King's *Ifa* god, and when the Ifa priests come every fifth day to worship and to consult it, she takes an active part in the ceremonies. She is the head of all the Babalawos (Ifa priests) in the city.

(3)—(8) as their names denote, are priestesses of the gods indicated by the title.

OTHER LADIES OF HIGH RANK

1. The Iyamodę
2. The Iya'le Oduduwa
3. The Odę
4. The Obaguntę

5. The Ęni-Ojà
6. The Iya'le-Agbo
7. The Iya-Otun

(1) *The Iyamodę.*—This high official resides in one of the out-houses of the palace, but her duties are not specially in the palace. She is the superior of those celibates living in the *Barà* and is styled by them " Baba " i.e. father.

Her office is to worship the spirits of the departed Kings, calling out their Egũguns in a room in her apartments set aside for that purpose, being screened off from view with a white cloth.

The King looks upon her as his father, and addresses her as such, being the worshipper of the spirits of his ancestors. He kneels in saluting her, and she also returns the salutation kneeling, never reclining on her elbow as is the custom of the women in saluting their superiors. The King kneels for no one else but her, and prostrates before the god Sango, and before those possessed with the deity, calling them " father." These are among those set apart for life-long service at the *Barà*. When any one of them is thus " possessed " by the spirit of deceased monarchs (it is said of them " Oba wa si ara wọn ") and comes raving from the Barà to the palace, she is immediately placed under the charge of the Iyamodę ; the possessed on such occasions prognosticates, and tells the people what sacrifice they are to offer to avert impending evils. The ceremony on such occasions is to pour some water into a mortar, covering it with a wide calabash, and this the other women in the palace beat vigorously as a drum ; the possessed and others infected with the excitement dancing to the sound of this drumming.

The Akunyungbas (the King's bards) are instructed in her apartments, their teacher comes there three times daily for three months or more until the learners are perfect in their studies. Small corporal punishments, twitchings of the ears, and cracks on the head are not spared on these occasions, if they are not quick at catching the words or if their memory fails them.

With the assumption of this office, the *Íyamọdẹ* is, of course, to be a celibate for life.

(2) *The Iya'le-Oduduwa* is the priestess of Oduduwa the supposed founder of the Yoruba nation. A special temple is built in the palace for him where his image is enshrined and worshipped. She is the head of all Oduduwa worshippers in the city. She resides in one of the out houses, and does not rank with the eight priestesses mentioned above.

(3) *The Qdẹ* is the head of all the worshippers of the god Osósi. On state occasions she appears dressed as a hunter (hence her name) wearing on her shoulder a bow ornamented with strings of cowries neatly strung.

(4) *The Ọbaguntẹ* is not regarded as having a very high position, although she represents the King in the Ogboni house on ordinary occasions, her work being strictly connected with that fraternity. She enters the Ogboni chamber on all occasions and acts in the King's name, reporting to his majesty the events of each day's sitting. Whenever the King wishes to entertain the Ogbonis, she has to undertake that duty.

(5) *The Ẹni-ọjà* is at the head of all the devil-worshippers in the town. She also has charge of the King's market, and enjoys all the perquisites accruing therefrom. She wears a gown like a man, on her arms the King leans on the day he goes to worship at the market, i.e. to propitiate the deity that presides over markets. She has under her (1) the Olosi who has joint responsibility with her for the market, and (2) the Arọja or market keeper, an officer whose duty it is to keep order, and arrange the manage-ment of the market, and who actually resides there.

(6) *The Iya'le-agbo* is a private attendant on the King, having charge of his private pharmacy. His *agunmu* (powders) and *agbo* (infusions) are all in her care : she is to see that they are in a condition fit for use when required.

All these ladies, except the *Ọbaguntẹ* and *Iya'le mọlẹ* although generally styled " Ilaris " are not really so, and that is known from the manner their hair is done up. They are really above the Ilaris.

The Iya-Ọba, and Iya mọdẹ are always shaven, the others plait their hair in small strips from the forehead to the top of the head and gather the rest from the back to the top, tying all into one knot with a string. This style is termed the Ikokoro.

The Ọdẹ, Eni-ọjà, Iyafin-Iku, Iya-Ọlọsun and the Iya'le Oduduwa adorn theirs with the red feathers of the parrot's tail.

The Ilaris.—The female Ilaris are somewhat differently shaved from the male, their incisions being made from the front to the back of the head along the middle line ; the hair is allowed to grow along the same line, and it is plaited into two horns front and back, being twined with a string or thread, and the sides of the head shaved alternately every fifth day.

The following are the names of the principal female Ilaris, every one of which is significant :—

1 Ọbaloyin	17 Irebe	33 Aronu
2 Majẹ-Ọba-koyẹ̀	18 Agbejo	34 Apa-ò-ká
3 Didun-l'Ọbafẹ	19 Awujalẹ	35 Ina-Ọba-kòkú
4 Ire-l'Ọba-iṣe	20 Ori're	36 Agbala
5 Igba-ewe	21 Oju're	37 Ọta-ko-ri-ayè
6 Ire k'aiye	22 Awigbá	38 Ma-dun-mi-de-inu
7 Ori-ogbo	23 Alògbo	39 Ọlẹdẹtu
8 Arọsin	24 Oridijo	40 Madajọ-l'Ọba
9 Ajinde	25 Tijotayọ	41 Ajijọfẹ
10 Oju're	26 Aiye f'ọbaṣe	42 Olu-f'ọba
11 Alosin	27 Aji gbohun	43 Iwàpẹ̀lẹ
12 Akọsin	28 Iwadẹrò	44 Ohungbogbo
13 Omi-su-yārin	29 Omuyè	45 Aiyedẹ̀rò
14 Bamwowò	30 Ajigbore	46 Ẹhin-wà
15 Afẹka	31 Ọbadarò	47 Maha-ro-t'ọba
16 Awoda	32 Alànù	48 Onjuwọn

These female Ilaris have the exclusive privilege of using the female head ties, or men's caps, the ordinary *Ayabas* or King's wives are distinguished by carrying their heads bare, always shaved, and their head ties used as a belt round the breasts.

At the demise of the King the whole of the Ilaris male and female go into mourning by dropping their official (Ilari) names, and letting their hair grow. At a new accession, the whole of them shave their heads. One of the earliest acts of the new sovereign after the coronation and the investiture of the Arẹmọ (Crown Prince) and just before the next great festival is to create all the Ilaris afresh by batches every 5 days, giving a new name to each and adding a new set of his own ; only the lances of the head are re-done, not those of the arm. Each batch is to remain seven days at the Ile Mọlẹ̀. This " distribution of honours " is eagerly sought after.

MEMBERS OF THE ROYAL FAMILY OCCUPYING RESPONSIBLE POSITIONS

As a rule, distinguished members of the Royal Family except those holding responsible positions do not reside in the metropolis, a great number of them may be found scattered all over the provinces especially in the *Ekùn Osi* or Metropolitan province, where each one resides as a lord of the town or village. They may take no part in the administration of affairs in the town, lest they over-shadow the chief of the town who is generally the founder or his descendant, but due deference is loyally accorded them, and certain privileges are granted them as befitting their rank. One such was Atiba the son of King ABIQDUN who resided in the town of Ago with Qja the founder, after whose death Atiba became practically the master of the town before he was subsequently elected King.

Some of the princes with a large family and a large following build their own town and become lord of the town. Such was Ayeijin who built the town of Surù near the ancient Qyq popularly known as Ile Gbagerè from the attributive of the founder.

There are those however, who hold high positions in the government such as the following :—

1. THE QNA ISOKUN. 2. THE QNA AKA. 3. THE QMQ-QLA.

These are known as the fathers of the King, hence the saying :—

" Qna-Isokun baba Qba,
Qna-Aka, baba Isokun." i.e.

The Qna-Isokun the King's father, the Qna-Aka, father to the Isokun. That is to say that they stand in the relation of a father to the King, who naturally cannot have a father living. To them it appertains to advise, admonish, or instruct the King, especially when he comes to the throne at a very early age, and as such lacks the experience indispensable for the due performance of his all-important duty. The titles are hereditary.

We have seen above that the nomination to the throne is in their hands. The QNA ISOKUN seems to be the most responsible of the three. We have seen that the King-elect is to sleep in his house the first night after his election, as the formal call to the throne comes from him. Lustrations, divinations, and propitiations for the new King are done in his house. Part also of the ceremony of creating the Aremo is performed in his house ; there all the princes are entertained in festivities, and there also all crown princes are buried if they die in that position.

Next to the above are those who are termed " brothers " to the King, they are :—

1. The Magaji Iyajin
2. The Olusami
3. The Arole Qba
4. The Atingisi
5. The Agunpopo
6. The Arole Iya Qba.

Officially, the Arẹmọ takes his rank among these princes, especially in public assemblies and is generally reckoned as the last of them in official order.

As the king must have official " father " and " mother " so also must he have official " brothers." Of these the Magaji Iyajin is the most distinguished. He is known as the King's elder brother, whose duty is to perform the part of an elder to a younger brother by defending his interests.

The term " Magaji " is the natural title of every heir to a great estate and is usually borne by the eldest son (or anyone in that relation) in the family. In this official royal circle the Iyajin is the eldest son. The term " Iyajin " implies the repelling of insults and indignities. The title therefore means the elder brother, who wards off insults and indignities.

This will often be found necessary when the King is young and inexperienced, and too conscious of his power, or sometimes rash. It is the Magaji's place to let the consequences of his action fall on himself rather than on the King who is the embodiment of the nation.

THE AROLE ỌBA is the official in whose house all the princes are to be buried, and in the month of July every year the whole of the princes and princesses, from the Ọna-Iṣokun downwards including the Arẹmọ repair to his house to worship the spirits of their deceased ancestors. A horse is usually offered in sacrifice, and all have to feed on the flesh of the same. The Iyajiu's portion is the head.

The ARẸMỌ as we have seen above is the Crown Prince. The term signifies an heir apparent, lit. *Chief of the sons*. How the title is formally conferred has been seen above.

The Arẹmọ practically reigns with his father, having nearly equal power, especially when the monarch is old and feeble.

From the period of the greatest prosperity of the nation to the time of the intertribal wars, the Arẹmọs were almost invariably tyrannical, and given to excess : they contributed largely to the disloyal explosion that caused the civil wars and the breaking up of the unity of the Yoruba kingdom ; they were,therefore, required to die with the father at his demise. Otherwise they expect to succeed to the throne as in earliest times, but they had to be elected thereto by the constitutional king-makers who would never elect one who has been infamous.

Since King Atiba in 1858 disallowed the practice in favour of his Arẹmọ Adelu, the custom has died out both for the Arẹmọ and the other princes.

THE NOBILITY

There are two classes of noblemen at Ọyọ; in the first, the title is hereditary; the second which is strictly military is the reward of merit alone, and not necessarily hereditary. In both, each member is styled " Iba " which means *a lord* being a dimunitive of " Ọba " *a king.*

A.   THE ỌYỌ MESI

The first class of noblemen consists of the most noble and most honourable councillors of state, termed the ỌYỌ MESI. They are also the king-makers. They are seven in number and of the following order :—

(1) The Ọṣọrun, (2) Agbakin, (3) Ṣamu, (4) Alapīni, (5) Laguna, (6) Akiniku, (7) Aṣipa.

The title of each (as above said) is hereditary in the same family but not necessarily from father to son ; it is within the King's prerogative to select which member of the family is to succeed to the title or he may alter the succession altogether.

They represent the voice of the nation ; on them devolves the chief duty of protecting the interests of the kingdom. The King must take counsel with them whenever any important matter affecting the state occurs. Each of them has his state duty to perform, and a special deputy at court every morning and afternoon and whom they send to the ALÂFIN at other times when their absence is unavoidable ; they are, however, required to attend court in person the first day of the (Yoruba) week, for the Jakuta (Sango) worship and to partake of the sacrificial feast.

(1) *The Ọṣọrun* or Iba Ọṣọrun (contr. to Baṣọrun i.e., the lord that performs the " Ọrun ") may be regarded as the Prime Minister and Chancellor of the kingdom and something more. He is not only the president of the council but his power and influence are immeasurably greater than those of the others put together. His is the chief voice in the election of a King, and although the King as supreme is vested with absolute power, yet that power must be exercised within the limit of the unwritten constitution, but if he is ultra-tyrannical and withal unconstitutional and unacceptable to the nation it is the Baṣọrun's prerogative as the mouth-piece of the people to move his rejection as a King in which case His Majesty has no alternative but to take poison and die.

His Highness being a prince is practically as absolute as a King in his own quarter of the town.

Next to the ALÂFIN in authority and power, he often performs the duties of a King. He takes precedence of all provincial kings and princes. There were times in the history of the nation when the Baṣoruns were more powerful than the ALÂFIN himself.

During the long course of history there have been several alliances between the two families so that, in the older line of Baṣoruns at any rate, the blood of the royal family runs also in their veins.

Several points of similarity may be noted between the ALÂFIN and his Baṣorun The ALÂFIN is Oba (a king) he is Iba (a lord). The ALÂFIN's wives are called Ayaba, the Baṣorun's Ayinba. They are similarly clothed, carrying their heads bare and shaven, and their head-bands used as belts ; but the Ayinbas are not equally avoided by men as the Ayabas are.

The *Iba Oṣorun* has *kobis* to his palace as well, but a limited number; those of the ALÂFIN being unlimited. He too has a number of Ilaris as a king, but they must be created for him by the ALÂFIN.

The ALÂFIN has his crown, his throne, his Ejigba round his neck. The Oṣorun has a specially made coronet of his own, a specially ornamented skin called the WABI on which he sits, and a string of beads round his neck also like the Ejigba.

We have seen that at the principal festivals of the ALÂFIN, the Baṣorun also has minor festivals to observe in conjunction and has his part to play at the main observance also.

When the ALÂFIN reigns long and peacefully enough to celebrate the *Bebe*, a festival akin to the royal jubilee, the Baṣorun must follow with the Owàrà.

But it is a peculiarity of the Baṣorun's children that the boys are never circumcised.

Although the title is hereditary in the same family yet it is within the King's power to change the line of succession when necessity demands that course.

Thus the whole unwritten constitution of the Yorubas seems to be a system of checks and counter-checks, and it has on the whole worked well for the country.

There have been five different families of the Baṣorun line, each one with its distinctive cognomen. The first and oldest belonged to the family totem of *Ogun* (the god of war) and have for appellatives *Moro, Maṣo, Mawò, Maja, Ogun*. This was the original line contemporary with the earliest Kings. It covers the reign of 18 Kings and ended with Baṣorun Yamba, in the reign of King OJIGI.

With the long lease of power and influence enjoyed by this family, it became as wealthy and great as, or even greater than the sovereign himself, especially as some of the Baṣoruns out-lived two or three successive Kings. Therefore King GBERU the successor of Ojigi transferred the succession to his friend Jambu of another line, whose appellatives were *Maja Maro*. This line embraced the reign of seven Kings and ended with Aṣamu in ABIODUN'S reign.

The third began with Alobitoki in Aole's reign, having the appellatives of *Maja Majo* of the totem of *Agan*.

This line was not allowed to continue,-it flourished during the reign of one King only, for Ojo Abuṛumaku the son of Oniṣigun and grandson of Baṣọrun Gâ was of the older line. The fourth line began with Akīoṣo in King MAJOTU'S reign, and also ended with himself in the reign of OLUEWU, the last of ancient ỌYỌ. This family was rather insignificant.

Oluyọle the first Baṣọrun of the new city was the grandson of Baṣọrun Yamba, and therefore of the older *Ogun* line.

The fifth and last line commenced with Gbenla in the reign of King ATIBA, the totem is *Ayẹ* and is the family now in office and has already lasted through the reign of three kings.

The Baṣọruns of Ibadan after Oluyọle are only honorary with no national duties attached to the office.

A SYNOPSIS OF THE BAṢỌRUN FAMILY

Baṣọruns.	Appellatives.	Family Totems.
1. Efufukofẹri to Yamba	Moro, Maṣo, Maja	Ogun
2. Jambu to Aṣamu	Maja Maro	(?)
3. Alobitoki	Maja Majo	Agan
4. Akioṣo	(?)	Ese
5. Gbenla to Layọde	(?)	Ayẹ

(2) *The Agbakin.*—The duties of this official are not so well-defined, but the present Agbakin has the charge of the worship of Ọrañyan.

(3) *Samu.* The duties of the Ṣamu are not clearly known.

(4) *The Alapini.*—He is the head of the Egūgun mysteries, and as such he is at the head of religious affairs in general. He has the charge of the famous JENJU, who is the head Egūgun of the country, and who executes witches ! He is at once a religious and a secular personage ; he shares with the priests all religious offerings, and in secular matters with the noblemen of his class. By virtue of his peculiar office he must be a *monorchis*.

(5) *The Laguna* is the state ambassador in critical times.

(6) *The Akiniku.*—The real duties of this officer are not known.

(7) *The Aṣipa* as the last of them performs the duties of the junior. He is called the " Ojuwa," i.e. the one who distributes whatever presents are given to the ỌYỌ MESI. The Baṣọrun in

these cases has always the lion's share viz., one half of the whole, the other half being equally divided between the rest of them.

The Aṣipa of the present Ọyọ being the son of Ọja the founder of the town, has the chief voice in all municipal affairs. He is thereby acknowledged to be the master of the town.

The provincial kings and ruling princes rank also as the noblemen of the first-class.

B. THE ẸSỌS

Next in importance to the Ọyọ MẸSI and of a rank below them are the Ẹsọs or guardians of the kingdom. These constitute the noblemen of the second class. They also are addressed as " Iba." It is a military title, not necessarily hereditary. It is the reward of merit alone, and none but tried and proved soldiers are selected for that rank.

First and foremost among them and apart by himself stands the Kakanfo, an Ẹsọ of the Ẹsọs. Then the 70 captains of the guard ten of whom are under each of the seven councillors. Each wears an Akoro (or coronet) and carries in his hand no weapon, but a baton or staff of war known as THE INVINCIBLE.

There is a common saying which runs thus :—

" Ohun meji l'o yẹ Ẹsọ
Ẹsọ jà O le ogun
Ẹsọ ja O ku si ogun."
One of two things befits an Ẹsọ
The Ẹsọ must fight and conquer (or)
The Ẹsọ must fight and perish (in war).

He is never to turn his back, he must be victorious or die in war. There is another saying :—

" Ẹsọ ki igba Ọfà lẹhin
Afi bi o ba gbọgbẹ niwaju gangan."
An Ẹsọ must never be shot in the back
His wounds must always be right in front.

Also another saying :—

" Alakoro ki isa ogun."
One who wears a coronet must never flee in battle.

They are of two ranks 16 superior and 54 inferior, 70 in all and they all must reside in the capital.

The following are the titles of the former, all of which are significant :—

Gbọnkâ	Ẹsọ Ọrañyan	Sagbẹdọ	Obago
Esiẹlẹ	Kogbonà	Ole	Ọruntọ̀
Owòta	Sakin	Odigbọn	Sagbua
Sadọẹ	Erukù	Gbọingbọin	Adàhá

So much is this title thought of by military men and others and so great is the enthusiasm it inspires, that even the children and grandchildren of an Eṣọ hold themselves bound to maintain the spirit and honour of their sires. The Eṣọ is above everything else noble in act and deed.

" Emi ọmọ Eṣọ " (me born of an Eṣọ) is a proud phrase generally used even to this day by any of their descendants to show their scorn for anything mean or low, or their contempt for any difficulty, danger, or even death itself.

Most of the Egba chiefs sprang from the Eṣọs of Ọyọ, Okukẹmu the first " king " of Abẹokuta was a Sagbua.

A special notice must now be taken of the Kakanfo who stands at the head of the Eṣọs.

THE KAKANFO. The title given in full is Arẹ-Ọna-Kakanfo. It is a title akin to a field-marshal, and is conferred upon the greatest soldier and tactician of the day.

This title was introduced into the Yoruba country by King AJACBO, one of the earliest and most renowned of Yoruba Kings.

Like the Ilaris, at the time of his taking office, he is first to shave his head completely, and 201 incisions are made on his occiput, with 201 different lancets and specially prepared ingredients from 201 viols are rubbed into the cuts, one for each. This is supposed to render him fearless and courageous. They are always shaved, but the hair on the inoculated part is allowed to grow long, and when plaited, forms a tuft or a sort of pigtail.

Kakanfos are generally very stubborn and obstinate. They have all been more or less troublesome, due it is supposed to the effect of the ingredients they were inoculated with. In war, they carry no weapon but a baton known as the " King's invincible staff." It is generally understood that they are to give way to no one not even to the King, their master. Hence Kakanfos are never created in the capital but in any other town in the kingdom.

There can be *but one* Kakanfo at a time. By virtue of his office he is to go to war once in 3 years to whatever place the King named, and, dead or alive, to return home a victor, or be brought home a corpse within three months.

The ensigns of office are :—

1. The Ojijiko. This is a cap made of the red feathers of the parrot's tail, with a projection behind reaching as far down as the waist.

2. An apron of leopard's skin, and a leopard's skin to sit on always.

3. The Àṣiṣó or pigtail as above described.

4. The Staff Invincible.

The following are the Kakanfos who have ever borne office in the Yoruba country :—

1. Kokoro gangan   of Iwòye
2. Oyatope   ,,   ,,
3. Oyabi   ,,   Ajase
4. Adeta   ,,   Jabata
5. Oku   ,,   Jabata
6. Afonja l'aiya l'okò   ,,   Ilorin
7. Toyeje   ,,   Ogbomoso
8. Edun   ,,   Gbogun
9. Amepò   ,,   Abemò
10. Kurūmi   ,,   Ijaye
11. Ojo Aburumaku   ,,   Ogbomoso (son of Toyeje)
12. Latosisa   ,,   Ibadan the last to hold office.

Nearly the whole of them were connected with stirring times and upheavals in the country. Afonja of Ilorin, Toyeje of Ogbomoso Kurūmi of Ijaye, and Latosisa of Ibadan being specially famous. Ojo Aburumaku of Ogbomoso fought no battles, there being no wars during the period ; the change that has taken place in the country left the Ibadans at this time masters of all warlike operations. But in order to keep his hand in, he fomented a civil war at Ogbomoso which he also repressed with vigour.

PROVINCIAL GOVERNMENTS AND TITLES

Every town, village or hamlet is under a responsible head, either a provincial " king " or a Bale (mayor). In every case the title is hereditary (excepting at Ibadan) as such heads are invariably the founder or descendants of the founder of their town.

The provincial kings are styled the lords of their town or district, and from it they take their title, e.g. :—

The Onikoyi, lord of Ikoyi ; Aseyin, lord of Iseyin ; Alake, lord or Ake ; Olowu, lord of Owu ; Oluiwo, lord of Iwo ; Alakija, lord of Ikija, etc. There are a few exceptions to this rule, where the first ruler had a distinctive name or title before he became the head of the town or district, e.g. :—

Timi of Ede, Atawoja of Osogbo, Awujale of Ijebu, Okere of Saki, Onibode of Igboho, etc., in which case the distinctive name becomes the hereditary title of the chief ruler.

A provincial king is, of course, higher than a Bale as a duke or an earl is higher than a mayor. They are privileged to build *kobis* to their palaces, and to create Ilaris which Bales are not entitled to do. They are also allowed an Akoro (coronet) which Bales are not allowed to have ; but few of them indulge in large state umbrellas. They are invested originally with power from Ọyọ whither they usually repair to obtain their titles, the sword of justice being given them by the ALÂFIN at their installation. Every one of them as well as every important Balẹ has an official at Ọyọ through whom they can communicate with the crown.

They are also invested with an *Ọpaga* by which they are empowered to make and keep an Ilari. The *Ọpaga* is an iron instrument of the shape of an *Ọsain*, but taller and is surmounted with the figure of a bird. This is the *Ọsain* worshipped by Ilaris. To be deprived of it is equivalent to being deprived of one's rank.

To dethrone a kingling, he is publicly divested of his robe and sandals and the announcement is made that XYZ having forfeited his title, he is deprived of it by AB his suzerain or feudal lord.

The following are the kinglings in the Ọyọ provinces.

1. In the Ekun Osi or Metropolitan province :—

The Onikoyi of Ikoyi ; Olugbọn of Igbọn ; Arẹsa of Irẹsa ; the Ompetu of Ijẹru ; Ọlọfa of Ọfa.

2. In the Ẹkun Ọtun province :—

Sabigana of Igana ; Ọniwere of Iwere ; [1]Alasia of Asia ; Onjọ of Oke'ho ; Bagijan of Igijan ; Ọkẹrẹ of Saki ; Alapata of Ibode ; Ona Onibode of Igboho ; Elerinpo of Ipapo ; Ikihisi of Kihisi ; Asẹyin of Isẹyin ; Alado of Ado ; Eleruwa of Eruwa ; Ọlọjẹ of Ọjẹ.

3. In the Ibọlọ province :—

The Akirun of Ikirun ; Olobu of Ilobu ; Timi of Ẹdẹ, the Atawọja of Ọsogbo ; Adimula of Ifẹ Ọdan.

4. In the Epo province :

The Oluiwo of Iwo ; Ọndẹsẹ of Idẹsẹ.

Of these vassal kings the Onikoyi, Olugbọn, the Arẹsa and the Timi are the most ancient.

Since the wave of Fulani invasion swept away the first three, those titles exist only in name. The Onikoyi has a quarter at Ibadan, the bulk of the Ikoyi people being at Ogbomọso, the family is still extant and the title kept up.[2] The same may be said of the Arẹsa at Ilọrin. But wherever the representative head of the family may be, he is completely subject to the ruler of the town, be he a Balẹ or a king. Thus the Olugbọn at Ogbomọso is subject to the Balẹ of Ogbomọso, the Arẹsa to the king or Emir

---

[1] The Alasia is the only man privileged not to prostrate before the Alâfin in salutation according to the custom of the country. He sits on a stool with his back turned towards him.

[2] The town has been rebuilt and the Onikoyi returned home in 1906.

of Ilọrin, and similarly the Olowu at Abẹọkuta is nominally subject to the Alake, the primus of the Ẹgba chiefs.

In the Ẹkun Osi and Ẹkun Ọtun provinces, no special remarks are called for in the arrangement of the titles in the government ; they are for the most part a modified form of the Ọyọ titles.

Ibọlọ titles.—Amongst the Ibọlọs the royal family is called Ọmọlaisin. The title next to that of the king which answers to the Basọrun is the Osa, next to the Osa comes the Aro, then the Ọdọfin and then the Ẹjẹmu. · These are the principal councillors. The other subordinate titles are chiefly military viz., the Jagun and his lieutenants the Olukọtun and Olukosi. Then the Agbakin, Gbọnkâ, Asipa which are Ọyọ titles that have been borrowed. Then the Saguna, Sakọtun, Sakosi, Asápẹ̀, Oladifi Esinkin, and the Ar'ogunyọ̀.

· The Elesijẹ is the chief physician.

Smaller towns are governed by the Balẹ, and the Jagun (or Balogun) is the next to him. In time of war, the Balẹ appoints the Jagun to go with the Kàkanfo to any expedition to which the ALÂFIN may send the latter ; but if it is a great expedition to which he appoints the Onikoyi, all the other vassal kings, and the Balẹs of every town were bound to go with him. The affairs of the town are then left to be administered by the Balẹ Agbẹ, i.e. the chief of the farmers. The duties of the Balẹ Agbẹ on ordinary occasions are to superintend the tax collectors, and to assist the Jagun who superintends the cleaning of the roads.

THE IYALODE, i.e. the queen of the ladies is a title bestowed upon the most distinguished lady in the town. She has also her lieutenants *Ọtun, Osi, Ẹkẹrin,* etc., as any of the other principal chiefs of the town. Some of these Iyalodes command a force of powerful warriors, and have a voice in the council of the chiefs. Through the Iyalode, the women of the town can make their voices heard in municipal and other affairs.

The King's civil officers judge all minor cases, but all important matters are transferred to the ALÂFIN of Ọyọ whose decision and laws were as unalterable as those of the ancient Medes and Persians.

THE ẸGBA PROVINCE

" Ẹgba kò l'Olu, gbogbo wọn ni nṣe bi Ọba (i.e. Ẹgbas have no king all of them act like a king), is a common saying. That is to say, they have no king that rules. The king is acknowledged as the head of the government, but only as a figure head. More marked was this when they lived in separate townships before their concentration at Abẹokuta. The Ogbonis constitute the town council, and they are also the executive, and even the

E

" king " was subject to them. The same rule holds good even at Abeokuta for each township.

Amongst the highest Ogboni titles are :—

The Aro, Oluwo, Apena, Ntowa, Bàla, Basálà Baki, Asipa, Asalu, Lajila, Apesi, Esinkin Ola, Bayimbo, Odofin.

The warriors rank next after the Ogbonis, the Balogun and the Seriki being the most important.

THE IJEBU PROVINCE

Among the Ijebus the civil authorities are of three divisions, viz., the Osugbos or Ogboni, 2, the Ipampa, and 3 the Lamurin. Without these acting in concert, no law can be enacted or repealed. Of these bodies, the Osugbos are the highest for even the king himself must be of that fraternity. The Lamurins are the lowest.

Amongst the Egbas and Ijebus, the Ogbonis are the chief executive, they have the power of life and death, and power to enact and to repeal laws : but in the Oyo provinces the Ogbonis have no such power ; they are rather a consultative and advisory body, the king or Bale being supreme, and only matters involving bloodshed are handed over to the Ogbonis for judgment or for execution as the king sees fit.

The actual executioners at Oyo are the Tetus, amongst the Ibolos, the Jagun, and in the Epo districts the Akodas or sword bearers of the principal chiefs, acting together.

THE IJESA AND EKITI PROVINCES

In the Ijesa and Ekiti provinces the form of government is more or less alike, with slight modifications. The tendency is to adopt the Oyo forms ; but they have some admirable systems of their own. The municipal arrangements of the Ijesas are quite excellent.

It has been mentioned above that there are 16 provincial kings recognised in the Ekiti province under four principal ones. The title of Owa is a generic term for them all, including that of Ilesa. The Owa of Ilesa stands by himself, for the Ekitis hold the Ijesas separate from themselves.

The Orangun of Ila is sometimes reckoned amongst the Ekitis ; but he is not an Ekiti although his sympathies are with them. He aims at being the head of the Igbomina tribes, but Ila seems to stand by itself.

Titles in ancient times may be obtained by competition, and it was not always the most worthy but the highest bidder that often obtained them.

CHAPTER V

YORUBA NAMES

The naming of a child is an important affair amongst the Yorubas; it is always attended with some ceremonies. These of course differ somewhat, amongst the different tribes.

The naming usually takes place on the 9th day of birth if a male, or on the 7th if a female; if they happen to be twins of both sexes, it will be on the 8th day. Moslem children of either sex are invariably named on the 8th day.

It is on that day the child is for the first time brought out of the room, hence the term applied to this event—Ko ọmọ jade (bringing out the child). The mother also is supposed to be in the lying-in room up to that day.

The ceremony is thus performed:—The principal members of the family and friends having assembled early in the morning of the day, the child and its mother being brought out of the chamber, a jugful of water is tossed up to the roof (all Yoruba houses being low-roofed), and the baby in the arms of the nurse or an elderly female member of the family, is brought under the eaves to catch the spray, the baby yells, and the relatives shout for joy. The child is now named by the parents and elderly members of the family, and festivities follow; with presents, however trifling, for the baby from every one interested in him.

This is evidently an ancient practice, a form of baptism which the ancestors of the Yorubas must have derived from the eastern lands, where tradition says they had their origin, and is another proof of the assertion that their ancestors had some knowledge of Christianity.

In some cases there is also the offering of sacrifice and consultation of the household oracle on the child's behalf.

For the sake of convenience we call this the *Christening* of the child. There are three sets of names a child can possibly have, although not every child need have the three; one at least will be inapplicable.

1. The *Amutọrunwa* i.e. the name the child is born with.
2. The *Abisọ* i.e. the christening name.
3. The *Oriki* i.e. the cognomen or attributive name.

A few remarks on each of these sets of names will serve to elucidate their meanings.

I. The Amutọrunwa

A child is said to be "born with a name" (*lit.* brought from heaven) when the peculiar circumstance of its birth may be expressed by a name which is applicable to all children born under like circumstances. The most important of these is twin-births. No condition is invested with an air of greater importance, or has a halo of deeper mystery about it, than that of twin-births; the influence is felt even upon children that may be born after them. Twins in Yoruba are almost credited with extra-human powers, although among some barbarous tribes they are regarded as monsters to be despatched at once.

Taiwo or Ebo.—The name of the first born of twins, applicable to either sex. It is a shortened form of Tọ-aiye-wò (have the first taste of the world). The idea is that the first born was sent forward to announce the coming of the latter, and he is considered the younger of the two. [Compare the stories of Esau and Jacob, and of Pharez and Zarah, in both of which the first born of the twins virtually became the younger of the two.]

Kẹhinde "He who lags behind," i.e. the second born.

Ídowu. The child born after twins, male or female, Idowus are always considered heady and stubborn, hence their usual appellation " Èṣu lẹhiu ibeji " (the d——l after twins). There is also a current superstition that the mother who has had twins and fails to get an Idowu in due course, may likely go mad; the wild and stubborn Idowu " flying into her head " will render her insane ! Hence all mothers of twins are never at ease until in due course the Idowu is born.

Ídogbe.—The child after Idowu if male.

Alaba.—The child after Idowu if female.

Thus we see the influence of the twins affecting the second and third births after themselves.

Ẹta Òkò.—The name given to the third of triplets.

The next to twins in importance is the child named *Oni Oni.* This name is given to a small neurotic child which at its birth cries incessantly day and night. The child after Oni is called *Òla*, the next *Òtunla*, and so on.

These names signify *to-day, to-morrow*, the *day after to-morrow*, etc. With a small tribe termed the Isin people, it is carried on as far as *Ijọni* i.e. the 8th day, if the mother have as many.

Asà or *Oroyè* are names applied under conditions similar to those of Oni by some clans. The latter is generally preferred by worshippers of the god *Oriṣa Oko.*

Igè is a child born with breech or footling presentation.

Ilọri is a child who was conceived during absence of menstruation.

Ọmọpẹ signfies " the child is late " that is, a child born later than the normal period of utero-gestation.

Ojo or *Aina* is a child born with the cord twined round its neck. The choice of name is a matter of preference partly clannish or by the decision of the family Oracle. Ojo, however, is never given to females, *Aina* may be male or female.

Ajayi is a child born " with face downwards " it is styled *Adojude*, that is to say, when rotation is absent during the exit of the shoulders.

Òke is a name given to a child which faints away on being fed in a horizontal position as is the custom of the country.

Ọkẹ (a bag) is a child born with membranes unruptured.

Salako (male), *Talabi* (female), a child born with the head and body covered with the caul, or ruptured membranes.

Dada is a curly-headed child styled " Olowo Ori."

Olugbodi is a child born with supernumerary digits.

Abiọna means " born by the way side," i.e. a child born when the mother is on a journey, or away from home.

Abiọdun born at the new year or any annual festival.

Abiọsẹ born on a holy day.

Babatunde means " father comes again," a name given to a male child born soon after the death of its grandfather. The sire is supposed to re-appear in the newly born.

Abiba is applied to a female under similar circumstances.

Yetunde means " mother comes again " a name given to a female child born soon after the death of its grandmother. The granny is supposed to re-appear in the newly born.

Babarimisa (father fled at my approach) is the name given to a posthumous child.

Jọ'hòjọ a child whose mother died at its birth (Ichabodlike) or during the puerperium.

II.—The Abisọ or Christening Name

All children need not be " born with a name " but all must be named. Names are not given at random because ot their euphony or merely because a distinguished member of the family or of the community was so named, but of a set purpose from circumstances connected with the child itself, or with reference to the family fortunes at the time etc. Hence the saying :—" Ile la iwò kia to sọ ọmọ l'oruko (the state of the house must first be considered before naming a child). The names then are always

significant of something, either with reference to the child itself
or to the family.

A child may have two or more christening names given it
one by each parent or grandparents if living or by any elderly
member of the family.   Whichever is most expressive of the present
circumstances of the family will be the one to stick.

(*a*) Names having reference to the child itself directly and indirectly
to the family :—

Ayọdele	Joy enters the house.
Onipẹde	The consoler is come.
Morẹnikẹ	I have some one to pet.
Moṣeb'ọlatan	Joy hitherto despaired of.
Ọmọteji	A child big enough for two.
Akinyẹle	A strong one befits the house.
Ibiyẹmi	Good birth becomes me.
Ibiyinka	Surrounded by children.
Ladipọ	Increase honour (of children born).

(*b*) Names having reference to the family directly and indirectly
to the child itself :—

Ogundalenu	Our home has been devastated by war.
Ọtẹgbẹyẹ	Warfare deprived us of our honours.
Ogunmọla	The river Ogun took away our honour.
Iyapọ̀	Many trials.
Ọlabisi	Increased honours.
Laniyọnu	Honour is full of troubles.
Kurũmi	Death has impoverished me.
Oyebisi	Increased titles.

(*c*) Names compounded of Ade, Ọla, Olu, Oye originally belonged
to one of high or princely birth, but are now used more or
less indiscriminately :—

Adebiyi	The crown has begotten this.
Adegbite	The crown demands a throne.
Ọlalẹyẹ	Honour comes fittingly, or is full of dignity.
Olubiyi	A chief has begotten this.
Oyeyẹmi	Title becomes me.
Oyewọle	Title enters the house i.e. where the parent has a title.

N.B.—Ade does not always signify a crown, it may be taken
from the verb *dé* to arrive, it may then mean coming, e.g.,

Adebisi or ⎱ Adewusi ⎰	My coming causes an increase.
Adeṣina	My coming opens the way.
Adepeju	My coming completes the number (of births)
Adepọju	The coming has become too much.

(*d*) Some names are compounded with fetish names showing the deity worshipped in the family :—

Ṣangobunmi	Sango (the god of thunder and lightning) gave me this.
Ogundipẹ	Ogun (the god of war) consoles me with this.
Ogunṣeyẹ	Ogun has done the becoming thing.
Omi yale	The god of streams visits the house.
Ọba-bunmi	The King (i.e. god of small pox) gave me this
Fabunni	Ifa has given me this.
Fatosin	Ifa is worthy to be worshipped.
Fafumkẹ	Ifa gave me this to pet.
Oṣuntoki	Oṣun is worthy of praise or honour.

It may be noted that names compounded with Ifa are very common amongst the Ijẹsas which shows that they are devoted Ifa worshippers.

(*e*) Compounds of Ọdẹ shows that the father is a worshipper of Ogun or Erinlẹ :—

Ọdẹwale	Ọdẹ comes to the house i.e. visits the family.
Ọdẹmuyiwa	Ọdẹ has brought me this.

These names are often confounded with Adewale and Ademuyiwa.

(*f*) Compounds of Oṣo or Ẹfun shows that the family is a worshipper of Oriṣa Oko i.e. the god of the fields :—

Oṣodipẹ	Oṣo has granted a consolation.
Oṣodẹkẹ	Oṣo has become a roof i.e. shield and shelter.
Ẹfunṣetan	Ẹfun has done it (by granting the child).
Ẹfunlabi	Ẹfun is the one born.

(*g*) Compounds of Ọje are peculiar to the children of Elewi of Ado. Names peculiar to the royal family of Ọyọ :—

Male : Afọnja, Tẹla, Ajuan.

Female :—Ogboja, Siyẹ, Akere.

Yoruba names are with few exceptions common to both genders. Ojo and Akerele, however, are never applied to females. Also names compounded of *Akin* which means strength ; and, of course, such names as Babatunde, Babarimisa can only apply to males, and Yetunde to females.

ABIKU NAMES

There are some peculiar names given to a certain class of children called " Abiku " i.e. born to die. These are supposed to belong to a fraternity of demons living in the woods, especially about and within large Iroko trees ; and each one of them coming into the world would have arranged beforehand the precise time he will return to his company.

Where a woman has lost several children in infancy, especially after a short period of illness, the deaths are attributed to this cause, and means are adopted to thwart the plans of these infants in order that they may stay ; for if they can only tide over the pre-arranged date, they may go no more, and thus entirely forget their company.

Besides charms that are usually tied on them and ugly marks they are branded with, in order that their old company may refuse the association of disfigured comrades which must oblige them to stay, certain significant names are also given to them in order to show that their object has been anticipated.

Such are the following names :—

Malomo	Do not go again.
Kosoko	There is no hoe (to dig a grave with).
Banjoko	Sit down (or stay) with me.
Durosinmi	Wait and bury me.
Jekiñiyin	Let me have a bit of respect.
Akisatan	No more rags (to bury you with).
Apara	One who comes and goes.
Oku	The dead.
Igbękòyi	Even the bush wont have this.
Ęnu-kun-onipę	The consoler is tired.
Akuji	Dead and awake.
Tiju-iku	Be ashamed to die.
Duro-ori-ikę	Wait and see how you will be petted.

Periodical feasts are usually made for these children of which beans and a liberal quantity of palm oil must form a principal dish.   To this children of their age and others are invited, and their company of demons, although unseen are supposed to be present and partake of these viands.   This is supposed to appease them and reconcile them to the permanent stay of their comrade, so that they may always have such to feed upon.

This superstition accounts for a rather high rate of infant mortality, for parents are thereby led away from the proper treatment of their ailments, while occupying themselves in making charms to defeat the purpose of imaginary demons !

It is fair, however to add that thoughtful men have begun to perceive the absurdity of this superstition, for many have been heard to say " There is really no such thing as *Abiku* ; disease and hereditary taints are the true causes of infantile mortality."

III.—THE ORIKI OR COGNOMEN OR PET NAMES

This is an attributive name, expressing what the child is, or what he or she is hoped to become. If a male it is always expressive of something heroic, brave, or strong; if a female, it is a term of endearment or of praise. In either case it is intended to have a stimulating effect on the individual.

Yorubas are always particular to distinguish between the Oruko (name) and the Oriki (cognomen or attributive).

Male attributive names :—

Ajamu	One who seizes after a fight.
Ajagbe	One who carries off after a contest.
Akunyun	One who buzzes to and fro
Ajani	One who possesses after a struggle.
Alawo	One who divides and smashes up.
Akande or Akanbi	One conceived after a single touch.
Alabi or Alade	Is a male that comes after several female births.

Female attributive names :—

Amoke	Whom to know is to pet.
Ayoka	One who causes joy all around.
Abebi	One born after a supplication.
Apinke	To be petted from hand to hand.
Akanke	To meet whom is to pet.
Asabi	One of select birth.
Awero	One to be washed and dressed up.
Alake	One to be petted if she survives.

The use of the attributive name is so common that many children are better known by it than by their real names. Some do not even know their own real names when the attributive is popular. But there is a method in the use of it ; as a rule, only children are addressed by their Oriki by their elders, especially when they wish to express a feeling of endearment for the child. It is considered impertinent for a younger person to call an elder by his Oriki or pet name.

Certain names carry their own attributive with them e.g. Adeniji (the crown has a shadow), the attributive to this is Apata (a rock). Hence Adeniji Apata, Apata ni iji i.e. Adeniji is a rock, a rock that casts out its shadow.

IV.—THE ORILE OR TOTEM

This is about the best place to take note of this singular system. The term Orile denotes the foundation or origin ; and is of an immense importance in the tracing of a pedigree. Each one denotes a parent stock. The Orilẹ is not a name, it denotes the family origin or Totem. The real meaning of this is lost in obscurity. Some say they were descended from the object named, which must be a myth; others that the object was the ancient god of the family, the giver of the children and other earthly blessings, or that the family is in some way connected with it.

The Totem represents every conceivable object e.g. Erin (the elephant), Ogun (the god of war), Opo (post), Agbo (a ram), etc. The number of totems of course is large, representing as each does a distinct family. Some families, however, have become extinct, and some obscure ones there are who have lost their totems.

A married woman cannot adopt her husband's totem, much less his name. Intermarriages within the same totem was originally not allowed, as coming within the degree of consanguinity but now the rule is not rigidly observed. The children both boys and girls take their father's totem, except in rare cases, where the father has lost his, or more usually when the mother's indicates a higher or nobler rank. Some girls of noble birth will marry below their rank, but would have their children brought up in their own home, and among their father's children, and adopt his totem. An illegitimate child if not acknowledged by the supposed father cannot adopt his totem but the mother's, especially if a female.

The following are some distinguished Totems :—

Erin, the elephant, the totem of the original line of the Kings.

Ogun, the god of war, the totem of the original line of the Baṣoruns.

Both were merged in King Abiọdun, who chose to adopt his mother's totem, the Baṣoruns being pre-eminent in those days. Hence the present line of ALÂFINS' is Ogun.

Opo (a post). The totem of a noble Ọyọ family.

Ọkin (the love bird) Totem of the Ọlọfa and the Oloro.

Ikọ	,,	Onigusun.
Agan	,,	Elese.
Ẹdu	,,	Onigbayi.
Ojo (rain)	,,	Ọlọgbin.
Agbe or Ade	,,	Olukoyi.
Agbo (a ram)	,,	Ajagusi father of Erinlẹ.
Ọgẹ	,,	Enira and the Onipẹ.
Ẹkan	,,	Olufan
Ẹlọ	,,	Elẹrin.
Eri	,,	Ọloyan
Iji	,,	Onigbẹti.
Ọgọ	,,	Ijẹṣa families.

When the Oruko (name) the Oriki (attributive) and the Orile (totem) are given, the individual becomes distinctive, the family is known; and he can at any time be traced.

Two men may be found with the same name, but rarely with the same cognomen together, and more rarely still with the same totem as well. The man is universally known by his Oruko (name) familiarly by his Oriki (attributive). The Oriki is always used in conjunction with his Orile (the family stock or totem) expressed or understood : always expressed when endearment or admiration is intended. The Orile of course is never used by itself as it would be meaningless.

A name given in full will appear thus :—

Male.			Female.		
Oruko	Oriki	Orile	Oruko	Oriki	Orile
Adewale	Agana	Erin	Ibiyemi	Abebi	Iko
Abiodun	Ajamu	Ogun	Olawale	Asabi	Opo
Adejumo	Ajagbe	Oguri	Morenike	Abeje	Agan
Oyebode	Akunyun	Opo	Mowumi	Agbeke	Agbò
Adegboye	Isola	Okin	Layemi	Atole	Ogun
Fagbemi	Akãwo	Ogo	Ibisoto	Akanke	Iji

Moslem children although named from the Arabic calendar yet must have their Oriki and Orile ; thus :—

Alihu	Isola	Opo	Fatumo	Akanke	Ojò

IRREGULARITIES INTRODUCED

The introduction of Christianity and the spread of British influence over the country have been the causes of great irregularities in names which one meets with now in the Yoruba country.

The early missionaries, notably those of Sierra Leone, abolished native names wholesale, considering them " heathenish," and substituted European names instead : such names are naturally transmitted to their children *anglice*, hence the incongruities of names that puzzle a foreigner on his first landing in West Africa.

But with more enlightenment and better knowledge, a gradual change is coming over this ; educated Yorubas cannot see why Philip Jones or Geoffrey Williams should be more Christian than Adewale or Ibiyemi ; he knows what these mean, the former to him are but mere sounds, nor are their meanings—even when known—an improvement on his own.

But nothing sticks so fast as a name, and nothing more difficult to eradicate ; for even in spite of the better knowledge Christians still give to their children foreign names although in conjunction with a Yoruba name. That an English name should be given at all can hardly be contended to be necessary, but the practice is defended by many who plead for it a universal custom, e.g. that a convert to Mohammedanism adopts a Moslem or Arabic name ; analogously therefore only Biblical names ought to be given, but in the British West African colonies, Yoruba and other tribes with Christian names include English, Scotch, Irish, Welsh, German and Dutch names !

But there is another consideration that helps to rivet the yoke. It invariably appears that most of those who have English or other foreign names, are in some way connected with English education and with Christianity, and are certainly in a way more enlightened than their pagan brethren, or considered to be so ; hence it comes to pass, that many who originally were free from the brand of a foreign name, nevertheless still regard it as a mark of enlightenment, and would voluntarily adopt one or more with their own real names in order to be considered " up-to-date ! " Nothing but a thoroughly sound education all round (and not limited to individuals here and there) can remedy this evil : but in the meantime educated Yorubas are losing the knowledge and the genius of the method of Yorubas in naming their children. Thus according to the system now prevailing, where one English name is given or adopted, it is used as the first name, and the Yoruba name as the second or surname, e.g. James Adeṣina. Where two English names are given the Yoruba is placed either in the middle as James Adeṣina Williams, or at the end, as James Williams Adeṣina. The reason for this want of system is due to the introduction of another element unknown to Yorubas and is, therefore, a complication, viz., the prefix of Mr. to the names. This is foreign to Yoruba genius and language and makes a hybrid mixture, as it would appear if attached to any historic Biblical name ! The essence of the incongruity in this matter lies in the conversion of Yoruba names into a surname or family name and it is in this particular that the most appalling absurdity occurs. Thus some retain their own Yoruba name as a family name to the exclusion of their father's. Others use their father's name as a surname and suppress their own native name or use it as a middle name. Some adopt a brother's name as a family name if he is considered more eminent, thus excluding the father's name and suppressing their own. Some use the father's " Amutorunwa " as Taiwo, Idowu, Ige. Some use the father's " Abiṣo " as Adejumọ Layọde, etc. Some use the father's Oriki as Akāwo, Alade, Ajasa, some use the father's title as Apena, Dawodu, Mọgaji, etc. All this in order— as is alleged—to make the individual distinctive but as a matter of fact to make the Yoruba conform to the English method, because that is considered more civilized! Some ridiculous results have thereby been obtained e.g. a woman is called Mrs. Taiwo, who was not twin-born, and probably her husband was not either, but it may be his father or his uncle! One fails to see how that system makes her distinctive among thousands of Taiwos in the land whilst it is so inappropriate.

A man was called Babarimisa because he was a posthumous child ; on his becoming " civilized " his children according to the English system of transmitting names became so many masters and misses "Babarimisas" with himself alive ! And yet these absurdities are supposed to be necessary to Christianity and civilization ! But when we remember that the fathers of western civilization, as also the founders of Christianity with the early Christians and martyrs have transmitted their names down to history in a simple form as Yoruba names, it becomes evident that the present method is not essential to Christianity or civilization.

And even now, we know that the familiar English method does not prevail all over Europe, not even all over Britain, for in the north of Scotland, it is usual for married women to retain their maiden names, and children take their father's Christian names for their own surnames, and yet, not only are the Scotch a highly civilized people, they are also intensely Christian. From all this we may learn that it is not necessary to do violence to an original language as the Yoruba in order to be considered civilized or Christian. Whatever incongruities may have been perpetrated in the past, it behoves those who are responsible for the keeping of the language in its purity to cease from inflicting these anomalies on those brought under their influence, especially among converts to Christianity.

Neither Christianity nor civilization requires a man's name to be given to his wife or children, considering the purpose for which children are named amongst the Yorubas.

On the coast, the corruption of the Yoruba language is proceeding at a rapid pace. What began with the names is now extending to phrases and expressions which are idiomatic English in Yoruba words. The writer thinks it will require a strong effort to preserve the Yoruba language in its purity.

CHAPTER VI

YORUBA TOWNS AND VILLAGES

All Yoruba towns with very few exceptions are built on one uniform plan, and the origin of most of them is more or less the same, and all have certain identical features. A cluster of huts around the farmstead of an enterprising farmer may be the starting point : perhaps a halting place for refreshments in a long line of march between two towns. In any case it is one individual that first attracts others to the spot ; if the site be on the highway to a large town, or in a caravan route, so much the better ; the wives of the farmers ever ready to cater refreshments for wearied travellers render the spot in time a recognised halting place : the more distant from a town, the more essential it necessarily must be as a resting place ; if a popular resort, a market soon springs up in the place, into which neighbouring farmers bring their wares for sale, and weekly fairs held : market sheds are built all over the place and it becomes a sort of caravanserai or sleeping place for travellers.

As soon as houses begin to spring up and a village or hamlet formed, the necessity for order and control becomes apparent. The men would thereupon assemble at the gate of the principal man who has attracted people to the place and formally recognise him as the Balẹ or Mayor of the village (lit. father of the land) and thenceforth the mayoralty becomes perpetuated in his family, with a member of the family either the son or the brother or a cousin, succeeding in perpetuity. This however is the only hereditary title in the village. The house of the Balẹ becomes the official residence, and is thenceforth kept in good repairs by the men of the town, and the frontage of his house becomes the principal market of the town.

The Balẹ having been elected, he in turn appoints his Ọtun (or right hand man), Osi (the left) and other civil officers of a town. Even in this early stage, the necessity for defence is felt ; the bravest man among them will be chosen as the Jagun or Balogun and he in turn picks out his lieutenants, so that in any matter that may spring up, either civil or military everybody knows his duty and whom to look up to.

The village must necessarily be answerable to the nearest town from which it sprang and thus an embryo town is formed. There are cases in which an influential personage with a large following deliberately built a town, and is from the beginning the recognised head of the same.

In fact if there are but half a dozen huts in the place, that of the headman or embryo Baḷę would be recognised.

From this we see how it is that the principal market of the town is always in the centre of the town and in the front of the house of the chief ruler. This rule is without an exception and hence the term Qloja (one having a market) is used as a generic term or title of all chief rulers of a town be he a King or a Baḷę.

Minor chiefs also have smaller markets in front of their houses. Market squares as a rule mark out the frontage of a chief or a distinguished man, and the principal entrance to his compound is marked out by its having a street verandah added to it right and left, and if a King two or more kọbis are added to the street verandah. The larger the town, the larger the principal market to which everyone resorts for morning and evening marketings and is the general rendezvous of the town on every national or municipal occasion. It is planted all over with shady trees for sellers and loungers of an evening. The central market also contains the principal mosque of the town, and the fetish temple of the chief ruler, if he be a pagan.

Every town is walled, deep trenches are dug all round it outside, the more exposed to attack the more substantial the wall and for the greater security of smaller towns a bush or thicket called Igbo Ile (home forest) is kept, about half to one mile from the walls right round the town. This forms a security against a sudden cavalry attack, and a safe ambush for defence, as well as hiding places in a defeat or sudden hostile irruption. The tall trees in them are sometimes used as a watch tower to observe the movements of the enemy : except in times of profound peace, it is penal to cut trees in the home forest. Highways are made through them straight to the town gate, and are always kept in excellent repair.

Towns in the plain that are greatly exposed to sudden attacks, or those that have had to stand long sieges have a second or outer wall enclosing a large area which is used for farming during a siege. This wall is called " Odi Amọlà " (wall of safety), sometimes it is called " Odi Amọnu " (wall of ruin) as the wall has been to them the means of safety, or has been unavailing for its purpose.

The town gates are always massive and a gateman lives in a house adjoining the town wall, he collects the tolls from passers by. Market people have a fixed amount to pay, varying from 40 to 200 cowries, and farm people contribute a trifle from whatever they are bringing home, a head or two of corn, a handful of beans, a yam or two, a few dry sticks and so forth, for his sustenance. The gates are named after the most important town they lead to. Each of these gates is in charge of a chief who is responsible to the town for whatever may occur there or along the route to which it leads right on to the frontier, also for keeping the walls of that part in good repairs, as well as the highway leading out of the town. This chief it is who is to put his servant there for collecting tolls, the amount to be collected from each person being fixed by the Town Council. This servant is expected to pay to his master a certain sum every 9 or 18 days, being the average of what the gate yields. Whatever surplus there may be in a brisk season, he appropriates to himself or if there is a deficit, he is expected to make it good.

In Yoruba Proper (including the Ẹgbas) streets are not properly made or named except large thoroughfares leading to town gates, and the squares and markets of chiefs.

It does not appear that any care is ever taken to choose the site of a town, as the neighbourhood of large streams : wells are sunk by individuals to supply drinking water. The streams that may be flowing through the town are fouled beyond degree, and are by no means fit for drinking purposes. For keeping the town clean every compound looks after its own frontage and surroundings, in the market place every seller sweeps the space around her stall.

The system of sanitary arrangements is the most primitive imaginable ; near every large thoroughfare or a market place is a spot selected as a dust heap for the disposal of all sorts of refuse and sweepings of the neighbourhood, and at intervals, fire is set to the pile of rubbish.

Here and there about the town are found leafy groves, usually clumps of fignut trees, the neighbourhood of which is unsavoury from the disposal of sewage. These sites are always infested by crowds of those keen-scented scavengers of nature, the hungry-looking vultures. Important chiefs have a large area of land enclosed within their compounds within which spots are selected for sanitary purposes.

Every chief is responsible to the town council for the quarter of the town in which he resides.

When a town has grown up to the town wall, the town council has to determine the amount of area to be taken in, and a new wall is built enclosing such area. The whole of the town participates in the work, even women and children also are engaged in fetching water to mix the swish and in providing refreshments for the men-folk ; the streets of the area simply follow the old line of the foot paths to the farms now enclosed within the town.

It must strike the most casual observer who has travelled over the Yoruba country that those portions of the country which are supposed to be more backward in intelligence viz. the Ijeṣa, Ekiti, Ifẹ and other provinces have better streets than the more intelligent ones. Old men attribute this fact to the effect of the intertribal wars. E.g. in the case of Abẹokuta, however well laid may have been the streets of the original farm villas, when the refugees began to flock in, attention could scarcely be paid to the alignment of the houses each one simply tried to find out the whereabouts of the members of his township, and thus they grouped themselves by their families in every available space around the chief of their town.

The same may be said of all the towns of Yoruba proper which have suffered from the vicissitudes of war. In later years the people seem to have lost altogether the art of laying out and naming streets as is the case in Ijeṣa and Ekiti towns.

Roads.—Before the period of the revolutionary and intertribal wars, the bulk of the Yoruba people lived in the towns of the plain, the towns in forest lands were small and unimportant, except the city of Owu, all below this being regarded as in the outskirts. Roads at that time were comparatively good. The country being flat was interspersed with hundreds of towns and villages, the inhabitants of which enjoyed the blessings of peace, and the fruits of their industry. Good roads were then made from one town to another, and were annually repaired at the time of the drummers' and Egũgun festivals. They were wide enough for the easy progress of the company of dancers at these festivals and also for nuptial processions.

But they are now neglected not only that they may impede the easy advance of invaders, but also to aid the concealment of the panic-stricken inhabitants, who at the first alarm disappear at once in the bushes surrounding their towns and villages.

§ 2 PECULIAR YORUBA TOWNS

There are some important towns which form exceptions to some of the rules above given ; in their case the cause is due to intertribal and the revolutionary wars as we shall find in detail in the second part of this book.

1. *Abẹokuta.*—This large town is a conglomeration of villages, to the number of 153 with Ake as the chief. Each township (as they are called) has its own organization. Ake can scarcely be said to have any authority over them in their own local affairs, except such authority as is granted by the Principal Chiefs or " Ogbonis " who form the chief political organization. Hence we see that there is not one central market for the town as such, in the frontage of

the chief ruler. There may be several Baloguns or Serikis, there are at least four kinglings, and several Ogboni houses, each section being jealous of its liberty and tenacious of its rights. Abeokuta in short was never organized as a single town : its peculiar political organization should be the subject of another chapter.

Ibadan.—This town was originally a small Ẹgba village around the site of the central market, but occupied by a portion of the army that destroyed the city of Owu and devastated the Egba villages. After the withdrawal of the Ẹgbas into Abeokuta, the motley crowd forming the army settled at Ibadan. Ibadan has since been the military encampment of Yoruba ; the titles, order of precedence, etc. are chiefly military. For that reason there is not one family in which the title of Balẹ is hereditary and no official residence for the Balẹ. The Balẹ is always chosen from old retired war-chiefs, always by sufferance of the Balogun, who has equal authority and more real power. But when the Balogun has become old and has already won his laurels, he is expected to be the next Balẹ. A young Balogun with his future to make yields the mayoralty to an older chief, usually the Ọtun Balẹ. This is the only town where such arrangement exists. Ibadan has no home forests. Attempts were made from time to time to form one, but always without success through the habit of firing the fields year by year at the dry season. They are in no fear of invasion. To be in Ibadan is to be in a place of safety. Hence the Ibadans style their town " Idi Ibọn " i.e. the butt end of the gun ; for the same reason also the town walls are very indifferently kept.

Ilọrin.—Ilọrin is in one respect different from the other Yoruba towns, in that the ruling powers are aliens to the place. How it came about that Ilọrin a pure Yoruba town, and one time the third city in the kingdom fell into the hands of aliens and to this day owns allegiance to other than its rightful sovereign, will be told in its place ; but to this day the principal market and the chief mosque of the town remain still in front of the house of the founder and rightful owner of Ilọrin.

These three towns, Abẹokuta, Ibadan, and Ilọrin are the largest towns in the Yoruba country, and probably in West Africa, and the three are the outcome of the revolutionary and intertribal wars.

CHAPTER VII

PRINCIPLES OF LAND LAW

THE Land laws of the Yoruba country are simple and effective, there being no need of any complicated or elaborate laws, as there is enough land for all the members of the various tribes. Whatever land is not effectively occupied is for the common benefit of all ; no one need own any land which he cannot utilize, except farm land left fallow for a short period.

Theoretically and traditionally we have seen above that Yoruba land belongs to the ALÂFIN of OYO as the supreme head of the race. " The land belongs to the King " has passed into a proverb. But it must be understood, that it is not meant that the land is the private property of the King, it is only his as representing the race, in other words, Yoruba land belongs to the Yoruba people and to no other, hence as the Yorubas are split into so many tribes, the head of each tribe, as representing the ALÂFIN is the King for that tribe, and he holds the land or division of the country for the benefit of the tribe, and even he has no power to alienate it permanently of his own accord, to an alien. All lands, therefore, including forests and the plain are owned by some tribe or other, and no one belonging to another race or another tribe can make use of the land without the permission of the king and chiefs who hold the land for their tribe. Members of the tribe have no difficulty at present in obtaining as much land as each requires for agricultural purposes in which every one is supposed to be engaged ; with the increase of population however, it is felt that some difficulties will arise in future, but the chiefs can cope with such cases.

Lands are never sold, but may be granted to outsiders for life, and to their heirs in perpetuity ; but where the land so granted had been under cultivation, it is understood in every case that the fruit-bearing trees, especially the palm trees, and kola-nut trees, etc., on the land are not included in the grant ; hence the common expression " The grantee is to look down not up," i.e. he is to confine his attention to plants he has cultivated and not on fruit-bearing trees he met on the spot.

Land once given is never taken back except under special circumstances as treason to the state which renders the grantee an outlaw, and he is driven altogether from that state or tribe, and his land confiscated. Even when left unutilized, if there are marks of occupation on it, such as trees planted, or a wall built, etc., it cannot be taken back without the consent of the owner.

There is no subject in which the Yoruba man is more sensitive than in that of land. This normally quiet and submissive people can be roused into violent action of desperation if once they perceive that it is intended to deprive them of their land.

We shall see in the course of this history that the non-alienation of their land forms one of the main conditions of their admitting a European officer among them by the Ibadans at the beginning of the British Protectorate.

The forests are under the direct guardianship of the hunters who form among themselves a fraternity recognized all over the land, subject of course to the town authorities. Any laws, rules, or regulations relating to forests that are to be made, must recognize the rights, privileges and services of the hunters, especially, as it is by them effect can be given to those laws. It is their duty to apprize the chiefs of any town, of any spies, expeditions, or raids that have that town or its farms for their objective. Crimes committed in the forests must be traced, and the authors tracked and unearthed by them. Any animal bearing traces or marks of their bullets or arrow-wounds must be restored to them. All information relating to forests must be given by the hunters to the chiefs of the town.

The forests are free to every member of the tribe for procuring building materials, medicinal herbs, firewood, etc.

Inheritance.—When a man dies, his farms are inherited by his children, and so from father to son in perpetuity, and, like the house are not subject to sale. If his children are females, they will pass on to the male relatives, unless the daughters are capable of seeing the farm kept up for their own benefit. If minors, they may be worked by their male relatives until the boys are of age to take up the keep of the farms.

No portion of such farms can be alienated from the family without the unanimous consent of all the members thereof.

These are the simple, fundamental and universal laws applicable to all the tribes in general, but subject to modifications and development according to the local exigencies of each place. These exigencies may be due to the proximity of large populations, and consequently higher value of land, the nature of the land, whether forests with economic plants in them or pasture land, and the locality whether near the coast where foreign intercourse affects local habits, or far inland where the tribes remain in their simplicity. But in every case the ruling of the local chiefs, and their councillors must necessarily be the law for that tribe since the fundamental laws are not violated.

None but citizens born or naturalized can own land permanently in this country.   Land granted to foreigners for a specific purpose reverts to the owner or the state on the grantee leaving the country.

These are the general laws, to be observed rather in the spirit than in the letter.

Chapter VIII

MANNERS AND CUSTOMS

§ (a) Social Polity

THE ancient Yorubas were very simple in their manners, their tastes, and habits. Their houses all on the ground floor are built in compounds called *Agbo Ile* (lit. a flock of houses), that is to say in the form of a hollow square, horse shoe or a circle, enclosing a large central area, with one principal gateway the house being divided into compartments to hold several families, all more or less related or united by ties of kinship, or friendship. One piazza runs right round the whole, and is used for all ordinary purposes by day, and for the reception of visitors. The central area is used in common by all the inmates for general purposes ; usually horses, sheep and goats are found tethered in it.

The compartment of the head of the house is usually opposite the main gateway or a little to the right. It is larger, the roof loftier and the piazza more spacious than the rest. Here the master is expected to be found at all times (during visiting hours) by a doorway which leads to his harem at the back of the house. This particular doorway is known as where the master " shows his face " (for the reception of visitors) ; it is an essential adjunct to the houses of chiefs or important personages, being used for no other purpose, for at all other times it is kept closed. A high wall often encloses a garden attached to the back of the building, the space enclosed is always in proportion to the size of the house, the rank, and the means of the owner. The houses of great men contain smaller compounds at the back attached to the main compound, these are called *Karà* or retiring quarters, each devoted to some purpose from a harem to stables for horses.

The houses of chiefs are distinguished by a " street verandah " (as it is called) on either side the main gateway on the outside, varying in length according to the taste and capacity of the owner ; the roof of which is an extension or projection of that of the main building. It is used for lounging in the afternoons, at the cool of the day. A small market is almost always to be found at the frontage of such houses. The walls of the houses rising from 7 to 8 feet in height are built of mud, the roof consequently is low, and is covered with a tall grass called Bẹrẹ or with Ṣẹgẹ or Ẹkan. In forest lands where these are not obtainable, a kind of broad leaf

called Gbòdògì is used instead.   The houses are without any decorations ; the walls are plastered and polished with black and
sometimes red earth by the women whose work it generally is.
The houses of Kings and Princes are embellished with a sort of
wash which is a decoction made from the skin of the locust
fruit.

Now and then attempts are found at artistic decorations, by
figures traced on the wall ; but more commonly the front posts of
the verandah consist of carved figures of various kinds, equestrians
swordsmen, hawkers, etc.   The floor is generally rubbed and
polished once a week.

The household furniture consists chiefly of cooking utensils,
waterpots, and a mortar with pestles, all of which are deposited in
the front and back piazzas of the house.

The use of bedsteads, tables and chairs being unknown, they
squat or lie on mats instead.   In modern times those who can
afford it keep a few chairs for the accommodation of visitors in
European garb, who find it difficult or are unaccustomed to squat
on the ground.   It is not unusual to find skins of buffaloes, leopard,
lion, or a large bullock hung up on the walls of the front piazza
which are taken down for distinguished visitors to sit on.

All their valuables are kept in pots or bags made of bamboo
fibres, and placed in one corner of the sleeping room, so that in all
cases of alarm, whether of fire, or night attack by robbers or slave-
hunters, everything of value is soon taken away to a place of
safety whenever possible.

As all the houses are invariably built with mud ceilings which
are themselves fire-proof, the losses in cases of fire are small, and
of hardly any account, especially if the doors are kept rigidly
closed.   The property of the women consists chiefly of cloths,
beads, with goats, sheep and poultry, these usually form a substantial part of their " dowry."

The head of the compound's principal wife is the mistress of
the compound, as himself is the master, and all heads of the
several families within the compound are bound to pay their
respects to them the first thing every morning, the men prostrating
on the ground, and the women sitting on the ground and reclining
on their left elbow.

[This is the ordinary mode of saluting a superior in this country;
but when greater respect is to be shown, or pardon asked for some
offence committed, the men while prostrating lay the right and
left cheek alternately on the ground, and the women wrap their
cloth lower down, loose their head tie, and recline alternately on
the right as well as on the left elbow.

Before Kings and great rulers, for a show of homage, they run
to the porch of the house and back three times, throwing dust on
their head or roll on the ground].

They are chiefs in their respective domains, where they transact
all business affecting the welfare or interest of the people in their
respective households. All important cases are judged and
decided in the master's piazza, and he is responsible to the town
authorities for the conduct of the inmates of his compound ; hence
the saying :—" Bāle ni ọlọran awo " (the master of the house
must be privy to all secrets). His word is law, and his authority
indisputable within his compound, hence also another saying,
" Ọbẹ̀ ti Bāle ile kì ijẹ Iyale ile kì isè e " (the sauce which the
master of the house cannot eat or which is unpalatable to him,
the mistress of the house must not cook), which when applied
simply means that no one should go contrary to the wishes of the
master of the house.

To this high authority belongs a leg of whatever is slaughtered
in the compound, from a chicken to a bullock ; whether killed for
sacrifice, or for a festival, or for any other purpose of whatever kind.

At the death of the master of the house, when the period of
mourning is over, his successor be it his son, or his brother or
cousin as the case may be, removes from his own compartment
into that of the master. He is installed into his place by his feudal
lord, or in case the deceased be a public man, by the Town Council,
with a title that attaches him to one of the senior chiefs. But
before the ceremony can take place, the roof over the late master's
compartment (be it old or recent) is taken down and rebuilt afresh ;
hence the term for a successor, Arole i.e. one who *roofs* the house.

Personal Appearance.—In early times very little regard was
paid to personal appearance. Boys and girls up to the age of 8
years walked about *in puris naturalibus* ; from that period up to
the age of puberty they were allowed the use of aprons, the cut and
shape for either sex being different, the one from the other, that
for boys being called *bantẹ*, that for girls *tòbi.* The whole period
was regarded as one of unencumbered freedom which ceases with
the act of marriage. It was not an uncommon thing to find girls
of the age of 15 when engaged in hard work whether at home or
in the farm with absolutely nothing on,· and even their mothers
on such occasions were but scantily clothed. This custom, however, excepting among some tribes as Ijẹṣa and Ẹfọn has completely
died out. The extreme poverty of the people in those early times
was probably the chief cause of such disregard of personal attire.
In modern times better attention is paid to their outward appearance, and although from the standpoint of an enlightened civiliz-

ation there may be much to be desired still among the ordinary class of people, yet on the whole, especially amongst the well-to-do, the Yorubas dress very decently and becomingly as compared with former generations of the same people.

Great regard, however, has always been paid to personal cleanliness, and for this the tribe is specially remarkable. The word Ọbùn (filthy) as applied to a person carries with it such a feeling of disgust which beggars description. The men are always shaved and hence, when one appears unshaven, unwashed, and with filthy garments on, you may safely conclude that he is mourning, for these are the signs of it. Children and youths are either entirely shaved or a strip of hair running from the forehead to the occiput along the top of the head is left which is sometimes made into circular patches. As it is considered decent and cleanly for men to carry their heads bald so on the contrary " the hair is the glory of the woman," and much attention is paid to it. Women have their hair done up in all sorts of ways dictated by their usual vanity ; the unmarried ones are distinguished by their hair being plaited into small strips (from 8 to 14) from the right to the left ear, the smaller and more numerous the plaited strips the more admired. Married women on the other hand adopt other forms of plaiting ; usually they commence on both sides and finish up in the middle in a sort of net-work running from the forehead to the occiput ; ornamental forms are adopted by some, such as stuffing the hair in the middle of the head after being gathered from all sides ; and others again as the Ijẹbus finish up theirs in the shape of a pair of horns.

Character.—As regards the social virtues, the ancient Ọyọs or Yorubas proper were very virtuous, loving and kind. Theft was rare as also fornication in spite of the scantiness or often times complete absence of clothing to which they were accustomed. Friendship was more sincere. Children were more dutiful to their parents, and inferiors respectful to their superiors in age or position. Liars were formerly punished by exclusion from society and from the clubs ; but as the whole people took delight in ambiguous forms of speech which were not understood by those unaccustomed to their habits they were regarded and spoken of as prevaricators. Now, as formerly they are remarkably patient of injuries, and would never resist or retaliate except in extreme cases when provocation became insupportable. They are characteristically unassuming in their manners and submissive to their superiors. They are very shrewd in driving bargains, and hence foreigners speak of them as " African Jews " in reference to their commercial instincts.

No nation is more remarkable for cautiousness and for putting themselves generally on the safe side.   When powerless they would submit to oppression and wrong to any extent so long as they find resistance useless ; but when an opportunity offers for asserting their rights and overthrowing their oppressors, they are never slow to embrace it.   The common proverb embodies this trait in their character :—" Bi ọwọ ẹni kò tẹ ekù idà a ki ibère iku ti o pa baba ẹni," i.e., if one has not grasped the handle of his sword he should not attempt to avenge the death of his father.

Intercourse with other nations has caused various forms of vice to creep in among modern Yorubas or Ọyọs ; their natural timidity and submissive spirit have produced a degeneracy of manners so as to be considered essentially lacking in straightforwardness ; they can effect by diplomacy what they cannot accomplish by force, in which proceeding the Ọyọs differ widely from the other tribes, some of whom are characterised by a proud and intractable spirit, but they are no less determined in carrying out their object although the means used to effect their purpose is essentially different.

Yorubas as a whole are social, polite, and proverbially hospitable.   Licentiousness is abhorred.   There are well attested cases where a member of a family would be condemned to slavery by a unanimous vote of all the relatives when he has brought disgrace on the family.   Sometimes forcible emasculation is resorted to as a punishment (as in cases of incest) or total banishment from the town and neighbourhood to where the offender is not likely to be known.

A peculiar custom was prevalent amongst the ancient Ọyọs. Young men were permitted to have intimate friends among the fair sex, and they were often the guests of each other.   At the annual festivals the young man and his female friend would meet and take an active part in the ceremonies, and render pecuniary services or manual assistance to each other. At the time of harvest the female friend with the full consent of her parents would go for about a week or a fortnight to assist her male friend in bringing home his harvest while he himself may be engaged on his father's farm.   Yet notwithstanding so much mutual intercourse strict chastity was the rule not the exception.   The practice, however, has long been discontinued, owing to the degeneracy of the present age.

Filial Duties.—It was the duty of every male child to serve his father although he might be married and have a family of his own unless he was exonerated from the obligation by the father himself.   As a general thing a small portion of farm work was allotted to him as his day's work after attending to which he may go and see after his own business. So while serving his father, every son had his own private farm also to manage ; and it was on his own portion of land that the female friend used to render assistance in time of harvest.

All married women were also engaged in their husband's farm and the harmony that usually prevailed between them and the young people was very remarkable.

Young men were not allowed to marry until they could give their father 10 heads of cowries, equal in those days to £10 sterling. They were seldom married before the age of 30 and the young women, not before 20. Promiscuous marriages were not allowed, freeborn must be married to freeborn, slaves to slaves, and foreigners to foreigners. Except amongst the Igbônas consanguineous affinity however remote was not allowed.

Privileges of the Great.—Kings and nobles who kept harems were exempted from this rule of affinity ; they were at liberty to multiply wives from any tribe, and these wives might be of any condition of life. It was the pride of Kings to fill their harems with women of every description, such as foreign women, slaves, hostages, daughters of criminals given as the price of redemption, or seized in confiscations ; dwarfs, albinoes, hunch-backs, and any other in whose persons there should appear any signs of *lusus naturæ*. Such beings, being considered unnatural, were the King's peculiar property. Hence the saying " Ọba ni ijẹ Ọrọ" (it is Kings who are to feed on the uncommon).

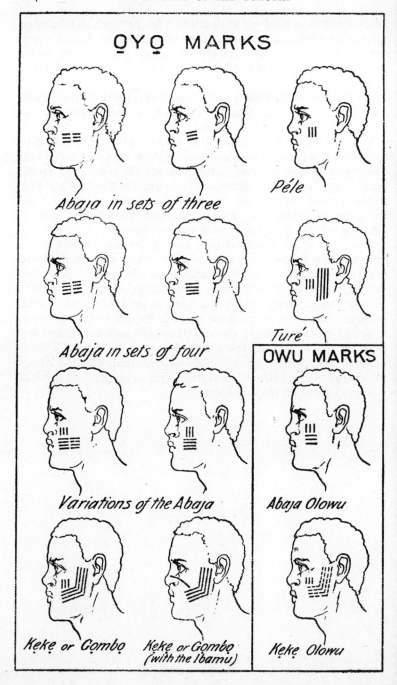

OYỌ MARKS

Abaja in sets of three

Péle

Abaja in sets of four

Turé

Variations of the Abaja

Kẹkẹ or Gọmbọ

Kẹkẹ or Gọmbọ
(with the Ibamu)

OWU MARKS

Abaja Olowu

Kẹkẹ Olowu

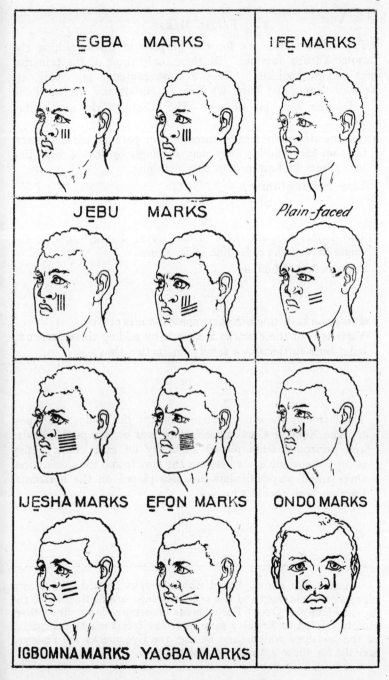

§ (b) FACIAL MARKS.

The facial marks are for the purpose of distinguishing the various Yoruba families. Of these, only those of the principal ones can be indicated. They are designated :—(a) Abajà, (b) Kẹ́kẹ́ or Gọmbọ, (c) Ture, (d) Pele, (e) Mandẹ and (f) Jamgbadi.

I. The Ọyọ marks are :—The Abaja, Kẹkẹ or Gọmbọ, Ture.

(a) The *Abaja* are sets of three or four parallel and horizontal lines on each cheek ; they may be single or double, each line being from half-an-inch to one inch long.

Lines in sets of three :—

$$\equiv\ \equiv \quad \text{or} \quad \equiv$$

The double sets are those of the Royal Family[1] of Ọyọ the single that of the older line of Basọruns.

Lines in sets of four :—

$$\equiv\ \equiv \quad \text{or} \quad \equiv$$

These marks distinguish some noble families of Ọyọ.

Variations of these marks are made by adding three perpendicular lines to them as a family distinction thus :—

$$\underset{\equiv\equiv}{|||}\ \_ \quad \text{or} \quad \underset{\equiv}{|||}$$

The latter of these is common amongst the Ibọlọs and Epos.

(b) The Kẹ́kẹ́ or Gọmbọ consists of four or five perpendicular and horizontal lines placed angularly on each cheek ; they occupy the whole space between the auricle and the cheek bone ; three small perpendiculars are also placed on the horizontal lines on both cheeks thus :—

---

[1] Besides the above, broad ribbon marks termed Ẹyọ drawn along the whole length of the arms and legs are distinctive of the Royal Family of Ọyọ. For whereas homeborn slaves and others closely related to Royalty may have the facial marks distinctive of the house to which they belong, the Ẹyọ marks are reserved strictly for those actually of Royal blood.

A variation of this is sometimes made by adding on the left cheek the *Ibamu* i.e. a line running aslant from the bridge of the nose to the horizontal lines. This also is for the purpose of distinguishing a family.

When the lines are rather bold, the mark is termed Kéké, when fine and faint it is termed Gombo. The Kéké or Gombo is a common mark of all Oyos and of the Egbado tribe.

(c) The *Ture* consists of four perpendicular lines somewhat like the Gombo, but longer, with the three small perpendiculars but without the horizontals.

(d) The *Pele* are three short perpendicular lines over the cheek bones, each about an inch long. They are not distinctive of any particular family, but are used generally by some men who disapprove of tribal distinctions, usually Moslems, but are loth to remain plain-faced, e.g.

(e) (f) The Mande and Jamgbadi are no longer in use; the latter is said to be distinctive of aliens naturalized amongst Yorubas.

These are the principal facial marks. The other principal Yoruba families are distinguished by a slight variation of these marks :—

II. Egba marks :—The *Abaja Òró* i.e. the upright *Abaja* is distinctive of the Egbas. They consist of three perpendicular lines each about 3 inches long on each cheek. The younger generations, however, have their lines rather faint or of shorter lengths undistinguishable from the Pele.

III. The Egbado marks are the same as the Oyo marks generally as this family remained in close connection with Oyo and in their allegiance to the Aláfin long after the break-up of the kingdom, and the establishment of tribal independence.

IV. Owu marks. These are of two kinds, both being variations of Ọyọ marks. They are :—(a) *Abaja Olowu* and (b) *Kẹkẹ Olowu*.

(a) The Abaja Olowu are three horizontal lines surmounted by three perpendiculars each about one and a-half inches long.

(b) The Kẹkẹ Olowu is like the Kẹkẹ or Gọmbọ with the lines discrete or interrupted.

V. Ijẹbu marks are also of two kinds (a) the first is much like the *Abaja Olowu* (the tribe from which they are partly descended) but with the horizontals curved.

(b) The other is the Abaja Òró of the Ẹgbas. The former is more distinctive of Ijẹbus.

VI. Ifẹ marks are three horizontal lines like those of the original Baṣọrun's marks, each being shorter, about half-inch long. Otherwise Ifẹs are usually plain faced.

VII. The Ondos and Idokos have only one bold line or rather a gash about one and a half inches to two inches long over each malar bone.

VIII. The Ijẹṣas as a rule have no distinctive marks ; they are mostly plain-faced ; some families, however, are distinguished by having on each cheek 5 or 6 horizontal lines. They are closely drawn, and much longer than any Ọyọ mark, e.g.

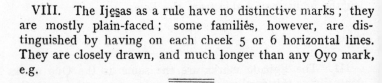

Amongst the Ẹfọns an Ekiti family, the lines are so many

and so closely drawn that the whole together form a dark patch on each cheek, e.g.

IX. The Yagbas are the most north-easterly tribes of Yoruba ; they are distinguished by three long lines on each cheek, far apart behind, but converging to a point at the angle of the mouth, e.g.

X. The Igbominas are by some classed with Ọyọs, and by others with Ekitis. It will, perhaps, be more correct to say they are Ọyọs with Ekiti sympathies. They occupy a midway position between the two ; and so their facial marks are parallel like those of Ọyọs, but long and far apart like those of Yagbas, yet not convergent in front e.g.

On the whole, speaking generally, the finer and more closely drawn lines, are more elegant than the same drawn bold, and too far apart.

We may note how each of the principal marks is indicated by a different verb signifying "to mark" :—

To be marked with the Pele	is	O kọ Pele
„ „ „ Abaja	„	O bu Abaja
„ „ „ Kẹkẹ	„	O ṣá Kẹkẹ
„ „ „ Gọmbọ	„	O wa Gọmbọ

§ (c) DIET

The diet of the common people is plain but substantial. The morning meal is a kind of gruel made from corn flour (maize or guinea corn) and taken between 7 and 8 a.m. with *Akàra* an oily cake made of beans, ground and fried. There are no fixed hours for meals. After midday, dinner is served, each family consulting its own convenience as to the precise time of eating. Supper is taken in the evening generally between 7 and 9 p.m.

In ancient times pounded yam is served out in a large bowl or earthenware vessel, and both the father and his children and grandchildren sit around it to partake of the food. Each one dips his hand into the dish and takes a morsel in strict order of seniority,

F

the youngest present acts the part of a servant and waits on his
seniors ; and whether the food be sufficient or not care was usually
taken to leave some portion for him.

The staple articles of diet are yam and yam flour, corn and
corn flour, beans of various kinds, cassava, sweet potatoes, etc.
Only the well-to-do can afford to indulge in flesh diet daily, the
poorer people are mostly vegetarians, except when animals are
slaughtered for sacrifice they seldom partake of meat ; game,
however, is plentiful. Dwellers on the coast have a plentiful
supply of fish.

Of fruits the principal are :—The shea fruit in the plain, the
Oro (*Irvinga Barteri Hook*) in forest lands. The *Òri* or black
plum (*verbenacea cuneata*), locust, bananas, plantains, pawpaws,
oranges, lime (citron), pine-apples, the well-known kola nut, and
the bitter kola (*garcinia kola-Heckel*), ground nuts (*Arachis hypogea*),
etc. Their drink consists of palm wine, bamboo wine, and beer
made from the guinea corn or from maize.

§ (d) Dress

The Yorubas clothe themselves in loose flowing robes like the
people of the East, whence indeed they trace their origin. The
men wear gowns, vests, and a very free and ample kind of trousers
called Ṣòkòtò. In lieu of the gown sometimes a sheet of cloth
three yards by two is thrown around the body for a covering,
passing under the right arm-pit, and overlapping over the left
shoulder.

In ancient times the gowns were made very plain and were
of purely native manufacture. They were without embroidery
on the breast and around the neck as at present ; only kings and
chiefs wore gowns made of superior stuffs richly embroidered.
The covering for the common people is called Ẹlẹgòdọ̀. The
weavers have a standard of breadths for all home-made cloths.
Men's coverings are made of 14 breadths, and women's of 10,
of about 5 inches each. Cloths of wide breadths—say about a
yard—were first imported from Oró or Ilá in the Igbomina
province, and were known as Akoko cloths being chiefly the production of Akoko women ; hence the practice spread all over the
country for women to manufacture broad width cloths, and men
narrow ones. Formerly only men were weavers and tailors, but
from intercourse with other nations the women now engage in the
same craft.

The vest spoken of above is known as *kukumọ* over which the
gown or loose cloth is thrown. It is sleeveless and without a collar,
and open in front ; it may be made of any kind of native stuff,

but that which is made of Alari (crimson dye) or of Sămayan (rough silk) is the most respectable, as it is at the same time most costly.

Another kind of vest is termed *Ewù*; this is much like the former, but with sleeves ; it is more commonly used in modern times ; in full dress it is often worn under the gown, and is always made of white stuff.

There is another form which seems to be of foreign importation used only by big men ; it is full of pleats below reaching to the calves, but the sleeves are very ample and long, about 12 inches longer than the arms, very wide at the end. It is called Dandogo, and is worn in lieu of the gown.

Togo is a sleeveless dress like kukumọ but smaller and simpler ; it is the soldier's dress and is often worn with a turban wrapped round for a belt.

There are three sorts of gowns, the Suliya, Agbada and Girike. The Suliya is the smallest, plainest and lightest ; always made of white material, it reaches much below the knee, open at the sides, with the arm stretched the sleeve would reach as far as the wrist, but long and pointed below. The Agbada is a larger form, always made of dyed or coloured stuff. It reaches as far as the ankles, much embroidered at the neck and breast, open at the sides, and quite covers the arms. The Girike is the largest and heaviest, it is like the Agbada but more ample ; it is much embroidered, reaching also as far as the ankles, and extends beyond the arms.

Trousers (called Ṣokoto) are made of different shapes and lengths, but all are kept round the waist by a strong cord. They are worn below the vests. They consist of the following :—

(*a*) *Ladugbo* is the commonest, worn by young and working men, it is quite free, but somewhat tight at the knee where it terminates. It is now out of fashion.

(*b*) *Aibọpo*, also common, worn by all classes. It is free but tightened towards the knee where it terminates.

(*c*) The *Alongo*. This is tight throughout, and is not unlike a bishop's gaiters. It reaches below the knee, and is used chiefly by sportsmen.

(*d*) The *Kàfo* is a tight-legged dress like the Alongo, but reaches as far down as the ankles. It is worn by warriors and ruffians generally.

(*e*) The *Kẹmbẹ*. This is made like the Aibọpo but richly embroidered about the legs with threads of crimson dye. This is the kind usually worn by nobles and gentlemen.

(*f*) The *Ẹfa* or *Abẹnugbangba*. The name (wide-mouthed) well describes the nature of the trousers. It is a kind that is very free, longer than the Aibopo, is somewhat shaped like European trousers, but stops short a little below the knee.

(g) The *Wondo* is made entirely like the European trousers. Though once fashionable, yet is now entirely out of use.

(h) The last is the *Agadanṣi*. This is adopted from the Nupes, by whom it is commonly used. It extends from the waist to the ankles ; it is very free throughout save at the ankles where it terminates and is heavily embroidered there. It is often made of two or three yards wide (sometimes more) so that when the feet are thrust in at either end, and the cord drawn above, it gathers into a large volume between the legs.

The men's head-gear is usually a cap (Filà) of which there are two kinds ; the ordinary filà which is about 10 inches long, rather close fitting, and is bent upon itself on the top. The turban is generally wound round it by Moslems and full-dressed gentlemen. The other kind is used generally by young folks, and is called *Filà Ab'eti* i.e. the ear-covering cap. It is shaped like the sector of a circle, the pointed ends being used—as its name denotes—for covering the ears in cold weather. But when used otherwise the pointed ends are turned fore and aft, the point on the forehead being tilted up in a sporting manner to show the under-surface prettily done up with cloths of bright colouring : it is then termed *Labànkadà*.

Hats made of straw, and ornamented with coloured leather are worn solely for protection from the sun : the crowns are large enough to accommodate the turbaned head.

The women's dress is much simpler, two or three wrappers and a head dress or circlet complete their toilet. Unmarried women generally use two wrappers, the under wrapper being fixed above the breasts. This is made of fine cloth and is heavier. The upper is fixed about the middle of the body ; and is made of lighter cloth. To these married women add a third, used as a shawl, or covering for the head and back. Underneath all these, and immediately next the body is worn from the age of puberty a short apron or petticoat reaching the knees, and tied round the waist with a strong cord or band. This is called Tòbi.

Female headgear consists of a band, of about 6 to 10 inches wide and 5 feet long (more or less). This is wound twice round the head and tucked on one side. It may be of plain cloth or costly, as she can afford. Well-to-do ladies use velvet cloths.

Hats are used only as sunshades ; the crown is small for the head but the rim is as wide as an open umbrella.

Camwood to the feet and stibium to the eyelids complete the female toilet.

§ (e) MARRIAGE

In ancient times the Yorubas were mostly monogamic ; not from any enlightened views on the subject however, but rather from necessity ; for, although polygamy was not actually forbidden, yet only rich folk could avai. themselves of indulgence in that condition of life.

Besides, in a community mainly pastoral and agricultural, where all were peaceful, and no one engaged in any occupation perilous to the lives of its male population e.g. warfare, sea-faring, deep mining, etc., where wants were few, and those easily satisfied, the young men married as soon as they were of an age to support a family, and therefore a superfluous female population was hardly ever known.

The marriage laws and customs have undergone changes brought about by intercourse with other peoples, but the chief features in them are still preserved.

Where all things are equal and normal, there are three stages to be observed, viz. 1, An early intimation. 2, A Formal Betrothal. 3, The Marriage.

1. *An early intimation.*—It is generally the duty of the female members of the family to look out for a wife for their male relative ; girls are generally marked out from childhood as intended for a particular young man, with or without her knowledge ; this is the first stage in the process. Mutual relations at this time are of an informal nature ; much depends upon subsequent events, especially on the girl's liking for the man when she is of age, and the consent of the parents. There are other important factors in the matter, but for the former, ways and means are found for the girl to make the acquaintance of the future husband. This period is also employed in making a close acquaintance with each other's family, for before a formal betrothal is made the relatives on both sides will first satisfy themselves that the family of the other side is free from the taint of any hereditary disease such as insanity, epilepsy, leprosy, etc. and also whether they be insolvent debtors. As mutual understanding becomes established, presents are usually given at the New Year, and at other annual festivals. This period will last until the girl is of marriageable age.

2. *The Betrothal.*—This is called the " Isihun " or formal consent. No girl will marry without the consent of her parents ; and it is rare for a girl to refuse the choice of her parents. The family oracles are invariably consulted before the final decision is arrived at.

The ceremony of betrothal is a very important one ; it is generally performed in the night, when all the most important members of the family on both sides will be at leisure to be present, as well as their intimate friends. The young man is to present 40 large kola nuts, some money, and several pots of beer for the entertainment of those present. The kola-nuts have to be split, and all present as well as important absentees must have a share of them, indicating thereby that they are witnesses of the betrothal. From this day, the girl is not to meet her fiancé or any member of his family without veiling or hiding her face.

Then follows what is known as the Anã or " dowry." The bridegroom-elect has to present to the parents of the intended bride, choice kola-nuts, some alligator pepper, and bitter kolas.[1] Also a fine wrapper of good quality, a large covering cloth, a head tie, and some money according to his ability. . Well-to-do families rarely require more than 10 heads of cowries in these days, in earlier times one head was considered ample—only as a token.

Whatever variations may be in these presents, the kola-nuts of both kinds and the alligator pepper are invariable and essential. If the girl happens to be doing debtors' service at the time, the young man will pay the debt and release her, before the marriage can take place.

This event (the betrothal) is also an occasion of rejoicing, feasting, and offering of sacrifices. The parties themselves are to carry special propitiatory sacrifices offered to the evil one. This is termed " Ẹbọ Iyawo " i.e. A bride's sacrifice.

3. *Marriage.* (Igbeyawo).—Marriages may be solemnized at any time of the year, except during the fasts, but the most usual time is after the season of harvest, and following the Egũgun festival.

The bride is conducted to her new home always in the night, attired in her best with a thin white cloth for a veil, and attended by her companions all well clothed, with drums, and singing and dancing. The bridal party is met at the entrance gate of the bridegroom's compound by a female band of the house specially selected for the purpose, and by them the ceremony of washing the bride's feet is performed, and then the bride is literally lifted and borne into the house. Hence the term for marriage " Gbe Iyawo " i.e. lifting or carrying the bride. She is then conducted into the bathroom where she is washed, rubbed down, perfumed,

---

[1] This is really not dowry but symbols of future relationship between both families.

and dressed up afresh, and then conducted into the apartment of the head lady of the house. She now becomes the inmate of that house for life.

The bride is usually brought with her idols, and furnished from her home with every thing that appertains to the female department of house-keeping, including cooking utensils, brooms, and other articles for house use.

If she gives satisfaction to her husband, and friends, presents are sent on the next day to her parents, she herself is covered with trinkets (consisting chiefly of corals and other costly beads, gold necklaces where they are obtainable, etc.) and the festivities continue for at least three days.

A bride who is found unchaste is rather hardly used and some times severely punished to the extent of having her tied[1] and severely flogged, thus compelling her to name her violator so as to have him severely fined. No ornaments are allowed her and she may be ordered to perform errands out of doors unveiled, the next day, or may be sent out with a pitcher for water ! Otherwise, a bride is never seen out of doors for 12 months at least after her marriage, except closely veiled, and with attendants.

In the case of Moslems, liturgical forms of ceremonies are performed by the priest in the house or in the mosque. This is termed *Isoyigi*. Such women alone in former times had the privilege of covering their head with a light shawl when out of doors ; but the practice has now been extended to all married women.

Widowhood and Remarriage.—Three months is the period of mourning in Yoruba, during which time widows remain closely indoors ; they may spin, dye, or do any home work, but must do nothing that will take them out of doors. Among other signs of widowhood is an entire absence of personal attention, they neither bathe nor do up their hair, nor change the cloth they had on at the time of the husband's death.

This period over, they are open to offer of marriage from members of the deceased husband's family. Where there are several women, the heir (usually the eldest son or younger brother) who succeeds to the headship of the house, usually inherits the majority of the women, except of course his own mother. The custom is for each man to send his chewing stick (tooth brush) round to the woman of his choice, she is expected modestly to decline

---

[1] This gave rise to the proverb " Tani dè o ti o nka oko " i.e. who has tied you that you begin to name a violator ? The equivalent of *Qui s'excuse s'accuse.*

it once or twice ; but if she refused it the third time, the refusal is taken as final.

The following peculiarities mark Yoruba wedded life :—

1. Women are never really married twice ; they may be inherited as widows, or taken for a wife outside the late husband's family, but the marriage ceremony is never gone over again under any circumstances.

2. Once married they are attached for ever to the house and family of their deceased husbands ; hence it is more usual for widows to choose another husband from the same family.

3. No woman is without a husband, except in extreme old age, but every woman must in any case have a male protector who is responsible for her.

4. Divorce is very rare ; so rare as to be practically considered as non-existing. It is by no means easily obtained especially when there are children of the union.

The causes that may lead to a divorce are :—Adultery with the husband's blood relation, kleptomania, repeated insolvency, especially such as may bring trouble to the house. A woman may apply for a divorce for extreme cruelty, which can be testified to, and ill-usage.

But these causes notwithstanding a divorce is never granted by the rulers of the town until all possible means of reclamation have been exhausted.

5. A woman divorced from her husband can never be married, or taken up legally by another man ; hence the saying A ki işu opo aláye (no one can inherit the *relict* of a living man).

Under purely Native Government the above rules still hold good.

OTHER RECOGNIZED FORMS OF MARRIAGE

There are cases in which all the above forms and ceremonies are not gone through, and yet the woman is regarded as the lawful wife of the man of her choice. Mutual consent is the only thing indispensable. Of such cases, some may be girls who when of age, will not accept the man chosen for them from childhood, except one of their own choice. Some may be widows who failed to be mated at the house of her late husband. Some may be slaves who have redeemed themselves, or a captive of war, or one bought to be made a wife of. In all such cases, the woman's free consent, and the recognition of her by the members of the man's family, are all that is required for her to be regarded as the man's lawful wife.

There is a third form of marriage which is more common among

Moslems of modern times.   In such cases, it is not usual to mark out a husband for the girls from childhood ; but when they are of age, the father, seeing a young man he delights in, or an elderly man with whom he desires to form a connection, if he expresses himself willing to accept the gift, the father after a very short notice will order his daughter to be washed and dressed up and taken over to the man in the evening, as a " Saráhà " i.e. a free gift of God ! The girl may not even know the man until she is taken to him !

In such cases a girl that is wild and unruly who is likely to bring disgrace on the family receives but a few hours' notice ; but a dutiful and obedient daughter will always have her feelings consulted, and her wishes granted as to her choice of the man and the time of the marriage.   Festivities are performed in these cases also.

These are the three forms of wedlock recognized by the Yorubas the first being far more binding than the latter two.

Moslems hold that the Koranic law limits them to four wives, and, therefore, the ceremony of *Isoyigi* is never performed for the same man above that number.

Other wives taken without the ceremony of *Isoyigi* are known as *Wahari* (a Hausa word) ; they are legal in every way and their children quite as legitimate, but both mother and children are regarded as somewhat inferior to those others.   Amongst pagans the " customs " detailed above take the place of *Isoyigi* with the status it confers upon both the mother and the children.

Only the products of an illicit intercourse are regarded as illegitimate.

§ (*f*) TRADES AND PROFESSIONS

The principal occupations of men are:—Agriculture, commerce, weaving, iron-smelting, smithing, tanning and leather working, carving on wood and on calabashes, music, medicine, barbing, and other minor employments.

Agriculture.—This is the most general occupation of the bulk of the people.   It is carried on with simple and primitive instruments, viz. a hoe and a cutlass, and nothing more, both of home manufacture.   Ploughing is unknown, and it is very doubtful indeed whether a plough would be of much service to them under present conditions ; experiments with that instrument by those who understand the use of it have not proved successful.

The principal articles of food and of commerce grown are :— Corn (guinea corn in the north and maize in the south), beans of several varieties, ground nuts (*arachis hypogea*), yams of various species, sweet potatoes, koko (colocasia antiquorum), pepper, piper, calabashes and other kinds of gourds, coffee, cocoa, kola nuts, vegetables of all sorts for home consumption, cotton for weaving, etc.

When a plot has been worked with rotation of crops for a few years, it is left to lie fallow for some years whilst contiguous plots are put under cultivation, and so on alternately ; manuring is unknown. The soil is remarkably fertile under present system.

Women and children assist in reaping and in bringing harvest home. No beasts of burden are employed in agricultural operations.

All farmers and men of any importance have generally smaller farms nearer home " *Oko Ètile* " and a more distant one generally in the forest " *Oko Egàn.*" When engaged in the nearer one, they work from 6 or 7 a.m. to 5 p.m., with intervals for meals, and then return home ; but at the distant farm, they invariably remain there for weeks and months before returning home. Regular farmers do so only at the annual festivals. In these farms, not only are fruits of the earth cultivated but also poultry and smaller cattle are reared for the market. Fairs are held periodically in some central farm markets where these products are disposed of to market women from surrounding towns and villages.

Although the soil is well adapted for raising fruits, yet fruit trees are rarely cultivated for the supply of markets.

Commerce.—Commerce comes next in the order of importance. Yorubas are keen traders, they are to be found in every part of neighbouring countries for that purpose. A large trade is carried on by barter. Cowry shells, the medium of exchange, being too clumsy for large transactions, are used only for small exchanges locally ; the very small species are used by travellers. Costly beads are used by many on distant journeys for trade, they are valued as precious stones. Thus the products of the north are given in exchange for those of the south, and those of Yoruba land for those of neighbouring states always by barter. Both sexes are engaged in trade but each in his own line.

Currency.—Metallic currency was unknown previously to the arrival of European traders, and even as lately as 1897 in places far off from the coast coins were regarded more or less as a curiosity. Silver was better appreciated than gold or copper, because it can be converted to ornaments. Silversmiths abound in the country whilst there were no goldsmiths. Shells then stood for money and are thus calculated :—

        40 cowries = 1 string
        50 strings = 1 head
        10 heads   = 1 bag

The value of a cowry was never fixed. Countries nearer the coast can obtain them with greater facility than those inland, and therefore they are of higher value in the interior ; but since the British occupation of Lagos the principal port of the Yoruba country, and English coins began to circulate in the country, the rate of exchange became practically fixed at 6d. for a " head " (the usual standard of calculation) i.e. 2,000 cowries ; hence 3d. = 1,000 cowries. But coppers being considered inferior in value, one penny is taken at 300 cowries each ; 3d. in coppers then would be 900 cowries. Cowries are an absolute necessity at the present stage of the country, and should be used *pari passu* with coins for purchases below one penny. Fruits, herbs, and small articles of food may be purchased for a few cowries, beggars collect them by two's and three's from passers by, and thereby earn enough to keep life going ; to what extent they are rare, to that extent the hardships of life are felt in the land.

The custom of stringing cowries was for the facility of counting large sums ; they were usually strung by 200 in 5 strings of 40 each, three of 66 or two of 100 each and with a discount of one per cent.

Esusu is a universal custom for the clubbing together of a number of persons for monetary aid. A fixed sum agreed upon is given by each at a fixed time (usually every week) and place, under a president ; the total amount is paid over to each member in rotation. This enables a poor man to do something worth while where a lump sum is required. There are laws regulating this system.

Weaving.—This also is carried on by both sexes but in different styles of manufacture. Men weave cloths of narrow breadths about 5½ inches wide called *Alawę*. The loom is operated upon with both hands and feet ; the threads of the warps are so arranged that they open and close by a mechanical contrivance worked by both feet moving alternately as the pedals of an harmonium, whilst the shuttle about 8 by 2 inches carrying the woof is tossed and caught by the right and left hand alternately through the opening, the disengaged hand being rapidly used in ramming in the thread. The cloth is woven in one long strip and then cut to the required lengths and tacked together.

Tailoring is done mostly by men only as it is only men's dress which requires a tailor. It includes embroidery made in the neck and breast of men's gowns. Women being wrapped in plain cloths hardly require tailoring. The stitches are made the contrary way to that of European tailors, the needle being pushed away from the seamster, and not toward himself.

Iron Smelting was carried on more largely in earlier than in modern times.   Certain districts are rich in iron ores, its iron production gave its name to the city of Ilọrin, from *Ilọ irin*, iron grinding, also to Eleta a district of Ibadan " *Eta* " being the term for iron ore.   Certain districts in the Ekiti province are also famous for their iron ores from which good steel was made, such as OKE MESI.   Charcoal from hard wood, and the shells of palm nuts are the materials generally used for generating the great heat required for the furnace (called *Ileru*) which is kept going all the year round. Iron rods and bars of European commerce being cheaper are fast displacing home-made products, and here and there all over the country the furnaces are being closed, and soon will doubts begin to be expressed as to whether Yorubas ever knew the art of smelting iron from the ores !

Other products of the mines e.g. gold, silver, tin, etc., are not known among the Yorubas.

Smithery is carried on largely.   Before the period of intercourse with Europeans, all articles made of iron and steel, from weapons of war to pins and needles were of home manufacture ; but the cheaper and more finished articles of European make, especially cutlery though less durable are fast displacing home-made wares.

There are also brass and copper smiths who make ornaments from these materials ; for this purpose brass and copper bars are imported from foreign parts.

Workers in leather were formerly their own tanners, each one learns to prepare for himself, whatever leather he wants to use ; black, white, green, yellow, and brown are the prevailing colours given to leather.   They are now largely imported from Hausa-land, principally from Kano.

Every worker is expected to know, and to be able to execute the various crafts performed with leather, e.g. saddlery, sheaths to swords and knives, leather ornaments on hats, waistbands for children, leather cushions, bolsters, boots and shoes, sandals, etc.

It may be remarked that shoes and boots are used only by riders on horseback, and therefore they are always made with spurs immovably fixed upon them.

Music is a favourite pastime and gives occupation to many, both men and boys.

Musicians also have first to learn how to manufacture the instruments they have to perform upon, hence each one can easily repair a damaged instrument.

Yoruba music has yet to be studied and reduced to a system by a competent musician ; how essential this is can easily be recognized when we consider how much time and trouble is spent in acquiring the art, and how much the practice of it enters into the varied life and conversation of the people. Having learnt how to make their instruments, they then begin to learn how to *speak* with them, an operation to which the Yoruba language readily lends itself, as it consists chiefly in modulation of the voice ; this the instruments try to imitate. The praises and attributes of great men and distinguished names are got up, and the various measures in dances are learnt. There is no sound more common in Yoruba towns than what Europeans term " tomtoms." Musicians are in requisition at weddings, funerals, in processions of all kinds religious and otherwise ; they are constant attendants on all great men, and many of them parade the streets asking alms on their drums.

Musical Instruments used by the Yorubas are of two classes only, viz. wind and percussion.

(*a*) The Ivory trumpet and the Kakaki introduced from the Hausa and Nupe are used for the ALÂFIN alone. The Fami fami, Okinkin, Igba, Tiyako fife and the Òge. These are the principal wind instruments.

(*b*) The Koso is the ALÂFIN's drum, and the Ogidigbo is used only on the occasion of the ALÂFIN and the Baṣọrun dancing on the annual festivals.

The Calabash drum—ornamented with strings of cowries— is called Sẹ̀kẹ̀rẹ̀. The Yangede, Dundun, Bàta, Àyé, Sâmi, Siki and the Apinti are all ancient drums. The Aro (cymbal) the Bẹmbẹ, introduced from Hausa, and the Gangan the noisiest but most popular are of recent invention. These are the percussion instruments.

Stringed instruments are rarely used, except by Hausa mendicants.

Medicine.—There are certain persons, doctors by profession (general practitioners) to whom people resort on an emergency. They are called *Adahunṣe*. There are no institutions like hospitals, but some of these doctors do keep on their premises a number of invalids suffering from chronic or constitutional diseases, e.g., leprosy, insanity, chronic ulcers, etc. Many of these patients being unable to pay the doctor's fees, style themselves " Gba mi o rá mi " i.e., help me and appropriate me. Such persons on being cured become the property (or perpetual house servant) of the doctor.

Formerly there were certain clans known as medicine people, and were licensed as such by the King. For instance, the inhabitants of the towns of Oguró, Ogidì, Abẹ, Agberi, Apatẹ̀, Arohungbé. They were remarkable for their skill in using secret poisons, and crimes committed by them generally went unpunished, they being under the special protection of the King. They are expected to be at the King's service when required, but it meant death to any of them if the poison given to the King for his use upon his enemies did not take fatal effect.

There was also a particular family of Ẹfọn descent living at one time at Ọyọ said to have belonged to the Ondasa tribe. Their great ancestor was said to have been invited to the capital by one of the early Kings of Ọyọ for medical advice when all his wives were barren. His prescriptions were successful, and so he was detained at Ọyọ and rewarded with a high rank and position in the palace amongst the household officers. His descendants are now distinguished from the citizens of Ọyọ by the totem Ọgọ̀ (a club) being affixed to their names.

The art of medicine is kept a profound secret by those who profess it ; an increase of knowledge can only be gained by an interchange of thoughts between brother professionals ; many die without imparting their secrets to others, and thus much valuable knowledge is entirely lost. But some do impart their secret to those of their children male or female who show special aptitude for such knowledge and whom they particularly love.

On the whole we can unhesitatingly assert that those men who are specialists in one or two particular branches but who do not make the practice of medicine a profession can be more confidently relied upon.

Carpentry is in a very backward condition. Of joinery they have no idea whatever. Carpenters are called Gbẹnagbẹna. They are the crudest and most primitive of handicraftsmen ; their services are not much in requisition.

Carving in wood is executed in a rather primitive way but such natural genius is displayed by some men, that it is a matter of surprise that such artistic achievements can be displayed by an illiterate person, and with tools so simple and primitive.

The Yorubas of the Egbadò district are said to be the best artists in the country. They certainly have in their forests wood most suitable for carving purposes.

Calabash dressers are always found in a row in market places plying their trade ; all sorts of geometrical figures are traced or cut in calabashes ; some designs are exquisitely correct and beautiful. Names, mottoes, and phrases are burnt into calabashes by educated artists, figures only by the uneducated. These designs are recently being imitated by Europeans under the term of *Poker Work*.

Seamanship.—There are very few large rivers in Yoruba land and nearly all of them fordable during the dry season, consequently only in coast towns and on the Niger are canoemen found who make any pretence to seamanship.

When the inland rivers are swollen by rains, large bowls and very large calabashes are used in ferrying passengers across. The passengers sit on them with their luggage, with the ferryman in the water, pushing the freight across.

All canoes are dug out from large trees. Our canoemen cannot really be called experts, as they rarely sail out of sight of land, and canoes can ill endure any storm or tempest; nevertheless, when war canoes are rigged up and manned, they are handled with no little skill in their fights, sham or real. In the title of Aromirẹ (i.e. one in friendly terms with water) we have preserved a chieftain who ranked as an admiral in the olden days of sea fights.

Fisheries.—Deep sea fishing is but little practised, the rivers and lagoons furnish all that they can harvest. Shrimps and oysters are plentiful in their season. The fishing industry is of course confined to coastal towns, and as there are no means of supplying inland towns the consumption of the fresh article is confined to the coast.

Building as a profession is almost unknown; houses as a rule are built by men clubbing together, but there are always a few experts among them in particular lines, either in building the mud walls or in roofing and they distribute themselves accordingly. These are always in requisition whenever they can be spared from their farms. Large works are undertaken and arranged for, when all hands can conveniently be spared from their farms.

Pastoral Work as a profession is carried on only in the northern provinces more suited for that purpose from the extensive plain and pasture land of those regions. But very few Yorubas are found engaged in it. Gambaris (i.e. Hausas) are generally engaged by the chiefs to tend their cattle.

The *barbers* and *ropemakers* are also mostly Hausas and Fulanis, these are crafts rarely practised by Yorubas.

These Hausas also perform some minor surgical operations such as cupping, bone-setting, tapping hydroceles, etc. Some are even oculists, and profess to be able to operate for cataract. It goes without saying that much mischief is often done by their crude performances. They are unskilled and the instruments used are rather clumsy. It is a wonder that more mischief is not done, or that they occasionally get good results at all.

OCCUPATIONS OF WOMEN

It is specially the province of women advanced in age to seed cotton and spin thread. The former is done by rolling out the

seeds from the wool between a smooth log of hard wood and a
polished iron rod, the latter by weighting a thin rod of about
12 inches long with a small ball of clay about 1 inch distant from one
end, attaching the cotton to the other end and setting the ball spinning like a top, the wool being rapidly drawn out to the required
fineness.   Seeded cotton is rendered fluffy for spinning by being
attached to the string of a bent bow, and the string constantly
pulled as if shooting an arrow.   These operations being an occupation of a sedentary nature, and more suitable for old women are
performed by them leisurely all day.   Reels of spun thread are
sold to dyers.

Aged women who reside in the farms also employ their time
in shelling the kernels from the palm nuts, and also tending
poultry, goats and sheep for the market.

Dyeing is done by women.   They buy a quantity of the yarn,
bleach and dye them in various colours, and sell them to the
weavers, male or female.   The commonest colour is blue or blue
black from the indigo dye.   The preparation of indigo balls for
the market is also an important industry.   Women are equally
with men engaged in trading and weaving ; but whereas men
weave in small breadths and carry on their occupation in courtyards
or secluded squares in the streets where they can stretch their
warp 20 yards or more, the women on the contrary fix their
looms in the piazza of the house, close to the door of their apartments where they may be seen sitting on the ground, with their
legs in a hole under the loom ; they weave the cloths in broad
pieces called Kijipa two or three breadths forming a covering.

The warp is wound round two stout bamboo poles fixed athwart
two strong upright posts, top and bottom.   There is a mechanism
by which the threads can be made to cross each other.   The
woof in rods of about a yard long is passed slowly right and left
as the warp is opened and separated one way and the other, being
rammed down each time by a flat smooth staff.

Besides indigo dyes of light blue and dark shades, the scarlet
called àlahárì and rough silk, Sãmãyan in grey are the prevailing
colours of Yoruba yarn.

Palm oil making and nut oil making from the kernels of the palm
nuts, as well as shea butter from the shea fruit are exclusively
female industries.

Beer-brewing from guinea corn or maize is done also by women ;
for this they have a sheltered place within or near the compound
to insure protection against fire.

A large class is engaged in preparing articles of food.   They are
purveyors of cooked food, keepers of refreshment stalls and other

branches of dietary for the market, especially to accommodate working men and caravans.

The manufacture of beads from the hard shells of palm nuts, or from the cocoa nut shells, is an important female industry. The former quality is more highly valued.

Pottery is also a female industry. Men may sometimes be seen assisting to dig up the clay and to perform some rough initial work, but as a rule the whole industry is in the hands of women. The drying, pulverising, sifting, mixing and moulding, are all done by women and girls.

Large pots for brewing beer, and for setting indigo dyes, and cooking Ẹkọ (the morning gruel) for sale are turned out with marvellous skill. Cooking utensils, dishes, water pots, etc., are also made for the markets. Some parts of the country furnish clay of superior quality, notably Ilọrin.

Although ignorant of the use of the wheel, or any such mechanical contrivance used in pottery, yet the figures, forms and shapes of the articles turned out are wonderfully correct.

Every woman whatever her trade may be, is expected to keep a few chickens and a goat or two from which she derives small income for house keeping and general " pin money." The rearing of poultry then must be reckoned among female occupations.

Hair dressing may also be mentioned among female occupations, for although the race has not much to boast of in that form of natural adornment, yet they often contrive to bring out styles and fashions which satisfy them ; but a marked distinction must always be made between that of married women and the unmarried ; this is a social law which on no account should ever be infringed.

On the whole the women seem to be far more industrious than the men, for whereas the men always contrive to have leisure hours and off days from work, the women seem to have none. Boys and young men certainly have more idle hours than the girls. The care of the children also devolves almost entirely upon their mother, an inevitable result of polygamy.

§ (g) LEARNING

As the Yorubas have no knowledge of letters, their learning consists chiefly in oral traditions. The historians are the King's cymballists and ballad singers, the chief of whom is called the OLOGBO or AROKIN. They may be compared to the rhapsodists of the Homeric age, as they perform almost precisely similar functions. They chant to the King the story of the nation, and history of former reigns, for his information and instruction. They

are kept in the royal service and are well supported.   The office
is hereditary.

Like many other heathen nations the Yorubas have their
tradition about the creation and the deluge.   It is their belief
that at the creation men fed on wood and water, that they had a
long projecting mouth ; that the bat was originally a creature in
human form, and was a black-smith by trade, and that with his
instrument he reduced men's mouths to their present shape, for
which cause he was condemned to lose the human form and to
assume that of a beast, and to use one and the same mouth for
receiving food as well as for evacuation.   The allegation that
water was the original food of man is supported by the fact that
it is the first thing taken by a new-born babe, as well as the last
thing taken at a man's dying moments.

§ (h) WEALTHY PERSONAGES

There were certain historical personages in Yoruba who were
noted for their great wealth, viz., Amolokú of Òró, Gẹdẹgbẹ of
Ọfà, Lapemọ of Ijọmu near Òró, Onibiyọ̀ of Guguru, Minimi
of Ẹrubu.   There is also a sixth spoken of who resided at Gbudu.
There was also a lady known as the Olowo of Ijẹbu.

§ (i) THE IWỌFA SYSTEM AND THE LAWS REGULATING IT

The term *Iwọfa* has no equivalent in English.   It denotes one
who serves another periodically in lieu of the interest on money
lent.   In short, it is one in service for interest.

It has been mistranslated a " pawn " by those who fancied
they saw a resemblance to it in that system, and are trying to
identify everything native with those that are foreign, and consequently, as in other similar cases, much mischief has been done
thereby.

The Yoruba man is simply shocked to hear of " pawning "
a man as is done with goods and chattels ; to pawn in Yoruba is
fi dogò which term is never applied to a human being.

It has also been compared to slavery by those ignorant of
the legal conditions ruling the system ; but an Iwọfa is a free
man, his social status remains the same, his civil and political rights
are intact, and he is only subject to his master in the same universal
sense that " a borrower is servant to the lender."

Iwọfas are held quite distinct from slaves ; the verbs applied
to each system mark the distinction e.g. *rà* to buy is applied to
a slave, *yá* to lend or engage (a hand) to an Iwọfa ; consequently
you can *buy* a slave, but engage an Iwọfa or service man.

The derivation of the term is probably from Iwọ̀ the entering into, and Ẹfà a period of six days ; hence an Iwọfa is one who enters into a recurrent sixth day service.

The Iwọfa system is a contract entered into in the presence of witnesses called Onigbọwọ i.e. sponsors, the money-lender is termed *Oluwa* i.e. master, and the worker Iwọfa, i.e. a service man.

It is a legal transaction recognized and protected by the laws of the country. Whatsoever the amount of money lent, it is the law that the service rendered goes for the interest, and only the principal is paid back whenever payment is made whether after a few days or after many years.

An Iwọfa may be a man or a woman, a boy or a girl, and the laws for each differ accordingly.

A man Iwọfa lives in his own house and plies his own trade, but he is required to clean a piece of land equal to 100 yam heaps or an equivalent in his master's farm once a week, the Yoruba week consisting of five days.

The people being mainly agricultural, farm-cleaning is the work of their daily life, and is the recognized ordinary system of labour.

Cleaning three hundred heaps is the ordinary amount of an average man's day's work, consequently a strong man often found it possible to work in three different farms on the same day, for different masters, or to do three week's work at a time in one farm, and have 14 off days at a stretch, in which he is free to follow his own trade without interruption. Special arrangements can also be made if a longer period is desired, but the Iwọfa is bound to make up for the number cf days lost.

This is the original law, but it is subject to slight modification or variation in various places, according to the local value, or the amount of money lent ; e.g. amongst the Ẹgbas, a whole day's work is required instead of a morning's work. But whatever modification of the original law is made in any particular locality, the law for that tribe is always fixed by authority, and never subject to the whims and caprice of an individual money-lender.

The master is to treat the service man as his social rank demands, he mingles freely with his equals in the house or in the field as a member of the household. A kind master often allows him his breakfast before he quits the field although he is not bound to do so, and if a master be too exacting or disagreeable, he may be changed any day without any previous notice, once the money lent is paid back in full.

Where the master is a great chief or a rich man, the service man may live under his protection and own him his feudal lord ; hence some men never troubled themselves to pay back the money, but may rather incur further obligations, being safe and free under the protection of a great name. Some men there are ,who are better able to do another man's work than their own.

An Iwọfa is never subject to punishment physical or otherwise, if he fail in his weekly service, the sponsors are called upon to make good the deficiencies.

In fine an Iwọfa differs from a slave in that a slave must live with his master, an Iwọfa in his own house. A slave can be compelled to work for his master every day, an Iwọfa for a limited amount of work for half a day in the week, and that not by compulsion but from obligations of honour. A slave can be punished, an Iwọfa cannot be. A slave has lost his independence and political rights, an Iwọfa retains both. A slave has no one responsible for him, an Iwọfa has two at least. In fine an Iwọfa can go and come as he likes, a slave cannot.

For women the same law holds good generally but with some modifications on account of their sex ; they work generally as char-women once a week, and have a meal in the house before returning home. In some cases they may live among the women folk in their master's house, carrying on their own work, and lending a helping hand in the housework and in harvest time do their own share of the day's work in the field along with the other women.

Some are engaged in trade, in which they sell for their master at the same time, and bring him the proceeds of his own articles as the allotted service rendered. When the trade is done in the home market, payments are made every nine days which are market days ; when out of town, at the return of the caravan.

If a service woman is tampered with by the master, the money is thereby considered absolutely paid, and the debt discharged. If forced against her will, not only is the debt cancelled, but he is also liable to prosecution and heavy fines besides to be paid both to the woman's husband as damages and to the town authorities as court fees.

If a young unmarried woman is tampered with, not only is the debt *ipso facto* discharged, but the master has to repay the *fiancé* all the money he has spent on her and also a betrothal " dowry " to the parents besides.

If the matter is not arranged amicably and the case has to go before the town authorities, the master has to pay, and heavy fines are inflicted on him besides. Often has a rich man been reduced to poverty by this means and consequently they are always very careful.

If a betrothed girl becomes marriageable whilst in service

and her *fiancé* wishes to get married at once, he has only to pay back the loan and lead his intended bride away. A woman cannot be married whilst doing service work.

A boy or a girl in service has to live entirely with the master or mistress as a domestic servant, inasmuch as their services are not worth much and they have to be trained besides, and the parent or whoever placed him there is supposed to have his whole time to ply his trade and withdraw his child as soon as possible ; therefore, the boy must give the master his whole time whatever that may be worth. The master is bound to feed him but not necessarily to clothe him, although many kind masters do that as well. They have a fixed time to visit their parents, usually once a week.

The boys generally tend horses and run errands, and the girls engage with the house-wives in domestic affairs. They are always with the boys and girls of their own age in the family.

The law protects such children very strongly. If the child refuse to stay any longer with the master or mistress for any cause whatever, they are never forced against their wish, but the parent or guardian must provide a substitute, or perform himself the weekly task.

If a child die during his or her service, the master must prove to the satisfaction of the parents and (if need be) of the town authorities that it was not due to any act of carelessness or neglect on his part, and that he provided ample medical aid for him.

The troubles accruing from young Iwọfas are often a deterrent to the acceptance of them for service ; some folks would expect and demand more comforts for their children in service than they can provide for them at home. Marriages and funerals are the two great causes of money borrowing.

But this system is not limited alone to the business of professional money-lenders, it enters much into other transactions of their everyday life.

The system of engaging domestic servants for service with a monthly wage is unknown in this country, the Iwọfa system is what is resorted to for that purpose. A parent will even put his child into service that way when there is no debt to pay in order to train him into habits of discipline and industry, and return the money when they feel that the child has been sufficiently trained.

Some would do so and put the money into trade and when satisfied with the profits made, return the principal and bring the child home.

The system is used also for apprenticeship. A man who wants

his son to learn a particular trade would put him under the crafts-
man for the purpose, and obtain from him a certain amount of
money ; the master, wishing to get his interest out of the boy
will see that he learns speedily and well, so as to be of some use
to him. In this way both are benefited.

A chief or a well-to-do gentleman with a wild and unruly son
whom he wishes to tame, or who is indulged at home, would also
resort to this method for training and discipline ; in such a case
the boy will remain with such a handicraftsman until he is able to
earn his own livelihood by his craft, then the money is paid back
and the boy returns home.

This method of lending money is the only one known for invest-
ment and is therefore resorted to as their banking system.

So the Iwọfa system may be regarded at one and the same
time as one for banking, apprenticeship, and domestic service.

Since the establishment of the British Protectorate there
has been more than one attempt made to abolish the system as
a "species of slavery!" The Yorubas themselves never at any
time regarded it as such ; to so regard it must be due either
to an ignorance of the laws regulating it, or because an exact
equivalent cannot be found in any European system. It can,
however, be imagined what chaos will result in any European
country if the banking system, apprenticeship, and domestic
service were abolished at a stroke—if that be possible. Like any
other system it may be reformed if given to abuse, that is more
reasonable and statesmanlike. But to abolish it outright because
it has no foreign analogue would be to disorganize the social life
of a people with no compensating advantage to borrower or lender.
If such were done in this case the greatest sufferers will be those
it was intended to benefit, viz., the service men themselves. But
with the country now settled, and everyone free to prosecute his
business, there must be less of money borrowing and service for
interest, and thus a gradual change or modification is naturally
effected in this system, with no tendency to abuse.

§ (j) DISTRAINING FOR DEBT

The Yorubas have a peculiar method of forcing payment out
of an incorrigible debtor. When a creditor who has obtained
judgment for debt finds it impossible to recover any thing out
of the debtor, he applies to the town authorities for a licensed
distrainor. This individual is called Ògò, he is said to d'ògò ti
i.e. to sit on the debtor (as it were). For that purpose, he enters
the premises, seeks out the debtor, or esconces himself in his
apartment until he makes his appearance, and then he makes

himself an intolerable nuisance to him and to the members of the house generally until the money is paid.

The distrainor is a man of imperturbable temper, but of a foul tongue, a veritable Thersites. He adopts any measures he likes, sometimes by inflicting his presence and attention on the debtor everywhere and anywhere he may go, denying him privacy of any kind, and in the meantime using his tongue most foully upon him, his own person being inviolable, for touching him implies doing violence to the person of the authorities who appoint him the task. He demands and obtains whatever diet he may require, however sumptuous and may help himself if not quickly served. If he thinks fit, he may lay hold on any poultry or cattle he finds in the premises, and prepare himself food, and all at the expense of the debtor. He must not take anything away but he may enjoy the use of anything he finds in the house.

Loud in his abuses, intolerable in his manners to all in the house whilst going in and out with the debtor, he goes on in this way all day, and from day to day if needs be, until even the inmates of the compound get tired of this, and then means will quickly be found of getting rid of the distrainor by paying off the debt.

§ (k) WAR

In early times war expeditions were sent out every other year by the ALÂFIN of Ọyọ to distant countries chiefly amongst the Popos. War then was for spoils and to keep their hands in, and not for captives ; the victors rarely pursued the vanquished ; those who concealed themselves behind heaps of rubbish, or in any hiding place in the town or in the fields were quite safe. When a town was taken the shade trees about the principal market—which is always in front of the official residence of the chief ruler of the town—are cut down as a sign of conquest. Slave-raiding and the traffic in human beings did not then exist. Long sieges were unknown, for whether victorious or defeated, the presence of the Kakanfo or his corpse was expected home within 60 days.

There never was or has been a standing army, nor any trained soldiers (except at Ibadan latterly where the idea began to germinate, and some of the chiefs had a number of their slaves trained solely for war ; some chiefs had also a corps of boys, not to bear arms, but to be attendant on them in battle, in order to familiarize them with the horrors of war !) But according to the custom of the country, every man capable of bearing arms is expected to serve in war ; but the law did not make it compulsory except for men of rank and title, and for home defence.

At the close of every war, each one goes away to his farm, and, except on an occasion of importance, as when the King's messengers are to be received, even the Balẹ and the Balogun could not be found at home during the day at the busy seasons.

Before the introduction of fire-arms (a comparatively recent affair) their weapons of war consisted of bow and poisoned arrows, a short sword called Jọmọ́ and Ògbó a kind of heavy cutlass used chiefly by the common people.

As sieges then were of short duration and always carried on in the dry season, there was no necessity to provide against severe weather ; the chieftains generally used awnings made of *Ayin* mats spread on four poles. Since sieges began to be carried on for more than 60 days, booths of palm branches have come into use, and in later times even these have given way to huts and houses built of swish.

The preserved food used in earlier expeditions consisted of parched beans, and a sort of hard bread made of beans and corn (maize) flour called *Akara-kuru*.

By the rules of warfare *piyẹ* or foraging was permitted. The Ibadans, who, more than any of the others carried on war operations for longer periods, and over wider regions, were accustomed to cultivate the lands all around their camps and in the neighbourhood whenever a long siege was anticipated.

WAR TITLES AND METHODS

War titles are of two grades, senior and junior, but both are modelled on one and the same plan.

Senior Grade :—The BALOGUN or Commander-in-Chief comes first with his principal lieutenants the Ọtun and Osi, that is Generals commanding the right and the left wings, then the (Aṣipa), Ẹkẹrin, Ẹkarun and Ẹkẹfa i.e. the fourth, fifth and sixth. These command the veterans.

Junior Grade :—The SERIKI with his principal lieutenants also, viz., the Ọtun, Osi, with the Ẹkẹrin, Ẹkarun, and Ẹkẹfa. These command the young warriors, and those not attached to any of the greater war-chiefs.

The ASAJU is the leader of the van, he too has his lieutenants.

The SARUMI or chief of the cavalry and his men form a class by themselves ; he also has his Balogun of the cavalry, with the Ọtun, Osi, etc.

These titles constitute what is termed " Oye Ilu " or " Town titles," because they are conferred by Balẹ or chief of the town and the town council, and they are all members of the town council with a right to speak and vote.

Among the senior war titles may be mentioned the Balẹ's war chiefs. The Balẹ himself does not go to war ordinarily, but he has his war-chiefs, the Ọtun Balẹ, Osi Balẹ, Ẹkẹrin, Ẹkarun, Ẹkẹfa as well, who represent him in war ; they are always chosen from among the older men who have past their best days.

SIGNIFICATION OF THE TITLES

The term *Balogun* is contracted from Iba-li-Ogun i.e. lord in war. In time of war, and generally in the camp, the Ibalogun is not only supreme, but he is also above all laws, he commands implicit obedience from all, and he can do whatever he likes.

The Balogun's Ọtun and Osi (right and left) are also the Ọtun and Osi of the town and of the army ; they command respectively the right and left wings, and they rank next after the Ibalogun.

The *Asipa* is a title borrowed from Ọyọ to satisfy any war-chief who, being equal by merit to the Ọtun and Osi, yet just missed becoming either.

The Ẹkẹrin, Ẹkarun, Ẹkafa are the fourth, fifth and sixth respectively of the senior generals.

Seriki is a Hausa word signifying a " king." He is practically like the Balogun, and is as important among the young warriors as the Balogun is among the veterans. A brave Seriki ranks himself next to the Balogun, the Ọtun and Osi Balogun notwithstanding ; for it often happens when he is exceptionally brave, that he skips over these and succeeds the Balogun, when a vacancy occurs. Otherwise the Ọtun succeeds.

All booty and perquisites that fall to the army are divided into two unequal parts, the larger portion belongs to the Balogun and his lieutenants and the lesser to the Seriki and his lieutenants also. The Balogun and the Seriki are each entitled to one half of the portion that falls to them, the other half being equally divided among the subordinate war chiefs of each respectively.

In every successful expedition each of the subordinate war chiefs is expected to give one half of his plunder or captives to his chief, the seniors to the Balogun, the juniors to the Seriki, and they themselves also receive the like from their subordinates.

Subordinate Titles :—Every one of the above chiefs, Senior and Junior had his own subordinate chiefs modelled on the same plan of Balogun, Ọtun, Osi, etc., in the same way, these also form their companies on the same plan, and so on throughout the whole army. By this system every man capable of bearing arms knows his right place in the army, so that what appears to be a motley crowd is really a well-organised body every man being in his right place at the front, the right or the left of his immediate chief, although they lack that co-ordination and precision of movements which are the outcome and advantages of discipline and drill.

Other subordinate titles Arẹagoro, Bada, Ajiyà.

Arẹagoro.—This is the first title borne by a young chief of great promise, who, as the heir of a great war chief has just succeeded to the headship of a great house. It is a stepping-stone to one of the senior grade titles. He is always attached to one of the senior chiefs, as his *alter ego ;* he represents his chief in the councils and other important assemblies in the absence of the latter, where he can speak and vote with equal right and authority ; hence the saying :   "Arẹagoro ti o ba gboju t'on ti Oluwa rẹ l'ẹgbẹ̀ra" i.e. an Arẹagoro who is bold is the equal of his master. An Arẹagoro remains as such only till a vacancy occurs in one of the higher titles suitable for him.

Bada.—The title of Bada answers in many respects to a knight of the middle ages. He is one who is expected to keep at least one or two war steeds and a few followers at his own charges, to be ready to take the field at a moment's notice, to be an accomplished horseman, a skilful swordsman or lancer, and to fight always on horse-back. All the principal chiefs have each at least a Bada. The Badas stand in the order of seniority of their respective masters and form a corps by themselves.

Ajiyà is a non-descript title borne by any junior war chief who cannot for the time being find a place among his peers. He is rather a free lance.

ARRANGEMENT OF THE WAR CHIEFS IN BATTLE

The Aṣaju or leader of the van comes first. His company begins the fight by skirmishing, and provoking the opposite party. He is supported by all the Badas.

The Seriki comes next with his lieutenants in their proper order, and then the real pitched battle begins. Last of all comes the Balogun with his lieutenants. The Balogun himself, however, does not take any active part at once, until later on, except to watch the various movements and generally to direct the fight.

The duties of the cavalry are to reconnoitre, to hover about the enemy watching for an opportunity they can take advantage of such as a weak or an unguarded point through which they can dash to break the ranks of the enemy, and throw them into confusion. Also to cover retreats on a defeat or to cut off stragglers when pursuing an enemy.

Occasionally at the height of the battle a brave horseman would demoralize the enemy by dashing suddenly into their midst, and return with a captive on his horse !

The usual method of a pitched battle is for all the war chiefs to be disposed, each in his right place, according to their rank and title, or as the commander-in-chief disposes, and then each in turn to march forward, company by company to the middle line of battle to discharge their arms, trying each time to gain more ground. This method they call Tawusi. But when later on, the Balogun himself rises to fight, that denotes a general *charge* throughout the whole host ; every man must be engaged in fight ; and wherever he fixes the war standard, every one is bound to dispose himself about it in due order. His going forward means that the whole army must push forward at whatever cost, for no one whose right place is in front dares fall to the rear of the Balogun except when *hors de combat.*

The Balẹ's war chiefs need not take any prominent part in the fight, but they guard the camp and baggage, support weak points, and make themselves useful generally as men who must keep cool heads while the others are engaged in the excitement of a fight. Their chief duty otherwise is to act the part of advisers and moderators of rash and hot-headed warriors.

A synopsis of the arrangement in battle :—

The Asaju

Supported by all the Badas

Osi Seriki   Seriki   Ọtun Seriki

Ekẹrin to Ekẹfa disposed as strategy requires

Osi Balogun   Balogun   Ọtun Balogun

Asipa, Ekẹrin to Ekẹfa disposed as strategy requires.

The Ọtun and Osi Balẹ and other older warriors are to guard the rear, camp, and baggage and support weak points.

War as a profession in this country was always said to date from the time of the Fulani invasion and seizure of Ilọrin when the necessity arose for an organized resistance but the Yorubas generally are not considered a fighting race, although they have now and again thrown up a general who would be considered distinguished in any race. In the later period of their history circumstances have brought things about that Ibadan became a centre for all warlike spirits of whatever tribe, and consequently it is to that place we have to turn, to see the development of warlike proceedings.

How war is declared.—Every expedition is supposed to be sent out by the King (Alâfin). It is in his name war was generally declared, and his permission or at any rate his assent must be obtained before an army can march out.

When it has become evident that a place is marked out for an attack, a system of exclusive dealings is first established between that town and its neighbours ; then follow preparations for attack and defence, and when plans are matured then, at the usual meeting of the town council in the house of the chief ruler, the announcement is made.

The Balogun (commander-in-chief) rising, would address the assembled crowd outside and end with " I leave (such and such a place) at your mercy." He is greeted with shouts of applause, and a day would be fixed when the war-staff will be taken outside the town walls. The marching out of the Balogun is always so denoted as the war-staff is always kept with him.

The War Staff or standard of war is a bamboo pole of about four feet in length, and 2½ inches in diameter. It is wrapped all over with charms and amulets, and finished up with a globular head, the size of a large cocoa-nut. The size of course varies with the cost. It is encased in leather with the charms hanging all over it. It is always an object of worship. To this day, proper standards of war are procured from Ile Ifẹ and are dedicated to Ọrañyan. Human sacrifices were usually offered to such standards before they are taken out to any campaign. Whenever war is declared, and it is to be worshipped, priests and priestesses are always required for the purpose of offering the sacrifice.

The Propitiation of Ọrañyan.—The victim is usually subjected to much inhuman treatment on these occasions before being despatched. With his hands tied behind his back, he is led to the market place, and there paraded from one spot to another, and made to do homage to the fetishes there, and to invoke blessings on the town and on the chiefs thereof. As he could not conveniently prostrate himself before the gods in his bound condition, he is assisted with a forked stick, with which he is pushed violently down from behind ! Bruised and bleeding, he is to receive three strokes on the back with a rod before he is helped up again !

In this way, the unfortunate one is soon exhausted ; he would then be literally dragged along into the grove sacred to Ọrañyan, and there beheaded.

The blood is considered sacred and hence the commander-in-chief of the army who must be present on such occasions with his staff of principal officers must come forward with each of them and have a touch of the blood to rub on their swords, and after them the common soldiers would all rush in for a drop to rub in their hands, for success in the war.

The corpse is not to putrefy before the Balogun leaves the town :

it is considered an ill omen if it does. Hence Qrauyan is never worshipped until they are quite ready to march out.

The corpse is exposed for seven days, and it is the duty of some of the priestesses to bathe it daily and smear it with camwood preparations, and pray for the speedy return of the victim to this world and to be born in their family !

We see in these revolting practices, not an act of studied cruelty, but one of supposed highest form of religious worship of a poor deluded people.

The blood of certain animals is forbidden to be used in the worship of Qrañyan e.g. the tortoise, he-goat, hen and pigeon.

§ (*l*) FUNERALS

The Yorubas do not bury their dead in graveyards or cemetries, but in their houses. Infants, however, are not buried in the house, but their dead bodies are either thrown away into the nearest bush or forest, or are partially buried with a bit of earth sprinkled over them, and are thus left a prey to jackals prowling by night.

Such children are called "Abiku" (born to die) and are supposed to belong to a company of young demons roaming about. They are believed to be capable of being born as young children, and (except forcibly detained by charms) of returning to their company at will, or at the instance of the members of their company.

The graves of aged people are dug generally in the piazza or in one of the sleeping rooms. In case of the wealthy dead, after the ground has been dug to a depth of about 6 feet in the piazza it is then carried on horizontally towards one of the bedrooms, so that the corpse is literally buried in the bedroom. It is then shut up in this horizontal hole with a piece of board plastered over with mud ; the whole grave is then filled up and the floor of the piazza levelled and polished, the rest of the earth being cast into the streets.

Only the well-to-do can afford a coffin, the workmanship of which is usually very rough and coarse, the many chinks and interstices being filled up with cotton-wool and soap. As a rule, coffins are made much larger than we should think necessary, but the superabundant space is filled up with some of the dresses belonging to the deceased, and with presents from all the relatives, it being a custom amongst them that all the nearest relatives should give each a piece of cloth for the burial. In the absence of cloths seeded cotton is put in to fill up the coffin tight, as they have a superstitious dislike of leaving any empty spaces in a coffin.

In the practice of filling up the coffin with cloths, one may catch a faint glimpse of the popular ideas in regard to another state of existence.

If the family is wealthy, after a couple of months another ceremony is gone through, consisting chiefly of feasting and dancing in honour of the dead, and this they term laying the dead upon its other side.

In cases where coffins cannot be had, after wrapping up the corpse in a mat like a mummy it is laid in the grave and a few sticks of the *Akoko* tree are laid across upon which a mat is spread. If a piece of board could be procured, it is laid over the corpse instead, and then earth is put upon it, and the grave filled up.

The funeral ceremonies are further continued by the following observances :—The wife or wives of the deceased are to lie on the bare ground over the grave without even a mat or cloth being spread for full three months from the date of the funeral. On the 7th day they are led out of their town wall by an Egũgun to a place where mounds of earth had been raised according to the number of the women with a yam placed on each mound. There is an extra mound raised, on which no yam is placed ; this represents the deceased. The widows are led out clad in rags with both hands on the opposite shoulders, their heads being left bare. Each takes a yam from the heap, and this is understood to be the last subsistence they should expect to receive from their dear departed. After this they return home weeping.

On the 13th or 17th day the final ceremony is thus performed : By the advice of the Alagbâ, they provide some heads of cowries, a dog, two dishes of pounded yam or cooked yam flour, two pots of native beer, kola nuts, parched corn, a hoe and a cutlass, and two coverings of native cloth for an Egũgun dress. At dead of night a man goes and sits on the roof of the house of the deceased ; another who is to personate the dead, is secreted at the back yard, but within hearing distance of the former ; a third is the Egũgun called Agan undressed, coming in the Alagbâ's company, speaking in a hollow, but thrilling tone of voice, crying out, " E gbe mi." (Do lift me up). Immediately several voices are heard " Lift here, lift there," as if they were carrying the Agan and found him rather heavy. As they enter the compound the widows and the other women are to rush into the rooms and extinguish all lights. The Agan is then conducted to the piazza of the deceased where the special ceremony is performed. He sings out distinctly the name of the deceased so that the substitute might hear him, at the same time warning him not to answer to his call, but to that of the man on the roof. The latter then strikes the hoe in his hand with the cutlass as a signal to attract the attention of the secreted substitute.

After this, he calls out in loud tones the name of the deceased as did the Agan. He calls out three times, and at the third call, which is also the last, a still small voice is heard from the counterfeit, simulating that of the dead. At this stage, the widows and all the other mourners begin to weep and wail for the dead ; the dog is then slaughtered and the flesh is taken to the Alagbâs.

On the following morning, the Egũgun of the deceased, appears in his usual dress, with an attendant Egũgun, both emerging from the Alagbâ's house. He proceeds to his old home where a mat is spread outside to receive him. He embraces all his children, sits them by turns on his knees, and blesses them, promising to bestow health, strength, long life, and the rest. He accepts presents from all the relatives, who are the mourners—of stringed cowries from the men, and unstringed from the women. After which they repair with all the presents received to the Egũgun grove or to the Alagbâ's where the Egũgun is undressed and a good feast is made of the flesh of the dog slaughtered on the previous evening. The stringed cowries contributed by the men are there returned to each of them, being participators in the organised imposture that was being practised. The unstringed cowries of their dupes, the women, are distributed amongst those who took part in the ceremony including of course the Alagbâ.

This is the last farewell between the deceased and his family if we except the supposed annual visits made by the former during the Egũgun festivals.

In case of a woman the ceremony is simpler. The same offerings are usually required, excepting the hoe and the cutlass. The relatives are ordered to procure a miniature hearth, and put it into a new calabash to meet the Egũgun of the deceased matron emerging from the Egũgun grove.

On the day appointed they proceed to the grove with drums, the orphans carrying each a horse's tail on his shoulder, as a sign of mourning. Then one of the Alagbâ's men calls out thrice the name of the dead matron, just as in the similar ceremony detailed above ; an Egũgun answers from the grove and the voice is drowned with drumming and singing. The Egũgun with the Paka (an attendant) now issues from the grove, and walks towards the orphan children to receive the new calabash containing the miniature hearth ; blesses the giver, and returns with it to the grove. The hearth is subsequently buried quietly by the river side or within the grove.

This is the last office of a dutiful child to its mother and this is understood as their last meeting in this world. The hearth presented to her is for her to cook with in the other world.

The period of mourning for either man or woman is as aforesaid, three months, during which time the men are to remain unwashed, unshaven and the women with dishevelled hair and dress unchanged. At the expiration of this term on a day appointed the whole of them shave for the dead, and their hair is thrown outside by the wall of the house. They then parade the streets, dressed in their best, singing and dancing in honour of the dead, and calling at one house after another to return thanks to the sympathizers. The children of the deceased, begotten or adopted, now carry the horses' tails in their hands by which they are distinguished from those who have no immediate connection with the family.

In the division of the property the widows as aforesaid pass into the possession of the children and the nearest relatives, the right to each being determined by ballot. Each male relative sends round his chewing stick (native tooth brush) with his name to the woman of his choice ; they are expected to reject the proposal twice as if they were resolved to remain widows all their life ; but at the third and last proposal, with tears in their eyes, they make their choice and are taken over. This concludes the final ceremony.

In the case of young men or young women, the proceedings are essentially different. The companions of him or her that is gone proceed in a body to a spot where two roads intersect each other, preceded by one of their number who stands at a great distance from them. The call as in the case of the Agan is made thrice, the usual answer follows, and then he or she is told by all the friends and companions " A yà ọ O ! " (we separate you from our companionship). The substitute returns home with the rest, and the simple ceremony comes to an end.

THE HISTORY OF THE YORUBAS

PART II.

YORUBA KINGS AND CONTEMPORARY EVENTS EMBRACING FOUR PERIODS.

I. THE MYTHOLOGICAL PERIOD: ODUDUWA TO AJAKA

II. THE PERIOD OF GROWTH AND PROSPERITY: AGANJU TO ABIODUN

III. THE DECLINE, REVOLUTIONARY WARS AND DISRUPTION: AOLE TO OLUEWU

IV. THE ARREST OF DISINTEGRATION, EFFORTS AT RESTORATION OF UNITY, TRIBAL WARS, THE BRITISH PROTECTORATE: ATIBA TO ADEYEMI

FIRST PERIOD—MYTHOLOGICAL KINGS AND DEIFIED HEROES

CHAPTER I

THE FOUNDERS OF THE YORUBA NATION.

§ 1. ODUDUWA

ODUDUWA the reputed founder and ancestor of the race is really a mythical personage. The Etymology of the term is from Odu (ti o) da Iwà. Whatever is unusually large as a large pot or container is termed Odù : the term then implies, the great container the author of existence. According to Ife mythology Oduduwa was the son of Olodù mare, i.e. the fatheŕ or Lord of Odu ; ma rè implies *cannot go beyond* i.e. the Almighty. Oduduwa was sent by Olodumare from heaven to create the earth. Olokun i.e. the goddess of the ocean was the wife of Oduduwa, Oranmiyan and Isedale their children, and Ogun a grand-child.

Such is the desire of most nations to find a mythical origin for themselves through their kings and ancestors.

All that was known of him has been told in Part I of this history, which gives an account of the emigration of the ancestors of the Yorubas from the east to Ile Ife where Oduduwa died in peace and was deified, being worshipped to this day by the Ifes, and up to the time of the British Protectorate, human sacrifices were offered to him at regular intervals. The soil of Ile Ife is said to be sacred to him. He was the grandfather and great-grandfather of renowned Kings and Princes who ruled and made history in the Yoruba country.

The number of years embraced by this period is unknown, but it includes the time during which the Yoruba kingdom was in prosperity, and the Kings despotic. The capital of the kingdom then was Ile Ife.

The Basorun of this reign was Olorunfun-mi.

§ 2. ORANYAN

Orañyan the grandson of Oduduwa succeeded his grandfather on the throne. He was a very brave and warlike Prince, and of an indomitable courage. He was the founder of the order of the Esos vide Pt. I page 73. His body-guard consisted of 150 well-tried soldiers.

How he headed his brothers on an abortive expedition to the
east to avenge the death of their great-grandfather, and how they
quarrelled at Igangan and dispersed from that place, has been
told in Part I.   After founding the city of Ọyọ where he resided
for a time he was said to have pushed on to a place called Òkò,
leaving Ọyọ in charge of one of the princes.   This is not unlikely
when we remember that that was not an age of settled government,
but that the warlike and restless King was engaged in extending
his dominions far and wide.   Much that was known of him has been
told in Part I.   He resided at Òkò for many years and according
to some died there, but others affirmed that he died at Ile Ifẹ,
where his grave is shown to this day.   But the Yorubas have a
custom whenever any one died away from home, to cut the hair
of his head and pare his nails, and these are taken to the place
where they would have him buried, and there ceremoniously
and religiously deposited.   It may thus have been the case here.
But an anecdote connected with his later years must here be told :

It was said that after a long period of reign an urgent necessity
made him revisit the city of Ile Ifẹ, which he had left for so long a
time ; perhaps to arrange some family affairs, or to possess himself
of some of his father's treasures left in charge of Adimu.   He left
his son Ajaka as Regent and went.   Having stayed much longer
than the time fixed for his return (communication between the
two places being then dangerous and difficult) the people thought
he was dead, or that at any rate he would no more return to Òkò ;
the ỌYỌ MESI who were the authorised rulers of the town consequently confirmed Ajaka on the throne, investing him with full
powers, and all the insignia of royalty.

But his father was returning ; and having come within a short
distance of the city, his attention was arrested by the sound of the
Kakaki trumpet—a trumpet blown for the sovereign alone.
Upon enquiry, he learnt what had taken place.   He thereupon
retraced his steps quietly to Ile Ifẹ where he spent the rest of his
days in peaceful retirement.   An obelisk termed Ọpa Ọrañyan
(Ọrañyan's staff) erected on the spot he was supposed to have been
buried is shown at Ile Ifẹ to this day.   This would seem to confirm
the view that he died and was buried at Ile Ifẹ and not at Òkò.

Ọpa Ọrañyan
Orañyan's Staff

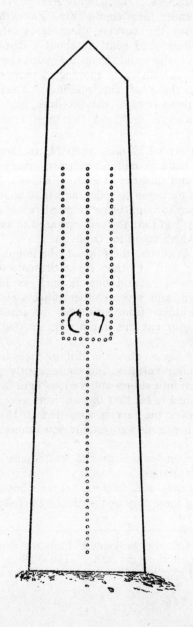

This obelisk is about 10 or 12 feet in height,[1] and about 4 feet square in width at its base ; it tapers to a point, and has upon one face of it, several spike nails driven into it, and some carvings as of ancient characters.   The nails are arranged in such an ordered manner as to render them significant.   First, there are 61 in a straight line from the bottom upwards at intervals of about 2 inches in midline; and next, at about a distance of 4 inches on either side of this, and from the same level on top, two parallel lines of 31 nails each running downwards and curving below to meet those of the midline.   Then in the space between these three rows of parallel lines, and about the level where they converge, is found the most conspicuous of the carvings, רד.

What is conjectured as most probable in these arrangements is that the 61 nails in midline represent the number of years Qrañyan lived, and that the 31 each on either side indicates that he was 31 when he began to reign, and that he reigned 31 years, the year he began to reign being counted twice as is the manner of the Yorubas ; and that the carvings are the ancient characters *Resh* and *Yod* which stand for Qrañyan.

Besides Qpa Qrañyan, there are to be found to this day, in groves at Ile Ife, and at other Ife settlements outside the city, carvings in stone of natural objects such as tongs and anvil, table, stool, fish, and several other objects of curiosity which are generally hidden from strangers, because they are held sacred ; they represent the handicrafts of the founders of the race.

The art of carving on stones or drilling holes in them has since become lost among Yorubas, and consequently, how nails could have been driven into stones and various figures cut out of them is usually explained to be, that these objects were once carved out of wood, and when the carvers were deified, their work became petrified ! As these gods were once men, so these stones were once wood !

The Ifes are the guardians and custodians of these sacred relics from ancient times.

Nearly all legends and folklore are attributed to the age of Qrañyan, among these may be mentioned the following told by an Ife :—

---

[1] About four feet was broken off from the top of this obelisk during a storm in the year 1884. The obelisk has since twice fallen down and inartistically re-erected. But a stump of it now remains.

The Legend of Moremi and her Son

" Moremi was the wife of one of the ancient heroes of Ile Ifẹ, probably Ọranmiyàn. She was a woman of great beauty and virtue, and had an only son named Ẹla or Olurogbo.

It happened that the city of Ifẹ was at one time in a state of frequent commotion and unrest, owing to the repeated raids of a tribe of people called the Igbos. This continued for a series of years. The Ifẹs attributed this affliction and distress to the displeasure of their gods, because those that attacked them from the Igbo territory appeared not to be human beings, but gods or demi gods, and consequently the Ifẹs felt they could not withstand them, and so these raiders used to make away with easy plunder, including their valuables, with their women and children. For this they propitiated and called upon their gods for help, but received no response.

Now, this Moremi, fired with zeal and patriotism was determined to do what she could to free her country from this calamity. She was resolved to find out what these Igbos really were, and how to fight them. To this end she repaired to a stream called Esinmirin, and there made a vow to the deity thereof, that if she was enabled to carry out her plans, and they proved successful, she would offer to the god the most costly sacrifice she could afford. Her plan was to expose herself to the raiders, and get caught, and be taken to their country where she could best learn their secrets : ' But,' she said, ' if I perish, I perish.'

At the time of the next raid she undertook to carry out her plans, she was caught by the Igbos and taken to their country ; and being a woman of great beauty, she was given up amongst others, and sundry booty to their king. Her beauty and virtue soon won her a place in the country and the confidence of the people ; she became familiar with all their customs, and learnt all their secrets: then she also learnt that those who were such objects of terror to her people were mere men, who covered themselves from head to foot with *Ekan* grass and bamboo fibres, making them appear extra human, and are nicknamed Eluyare. She extracted from her husband also the secret of attacking them successfully. ' If your people know how to make a torch, and have the courage to rush amongst them with lighted torches, they cannot stand that.'

Moremi feeling she was now conversant with everything amongst the Igbos, having disarmed any suspicion they may have entertained of her as a captive, suddenly escaped one day to her native land, and by making use of the secrets she had learnt, freed her country for ever from the raids of the men once their terror. It remained now for her to fulfil her vows.

She repaired to the stream with her offerings of lambs, rams, and goats for sacrifice, but the god would not accept any of these. She then offered a bullock, which the god also refused to accept, then she prayed the priests to divine for her what would be acceptable; this was done, and the god demanded of her, her only son !

She then gave up her only son in sacrifice to the gods in the fulfilment of her vows. The Ifẹ nation bewailed her loss and promised to be to her sons and daughters, for the loss she had sustained for the salvation of her country.

Olurogbo however, when supposed to be killed, was but half dead; he afterwards revived and rose again, and made a rope with which he climbed up into heaven; and all Ifẹs to this day have a full hope that he will come again to this world, and reap the full reward of his good deeds."

We may discern in this legend a confused idea of the story of Jephtha, and that of the Blessed Virgin and her Son perverted.

Ọrañyan was the father of all Ọyọs or Yorubas proper, and was the universal conqueror of the land. He left behind him two renowned sons, Ajaka and Sango, both of whom succeeded him in turns, and both of whom became famous in Yoruba history, and were deified after death.

The Baṣọrun of this reign was Ẹfufu-kò-fẹ-ori.

§ 3. Ajuan *alias* Ajaka

Ajuan *alias* Ọba Ajaka was at first only a Regent when his father left for Ile Ifẹ, but was subsequently confirmed on the throne as was mentioned above. He alone of all the Yoruba Kings had the singular fortune (or misfortune) of being called to the throne twice, being once deposed, but afterwards recalled to the throne.

Very little was known of his earlier reign, except that, unlike his father, he was of a peaceful disposition, loved husbandry and encouraged it.

Being too mild for the warlike spirit of the age, and tamely suffering the encroachments of provincial kings, he was dethroned, and he went to Igbodo where he remained in retirement seven years during which period his brother Sango reigned in his stead. His Baṣọrun was nick-named Ẹrin-din-logun-Agbọn kò ṣe da ni Ifa (i.e. sixteen cocoa nuts is unsuitable for Ifa divination). That is to say cocoa nuts are not suitable substitutes for palm nuts. The reason for this sobriquet is not known.

§ 4. SANGO OR OLUFIRAN

Sango son of Ọrañyan, and brother of Ajàka was the fourth King of Yoruba. He was of a very wild disposition, fiery temper, and skilful in sleight of hand tricks. He had a habit of emitting fire and smoke out of his mouth, by which he greatly increased the dread his subjects had of him.

The Olowu at this time appeared to have been more powerful than the King of Ọyọ, for after the death of the uncle Ọrañyan, he compelled his cousin the peaceful Ajaka to pay tribute to him. This was probably the reason why Ajaka was deposed.

On Sango's coming to the throne, being a much younger man, the Olowu meant to take advantage of his youth ; he demanded the tribute of him, but Sango refused to acknowledge his primacy, notwithstanding the Olowu's threat to deprive him of his wives and children ; consequently his capital was besieged and a sharp fight ensued. Sango there displayed his wonted bravery as well as his tricks ; volumes of smoke issuing from his mouth and nostrils so terrified the Olowu and his army that they became panic stricken and were completely routed and put to flight.

Sango pushed on his advantage, and with every fresh victory he was the more firmly established on the throne ; he thereby became elated and was tyrannical.

It was his ambition now to remove the seat of government from Òkò to Ọyọ then called Ọyọkóró, he knew he would meet with strong opposition from the prince of that city and so he set upon devising plans by which he could effect his purpose with as little fighting as possible.

Sango was now possessed with a desire of performing an act of filial piety. He wished to worship at the grave of his dead mother, but he did not so much as remember her name for she died when he was but a babe. She was the daughter of Elempe a Nupe king, who formed an alliance with Ọrañyan by giving him his daughter to wife, of which marriage Sango was the issue. Sango therefore commissioned a Tẹtu and a Hausa slave to proceed to the Tapa country, to his maternal grandfather Elempe for the purpose giving them a horse and a cow for the sacrifice.

The King's charge to these messengers was, that they should listen carefully to the first name uttered in the invocation which evidently will be his mother's name.

The messengers were heartily welcomed and highly entertained by Elempe, their King's grandfather, so much so that the Hausa forgot himself and the duty he was charged with. At the time of the sacrifice, the priest said at the grave " Torôsi, Iya gbodo, listen to us, thy son Sango is come to worship thee." The Tẹtu noted the name Torôsi, but the Hausa, being far from sober paid no heed to what was said; therefore, on their return home, the Tẹtu who had faithfully carried out his orders was highly rewarded, and the Hausa slave severely punished. The punishment meted out to him was 122 razor cuts slashed all over his body as a lasting warning for all time.

The scars left by these wounds strangely took the fancy of the King's wives who thought that they added comeliness and beauty to the man, and therefore they advised that in future such marks should not be performed upon a slave, but on actual members of the royal family as distinctive of royalty.

Sango took this advice, and placed himself first in the hands of the " Olowolas " (the markers) named Babajẹgbe Ọsan and Babajẹgbe Oru ; but he could stand only two cuts on each arm, and forbade them to proceed any further. This is what is termed Ẹyọ̀. The marks are to this day retained in the royal family, as a dis.inctive badge of royalty, and hence members of the royal family are termed Akẹyọ̀. They are two broad ribbon marks on the arms from the shoulder to the wrist.

When the King had determined upon taking Ọyọkoro, it occurred to him to employ this as a device by which he could effect his purpose easily without loss of lives. He thereupon sent the Hausa slave to Ọlọyọ-koro for him to see how beautiful this slave looks with these marks, and that it has been resolved to use the same as a mark of royalty ; he therefore advised the Ọlọyọ-koro to submit himself to be thus marked, with his principal chiefs for rank and beauty, stating that he himself had done so. To this they consented, Babajẹgbe Ọsan and Babajẹgbe Oru were sent over there, and admirably did they perform their tasks.

But on the third day, when the Ọlọyọ-koro and his chiefs were very sore, Sango appeared with his forces against them ; no resistance could be offered, and the city fell easily into his hands : shamefully and brutally he put to death the prince and his chiefs, the dupes of his stratagem.

Thus the seat of government was permanently removed from Òkò (or as some would have it, from Ile Ifẹ) to Ọyọ the ancient " Eyeo or Katunga."

Sango reigned for seven years, the whole of which period was marked by his restlessness. He fought many battles and was fond of making charms. He was said to have the knowledge of some preparation by which he could attract lightning. The palace at Ọyọ was built at the foot of a hill called Òkè Ajaka (Ajaka's hill). One day the King ascended this hill accompanied by his courtiers and some of his slaves, among whom were two favourites, Biri and Omiran ; some of his cousins went with him, but none of his children. He was minded to try the preparation he had in hand ; thinking it might have been damp and useless, he first made the experiment on his own house. But it took effect, a storm was immediately raised and the lightning had struck the palace before they came down the hill, and the buildings were on fire. Many of Sango's wives and his children perished in this catastrophe.

Sango who was the author of his own misfortunes became alarmed and dismayed at what had happened and from a broken heart he was resolved to abdicate the throne and retire to the court of his maternal grandfather, Elempe king of the Nupes.

All Ọyọ was now astir, not only to sympathize with the King, but also to dissuade him from carrying out his resolution ; but he could not bear any opposition, and so mad was he, that he even used his sword against some of his loyal subjects who ventured to remonstrate with him, and who promised to replace for him his dead wives by others, by whom he might beget children, and so in time make good his present losses.

According to other accounts, he did not abdicate of his own freewill, but was asked to do so by a strong party in the state. Both accounts may be true, there may have been two parties, for to this day, Yorubas have an abhorence of a King given to making deadly charms ; because for one who already has absolute power invested in him by law, this strange power can only be used spitefully, so that no one near him would be safe.

He was said to have caused 160 persons to be slain in a fit of anger, of those who were showing much concern and over-anxiety on his behalf, and who would prevent him by force from carrying out his resolve.

Thus determined he set out on his fateful journey with a few followers. Biri his head slave and favourite was the first to regret the step taken, and to urge on his master to yield to the entreaties of those citizens of Ọyọ, who with all loyalty promised to replace his losses, as far as man can do it, and to rebuild the palace ; but finding the King inexorable, he forsook him and returned to the city with all his followers ; Omiran likewise followed his example, and the King was thus left alone. He now repented his rashness, especially when he found himself deserted by his favourite Biri. He could not proceed alone, and for shame he could not return home, and so he was resolved to put an end to his own life ; and climbing on a shea butter tree, he hanged himself.

His friends hearing of this tragedy went immediately and

performed for him the last act of kindness, by burying his remains under the same tree.

On hearing of the King's death, his personal friends followed his example, and died with him. Biri committed suicide at Koso (where the King died), Omiran did the same. His cousin Ọmọ Sàndà committed suicide at Papo, Babayanmi at Sẹlẹ, Obei at Jakuta and Ọya his favourite wife at Irá.

Thus ended the life of this remarkable personage, who once ruled over all the Yorubas and Popos. He was afterwards deified, and is still worshipped by all of the Yoruba race as the god of thunder and lightning.

In every Yoruba and Popo town to this day, whenever there is a flash of lightning followed by a peal of thunder, it is usual to hear from the populace shouts of " Ka wo o," " ka biye si " (welcome to your majesty, long live the King.)

Ajaka his brother was now recalled from exile, and he once more held the reins of government.

Salekuodi was the Basọrun of this reign.

§ 5. AJAKA'S SECOND REIGN

King AJAKA who was dethroned for being too peaceful was now recalled to the throne. He proved after his re-instatement a totally different man to what he had been before, and showed himself more warlike than even his brother Sango.

He led an expedition into the Tapa country. Tradition has it, that he employed large and well-trained birds, armed with arrows, and after crossing the Niger they showered down these deadly weapons upon the maternal relations of his brother Sango.

What is certain is, that the expedition was successful but by what means, it is not really known. But thus it was with the Yorubas (as with all superstitious people) that brave deeds and extraordinary acts of daring are always attributed to the supernatural.

He spent the latter part of his years in waging intestine wars with his subjects. He was said to have been engaged in civil wars with 1060 of his chiefs and princes among whom were the principal vassal or provincial kings, the Onikoyi, the Olugbọn, and the Arẹsa.

He had in his service certain " medicine men," who made charms for him, viz., Atagbọin, Ọmọ-onikòkò, Abitibiti Onisẹgun, Paku, Tẹtẹoniru, Yănà, Ọkọ-adán Ẹgbẹji, Alari baba isẹgun, and Elenre.

The following fable was related of him :—

After his wars, some of these " medicine men " went up to him,

and humbly prayed to be allowed to return home ; but the King
refused to grant them leave, fearing lest their services might be
required by some other kings, and in that way, others might be in
possession of the charms they made for him. As they were
determined to go home they showed the King by demonstrative
proofs, that they made the request simply out of courtesy but
that the King could not detain them.   Paku fell down before him,
and disappeared.   Tẹtẹ oniru, Abitibiti Oniṣegun, and Alari
baba Iṣegun performed the same feat and vanished. Ẹgbẹji
threw up a ball of thread which hung suspended in space, and he
climbed up it and disappeared. Elenre alone remained standing
before him. Then said the King to him " Elenre, you had better
follow the examples of your colleagues and vanish, or I shall
wreak my vengeance upon you for their disobedience." " Kill
me if you can " replied Elenre. The King thereupon ordered him
to be decapitated ; but the sword was broken in two on the
attempt. He then ordered him to be speared but the spear
became bent and the spearman's arm withered ! He ordered a
large stone to be rolled over him to crush him to death but it
fell on him as light as a ball of cotton-wool.

The King and the executioners were now at their wits' end,
and then it occurred to one of them to " plough with his heifer."
His wife Ijaehin being prevailed upon, told them that no iron or
steel can affect him: " Pull off a single blade of grass from the
thatch of the house, and with that you can decapitate him."
This was done, and the head was struck off, but instead of
falling to the ground, it fell into the King's hand, and he
involuntarily grasped it. The King tried all his best to drop it
off, but to no avail. Any food brought to the King the head
devoured, and drank all the water likewise. The King soon
became famished, he was losing flesh, and was really dying from
hunger.

All the " medicine-men " of every tribe in the kingdom were
sent for, to disenchant this alarming phenomenon : as soon as
anyone entered, the head would call him by name, tell out the
composition of his charms, and then ask " Do you think that
can affect me ? " Thus many were baffled, until at last came one
Aṣawo ; this man at once prostrated at a distance and entreated
the head to forbear with him, saying :—" Who am I to oppose
you ? In what am I better than my predecessors whom you have
already foiled ? I came only in obedience to the King's commands
as I dare not refuse to come."   The head replied " I will respect
you because you are wise and respect yourself ; I yield to your
entreaties."   Then, falling suddenly from the King's hands,

Elenre's head became a flowing river known at Ọyọ to this day as Odo Elenre (Elenre's river).

His wife Ijaehin who disclosed the secret of his strength was also converted into a stream, but Elenre's head said to it " Thou shalt not flow," therefore Ijaehin became a stagnant pool at Ọyọ unto this day.

From this incident King AJAKA made it a rule that from henceforth no King should be present in person at an execution.

He put to death all the vassal kings 1060 in number taken in war ; the relics of their skulls were put together and are worshipped under the name of Orisạ'la to this day. This is the probable origin of that worship.

The reign of the mythological heroes abound in garbled forms of scriptural stories, showing as was remarked in the earlier part of this history that the ancestors of the Yorubas were acquainted with Christianity in the land of their origin. The fable here related is evidently the story of Elijah in a perverted form. His putting to death so many priests of Baal has been perverted into Ajaka slaying all his vassal kings and their skulls converted to an object of worship. His judgment of fire on those sent to arrest him finds a counterpart in Elenre's head anticipating those who came to exorcise it, both yielded to a wiser delegate who substituted entreaties for authority. The name Asạwo (i.e. one who deals in mysteries) is very significant ; it is evidently a mythological rather than a real name. Elijah going up to heaven became Egbẹji climbing up a cord and disappearing as the saying goes " Egbẹji ta 'kun O lọ si Ọrun," i.e. Egbẹji suspended a cord and by it went up to heaven. The river Jordan crossed by Elijah suggested Elenre's head becoming a river, etc.

The Ogidigbo drum was introduced into Ọyọ during this reign. It is of all drums the most inartistic, and is totally devoid of any embellishment. It consists of a block of wood about 3ft. in length hollowed out from the centre to about 6 inches of both extremities, and is beaten with a rod.

It is used only for the King and the Basọrun at the great festivals when they dance together at his public appearance.

Nothing is known of the end of Ajaka, probably he died in peace.

Salekuodi continued as the Basọrun of this reign also.

SECOND PERIOD.—THE PERIOD OF GROWTH AND PROSPERITY AND OPPRESSION.

CHAPTER II

HISTORICAL KINGS

§ 1. AGANJU

As Sango left no issue, the crown fell to Ajaka's son Aganju without any dispute. His reign was long and very prosperous. He had a remarkable faculty of taming wild animals and venomous reptiles, several of which may be seen crawling about him. He had also in his house a tame leopard.

He greatly beautified the palace adding piazzas in front and back, with rows of brazen posts. He originated the custom of decorating the palace with hangings on state occasions, being a sovereign of accomplished taste.

Towards the end of his reign, he waged war with a namesake of his, Aganju the Onisambo, for refusing him the hand of his daughter Iyayun. In this war, four chiefs, viz. the Onisambo and his allies the Onitede the Onimeri and the Alagbọna were captured, their towns destroyed, and the bride forcibly secured.

The close of his reign was clouded by great domestic troubles. His only son Lubẹgọ was discovered having illicit intercourse with his beloved Iyayun, on whose account so many princes and people have lost their lives. The stern father was enraged beyond words, the sentence pronounced on him was the extreme penalty of the law, and it was rigidly carried out. But the King was overcome with grief, he died not long after this, even before the birth of a successor to the throne. The name of his Basọrun was Banija, succeeded by Ẹrankogbina.

§ 2. KỌRI

The late King having no surviving son Ẹrankogbina the Basọrun was left to manage the affairs of the kingdom. The only hope of a direct successor to the throne was the child of Iyayun still *in utero* ; hence sacrifices were offered frequently on the grave of Aganju praying him to grant Iyayun a son if his name is not to be forgotten, and the dynasty end with him. When in due course therefore Iyayun gave birth to a son, the joy of the populace was unbounded. He was named Kọri.

During Kọri's minority, Iyayun was declared Regent ; she wore the crown, and put on the royal robes, and was invested with the *Ejigba*, the *Ọpa ilẹkẹ* and other royal insignia, and ruled the kingdom as a man until her son was of age.

It was during this reign that Timi was sent to Ẹdẹ and not in Sango's reign as was supposed.[1]

The Ijẹṣas proving very troublesome to their neighbours by kidnapping them in their farms, and molesting caravans to and from Apomu a frontier town where a large fair is periodically held for the exchange of goods with the Ijẹbus, and also getting frequently embroiled with the king of Ido their neighbour, complaints from time to time reached the ALÂFIN of Ọyọ. It was now determined that a stop be put to these inroads ; for this purpose the King sent a notable hunter to that district who succeeded in checking these marauders. He took up a position at a place called Ẹdẹ as his headquarters, and there he subsequently established himself as a kinglet with the title of Timi.

Timi was a famous archer, notable for his deadly arrows, and he more than justified his appointment. The Ọwa of Ilesa imitating the same appointment, posted an opposition kinglet at Oṣogbo named Atawọja ; but his chief duty was to worship the fish in the river Ọṣun.

As the Timi's duties required all his time, skill and valour, he had no time left to provide for himself and family ; the traders and caravans being now well protected, he obtained permission from the ALÂFIN to levy a toll of 5 cowries each on every trader ; by this means he soon had more than enough for the support of his family, and as a good and loyal subject, he paid the surplus into the royal treasury.

After some years of this act of loyalty, he regretted this self-imposed tribute, taking another view of the matter, that whatever he could collect this way should be his own by right as a compensation for the loss of the advantages of a city life, as well as a reward for his labours. So he abruptly stopped the tribute.

When the King missed the usual tribute, he sent to demand the same, but Timi refused to pay it, and gave his reasons for not doing so. This did not satisfy the King, so a more peremptory order was sent to Timi to deliver up what he had withheld. This order was also disobeyed, and so the King resorted to force, a body of troops was sent to arrest him, and to seize all his belongings. But Timi was prepared for this, he resisted with all his might, and routed the King's forces.

---

[1] Vide *Yoruba Reading Book.*

But the King was resolved to punish Timi as a warning to others who might follow his example. Ẹliri-onigbajo the Gbọnkâ was proposed to him as the only man equal to the task. But the Gbọnkâ was already a powerful subject at Ọyọ, being the only man who dared to oppose the King's encroachments upon the liberties of the people, therefore, he was at first loth to accede to this proposal, lest a success might add an additional lustre to the Gbọnkâ's glory, and make him more elated than before ; but on second consideration he consented, secretly hoping he might fall by the hand of his brave antagonist. So the Gbọnkâ was appointed.

The fight was limited to a single combat between the two chieftains, Timi armed himself with his bow and arrows, but the Gbọnka carried a shield with which to defend himself against the powerful darts of his assailant. His own weapon of offence was a viol containing a drug with strong narcotic properties when inhaled, and by means of this Timi was soon rendered unconscious, and in this state, he was dispossessed of his weapons, and taken bound to Ọyọ.

The King received the tidings with mixed feelings of joy and disappointment that neither of them fell in the combat, especially the Gbọnkâ whom he wished to get rid of. When the illustrious captive was brought before him, the King pretended to be dissatisfied with the issue of the contest, doubting its fairness, except the same could be repeated in his presence, so that he may witness it personally, secretly hoping that Timi might have a better chance this time, and that the Gbọnkâ might fall. This desire was apparent to all present, and to the Gbọnkâ himself ; however, he addressed himself to the renewed combat. The King ordered the Timi's weapons to be restored to him, and the fight resumed. To his mortification the Gbọnkâ was again victorious amid shouts of applause from the people. Timi was not only subdued but was also instantaneously killed by the victor before the King and without his orders.

The Gbọnkâ to show further what he could do, and to strike terror into the King, ordered a pile to be made, and pots of palm oil, nut oil, and shea butter to be poured on it ; he then went coolly and sat on the top of it, and ordered it to be set on fire. All present were anxious for the consequence ; but when the pile was ablaze, the Gbọnkâ disappeared.

Courtiers now began to congratulate the King on the fall of his enemy by his own hands ; but he was apprehensive of some other issues " Not too fast " said he, " we must first wait and see." Tidings soon reached the court that the Gbọnkâ followed by drummers, was seen dancing about the town.

The Gbǫnkâ knowing the public feeling towards the King, and his unpopularity, entered the palace and challenged His Majesty to display feats similar to his own and said if he could not, he would be rejected. There being no alternative, the King took poison and died.

Esugbiri succeeded Erankogbina as Basǫrun during this reign.

§ 3. OLUASǪ

The unfortunate King was succeeded by a handsome and amiable prince called Oluasǫ, who was remarkable for his longevity and peaceful reign. His agnomen was Ǫsarǫwa S'akin i.e., handsome but strong. He was a wise and affable sovereign fabled to have reigned for 320 years, and had 1460 children ! Three times did nine of his wives bear him male twins in one day. The first set he named Ǫmǫla, the second Ǫna-aka, and the third Ǫna-isokùn. Of these three sets of twins the last (Ǫna-isokun) were the most popular and Kings were chosen from amongst them and their descendants. These names have become hereditary titles unto this day. The King built 54 palaces for these 54 princes all of whom rose to positions of trust and responsibility by their own merits.

He originated and built 120 *kǫbis* to the royal palace. He was ably assisted by his Basǫrun, Esugbiri-ǫlu. He lived to a good old age, and died full of days and honour, and his longevity has passed into a proverb. " O ni ki o gbo ogbo Oluasǫ, o le jiya Oluasǫ ? " You pray to live as long as Oluasǫ, can you endure the trials of Oluasǫ ? Old age has its own trials and sufferings. His son Onigbogi succeeded him on the throne. Esugbiri was the Basǫrun of this reign also.

§ 4. ONIGBOGI

Onigbogi was one of the sons of Oluasǫ by Aruigba-ifa an Ǫta woman. She had left Ǫyǫ during the previous reign for her own native town, but on hearing that her son ascended the throne, she returned to Ǫyǫ in order to assist him in his government by her advice. She was a very superstitious woman. Wishing her son to have a long and prosperous reign, she advised him to introduce the worship of Ifa into Ǫyǫ as a national deity. The Ǫyǫ citizens asked the King and his mother what offerings are required with which to propitiate Ifa. She replied, 16 rats, 16 bags of cowries, 16 fishes, 16 fowls, 16 arm lengths of cloth and 16 ground pigs. The Ǫyǫ citizens answered that they were prepared to give the offerings, but they could not worship palm nuts. Thus the advice of the King's mother was rejected and the worship of Ifa cancelled.

When Aruigba-ifa was going to Ọyọ she was accompanied by the personification of several common objects used in fetish worship e.g. *Ajc, Opon, Ajere, Osun, Ẹlẹgbara,* and *Irọkẹ.* When the citizens of Ọyọ rejected her god, she returned on her way to Ọta with all her followers, weeping as they went. On reaching the foot of the Ado hill, the Alado's wife came out to see the cause of a company of people weeping and wailing, saying " We are driven out of the country." She reported this at home, and the Alado came out and invited the party to lodge with him. His inquisitiveness led him to ask why such august personages should be driven out of the city ; when he had learnt the whole story, he sympathized with Arugba, and asked her to stay, promising to give some of the things required, as they were too poor to be able to afford all. This was done, and Arugba not only initiated him into the mysteries, but also conferred upon him the right of initiating others. Hence in the subsequent reign when the Ọyọs decided to adopt Ifa worship, it was this Alado who went to the city to initiate them into all the mysteries, rites and ceremonies of Ifa worship.

A war broke out after these events, and the King sent out the Basọrun at the head of his army to Ita-ibidun with all the war chiefs. The king of the Tapas (Nupe) between whom and the Yorubas there have been strained relations since the death of Sango, seized this opportunity for crossing the river, and pouring his army into the Yoruba country, carried everything before him, until he stood before the gate of Ọyọ. There being no available force to oppose him, the city was soon taken. The King fled to Gbere in the Bariba country, and there he died not being used to the hardships incidental to the life of an exile ; leaving his son Ofinran a refugee in a strange land. In the land of his exile, King Onigbogi made it a law that only 35 of the Ẹsọs should be absent from home at any time, leaving 35 for the defence of the city and country, the Tapa King having entered Ọyọ practically without any opposition.

Ayangbagi Aro was the Basọrun of this period.

§ 5. OFINRAN

The Ọyọ refugees were at first received with open arms by the King Eleduwẹ and his Balogun Bọkọyọ because Ofinran's mother was a Bariba woman. The refugees having no regular employment here, joined the Baribas, who are a race of marauders, in all their expeditions. In one of these expeditions Irawọ in the Yoruba country was taken, and also Oke Iṣero where died the famous warchief Gbọnkâ Eleri-onigbajo.

After this, the Baribas began to ill-treat the refugees, but the young prince proved himself equal to the occasion ; he collected his people together, and set out at their head for Ọyọ.

When they arrived at a place called Kuṣu, they encamped there to complete their preparations for the journey to Ọyọ. From Kuṣu the King sent delegates to Ọta for Ifa priests, as he and his chiefs superstitiously believed that their misfortunes arose from their rejecting the worship of Ifa ; the Alado then came to initiate the ALÂFIN and his people into the mysteries of the Ifa worship. Thus Ifa was accepted by Yoruba proper among the gods of the land.

The Egũgun mysteries also were hitherto unknown to the Yorubas, by this means the Tapas have long imposed upon them, they believing in the reality of the so-called apparitions. On the hill Sanda at Kuṣu the secret was made known to Sàhá the King's head slave.

The first Alapĩñi with the other Egũgun priests the Elẹfi, Olọhan, Ọlọba, Aladafa, and the Ọlọjẹ, emigrated from the Tapa country to Yoruba, joining the remnants returning from the Bariba country. These became the first priests, and instructed the Yorubas further in the Egũgun worship ; therefore the honours and emoluments to be enjoyed in this worship by right belong to them and their successors unto this day.

Before the encampment at Kuṣu was broken up, the King died, and was succeeded by his son Egugũoju. The deceased King's body was wrapped in an ass's skin to be taken to Ọyọ. At a place called Okutu-gbogbo the cord broke, and the body had to be bound up afresh before they could proceed. On the very spot in which this happened, the palace at Ṣaki was built.

Sokia " ti iwọ ẹwn irin " (clad with a coat of mail) was the Baṣọrun of this period.

CHAPTER III

THE KINGS OF ỌYỌ IGBOHO

§ 1. EGUGUOJU

EGUGUOJU having succeeded his father, became the leader of his people to Ọyọ; the camp at Kuṣu was broken up and they carried the remains of the late King with them for state funeral at home.

They encamped next at Ìju Sanya, a desert place. Whilst there two large birds an Igbò and an Òyó were seen fighting, and they chased each other from the bough of the tree under which the King sat until they came down to the ground, and he ordered both to be caught and killed.

This occurrence was regarded by him as a happy omen; he therefore resolved to build a city there and to remove the seat of government to that place. From the example of the birds, he was resolved to fight to the last drop of blood in his veins any army that came against him there, never showing the " white feather." The city was accordingly built there, and was named Ọyọ Igboho, after the two birds, Igbo and Òyó, and there he buried the remains of his father.

Nothing remarkable was recorded of this King except that he built Igboho, which became the last resting-place of four Yoruba Kings before the government was again removed to the ancient capital.

Ọbalohun was the Baṣọrun of this reign.

§ 2. ỌROMPOTỌ

Prince Ọrompoto, brother of Eguguoju, and son of Ofinran succeeded to the throne. Shortly after his accession, troubles began to assail him; he, however, proved himself to be a skilful and experienced commander, and as a statesman, he was unrivalled. In his reign Ọyọ regained the military fame it had lost. He was swift in action, darting upon his enemies as an eagle upon his prey, when they least expected his approach. He used all skill to conceal his movements from the enemy. His rearguard consisted of 1,000 foot and 1,000 horse, for each of whom he provided a broad *gbaju* leaf to sweep and obliterate the foot prints of his army on the march, the horsemen tying the leaves to the tails of their horses.

But at the battle of Ilayi the King's army was routed although he fought with unusual bravery. He lost in this battle, three Gbonkâs, leaders of the van. When the first fell, he there and then created another ; he also fell, and he created a third who also fell, but whose fall converted the rout to victory under a peculiar circumstance

As he fell under showers of arrows in a kneeling posture his mouth remained fixed in a state as if grinning; the Baribas observing two white rows of teeth under his helmet thought he was playing them a trick, and that he was laughing at their fruitless attempts to kill him and put his army to flight, not knowing that he was stiff dead and that the Oyos were on the point of retreating. A sort of dread overcame them for a man it was impossible to kill notwithstanding showers of arrows hanging on him ! so they retreated thinking they had lost the day, and the Oyos remaining in the field claimed the victory. Hence it was commonly said of this man " Gbonkâ Orògbori ti o fi ehin le ogun." (The Gbonkâ of the ghostly head who routed an army with his teeth).

How long this King reigned is not known but he was the third buried at Igboho.

Asamu was the Basorun of this reign.

§ 3. AJIBOYEDE

Ajiboyede succeeded to the throne. He was a most successful King but he was a tyrant.

During this reign, the country was invaded by Lajomo, king of the Tapas. The King marched against him ; brave deeds were done on both sides; at last, however, the Yorubas were routed, and the King would have been slain but for a circumstance which not only saved his life, but also turned the tide of victory in his favour.

When it became apparent that the battle was lost, Ajanlapa the Osi'wefa hastily exchanged dress with the King, and told him to escape for his life. He put on the King's crown and his robes, and the Tapas supposing him to be the King turned their attention chiefly on him, and showered upon him such a number of darts, that in falling his body was propped up by the shafts of the arrows. As the crown fell off his head (like Gbonkâ Orogbori of the preceding reign) a coward observed his teeth with the face set as if he were grinning ; thinking he was laughing at their futile efforts he concluded at once that they had supernatural beings opposed to them ! He was alarmed, communicated his fears to his comrades, and panic immediately spread throughout the Tapa host ; and before they could be rallied, the stampede had become general, and he pursued now became the pursuers ; the Yorubas returned to the charge, and the Tapas were completely routed, and put to the sword. Lajọmọ their King was taken and the victory was complete.

The King was so grateful for his life being saved by the devoted Osi'wẹfa, that he took counsel of all the Ọyọ nobles as to what honours he should bestow on Ajanlapa's son. He wished him to be his constant attendant, to be about him night and day, and that he should be free of any part of the palace. But such a post cannot be held by any other than a eunuch and to make him so would seem cruel and ungrateful ; but the Ọyọs counselled that unless he is so, he cannot enjoy the full liberty desired by the King. A painful necessity that seemed to be, but the King yielded to that advice, and he was emasculated.

This circumstance accounts for the great honours attached to that office to this day, vide p. 59. The Osi'wẹfa is always the first as well as the last in the King's bed chamber. If the King is ill, he takes his place on state occasions, putting on his robes and the crown ; in war, he often appears as the King's deputy, invested with all the paraphernalia of royalty, including the state umbrellas, the kakaki trumpet, etc. Thus Ajanlapa by sacrificing his life converted what would have been a crushing defeat into a triumphant victory, and so saved his country from humiliation, and purchased royal honours for his family and for his official successors for ever. To mark this victory as well as his long reign, Ajiboyede celebrated the Bẹbẹ festival.

The Bẹbẹ is akin to a jubilee or golden age of a king's reign. There have been but few such in the history of the Yorubas. It lasts for 3 years, and during this period liberty of speech and action is granted to everyone, high and low, rich and poor throughout the kingdom, without any fear of being accused of sedition or treason. No riot or fighting is to be heard of anywhere, all provocations must be suppressed while the Bẹbẹ lasts, for no one is to be prosecuted during that period. All is peace. The King's Ilaris are rarely seen about on duty at this time, and when met, need not command that worship and deference usually accorded them. No toll or tribute is paid. Everyone appears in his holiday dress. Country folks go to Ọyọ to enjoy themselves without fear. Festivities mark the occasion. Provincial and feudatory kings and princes, and those of adjacent countries pay visits to Ọyọ to offer congratulations ; presents are given and received in a lavish manner. The corridors and courtyards of the palace, and all the trees in the King's market used to be decorated with hangings of cloth of various hues, native and foreign make, as with bunting. One deplorable act, however, is a blot on the Bẹbẹ celebration ; it is always accompanied with human sacrifices offered to the memory of all preceding Kings from ODUDUWA downwards ; two to each, and their blood mingled with those of animals slaughtered without number is poured out, for the King and his courtiers are required to have a religious dance upon it ; and this part of the ceremony is regarded as the highest act of worship, and of thanksgiving.

The Bẹbẹ is sometimes termed the *Iku* or funeral rites, as if intended to mark the close of a long reign, from the fact that the few Kings who celebrated it died a short time after.

The three years festivities of the Bẹbẹ being over, the Baṣọrun celebrates a minor form of festival termed the Qwara, and this lasts three months.

A short time after these festivitives were over, the King lost by death his first-born son, Ọsẹmolu to his inexpressible grief. All the Ọyọ nobles who came to sympathize with him were by his orders put to death, alleging that their feigned condolence was but a mock sympathy, for since he was fasting from grief, their hands smelt of food recently partaken. An insurrection against him was quite ripe when a Moslem priest from the Tapa country called "Baba-kewu" sent his son "Baba-Yigi" to remonstrate with him for his unjust and cruel acts in avenging his son's death on innocent people, when his son had died a natural death. "This," said he, "is a sin against God who took away the life of your son."

The King pondered seriously over this message, and became convinced of his tyranny. He convened an assembly of the Ọyọ citizens, and publicly asked their pardon for his unjust acts.

He was making preparations for removing the seat of government back to Ọyọ when he died.

This is the fourth and last King buried at Igboho.

The Baṣọrun of this reign was Ibatẹ̀.

§ 4. ABIPA OR " ỌBA M'ọRọ " (the ghost catcher)

Prince Abipa succeeded to the throne, being the fourth and last King who reigned at Gboho.

His first effort was to carry out the last wishes of his father, viz., to remove the seat of government back to the ancient capital.

The Nobles however, and those born at Gboho were strongly opposed to the removal, but could not prevent or dissuade the King from carrying out his purpose ; they therefore had recourse to a stratagem by which they hoped to thwart his purpose.

When they knew that the King was about to send to inspect the old sites, and to propitiate the gods as a preliminary to re-occupation, emissaries were secretly despatched by them to precede the King's messengers. The Baṣọrun sent a hunchback, the Alapīni an albino, the Aṣipa a leper, the Samu a prognathi, the Laguna a dwarf, the Akiniku a cripple. All these emissaries are considered in this country as unnatural beings, suffering the vengeance of the gods, hence they are termed " Eni Oriṣa " (the belongings of the gods). They are usually kept as priests and priestesses to Qbatala and other gods, especially the albinoes, dwarfs, and hunchbacks.

As the King's messengers were about to offer the sacrifices at the place appointed, these counterfeit apparitions who, according to instructions had posted themselves on the hill Ajaka, at the foot of which the palace was built, by a preconcerted plan suddenly began to shout " Ko si aye, ko si aye " (no room, no room).

At night they roamed about the hill, hooting and cooing with lighted torches in hand, and they were taken for the spirits of the hill refusing them readmission to Qyọ.

This report was very distressing to the King, and he was at a loss what to do. The Ologbo or Arọkin (chief cymbalist) shrewdly suspecting the real facts of the case advised his master to send hunters to investigate the truth of the matter. Bọni, Igiṣubu, Alegbàtà, Lọkọ, Gbandan, and Qlọmọ were the six famous hunters sent. They armed themselves with weapons and with charms to meet any contingency for self-defence.

When these hunters discovered that they were human beings they came upon them, and one of them took his aim and would have shot one of the deformed beings, had he not cried out and begged for his life. They were all taken alive and brought before the King ; and being questioned they were obliged to betray their masters who were at this time ignorant of what had taken place. The King adopted a most characteristic way of administering to his Nobles a silent rebuke which told.

At the weekly meeting of the King and the noblemen for the Jakuta sacrifices (which occur every 5 days) after the usual proceedings and religious ceremonies of the day were over, and they retired into the banqueting hall for refreshment as was their wont, the King on this occasion sent to each of the noblemen a calabash full of beer by the hands of his own emissary the " apparition " of Qyọ ! The Baṣọrun saw with ineffable surprise his hunchback whom he thought was playing the ghost at distant Qyọ emerging from the King's inner apartment with a calabash full of beer for him, the Alapīni his albino, and so with all the others, each one being waited upon by his own emissary ! Instantly a deep silence pervaded the room and the rest of the time was passed in an ominous stillness. The King and his Nobles parted without a word being spoken on the subject. The noblemen, however, showed their resentment by poisoning the *Ologbo* the King's adviser; but he, in order to show his love and esteem for the deceased, ordered for him a semi-state funeral, and had his body wrapped in ass's skin to be taken to Ọyọ for interment.

From this incident, King ABIPA was nick-named Ọba M'ọrọ (the King who caught ghosts).

Another nickname given to the King that had connection with this event was derived from his head slave Bisa, a Bariba, who was his favourite, and one time had great influence with his master. The King found out that Bisa was an accomplice with the Nobles in thwarting his designs. His Majesty now adopted a characteristic method of administering him a very sharp rebuke which he never forgot.

He one day called Bisa, and told him that the Eleduwẹ (the king of his native country) was dead, and that the Baribas have sent to him to pay the ransom of Bisa, who has been elected to the vacant throne. " Now Bisa, will you go ? " " Yes, your Majesty " replied Bisa, " and your majesty may be sure of this, that when I ascend the throne, the Bariba country to its utmost limits will be free and open to all Yorubas." The King then rejoined " Why do you wish to go to your country and yet you were trying to prevent me going to my birthplace and ancestral home ? Therefore, *you shall not go*." Bisa begged hard, but his master remained resolute, hence he was nicknamed " Ogbolu Akọhun, Akọhun Bisa jalẹ " Ogbolu the Refuser who totally refused Bisa's entreaties.

From this time Bisa lost all influence with the King. The design of removing the seat of Government to Ọyọ was now carried out, and Ọyọ from that time was known as Ọyọ Ọrọ̀ i.e. Ọyọ of the ghosts.[1]

Those famous hunters remained three years with the King in the capital as his guests, until he was perfectly settled. When they were about to return home, the King in order to do them honour, sent a special messenger with them as his representative, and lest this servant of his should prove a source of expense to them, he was allowed the privilege of receiving tolls for his livelihood. He became really the new Governor of the town with the title of Onibode (receiver of customs). Hence that title is bestowed on the chief ruler of Gboho to this day.

The remaining act of this King was the consolidation of his

---

[1] Ọyọ is also sometimes called Ọyọ Egboro from the name of the prince from whom Sango seized it.

kingdom. He buried charms in several places in the city that it might never be destroyed by war.

When his " medicine men " asked for a new born babe to be used as an ingredient in the composition of the charm, it happened that one of his wives had just then been confined ; this being reported to him, he ordered the new born babe to be brought in its blood as it was, and he handed it over to the men to be pulverized and used for their purpose. This act is to this day highly commended by the people, and the King accounted a great public benefactor who so loved his country, that he sacrificed his son for the welfare of his people.

Ọyọ was never destroyed *by war* after this event, but all the same, when the hour of retribution came, the blood of the innocents was avenged, for she suffered the fate of all cities destroyed by war. She was deserted, and thus she is in ruins unto this day.

Ibatẹ continued as the Baṣorun of this reign also.

CHAPTER IV

A SUCCESSION OF DESPOTIC AND SHORT-LIVED KINGS

§ 1. Ọbalokun Agana Erin

Ọbalokun succeeded to the throne of his fathers. His mother was the daughter of the Alake, the Primus of the Ẹgba chiefs.

The most memorable event of this reign was the introduction of salt into the Yoruba country. The article hitherto used for it was an insipid rock salt known as *Obu.* Salt now known as *iyọ* was at first called *dùn-mọ́mọ́.*

This King was said to be in friendly relations with the King of France (probably Portugal) with whom he had direct communication. It was said that the King sent 800 messengers with presents to that European sovereign, but that they were never heard of again. Tradition says that the sounds of bells ringing in the skies was plainly heard in the Akẹsan (King's) market, and it was conjectured that it was the voices of the unfortunates speaking to them from the other world to tell their fate.

What natural phenomenon this may have been due to which was interpreted thus, we do not know, but so it was believed at the time, and similar omens are not unknown to history.

It was said that a white traveller visited Ọyọ during this reign.

This King placed the first Ajẹlẹ (political resident) at Ij̃ana near Ilaro, with the title of Onisārè. The appointment of an Onisārè was regularly from Ọyọ and he must be a Tapà by birth. More of this will be noted hereafter.

He sent an expedition into the Ijẹsa country which was ambushed and defeated by the tribe known as Ijẹsa Arẹra, the Ọyọs being then unaccustomed to bush fighting. So great was the loss of life in this expedition that the *Ologbo* was sent out as a town crier to inform the bereaved of their losses in this war.

During this reign Sabigãna emigrated from the Sabẹ to the Yoruba country.

The Baṣọrun of this reign was Iba Magaji.

§ 2. Ajagbo

Ajagbo who succeeded Ọbalokun was remarkable for a long reign. He was said to have reigned 140 years and is an exception to the recent rule.

He was born a twin, and so striking was the resemblance

168

between himself and his brother Ajampati that the one was often mistaken for the other, and very often royal honours were paid to the latter as to his brother.

Ajagbo was also a warlike prince ; several expeditions were sent out by him.

He had a friend at Iwoye called Kókoro-gangan whom he made his Kakanfo (vide p. 74). This was the first Kakanfo in the Yoruba country.

It was his custom to send out four expeditions at the same time under four commanders. One under the Basǫrun, the next under the Agbakin, the third under the Kakanfo, the fourth under the Asipa. Those under this last consisted of the youths of the metropolis.

He destroyed Iwemę in the Popo country, Ile Ǫlǫpa, Onkò and his maternal town Ikereku-were an Ẹgba town. The rest of his reign was peaceful.

The Basǫrun of this reign was Akidain.

§ 3. ODARAWU

Odarawu was the successor. His reign was very short. He had a bad temper which was the cause of his being rejected. His short reign became a proverb, and often used to point a moral, and as a warning to succeeding Kings and also to inculcate a lesson of patience and forbearance.

On his accession he was asked according to custom who was his enemy ; he replied Ojo sęgi, i.e. a town in the kingdom named after the Balę thereof.

The reason he gave for this was that when a private man, he was once insulted by the Balę's wife. The alleged insult was under the following circumstances : —

He was accustomed then to trade in the provinces, and on one occasion he went to the market to buy *ękǫ* for his dinner, the seller whom he approached happened to be the Balę's wife ; both buyer and seller were ignorant of each other's position. *Ękǫ* then was sold for one cowry each ; he bought six and paid five cowries as a privilege of his birth. The seller not knowing that he was an *Akęyo* (prince) and considering herself insulted thereby, in the heat of passion gave him a slap, and called him a thief for the one cowry withheld !

The King's order for the destruction of the town was obeyed, but the Ǫyǫ people surmised that this would be a heartless tyrant, who, on account of a single cowry harboured such malice and resentment within him as subsequently to order the destruction of so many lives of his peaceful and loyal subjects. On this account, having fulfilled his wishes, he was rejected. He, therefore committed suicide.

Akidain survived the late King and was the Baṣọrun of this reign also.

§ 4. KARAN

Kãran succeeded Odarawu, but he proved to be an unmitigated tyrant. He tortured many of his subjects by ordering them to be scourged front and back until they expired ; so great were his cruelties that his name has passed into a proverb " as cruel as Kãran " and this led to a speedy termination of his reign.

He sent out an expedition against Aga Oibo, and there the conspiracy against him was quickly developed.

When the insurrection was ripe for execution, they sent a message home to him craving for his fan, as it has been told them by divination that the town cannot be taken except the King's fan be offered in sacrifice to the gods. This was complied with, and a portion of the sacrificial meat was sent him to partake of.

As soon as he had tasted thereof, it was said to him " The King has eaten his own fan, his word is now of no value, " i.é., his commands have returned to his own mouth. This is a characteristic round about method the Yorubas have of conveying intimations of what they intend to do. The army is now absolved from a charge of disobedience if they withdraw from the siege for the King has recalled his words ! All those who would stand by him were included in the plot. Iba Biri was elected to be the Baṣọrun in place of Woruda who had succeeded Akidain. The Agbakin's son was chosen to succeed his father, and so on with the other titles. This done, they raised the siege and encamped against the city demanding the King's abdication or death.

The King unwilling to die offered a stout resistance. He was personally courageous and brave, but he had the whole of his army against him. When they entered the city, he held out against them in the palace ; overcome by odds, he shot arrows until his hands were swollen. Dislodged from within the courtyard he climbed to the top of the roof, and there he sat fighting until the palace was set on fire and he perished in the flames.

Thus ended a short and an inglorious reign. He was succeeded by his son, Jayin.

Woruda was the Baṣọrun of this reign.

§ 5. JAYIN

Jayin was the son of the late King Kãran. He was an effeminate and dissolute prince. He had his harem full of all sorts of characters. His son Olusi was kind and generous ; he was the idol of the nation, and on him they built their hopes for a better future for the country.

Brought up amidst such demoralizing influences, in an evil hour, he fell under the charms of one of his father's numerous wives and was caught in her embraces. The father already jealous of the son's popularity with the people never forgave this offence. According to one account he summoned the prince before him, and whilst reprimanding him for his conduct, he was for a moment off his guard and thus betrayed himself by letting out the feeling rankling in his breast. " Villain " said he, " the citizens of Ọyọ prefer you to myself, and you are at one with them against me." Whilst speaking thus to him, he had in hand a club, the top of which was spiked and tipped with poison ; this he pressed upon his head to the point of bleeding, and the poison proved fatal to him.

According to another account, it was a poisoned cake made of beans that his father gave him, and of which he partook that caused his death. Anyhow, it was certain that he died of poison by the hand of his father.

He was universally mourned. The Ọyọ chiefs were determined to find out the cause of his death. They had a strong suspicion of foul play and were determined to avenge it.

The King gave it out that his death was due to an accident from the kick of his horse. The secret however, was divulged by one of his wives, and the disappointed citizens became much disaffected towards their King.

The late Olusi had a public funeral, a national mourning was proclaimed, and the public undertook to perform his funeral obsequies. His *Egugun* was brought out, i.e. an appearance of his apparition clothed with the cloths with which he was known to have been buried.

The Egũgun was said to have repaired to the palace, as was usual to pay honours to the chief ruler of the town, and as soon as the King showed his face, he was grasped by it. He was then told to die, having been touched by an Egũgun.

But according to another and a more probable account, when the King heard that his late son's Egũgun in the company of others was coming to the palace, knowing what the most probable outcome of such a visit must be, he hastily took poison and died. And this has passed into proverb " O ku dẹdẹ ki a ko iwi wọ Akẹsan, Ọba, Jayin tẹ ori gba aṣọ. (At the approach to Akẹsan of a company of chanting Egũguns, King JAYIN buried his head in a shroud.) Used of one who anticipates the inevitable.

It was during this reign that an Ilari " Agbeja-ilẹ̀ " was sent to settle a land dispute between the Aseyin ᴄdo, and the Olowu Ipolé ; he became the first Awujalẹ of the Ijẹbus.

Iba Biri was appointed Basọrun in place of Woruda deposed.

§ 6. AYIBI

An inter-regnum of some years followed the last reign, the affairs of the kingdom being left in the hands of the Basọrun. The heir to the throne, was the late King's grandson, the infant son of the lamented Olusi, who was too young to administer the government. The ỌYỌ MESI elected him in order to do honour to the memory of his deceased father. Ayibi was crowned when he came of age. Unfortunately he proved unworthy of the honour and respect done him ; he greatly disappointed the hopes of the nation. This may have been due to a great defect in his training when a minor, over-indulgence taking the place of strict discipline. He proved to be a tyrant who took delight in shedding blood.

When any suit was brought to court for his decision he often gave judgment by ordering both complainant and defendant to be executed. He had no respect for age, or rank, but terribly abused his power.

As an example of his cruelty and arbitrariness, the following story was told of him :—

He was one day in his bath, being attended by one of his favourite wives ; and she, in a moment of self-forgetfulness (or rather of amorous regard) said jocularly to him, " And this is all of the man so much dreaded by all ! " He took offence at this remark, but disguised his displeasure by a smile, but inwardly he was determined to convince her practically of the power which made him an object of dread to all.

After leaving his bathroom, he gave an order to a Tẹtu (executioner) privately to fetch the heads of the wife's father and mother each in a calabash, and decently covered up. This order was promptly executed The wife had by this time forgotten her remarks in the bathroom, as she had no reason to be apprehensive of any evil consequences arising therefrom. The calabashes being brought and set before him, he sent for her from her apartment, and asked her to uncover those .calabashes and tell the contents of them ! " Do you know them ? " asked he, " Yes I do," she replied trembling. " Then," rejoined he " that is the secret why I am so much dreaded by all, although to you I seem but commonplace and ordinary." She fully expected her own execution to follow, but he was satisfied with the pain and misery into which he had thrown her, and he graciously pardonéd (sic) her.

For this and similar acts of cruelty, an insurrection was stirred up against him by all the people, and being rejected he committed suicide.

Oluaja, and after him Yabi were the Baṣọruns of this reign.

The reason why these Kings after rejection invariably committed suicide is this. The person of a King is regarded as sacred. Kings are venerated as gods, indeed many of them have been actually deified; but the moment a king's enormities provoke an open rebuke, or on being told publicly " We reject you," by the constitution of the country he must die that day. He cannot from the sanctity with which he has been regarded abdicate and continue to live as a private individual, or continue to reign by sufferance, by the clemency of aggrieved subjects. Hence he must die; and by his own hands, for it is an unthinkable horror among the Yorubas for any man to lay hands upon a being regarded as sacred. It is the prerogative of the Baṣọrun to utter the sentence of rejection when the people are determined on it.

Even Noblemen also from their exalted positions are never ordered to execution. " The King rejects you. The ancient Kings Oduduwa, Ọrañyan, Aganju, and others, reject you." He must then take poison and die. Such deaths are accounted honourable, public and decent funerals are accorded them.

If any one allows himself to be executed his carcase will be treated like that of a common felon, and his house pulled down. Therefore a faint-hearted individual would be despatched by his nearest relatives to save themselves from indelible disgrace. An honourable burial will then be accorded to the illustrious dead.

§ 7. Ọsinyago

Ọsiñyago who succeeded to the throne was equally worthless. He was an avaricious man who by exactions, massacre, and confiscations amassed wealth which he did not live long to enjoy.

His firstborn son, like his father, was of a grasping propensity, which led to his early death. The second child Ọmọsún, although a female, was of a masculine character, and she considered the rank and privileges of the Arẹmọ (Crown Prince) her own ; but the King adopted a cousin Woruale (contracted to Wurale or Irale) son of Gbagba, a physician, his maternal uncle, as the Arẹmọ, and this Ọmọsún resented.

It happened that a dispute arose between these two as to the right of appointing a new Asẹyin at the death of the then king of Isẹyin, and Ọmọsún from wounded pride that she was opposed by a commoner, in the heat of passion slew Irale !

H

Irale's father Gbagba the physician was determined to avenge the death of his son, and this he did by poison said to have been extracted from one cowry worth of shea butter, 200 grains of beniseed, and other ingredients by which he effected the deaths of the King, Ọmọsún, Apala the Baṣọrun, and other notabilities of Ọyọ who were concerned with the misgovernment that was going on.

He was said to have escaped to his own country by means of charms. One report says, he flew away like a bird, and was found at Ẹdẹ ; another says he died and was buried, but his corpse became a red monkey which escaped into the bush. What was more probable was, that from the dread he inspired by his powers, he had an opportunity of escape, and was not slow to make use of it. The country was bereft of King and Baṣọrun simultaneously.

The Baṣọrun of this reign was Apalà.

§ 8. Ojigi

Ojigi who was elected to the vacant throne, was a powerful and warlike King. He extended his conquests to the Dahomian territory. In three expeditions headed by the Baṣọrun and the Gbọnkâ Latoyọ̀, the Dahomians were brought fully under subjection.

Yansumi an Idahomian town was taken and destroyed. He sent an expedition also against the Igbônas.

This King in order to show his undisputed sovereignty over the whole of the Yoruba country, including Benin, sent out a large expedition which struck the Niger in the north, near the Ibaribas, and coasted along the right bank until they arrived at the coast and returned to Ọyọ by the Popo country. Great exploits were reported of the leaders.

Personally, he was a very good man, but a too indulgent father. The Arẹmọ by his cruelties and excesses brought about the father's rejection and death. He ordered Olukẹ the Baṣọrun's son to be unlawfully beaten. As this wrong could not be avenged without serious consequences, and as the King did not punish the wrong doer, it was thought more expeditious to effect the King's death ; for about this time the custom began to prevail for the Arẹmọs to die with the father, as they enjoy unrestrained liberty with the father. A pretext was soon found for rejecting the King and fond father, and consequently he died, and his eldest son with him.

One of the most famous men in Yoruba history YAMBA was the Baṣọrun of this reign.

§ 9. GBERU

Prince Gberu who now succeeded to the throne was a wicked and superstitious King, much given to making charms. Before his accession to the throne he had a friend called Jambu whom he afterwards raised to the high rank of Basọrun. But it was not long before these former friends became disaffected towards each other. Both of them were one day sitting under a large Osè tree (the Adamsonia digitata) at Ọyọ. The Basọrun remarked on the magnificence of the tree which " bade fair to last for ever." The King made no reply, but afterwards poisoned the tree in order to cast the suspicion on the Basọrun who had made remarks on it ; and before the next morning it had withered.

Ọyọ we may remark is situated in a vast plain where trees are rarely seen. This was one of the few that grew there and it was much thought of, and was highly prized for its magnificence when in full bloom.

This circumstance caused a great sensation in the city among all who saw the tree flourishing in all its glory only the day before ! Enquiries as to the cause were keen and close ; it was at first thought this deed was done by the Basọrun in order to frame an accusation against the King as both were seeking each other's life ; but the author of the deed was soon known.

The chiefs of the town now grew suspicious and apprehensive of their own safety should the King add the use of secret poison to his unlimited regal power. They soon found a pretext for rejecting him, and he had to put an end to his own life. His quondam friend Jambu the Basọrun who divulged the secret was not spared either, he soon shared the fate of his friend and sovereign.

Gberu's reign was short and inglorious. He was succeeded by Amuniwaiye.

Jambu was the Basọrun of this reign.

§ 10. AMUNIWAIYE

Prince Amuniwaiye who now ascended the throne promised well at first, by his clemency and grace; but subsequently his low morals rendered him weak and despicable, and, as such, a disgrace to his high office.

He had for mistress the wife of his principal " medicine man " Olukoyisi, with whom he became acquainted under the following circumstances :—

The King engaged this " medicine man " to help him against the friends of Jambu the powerful Basọrun who effected the death of the former King. Being afraid that if his services to the King were known, his own life would be in danger, he worked warily by sending his wife Ololo with the pots instead of going himself personally. In this way the King had the opportunity of coming into contact with her, which he disgracefully abused, and the husband got to know it.

He could not bring an open charge against the King nor had he any other means of obtaining redress but by secret revenge, and this he effected terribly!

Olukoyisi prepared certain ingredients from the root of the Ọpọki tree which he applied to his wife unsuspected; it was a fatal " tell-tale," for when next she was being indulged in the royal embraces, the pair of them got so inextricably adhered together, that it became necessary to resort to a surgical operation in order to separate them! Thus both of them died in the act. Thus ended this inglorious reign.

The Baṣọrun of this reign was Kogbọ̀n son of the late Jambu.

§ 11. Oniṣile

Oniṣile who now ascended the throne was quite a different man from the former occupant. He was a great warrior, and for his exploits was nicknamed " Gbagida ! Wọwọ l'ẹ́wọn ab'ẹsin fo odi " (Gbagida [an expression of admiration] a man with clanging chains [for prisoners] whose horse can leap over a town wall.)

He was remarkable for his indomitable courage and lion-hearted spirit. He was moreover very artistic, and was said to have made seven silver doors to the seven entrances of his sleeping apartment.

During this reign the Ṣẹkẹrẹ (calabash) drum was ornamented, not only with cowries, but also with costly beads e.g. Iyùn (corals) Okún (stone beads, Benin) Ẹrinla (striped yellow pipe beads) and Ṣẹgi (blue pipe beads), strung with silk thread dyed red ; all of native manufacture.

His rashness and fearlessness was the ultimate cause of his death. He was cautioned against experimenting with the " sun leaf " a plant known to possess electrical properties, by which lightning can be attracted ; but he was not the man to heed any such remonstrance. The consequence was that the Sango worshippers managed to attract lightning on the palace, the King was struck, and from the shock he became paralysed. Thus he was incapacitated from performing the duties of his office.

The chiefs of Ọyọ then assembled and waited on him, and told him that as he had challenged Sango to a single combat and had been worsted, he could no longer continue to live.   Thus he was rejected, and he had to die.

The feeling had gained ground by this time that Kings should not be allowed to die a natural death. Unchecked despotism, unrestrained licence, insatiable greed, and wanton voluptuousness should not be allowed to flourish throughout the full term of a natural lifetime.   The excesses of the Crown Prince also were unendurable hence the earliest opportunity was usually sought, for putting an end to their reign.

His Baṣọrun's name was Soyiki alias Èṣùògbó.

Chapter V

BAṢỌRUN GAHÀ AND HIS ATROCITIES, HIS FALL, AND ABIỌDUN'S PEACEFUL REIGN

§ 1. Labisi

This unfortunate Prince was nominated to the vacant throne, but was never crowned. Only 17 days after he commenced the preliminary ceremonies, the new Baṣọrun Gáhà rose to power, and commenced those series of atrocities which made him notorious in Yoruba history.

Olubọ and Ajibadu the King-elect's friends were summarily put to death, and he, having no supporters was not even allowed to enter the palace, much less to sit on the throne. He had to put an end to his own life.

Gáhà had great influence with the people, and a great many followers who considered themselves safe under his protection, from the dread in which they stood of the Kings, because of their cruel and despotic rule.

Gáhà was also famous for his " charms ; " he was credited with the power of being able to convert himself into a leopard or an elephant, and on this account was much feared. He lived to a good old age, and wielded his power mercilessly. He was noted for having raised five Kings to the throne, of whom he murdered four, and was himself murdered by the fifth.

§ 2. Awọnbioju *alias* Oduboye

Gáhà the Baṣọrun had by this time attained to great power and influence. He made himself the King maker and King destroyer. He did not aspire to the throne, for that was impossible of attainment, but he demanded the homage of all the Kings he raised to the throne. He raised Awọnbioju into the place of Labisi. His reign was very short, having wielded the sceptre for only 130 days. He was murdered by the all-powerful Baṣọrun for nobly refusing to prostrate before him, his own Chancellor.

§ 3. Agboluaje

Agboluaje who succeeded the late King on the throne was a very handsome and prepossessing Prince, and as he submitted to the powerful Baṣọrun, he was allowed to reign for a longer period than the two preceding Kings. He was not as ambitious

as some of his predecessors, he had no wars, the kingdom had
extended to its utmost limits, bounded by the river Niger on the
north and a portion of the Tapa and Bariba countries, on the
East by the lower Niger, on the South by the seacoast, and on the
West it includes the Popos and Dahomey.   From all the provinces
included within these boundaries, and by some including the Gās
and Ashanti, tributes were paid to Oyo.   Tranquility prevailed
all over the land.

The King thought this a fitting opportunity for celebrating
the Bebe, not so much for the length of his reign, but for the
peace and prosperity that prevailed all over the Kingdom.

During the three years celebration, visitors from all parts
thronged Oyo as was usual, but the most distinguished guest was
the Elewi-odo, a Popo king, who visited Oyo in state and had a
reception befitting his rank.   He was a particular friend of the
ALÂFIN'S, and usually supplied him with cloths and other articles
of European manufacture, being nearer the coast and having dealings with European traders of those days.

As on such occasions everybody visited Oyo in his best holiday
dress, so the Elewi-odo who was accounted proverbially rich
appeared at this time.   On public occasions the Elewi-odo sat
on a throne opposite the King ;   as often as the King changed
his robes, he changed his covering cloth to one of the same
material ; when the King puts on a robe of silk or velvet, he covers
with a cloth of the same material.   Both Kings were an object
of interest and admiration by the 1060 vassal kings and chiefs
of Yoruba, with the populace who were present on that occasion.

But the citizens of Oyo grew jealous for the honour and glory
of their King and wished him to appear superior to the Elewi-odo
by robing himself with something the like of which even the Elewi
had not ; but they found that he had nothing the like of which his
friend had not ; so they had recourse to a device.   The manu-
facturers were summoned and the case put before them, and they
promised to rise to the occasion.   A simple gown was thereupon
woven, of common stuff indeed, but embossed all over with the
silken wool of the large cotton tree ; seen at a distance the nature
of the cloth could not be made out by the crowd ; when the sun
shone upon it, it reflected a silken hue to the admiration of all ;
when the breeze blew, detached flosses of silk floated all around
his majesty.   Even the Elewi-odo and the provincial kings could
not help admiring the curious robe which they took for something
so superior, that none but the great ALÂFIN of Oyo alone possessed!
The crowd went into ecstatic frenzy about it, and shouted an
applause.

But the conduct of the Elewi on this occasion offended the Baṣọrun because he vied with his sovereign. Therefore, after his return home at the expiration of the *Bẹbẹ* and the Baṣọrun had celebrated his *Owara* as usual, he denounced the Elewi before His Majesty in the severest terms : that he came, not to honour the King but to disgrace him, to show off his wealth to the King's disadvantage, and, therefore, he was determined to punish him for his conduct.

The King pleaded hard for his friend but in vain. " Every one " said he, " is allowed by custom to appear at Ọyọ during *Bẹbẹ* in his best, how much more should a king do so ? His action in this matter is pardonable, and therefore, should be overlooked." But Gáhà was inexorable, and war was declared.

The Elewi having been privately forewarned, attempted no resistance, but sent a private message to the King not to be anxious on his account, and that his safety was assured. He speedily crossed the Esuogbo river and escaped to the Tapa country.

Unfortunately the private messenger arrived at Ọyọ too late to meet the King alive. Unwilling that the head of his friend the Elewi should be brought in triumph to him at Ọyọ, he took poison and died before the return home of the expedition. His brother Majẹogbe was placed on the throne by the all-powerful Baṣọrun Gáhà.

§ 4. Majẹogbe

Majẹogbe did not fare any better than his immediate predecessors. His first care was to find means of checking the ambition of the Baṣọrun. He could not order his execution, and the Baṣọrun was too much on the alert to be taken off by poison ; but he set about making charms offensive and defensive in order to rid himself of this terror.

Gáhà had by this time attained the zenith of his glory ; his sons were scattered all over the length and breadth of the kingdom, they resided in the principal towns and all the tributes of those towns and their suburbs were paid to them. No tribute was now paid to the ALÂFIN ; Gáhà's sons were as ambitious and as cruel as their father.

Several anecdotes illustrating their wanton cruelties were told of them, e.g. :

One of them once engaged a carrier to whom he gave a load too heavy for him to carry, but he dared not refuse to do so. He walked behind the man amusing himself with the sight of the man's sufferings from the weight of the load. He remarked in jest that the man's neck had become so thick that he doubted whether a sword could cut through. He suited his action to his words, drew his sword, and actually tried it ! The man was decapitated, and his body was left wallowing in his blood, and another man was compelled to take up the load.

Another of his sons was said to have shot a farmer dead, whilst engaged in making heaps for planting yam, wantonly charging him with disfiguring the King's ground by making horns on it !

Another similarly shot a farmer dead whilst hoeing the ground, pretending that he mistook him for an ape on all fours !

Thus Gáhà and his sons usurped all power of the government the King himself living in dread of his own fate at the pleasure of the notorious regicide.

The King's own " medicine men " were not idle either. A lighted lamp was said to have been placed in one of his inner apartments which was kept burning for three years untrimmed, and while it was burning there can be no peace to the regicide.

A horse was said to be in one of the stables and was heard neighing every day, and yet was kept there 3 years without fodder !

The ALÂFIN's death was brought about by one of his sons quarrelling in the Basorun's quarter of the town ; this act Gáhà resented as a daring affront which the father's life must atone for, the son being too insignificant for him to take any notice of. But the ALÂFIN had succeeded by this time in poisoning the Basorun that he became paralysed in both his legs. On the other hand the nature of the charms in the King's apartment had been made known to Gáhà, who now bent all his energies to extinguish the ever-burning lamp. Its effect was so great that all who approached that apartment instantly dropped down dead. All the " medicine-men " in the kingdom were summoned by Gáhà but none succeeded, and it cost many their lives. At last an Agberi man appeared, who sacrificed the life of his slave in order to gain the honour, nor did he survive it himself. In this service the Agberi tribes gained the pre-eminence over others of the same craft, and became friends of the Basorun. And thus the King died.

But from this time the power of Gáhà began to decline, old age set in, and impaired his strength of body and mind. His wives began to desert his harem, but some faithful domestics stood by him and they concealed from the general public the fact of his being lame. The door opening to the audience chamber was always kept shut whilst the King and the other noblemen were in waiting every morning to pay their respects to him. The opening and closing of the doors of the inner apartments announce the approach of his supernal highness. He crawled on all fours, and was usually

seated before the door of the audience chamber was slid back,
so that he was never seen on the move ; but in order to inspire
dread, his drummer used to beat " Iba kanbọ, irin ija ni nrin."
His Highness comes majestic, striding as one spoiling for a fight.

§ 5. Abiọdun *alias* Adegolu

Abiọdun, whose peaceful reign has passed into a proverb was
described as a tall and slender prince, of a very dark complexion,
a comely person, of dignified manners, and altogether fit to wear
a crown.   He also was raised to the throne by the order and
influence of the Baṣọrun.

The young King was wise and prudent, and at first made no
attempt at any opposition to the powerful Baṣọrun.   He went
regularly every morning to pay him his respects, and invariably,
received his presents of 10 heads of cowries (which as a matter of
fact, never exceeded 6 heads, not with the knowledge of the
Baṣọrun however, but by the action of the attendants).

This state of things continued for many years so much so that
even the Baṣọrun himself was becoming tired of this abject
submission, and wanted but a decent pretext for which he might
kill him, just for a change !   This man of blood was often heard
to say " Who taught this King to be so wise? These daily presents
are getting to be too heavy a charge on my exchequer now."
All power was in his hands and so were the responsibilities.   His
lust for power drained his exchequer, for his sons lording it all
over the country deprived him of the revenues which might have
come to him.

That he was in great straits for money seemed evident from the
fact that he requested his " medicine men " to make him charms
to get him plenty of cowries.   " Of all that constitutes wealth
or power," said he, " I have, save money (cowries) enough to
support my position."

One of his " medicine men " assured him that he can make
him a soap to wash with, and before sunset, his wish will be
realized.   He made the soap, and His Supernal Highness used it
according to directions, and strange to say, it took effect, but in a
way no one anticipated.   Whatever the cause was due to, nobody
knew, but fire broke out in the Baṣọrun's house that afternoon,
and all efforts to extinguish it failed, and so the palace was burnt
to the ground.   Owing to His Highness' influence and power,
and the dread all had of him, every rank and station, from the
Alâfin downwards now vied to be the foremost in contributing to
repair his losses, 10, 15, 20 bags of cowries came in from all quarters.

The heads of the different wards of the city, the Modade, Mǫlàbà, Nṣiṣe-oguǹ, Ntẹtu, T'onṣẹ-Awo, Arẹmu, Ita-Ologbo, Ajǫfà, and the Ǫgẹdẹ quarters, all brought presents in cowries.

Then the provincial kings and chiefs from the Onikoyi down-wards brought building materials, and also their own contributions in cowries, which greatly augmented his store. The Baṣǫrun then asked the " medicine man " " Is this the way you promised to get me cowries ? " He replied, " Yes, your Highness ; by what other means could you have amassed such an abundance in so short a time? "

But the Baṣǫrun was still thirsting for the blood of the ALÂFIN, and he was never so wise in his dealings with him, till at length, King ABIǪDUN took a bold step, upon which he had devoted no little consideration. Having given orders to his courtiers and his wives privately to report to the Baṣǫrun that he was suffering from indisposition he left Ǫyǫ privately in the night for a town called Akálà to his namesake Adegolu the powerful chief of that place. Being in disguise, he was not recognised by the Balẹ's wife, who told him her husband had gone to his farm. The feigned poor stranger asked the lady kindly to fetch him home in haste, as he had an important message for him. The kind hostess did so, and Chief Adegolu came home immediately, wondering what the message could be.

" Who are you? Where from? And what is your message? " weie the eager questions the Balẹ put to the stranger. " I want a private interview " was the reply. Both of them retired to a convenient place, and the Balẹ was startled, and was scarcely himself when he heard from this humble stranger " I am your namesake Adegôlu the ALÂFIN of Ǫyǫ." It was with some difficulty he could restrain the Balẹ from doing homage there and then with earth on his head, etc. " No, no," said the King, " another time will do for that. I am come to confer with you upon the present crisis, how to rid the throne of Ǫyǫ of the great usurper, the King maker and King destroyer. You know very well, that in all the 6,600 towns and villages of the Yoruba kingdom, Gáhà and his sons have the dominant 1ule."

After conference, Chief Adegolu went with the stranger to che powerful Kakanfo (Field Marshal) Ǫyabi at Ajaṣẹ ; here the plot was matured, of a strong and secret combination against the Baṣǫrun and his sons. This was communicated by swift posts to all the principal kings and chiefs in the country, and it was arranged that on a fixed day, they should all rise and destroy all Gáhà's children.

The arrangement being complete King Adegolu returned home

as he came out ; and next morning paid his respects to the Baṣọrun as before.

At the day appointed, the whole country rose up against Gáhà's children, and butchered them to pieces ; and in order to exterminate the seed *in toto*, those of their wives who were *enceinte* were ripped open, and the embryo chopped in pieces !

The whole army of the country headed by Ọyabi, and Adegolu now marched for Ọyọ according to the secret arrangement, and the Ọyọ chiefs with the ALÂFIN opened the gates to them.

Gáhà's people single-handed were preparing to resist, but it was evident that his time was come and nothing could stop the inevitable and fatal end. Gáhà summoned his relatives together, and handed to them a bundle of bẹrẹ grass, well tied, and asked them to break it ; when all had tried and failed, he had it loosed, handing round a few blades to each ; that was easily crunched ; then said he to them " Combined we shall stand, but if disunited we shall be broken to pieces like the blades of bèrè in your hands." But his brother Olúbú who might have offered the stoutest resistance, had been won over by the Ọyọ chiefs, who promised him his brother's title when all shall have been over ; but this turned out to be a ruse, devised to weaken the Baṣọrun's resistance, for Olúbú never escaped the fate of all Gáhà's people, but was butchered in the general massacre of the great man's adherents and relatives. To the last, Ọlaotan, Gáhà's eldest son, stood by his father. The troops from the country poured in from all quarters and were joined by those of the city, all equally tired of the iron rule of Gáhà and of the enormities being perpetrated by his children. His palace was surrounded, and attempts were made to beat down the walls thereof ; but they were heroically defended by his trusty domestics, and the few faithful adherents.

Gáhà in vain tried to transform himself into an elephant as of yore. He ordered four mortars to be placed in position for the fore and hind legs, and two pestles for the tusks ; old and feeble and lame, he could not even help himself up the mortars, and when helped to them, his trembling limbs could not support his body weight : his incantations proved a failure. At the sight of this failure Ọlaotan groaned with disappointment and said, " Father, have I not always said it were better you should secure a charm for ensuring perpetual youth ? It was because I was strongly convinced that these charms will be of little avail to you, when old age has set in."

From the walls and from the roofs of his palace, the Baṣọrun's men kept the army of the Kakanfo at bay. A sharp shooter in particular did havoc amongst them ; but a certain young man,

bold and astute, observing this, ran close to the wall at some
distance from the spot where he was, and walked along so close
under it right on to the spot, that he was not seen from above or
within, and as soon as the marksman put his head out again for
another shot, he grasped and dragged him down, and immediately
the men rushed forward and beat down the wall. The house was
immediately fired, and all the domestics found within were put
to the sword. The Basorun and Gbagi a faithful and favourite
Ilari were taken alive and brought before the King. He was
soon on his chair of state with all insignia of royalty in full display
about him, and the fallen minister made to prostrate at a distance
before him, under a hot burning sun. The old man pleaded for
his life, and even asked to be degraded and made the keeper of
His Majesty's poultry yard, but it was felt that no quarters could
be granted to him now. Being bulky in size, the ground under him
where he lay prostrate under the mid-day sun became saturated
with the profuse perspiration oozing from him. He neither deserved
nor received pity of any one. There were great rejoicings in the
city and in the King's palace, and especially among the King's
wives.

So great were the indignities and contempt this fallen minister
was subjected to, that even children could approach him now
and pull at a pedunculated tumour in his forehead, hanging down
his face, which the fear and dread of him did not allow people to
notice before, for who could approach so near as to gaze on him ?
But the fate awaiting him was of greater concern to him now, than
to take notice of these trifling jests.

By the order of the ALÂFIN, the posts of his house and everything
that could be used as firewood, which had escaped the burning,
were brought together and piled as a stake ; pots of palm oil,
nut oil, and shea butter were poured on it, and set alight ; he was
then approached by a menial saying in mockery " Master, the fire
is alight, will you not warm yourself a bit in such a weather as
this ? " Then he was lifted up to the top of the stake and made
secure, together with Gbagi, his faithful *Ilari*.

His fate has been a lesson to all usurpers and abusers of power.
It has passed into a proverb " Bi o l'aiya Osika, bi o ri iku Gáhà,
o yio so otito. If you have the heart of a cruel man, take note of
Gáhà's death and be true."

A one day *bebe* i.e. a public holiday with the freedom of a
Bebe (vide p. 163) was proclaimed, after which Oyabi the Kakanfo
returned home with the thanks and good wishes of the King and
nation.

ABIODUN now commenced the work of reformation beginning

from the capital.   In order to make himself secure on the throne, he suppressed or executed all those known or suspected to have been Gáhà's friends secretly, and who might raise an insurrection against him, for Gáhà was not without friends even among the chiefs, such as the Ẹsiẹlẹ, the Sakin, and the Sàhádọ́wẹ̀.

From this time commenced that period of peace and prosperity for which King ABIỌDUN's reign was famous.   Tributes poured into Ọyọ from the remote states and from Dahomey, agriculture and commerce flourished, and the people to the remotest part of the kingdom were so far happy and contented.

The Kakanfo Ọyabi did not live long to enjoy the peace he was so instrumental in effecting ; two years later, the ALẢFIN invited him to Ọyọ in order to bestow on him special honours, and marks of favour in recognition of his services to King and country, but unfortunately, his health was in a precarious condition, and in obeying the commands of his sovereign, he died on his way to Ọyọ.

§ 6. ABIỌDUN'S PEACEFUL REIGN

King ABIỌDUN had a long and prosperous reign.   He was said to have been the father of 660 children ·!   The firstborn Agunpopo was said to have been the issue of an illicit intercourse with one of his father's wives, during the father's lifetime : hence the Ọyọ citizens refused to have him as the Arẹmọ (Crown Prince). Ige Gbengberu his legitimate firstborn was accepted for that title, but he was of a delicate constitution, and died prematurely ; the office of Arẹmọ now devolved upon the next prince Adeṣina.

When ABIỌDUN was fully established on the throne he found out that a Mohammedan had hidden one of Gáhà's children for about 40 years[1] !   The King not only graciously spared the young man, but also amply rewarded his preserver for his generous act, and confirmed his goodwill by giving one of his daughters to the Moslem for wife ; " for surely," said the King, " you would have done the same for myself also."

Towards the latter part of the King's reign, certain of the Popo tribes had a quarrel among themselves, and two of their kings came to Ọyọ with a large retinue of about 4,000 people for an appeal.   They were detained for 3 years without their case being heard, and in the end they were informed that they were no more to return to their own country, but kept as the

---

[1] The Yorubas always exaggerate their time period by a bad method of calculation.   If, for instance, a child is born 5 days before the new moon appears, he is then 2 months old, and at the next new moon he is 3 months, when in reality he is only a month and some days.   So also is the calculation for years.

King's body guard under the command of his son Agunpopo whom the Oyọ citizens insisted upon reckoning among his brothers the Olusami, Atingisi, and Iyajin for the reason stated above.

One act of revenge marred this distinguished sovereign's reputation. Long before his accession, he was a trader in potash. He once had a quarrel at Ijaye with the Balẹ's son but the Balẹ, out of deference to his high birth interposed and sharply reprimanded his son. Upon his accession he avenged the alleged insult by ordering the destruction of the town. Ijaye was then an Ẹgba town.

This fact is noted because this was the first time Ijaye was taken, a town which was destined hereafter to play a notable part in Yoruba history. His other wars were against the Popos every other year. They were completely subdued.

The Crown Prince Adesina turned out to be a very vain and extravagant young man, weak in character, yielding to flattery. E.g., it was said that some of his followers used to say to him " Prince, you can give me 10 heads of cowries now (equivalent to £10 in those days), if only you wish ; why, you have only to say the word and it would be done ; come now, why be reluctant about it ? It is only to speak, etc." The Prince would yield, and order the money to be given.

King ABIODUN attained to a good old age, full of honours, having subdued all his enemies. The Aremọ had hoped to succeed his father. Not satisfied with the high honour and unrestricted liberty he was enjoying, he was too eager to occupy the throne, and so he hastened his father's death by poison.

The end of this reign marked an important epoch in Yoruba history. With the death of ABIODUN ended the universal and despotic rule of the ALÂFINS of Oyọ in the Yoruba country. He was the last of the Kings that held the different parts of the Kingdom together in one universal sway and with him ended the tranquility and prosperity of the Yoruba country. The revolution ensued, and the tribal independence, with the loss to Yoruba of the Tapa and Bariba, and Dahomey provinces, and the Popos later on, which has continued to our own day. In a word, with Abiọdun ended the unity of the Yoruba kingdom.

Kangidi succeeded Gáhà as the Basọrun of this reign.

THE THIRD PERIOD.

In which revolutionary wars devastated the whole of Yorubaland, ending in the Fulani usurpation and tribal independence. It embraced a period of the reigns of five Kings, from the accession of AOLE to the death of OLUEWU, the last of the Kings, who reigned at the ancient Oyọ.

CHAPTER VI

THE REVOLUTION

§ 1. AOLE SURNAMED AROGANGAN

NONE of Abiọdun's numerous children succeeded him on the throne. Aolẹ̀, a tall and handsome Prince, a cousin of the late King was elected in his stead. But unfortunately, his reign was a very unhappy one ; it marked the commencement of the decline of the nation until it terminated in the tragic end of the fifth King after him. The cup of iniquity of the nation was full ; cruelty, usurpation, and treachery were rife, especially in the capital ; and the provinces were groaning under the yoke of oppression. Confiscation and slavery for the slightest offence became matters of daily occurrence, and the tyranny, exactions, and lawlessness of the Princes and other members of the royal family, were simply insupportable. Oaths were no more taken in the name of the gods, who were now considered too lenient and indifferent ; but rather in the name of the King who was more dreaded. " Idà Ọba ni yio jẹ mi " (may the King's sword destroy me) was the new form of oath ! Aolẹ̀ was unfortunately saddled with the ill fate of the nation, as the following ditty commonly sung would show :—

> " Laiye Abiọdun l'afi igba wọn 'wo
> Laiye Aolẹ̀ l'adi adikalẹ̀."

(In Abiọdun's reign money we weighed by bushels. [Lit. with calabashes.] In Aolẹ's reign, we packed up to flee).

But there was nothing more in his actions than in those of his predecessors to warrant this saying, on the contrary, he was probably too weak and mild for the times. The nation was ripe for judgment, and the impending wrath of God was about to fall upon it ; hence trouble from every quarter, one after another.

On the King's accession, according to custom when the time came for him to send out his first expedition, he was asked who was his enemy, that they should fight him. He named the Balẹ of Apomu, and hence Apomu was doomed.

The alleged cause of offence will clearly show how much of corruption there was at the fountain head in those days.

Apomu was the market town where Ọyọs, Ifẹs, Owus, and Ijẹbus met for trade. It was situated in Ifẹ territory, and in the border of the Olowu's dominion. Raiding and man-stealing were rife at those times. Ọyọs particularly were in greater danger, as they came from afar. During the last reign several Ọyọs were stolen and sold here, and hence King ABIỌDUN sent orders to both the Olowu and the Ọwọni of Ifẹ to keep a strict watch and prevent the recurrence of these practices. The Ọwọni and the Olowu in turn sent strict orders to the Balẹ of Apomu to be on the watch, and arrest any offender.

Aolẹ who was then a private man used to trade in these parts with a friend who was also his attendant ; and on one occasion, he bartered away his friend for merchandise ! So faithless and heartless were the princes in those days. The Ijẹbus were actually taking him away when it was reported to the Balẹ of Apomu that an Ọyọ man was being sold away. Fortunately for the man by the prompt action of the Balẹ he was rescued at a certain spot named Apata Ọdaju (the rock of the heartless), perhaps so named from this circumstance, and brought before the Balẹ. Investigation soon showed who the slave-dealer was ; but as Aolẹ was an Akẹyọ (Prince) and could not more severely be dealt with, in order that justice may not miscarry, he was ordered by the Balẹ to be severely flogged. This was the reason why AOLE now named the Balẹ of Apomu as his enemy.

When the Balẹ of Apomu heard that war was declared against his town on his account he took refuge in the court of the Ọwọni of Ifẹ his over-lord, and whose orders he had obeyed. But as the offence was against the Suzerain, even the Ọwọni could not save him ; so this faithful chief, in order to save his town and his people from destruction, committed suicide, and his head was cut off and sent to Ọyọ to appease the offended monarch !

But an expedition must in any case be sent out, the King was, therefore, approached again and asked to name his enemy. But he replied, " My enemy is too formidable for me." Being pressed, he named the powerful chief Afọnja the Kakanfo residing at Ilọrin with great reluctance, as he foresaw evil ahead.

§ 2. THE KING'S ENEMIES

After the death of the Kakanfo Ọyabi, Afọnja of Ilọrin demanded the title ; but as a Prince (through the mother) the title was below his rank, for the Kakanfo ranks after the Baṣọrun, but being the highest military title, it suited his restless nature best, and so he obtained it, almost by force.

But King AOLE was unwilling to initiate any civil war, and refused to take any action against Afọnja after he had granted him the title.

Hitherto, Afọnja alone was his enemy, the other chiefs were as yet loyal to him, but circumstances occurred, one after the other which created a disaffection between him and the Baṣọrun and the other chiefs, fanning into a flame the destructive fire already smouldering in its embers.

The cause of quarrel between the King and Aṣamu the Baṣọrun was this :—

One Alaja-ẹta a Hausa trader at Ọyọ was plundered of his goods, under the pretext that he was bringing bad charms into the city.   Among his confiscated goods was his Koran which he prized more than all his other stolen property.   He appealed to the King, and he, from a sense of justice ordered that all his goods be restored to him.   All but the Koran were accordingly restored. The Hausa again appealed to the King for this his most valued treasure ; the King insisted that search should be made and the lost Koran be restored.

The Baṣọrun in whose possession it probably was, or who at any rate knew where it could be found, refused to restore it and told the King it could *not* be found !   His Majesty felt this keenly as an insult to his dignity ; he was heard to say " Is it come to this that my commands cannot be obeyed in my own capital ?   Must it be said that I failed to redress the grievance of a stranger in my town ?   That he appealed to me in vain ? " Turning to the Baṣọrun and pointing upwards he said, " Very well then, if you cannot find it my father (meaning the deified Sango) will find the Koran for me."

As the god Sango is reputed to take vengeance on thieves and liars by burning their houses, so the next day, when lightning struck the Baṣọrun's house, great was his rage against the King for being instrumental in convicting him of theft and lying !

The ceremony of appeasing the god by the devotees, entailed heavy expenses on the Baṣọrun who, had it been another man's house might have gone shares with the ALÂFIN in the fines imposed upon the sufferers.   He knew where the trouble came from, for he noted the King's words " My father will find it for me."   In this way be became the King's enemy.

Another circumstance occurred which added the Ȯwȯta one of the Ẹsọs to the list of the King's enemies.

One Jankalawa who had offended the late King and who had escaped to the Bariba country when he sought to kill him, now returned after the King's death and was flaunting about the streets of Ọyọ under the protection of Lafianu the Ȯwȯta.   The late King's wives were angry at this and complained to Aolẹ against Jankalawa.   Said they " You have inherited our late husband's wives, his treasures, slaves and his throne. Why not make his cause your cause and his enemies yours as well ? Why do you allow this Jankalawa to stalk so defiantly about the streets of Ọyọ ?"

By thus appealing to him from day to day, he yielded to their entreaties and remonstrances, and ordered the arrest and subsequent execution of Jankalawa.

The Owòta's pride was wounded, because he was not respected by the King, in that one known to be under his protection should be so summarily dealt with. Thus the Baṣọrun and the Kakanfo found an accomplice in the powerful Owòta. A conspiracy was formed but not being ripe for execution, they awaited a favourable opportunity.

At length the time arrived when an expedition must be sent out, and the King was again asked "Who is your Majesty's enemy?" He replied, " I have told you that my enemy is too formidable for me, and besides we are the same kith and kin." However, he advised that as the last campaign ended at Gbeji, the war should be prosecuted from that place.

But in order to gain their object in view, viz., the removal of the Kakanfo, the King's counsellors advised that the Kakanfo and the army should be sent against Iwere, a place fortified by nature and by art, and impregnable to the simple weapons of those days, and as the Kakanfo by the oaths of his office must either conquer within three months or die, and Iwere is impregnable, he will have no other alternative, but as in honour bound to make away with himself.

It was, however, arranged that he should not be forewarned, but decoyed as it were to that place until he found himself at the foot of the hill on which Iwere was built ; hence it was given out that war was declared against Gbeji.

But the royal party leading the army received private instructions to lead the army to Iwere and when there to inform the Kakanfo that that was the place he was sent against.

But private intelligence had reached the Kakanfo at Ilọrin, of all the plots and intrigues going on in the capital. However, he with his accomplices in the city deferred the execution of their design till after their arrival at the seat of war.

The army at length stood before Iwere and the Royal party, consisting of the King's brother, the Eunuchs, and the principal slaves, and their men, pointing to it said " This is the town to be taken by the order of the ALÂFIN."

The time was now come for the mutiny to break out. The Baṣọrun and the Òwòta at the head of the troops from the city, the Onikoyi and the Kakanfo leading those from the provinces now alleged as a pretext for the mutiny that " If the King had not aimed at our destruction, he would not have ordered us to this impregnable town. And besides, is not this the maternal town of King AJAGBO ? Are there not Kobis in the Queen Mother's palace there ? "

The watchword was now given " O yá " (now is the time) and so the whole army turned their swords upon the royal party and massacred them ! Chief Opele of Gbogun in particular was famous as a swordsman ; he made himself notorious on that occasion, and took to himself a name " A ri agada pa aburo Oba " (one who has a blade for slaying the King's brother).

The siege was immediately raised, and the whole army stood before the city for forty and two days. The King sent word to say if they have returned from the expedition, whether successful or unsuccessful, let them come in for an interview. The insurgent chiefs sent word back to say that the royal party had offended them and that the result had proved unfortunate. " Very well," said the King, " in any case, come in for an interview." Several weeks passed, and they were still encamped before Oyo irresolute as to what they should do next. At last an empty covered calabash was sent to the King—for his head ! A plain indication that he was rejected. He had suspected this all along and was not unprepared for it. There being no alternative His Majesty set his house in order ; but before he committed suicide, he stepped out into the palace quadrangle with face stern and resolute, carrying in his hands an earthenware dish and three arrows. He shot one to the North, one to the South, and one to the West uttering those ever-memorable imprecations, " My curse be on ye for your disloyalty and disobedience, so let your children disobey you. If you send them on an errand, let them never return to bring you word again. To all the points I shot my arrows will ye be carried as slaves. My curse will carry you to the sea and beyond the seas, slaves will rule over you, and you their masters will become slaves."

With this he raised and dashed the earthenware dish on the ground smashing it into pieces, saying " Igba la iso a ki iso awo, beheni ki oro mi o se to ! to ! " (a broken calabash can be mended, but not a broken dish ; so let my words be—irrevocable !)

He then took poison and died, after which the camp was broken up, and each of the chiefs repaired to his own place.

Thus ended an unhappy reign of about seven years, and Prince Adebo succeeded him on the throne.

Asamu Agba-o lêkan was the Basorun of this reign.

§ 3. The Rebellion of the Ọyọ Chiefs

The death of the late King was all that the rebel chiefs demanded, after which, the army entered the city, pillaged the palace and then dispersed each to his own place. From this time the spirit of rebellion and independence began to spread throughout the kingdom. Adebọ was placed on the throne with the nominal title of King, but without the authority and power of a King. It was his misfortune to have come to the throne at such a time, and he held the sceptre for only 130 days.

Afọnja the Kakanfo of Ilọrin and Ọpẹlẹ the Balẹ of Gbogun were the first to proclaim their independence, other chiefs soon followed their examples. This was the commencement of the break-up of the unity of the Yoruba kingdom, and the beginning of the tribal independence. Tribute was no longer paid to the King. The King's messengers and Ilaris no longer carried that dread as before, nor were they allowed to oppress people or enrich themselves with their goods as before.

As the King's authority waned, so also the respect and deference hitherto paid to the citizens of the capital ceased ; they were even treated disrespectfully and became the subjects of vulgar songs all over the country, a thing unheard of before ! Law and order were subverted, might triumphed over right, and the powerful chieftains turned their arms towards subverting town after town in the kingdom in order to increase their own wealth and power. Chief Ọpẹlẹ of Gbogun took Dofian and Igbo-Owu; he besieged Gboho but fell in that place, being shot with an arrow by the brave defenders.

Ọpẹlẹ was the only powerful chief Afọnja respected and having now no rival he resolved upon a scheme to reduce the provinces under his own sway, leaving the capital severely alone in complete isolation. He made no attempt on Ọyọ, had no aspiration after the throne knowing that was impossible of attainment ; it was sufficient for him that the King was powerless to check his ambition. In order to strengthen his hands in the enterprise he was about to undertake, he invited a Fulah Moslem Priest named Alimi to Ilọrin to act as his priest. Alimi in responding to his call came with his Hausa slaves and made Ilọrin his home. These Hausa slaves Afọnja found to be useful as soldiers. He also invited to Ilọrin a rich and powerful Yoruba friend at Kurwọ named Ṣọlagberu, who quartered himself at the outskirts of the town.

All the Hausa slaves in the adjacent towns hitherto employed as barbers, rope-makers, and cowherds, now deserted their masters and flocked to Ilọrin under the standard of Afọnja the Kakanfo, and were protected against their masters.

Under Ṣọlagberu's standard also flocked Mohammedans from Gbandạ, Kọbayi, Agoho, Kuwọ, and Kọbẹ. All in his quarter being Moslems, he named that part of the town OKE SUNA, i.e., the quarter of the faithful. They held themselves separate not only from the pagans, but also from the Fulahs or Fulanis their co-religionists.

From this time began the Jehad or religious war in the Yoruba country. Those who were enlisted as soldiers called themselves Jamâ (a Hausa word for the rank and file, as distinguished from the leaders). The mark of distinction between themselves and others was the *Kendé*, two large iron rings one on the thumb, the other on the 3rd or 4th finger of the left hand ; with this they welcome each other, striking the rings against each other to produce a sound. This is the sign of brotherhood ; hence they often say " O re kendé si mi, ọkan na ni wa," (he welcomed me with the Kende, we both are one).

The operations of the Jamâs were directed against the Igbôna tribe. The only towns of Yoruba proper destroyed were amongst the Ibọlọs viz., Irẹsà, Ejigbo, and Ilobu. The reason why these towns were destroyed we shall notice afterwards.

§ 4. THE RISING OF OJO AGUNBAMBARU

OJO surnamed AGUNBAMBARU was one of the surviving sons of the renowned Baṣọrun Gáhà. He had escaped to the Bariba country at the general massacre of Gáhà's children and relatives in the reign of King Abiọdun. Hearing of the present state of the country, he thought there could never be a more favourable opportunity for him both to avenge his father's death, and also to obtain his title without opposition.

He returned from the Bariba country with an immense army, entered Ọyọ, and under the pretext of espousing the King's cause, he put to death indiscriminately most of the influential citizens who were named as Afọnja's friends and allies. The Òwòta was the first victim of his ambition and revenge. On the whole, about 100 chiefs were despatched, who were either his father's enemies, or who might have opposed him in his main object.

He now set off for Ilọrin to measure strength with Afọnja the powerful Kakanfo, whose father was one of those who swelled Ọyabi's army for the overthrow of his father the Baṣọrun Gáhà, and who had succeeded the same Ọyabi in his title as Kakanfo. These were his grievances against Afọnja ; but besides these, Afọnja was the only person in the land after Ọpẹlẹ of Gbogun, who might have opposed him in his designs.

If Ojo had acted with prudence, he might have succeeded without the slightest doubt ; but his indiscriminate slaughter of the Oyo chiefs and others in his track, and his threats against the Onikoyi, tended to weaken his own strength on the outset. Fire and the sword marked his path to Ilorin, and so great was the dread of him, that such towns as Ogidi, Ogele and others, were deserted at his approach.

Adegun the Onikoyi being one of Afonja's secret friends, was on his list for destruction but he was reserved till after the war. Both were kept informed of all Ojo's movements, policy, and designs by the Oyo people who followed him trembling, not really as friends, but rather as traitors, their minds having been prejudiced against him, on account of his excesses, and a secret combination was formed between them and the Onikoyi, to desert Ojo at the most ciitical moment.

Ojo's army was further swelled by recruits from all the Yoruba towns who feared his vengeance should victory crown his efforts without their help ; and even the Onikoyi who knew himself to be a marked man, declared for him and swelled his army.

Afonja met this large army a great way off but he was defeated on three successive engagements. His army being completely routed he fled precipitately to Ilorin to fortify the town against the approach of the conqueror. Ilorin had not been walled, and there was no time to think of doing so now, so he had to extemporise fortifications, erecting stockades with the locust and shea-butter trees.

Ilorin was soon besieged and was nearly taken, as Afonja's courage was failing from repeated reverses, when private messages from the enemy's camp were sent to encourage him to hold out a little longer.

At last, the final decisive battle was to be fought, Afonja and his army were hard pressed on every side, being shut up within their forts, and the town was on the point of being taken when Adegun the Onikoyi and his accomplices suddenly gave way, in the heat of the battle, and the great conqueror irretrievably lost the day !

The traitors fled away in confusion, but Ojo and his trusty Bariba troops retreated orderly ; the Kakanfo could not follow up the victory by pursuing him from the dread he had of the Baribas, who were renowned for being good archers, and for their poisoned arrows. Ojo made good his escape with the remnant of his army. Being thus deserted by those whose cause he professed to espouse, Agunbambaru considered himself unsafe among them, and therefore returned to the Bariba country with the wreck of his army watching for another favourable opportunity.

After the fall of Ọpẹlẹ of Gbogun, King ADEBỌ declared war against the town of Gbogun, but he died at home during the progress of the siege. His reign was short and specially marked by troubles. The people now longed for peace, hence their pathetic songs :—

> " A pete, a pero, a fi Adebọ jọba,
> Abiọdun, pada wa jọba o ! "

(With deliberation and thought we made Adebọ King, O Abiọdun, do thou return to reign !)

Aṣamu was also the Baṣọrun of this reign.

§ 5. MAKU

Afọnja by new conquests and especially by his recent victory over Ojo became mightier still. The Igbônas having already been subjugated, he now proceeded to punish Irẹsa for being in league with Ojo, because no private message came to him from that place during the war.

Prince Maku ascended the throne without Afọnja's being consulted, and therefore he never sent any congratulations, nor repaired to Ọyọ to do homage as usual. A deputation was therefore sent to inform him that " The New Moon has appeared," meaning a new King has ascended the throne ; and he sent back this arrogant reply " Let that New Moon speedily set."

Maku's reign was very short, not exceeding two months (or *three moons* as Yorubas reckoned it).

He declared war against Iworo, and took the field in person. He suffered a defeat and retreated to Iwo (in the Metropolitan district). From shame he did not return to Ọyọ till the Ọyọ MESI sent word to him that he should not think of removing the seat of government to Iwo, or else why did he remain there ? His Majesty thereupon returned to the capital, and then he was politely told that no Yoruba King must survive a defeat. He thereupon committed suicide.

The Baṣọrun of this reign was the same Aṣamu.

CHAPTER VII

THE RISE OF THE FULANIS TO POWER

§ 1. THE SPREAD OF ANARCHY AND FALL OF AFONJA

AN interregnum followed the last reign but for how long, it is not known ; after which Májotu was placed on the throne. The whole country was at this time in the greatest disorder, wars and rumours of war being the order of the day. The tocsin of war resounded from every quarter, and the new King found himself incapable of coping with the situation.

The Epos, imitating the Kakanfo at Ilọrin organized a military band which they called *Ogo Wẹrẹ* (i.e. the Jackals) at the head of which was the Arẹsà but with what object in view, it was not known. The Kakanfo received the news with mixed feelings of jealousy and suspicion ; he sent and enquired of Toyejẹ the Balẹ of Ogbomọsọ his Ọtun i.e. commander of his right, what he understood by that movement. Toyejẹ could not say. War was in consequence declared against the Epcs, and several towns in that province were taken, only Ọgbàhágbàhá and Iwo amongst the principal towns escaped. Ilobu and Ejigbo amongst the Ibọlọs were also taken, and the *Ogo Wẹrẹ* suppressed.

Afọnja was now the sole power in the kingdom ; the King and the capital were left to manage their own affairs by themselves.

The Jamâs were increasing in number and in rapacity, to the utter distress and ruin of the country. When there was no war in hand they usually scattered themselves all over the land plundering the people and committing outrages. They would enter any house, make it their headquarters, from which they would pillage the neighbourhood and surrounding districts. They fed upon the cattle of the house and led the rest away at their leisure and pleasure.

Knowing the consequences to themselves and to the town if they were to attack these marauders, the country folk became rather disinclined to rear up any cattle or poultry to feed these thieves ; every one helped himself and family to whatever remained of their livestock, so that at one time there was not a single livestock to be found in country towns.

To further illustrate the gross licences of these Jamâs, slaves who had deserted their masters often returned to the same town, and even to the very house as a Jamâ, making their former master's house their headquarters for their rapine : masters who were kind to them formerly were now repaid by protection against the rapacities of their comrades ; unkind ones were now treated with heartless revenge. These fellows were not regarded now as slaves but as the Kakanfo's servants.

Thoughtful men were now apprehensive of the evils to the nation which the unrestrained licences of these Jamâs portended, but no one was bold enough to remonstrate with the Kakanfo, or even to appeal to him against their rapacities. Fagbohun the chief of Jabata alone had the courage to do so by virtue of his office as the commander of the left wing of the Kakanfo's army, and he incurred his displeasure for his boldness.

In order to get Fagbohun into his grasp, Afọnja summoned all the provincial Balẹs to him at Ilọrin, but Fagbohun having got wind of his intention escaped back to his town.

But Afọnja perceived his error when it was too late. Haughty and passionate, his very egotism was the cause of his fall. Fortune had carried him to such a high pitch of glory, he thought his fall was impossible ; besides, he had unlimited confidence in his Jamâs, and was not aware of their growing disaffection and disloyalty towards himself. He thought he could put them down whenever he liked, and was sometimes very severe with any act of insubordination, openly threatening them with suppression and annihilation. This threat only served to increase their disaffection. Too late, he saw what Fagbohun had warned him against. He failed completely to check their ambition, rapine and lawlessness. His threats and warnings were not heeded. Long impunity had increased their boldness.

At last, the Kakanfo was resolved to give effect to his threats and to disband the Jamâs, but he miscalculated his own strength. By the death of his brother Agbọnrin, and his head slave Lasipa he had lost his mainstay for these were men of power. He had offended all the powerful chiefs in the kingdom including his former friend and ally Sọlagberu of Oke Suna, and his priest Alimi by his high-handedness, lofty airs and haughty spirit.

Fearing lest these Jamâs should attack him suddenly if he were to delay their destruction, he sent a private message to the Onikoyi and other powerful chiefs in the country inviting them to make their appearance in Ilọrin suddenly, and to assist him in annihilating these Jamâs.

But the secret was divulged to the Jamâs, and they, losing no time, being headed by Alimi the priest, rose up against him before he could obtain help from abroad. Sọlagberu being a Yoruba, professed neutrality. The Kakanfo was closely besieged in his quarters, but he fought with his characteristic bravery. When he found himself overwhelmed by numbers, he despatched Bugare his head slave to solicit the aid of Sọlagberu ; but Sọlagberu treacherously detained him, saying, " Your Master has hitherto looked down upon us as his menials, and why does he now require our aid ? " This treachery, he lived to regret.   The great Kakanfo was disappointed on all sides.   As neither Bugare nor Sọlagberu made an appearance, he could not hold out till the Onikoyi's arrival ; he was compelled to fight within the walls of his house ; but when the house was set on fire, he rushed out again into the streets surrounded by his faithful few.   The insurgents surrounded them, charged again and again, but could not break their ranks. Afọnja himself in the midst of them was fighting most desperately, surrounded by the corpses of some of his faithful attendants. Seeing the day was lost, some of his followers became disheartened and deserted him, but the rest chose to die with him.   He fell indeed like a hero.   So covered was he with darts that his body was supported in an erect position upon the shafts of spears and arrows showered upon him.

So much dread had his personality inspired that these treacherous Jamâs whom he had so often led to victory could not believe he was really dead ; they continued to shower darts upon him long after he had ceased fighting.   They were afraid to approach his body as if he would suddenly spring up and shake himself for the conflict afresh ; not till one of them, bolder than the rest cautiously went near and placed an arrow in his hand and they saw he could no longer grasp it, that they believed he was really dead ! His corpse was taken up and burnt to ashes.

The crafty Alimi his treacherous friend took his helpless children and family under his own protection, alleging that it was a misunderstanding that led to the civil fight between himself and his old friend, in which the latter unhappily lost his life.   His house was rebuilt, and the remnant of his people were permitted to occupy it, but the government of the town passed over to the conqueror. His family, however, are highly respected at Ilọrin to this day. Thus passed away one who will always be remembered in the annals of the Yoruba country as the leader of the revolution which ended in the dismemberment of the Yoruba country.

The late Afọnja was a native of Ilọrin.   The city was built by his great grandfather, Laderin, whose posterity bore rule in her in succession to the fourth generation.   Laderin the founder, was succeeded by Pasịn, his son, a valiant chiet who opposed the renowned Gáhà when he was in the zenith of his glory.   Fearing his rising power, Gáhà drove him out of Ilọrin and he escaped to

Ọlà. He sent an army after him there which reduced the town and Paṣin was taken and slain. Alagbin the son of Paṣin succeeded his father, and in turn handed the government to his valiant son Afọnja with whom the rule ended.

Ilọrin is sometimes spoken of as Afọnja's Ilọrin. This is because he was the most renowned of her rulers, and not only so, but also because it was he who made it into the large city it now is.

There were several towns and villages around at no very great distance from Ilọrin e.g. Kanla, Oke Suna, Ganma, Ẹlẹhinjare, Idofian, Oke Oyi, Ibarẹ, Igbọn, Irẹsa etc. Most of them this restless warrior captured one by one and resettled them around Ilọrin so as to make it into what it has become. The able-bodied men he enrolled among his soldiers, and several women and children he sold into slavery, in order to have wherewith to maintain and supply arms to his war boys.

He was not actually of the royal family although often reckoned as such, but his mother was said to have been a home born slave of the palace, and he was brought up among the children of the royal family, hence the Ibàmu facial mark across the face seen in his descendants to this day.

Ilọrin now passed into the hands of foreigners, the Fulanis who had been invited there as friends and allies. These being far more astute than the Yorubas, having studied their weak points and observed their misrule, planned to grasp the whole kingdom into their own hands by playing one chief against another and weakening the whole. Their more generous treatment of fallen foes and artful method of conciliating a power they could not openly crush, marked them out as a superior people in the art of government.

§ 2. THE FIRST ATTEMPT TO RECOVER ILỌRIN FROM THE FULANIS

THE BATTLE OF OGELE

The tragic end of Afọnja the Kakanfo by the hands of his Jamâs had long been anticipated by thoughtful men who deprecated their formation, and had predicted the worst for the nation when slaves became masters.

The death of the Kakanfo struck the whole nation with such awe and bewilderment that it took the people nearly a whole year to bring them to their right mind. Seeing that the fate of the whole nation was trembling in the balance as it were, all the people united to avenge the death of Afọnja, while in the meantime, the crafty Fulani had been strengthening himself for the conflict. He had studied the Yorubas and knew how to circumvent them.

Toyejẹ the Balẹ of Ogbomọsọ and commander of the late Kakanfo's right, was promoted to the post of Kakanfo, and the whole nation was united under his standard to expel the Fulanis from Ilọrin. They encamped at a place called Ogele, where they were met by the Fulani horse aided by the powerful Yoruba Moslem Chief Sọlagberu of Oke Suna. Another fatal mistake of Sọlagberu's.

A sanguinary battle was fought in which the Fulanis were victorious. They routed the Yorubas and followed up their victory, which resulted in the desertion or destruction of a great many towns in the Ibọlọ province. The only important towns left in that part were Ọfa, Igbọna, Ilẹmọna, Ẹrin, and a few others.

The refugees could only carry away such of their personal effects which could be snatched away in a hasty flight, as the Fulani horse kept hovering in their rear. They found temporary refuge in any walled town where a powerful chief happened to be, there, it may be, to await another siege by the conqueror.

The distress caused by this calamity cannot be described. Aged people who could not be carried away were left to perish. The doleful lamentations of parents who had lost their children, and of thousands of widows and orphans were heartrending. Bereft of every thing, without money, or anything that could be converted into money in such hasty and sudden flight, they were reduced to abject misery and poverty among strangers, and could only support life by doing menial work by procuring firewood or leaves for sale and such like. A people who until recently lived in what for them was affluence and plenty, are now oppressed with want and misery brought about by the want of foresight, and the vaulting ambition of their rulers.

§ 3. THE SECOND ATTEMPT TO EXPEL THE FULANIS AND RECOVER ILORIN

THE MÙGBAMÙGBA WAR

After a short respite the Yorubas again rallied and resolving to rid the country of these hordes of marauders the Jamâs, made an alliance with Monjia, the King of Rabbah, that he may help them to extirpate the pests. The war took place somewhere between March and April at the time when the locust fruit was ripe for harvest.

The country was already devastated by the late wars, many towns were left desolate, and consequently there were no farms for foraging. What food there was in the Ilọrin farms were soon eaten up, and both the besiegers and the besieged were without provisions and had to live on the locust fruit (igbá). Hence the war was termed Mùgbámùgbá.

The Yorubas were again unsuccessful in this expedition. They had not yet learnt how to cope with cavalry and the Fulanis were expert horsemen. From successive deféats the Yorubas lost all courage, and victories one after another made the Ilọrins more confident, so that in the open fields they gained easy victories over the Yorubas ; and when they were protected within walled towns they reduced them by long sieges and famine.

On this occasion, the Ilọrins attacked the allies to advantage. They hid their horses in the rear of the allied armies and while a party of horsemen engaged them in front the main body of the cavalry suddenly bore down upon them from the rear and routed them. Monjia fled precipitately to his own country, leaving the Yorubas at the mercy of the victors. The Ilọrins followed up their victory and swept away all the towns in the direction of Ọfa, Erin, Igbọna etc. The Ọlọfa with Asẹgbe his favourite and wise Ilari escaped to Ikoyi.

§ 4. THE BATTLE OF PAMỌ

Alimi the Moslem priest, who was at the head of the foreigners at Ilọrin died after the last war and was succeeded by his son Abudusalami, who became the first King, or Emir, of Ilọrin. Ilọrin now passes definitely into the hands of the Fulanis as rulers, and affords a home for the Gambaris (Hausas) from whom the Jamâs were recruited.

The late Alimi was much respected at Ilọrin from his arrival there as a mere priest. At first he had no intention of making Ilọrin his home much less to embark upon a career of conquest ; and indeed when Afọnja and his Jamâs commenced their excesses he was prepared to return to his own country from disgust, but the elders of the Yorubas prayed him to stay and act as a check on Afọnja for there was no one else to whom he would defer and there was no telling how far he would go without someone to put the fear of God into him. The Kakanfo and the people of Ilọrin prevailed upon him to send for his family and make Ilọrin his home.

Alimi was a pure Fulani by birth and his wife also a Fulani lady. They lived together for a considerable time without any issue. The wife then consulted a Moslem priest as to her state of childlessness, and she was told to give out of her abundance to a distinguished Moslem priest a slave as an alms to the glory of of God, and she was sure to have children.

Having considered this matter over, she came to the conclusion within herself that she knew of no distinguished Moslem priest greater than her own husband, and therefore she gave to her husband one of her maidens as " an alms to the glory of God."

This maiden as Alimi's secondary wife became the mother of Abudusalami and Shitta his two eldest sons. The Fulani lady herself subsequently gave birth to a son named Sumọnu, who was nick-named Bẹribẹpo (one who cuts off head and post). Alimi afterwards took to himself a third wife by whom he also had a son, and, therefore at his death he left four sons to inherit his property. As will be seen below however, no advantage in the matter of government accrued to the son of the real wife (who was a pure white Fulani) above those of the slave wife who were coloured. Hence in the third generation, the chief rulers of Ilọrin have become black.

The power of the Fulanis was now very great, and they aimed at nothing short of the subversion of the whole Yoruba country, and the short sighted Yoruba war-chiefs were playing the game for them by their mutual jealousy of one another. One expedition followed after another and the result was the devastation and depopulation of the country. Far seeing men had predicted all this, if the various Yoruba families did not unite and expel the foreigners ; but jealousy and rivalry among the chiefs prevented unity of purpose. Allegiance was no longer paid to the King, not even in the capital. Intestine wars not only weakened the country, but offered it an easy prey to the common enemy.

Thus Toyejẹ the Kakanfo at Ogbomọsọ had a difference with Adegun the Onikoyi which at length broke out into an open war, each of them being now independent, and neither would submit to the other. The Kakanfo formed an alliance with the Oluiwo of Iwo, the Timi of Ẹdẹ and Sọlagberu of Ilọrin, and besieged the Onikoyi in his city of Ikoyi.

Sọlagberu had his own personal grievance to vent because the Onikoyi did not do homage to him or pay him tribute ; so he came with all the Ilọrin forces at his command. Abudusalami the Emir alone remained at home. The combined forces encamped at a place called Pamọ̀. The conflict was very fierce, and Ikoyi, hemmed in on all sides, was nearly taken, when Asegbe the Ọlọfa's Ilari, who was then with his master, a refugee at Ikoyi, saved the city by wise and judicious measures. He told his master and it also came to the Onikoyi's hearing that if he could be allowed to use his wisdom without being forbidden or thwarted, he could save the city. The besieged who were prepared to agree to any terms in order to obtain peace accepted the offer, although reluctantly, as Asegbe kept his plans to himself.

He sent a private messenger to Abudusalami the Emir of Ilọrin in the name of the Onikoyi, that he was besieged in his city, for the sole reason that he declared himself for the Emir of Ilọrin. The Emir again questioned the messenger " Is it true the Onikoyi declared for me ? " " Quite true, your Majesty," was his reply. " Then the siege must be raised," said the Emir.

Orders were now sent to recall Sọlagberu with all the Ilọrin forces, but he refused to obey orders. Again and again peremptory orders were sent, with the same result. The fifth and last message was to the Princes and other chiefs, to the effect that whoever would prove himself loyal should return home at once by the order of the Emir. The Ilọrin army now left the camp, leaving Sọlagberu alone behind together with the allies.

The next effort of the Emir of Ilọrin was to raise the siege at all cost, and hence he sent his army to reinforce Ikoyi. These Ilọrin troops entered Ikoyi, but for ten days did nothing but help themselves to every thing they could lay hands on, eating and drinking to excess. On the eleventh day they asked to be conducted to the scene of action. Then they joined battle, and completely routed the Kakanfo's army. Sọlagberu fled back to his quarters at Ilọrin, and the Yorubas were dispersed. Sọlagberu's feelings towards Abudusalami, can better be imagined than described. The men of note who fell in this war were,— The Timi of Ẹdẹ, the king of Ẹrìn, the Chief Aina-Abutu-Ṣogun, and Ayọpe.

Although Sọlagberu was allowed to remain in his quarters, yet the disaffection between him and the Emir of Ilọrin was very great, and every incident served but to heighten it. It grew from jealousy and illwill to opposition and resentment, and at length into a civil war. The Emir's party besieged Oke Suna, desperate battles were fought, but the besieged held out for a long time until they were reduced by famine. They were hard put to it in order to sustain life, living on frogs, lizards, barks of trees, etc., till no green thing could be found at Oke Suna. Sọlagberu had cause to remember with regret his treachery towards his friend Afọnja, in his hour of need, at the hands of these very Jamâs. At last, Oke Suna was reduced and Sọlagberu slain.

Abudusalami the Fulani Emir having now no rival in any Yoruba King or Chief, the Onikoyi having declared for him, the Kakanfo's army shattered, and Sọlagberu slain, resolved upon subverting the whole kingdom, and making himself the King of the Yoruba country. The remaining Yoruba towns spared were placed under tribute. He was aided in his enterprise by the Jamâs whose tyrannies and oppression greatly exceeded those which they practised in the days of Afọnja, which were so galling to the Yorubas : formerly it was only the livestock that were freely taken away, but now, they entered houses and led away women and young persons at their pleasure. It was literally enslaving the people !

To such a wretched and miserable condition were the people reduced, especially in the provinces.

CHAPTER VIII

THE CONSEQUENCES OF THE REVOLUTION IN THE SOUTH

§ 1. The Owu War

THE kingdom being now in a disorganized condition each tribal unit constituted itself an independent state. The Ifẹs in the east, and the Ijẹbus in the south formed an alliance against the Owus to the south-west of the former and north-west of the latter.

The Owus (although now domiciled with the Ẹgbas) are a family quite distinct from Ẹgbas or Ọyọs. Hardihood, stubbornness, immorality, and haughtiness are marked traits in their character, so much so that it has passed into a proverb " A bi ọmọ l'Owu, o ni akọ tabi abo ni, ewo ni yio ṣe ọmọ nibẹ ? " (a child is born at Owu, and you ask male or female: which will be a proper child ?) Either sex when roused by passion would sooner die than not take dire revenge. Their manners were totally different from those of the Ọyọs, but from the days of Sango they have been very loyal to the ALÁFIN of Ọyọ.

As warriors, the Owus were hardy, brave, and courageous, they had no guns, their weapons consisting of the Agedengbe (a long heavy cutlass) with bows and arrows. Coming to close quarters with cutlass in hand was the mode of fighting characteristic of these brave people.

The cause of the war between these three families was this :— We have already stated above that during the reign of King ABIỌDUN, express orders were sent from Ọyọ to the Ọwọ̀ni of Ifẹ, and the Olowu to prevent Ọyọs being kidnapped and sold at Apomu, the great market town where the interior and the coast people met for trade. Now, since the commencement of the revolution, and the disorganized state of the kingdom, the practice was revived. The rebellion has rendered the Central Authority powerless, but there were still some men of considerable power and influence in the land, such as Adegun the Onikoyi who was the premier provincial king, Toyejẹ the Balẹ of Ogbomọṣọ the Kakanfo, and Ẹdun of Gbogun.

A message similar to that sent by King ABIỌDUN was now sent by the Onikoyi and the Kakanfo conjointly to the Olowu, and he in carrying out his orders had to chastise several towns ; hence

Ikoyi Igbo, Apomu, Ikire, Iràn, Ile Olupọ̀mi, Itahakun, Isẹyin Odò, Iwàtá, Akinbọtọ, Gbàngán, Isọpẹ, Iwarọ̀, and Jagun, were destroyed by war, all in Ifẹ territory.

The Ọwọ̀ni of Ifẹ was highly incensed at this and declared war against Owu. The command of the war was entrusted into the hands of his commander-in-chief Singunsin. Other war-chiefs associated with him were:—Ọkansà, Gbogbo Olu, Wasin, Alọdẹloko, etc. Their first encampment was at a place called Dariagbọn a farm village of one Olupọ̀na, next at Sifirin at the confluence of the Ọsun and Ọbà rivers.

The Ifẹs thought they would make an easy conquest of Owu for they themselves arẹ a brave people, and hence this war song in their peculiar dialect :—

Ẹ maha ja (a) gba,	Let us cut ropes,
Igbekùn ia mu a di	Our captives to bind.
Ifa Olowu	The Olowu's Ifa (god of palm nut)
Èwa la mu a se	With our. corn we'll cook.

The Owus received the news that war was declared against them with great indignation. They considered themselves *the* power in these southern regions, and what infatuation has led the Ifẹs to this presumption ? With one consent they immediately marched out to meet them at this great distance. The engagement was a hand to hand fight in which the Ifẹs were completely routed ; their army was all but totally annihilated, only about 200 escaped to tell the tale of their dire misfortune !

The King of Iwo, in whose territory this disaster took place did not admit the survivors into his town for fear of incurring the displeasure of his formidable neighbours the Owus, whom he dreaded and of whom he was jealous, but he so far sympathized with them that he advised that they should not undergo the humiliation of returning home, and he allowed them to rendezvous in a place called Adunbiẹiyẹ for the purpose of recruiting their army and to try another chance, secretly hoping that fortune may favour them next time, and being ill at ease with such a formidable neighbour as the Owus.

This small army remained in this place for about 5 years, unable to return home from shame, and yet could not obtain re-inforcement adequate for the great enterprise.

Just at this crisis the Owus and the Ijẹbu traders had a serious complication at the Apomu market. The dispute arose from the sale of alligator pepper, and it resulted in the rash expedition against Apomu by the haughty Owus ; the town was destroyed, and many Ijẹbu traders and residents lost their lives or their all.

The king of Iwo thereupon advised the Ifẹs to form an alliance with the Ijẹbus, who, like them, have now a grievance against Owu. When this was done, the Ifẹs at home were now willing to re-inforce their wrecked army for a conjoint attack upon Owu.

The Ijẹbus now declared war against Owu, and crossing the Ọṣun river, encamped at the farm of one Ọṣọ.

The Ijẹbus were better armed than either their allies or their foes, and indeed, than any of the interior tribes, for, being nearest to the coast, they had the advantage of obtaining guns and gun-powder from Europeans in exchange for slaves. They were remarkable marksmen. The older men with their cloths tied round their waists, and the ends left flowing behind, constituted the regular fighting column : being too old or too heavy to run away, they were obliged to be courageous.

The Owus were mad with rage at the receipt of the news that anyone, such as the Ijẹbus, had presumed to declare war against them who (as they considered themselves) were the first power in these parts (southern Yoruba). They rushed out to check the progress of the Ijẹbus as they did that of the Ifẹs, and attacked them furiously cutlass in hand. But they were compelled to fall back from the steady fire of the Ijẹbus which did great havoc amongst them. Summoning courage, the Owus offered another obstinate battle, but they were again repulsed with a heavy slaughter, having lost in the first and second engagements about 40 of their leaders. This was the first check to their pride. They rallied, however, and retreated to a short distance, and then again ventured upon another attack, the Ijẹbus advancing as they were retreating : they finally met, and once more fortune was against the Owus, and they fled precipitately to fortify their city against the expected siege.

The Ijẹbus with their allies the Ifẹs encamped to the west of the city of Owu, under a large tree called the Ògùngun, east of the town of Oje. We may here remark that although the Egba towns of Ọfa and Oje were about a mile and two miles respectively from Owu, yet so bitter was the animosity between them that not only did these towns refuse their aid to Owu, but rather rejoiced at its misfortunes !

The Owus fought with their accustomed bravery, and in one furious assault, routed the allies, and pursued them to Oje, Ọfa, and Ibadan. The first two places were deserted in the general confusion and panic, and all sought refuge at Ibadan. Here the allies received reinforcements from the Egbas, and from the Ọyọ refugees from the north whose homes had been devastated by the Fulanis and who were now scattered about the provinces homeless, and without occupation. Glad to find some occupation in arms, these refugees flocked to the standard of the allies in numbers ; and thus strengthened, the war was renewed. The siege lasted about 5 years (usually reckoned as 7). The city was obstinately defended by the brave inhabitants from the walls, and from the forts built on the walls of the city. One Sàkúlà was an expert sharp shooter who was never known to miss his aim ; he contributed much to the defence of the town. But he was at the same time a good-natured man, kind and merciful to his enemies. Whenever he saw a young man hazarding his life too close to the forts in order to show valour, pitying his youth, he used to hail at him from the fort, and warn him as follows :—" I give you your life for to-day, but do not venture here to-morrow or you shall die." And he was always as good as his word. Thus Sàkúlà defended the city heroically and killed many a valiant warrior.

At last, the allies held a council of war, and were determined to get rid of Sàkúlà on the next day. The Ijẹbus, who had guns were the foremost, and the whole army directed their fire and showers of darts at the fort where Sàkúlà was fighting, all kept shooting at that one spot, until they saw Sàkúlà fall, suspending from the fort !

Owu was now deprived of her bravest defender, and famine also began its fatal work within its walls.

It was at this time the Owus began for the first time to eat those large beans called popondo (or awujẹ) hitherto considered unfit for food ; hence the taunting songs of the allies :—

Popondo l'ara Owu njẹ,   The Owus now live on propondo,
Àjẹ f'ajaga bọ 'rùn.   That done, their necks for the yoke.

Unto this day, whoever would hum this ditty within the hearing of an Owu man, must look out for an accident to his own person.

For all the famine within, the besiegers could neither scale the walls, nor force the gates open, until Akinjọbi the Olowu opened a gate, and escaped to Ẹrunmu, one of the principal towns in his territory. The chief of this place was one Oluroko who was nearly related to the Ọwọni of Ifẹ. Oluroko protected his overlord. The allies pursued the Olowu to this place, but Oluroko when called upon to answer for his conduct, submitted himself, and asked for pardon, showing that he could not have acted otherwise and be blameless. The allies saw with him, and pardon was accordingly granted him.

Ikija was the only Ẹgba town which befriended the city of Owu in her straits hence after the fall of the latter town, the combined armies went to punish her for supplying Owu with provisions during the siege. Being a much smaller town, they soon made short work of it.   After the destruction of Ikija,[1] the allies returned to their former camp at Idi Ògùngun (under the Ògùngun tree).

Owu was thenceforth placed under an interdict, never to be rebuilt ; and it was resolved that in future, however great might be the population of Oje—the nearest town to it—the town walls should not extend as far as the Ògùngun tree, where the camp was pitched. Consequently to this day, although the land may be cultivated yet no one is allowed to build a house on it.

[In the year 1873 Akinyẹmi one of the sons of one Bolude of Ibadan happened to build a substantial farm house at Owu. Latòsisà then the Kakanfo at Ibadan ordered it to be pulled down immediately, and Akinyẹmi was fined besides].

After the fall of Owu and Ikija, the army was not disbanded, but the commanders of the Ifẹ and of the Ijẹbu armies returned home to give an account of the war to their respective masters, but the remnants still in the camp were continually swelled by recruits from Ọyọ refugees whom the Fulanis had rendered homeless.

After a time the Ijẹbus in the camp invited the allies home to their country as friends ; then they broke up the camp at " Idi Ògùngun " and withdrew to Ipara in the south.

It should be noted that the Owu war marked a definite period in Yoruba history. It was here for the first time gunpowder was used in war in this country, and it was followed by the devastation of the Ẹgba townships and the foundation of modern Abẹokuta and Ibadan, to be related in due course.

§ 2. Consequences of the Revoution :—The Lasinmi War

Whilst the Owu war was raging in the south, the northern provinces were in no less disturbed condition.   The Onikoyi, not content with being the first and greatest of the provincial kings took advantage of the disturbed state of the country to usurp the King's prerogative and aimed at subjugating the other chiefs under his own authority.   Toyẹjẹ the Kakanfo at Ogbomọsọ was alone his rival and in order to oppose him, the Onikoyi created Ẹdun of Gbogun an opposition Kakanfo to him.   But Toyẹjẹ continued in office, and so there were two Kakanfos at this period, a thing quite unprecedented.

During this reign, it was said that a European traveller visited Ọyọ to whom the King granted an interview.   This was most probably Clapperton (vide Clapperton's *Last Expedition to Africa*,

---

[1] The site of Ikija is now an Ibadan farmstead known as Karaole.

Vol. I., Chap. IV.).   The King was said to have complained bitterly of the rebellion of his subjects, and that he was King only in name : he craved for military assistance in order to reduce his rebellious chiefs ; but as it was impossible for the stranger to afford this, he tried persuasive measures. He visited the several powerful chiefs in the country, remonstrated with them pointing out forcibly how " Unity is strength." His advice was favourably received and the result was a congress held at Ikoyi in which all the principal chiefs were present, and to which the King sent an Ilari.

After a prolonged deliberation they came to an agreement to return to their former loyalty and allegiance. The Onikoyi then asked that the Ilari be called in to bear the good tidings to his master ; but when called aloud by his official (Ilari) name " Kafilegboin," the chiefs all gave a start and were much surprised to hear the name of the Ilari sent to them. " What ! Kafilegboin ! (i.e. let's have it on stiff)   Is that then the King's intention ? A name which implies implacability, resolute determination and inexorableness! Very well then, let the rebellion continue. No one among us can consider himself safe at the hands of the King should we return to our allegiance, since he can send us such an Ilari at a time as this when he wants to win us back!"   The congress was then dissolved.

Whether the King did this intentionally or not, we cannot say; but Yorubas being very diplomatic, and very suspicious of one another, he should have sent one whose name implies conciliation or harmony if he wished to win back the chiefs.

But we consider all this from God in order that the sins of the nation may be purged by judgment from above.

Shortly after this, there was a serious complication between the Kakanfo at Ogbomoso and the Timi of Ede. Ede had been tributary to Ogbomoso, but after the Pamo war it threw off its allegiance, and the Kakanfo had long been seeking for an opportunity to reduce it again to subjection. One cannot say what was the real cause of the war, but there can be no doubt that the Kakanfo made something or other a pretext for commencing hostilities. The Kakanfo, however, did not take the field in person as he considered it only a small affair ; he sent Lasinmi his Balogun to reduce the town.

Ede was beseiged, and for 15 days desperate battles were fought, but the town was defended heroically.

Bamgbaiye the Timi of Ede at that time, was one of the richest of the provincial kings, and it was due to his largesses that the town was able to hold out so long. Every morning he ordered bushels of corn (maize) to be well cooked, and placing large earthenware pots at certain intervals right round the walls of the town, he filled them alternately with the cooked corn and cool drink (well-mashed Ẹkọ) or pure water, for the combatants, so that no one need complain of hunger or find an excuse for leaving his post by day or by night.

The strength of the besiegers and the besieged was well-nigh spent, when Asegbe the Qlofa's wise Ilari appeared again on the scene to prevent further bloodshed and to save the town. With a small body guard, he approached the walls of the town, so as to be heard. With his usual persuasive eloquence he induced the people to surrender in order to avoid further bloodshed. " We are all the same tribe and one family, and why should we destroy one another in the very face of our common enemy, destroying us from without ? I give you my word, that if you capitulate the siege will be instantly raised. "

These words were soon conveyed to the Timi, and so glad was he that he sent Asegbe a bottle of gin, which he and his attendants drank on the spot and the empty bottle was sent back as a token of good-will, that the gift was accepted.

The Timi sent again to enquire how the negotiations might best be carried on. Asegbe advised him to send 10 bags of cowries and 10 goats, and to capitulate and the siege would be raised. Asegbe returned to the camp to report his success, and the chiefs were all glad and thankful. Towards the evening the Timi paid the fines imposed and capitulated and the siege was raised.

Bamgbaiye was the richest Timi that ever ruled Ẹdẹ. His large garden was full of goats and sheep without number so that all the green grass in the garden was eaten up. But the creatures were all miserable looking as they were more in number than could be properly fed at home ; they should have been driven by herdsmen to the pastures to graze, but the war without prevented this. It was even said that they were so hungry that any one entering the garden would have to defend himself with a stick to prevent his clothes being eaten off his body! When presents had to be given, or fines and indemnities paid in token of subjection, or to purchase peace as above related, selections were made from the well-favoured ones among them and the enemy appeased. He could afterwards recoup himself by taxation.

Ẹdẹ prospered under the rule of this king.

§ 3. State of the Capital During this Period

King Majotu was well advanced in age, before he was called to the throne, and consequently the business of state was for the most part left in the hands of the Crown Prince Adewusi surnamed

Fùhúnijì : unfortunately, he was neither wise nor prudent but rather a dissolute and licentious prince, extravagant and cruel to a degree. His weak qualities were, however, eclipsed by his largess. He acted more like a monomaniac than like a rational being. His father was too old and weak to check him. Notwithstanding his exalted position he usually spent days and nights out-of-doors, roaming from one quarter of the town to another without returning home.

Whenever he was going to spend a night in a house in any quarter of the town, he usually gave orders that his suite should start about half-an-hour after he had preceded them. He would clothe himself in tatters, carrying an axe, a club, or a stick just like a madman ! He would reach the gate of the chief whose guest he intends to be, long before the arrival of his suite, and mingle with the crowd of spectators who were there waiting to see the sight of a royal equipage, listening to their remarks and especially to those of his intended host.

If the host were to complain of the undesired visit of an unprincipled coxcomb putting him to unnecessary trouble and expense, and that he would rather do without the honour of his visit, or any other such remarks that he might make, he would hear it all with his own ears. As soon as his attendants arrived he would instantly get himself into the midst of them, change his rags for a magnificent robe, and step forth as becomes a prince. When the host now rushed forward to show his respect, and bid him a hearty welcome, etc., he would burst out "You hypocrite, did you not say *so and so*, when you heard I was coming to you on a visit ? I'll curb your lying tongue." When the host lay prostrate and trembling, conscious of guilt and pleading for mercy, he would deal him heavy blows with his club, which more often than not killed or disabled him for life, and in some cases, if he survived, he would order him to be sold into slavery.

But if the host were really solicitous about giving him a loyal welcome, and showed himself desirous of giving him an entertainment worthy of his rank, he would hear and know for himself, so that when he joined his attendants and came forward to greet his host, he would accept his welcome and bid him not to care about how he should entertain him, but would himself order refreshments and entertain the host and all present out of his own bounty, and give him presents lavishly besides. If this prince is spoken of as cruel, and as having killed or sold into slavery several of his father's subjects, it was in this way.

An instance related of his liberality was as follows :—
Upon a festival called Isulẹ̀ customarily held in the month of

July, all the members of the royal family gorgeously dressed go in procession to a certain place to worship the spirits of their dead ancestors. The demonstrations on these occasions are very imposing, and usually end with gifts from the Crown Prince.

On one such occasion, this Prince gave the Ologbo who accompanied him a common gown, but the latter refused to accept it, saying it was not worthy of the dignity of His Royal Highness. The Crown Prince thereupon took off his robes in which he went to the Isulè, and gave them to the Ologbo, and ordered other members of the royal family to do the same.

Adewusi had his own good qualities but his enormities were revolting ! He accounted it a privilege to commit indecencies under the open sky, surrounded by his attendants and Eunuchs holding large cloths in the four corners as a curtain to shield him from sight. In his train were always some of his wives and mistresses.

He would commit rape with impunity, and whether to show that he was above law, or out of pure spite to the chiefs, in his visits to any of them it was his custom on entering their houses, to perform the same act in the open court-yard before he took his seat in the piazza !

This beastly conduct bemeaned him in the estimation of the Ọyọ chiefs, and not only had he lost all respect from them on that account, but, on one occasion, he very nearly lost his life at the hands of the Baṣọrun, in whose palace he had the temerity to venture on the same action ! On his arrival, his supernal highness came out to receive him as his guest, but was shocked to find that Adewusi made no exception in his lewd practices in regard to himself. He returned in a rage to his inner apartment, to reappear with a drawn sword, and would have despatched him and his mistress on the spot had not the Prince and all his attendants fled away in confusion. The Baṣọrun's servants pursued after them with clubs and dispersed them.

Adewusi had no one among all the chiefs to appeal to for sympathy, as he had offended every one of them in the same way, although none but the Baṣọrun was able to resent it; hence their sympathy was rather on the side of the Baṣọrun.

But the ultimate result of this would have been serious for the Prince had not his wise and aged father conciliated the chiefs.

Knowing what the outcome would probably be, His Majesty summoned a meeting of the chiefs, noblemen, and other important personages in the city and said to them in a parable :—" The Crown Prince was my creditor when we were in the other world, and when I could not pay the debt, I escaped to this world. He pursued me hither demanding payment, and being born of royalty, I was able to pay off my debt.

But my difficulty is this—for the purpose of which I have summoned you all my chiefs for your advice and help.   The Crown Prince not content with the payment, demanded that I should carry back the amount paid to the other world ; and for this I crave your advice and help."

The Ọyọ chiefs asked His Majesty for an explanation of the parable and his reply was as follows :—

" The enormities of the Crown Prince in your quarters and in your houses, I have heard of, and what would have been the result, if the Baṣọrun had killed him in his house, we all know. Would it not have cost me my own life also ? What I crave of you is that in future I should be exonerated, and not be charged with his conduct." The Ọyọ chiefs were appeased and promised not to implicate the father in the crimes of his son.

Added to the scourge of the sword, divine judgment fell upon the nation in famine also and pestilence.   Towards the end of this reign there was a famine in the land for two years which obliterated every trace of the plenty they revelled in when there was peace and prosperity.   Many died from it.   It was a struggle for many to be able to support their family, especially those in exile ; but the richness of the soil enabled those whose towns were not destroyed to render great assistance to their guests the refugees. But unfortunately there was a dearth of the latter rains and the dry season crops could not be planted.   This following closely after the Lasinmi war caused the distress to be more severe.

Gbogi, an Ijẹṣa town was attacked and destroyed only for the sake of the provisions it contained, no one caring for slaves or booty.   The staple of the Ijẹṣas being yam and not corn, the famine was less felt amongst them, as the yam crop does not depend upon the latter rain.   This famine was called Iyan Yāmọrọ.

It was said that a subscription was made by several families to the amount of 6 heads of cowries, and a special messenger was sent to the Ẹgba territory to buy corn. The return of the messenger was eagerly looked forward to, and at length he returned with a merry heart whistling as he walked along : but there was no load on his head, the 6 heads worth of corn was carried in a bag slung on his shoulders ! and he protected it beneath the cloth he wrapped himself with, so that no one may know what he had with him. It was a treasure ! It was shared by the subscribers by counting the grains.

This calamity was followed by a pestilence called the Pẹhẹ,

a disease of the respiratory organs like the recent (1892) fatal epidemic of Influenza ; thousands were swept away by it, and King MAJOTU was among its victims. Of a long succession of Kings, it was his good fortune to have died a natural death.

At the death of the King, the Crown Prince was told to die with his father, according to the custom now prevailing. But he was unwilling to do so, and was giving out bribes liberally to the chiefs that they should give him their support ; and trusting to his former largess to the people, he was determined upon a civil fight, hoping for a general rising in his favour ; but Akāwo, his bosom friend quietly undeceived him, and advised him to die honourably, or he would have the mortification of seeing himself deserted at the most critical moment by those on whom he counted most to espouse his cause. Adewusi then committed suicide, and Prince Àmọdo was placed on the throne.

CHAPTER IX

FURTHER DEVELOPMENT OF THE ANARCHY

§ 1. Evil Days for the Capital

Prince Amodó was one of the grandchildren of Ajampati the twin brother of King Ajagbó. He came to the throne at a time when the kingdom was distracted by anarchy and confusion. The Fulanis having an eye on the capital of Yoruba-land, but not being confident enough to make an attack on the city whilst there were so many powerful chiefs in the land, who might suddenly return to their allegiance, were using prudence and astuteness to spread the disaffection. They were fanning the flames of discord by allying themselves with one or other of the chiefs known to be rebellious against their lawful sovereign. None of the provincial kings now paid tribute to Oyo or acknowledged the authority of the King. He was virtually King of the capital only.

In order to have a powerful friend and ally in whom he could confide in time of emergency, King Amodó made an alliance with Lanloke the chief of Ogodo, a market town, at the confluence of the river Niger, where Yorubas and Tapas met for an exchange of merchandise. Ogodo was originally a Tapa town, but subsequently the Yoruba population predominated, nearly all the children of influential Oyo chiefs resided there permanently for the purpose of trade. King Amodó cemented and strengthened this alliance by giving his daughter to Lanloke to wife, and treating him as an independent sovereign.

To show how weak and contemptible the Aláfin has become, Lanloke most brutally and cowardly beat the princess his wife actually to death, and boasting over it, took to himself the nickname, " My name is Amodó, and I put Amodó to death. My name is Ajẹbaba, and I enslaved Ajẹbaba."

Fearing the resentment and vengeance of Oyo for this act, he hastily formed an alliance with the Ilorins, and assumed the aggressive, and so besieged Oyo. Oyo at length capitulated and the Ilorin troops entered and sacked the city. Oyo was plundered of nearly everything, but no captives were made excepting some Oyo beauties who were carried away with the spoils.

Jimba, one of the head slaves of the Ilorin Emir was the chief spoiler. He took away all the Egúgun dress, and forced the citizens to accept the Koran, which necessitated every one to change his name for an Arabic name, the only alternative being the sword.

Thus at length Ọyọ became tributary to Ilọrin !

§ 2. THE THIRD ATTEMPT TO EXPEL THE FULANIS

THE KANLA EXPEDITION

AMODÓ was ill at ease under the yoke of the Fulani Emir of Ilọrin, and he prevailed upon all the Yoruba chiefs throughout the country to unite and rid themselves of their common enemy. Apparently they were united, but between the capital and the provinces, the spirit of disaffection and jealousy was strong. It was understood full well that the King's policy was to use them together to rid himself first of the common enemy, and then to subdue the rebel chiefs one after another, by force of arms.

But the Ilọrins on the other hand were more diplomatic. In order to facilitate their plans, they made friendship with some of the Yoruba chiefs who were men of power, and who, if united, would be able to oppose them successfully ; such were Prince Atiba of Agọ Ọja, Ẹdun chief of Gbogun, the most powerful Yoruba general of the day, and Adegun the Onikoyi the premier provincial king.

Whenever there was war with the Ilọrins these chiefs usually acted against their own real and national interests, either by betraying their own nation and people, or by giving their backs to the enemy without shooting an arrow, and thus allowing the Ilọrin horse the advantage of out-flanking their foes.

King AMODÓ having prevailed upon all the chiefs to come together, declared war against the Fulanis, and Ilọrin was besieged by a formidable army raised throughout the country.

Adegun the Onikoyi was suffering from indisposition and was really unfit to take the field ; but Ẹdun of Gbogun his rival, forced him to go to the war, secretly planning with the Ilọrins that he would give way in the heat of the battle, in order that Adegun might be taken alive ! This battle took place at Kanla from which the expedition was named.

Ẹdun having carried out his act of treachery, the Onikoyi was surrounded by the Ilọrin horse ; but he fought, and fought bravely and fell like a hero. Thus the ALÂFIN's army was routed, and the people fled away in confusion.

It was at the time when the rivers overflowed their banks, and a number of people were drowned at the river Ogun. The most notable chief drowned on this occasion was Ọja the founder of Agọ́ (the present Ọyọ). Prince Atiba, one of the rising power, rode his powerful horse into the river, and narrowly escaped being drowned.

The Yoruba towns deserted at this defeat were Eṣiẹlẹ and Popó.

§ 3. THE VICISSITUDES OF IKOYI

The fall of Adegun at the Kanla war left the kingship of Ikoyi vacant. There were two aspirants to the title, viz., Siyẹnbọla, the son of the late Adegun, and Ojo, the son of Adegun's prede-cessor. The majority of the people was for Siyẹnbọla, and Ojo's partisans were but few. Ojo, however, went to Ọyọ to have the title conferred on him by the Suzerain as of yore, and he succeeded in obtaining the ALÂFIN's favour in his claim.

King AMODÓ was glad for this mark of recognition and hoped for the gradual return of the provincial kings to their allegiance. He therefore made Ojo take a solemn oath that he would ever be loyal to him. His Majesty strictly charged him against making any league with Ẹdun the rebel chief of Gbogun through whose town he must pass to reach his home at Ikoyi. This charge was occasioned by the treacherous conduct of Ẹdun at the Kanla war by which the ALÂFIN lost the day. " I am a King," said Amodó, " and you are now a king. Kings should form alliance with kings and not with a commoner."

The King justly anticipated what would happen, for when Ojo the new Onikoyi reached Gbogun on his way home, Ẹdun sought his friendship and alliance, and pressed him to take an oath with him, that they would always be faithful to each other. Ojo stoutly refused to take the oath, alleging that it was unbecoming for a king to take an oath with one not of royal blood. But Ẹdun was a man of power, and the Onikoyi was already in his clutches being in his town and he felt he could do whatever he liked with him ;, he therefore insisted that the oath should be taken before the Onikoyi could leave his town. Ojo was in a dilemma, his oath of allegiance to the ALÂFIN forbade him to dis-obey the King's charge, and now he was at the mercy of this miscreant. He had now no option, the oath must be taken and the only way out of it the Onikoyi could find was to delegate one of his attendants to perform the business for him, as the fitness of things required from the inequality of their respective ranks. The Kakanfo considered this an insult to his dignity, and he resented it by ordering Atàndá one of his own attendants to take the oath with the Onikoyi's delegate.

Whilst this was taking place at Gbogun, tidings reached Ikoyi that Ojo had succeeded in obtaining the title from the ALÂFIN, and Siyẹnbọla who had usurped it therefore fled from the town with all his party to Ilọrin.

The remnant of Ojo's party at home who did not accompany him to Ọyọ met him at Ẹsiẹlẹ with the news that the town had been deserted from disgust that he should reign over them. The Onikoyi was too weak to proceed to occupy Ikoyi with his small party, he therefore remained at Ẹsiẹlẹ.

A week after this, the Ilọrin horse came against Ẹsiẹlẹ to espouse the cause of Siyẹnbọla, and they had seven days of hard fighting, but finding it not such an easy business to rush the town, as they had supposed, they retreated home to make full preparation for a regular siege at the ensuing year.

The siege was accordingly laid in the following year. Ẹsiẹlẹ held out for a long time, being heroically defended by its balogun Kurumi, and another notable war-chief Dadò (of both of whom we shall hear more afterwards). When they could hold out no longer, the war-chiefs deserted the town, leaving mostly the women and children at the mercy of the conquerors. Ojo the Onikoyi was slain, and Siyẹnbọla having now no rival obtained the title of Onikoyi from the Emir of Ilọrin, and returned with those of his party who went with him to Ilọrin to re-occupy the town. Thus Ikoyi was re-peopled but no longer as a vassal state of Ọyọ but of Ilọrin. The city was rapidly refilled by those of Ojo's party that escaped the fall of Ẹsiẹlẹ and they now acknowledged Siyẹnbọla as their king.

Ẹsiẹlẹ also was again re-peopled, as it was not actually destroyed by war but deserted under stress. The inhabitants were permitted to remain as they were because the siege was laid against the town on account of the late Onikoyi—no longer alive.

Shortly after this there was a serious complication between Ẹdun of Gbogun the Kakanfo and Dada the Balẹ of Adeyi which broke out into a war. Edun marched his army through Ẹsiẹlẹ to besiege Adeyi, but Fasọla the Balẹ of Ẹsiẹlẹ hearing that the Kakanfo's army was to pass through his town having hardly recovered from the effects of the late war, and dreading the devastation and pillaging of farms consequent on such a march, deserted the town. So Ẹsiẹlẹ was again desolate, the people finding refuge at Ogbomọsọ and Ikoyi.

The expedition, however, was unsuccessful. The Kakanfo's army suffering many reverses, it had to be given up.

§ 4. THE GBOGUN WAR AND FALL OF ẸDUN THE KAKANFO

Gbogun was the last of the powerful towns in the country and as the aim of the Fulanis was the subversion of the whole country, a pretext for war was soon found in order to lay siege against her.

Abudusalami the Emir of Ilọrin threatened the Kakanfo with war if he refused to pay allegiance to him ; Ẹdun accepted the challenge and began at once to make a vast preparation, offensive and defensive.

Ikoyi being already a vassalage of Ilọrin and a neighbouring town, Ẹdun regarded her as an enemy and insisted that it should be deserted at once or he would take her by surprise. Siyẹnbọla the Onikoyi sent ambassadors to Gbogun to arrange terms of peace but Ẹdun refused to hear of any such thing and threatened to destroy the town the next day, if not deserted at once, as he would not afford the Ilọrins a base of operation against him at such close quarters. There being no alternative, Ikoyi was a second time deserted and Siyẹnbọla escaped to Ilọrin.

Gbogun was soon besieged by the Ilọrins and desperate battles were fought, the defenders fighting heroically and could not be overwhelmed until at last the city was reduced by famine and thus Gbogun fell, the last of the powerful towns of Yoruba.

Ẹdun the greatest Yoruba general of the day escaped by way of Gbodo where he was overtaken, being hotly pursued by the Ilọrin horse. He had with him a handful of veterans and such was the terror his very name inspired that the pursuers did not dare to offer him battle.

The men of Gbodo were torn between two opinions whether they should afford protection to their fallen general, or allow him to escape in peace. But the pursuers insisted on his destruction, saying " If you allow him to escape, your lives will go for his life as you will show yourselves thereby to be an enemy to the Emir of Ilọrin." This decided the men of Gbodo ; in order to save themselves they took up arms against the fallen general and overwhelmed him and his faithful few, the brave man himself falling under a shower of darts fighting gallantly at the head of his little band. His head was taken off, raised upon a pole and carried in triumph to the camp and from thence to Ilọrin ; Ọdūewu his eldest son and some of the distinguished war-chiefs who were taken being compelled to ride behind it in order to grace the triumph of the conquerors.

On the 3rd day after their arrival at Ilọrin Ọdūewu succeeded in purchasing the head of his father and had it decently buried to save himself from disgrace.

After the fall of Gbogun, Siyẹnbọla returned the second time to Ikoyi. Faṣọla the Balẹ of Eṣiẹlẹ, who had escaped with his family and a few followers to Ogbomọṣọ, also returned to his town. On his way to Eṣiẹlẹ, he was the guest of Siyẹnbọla the Onikoyi for three days. He and his sons Siñolu and Abọsẹde and his eldest daughter Ọmọtajò were feasted on the flesh of an elephant just killed and brought to the Onikoyi. This was regarded as an auspicious omen.

§ 5. The Polẹ War and the Death of the Abuousalami

The Fulanis having subdued all the chiefs in Yoruba proper and reduced the large towns by conquest or annexation, his ambition led Abudusalami to turn his attention to the Ijẹsa tribes for conquest, and hence he sent an expedition to that province.

The Fulanis depended more on their cavalry than on their infantry, the latter being armed with only a sword and a club. In a country with primitive forests like those in the Ijẹsa province horses were of no avail, and hence the Ijẹsas chased the enemy in their mountain tracks and cut in pieces the greater part of their horsemen. In pursuing their foot soldiers, they cry after them " Polẹ, Polẹ," which in their dialect means *Down, Down*. From this circumstance this expedition was termed the Polẹ war.

After the return of this expedition Abudusalami fell sick and died. He was a successful king who raised the Fulani power to that pitch of glory which Ilọrin has attained.

The late Abudusalami and Shitta were the children of the slave wife of Alimi and being the two eldest they naturally took the lead.

On their father's death Abudusalami divided his property into four equal parts, called all his brothers to take each one his portion beginning from the youngest. His half brothers took theirs and went away, but as Shitta was about to take his Abudusalami stopped him and sent him away with a walking stick. With the slaves and riches of himself and his brother, he kept up his royal estate and had sufficient means to carry on the war and to effect the conquest of Yoruba proper and hence at his death the throne and the property devolved upon Shitta, the half brothers having no longer any claim. Abudusalami hereby secured the throne of Ilọrin to his own and his brother's descendants to the total exclusion of the half brothers and the succession to this day alternates between the family of the two.

The children of the lawful wives (especially those of the Fulani lady) considered the throne theirs by right, but as they could not claim anything of the royal estates they were excluded from the throne as well. Abudusalami was succeeded by his brother Shitta. Olusi the Balẹ of Ogbomọsọ also died about this time.

CHAPTER X

THE SPREAD OF ANARCHY AND POLITICAL DISPLACEMENTS

§ 1. THE DESTRUCTION OF ẸGBA TOWNS

We have seen above (Chap. VII) that after the fall of Owu, and the punishment inflicted upon some Ẹgba towns for secretly befriending the beleagured city, the camp at Idi Ogũgun broke up, and the leading Ifẹ and Ijẹbu generals returned home to their respective masters, but the rest of the allied armies with the Ọyọ refugees were invited by the Ijẹbus to Ipara, a town of Ijẹbu Rẹmọ. Making this place their headquarters, these restless bands of marauders found occupation for their arms in conquering and subjugating several towns in Ijẹbu Rẹmọ under the Awujalẹ of Ijebu Ode, viz Odè, Ipẹru, Ogérè and Makun.

Pretext was soon found for waging war with the Ẹgbas who were then living in small villages scattered all over the area between Ipara and Ibadan. Several expeditions were made from their base at Ipara, and Iporo, Eruwọn, Ọbà, Itoko, Itẹsi, Imọ, Ikereku, Itoku, etc., were taken.

The following are the names of the distinguished war-chiefs in this campaign :—Ọyọ chiefs—Oluyedun, Lakanlẹ, Oluyọle, Adelakùn, Ọpẹagbe, Abitiko, Yămati, Oluọyọ, Koseikò, Abidogun, Apàsá, Ọsun, Laleitan, Bankọle, Fadeyi Ọgani-ija, Agbeni, etc.

All these chiefs joined the allied army as private soldiers, but the fortunes of war raised them to positions of great distinction. Notwithstanding this, they were looked down upon by the Ifẹ and Ijẹbu leaders under whose auspices they joined the war against Owu, and had no voice in their councils. But they were soon to show their superiority.

Ifẹ chiefs—Mayẹ (the generalissimo in the absence of Singũsin) Ogũgú, Derin-Okùn, Labọsinde, Ọgini, Arẹgbẹ, Olufadi, Degòkè, Kugbayigbe, Oluyọde, Epo, Kudayisi.

Ijèbu chiefs—Kalẹjaiye, Amoibo, Ọsunlalu, Ogũade, Arọwọsanlẹ, etc.

Rich with the booty of these expeditions, and finding no fresh fields of operation for their arms they decided to disband the army. The Ijẹbu war chiefs returned home and the Ifẹs set out to return by way of Oòrùn ; the Ọyọs who had nowhere to go to accompanied them. There were thousands of Ọyọs already in Ifẹ districts.

At Oòrùn (a Gbagura town) they found fresh employment for their arms when the men of that place refused them a passage. Another circumstance also occurred which hastened the siege of Oòrùn and the fall of the remaining Ẹgba townships.

A dispute arose between the people of Idomapa a neighbouring town and the Gbaguras about territorial limits which at length broke out into war and Oluwọlẹ the king of Idomapa who was the weaker of the two combatants asked the aid of Labọsinde one of the leading Ifẹ war-chiefs, and through him the rest of the Ifẹ and Ọyọ war-chiefs against Ajibọsọ the king of the Gbaguras. The allies encamped at Idomapa and Oòrùn was the scene of conflict, where the Gbaguras concentrated all their forces to oppose the Idomapas and their allies.

The Gbagura army was swelled by re-inforcement from Ika, Ọwẹ Ikija, Iwokoto. The contest was furious and one Ọga Ọhọrọ a gallant war-chief greatly distinguished himself in the defence of Oòrùn. As long as he could handle his bow and arrows, the enemy was kept at bay ; but he fell in an engagement, and at the same time famine had commenced its direful work, and so the assailants successfully reduced the town.

As their fighting men had all fallen at Oòrùn the conquest of all the rest of the Gbagura towns was complete. Oòrùn when captured was fired ; being a town situated on a high hill, the conquerors were able by the aid of the light to pursue their victory to the next town which they found deserted, and so on to the next and the next until they reached Ọjọhọ.

The towns deserted and overrun that night were Oòrùn, Ijaiye-maja, Kosi-kosi, Ikerekuiwere, Ọra, Ibadan. Ọfa and Oje were also deserted, but the conquerors did not know of this till three days after as they lay outside their line of march.

From Ibadan they followed up the conquest to Ojokodo Iwohahá, and Egũoto ; all these places were deserted and plundered in one night and by the dawn of day they were before Ọjọhọ. Ọjọhọ offered a stout resistance and being weary from long marches the conquerors retired to find a resting place. Of all the towns overrun the previous night, Ibadan alone they found not destroyed by fire, and so this marauding band hastily occupied it, the war-chiefs taking possession of any compound they chose, and their men with them and thus Ibadan was again re-peopled but not by the owners of the town, but by a composite band of marauders, consisting of Ọyọs, Ifẹs, Ijẹbus, and some friendly Ẹgbas, Mayẹ a bold and brave Ifẹ chieftain being their leader. Next to him was Labọsinde also an Ifẹ, but, through his mother, of Ọyọ descent. These two leaders were men of different character and opposite temperament. Mayẹ was of an irritable temper, in manners rough and domineering, and never failed at all times to show his contempt for the Ọyọs, chiefly because they were homeless refugees. At the head of the Ọyọs was Lakanlẹ a bold and brave leader who alone of all the Ọyọ war-chiefs could venture to open his mouth when Mayẹ spoke. Labọsinde on the contrary was most agreeable and very fatherly in his manners and therefore much respected by all.

Ibadan now became the headquarters of these marauders from which place Ọjọ́họ̀ was besieged and at length taken. At this time also Ikẹiyẹ Ọwẹ and a part of Ika were deserted ; the Ika people escaping to Iwokoto. All these werẹ Ẹgba villages of the Gbagura section.

§ 2. Foundation of the Present Abẹọkuta

As stated in the preceding section there were some friendly Ẹgba chiefs who joined the marauders at Idi Ogũgun and at Ipara, and now they were all living together at Ibadan. The most influential among them were :—Lamọdi, Apáti, Ogunbọna, Oṣo, Gbewiri, and Inakoju. Ogũdipẹ, who afterwards became a notable chief at Abẹokuta was then but a blacksmith and a private soldier.

Rivalry was so rife among these various tribes that altercations were frequent, and one led to a civil war. In a public meeting held at the Isalẹ Ijẹbu quarter of the town, Lamọdi an Ẹgba chief shot Ẹgẹ an influential Ifẹ chief down dead with a pistol, and in the commotion which ensued Lamọdi himself was slain. For fear of the Ifẹs avenging the death of Ẹgẹ the Ẹgbas withdrew in a body from Ibadan and encamped on the other side of the Ọnà river, about 3 or 4 miles distant. Here also they were ill at ease and after divination they sent for one Sodẹkẹ to be their leader, and they escaped to Abẹokuta then a farm village of an Itoko man, and a resting place for traders to and from the Okè Ogun districts. Sodẹkẹ was at the head of this new colony until his death. This was about the year 1830 They were continually swelled by Ẹgba refugees from all parts of the country, and also by Ẹgba slaves who had deserted their masters. At Abẹokuta the refugees kept together according to their family distinctions, viz.:—

1. The Ẹgba Agbẹyin comprising Ake the chief town, Ijeun, Kemta, Imọ, Igbore, etc. These were under the Alake as chief.

2. Ẹgba Agura (or Gbagura) comprising Agura the chief town Ilugun, Ibadan, Ọjọ́họ̀, Ika, etc., under the Agura as chief.

3. Egba Oke Ọna with Òkò the chief town. Ikija, Ikereku, Idomapa, Odo, Podo, etc., under the Ọṣilẹ as chief.

Here also the Owus joined them, one common calamity throwing them together. It was some considerable time after that Ijaiye joined them, and so by degrees all the Egba townships about 153 became concentrated at Abeokuta, the new town comprising Ijemo Itoko and a few others who were already on the spot.

Until the death of Sodeke in A.D. 1844 the Egbas never spoke of having a king over them, Sodeke wielding supreme power in a very paternal way. Of external relations, very little (if any) existed, each of these families managed its own affairs, and there was no properly organized central government.

Even after the foundation of Abeokuta there were still some Egbas residing at Ibadan. Egba women also who were unable or unwilling to go with their husbands to the new settlement were taken as wives by the new colonists at Ibadan and they became the mothers of most of the children of the first generation of the new Ibadan.

From this it will be seen that the current tale of the Egbas being driven from Ibadan by the Oyos is lacking in accuracy. Such then is the foundation of the present Abeokuta.

§ 3. The Egbado Tribes

The Egbados are a Yoruba family bordering on the coast. They were very loyal subjects of the ALÂFIN[1] before the revolution that altered the political state of the country. The Olu or king of Ilaro was the greatest king of the Egbados, having about 443 ruling chiefs under him, himself a crowned vassal of Oyo. The ancient custom was for the ALÂFIN to crown a new Olu every three years. After the expiration of his term of office the retiring Olu was to take 10 of his young wives, and whatever else he chose and proceed to the metropolis, and there to spend the rest of his days in peace. There was a quarter of the city assigned to them known as Oke Olu (the quarter of the Olus).

The parting between these young wives and their mothers was most touching. The relatives generally accompanied them as far as to Jiga or Jako, and the wailings and lamentations on such occasions were as one mourning for the dead. Hence the saying

---

[1] In the year 1902 the head chief of Ifo died, an Egbado town about 6 hours distant from Ilaro. Sir Wm. MacGregor, then Governor of Lagos, asked the chiefs of the town who their overlord was, to appoint a successor, they replied the Alâfin of Oyo. He was much puzzled at this. He told them he was too far, they had better apply to the Alake of Abeokuta. Evidently they at least were not affected by the revolution.

" À ri ẹrinkan l'Ẹgba iri Olu " (the Olu is seen by the Ẹgbas but once in a life time).

Next to the Olu of Ilaro came the Onisarẹ or king of Ijăna, but his was not a crowned head.   The appointment of the Onisarẹ was also from Ọyọ, and a Tapa was always selected for that office. The reason for this is not known.   The Olu and the people of Ilaro, as well as the Onisarẹ and the people of Ijăna were so to speak but one people; they observed the same national customs, and the same laws, their national deity was the god Ifa and the annual festivals in its honour were observed in both places one after the other in the same month, each lasting for a week, the one commencing the day after the completion of the other so as to give the people of both places an opportunity of taking part in each other's festivities.

The following ceremony usually brought the anniversary to a close :—Both these kings were to meet in a certain place in the open field midway between the two towns : two mounds of earth previously raised opposite each other served for each king to enthrone himself upon, the one turning his back to the other as they were not to see each other's face.   The one to reach the spot first would sit with his face turned homewards, the other on his arrival does the same, and thus they sit back to back, each one looking homewards ; communication with each other was by messengers.   A numerous retinue always attended either to take an active part in the proceedings or as mere spectators.

This custom served as a bond of union and friendship between them, a people having identical interests.

The kings of Ijakọ and Jiga are called Abẹpa: they had a strange custom of standing seven days and seven nights in the seventh month of the year during the anniversary of their national deity, after which they may sit down.

The Ẹgbados were a commercial people and of a quiet and peaceful disposition and, as a result, were considered very wealthy. They termed themselves " Ẹgbaluwẹ " to distinguish them from the Ẹgbas in forest lands (now inhabiting Abẹokuta) whom they designated " Ẹgbalugbo." They traded in kola nuts, palm oil, and fish.   They had very few slaves, and their wealth consisted in beads and native cloths.   From Kano and Sokoto they imported what they termed Ẹrinla and Esuru beads in quantities, as they esteemed them very valuable.

THE BEGINNING OF DISTURBANCE IN THE ẸGBADO DISTRICTS.

The Ijaka War.   A serious complication arose between the people of Ijăna and Ijaka which ended in the conquest and fall of this peaceful tribe. War was very foolishly declared against Ijaka by the Onisarẹ of Ijăna which resulted in the defeat of the aggressor.

There was a rich and influential chief at Ijăna called Dẹkun, in whom the Ijănas trusted when they rashly declared war, not knowing that he was a great coward. At the height of the battle Dẹkun dastardly gave way and the Ijănas were completely routed. He escaped to Oniyẹfun and those who like himself escaped with their lives murmured against him, and even insulted him to his face, calling him " white-feathered," " a poltroon," " the cause of their defeat." Dẹkun was offended at this, and more from shame than from the insult he resolved never to return to Ijăna. He remained at Oniyẹfun for a considerable time, until a war (which we shall notice afterwards) met him there.

On the return home of the remnants of the defeated Ijănas Dẹkun's house was plundered.

Dẹkun afterwards spent several years at Ijaka with whose king he contracted friendship, and later perhaps in order to avenge the insults received, he took refuge with the king of Dahomey whom he asked to espouse his cause. The king of Dahomey destroyed Inùbi where thousands of Ọyọ refugees made their home ; of these about 13,000 were children or grandchildren of Ọyọ nobles or well-to-do people " whose fathers had kept horses " before the devastation of the Yoruba country by the Fulanis. They were all put to the sword by the Dahomians with the exception of one Ẹkũọla to whom Dẹkun was under some obligation, and he evidently interposed and had his life spared. Thus did Dẹkun resent his so-called insult. Such was the beginning of the fall of this peaceful Ẹgbaluwẹ tribe, and the inroads of the Dahomians into the Yoruba country.

Two years after the destruction of Inùbi, the king of Dahomey took Rẹfurẹfu by capture in war.

A Short Account of Dẹkun. Dẹkun was an Ilari of Ọyọ, placed at Ijăna by one of the ALÂFINS as the King's representative. Instead of upholding the King's interests when the great chiefs of the kingdom rebelled against their sovereign, he also rebelled against his master, and made himself great at Ijăna, by appropriating all taxes and tributes he should have forwarded to Ọyọ. He joined the marauders at Ipara in the devastation of the Ẹgba principalities, but at the occupation and settlement of Ibadan he returned to Ijăna, and did not reside with the new settlers. In one of their expeditions Sodẹkẹ was captured by him, and served him for years as his horse boy. But providence destined Sodẹkẹ for a great position in life and hence he eventually became the renowned leader of the Ẹgbas to Abẹokuta.

Dẹkun was rich but childless, although he kept a numerous harem.   There is a story told in connection with him which is worth recording :—

A woman of an abandoned character called Iṣokun had left her husband and children at Ipokia to become Dẹkun's mistress. This woman on one occasion went on a long journey and required some justification for her prolonged absence ; on her way home, she saw at the last sleeping place of the caravan, a mother with her new born babe 3 days old, she quietly stole this babe from its mother's side while she was fast asleep, and immediately went off with it.   On reaching home she gave it as an excuse for her long absence that she was *enceinte* of this child before she left home, and when she might have returned she was unfit for travelling but immediately after delivery she was able to hasten home.

Dẹkun rejoiced that after all he was now a father and to demonstrate his joy he invited all the principal men and chiefs of Ijãna and of the adjacent towns to a feast held in honour of the event.   Presents poured in from every rank and station for the child and the supposed mother according to the father's dignity and every care and attention were bestowed on them.

Meanwhile the real mother was in eager search for her lost baby.   She at first supposed that it might have been a wolf that snatched it away from her side, and consequently she explored the surrounding woods if haply she might find the bones.   Failing in this she was resolved to seek for it in the town ; and taking it quarter by quarter she entered every house asking the mothers to produce their babies, in order to identify her own.   On the 18th day of search she reached Dẹkun's house and discovered her baby with Iṣokun.   Then there arose an uproar about the child and a regular " to do " about the whole affair with assertions and denials on either side.   A proper investigation of the case having been instituted, and signs of recent delivery not found in Iṣokun she was thus brought to book ; the whole truth was at length extorted from her when her arms were bound behind her back with a new rope, till both elbows and wrists met.

From shame she escaped from Ijãna to her former home at Ipokia where she had left her sons and daughters to become Dẹkun's mistress.   Her name was put to vulgar street songs, being branded as a man-stealer.

Dẹkun lived in Dahomey till the accession of King ATIBA of the present Ọyọ who demanded him from the King of Dahomey, and he was given up.   He was charged as a rebel and a traitor, condemned, and publicly executed at the market-place.   The sentence was universally held to be a just one.

Dẹkun it seems had a son called Onibudo ; perhaps an adopted one as is customary with childless chiefs ; his life was spared, but he was degraded by the ALÂFIN and the mean title of Agbọmọpa was conferred on him and his descendants.

§ 4. THE FOUNDING OF MODAKẸKẸ

By the Fulani conquest of all the principal towns in Yoruba proper, fugitives from all parts escaped southwards and settled in all Ifẹ towns except at Ile Ifẹ the chief town. They were in great numbers at Mòro, Ipetumodù, Ọdũabọn, Yàkioyó, Ifa-lende, Sọpẹ, Warọ̀, Ogi as well as in Apomu and Ikirè.

Just about the time of the Lasinmi war a Mohammedan at Iwo called Mọhọmi invited the Fulanis of Ilọrin to extend their conquest to the towns of these Eastern districts, as the Ọyọs were then engaged in a civil war. The Ilọrin army accordingly came and overran the above mentioned towns. The latter made no attempt at resistance but simply deserted their towns and with all the Ọyọ refugees escaped to Ile Ifẹ their chief town and were well received and protected by Akinmọyerò (alias Ọdunle) the then reigning Ọwọ̀ni of Ifẹ. The most important Ọyọ chief amongst the refugees was the Aṣirawo, the king of Irawọ̀.

Before long, a feeling of disaffection became evident between the Ifẹ citizens and the exiles. The Ọwọ̀ni spared the Ifẹ refugees, but enslaved all the Ọyọs making them " hewers of wood and drawers of water " after having murdered the Aṣirawọ their chief. One of the Aṣirawọ's sons enslaved was the afterwards renowned chieftain of Modakẹkẹ, Ojo Akitikori by name.

The Ọyọs built their houses, cleaned their farms and performed all sorts of menial work for them. This was towards the close of Akinmọyerò's reign. Gbanlarè who succeeded him was more favourably disposed towards the Ọyọs, and they now received better treatment, but this was not for long. Gbegbaaje succeeded Gbanlare, and the bad feeling and cruelty against Ọyọs were revived ; many of them were even sold into slavery. This king also was soon murdered.

Winmọlajè who succeeded Gbegbaaje utilized the services of these Ọyọs in repelling the inroads of the Ijẹṣas into his territory. From appreciation of their services, he was kindly disposed toward them ; but the hatred and malice of the Ifẹ citizens generally was so strong that not even the well-disposed could curb the virulence of the opposite party.

A pretext was soon found again for murdering the well disposed Ọwọ̀ni. Adegunle succeeded to the throne : he was partly of

Yoruba descent on the mother's side and hence was the benefactor of the Ọyọs all his days.

Before he accepted the crown of Ifẹ he made the chiefs take an oath that they would not find a pretext for murdering him as they did his predecessors, but would allow him to die a natural death; they readily agreed to this request. Soon after his accession knowing full well the disposition of his people, he took the precaution at once of accumulating ammunition of war, in order to make himself strong against any attack from the populace. He was not of a warlike disposition but was rather given to agricultural pursuits ; hence his nickname " Ab'ewe ila gbàgàdà gbagada " (one whose okra leaves are very broad) from his garden plantations.

The Ọyọs were by this time growing to be an important section in the community, having for their chief one Wingbolu a smelter of iron.

The Ifẹ nature and spirit of the times soon became evident. Notwithstanding the oath, a pretext was soon found for a civil war against their king, but he was too strong for them; he defeated and suppressed all the refractory chiefs among them.

After the civil fight the Ọwọ̀ni called Wingbolu and asked him why he and the Ọyọs were neutral at the time of the insurrection. He replied boldly " Had I been invited by your opponents, does your majesty think you would have proved victorious ? Or if you had invited us, would not your victory have been more complete? "

Thinking over these significant remarks the Ọwọ̀ni who had some strains of Ọyọ blood in him was resolved not on exterminating these Ọyọs as some others would have done but rather on emancipating them. He appointed them a settlement outside the walls of the city deputing one Adewọrò to accompany Wingbolu to the site and mark out the settlement. On the Ọyọ chief himself he conferred the title of Ogunsùwa signifying One whom Ogun (the god of war) has blessed with a fortune. That has become the title of all the chief rulers of Modakẹkẹ to this day.

By a royal proclamation all Ọyọs were to leave the city of Ile Ifẹ for the new settlement, and accordingly the settlement grew rapidly from new arrivals every day. The new settlement was named Modakẹkẹ, a term said to have been derived from the cry of a nest of storks on a large tree near the site.

Modakẹkẹ was first built in a circular form as a single vast compound of about 2 miles in circumference ; the enclosed area was left covered with trees and high grass, each individual clearing out a small space in front of his dwelling. This was done for the sake of mutual protection as no one need to go out of the compound for sticks or thatch for roofing purposes. Modakẹkẹ was in 1884 a town of between 50,000 and 60,000 inhabitants.

By dwelling in a separate settlement it was not meant that they should hold themselves independent of the Ifẹs. They were still loyal to the Ọwọni.

A sedition was again raised for the purpose of murdering the Ọwọni for emancipating the Ọyọs, but he receiving help from the new settlement crushed the rising completely, and all the ringleaders were put to death among whom was the son of a rich lady called Olugboka.

As Ab'ewe-ila could not be murdered by force of arms, the Ifẹs finally succeeded in poisoning him and the first intimation the settlers had of the death of their benefactor was from the street song of the Ifẹs " They are deprived of their King, woe betide the Ọyọs."

The late king was denied a royal funeral, and was buried like any common man and all his slaves were seized by the Ifẹs, but the Ọyọs amongst them went over in a body to the new settlement.

Modakẹkẹ was soon besieged by the Ifẹs, but they were repulsed with a heavy loss in dead, wounded, and captives. The Modakẹkẹs captured about 12070 of them, but they had not the heart to enslave their former masters and benefactors and hence all were released. Thirty days after this defeat, one Ogunmakin an Ifẹ chief receiving re-inforcement from Oke Igbo, Modakẹkẹ was again attacked. The Ifẹs were again badly beaten and they were pursued right home, and the city of Ifẹ taken by an assault. The victors now ventured to sell their Ifẹ captives as slaves, but reserved of their women-folks for wives. The Ifẹs escaped to Isọya, Oke Igbo, and other Ifẹ towns where they remained for many years till about the year 1854 when the Ibadans were engaged in the Ijẹbu Ẹrẹ war. Chief Ogunmọla of Ibadan sent messengers from the camp to negotiate terms of peace and bring the Ifẹs home, as it would never do to let the cradle of the race remain perpetually in desolation and the ancestral gods not worshipped. Kubusi was the then reigning Ọwọni who could no longer remain in exile, but promised that if allowed to return home the past would be obliterated ; no restitution of anything will be demanded of the Modakẹkẹs, not even of their wives who might have been appropriated.

But no sooner did they return home than all the Ifẹ women deserted their present husbands with all the children born to them and returned to Ile Ifẹ.

Notwithstanding their present relations the Modakẹkẹs still acknowledged the supremacy of the Ifẹs and by mutual arrangement they had their representatives in the Ifẹ assembly. Thus they lived together harmoniously till the year 1878 when the whole of the Yoruba country was again embroiled in war, and the latent animosity broke out afresh in an open fight, and the Ifẹs weie again worsted as we shall noti e hereafter.

THE REVOLUTION IN THE EPO DISTRICTS

§ 1. The Destruction of the Epos and the Death of Ojo Amepo

Notwithstanding the Fulani devastations, there were not wanting still among the Yorubas powerful generals, who could successfully oppose them if only they would act together. One such was Ojo Amepo the Kakanfo.

Ojo Amepo was one of the generals of the late Kakanfo Afọnja of Ilọrin ; he inherited the lion-like spirit of his chief. After the fall of Afọnja he resided at Akesẹ̀, where he found employment for his enterprising spirit in waging intestine wars with the Epọs, and became a great man and a terror in that district. Thus Ojo Amepo usurped the prerogatives of the ALÂFIN in that district. ` He took Iwàre, Okiti, Ajerun, Koto, Ajabẹ, towns near Ijaye, and he assumed the title of Kakanfo in opposition to Ẹdun of Gbogun whom, however, he survived (as Ẹdun himself formerly did in opposition to Toyejẹ of Ogbomọṣọ) showing the state of anarchy in the kingdom as there can be but one Kakanfo at a time.

Amepo was a good horseman and an intrepid warrior. Agọ was one of the towns in the Epo district. Ọja the founder perished at the Kanla war as we have already noticed, and the only man of power then in that town was Prince Atiba formerly of Gudugbu, and he was in friendly alliance with the Ilọrins and abetted them, when they were resolved upon subjugating the Epọs.

Chiefs Amepo, Salakọ, and Ojomgbodu were opposed to the Ilọrins, and the latter soon found a pretext to wage war upon them and to destroy their towns.

The Ilọrins encamped at Agọ Ọja against Ojomgbodu which was about 6 or 7 miles distant. The Kakanfo at Akesẹ̀ sent Dadò his commander-in-chief at the head of a detachment to reinforce the beleaguered town ; associated with Dado were Adekambi, Sọṣọ, Desẹ and Lagbayi, all distinguished men. A portion of the Ilọrin army was encamped against Wònwòro at the same time, and the Kakanfo also sent Ayò another distinguished war chief to protect the place. Both these places were obstinately defended and, but for the tragedy which befell the Kakanfo at home, they might have held out longer even if they could not repel the enemy eventually.

Amepo the Kakanfo being anxious about his men when he heard no news from the seat of war, rode out one morning dressed in his red uniform with only about 20 boys as his attendants. He took the path leading to the seat of conflict to listen if perchance he would hear the sound of musketry showing that his people were still holding out and the town not yet taken.

He dismounted under a large tree in the fields, and most unfortunately for him was discovered from afar by a company of Ilọrin horsemen, who had made excursion into the Wònwòro farms, and were returning to their camp at Agọ-Ọja by way of Akesẹ̀. He found himself in a predicament all too late, his body guards were, alas! too young to defend him, and his corpulency prevented him from springing at once upon his horse and making good his escape. So he was slain there under the tree, and his head and hands were cut off and carried in triumph to the camp before Ojomgbodu. But before doing so, the Ilọrin horsemen rode back to Akesẹ and called upon the town to surrender under threats of immediate destruction. The Kakanfo being slain, and the war-chiefs absent at Ojomgbodu, the town Akesẹ surrendered at discretion ; but as soon as the horsemen were gone the inhabitants packed up and deserted the town.

The Kakanfo's army at Ojomgbodu of course did not know of the tragedy that had befallen their master at home until they were informed the next morning in the battlefield by the Ilọrin horsemen taunting them. To confirm the truth of their statement, Amepo's speckled hand which was cut off was thrown to them within the town wall for identification. " Know ye whose hand that was ? We have slain your master ! What is the use of further fighting ? Woe betide you if you do not surrender at once." The men were panic stricken and would have fled there and then but for the presence of mind and brave speech of Dado the commander-in-chief. He said to them " The death of our master is no reason why we should give way, let us fight like brave men and not show the white feather." Turning to the besiegers he said " We are here to defend the town not our master whose misfortune is only an incident though a lamentable one. You prepare yourself for a battle to-morrow, for you shall receive such a severe encounter as you have never experienced before ; you will then know how brave men can resent treachery." This speech created order among the troops and the Ojomgbodu people also were re-assured ; but it was only a ruse in order to make good their escape, for by daybreak, before the Ojomgbodu people knew that they were deserted, Dado had retreated with his army in good order and escaped to Ika-Ọdan.

§ 2. THE OCCUPATION OF IJAYE AND END OF DADO

Ika-Ọdan now became the home of the flower of the army from the Ọyọ provinces. The leaders here were the only brave generals who would not submit under the yoke of the Ilọrins, and who held out still until such time that fortune would veer round to their side.

These refugees soon became masters of the town, the wives and daughters of their hosts became theirs, and the hosts themselves practically their menials.

Everything at home and in the farms was soon devoured as they lived only by foraging. When nothing remained in the Ika-Ọdan farms they extended their operations into the Ijaye farms. When the Ijayes could no longer endure it, and their farms were nearly all eaten up they attacked these marauders ; a skirmish ensued and the foragers finding the men of Ijaye too strong for them, sent home for re-inforcements.

Kurūmi's advice was for conciliatory measures, considering that these proceedings were rather hard on the people, who really could not help attacking the foragers. But Dado their leader was for opposition. " Cowards " said he, " what can the Ijayes do ? " Saying this, he hastily put on his armour and rushed on to the scene of the conflict. He was allowed to go on alone, none of the other war-chiefs followed him.

The foragers seeing their leader coming were inspirited and put forth more efforts, and he led them to victory. They drove the Ijayes home, and pressed so closely on their heels that the latter could not rally to defend the town, but deserted it and fled on, till they escaped to Ika-Igbo. Ijaye now fell into the possession of the assailants who did not fire it, but simply occupied it as was done at Ibadan, each one taking possession of the finest compound he could get.

Dado now sent to invite Kurūmi and the rest of the war-chiefs at Ika-Ọdan, and they came and took possession of Ijaye. Thus that town passed out of the hands of the Egbas, and became an Ọyọ town to this day.

At a special meeting convened to consider their future course it was resolved that they should make Ijaye their home at least for the present until they could see a brighter prospect of dislodging the Fulanis from Ilọrin and then return to their own homes. They therefore took possession of the lands and farms along with the houses and proceeded to sow the farms, lest famine should follow the present abundance. Thus they became proprietors of houses, lands and farms not their own. The fields were extensively cultivated, all the war-chiefs with the sole exception of Dado their leader, paid great attention to agriculture, going to their farms daily.

Dado was of a more restless spirit and was indifferent to agriculture. Nothing delighted him more than the rattle of musketry, for he was never in his element unless he was at the head of his army directing a battle. He often frightened his people home from farm, mistaking the volleys Dado ordered to be fired for an attack on the town. The other war-chiefs petitioned him again and again not to cause such an alarm, but he usually replied in a haughty manner: " Cowards, were I such as you I could not have brought you here, when you wished to negotiate peace with the aborigines."

Casting this at their teeth day by day, his colleagues felt hurt but were afraid of opposing him till one day Kurūmi summoned up courage to do so and was backed by the other chiefs, a civil war ensued and Dado was expelled the town.

Dado's Later Career.—To trace the subsequent career of Dado we have to anticipate some events of history yet to be narrated.

Dado was bold and brave as a warrior, but in his disposition, he was irritable and very proud. On his expulsion from Ijaye he went first to Iwàre, and from thence he crossed the river Ogun going to a small town near Iṣẹdẹ called Tọbalogbo. He encamped outside the town walls with his few followers, and sent to apprise the Balẹ of his arrival. His fame as a great warrior having travelled far and wide the Tọbalogbo treated him with every mark of respect, supplying him and his followers with provisions, and on the next day he came out with his chiefs to pay his respects to the fallen general.

Whilst the Balẹ and chiefs prostrated before this monster in the act of salutation, he ordered them all to be decapitated ! He and his men then rushed into the town and captured it. He cared only for the booty and not for making it his residence ; he, therefore, passed on to the town of Aborẹrin near Ibẹrẹkodo and there he built a house and resided with his family and about 400 men. Subsequently he left Aborẹrin with his family and belongings and wishing to try the fortunes of war once more, he joined an Ibadan contingent under Oṣun the chief of the Ibadan cavalry in an expedition in aid of Oniyẹfun. When Oṣun fell in battle, and Oniyẹfun was reduced by the Ẹgbas, he narrowly escaped with a handful of his men, leaving his wives and children at the mercy of the conquerors and escaped to Ijaka. Divine retribution now began to overtake him for his cruelties and for his heartless treachery and cold-blooded murder of Tọbalogbo and

K

his chiefs. He lost everything at Oniyẹfun, and from that time he went up and down the country as a " fugitive and vagabond." After some time spent at Ijaka he came to Ibadan ; he accompanied Lakanlẹ the Ibadan commander-in-chief to the Arakanga war (to be related afterwards) ; on their return he went to Ilọrin and returned again to Ibadan. Fortune was altogether against him He outlived his fame and glory, suffered from penury and want and was reduced to a nonentity.

After Lakanlẹ's death, having no one to befriend him at Ibadan again, he went once more to Ijaye. Kurūmi was then at the zenith of his glory, with the old animosity against Dado still rankling in his breast. He sent for him one day and as Dado lay prostrate before him Kurūmi ordered him to be decapitated !

Thus the same measure was meted to him, as he once meted to his hosts of Tọbalogbo.

The Occupation of Abemo.—Kurūmi of Ijaye was an arbitrary and domineering chief, and moreover tribal jealousies and clanship were rife among the chiefs who now occupy Ijaye as they were from different provinces and townships brought together here by one common calamity. Kurūmi and the Ikoyi chiefs with him were from the Metropolitan province.

The notable war-chiefs from Akesè were :—Ayọ̀, Adekambi, Ajadi, Sukọtọ, Bankọle, Lahàn, Arunọ-agba-ni-igbe and Oluwọlẹ. These chiefs from the Epò districts could not endure the hauteur of Kurūmi who was backed up by the Ikoyi chiefs. They hold themselves superior to the Akesè chiefs. Ikoyi was indeed the premier provincial city next to the Metropolis, and the Onikoyi the ALÂFIN's viceregent, but these chiefs seem to have forgotten that they were no longer worthy of the honour they now claimed since they have become disloyal to the Crown.

However, in order to avoid a civil war from constant friction the above-mentioned Akesè chiefs with their men left Ijaye in a body and retired to Abemò, a town 12 miles distant (midway between Ijaye and the present Ọyọ) under the leadership of chief Ayọ̀. We now have two rival towns, Ijaye occupied by the Ikoyi chiefs, and Abemọ by the Akesè chiefs.

§ 3. How Ibadan Finally Became a Yoruba Town
The Fall of Maye

The marauders who settled at Ibadan after the fall of Oorùn and all the Gbagura towns (as we have mentioned above) comprised the Ifẹ, Ijẹbu, Ọyọ, and Egba chiefs with their men. Chief Maye an Ifẹ was the acknowledged head of them all. He was a proud, haughty, and irritable man, overbearing to all ; Lakanlẹ the Ọyọ leader (as above mentioned) was the only man who could speak when Mayẹ was in a rage.   The Ifẹs generally regarded the Ọyọs of the settlement as slaves because they were homeless refugees ; they treated them little better than they would dogs. Mayẹ handled them with an iron hand, and denied them every security either of their goods or of their lives ; they were oppressed and beaten with impunity.

The Ọyọs, groaning under this yoke of bondage sought every opportunity for lifting up their heads, but the very name of Mayẹ inspired such a dread in all, that no plan could be acted upon. The bards sang of him as the greatest general of the day, a man who commanded an amount of dread and respect, unsurpassed by any, etc. But, like Napoleon after Moscow, " From the highest to the lowest, there is but one ṣtep ;" so it was with Mayẹ. His fall was sudden and complete.

Two neighbours were quarrelling over a piece of ground used in common as a dunghill, one was an Owu man, Amejiogbe by name, one of Mayẹ's soldiers, the other an Ọyọ man ; both of them private soldiers. But as Ọyọs were treated like dogs, when Mayẹ came out, he asked no questions about the case, but sided with the Owu man and simply drew his sword and cut off the head of the Ọyọ man. Instantly a hue and cry was raised, and an alarm given that Mayẹ was putting all Ọyọs to death ! The Ọyọs became desperate, and all flew to arms. Mayẹ was taken aback with surprise to see them making a dead set at him.. They refused to hear his plea for self-defence, and would not allow him to re-enter his house ; he was beset on every side and driven out of the town.   He escaped on foot by the way of the present Abẹokuta gate and crossed the river Ọnà followed by some of the Ifẹ chiefs e.g. Apọnju-olosùn, Arẹgbẹ Derĩokun, etc.

After this, the Ọyọ chiefs began to feel ill at ease, and were the first to offer him terms of reconciliation. They knew his fame and valour and were trembling for the possible consequences. In the afternoon an embassy was sent to him with a humble apology and petition saying " Our Father should return home, our Father should not spend the night in the bush." He answered the messengers roughly and swore by the gods that he would surely destroy the town and that before long.

The next day higher grades of ambassadors were sent to sue for peace, and with them large baskets of provisions for himself and his followers because "Father must be hungry since yesterday." These were not even allowed to approach his camp, and some of the Ọyọs who accompanied him as personal friends sent privately to apprise their country-men that it was of no use their waiting for an answer, the great chief would neither listen to them nor even grant them an interview and it was in vain to hope that he would agree to return to Ibadan.

The ambassadors had to return home to report their ill success but they left behind all the provisions they took with them in hopes that his followers would take them away after they had gone.

The chiefs were much disappointed at this turn of affairs and blamed themselves for their rashness and instructed the ambassadors not to wait for further orders but that by early dawn they should proceed once more and offer their humble submission and say that they would agree to any fine he would be pleased to impose upon them as a condition of his returning home.

In the meantime a meeting was convened to consider what further steps should be taken ; they decided to levy a tax upon all the people in order to raise money for the fine. But the messengers soon returned with a distressing report :—" The master's camp, has been broken up, the food they carried the previous day was left untouched, for hawks, crows, and vultures to feed upon, nor could anyone tell his route or destination ! "

It was surmised that he probably went to join the Egbas at Abeokuta to raise an army to fight them : but a few days after, a farmer reported that he saw a broad path leading to Idomapa in the south. Maye then was the guest of Oluwolè of Idomapa, but the people of Erūmu invited him to Erūmu, offering him their support and friendship because his calamity was caused by his espousing the cause of an Owu man. We have seen above, that Erūmu was the chief vassal state of Owu and that to this place the Olowu and his people escaped when the city of Owu was taken.

They were determined to avenge Maye's wrongs, and with such a distinguished commander on their side, they hoped to be able to annihilate these Oyo marauders, the principal agents in the destruction of their capital city.

Before they were prepared to lay siege to Ibadan, the Erūmu people and their guests began at once to make predatory incursions into the Ibadan farms, kidnapping also the caravans with corn and other foodstuffs from Ikirè so as to cut off their food supplies and distress them by starvation before reducing them by war at the ensuing dry season.

This state of things continued nearly a whole year and during that time vast preparations were made to crush Ibadan by an overwhelming force. An alliance was formed with the Ife towns of Ikirè, Apomu, Ipetumodu and other towns in their neighbourhood, and a large army was raised against Ibadan. The Egbas also were invited as allies, as all have their grievances to avenge on the new occupants of Ibadan. Two famous commanders Degẹsin and Ogini led the Ẹgba contingents ; they marched through the Ibadan farms in the south to join the main army at Idomapa.

The Gbanamu War. The Ibadan chiefs met this overwhelming force with courage and determination but the odds were against them ; at every battle in spite of all they could do, they lost ground and the assailants advanced to within a mile or a mile and a half of the town. The Ibadans in their extremity were obliged to ask help from Kurūmi of Ijaye who readily responded to their call. They were all one people whom a common calamity compelled to these parts, and they had to make a new home and defend it. Kurūmi arrived at Ibadan on a Friday, but as Fridays were considered inauspicious days the Ibadan chiefs suggested that the fight should be postponed till the next day. Kurūmi replied, "It is true Fridays are inauspicious, but it is only so to aggressors, not to defenders of hearth and home." The last decisive battle then was fought on that day. It was a bloody day. Equal courage and valour were displayed on both sides, but in the end, though outnumbered by far, the superior military skill of Kurūmi and the Ibadans won the day. For the Ibadans it was a life and death struggle, and because it was mostly a hand to hand fight in which swordsmen proved themselves a match for those with fire-arms the battle was named " Gba'namu " (grasping fire). Rushing upon their assailants sword in hand and grasping the barrel of the gun, the Ibadans averted the fatal discharge of the weapon while using their swords and cutlasses with effect. Thus the Ifẹ, Owu, and Ẹgba allies were completely routed. Several of their leaders were made prisoners and put to death. Mayẹ the great commander was taken prisoner by a common soldier, and as he was being led to the town all the war-chiefs refused to see his face.

It is a common belief amongst warriors in this country that any war-chief, who ordered a brother war-chief, his equal in arms, to execution, will surely meet with the same fate at no distant date. Therefore, although the whole of the chiefs desired his execution yet no one was bold enough to show his face and order it, and take upon himself the responsibility for what all desired. Both the captor and the captive fully understood the import of the phrase " Let him not see my face." It meant his death warrant. Mayẹ therefore cried out : " Ẹ má da a sẹ, Ẹ fi oju mi kan alagbà ! Ẹ má da a sẹ, Ẹ fi oju mi kan Lakanlẹ. (Do not take the responsibility, bring me before a chief ; do not take the responsibility, bring me before Lakanlẹ). But all in vain, his fate had been sealed by the chiefs declining to see him, and so the great Mayẹ was beheaded by a common soldier. Degẹsin and Ọgini the Ẹgba commanders also shared his fate.

Chief Kurũmi claimed the honour of the victory and hence his bards sang to his praise "O pa Maye, o pa Ọgini, O pa Degẹsin, O fi ọkọ ti Ifẹ laiyà" (he slew Maye, he slew Ọgini and Degẹsin and thrust his spear into the breasts of the Ifẹs).

By this victory the remnant of the Ọyọ refugees was saved.

THE ẸRUMU WAR

The victors followed up their victory and encamped against Ẹrũmu. Reinforcements came for them from Iwo, Ẹdẹ, Apomu and other places ; the Ọyọ refugees in those parts joining their brethren at the siege of Ẹrũmu so that the doomed town was hemmed in on every side : indeed they had to fight from within their walls. As the besiegers could neither force the gates nor scale or beat down the walls, they were content to reduce the town by famine. The most disgusting creatures were used for food, and even greedily devoured in order to sustain life ! It passed into a proverb " When the price of a frog came to 120 cowries then Ẹrũmu was taken."

The siege of Ẹrũmu recalled that of Oke Suna in the fight between Ṣolagberu and Abudusalami.

The following anecdotes illustrative of the horrors of the siege of Ẹrũmu were told by eye-witnesses :—

Corn planted within the walls of the town wanted but a few weeks for ripening when the famished inhabitants could no longer wait for a full corn, everyone helping himself not only to the immature corn but also the corn-stalks. It was so much relished that one of them was heard to say that he did not know before that corn stalks were so delicious and that henceforth he would ever be using it as an article of food.

Another reported the case of a good-looking and well-to-do young woman, a snuff seller, at Ẹrũmu. Before the war broke out, her beauty and style always attracted young men to her side in the shed where she was grinding and retailing snuff. Her stall was so clean and so well-polished that they required no mats to sit upon, they would just squat on the ground about her. This well-to-do woman was so famished that she died of starvation at her stall in the open thoroughfare, and of all her admirers not one was found to do her the honour of a burial !

Again, another eye-witness among the besiegers related that whilst bathing in a stream which flowed through the town to the camp, he often saw myriads of maggots which he could not account for as if the water bred them, but when Ẹrũmu was taken he saw hundreds of putrefying bodies in the stream within the town and this accounted for the maggots he saw in such abundance lower down as the stream flowed by the camp.

On the town being taken the Oluroko (or king) of Ẹrūmu and the king of Idomapa were caught and slain. Also the Olowu was now caught who (as was related above) escaped thither when the city of Owu was destroyed. Now, he was a provincial King of great importance, a real crowned head, and his case caused the victors some embarrassment. No pure Yoruba would venture to lay hands on a king even if worthy of death ; in such an event the king would simply be told that he was rejected and, *noblesse oblige*, he would commit suicide by poison.

The Olowu, although now a prisoner of war, was regarded with so much reverence that none of the chiefs would dare order his execution, and yet they could not keep him nor would they let him go. His death was compassed in a diplomatic manner.

The conquerors pretended to be sending him to the Ọwọ̀ni of Ifẹ, who alone may be regarded as his peer in this part of the country, and he was to be accompanied by one of his own slaves as a personal attendant and by some messengers to the Ọwọ̀ni as his escort. But the slave, who was supplied with a loaded gun as his master's bodyguard, had been privately instructed that at a given signal from the escort he was to shoot his master dead, and that he would be granted his freedom and loaded with riches as well. Thus they proceeded on their way until they came to the bank of the river Ọṣun when the signal was given and the slave shot his master dead on the spot ! These "messengers" now set up a hue and cry of horror and surprise: "What ! You slave ! How dare you kill your royal master ? Death is even too good for you." And in order to exonerate themselves of all complicity in the matter, they set upon the poor slave attacking him on all sides and clubbed him to death saying " The murder of the king must be avenged." They then dammed up the river in its course and dug the king's grave deep in the bed of it, and there they buried the corpse whilst uttering this disclaimer :—

" O King, we have no hands in your cruel murder. The onus of it rests with your slave and we have avenged you by putting him to death, and he is to be your attendant in the other world."

They then allowed the river to flow on in its channel over the grave. Burying the king in the bed of the river was regarded as an expiation made for his murder, because they were conscious of guilt although they attributed the act to the slave. With such reverence and sanctity was the person of a king regarded. The divine right of kings is an article of belief among the Yorubas.

Such was the end of the last king of the famous city of Owu. The title is continued by a representative of the family at Abẹokuta.

§ 4. THE SETTLEMENT OF IBADAN

After the fall of Ẹrūmu the war chiefs returned to Ibadan and the rest of the people who joined the war as volunteers returned to their respective homes. It was not till this time that Ibadan was peopled by Ọyọs chiefly. Everyone of these war-chiefs entered the allied army of Ifẹ and Ijẹbu at Idi Ogūgun as a private volunteer, but they soon showed their capabilities in the various wars. Oppressed and enslaved by the Ifẹs, scorned by the Ijẹbus, in pure self-defence they banded themselves together under a leader for mutual protection and notwithstanding the great disadvantage under which they were placed, they vindicated their superiority and at last obtained the ascendancy in the town.

Under such circumstances did the Ọyọs become masters of Ibadan. Hence the allegation that it was they who expelled the Egbas from their original home and took possession of the same is wholly inaccurate, and the bad feeling which this impression has created and perpetuated between the two peoples unto this day is hereby shown to be groundless.

Ibadan then consisted of the central market and about half a mile of houses around. The town wall was where the principal mosque now stands.

Hitherto Ibadan has been occupied as a military headquarter for marauding and other expeditions, but after this war, at a public meeting held to consider their future course, it was resolved that as they now intend to make this place their home they should arrange for a settled government and take titles. Oluyedun came first. He was the son of the late Afọnja of Ilọrin, and as such, the scion of a noble house. He was honoured and respected by all. He might have been the Balẹ, but he preferred to adopt his father's title of Kakanfo and it was conceded him, not for his valour, but for his age and dignity, being a survivor of the men of the preceding generation.

Next came Lakanlẹ "the bravest of the brave." He might have taken the title of Balogun or commander-in-chief, as he had hitherto been their principal leader in war, but Kakanfo being a military title, that of Balogun would be superfluous. He then became the *Ọtun* Kakanfo and Oluyọle the *Osi* Kakanfo.

The others were: Adelakun the *Ekẹrin* (fourth), Olumaiye the *Ekarun* (fifth) Abitiko *Ekẹfa* (sixth) Keji the *Arẹ Abẹsẹ*. To Ọsun was the honour given to confer these titles, and he in turn was created the *Sarumi* (chief of the cavalry). Only a single Ifẹ

chief remained at Ibadan and that was Labosinde, and even he
(as was mentioned above) had Oyo blood in his veins through
his mother. He was very gentle, good-natured and fatherly to
all. Even during the days of Maye the Oyo chiefs had an
affection and great respect for him as a father. At the expulsion
of Maye when the other Ife chiefs joined him, he took no sides and
hence he was allowed to remain. After Maye's fall he did not
aspire to the leadership of the people, preferring private life to
the responsibilities of government. He was a man who loved
peace; he would never carry arms nor allow any to be carried before
him even in those turbulent days, except in the battlefield. A
bundle of whips was all usually carried before him, as used to be
done before the Roman Tribunes of old, and with this token of
authority he was able several times to disband men in arms
and put an end to civil fights. The combatants as soon as
they saw the bundle of whips coming would cease firing,
saying to one another ": Baba mbò " " baba mbò " (father is
coming, father is coming). His title now is *Baba Isale* i.e. chief
adviser, *lit* father underneath (for counsel).

It will be noticed that (except this last) all the principal titles
were military titles. Ibadan has kept that up unto this day.

Although they seemed to be now settled, yet they really lived
by plunder and rapine. A single stalk of corn could scarcely
be seen in an Ibadan farm in the days of Maye, and although
Lakanle encouraged husbandry, yet the people were so much
given to slave hunting that they could not grow corn enough
for home consumption. The women of those days were as hardy
as the men, and often went in a body—as caravans—to Ikirè and
Apomu for corn and other foodstuffs although the road was unsafe
from kidnappers. They supplied the town with food whilst the
men were engaged in slave hunting. One company returning
would meet another just going out, and often, an unsuccessful
individual returning would go back with the outgoing company to
try another chance without first reaching home. Ill-luck of one
did not prevent another company venturing out.

At home violence, oppression, robbery, man-stealing were
the order of the day. A special gag was invented for the mouth
of human beings to prevent any one stolen from crying out and
being discovered by his friends. No one dared go out at dusk for the
men-stealers were out already prowling about for their prey.
Thus even the great Maye was once stolen on going out
one night. He offered no resistance but went quietly with
the man-stealer, who, on reaching home, called for a light to
inspect his victim. Finding to his dismay that it was the great

chief Mayẹ himself, he nearly died of fright.   Quaking and trembling he prostrated at his feet and begged for his life.   So bad were
those days at Ibadan and so callous had the people become that
if a woman or a child was heard to cry out "Ẹ gbà mi, wọn mu mi
o " (O help me, I am taken) the usual answer from indoors was
" Maha ba a lọ " (you can go along with him).   The moral and
social atmosphere of such a place as has been described could
easily be imagined.   Yet they were destined by God to play a most
important part in the history of the Yorubas, to break the Fulani
yoke and save the rest of the country from foreign domination ;
in short to be a protector as well as a scourge in the land as we
shall see hereafter.

A nation born under such strenuous circumstances cannot but
leave the impress of its hardihood and warlike spirit on succeeding
generations, and so we find it at Ibadan to this day.   It being
the Divine prerogative to use whomsoever He will to effect His
Divine purpose, God uses a certain nation or individual as the
scourge of another nation and when His purposes are fulfilled He
casts the scourge away.

WARS FOR THE CONSOLIDATION AND BALANCE OF POWER BETWEEN IBADANS, EGBAS AND IJEBUS

§ 1. THE EVACUATION OF APOMU

WE have seen above that the people ot Apomu being Ifes allied themselves with Maye at the Gbanamu war, hence after the destruction of Erunmu, they were afraid that the next wave will overwhelm themselves. They therefore sent an Oyo resident at Apomu, chief Agbeni by name, to encamp on the further side of the river Osun as an outpost, to watch and report upon the movements of the Ibadan army.

But the Ibadans were not meditating any revenge on them; yet they were so ill at ease that they would not even wait for a report from their outpost, but one chief after another, one master of a large compound after another deserted the town for Ipetumodu till only the Oyo refugees remained at Apomu.

At Ipetumodu they were however restless ; it seemed unreasonable that they should be famishing in another town when food could be obtained in their own farms ; therefore bands of pillagers and kidnappers issued daily from Ipetumodu to the Apomu farms destroying whatever they could not carry away. They also grew suspicious of Agbeni and sent a strong force to drive him away from the post where they had located him. But Agbeni was determined to maintain his ground, and he therefore despatched messengers to Ibadan to ask for help. Only one desperate battle was fought between them, and the Ipetumodu men apprehending danger to themselves if they should wait to offer a second, as by that time reinforcements from Ibadan might have come, they retreated hastily home.

The Ibadan army arrived too late and were disappointed to find the Apomu army gone ; they were loth to return home empty handed as they lived by plunder, they therefore began to loot the houses of the residents at Apomu. But these were their kinsmen, the Oyo refugees who were left behind by the townsmen, and nearly every one of them saw a friend or a relative whom he was in duty bound to protect from violence and robbery. These relatives went over to them and with them to Ibadan. Lakanlè their leader took away all his, and his friend Agbeni came over also with him. Lanáṣẹ went over with all his belongings to Ọṣun the chief of the cavalry, and so Apomu became deserted.

Agbeni was located in Lakanlẹ's farm and the site has since been included in the overgrown town and known as Agbeni's quarter to this day with a market in front ot his house. Chief Agbeni survived Lakanlẹ and all his contemporaries and died at a good old age in May 1860.

Thus the Ọyọ refugees at Apomu were merged with the Ibadan settlers, and helped to swell the population of that important town.

THE IPETUMODU AND OWIWI WARS ABOUT A.D. 1819

The Apomu and Ipetumodu people having drawn attention to themselves, after a short respite the restless Ibadan chiefs declared war against Ipetumodu for allying with Apomu to kidnap the Ibadan caravans, who went to buy corn at Ikire, Iwo, Ile Igbo before the Ẹrūmu wars. Any pretext, however flimsy, would do when they were on mischief bent.

It was just at this time that ·the Ijẹbus declared war against Abẹokuta, and sought the alliance of the Ibadans. But they could not send them adequate help and advised the Ijẹbus rather to wait a while and let them get Ipetumodu off their hands. But the Ijẹbus would not wait, the Ibadans, therefore had to send them a small contingent under one Olugūnà. The last decisive battle between the Ijẹbus and the Ẹgbas was the celebrated battle of Owiwi (a stream so called) where the Ijẹbus were sorely defeated; they lost all their principal fighting men and their power was completely crushed! Olugūnà with his small force escapéd to Oniyẹfun a town on the right bank of the river Ogun where he remained for a long time, apparently seeking for an opportunity to return home.

The Ibadans on the other hand were successful in their own expedition, Ipetumodu was taken and those who escaped fled to Ile Ifẹ their chief town.

§ 2. THE FALL OF ILARO AND IJANA

During the siege at Owiwi the Ijẹbus sought and obtained the alliance of the Ẹgbaluwẹ kings. Abinuwọgbo the Onisarẹ of Ijãna sent his forces under the command of two of his war-chiefs Lapala and Ajiṣẹ; the only war-chief remaining at home was Akère the Arẹagoro. Lapala fell in battle and the command devolved upon Ajiṣẹ alone.

The Ilaros sent no re-inforcement because of a great disaffection among the people towards their Olu on account of his·tyrannies.

For a small matter which he might very well pass over, he would impose exorbitant fines, hence the affection of his people was alienated from him and they were seeking an opportunity for his overthrow. His was a long reign, for this age of anarchy, and he did not retire to Ọyọ after three years, like his predecessors, to spend the rest of his days there as was customary. He became lame on both his feet, from poison by his people as was alleged.

A private message was sent to the Egbas by the people inviting them to come and rid them of their tyrant, thinking they would come and simply remove the Olu and leave them in peace. The Egbas thereupon sent from Owiwi a detachment of 134 men under chief Anọba who entered Ilaro without opposition, fired it, and began to kill and plunder indiscriminately ! As the Egbas cared more for booty than for captives the Olu (their principal objective) had an opportunity for making his escape to Ifọin, being borne on a litter by his slaves, while most of the Ilaro people escaped to Ijãna. A bride was said to be so frightened by the hasty flight that she fell down dead at the gate of Ijãna, and was buried behind the house of one Tagi the gate-keeper.

They had scarcely had breathing time here when news came that the Egbas had gained a victory over the Ijẹbus at Owiwi and a rumour gained ground that they were coming to take vengeance on the 'Luwẹs of Ijãna for allying themselves with the Ijẹbus. The consternation became general when Ajisẹ the surviving war-chief arrived home. Neither the Ilaro refugees, nor the Ijãna people themselves could stay in the town any longer, all sought safety in flight, and so Ijãna was deserted. The flight took place on a dark and stormy night, and hundreds of people were groping in darkness trying to find the way to the town gate. Fortunately it was only a rumour or the Egbas might have met them within the town for at break of day the dawn found them at Dekun's quarters late of Ijãna.

Akère the Arẹagoro the only war-chief left at home instead of preparing for the defence of the town deluded the people by having three lighted lamps burning at the three entrances to his house making it appear as if he was still at home whereas he had already escaped.

An incident of interest occurred during this flight. A child of about 3 years of age was found the next day at Afẹhintẹ weeping, its mother having disencumbered herself of it in her flight. A kind-hearted man Ajayi by name took it up from pity and carried it in his arms wherever he went. They did not meet the Arẹagoro at Rẹfurẹfu but joined him at Osoro ; there the heartless mother seeing the child with Ajayi, claimed it but Ajayi refused to give it up till it was duly ransomed.

The refugees left Ọsoro for Ifọin where they met the Olu and here they were resolved to wait and offer some resistance in case of an attack, as they were afraid to proceed to Porto Novo. The Olu, however, left Ifọin for Itọhọ his maternal town, where he would wish to die ; here Sodẹkẹ with an Ẹgba army met him and he was taken with his family and slain. One Okete the executioner carried the head about at Rẹfurẹfu for money ; at the gate of whomsoever the Olu's head was placed Okete received 3 heads of cowries before removing it. It was brought to Abẹokuta and was buried at the threshold of the main entrance to Sodẹkẹ's house.

Sodẹkẹ took Ayawo the Olu's daughter to wife, but she had no child by him. After Sodẹkẹ's death she was " inherited " by Somoye, who subsequently became the Baṣọrun of Abẹokuta. She went with him to the late Ijaye war and was taken captive when Ijaye fell on the 31st March, 1862. The captor gave her up to Chief Ogũmọla. She was sent back to her husband in the year 1865 and was the means of reconciliation between Ibadan and Abẹokuta, after the return of the latter from the Ikorodu war. The accounts of these wars will be given below in due course. After Somoye's death Ayawo refused the hand of Chief Ogundipẹ and went back to her early home at Ilaro where she died.

After the death of the Olu Aṣade at Itọhọ the Ilaro refugees at Idọgọ near Igbeji created another Olu, Ojo Kosiwọn by name. For 19 years he reigned at Idọgọ and after his death there was an interregnum of many years.

Ilaro was, however, again repeopled but under Ẹgba suzerainty, who created one Tẹla the Olu in 1857. Ilaro continued under the Ẹgbas till the year 1891 when they gave themselves over to the British Government on account of the incessant raids and molestations of the Dahomians from which their Suzerain failed to protect them. They now form a Protectorate in the " Western Waters " of Lagos.

§ 3. THE ONIYEFUN WAR

After the return of the Ibadans from the Ipetumodu war, hearing of the disaster at Owiwi, and that their contingent under Olugũna had escaped to Oniyẹfun and was there hemmed in by the Ẹgbas, some of the war-chiefs headed by Ọṣun the chief of the cavalry, and Elẹpo also a great warrior, decided to go to their rescue. But Olugũna was met rather on the offensive, waging a desultory warfare in Ẹgba territory. Being now re-inforced from home he commenced regular operations against the small and weaker Egba towns such as Imosai, Iboro, and Jiga. Jako was deserted and these marauders were infesting the Isaga farms and would have taken Isaga had not the Egbas sent a strong force to protect the place.

After a short time, however, Elêpo left them and returned to Ibadan and with him nearly all the other war-chiefs, as he was a man of great power and influence.

The army at Oniyefun being now considerably reduced in number, the Egbas attacked it in full force; several battles were fought and the Egbas gained an advantage at every engagement. They succeeded in cutting off all supplies and in laying a close siege against Oniyefun. All the Ibadan common soldiers under colour of going foraging escaped from the doomed town one by one never to return, but the war-chiefs themselves, with their immediate followers and bodyguards, could not leave without attracting attention or creating a panic and a rush, with an immediate destruction of the town. Osun fell in an engagement; being shot through the head he tumbled off his horse. Sogunro was wounded and Dado—late of Ijaye—who was also there, prevented Sogunro being taken to Jako as an invalid, lest they should lose the services of his fighting men. Dado remained the only war-chief in command, but he was no longer the commander he once was before his fall. He held out for only five days longer, and then left Oniyefun secretly with the other war-chiefs and escaped to Ibadan, leaving Oniyefun at the mercy of the invaders.

The Ibadan war-chiefs who fell at Oniyefun besides Osun were: Sogunro, Keji, Ilupakin, Iyanburu, Otopo, and Esan.

§ 4. The Arakanga or Jabara War

The Ibadan war-chiefs were indignant at the fall of their comrades at Oniyefun, especially Osun who was held in high esteem, and were bent on avenging his death. This was really the cause of the Arakanga war, and not in order to show that they were more powerful than the Ijebus as some have erroneously averred.

In this expedition they secured the alliance of Kurũmi of Ijaye and Ayo of Abemo, whose contingent met the Ibadan army at Olokemeji.

This expedition was one of the most stupid ever undertaken by the Ibadans. Divided counsels prevailed and therefore no adequate preparation was made, one half of the so-called kegs of gunpowder carried before the chiefs contained nothing but yam flour, thereby deceiving the people who followed them. Some asserted that the Egbas were more afraid of poisoned arrows than of bullets and therefore never supplied themselves with fire-arms.

Others went just mechanically because they were obliged to go, but without any preparation. We may here notice that this is how the junior chiefs behave when the war is unpopular, for they dare not remain behind when the head-chiefs march out.

They marched out through the Ido gate and encamped by the Ogun river at Olokemeji for a long time till their stores were exhausted, and before the enemy was in sight ! Meantime their wives used the empty kegs as water pots.

After a long time they pushed forward towards Abẹokuta, and the Ẹgbas met them a great way off. Four hard battles were fought and the Ẹgbas retreated to Arakanga, a river behind their town wall. Here the Ibadans found themselves with their powder exhausted and no time to procure more from Porto Novo or Ado ; the arrows some depended upon were found to be of little use. Adekambi the war-chief sent from Abemọ was the first to return home being disgusted at the conduct of the war. With him went a good many war-chiefs, and recruits which they met on their way back also returned home when they heard the ill report of the campaign.

Five days after Adekambi had left the Ẹgbas appeared in full force, determined on death or victory. At a given signal by the sound of their god Orò to which they responded with a shout, they made a sudden dash and attacked the enemy vigorously, cutlass in hand.

With their powder exhausted some of the Ibadans resorted to the gourd bàrà planted all over the battlefield, and with this they pelted their assailants. From this circumstance the campaign was termed the " Jabara war." At the height of the battle, Bada Akẹyan one of the chief swordsmen fell ; and when another chief named Adelakun was mortally wounded, the Ibadans gave way and the rout was general and complete.

This desperate method of attack—cutlass in hand—is the peculiar method of the Owus, the bravest element in the new settlement, and the honour of the victory was theirs.

The Ẹgbas however had not the courage to pursue their victory to any extent seeing amongst the war-chiefs many of those who had but recently driven them to Abeokuta : " a lion at bay " may prove a dangerous customer to tackle. The Ibadans instead of escaping home by the direct route went by way of Ijaye, being suspicious of the Ijẹbus.

§ 5. The Onidẹsẹ and Oke Iṣero Wars

After a short period of rest Kurūmi the chief of Ijaye invited the Ibadans to an expedition against Onidẹsẹ. He gave as a reason for this war that they were troublesome to him, but as a matter of fact, it was from pure jealousy at the growing importance of the people of that place and that of their neighbours of Ile Ọdẹ famous for their poisoned arrows.

Seeing the overwhelming force from Ibadan and Ijaye, Ọwọkọ the chief of Ọdẹ was so terrified that he deserted the town with his people and escaped to Onidẹsẹ, but this place was besieged and taken.   Sẹjo the chief of Onidẹsẹ and Ọwọkọ of Ile Ọdẹ were both taken together.

Oke Iṣero.—The following dry season the Ibadans captured Oke Iṣero for no alleged cause of grievance but simply out of a desire for slave raiding.   The people of this place were quiet agriculturists. Ibadan and other towns were fed with yam flour exported from this place.

§ 6.   The Iperu War

After the defeat of the Ijẹbus by the Ẹgbas at Owiwi there was a series of desultory warfare between them with little or no success. Neither of them could encamp or take a town from the other, neither would yield though both were tired.   Whereupon the Ẹgbas had resort to a cowardly trick, at once disgraceful and perfidious. They proposed to the Ijẹbus of the Rẹmọ district who were their neighbours, terms of peace which these gladly accepted, being tired of the war, and a treaty was made between them.   But while the Ijẹbus were rejoicing and congratulating one another in songs and dances :—

> " Ọmọde Ijẹbu, Ẹ ku ewu
> Agba Ijẹbu, Ẹ ku ewu
> Ọtẹ yi jaja pari o ! "

(Young folks of Ijẹbu, we congratulate you
Old folks of Ijẹbu, we congratulate you.
This long-drawn war is at an end at last).

Suddenly, the Ẹgbas who had lain in ambush sprang upon them and began to make captives of them.   Makun and other towns were taken and destroyed and Iperu was besieged.   The Ijẹbus being harassed and greatly straitened sent to Ibadan for help. All the war-chiefs were sent forward except Lakanlẹ the Commander-in-chief, who remained at home with the aged Oluyedun the Kakanfo, and the venerable Labọsinde the Baba Isalẹ.

The Ẹgbas proved too strong for the allies, and all their efforts to raise the siege of Iperu were fruitless.   The difficulty of provisioning a besieged town without stores at the best of times and with a large access of auxiliaries proved insurmountable.   The allies lost several battles and the Egbas hemmed them in very closely. Iperu was nearly taken when the Ibadan allies sent home to their commander to come at once to their rescue as all hopes of defeating the Egbas were gone.

Lakanle responded to the call of his people and took the field in person. On his arrival at Iperu he assumed no lofty airs nor did he allow one word of reproach to fall from his lips. On the contrary he praised the war-chiefs and harangued the men as follows :—" Fellow countrymen and companions in arms, I am not more surprised at your valour and prowess than at your chivalry in inviting me to share with you the honours of the field. For what can I do singly without your aid ? I know your love and esteem for me and that you only wish for me the honour and fruits of the victory ; I am come therefore to grant you your hearts' desire and lead you on to victory. Be assured also that I reciprocate your feelings of love towards me, for since your absence from home I have entered every compound now and again to ask after the welfare of your families and I am this day able to assure you that they are in good health.

I have gone the round of all the farms and when I saw any overgrown with weeds and learnt that the owner was at the seat of war, I ordered the farm to be immediately cleaned. I am now able to assure you also that your farms are in good order and your families in good health. Be of good cheer my brave men and by this time to-morrow let victory crown our efforts."

The soldiers gave long and loud shouts of "Muso, Muso, Muso." They made the heavens reverberate with their shouts and were heard at a very great distance.

When the Egbas heard that Lakanlè had reached the camp they extemporized a ditty including his name :—

" Nigbati a ba pade t'awa ti Lakanlè
Igi t'o ba ṣè oju rè a wi o ! "

(When we do meet, ourselves and Lakanlè
The trees that witness the sight shall tell the tale.)

And so it was. It must here be admitted that since the Egbas have been driven to Abeokuta and have had almost constantly to engage in wars both offensive and defensive against the Ọyọs in one direction, Ijebus in another, and the Egbaluwe provinces, they have developed a wonderful aptitude for fighting, and capable generals have been thrown up amongst them. A most sanguinary battle was fought the next day, and so great was the courage which the presence of their commander-in-chief infused into the Ibadan soldiers, and with such skill were they led that the tide of victory turned in their favour that day.   The Egbas were utterly defeated but their skilful commanders encouraged them to keep up the fire until sunset so as to be able to retreat in good order.   Moreover they also tried to prevent a panic among their soldiers by not allowing the bodies of the wounded and the slain to be taken to the camp or to lie scattered about in the battlefield, and so they made a pile of the corpses so as to have the field cleared up.   But in spite of it all, the Egbas could not hold on till the evening ; they were completely routed and Lakanlè's victory was decisive.

In the pursuit, Lakanlè's attention was drawn to the pile of corpses, and for the first time his lion-like heart was melted by the dreadful carnage, and the following exclamation escaped from his lips "Are these the bodies of mortals once born of women?" " Of course they are " retorted a private soldier " and whose work it was but yours? Was there any such butchery seen before you came into the camp ? " The great general turned away quietly without uttering a word more.

Thus Iperu was saved to the great disappointment of the Egbas and this they afterwards expressed in their street songs :—

> Ki a kó Iperu ki a kó Odè
> Ni Barapa ru imu rè de
> (Iperu and Ode we had all but taken,
> When officious Barapas came poking their noses.)

§ 7.   The Fall of Ọta

The Egbas at this time were equally as restless as the Ibadans waging a series of wars with the surrounding tribes. A serious complication arose between them and the Ọtas about this time which resulted in the latter place being besieged by them.

Ọta is the name given to a small town and clan of the Awori tribes situated about 24 miles north of Lagos. They are usually reckoned amongst the Egbaluwẹs.

Prince Kosọkọ of Lagos was an ally of the Ọtas and it was he who asked the help of the Ibadans in defence of Ọta.

A force was sent from Ibadan under the command of Oluyọle the Òsi. He made Ipara his headquarters and sent two war-chiefs Elêpo his own lieutenant and Inakoju the Seriki with some minor war-chiefs to the scene of conflict ; these encamped at Agerige, Lagosward, from which place they marched to Ọta when there was to be a fight.

The Egbas fought bravely but the besieged defended their town most heroically assisted by their ally. The Egbas in order to harass the allies began kidnapping the Ibadan caravans, who were supplying them with provisions from home, as there was none to be got locally, so that the station at Ipara could not supply that at Agerige. Lakanlẹ hearing this at home left the town and stationed himself at Ikija, from which place he sent escorts with the weekly caravans to Ipara ; by this means Agerige was also relieved and communication established with Ibadan.

The Ọtas are known to be an obstinate people, and in the defence of their homes every man amongst them was a hero ! The Egbas had nearly given up the campaign in despair ; a good many of the war-chiefs had returned home and others became rather listless, but for the shame of being baulked by such a small clan which kept them in the field, the whole undertaking would have collapsed. But the situation was improved by the diplomacy of one of the Egba chiefs ; he advised that unbounded licence be granted to the soldiery in the field to gratify their passions in any manner they liked with impunity, himself setting the example : the amount of bravery displayed under fire, was to be the measure of indulgence in the camp. The device proved successful, the camp was refilled with characters of all sorts, and the campaign was prosecuted with renewed vigour. The small town was hemmed in on all sides and famine effected what the sword failed to accomplish.

When their Ibadan allies saw that the Ọtas were not likely to hold out much longer, and that it was with difficulty they could obtain supplies from home, they left Agerige secretly and hastened homewards.

Ọta was at length taken by the Egbas and they wreaked their vengeance on the inhabitants so mercilessly, especially on the men for their obstinate resistance, that the clan was nearly extinguished altogether. From that time to this Ọta has been subjected to the Egbas.

The Ibadan contingent under Elẹpo and Inakoju met Oluyọle at Ipara. Whilst here, a most pernicious plot was hatched with consequences so far-reaching and so disastrous resulting in repeated civil fights at home, until nearly the whole of the important war-chiefs perished one after another. Oluyọle aspiring to the position of commander-in-chief planned a scheme by which Lakanlẹ and Bankọle his lieutenant should be wiped out, but the plot was discovered and it aroused great indignation at Ibadan. There was a determination that he should not be allowed to re-enter the town and steps were taken to prevent it. All the other chiefs returned one by one.

It was due to his friend Elẹpo alone that Oluyọle re-entered Ibadan. He kept him informed of all that was taking place at home. Oluyọle remained out but kept advancing by small stages, with the connivance of Elẹpo, till one night he entered by the town gate from another direction. Once at home Elêpo prevailed on all the senior Chiefs to forbear with him and pardon him.

Then Oluyọle's men began firing a *feu de joie* but with guns charged with bullets, directing them towards Lakanlẹ's house, and Lakanlẹ's men returning the compliment did the same towards Oluyọle's, the houses of the principal war-chiefs ranging round the central market. This continued for several days, the chiefs of both sides taking no part, but leaving the skirmishing to their boys. The tension of affairs affected the whole town, all business was at a standstill, till Labọsinde the Baba-Isalẹ came forward with some elderly chiefs and put a stop to these proceedings.

This pacification however lasted but a short time, for soon afterwards there arose a complication between Oluwaiye, one of Lakanlẹ's lieutenants and one of Oluyọle's men. This developed into something approaching a civil fight, the town was soon in an uproar. Then Bankọle unarmed approached Oluyọle's men, and with soothing words was urging them to desist, and not to disturb the recently made peace, when one of Oluyọle's men levelled his gun at him for interfering and shot him down dead ! This was a signal for a civil fight in the heat of which Oluwaiye fell. Thus Lakanlẹ was deprived of both his lieutenants, and Oluyọle's party gained the upper hand ; Lakanlẹ had to take refuge with his old friend Agbeni at his quarters.

Oluyọle now obtained the object of his ambition, and would not listen to any adjustment of affairs except the death or expulsion of Lakanlẹ. The brave man hearing this put an end to his own life by ripping his bowels open with a jack-knife, and passing the entrails around his own neck. In a few minutes he expired in the arms of one of his men.

Thus Oluyọle became supreme at Ibadan.

CHAPTER XIII

THE LAST OF KATUNGA THE GREAT METROPOLIS AND THE END OF A DYNASTY

§ 1. Final Efforts to Throw off the Fulani Yoke

The Metropolis had long been left to herself whilst great and stirring events had been taking place all over the country. The outcome of the rebellion of the chiefs and the revolution was the foundation of modern Ibadan, Abẹokuta, Modakẹkẹ, the occupation of Ijaye, Abemọ, the destruction of the city of Owu, and the fall of many ancient towns in the plain, and above all the ascendancy of Ilọrin under the ravaging foreigners.

That such important events as these should take place, one after another, altering the face of the country, and the King not be able to promote or retard the accomplishment of any— a King only in name, the direct descendant of absolute monarchs and deified heroes—could not but be a matter of pain and grief to the sovereign. Added to all this was a great calamity which befel him at home, one that distressed him sore and accelerated his death. A fire broke out in the palace and all efforts to arrest its ravages failed, and most of the accumulated treasures of his ancestors were consumed in the conflagration! Great efforts were made to remove some to out-houses away from the direction of the flames, but unfortunately by a turn of the wind, those out-houses also caught fire and everything was lost!

Between the distress caused by the Ilọrins now masters of the country, and the destructive fires the King died of a broken heart. Prince Oluewu was elected his successor with the general consent of the nobles and the King-makers.

Oluewu was said to be a prince comely in person, but all too conscious of his own dignity and importance ; haughty and irritable in temperament. His one aim and determination was to recover his dominions from the Fulanis first, and then subdue all his refractory chiefs.

Soon after Oluewu's accession, Shitta the King of Ilọrin, required him to come to Ilọrin in person to pay homage to him as his vassal. But Oluewu was unwilling to go ; however, his great chiefs, and especially Prince Atiba of Agọ Ọja brought pressure and entreaties to bear upon him, and he was prevailed upon to accede to the wishes of the conqueror in order to save the capital and the remnant of the towns that still paid their allegiance to Ọyọ.

Shitta received him with every mark of honour and distinction; but all the same, the shame and disgrace of it all, with unutterable resentment rankled in the breast of King OLUEWU. The Gbẹdu drum was beaten before him as he went, and also on his returning. Shitta's attention was drawn to that particular drum and he asked some questions about it. When he was told it was a royal drum beaten before the King alone, he ordered it to be taken away, saying " There cannot be two Kings in my dominion but one only, and that is myself."

OLUEWU felt his humiliation keenly and was resolved to resent it at all cost or die in the attempt. But that was not all; the Emir of Ilọrin sent Jimba one of his head slaves after OLUEWU to ransack the palace at Ọyọ and to bring away anything of value he could lay his hands upon so that Ọyọ may not be said to have anything which Ilọrin has not. This Jimba did, and among other things removed were the 100 brass posts in the long corridor of the palace erected by King AGANJU.

Again, a short time after, Shitta required the ALÂFIN of Ọyọ to come over to Ilọrin to perform the ceremony known as " tapping the Koran," in order to become a true Moslem, but the ALÂFIN was resolved never to go to Ilọrin a second time come what may. The chiefs urged him to do so in vain. However, Akīoṣo the Baṣọrun and Ailumọ the Aṣipa went, against the express order of the King forbidding them to go ; and on account of this he was resolved to punish them, although they were too powerful for him to order their execution at once.

The ALÂFIN's refusal to go to Ilọrin being considered an offence to Shitta, the latter sent an army with Lanloke the chief of Ogodo, which ravaged the suburbs of Ọyọ and the city itself was threatened. At this crisis the ALÂFIN invited the aid of the Baribas, to assist him in subduing his enemies " within and without." Those within were the Baṣọrun and the Aṣipa who went to Ilọrin against his commands.

On a fatal morning the Baṣọrun and the Aṣipa went with the other noblemen to a council at the palace gate, for consultation about the impending Ilọrin war, and the defence of the city. Whilst there, they heard that the Baribas were entering the city by the Modahade gate. Thinking that they were invited by the King merely to help to defend the city, the Aṣipa rode to meet them and was according them a hearty welcome in the usual manner of men on horseback shaking the fist, when all of a sudden a shower of darts came pouring down upon him, and the son of one Fagbayibi shot him dead on horseback!

The Baribas then pursued after the Baṣọrun who fled to the palace begging the King to spare his life. " Ah," said the King, " why should you beg me now, are you not the master and I the subordinate ? Why crave your life from your servant ? "

In the noise and confusion that ensued with the entrance of the Baribas, the Baṣọrun managed to escape to his own house ; express messengers were thereupon sent to his relatives that he should be kept under strict surveillance whilst the King and his allies were engaged in the defence of the city, and that they would be held responsible for his escape. But a family council was held and in order to save him from a disgraceful death in public, his relatives put an end to his life by strangling.

The forces of nature came to the defence of Ọyọ on this occasion. There was a great storm, and whether it was due to the great number of glittering swords and spears brandished, or whatever may have been the cause, lightning was attracted and so large a number of men were struck in the Ilọrin host that their army was discomfited, and the men fled away in terror. Ọyọ was a great city, which could not be rushed by the Ilọrins nor could it be invested and reduced by a long siege, for there was always the fear that a prolonged siege of their metropolis by aliens might rouse the great chiefs of the country to its aid. Thus failing to take the city, Shitta's next tactics were the subversion of the remaining large Yoruba towns that still showed any allegiance to Ọyọ, and hence Gbodo was besieged. He also succeeded in securing the alliance of some powerful Yoruba chiefs among whom were the Onikoyi, Chief Ẹlẹbu of Agọ Ọja, and Prince Atiba of the same place. This last named having resided at Ilọrin for some time was well known to the Fulanis.

The ALÂFIN again secured the help of the Baribas. Eleduwẹ the Bariba king promised to help him not only to conquer the Ilọrins but also to subdue his rebel chiefs. Gbodo which was closely besieged by the Ilọrins was well nigh taken when timely help arrived in the person of the Eleduwẹ and his Bariba hordes. Some of the Yoruba chiefs were serving in the Ilọrin army at the time, notably those of Agọ Ọja mentioned above, but be it said to the praise of Prince Atiba that he was acting merely out of policy, for his soldiers, from private instructions previously received, were firing only gunpowder. This was suspected when in spite of the vigorous attacks of Atiba, his fire never killed or wounded anyone ; the guns of his men were thereupon examined, and the truth had to be confessed.

The Baribas were good archers, the siege of Gbodo was raised and the defeated Ilọrins and their allies were hotly pursued.

It was about the month of June, when the rivers were swollen by rain, and thousands of Ilọrin horse and foot were driven into the river Ogun and were drowned.   Ẹlẹbu the brother and successor of Ọja the founder of Ago found here a watery grave. He would have escaped death but for the plot against his life. It is said that the late Ọja was a dear friend to Prince Atiba and the friendship continued all through his life until he perished at the Kanla expedition ; but Ẹlẹbu his brother begrudged that friendship : he always suspected the influence and good faith of the prince, regarding him as a potential usurper of his family rights ; and when he succeeded his brother as the Balẹ of Ago, there was always friction between them.   Consequently on this occasion as Ẹlẹbu plunged into the river during the flight and with great difficulty swam across he caught hold of a Gbingbin tree that stretched its branches far out into the river, but one Lọhọsà who had preceded him and got on to the tree, seeing Ẹlẹbu in his exhausted condition, and in order to do good service to Prince Atiba, cut off that branch of the tree and Ẹlẹbu was swept away and was drowned.

Prince Atiba himself nearly lost his life there also, had not Yesufu his uncle, carried him across on his back and given him his horse on the other side to ride home.

But the prince and many others owed their life really to Majẹ his balogun. The Baribas would have overtaken them at the banks of the river before they could cross had he not kept them at bay whilst horses and men were struggling across, and so he gave up his life to save theirs, for he fell there.

The wreck of the Ilọrin army gathered at Bàlà and Iwò from which places they returned home.

But the Eleduwẹ was not satisfied with raising the seige of Gbodo, he was determined to free the country entirely of these foreigners, and hence he was resolved to conquer Ilọrin.   OLUEWU the ALÂFIN, whose cause he was espousing was right glad and sent round to invite the co-operation of all his subjects including those who were allies of the Ilọrins, knowing that they were allies only out of policy, but not willingly, and that they would be glad to be free from the foreign yoke.

But matters were complicated by the fact that most of the Ọyọ chief towns in the eastern and western provinces had been subjugated by the Ilọrins and were vassals of that state. Hence at a council of war held by the two Kings it was decided that they should not march straight from Ọyọ to Ilọrin, but make a detour

by the western province, in order to secure the alliance and good
faith of these vassal states, and thus to collect an overwhelming
army against Ilọrin. Accordingly the Eleduwẹ sent Jankọrọ
one of his war-chiefs to garrison Ago Ọja, whose chief was an Ilọrin
ally, and Jẹgẹdẹ another war-chief to garrison Ọtẹfan whilst he
himself was following with his invincible army in their wake.

The Ilọrins hearing of the threatened invasion were not idle
either, but were making full preparations offensive and defensive.

Jimba the head slave of the king of Ilọrin headed an expedition
of horse and foot to the Ọtẹfan farms when they heard of the
garrison there, and brought away several captives. Jimba's
route in going was through the Ẹsiẹlẹ farms, but was so far from
the town that his company was not seen. On his return he came
through the town and halted at the gate to receive Fasọla the
Balẹ, who came to pay him his respects. Jimba did not dismount
as he was in a hurry to get away with his captives lest he be overtaken, for he was sure of a pursuit. On horseback he accepted
the hospitality of a drink of cold water, and before hurrying away
gave the following advice to Fasọla " You are between two fires
and you would be wise to vacate this town at once. I am
just returning as you see with captives from the Ọtẹfan farms.
Although you were not aware of my passing through your farms
yet had I been detected, I would have suspected you as a traitor,
and would have punished you on my return although you may be
innocent. And now as I return through your town the Ọtẹfan
pursuers will track me to this place and you may likely suffer for
it and we have no means of protecting you, hence I advise you
speedily to vacate this place."

The Ẹsiẹlẹ people after consultation together decided at
once to follow his advice. Ọtẹfan being the nearest large town
and wishing to cast in their lot with the new conqueror, they
decided to escape thither and accordingly despatched one Bankọle
to apprise Idowu the Balẹ of Ọtẹfan of their intentions. At
Bankọle's instance they promised not to desert their home before
his return as they treated him on a previous occasion; but their
cowardice got the better of them. On returning Bankọle met the
fugitives by the way and this was the third and last time Ẹsiẹlẹ
was deserted, and is to this day an uninhabited desert.

It was in the month of March 1830, that the Eleduwẹ accompanied by Prince Atiba of Ago Ọja and Jato, Eleduwẹ's general,
joined the garrison at Ọtẹfan the rendezvous of the Ọyọ army.
Kurũmi of Ijaye, the Asẹyin of Isẹyin, the Sabigana of Igana,
the Ọkẹrẹ of Saki and others of the western province met them
there. Here King OLUEWU and the Eleduwẹ pledged the confidence

of all the Ọyọ war-chiefs save the Balẹ of Ogbomọsọ and the
Onikoyi, both of whom were in secret alliance with the Ilọrins,
although they outwardly professed loyalty to their lawful
sovereign.

Meanwhile, the Emir of Ilọrin alarmed by this great host sent
to the Sultan of Sokoto his suzerain for help. The Sultan sent
17 kings under Esugoyi of Rabbah to his aid, and they came
with such an overwhelming force that those of the two kings were
as a mere handful before them. The two kings were besieged at
Ọtẹfan by the Ilọrin and Niger hosts, several battles were fought,
and they were nearly overwhelmed by numbers. At the last great
battle, but for the courage, wisdom and experience of Eleduwẹ
the Bariba King, the fate of the whole expedition would have been
decided on that day. He fought in the centre, the ALÂFIN and
Ọyọ chiefs in the right and left wings. He sent aid to those
fighting in both wings, so that they forced the enemy into the
centre, and in one furious charge he bore down upon them and
dispersed them. Esugoyi's army was routed with great slaughter
and fled away in confusion. The victory however, was dearly
bought, for Yenibini, King Eleduwẹ's first-born son fell in the
battle.

The Ọyọs pursued their victory too far till they met with a
disaster. They dearly learnt the lesson that in the pursuit of a
foe footmen are no match for horsemen. The Ilọrins having
recovered from the panic of their defeat, a body of horsemen
suddenly wheeled round and charged upon their pursuers and
speared about 400 of them, thereby forcing them to desist from
the pursuit. They were then able to retreat in good order, and
made good their escape.

§ 2. FAILURE. THE ELEDUWE WAR

About the month of June, 1830, the two Kings left Ọtẹfan for
Adeyi, and thence proceeded to Ogbomọsọ. Here King OLUEWU
sent round to the whole of the Yoruba chiefs to join him in the last
effort to throw off the Fulani yoke. There responded to his call
Oluyọle of Ibadan with several Ẹgba war-chiefs, Kurũmi of
Ijaye, Ayọ of Abemọ́, Timi of Ẹde and others. This mighty host
remained here for about six months wasting time. They were
holding councils almost every day as to how best they might
attack Ilọrin with success. But here also the future of the expedition was foreshadowed and the doom of the allied Kings was
sealed. There were two principal causes for this, viz., the rapacity
of the Bariba soldiers, and the imprudence of the Kings.

The excesses of the Baribas made the Yoruba chiefs and

people fear lest they pass from one master to another and a worse. The Fulanis were after all a superior race, but the Baribas, a race of bandits, as masters would be more intolerable. The country was literally being ravaged by them. They considered themselves licensed to all the goats in the country. Even when kept in the inner apartment of the houses, they would get at them and devour them. Sheep they did not care for, but goats, say they are traitors and must be devoured. For this reason the Yorubas termed them "Arun-ẹran" (cattle devourers) while the Iḷọrins termed them Ikòrikò (wolves).

Their excesses consisted not only in devouring cattle, but also in stripping and depriving helpless ones of their cloths ; at length they spared not even men though they might be armed. Organized bands would attack and deprive men of all their valuables.

The Ọyọs could offer little or no resistance because the persons of the Baribas were held sacred, already being considered the deliverers of the country.

The following instance will show how sacred their persons were regarded. One of them attacked an Ọyọ man, who was not willing to give way lightly and the Bariba was shot dead by him. The Ọyọ man ran away. So much noise and hubbub were raised about this, that both Kings rode in person to the spot to see the corpse. The converse to this might have happened every day without provoking any comment. But the eyewitnesses of the affray were so much in sympathy with the murderer that he was not betrayed, so disgusted was everybody with the excesses of the Baribas. All this might have been avoided if instead of wasting time at Ogbomọsọ they had given the soldiers work to do by marching at once on Iḷọrin, half demoralized by two successive defeats. On the contrary they allowed them time to regain their confidence and perfect their defences. Small blame indeed to the soldiers as each one had to provide for himself, however prolonged the campaign.

The two Kings were imprudent enough to betray their feelings. It leaked out that after the conquest of Iḷọrin all the refractory Yoruba chiefs who had usurped the King's prerogative would be murdered by the help of the Bariba king ; and the kingdom would again be one under the ALÂFIN.

One or two instances might be given of how the Kings betrayed themselves.

1. Timi Bamgbaiye of Ẹdẹ on his arrival at the camp went straight to pay his homage to the King. Being a corpulent man the Eleduwẹ was heard to remark " See this corpulent fellow, one of those who have made themselves fat upon the King's

diverted revenues. Never mind, he also will be dealt with after
the war as he deserves."

2. Above all the others the one who appeared the most offensive
to the Bariba king was Prince Atiba of Ago Oja. He was all
Fulani in his manners. He had resided at Ilorin for some time
and adopted the Fulani custom of being lifted up and helped
off his horse by his attendants, and one of his menials ready
with his sandals so that he might not have to walk barefoot when
his riding boots were off.

The two Kings were one day sitting at a public meeting, and
Prince Atiba arrived late with an august pageantry to the disgust
of the kings and chiefs present, who could not afford as much.
He was preceded by his Junior war-chiefs mounted on strong
ponies, with their attendant footmen ; then those mounted on
larger horses came after, then himself followed on a specially
powerful animal richly caparisoned, with a large retinue. He
was lifted off his horse his sandals being ready for him to
put on, contrary to the etiquette of the country to be shod before
a king. This was disgusting to both Kings and to many of the
Oyo chiefs present, who, notwithstanding the rebellion and
revolution still going on, have yet full respect for royalty.

Olurinde the chief of Sepeteri in the eastern province, could
not bear to see this act of disrespect pass unreproved, so he
went near and pulled off the sandals from Atiba's feet, and thus
reprimanded him : " Know you not before whom you are ? How
dare you be shod in the presence of our King ? " Atiba could
not brook a reproof from a commoner and from wounded pride
fiercely retorted; "And who are you ? And what is that to you ?
The King is my father and, as a prince, I have privileges which
the likes of you can never aspire to. I can even pass by him into
the harem which none of you can dare do ; but who are you ? "
The contention was so sharp that Kitoyi the Okere of Saki had
to interpose begging Prince Atiba to have respect for the two
Kings, to take off the sandals, and not to persist merely for the
purpose of spiting the Sepeteri chief.

The Kings noticed all this and marked Prince Atiba out as one
of those to be dealt with after the war.

Lastly the disaffection towards OLUEWU was increased by the
unreasoning stubbornness he displayed to whatever advice was
given him, however good. The Oyo chiefs who were left to guard
the city were kept informed of everything that transpired. They
were very anxious as to the fate of the expedition ; their own
interests were chiefly involved in the fate of the capital. They
were sure the offended chiefs would take revenge and wreck the army

of which they formed a part. Consequently they sent message after message to advise the King not to advance on Ilọrin direct from Ogbomọṣọ but to come by way of Ikoyi, Iwò, Gbogun, and Saho making the attack from the north so that having the capital and the Niger provinces behind him he might in case of defeat have safe places within easy reach to retire upon. And in order to give strength and force to the advice, they represented it as the express advice of the god Ifa by divination. Knowing his haughtiness they sent their messages through the Bariba king, to whom alone he might perhaps listen ; but as they anticipated, not even from the Eleduwẹ would he brook any such advice. He was for marching straight on Ilọrin from Ogbomọṣọ.

Before the army marched out of Ogbomọṣọ the disaffected Yoruba provincial kings and chiefs entered into a conspiracy to desert the King and his ally at a critical moment and therefore in order to apprise the Ilọrins of their intentions they sent them a parabolic message in soap, camwood, and kărinkan (flesh brush) implying " We are attending the bride to the bridegroom's house." This was fully understood at Ilọrin.

The huge host left Ogbomọṣọ in December 1830 by slow stages encamping first at Aduin, where they were for nine days. (Ilọrin is but one good day's walk from Ogbomọṣọ). On the tenth day they advanced to Jayin, thence to Ogele, and from Ogele they encamped at the farm of one Ajiya of Ilọrin. Never before was Ilọrin threatened by so large a force, consequently the consternation there was great, and vast preparations were made for battle, offensive and defensive. The face of every man was marked by grim determination to do his best. The Moslem priests were very busy making charms and amulets not only for individual self-protection but also in order to defeat the enemy completely. A crow, a cat, and a crown bird (the Agufan) with charms tied round their necks were sent by special messengers to be left in the camp of the allied armies. These messengers were caught and when threatened they boldly showed that they despised death and said to their captors " Take our advice and decamp at once for as for the yams you are now cooking in our farms it is a question whether you will be able to eat them before you are defeated, and even if you should, we are quite sure that the survivors will evacuate them at the Ogbomọṣọ farms."

Shortly after this a company of Ilọrin horse surprised a body of men who went foraging, and the Bariba troops who went out against them were repulsed, but Prince Atiba whose men were armed with guns came to their timely aid, drove back the horsemen and captured a horse.

To show the wanton excesses of these Baribas, even after this skirmish in which they figured so badly, they went unceremoniously to Prince Atiba's tent and coolly loosed the horse that was captured and were taking it away ! They laid claim to it not because it was captured by them, but because they considered themselves now the masters as it was they who had the first brush with the enemy. But the Prince was not the man to forego his claims easily, he pointed out forcibly how, but for his timely succour there could not have been any question as to the ownership of the horse, for instead of capturing, they themselves would all have been killed. or captured. The contention was so fierce between them that the ALÂFIN had to send a special message to Atiba to forego his claims and give up the horse for the sake of peace.

The following day being Friday the Kings did not take the field until 2 p.m., Fridays being considered unlucky up to that hour.

The Kings again fought in the centre in the highway called the Pàkábà road, and located the Yoruba war-chiefs on the right and left wings of the army.

But Prince Atiba of Agọ and the Timi Bamgbaiye of Ẹdẹ did not fire a shot or shoot an arrow before they gave way, affording the enemy an advantage to surround the two Kings. It was Oluyọle of Ibadan alone who seemed not to have been apprised of the plot, for he fought for some time on the road leading to Oke Suna and pressed the Ilọrins hard towards the town wall. The camp was taken behind them and fired before the Kings were aware of the perfidy of the Yoruba chiefs. There was no alternative now for them but to fight desperately and sell their lives as dearly as possible. The Eleduwẹ fought with his usual bravery and exhausted all his skill to retrieve the position if possible, but he was overpowered by numbers and fell among the slain. His head was taken off and carried in triumph to the town and exposed upon the town wall.

King OLUEWU's heir seeing that the day was lost rode up to his father and bade him farewell, to meet again in the other world. Putting spurs into his horse he galloped to meet the enemy and fought gallantly until he fell among those he had slain.

The Ilọrin horse and foot were in pursuit all night and unfortunately for the wreck of the Ọyọ army whilst escaping to Ogbomọsọ they missed the way taking one that led back to Ilọrin ; they met the pursuers at a short distance and were all either captured or slain.

Thus was fulfilled the prophecy of the charm bearers who were caught, that the yams they were then cooking might be eaten at the Ilọrin farms but would be evacuated in the Ogbomọsọ farms.

Lanloke the chief of Ogodo who had always been an inveterate enemy of Ọyọ and an active ally of Ilọrin, taking advantage of the absence of the King and principal war-chiefs from the city, came and attacked Ọyọ, but he was repulsed by the Òhota nick-named Ari-ibọn-peji eyin, (one whose gun can create a gap in the upper front teeth), who was left in charge.

When the news of the disaster reached Ọyọ and that both Kings had perished, Lanloke again attacked the city but was again repulsed. The citizens fearing that he would receive re-inforce-ment from Ilọrin did not wait to try any further conclusions ; the great metropolis was deserted, some fled to Kihisi, some to Igboho, and some even to Ilọrin. As it was not a flight from an enemy in pursuit many who reached Kihisi and Igboho safely with their family returned again and again for their household goods and chattels till one Agandangban went and told Lanloke that Ọyọ had been deserted, and the latter proceeded immediately to plunder, and carry away what was left by the citizens.

Thus failed the fourth and last campaign against Ilọrin, and such was the fall of the great Metropolis " Eyeo or Katunga," the ancient Ọyọ, still in ruins.

THE INTERREGNUM

§ 1. CIVIL WAR AT ABEMǪ

BEFORE the Eleduwẹ war broke out, a marked disaffection and rivalry was rife between the two leading chiefs of Abemǫ, Ayǫ the Balẹ and Okoyan *alias* Lahan the next man to him.

The latter claimed relationship to Ǫyabi the late Kakanfo at Ajasẹ and hence to Kurūmi of Ijaye also. This rivalry became apparent during the expedition, for Lahan out of spite to his chief Ayǫ, went over to Kurūmi, encamped with him and fought under his standard as if he was an Ijaye man. The disaffection now became an open rupture and it was evident to all that Lahan was secretly abetted by chief Kurūmi of Ijaye. It subsequently became known that Lahan and Kurūmi were plotting to fall upon Ayǫ suddenly and despatch him after their retreat, before reaching home. Ayǫ apprised of this, suddenly broke up his encampment, and by forced marches reached home a considerable time before Lahan who followed hard after him.

But Ayǫ instead of entering his house remained squatting on a mat in the square in front of his compound, close by the spot where his women folk were dyeing cloths, his horse standing by his side, and his spear stuck in the ground close by him.

Lahan halted outside the town walls, afraid to enter. When Ayǫ heard of it he sent to invite him to return to his house in peace, but Lahan suspicious and afraid to enter by the main gate took a circuitous route and entered by the one nearest to his quarter of the town where he commanded about 200 compounds. Their designs having now failed Kurūmi became very anxious about the safety of his friend Lahan, and not wishing to leave him thus at the mercy of Ayǫ he attempted to bring about a reconciliation between them before proceeding home to Ijaye; but Ayǫ politely declined his interference saying that having just returned home from this great war it was too early to talk about such matters. Kurūmi thus disappointed proceeded homewards but first despatched Amǫdu one of his distinguished captains on horseback to bid Ayǫ good bye and to say he would return in a short time to settle their difference.

Amǫdu met Ayǫ on the same spot his horse still unsaddled but all his men had dispersed, only about 5 attendants remained

L

with him. Amọdu having delivered his message returned to his master, and suggested to him that a better opportunity than this cannot be had of making short work of the whole affair ; Ayọ's men having dispersed he could easily be surprised and killed.

Kurũni took the hint and made for Ayọ ; the latter surprised to see an armed force coming on towards him, hastily jumped upon his horse and was ready for action. Kurũmi perceiving it would not be an easy matter to accomplish his purpose, did not venture upon an attack but speedily wheeled round and left the town by another gate.

Ayọ and his men thereupon became mad with rage and they fell upon Lahan, fired his quarter of the town, took his men with their wives and children as captives of war ! Lahan himself was spared with but a few attendants, and allowed to shelter himself in a small house in that quarter which had escaped the conflagration. Here he spent a most miserable night of grief, remorse and disappointment, having lost all his family and all his property.

Chief Oluyọle of Ibadan arrived at Abemọ̀ only a day too late to be of any service to his friends, and was very sorry that this had happened, especially at this crisis. He visited Lahan where he was to sympathize with him for his misfortunes having a reminiscence of his own troubles on his return from the Ọta war. He went straight from Lahan to Ayọ to effect a reconciliation between them and the release of those who were seized, contending that they cannot be regarded as prisoners of war but fellow townsmen and victims of a civil fight. He further showed the impolicy of having one part of the town desolate. He succeeded with Ayọ and with some of his chiefs ; some had even set free their own captives. Thus, in order to assure Oluyọle, one Ọga appealed to Kukomi one of his followers in the presence of them all, "Have I not released mine ? " In the same way one Ẹkũòdebẹ appealed to one Bankọle. The reply in both cases was in the affirmative. Thereupon one Akilapa and Agidi-kò-kọ-iku who had not yet done so asked leave to go home and release theirs at once. Everything now seemed to make for a peaceful settlement, when one Ogungbade an Owu man then residing at Abemọ̀ raised a strong objection to the proceedings ; he declined to set his captives free and declared himself unconcerned as to the results even if it be the destruction of Abemọ̀ and the loss of his own liberty. Said he " I am an Owu man by birth, my parents came from the ancient Owu Ipole to the city of Owu where I was born. The same fortune that smiled on my parents at Owu Ipole, smiled on them at the city of Owu. Here am I, fortune is smiling on me to-day although

I was taken captive at the fall of the city of Owu. Let Abemọ̀
be destroyed to-day and let me lose all I have and be taken captive,
I shall still be a great man wherever I may be. 'Tis enough, Abemọ̀
may be destroyed in part or in whole ; it matters nothing. We
shall not release our prisoners."

Unfortunately at such a crisis as this, Chief Ayọ was in an
inebriated condition, although he was conscious of what was going
on and was able to signify his acquiescence to Chief Oluyọle ; yet
throughout all the proceedings and the wicked proposals of the
Owu man he remained silent, and further, he displayed in the
presence of Oluyọle some of those disgusting habits customary
with him of soiling himself while in that state.

Oluyọle was indignant with Ayọ and his councillors and looked
upon them all as a number of fools ; he, however, concealed his
anger, but the whole affair was terminated abruptly and unsatis-
factorily.

About the time of Oluyọle's departure however, Ayọ was
able to thank him for the interest he kindly took in the affairs
of the town, and presented him with a young woman among the
captives. Oluyọle was delighted with this acquisition to his
harem. She was described as a young woman of great beauty,
of a fair complexion and a slim figure. But the mother hastened
forward with a tender appeal to Oluyọle, and prostrating (after the
manner of men) before him, said " She cannot be your wife,
for she is your relative ; we also are of the Baṣọrun descent like
yourself." Oluyọle yielded to her entreaties but demanded 15
heads of cowries for her release ; this was paid and the girl was
handed to her mother.

Oluyọle left Abemọ for Ibadan by way of Ijaye where he spent
5 days with Kurūmi, and both of them being offended at Ayọ's
conduct the fate of Abemọ was thereupon settled and sealed.

§ 2. THE DESTRUCTION OF ABEMỌ̀

According to the settled arrangement between Kurūmi and
Oluyọle during the stay of the latter at Ijaye, their movements
were to be kept private as much as possible. Abemọ̀ was to be
taken by surprise in order to avoid the necessity of a siege. The
Ibadan forces were to join those of Ijaye and in order to do this
without their objective being known, Oluyọle gave it out that the
Aṣẹyin was paying a visit to Ibadan and that they should go out
and escort him to the town.

As the head chief went outside the town wall, no war-chief
dared remain behind ; hence, all went out according to custom.

They went as far as Ijaye but when they saw the Ijaye army

also marshalled forth then they knew that they were going against Abemọ̀.

It was quite late before Ayọ knew that evil was determined against him. He went out that morning to review his troops. Two of his generals Aruna and Ajadi being accused of treason were before him, and whilst he was enquiring into the charge they were interrupted by the approach of the enemy. The intrepid warrior at once jumped upon his horse, and dashed into the ranks of the enemy. He performed feats of valour that day, he broke through their ranks, had his horse shot under him and himself wounded in the leg. But he was not dispirited ; he called for another horse and fought bravely at the head of his people. The men of Abemọ̀, however were overpowered by numbers, for whilst fighting bravely at one gate of the town, the Ibadans entered by another and set fire to the town. All hopes being now lost, Ayọ escaped with a few horsemen and followers to Agọ Ọja (the present Ọyọ) being hotly pursued by Ijaye and Ibadan troops.

In order not to incur the displeasure of Kurūmi and Oluyọle the two leading chiefs of the country whom he hoped hereafter would be his back stay, Prince Atiba of Agọ Ọja told Ayọ that he could not protect him and consequently he should leave the town before his pursuers arrived there. Ayọ took the way to Ojomgbodu on his way to Ilọrin, but after a while on considering the humiliation of it all and the grave probabilities that lay before him, he chose death rather than dishonour.

He dismounted at a certain spot and sat under a tree, his horse standing by him. He sent away his little band of devoted followers in order to die alone like a soldier. Here he calmly awaited his pursuers.

According to one account, at the sight of them he sprang again upon his horse and made for them. He threw one Lakonu off his steed and brandishing his spear round and round him, exclaimed " But for Atiba you are a dead man," then the men opened fire upon him and he dropped down dead.

But another account says he sat with calm dignity under the tree and offered no resistance whilst they showered their deadly weapons upon him and he dropped down dead.

Thus perished one of the best and ablest of the Ọyọ or Yoruba generals. His remains were brought back to Agọ Ọja and interred there.

Ayọ like the late Ojo Amepo was a good horseman and one of the best generals of the day, but drink was his greatest vice, and to that may be attributed the cause of his ruin as well as that of Abemọ̀. His aide-de-camp was nick-named Amu-igba-lẹgbẹ-giri, i.e., one who grasps tight the sides of a drinking bowl ; because he himself was hardly inferior to his master in that respect as the name implies.

Although the ruler of the town yet he often spent as much as three days and nights out of home attending " wakes " at night wherever he was invited, and during daytime dancing to the bàta drum in various quarters of the town like the commonest citizen. He offered the right hand of fellowship to anyone who could drink like himself.

He was by nature generous and merciful, in which respect he was most unlike his bloodthirsty peers of that age. As an instance of this a story was told of his favourite Amu-igba-lẹgbẹ who on leaving the Balẹ's house quite late one night the worse for drink missed his way into his chief's harem, and slept by the side of one of his wives thinking he had got home ! When the woman awoke in the early hours of the morning, and saw a stranger by her side she cried out and roused the whole establishment.

Amugba starting from his sleep being now sober, took in the situation at once and resigned himself to the only fate he felt sure was awaiting him under the circumstances.

Overcome with fear he went home in great distress and when the matter was known in the house the whole compound was deserted for fear of the usual confiscation and punishment in such a case. Amugba expected nothing but death and when about noon he heard his chief's drum coming towards his house, he thought the fatal hour was come. Ayọ entered and saw him trembling and attempting an apology ; he simply jeered at him and said : " Why are you looking so dejected ? Is it because you missed your way last night ? Never mind the mistake, let's go out and drink away yesterday's occurrence."

Amugba thought it was only a stratagem to get him out of his house to be arrested and executed; he followed, however, but was still dejected. Whilst drinking in a friend's house Ayọ observed him still in that mood, and said to him with surprise, " Are you still downcast on account of yesterday's affair ? Why that is past and gone ; it only proved I can beat you in drink, for I drank far more than you did on that occasion, but was not in the least affected, whilst you could not find your way home." So the matter passed off in jokes.

Abemọ and Ijaye were rival towns and the former had the sobriquet of " Abemọ ṣúrú ọkọ ilu bàntàtà " (Abemọ small and compact, but the husband of a huge town) meaning Ijaye.

FOURTH PERIOD. — ARREST OF DISINTEGRATION —
ILORINS CHECKMATED—ATTEMPTS AT RECONSTRUC-
TION—INTERTRIBAL WARS—BRITISH PROTECTORATE.

CHAPTER XV

THE NEW CITY AND NEW GOVERNMENT

§ 1. PRINCE ATIBA : HIS EARLY LIFE AND HISTORY

PRINCE ATIBA was the son of King ABIODUN by an Akeitan
woman. According to one account, he was born in the city of
Ọyọ, his father died when he was but a child, and when ABIODUN'S
children were being ill-treated by King AOLE his mother fled with
him to her own town in the country.

But another account was of a more romantic interest and is
more probable, as being characteristic of that age. According to
this account, his mother, a slave at Gudugbu, was given as a hostage
to the ALÂFIN of Ọyọ. She had an intimate friend who was much
distressed by this separation. After 8 or 10 weary months, she
was resolved at all costs to go up to the city to visit her friend with
whom she had been associated from childhood.

The Gudugbu hostage was too insignificant to be noticed among
the crowd of women in the King's harem until this strange visit
of her friend drew the King's attention to her. The visitor from
the country loitering within the precincts of the palace was asking
all whom she saw coming from the women's quarters to call her
Ẹni-Olufan one of the King's wives, but no one knew who that
was. At length King ABIODUN was told that a woman from the
country was asking for one of his wives, and this unusual incident
aroused the King's curiosity. The Gudugbu woman was called
to his presence to state the object of her visit. She replied :—
" May your majesty live long. The young woman from Gudugbu
given as a hostage was my bosom friend, and for the past 8 months
or more I have had no one to talk to, and hence I was resolved to
visit her."

The King then said to her, " Are you not afraid to come here
and to enquire for my wife ? Suppose I add yourself to the harem
or kill you or sell you ? " She replied, " For my friend's sake I am
prepared to undergo any treatment, and if your majesty make a
wife of me I shall be happy as my friend and I will see each other
every day."

The King greatly admired their friendship ; he gave permission for her to be lodged with her friend, and was by this led to pay some attention to the Gudugbu hostage.

For three months these two friends enjoyed each other's company and as the King's wife was now in the way of becoming a mother, he was graciously pleased to send them home. He sent for both of them one morning, and after a few approbatory remarks on their friendship, he loaded them with presents, and said to his wife's friend, "I am sending your friend home with you in order that you may not fail to have some one to unbosom your mind to as hitherto. I make you both my deputy for that part of the country. All matters to be referred to Ọyọ will henceforth be brought to you for decision, all the tribute monies will be paid to you also, and as my wife will be unable to undertake a journey, I expect your visit here as often as you can come." With this instruction he dismissed them and sent several Eunuchs and Ilaris with them as escort and to commend them formally to the care and protection of the Balẹ of Gudugbu. Both these women returned to Gudugbu in quite a different capacity from that in which they left it. The little town was all astir on their arrival, and many were the private murmurs against Ẹni-Olufan's friend for the heavy responsibilities she had brought upon them. Great deference, however, was paid to them both, and they became practically the supreme rulers and judges of that district. The King's wife in course of time gave birth to a son who was named Atibà ; her friend also (who was a married woman) gave birth to a son named Onipẹde. The intimacy existing between the two mothers re-appeared also in the boys from childhood up to manhood.

[This account is reconcilable with the first as it is possible that as an infant, Atiba may have been taken to Ọyọ to see his father, and may have been there till Aolẹ's reign when the mother had to flee with him back to the country as stated above].

Atiba grew up a wild and reckless lad. When he was of age, his father ordered that the mother should apportion to him the tribute money of that district, this continued until the succeeding reign when the country was thrown into confusion and anarchy.

This circumstance probably led his mother to remove with him from Gudugbu to Akeitan her own home. Here Atiba was under the care of his maternal uncle who was now head of the house and the family estate.

Atiba was brought up as a tailor, but he preferred a wild and predatory life, for which the circumstances of the times afforded great opportunities. A story was told of him that once being very hungry, he asked his uncle for a yam, and the uncle not only refused it him, but took the opportunity of reprimanding him sharply for living the idle life of a kidnapper. " If I had lived on man-stealing like you," said he, " I could not have got any yam." But Yesufu the younger uncle felt sorry for his nephew and said to Atiba that whilst he (the uncle) was living, he (Atiba) would never suffer the pinch of hunger. This incident had its reward hereafter as will be noticed in its place.

From Akeitan Prince Atiba made several incursions into the Gudugbu farms, and was generally a pest to the country round about.

In order not to bring trouble on the Akeitan people, Atiba was urged to remove his residence to the town of Agọ where he would find in Ọja the chief of that place a man of a like spirit to his own, of a warlike disposition, and he did so.

But when Atiba arrived at Agọ, Ọja was strongly advised not to let him settle down there, because a man like him would eventually become master of the town. Elẹbu, Ọja's brother was the chief opponent. But Ọja did not follow this advice. " How can I," said he "an officer on the staff of the Kakanfo, and a title-bearer in the kingdom, turn away my prince ? " Ọja continued friendly to him until his fall in the Kanla expedition.

Their kidnapping expeditions were at that time chiefly directed against the Ẹgbas in the Oke Ogun districts near Sagaun. They found them so simple and unsophisticated in those days that when a kidnapper had captured several of them and was in quest for more he had only to leave his cap or his spear or any other personal property by the side of them, and bid them wait for him there, and should another kidnapper fall in with them he was to be shown the sign of prepossession, and thus they would be left untouched until their captor returned. These captives never made any effort to escape.

Atiba rose to importance by committing acts of violence and extortion with impunity, from the great deference paid to his high birth. In that age of anarchy and confusion he collected around himself all lawless men, insolvent debtors, slaves who had deserted their masters. His wealth was continually augmented by fresh marauding expeditions, his men behaving like the Jamâs, himself at the head of them.

By his address and largess Atiba won to himself the following chiefs of Ọyọ, viz., Aderinko, Ladejọbi, Olumọlẹ, Oluwajò, Lọsà Oluwaiye (the Alagbâ), Adefūmi, Lakonu, Toki Majẹ, Falade, and Gbenla.

His slaves who had horses and a large retinue each were :—

Ẹni-d'Ọlọrun (who subsequently became the Apeka), Galajimọ, Ọtẹlọwọ and Ọgboinu his mounted trumpeter.

Ẹlẹbu succeeded his brother as the Balẹ of Agọ. As might be expected he was not on good terms with Atiba; but the latter had already risen to such a height of greatness and popularity that Ẹlẹbu could neither crush him nor turn him out of the town; they remained antagonists till Ẹlẹbu was drowned in the river during the Gbodo war, as related above.

Before Ẹlẹbu's death, Ajanaku of Ilọrin to whom Agọ Ọja paid tribute summoned them both to Ilọrin and asked Shitta his sovereign to effect a reconciliation between them. The turban was given to both as a sign of brotherhood in the Moslem faith. This reconciliation was only on the surface, but by no means real. It was at this time that all children born at Agọ had Moslem names given to them and many adults and aged people changed theirs in order to be in good favour with the Jamâs of Ilọrin, who then infested the country.

Atiba had nearly lost his life in the Gbodo expedition; his horse was shot dead under him and the Baribas were pressing hard behind him in pursuit. His life-long friend Onipẹde galloped past him paying no heed to the despairing cry of his friend and master: " Onipẹde here am I, will you leave me behind to perish ? " Onipẹde notwithstanding this rushed on into the river Ogun and swam across safe to the other side. But when Atiba's uncle, Yesufu came up and saw him in such straits he dismounted and offered him his horse. Atiba declined to take it, but Yesufu forced him to accept it, saying " Even if I perish in this war I know that you will take care of my children." Yesufu was a powerful swimmer and he assisted both the horse and the rider safe to the other side. Adekidero the Lemọmu also offered his own horse to be used alternately with Yesufu's until they reached home.

Onipẹde did not wait for him although he was riding on a horse bought for him by the very Prince he now deserted. It was even reported of him that after he had reached the other side of the river, he halted to watch with amusement the distress and danger of his friend battling with the swift current until Yesufu came to his assistance, and that on the Prince's reaching the other side Onipẹde came up with a smile and an untimely joke saying " The intrepid warrior that you are, I did not know that a river current could conquer you." The Prince said nothing, and showed no sign of resentment, but Onipẹde from that day became a marked man, because it was evident to Atiba that his death would have excited no feelings of sympathy and regret in Onipẹde.

Up to this time Onipẹde enjoyed his entire confidence. Whatever he said or did was indisputable ; any criminal pardoned by him was free, and latterly he would not even take the trouble of acquainting the Prince with all that he did. He was known beyond the confines of the kingdom as the confidant of the Prince and all foreigners residing at Agọ were under his protection. He was always attended by a large retinue of foot and of horsemen as a Prince, whenever he paid visits in town or in going to his farm. He was the greatest favourite at the Prince's palace ; no one was allowed to see the Prince or obtain favours from him except through Onipẹde. The love Atiba had for this companion of his childhood and youth made him blind to all his faults until his eyes were opened by the incident narrated above.

Onipẹde at the zenith of his popularity quite forgot himself and regarded the Prince rather as his equal or co-partner, although as a matter of fact he was in no way equal to one of his war-chiefs or his notable slaves enumerated above. Still all of them used to show him due respect and pay him marked deference as one above them, so he came to set himself as a rival of his master ; but the incident of the Gbodo disaster was the means of his fall.

On their arrival home from the unsuccessful war, they hastened to fortify the town against an expected invasion. Atiba attended by all his great warriors was digging a trench right round the town, when Onipẹde rode up attended by a retinue of mounted servants. Atiba could no longer suppress his anger but ordered him to take up a digger and work like any of the common labourers. For one who had always lived an easy life Onipẹde's hands became blistered and sore. There are two accounts given of his death : one was that after this Atiba ordered him to be slain and buried in an upright posture when they returned home ; and that his slaves carried out his orders by showering darts upon Onipẹde, cut off his head and buried him in a house near the present Akẹsan market.

But a more probable account given of his death was as follows : The Prince and his servants began by slighting him, the latter losing no opportunity of showing him marks of disrespect. He now observed that he was no longer in favour but the exalted position he had already attained placed him above fear ; and indeed the Prince could not attack him in an open civil fight without dire results, for he was the commander of some of the greatest war-chiefs in the town. An opportunity at length was offered when he was unattended. He met Atiba where he was busy with his servants storing up his Bẹrẹ grass, and there and then he ordered his slaves to club him to death. Such was the end of Onipẹdẹ.

By the death of Ẹlẹbu, Ọja's children lost their natural protector and guardian, and the people their chief. Prince Atiba who was aiming at the supreme power placed none of Ọja's children who were capable as head of the house and chief of the town, but rather his younger brother Ailumọ, whom he knew to be weak in intellect. He placed him over the house with the title of Mọgaji till after the Eleduwẹ war, he should be formally installed as Balẹ of Agọ. In the meantime Atiba constituted himself the administrator of the affairs of the town in the place of Ọja's children and overshadowed even the Mọgaji himself. Thus the fears of the late Ẹlẹbu were fully realized and the town of Agọ practically passed out of the hands of the children of Ọja the founder.

§ 2. Atiba's Accession to the Throne

That Atiba was aspiring to the throne was evident to all when they were assembled for the Eleduwẹ war. He was even then far more powerful than the King and all eyes were turned upon him as the one who would eventually save the country from the Fulani yoke, In order to obtain the object of his ambition he plotted with others to bring about the downfall of the King. He bought the support of the two most powerful war-chiefs left in the land, viz., Oluyọle of Ibadan by promising him the title of Ibasọrun, and Kurūmi of Ijaye by promising him that of Kakanfo.

After the fall of the ancient capital and the death of King Oluewu the crown was offered to Lagūade, but he declined it and advised that it should be offered to that powerful aspirant Prince Atiba, of Agọ Ọja; the only one with men and means, who seemed able to cope with the Ilọrins and save the country from tyranny and oppression. This was done, and Atiba accepted it with the general consent and approval of all, but it was with the distinct understanding that he would lead the people home from Saki, Gboho, Kihisi, Ilọrin and other places whither they had taken refuge. For this purpose Prince Lajide, son of Onsọlu, and Fabiyi with 32 other messengers were sent by the Ọyọ Mesi at Kihisi and Igboho to invite him home to the ancient capital. They were his guests till the coronation, after which he detained them permanently at Agọ and conferred on Prince Lajide the title of Ọna'sokun.

After he was established on the throne, he sent Lakọnu one of his powerful chiefs to Kihisi and Gboho for the remnant of the Kings' wives, and the eunuchs and other court officials that could be found in those regions.

Thus Agọ passed out of the hands of Ọja's family and became

the royal city of Yoruba and as such it was no longer called Ago-Oja but Oyo as the ALÂFIN now resides there. And hence it is often styled by way of disparagement Ago-d'Oyo (Ago which became Oyo). This is the present city of Oyo.

§ 3. CONFERRING OF TITLES

At the conferring of titles and re-organization of the kingdom the ALÂFIN confirmed on those who came to him from Kihisi and Gboho the titles they had formerly borne. Those who did not care to leave the more salubrious north for forest lands were superseded in their offices.

The following are those who were confirmed in their titles.

Name.	Title.
Makãaiye	Òhòta
Odusola	Agbakin
Ariori	Sàmu

The following were those newly conferred at the present Oyo.

Obagbolu	Ona-modekè
Gbenla	Lagũnà
Aiyewun (from Iseyin)	Alapīni
Ailesò	Tetu
Adefalu	Olokũesin
Ailumo (Oja's brother)	Asipa
Yesufu (Atiba's uncle)	Parakoyi[1]

The following were titles conferred on members of the royal family, not all of whom however were deserving.

Olukokun (grandson of King Onisile)	Atingisi
Telaòkòki	Magaji Iyajin
Abioro (son of King Ajagbo)	Arole Oba
Idowu (son of King Ojigi)	Olusami

The following were commoners, but favourites and formerly companions-in-arms of Atiba, on whom were conferred titles usually borne by members of the Royal Family exclusively:—

Falade	Agunpopo
Lákonu	Ogìgìmagi
Ladejobi	Olosun
Toki	Ladilù

Eniaiyewu the Alapīni of the ancient city was still alive when Aiyewun was brought from Iseyin for the same office. The former remained and died at Saki.

---

[1] In recognition of his kind services to him at the Gbodo Expedition.

Ailẹsọ had been created chief of the Tẹtus (they are 150 in number) before those from the ancient city arrived to claim their rights ; they had to be satisfied wth minor ranks.

Ancient Ọyọ was a very large city comprising the following wards :—Oke Ẹso, Modade, Molaba, Nsisẹ-Ọgan, Ntẹtu, Ondasa, Onsẹ-awo, Arẹmu, Ile-Ologbo, Ajọfa, Isalẹ-Ọgẹdẹ.

Now, Ago d'Ọyọ was very small in comparison, and hence the ALÂFIN adopted forcible means to enlarge it. Several of the surrounding towns and villages were depopulated and the inhabitants transported to the new city e.g. Akeitan, Apara, Idodẹ, Ajagba Ṣẹkẹ, Gudugbu, Jabàtà, Ojomgbodu, Aguwọ, Ọpapa and Ijoga. These places were all within 10 or 20 miles from Ago. The King's army would surround each of them by night, and at break of day, the inhabitants were offered the choice of a peaceable migration to the new city or (in case of resistance) the town would be destroyed. Thus they were transported with all their household effects and as they arrived the King assigned to each a quarter of the town for their residence. Thus Igaga was taken in the month of May during the Egũgun festival.

HIGHER TITLES

(a) *The Baṣọrun.*—Oluyọle of Ibadan received the title of Ibaṣọrun as was conditionally promised him at the Eleduwẹ war. He based his claim on his descent from Baṣọrun Yamba whose cognomen was Òkòlo Ogun. His father's name was Olokũoye, his mother was Agbọnrin daughter of King ABIQDUN and thus he was the ALÂFIN'S nephew.

Oluyọle now came to Ọyọ to have his title conferred upon him by the King.

This was a new departure from the old custom for the Baṣọrun to reside in the country. His right place is in the city being the next man to the King, and the chief of the seven principal councillors of state comprising the Ọyọ MESI. He, moreover, has distinct official duties to perform at the principal annual festivals especially at the Bẹrẹ at which he is the chief actor.

But this new departure must be allowed in order to meet the exigencies of the times. The King could not be secure on his throne if he were to cause a disaffection to arise between himself and the powerful war-chiefs of Ibadan and Ijaye by denying them the titles of their ancestors which they were so ambitious to obtain.

But a provision had already been made in the constitution for performing the state ceremonies in the absence of the Baṣọrun : his place could be filled by either the Ọtun'wẹfa, the Ọna Onsẹ-

Awo, or the Ariwo. Thus what would have proved a serious constitutional difficulty had already been obviated by past experience, and adequately provided for.

(b) The *Arẹ-ọna-Kakanfo* or Yoruba Field Marshal. This title was now conferred upon Kurũmi of Ijaye according to the conditional promise made to him also at the Eleduwẹ war by Prince Atiba. He was undoubtedly the greatest Yoruba general and tactician of the day in the Yoruba country. He was a great friend of the King and during his term of office he shielded the sovereign against the encroachment on his prerogatives of his nephew of Ibadan for he was by no means loyal to him. He also on this occasion went to Ọyọ to have the title conferred on him. Thus it came to pass that the two most distinguished titles next to the sovereign were held by the chiefs of the two largest towns in the south, viz. that of Basọrun the head of all civil affairs, and that of Kakanfo the head of the military department.

State Policy.—In order that a collision may not take place between these two warlike towns, so contiguous to each other, a compact was now arrived at between the ALÂFIN and his principal chiefs :—

1. That they should make it their primary aim to defend what was left of the Yoruba country, and gradually regain if they could their lost provinces under the Fulanis of Ilọrin.

2. As the last King died in war, the sovereign should not be allowed to go to war any more, but confine himself to all religious, civil, and political matters (external relations) on behalf of the nation.

3. That the Ibadans were to protect all Yoruba towns to the north and north-east, and meet whatever danger might arise in those quarters, to have a free hand over all Ijẹsas and Ekitis, and the eastern provinces generally, to reduce them to subjection.

4. That the Ijayes should protect all Yoruba towns of the western provinces, and meet whatever danger appeared in that direction and carry on their operations against the Sabẹs and disloyal Popos.

Thus the disintegration of the country would be arrested.

But the ancient cities of Iluku, Ṣaki, Gboho and Kihisi with their towns, containing the remnant of the citizens of the ancient Ọyọ and members of the royal family preferred not to be placed under the protection of either of these powers, but under the King direct ; and this was allowed. Thus it was hoped that in time the unity of the kingdom would be regained, and those who still longed for their old homes would be able to return thither.

In this way it appeared latterly that the province under the

ALÂFIN is small, and foreigners ignorant of the history of the country are apt to consider Ibadan of more importance than Ọyọ especially when by the destruction of Ijaye the former claimed the overlordship of the territories formerly under Ijaye.

PROVINCIAL AFFAIRS

The affairs of the new Metropolis having been settled both the Baṣọrun and the Kakanfo returned home to arrange their own local affairs.

Ibadan. At this time the war-chief next to the Iba himself who was head and shoulders above all his compeers at Ibadan was chief Elêpo, consequently the title of Ibalogun was offered him ; but he declined it, for reasons which no one could tell. He was urged over and over again in public as well as in private, both by the Baṣọrun and his brother chiefs to accept it, but he declined, saying his name Elêpo alone was enough for him. And yet he would submit to no one but the Baṣọrun alone who was his old colleague. The title of Balogun was, therefore, conferred upon Ọderinlọ.

The following were the titles conferred upon distinguished war-chiefs :—

Names.	Titles.
Ọderinlọ	Balogun or commander-in-chief.
Lajumokẹ	Ọtun i.e. general commanding the right
Ọpẹagbe	Osi i.e. general commanding the left wing
Toki	Seriki
Babalọla	Asipa
Oyeṣilẹ	Abẹṣẹ
Ogunrẹnu	Sarumi or chief of the cavalry
Yerombi	Agbakin
Dele	Arẹagoró

Ijaye.—The Arẹ-ona-Kakanfo of Ijaye was a bloodthirsty tyrant. He put to death all the chiefs rising into power who might become his rivals. His Balogun's name was Ọlaṣilọ alias Ogun-koroju, a Mohammedan, and the friend of Balogun Ọderinlẹ of Ibadan. He was the only man at Ijaye for whom Kurûmi entertained any regard. One Ajayi was his Arẹagoro, and this was about all the titles given at Ijaye. Nevertheless there were other powerful men at Ijaye such as Lakusà, Agãna Epo, Fanyàka, Akiọla, Aṣegbe, Amọdu and Labudanu. Lahan after the destruction of Abemọ came to reside at Ijaye.

Kurûmi usurped all power both civil and religious ; all were centred on him or his family, and all the profits accruing from them flowed to his exchequer. His brother Popoola was the Alagbâ or Egũgun high priest, himself the Mọgba or head Ṣango priest. His chief executioner was one Jòmgban. The Kakanfo was more dreaded at Ijaye than even the gods as the common saying shows " Arẹ npe ọ o ndifa ? Bi Ifa fọ rere ti Arẹ fọ ibi nkọ ? (You receive the Arẹ's summons and you are divining with your Ifa ? What if Ifa is propitious and the Arẹ is not ?) He did not value the life of a human being more than that of a dog. For the least offence he ordered the offender to execution and plundered his house. But he was more of a terror to rank and station, for to the poor, he granted liberty and redress.

THE AGBAMAJA WAR

It has become the custom at Ibadan that a newly created Balogun should lead the army out on an expedition in order to prove his worth to the title and thereby commend himself to the respect of the soldiery. But no town at this time gave any cause of offence for an attack, all the same the Balogun was sent against Ẹdẹ—a town under their own protection. But it would appear that Elêpo vetoed the destruction of Ẹdẹ and so they marched on towards Ilobu.

The people of Ilobu became alarmed. They had not committed any offence, but although they were assured of peaceful measures yet they brought a large amount of presents to the Ibadan camp to buy off their hostility, and showed every sign of submission. All the same, the soldiery becoming restive from inaction would have sacked the town but for Elêpo, especially when it happened that lightning struck a house in the town and the war boys became wild, and rushed to the spot under pretext of doing homage to Sango, while others were already scaling the walls when Elêpo and his men undertook to beat them off and save Ilobu. From that town and the surrounding villages presents came pouring into the Ibadan camp but instead of going to the Balogun all went to Elêpo, before whose tents all the presents were piled up. He neither directed them to the commander-in-chief nor made use of them for himself. He ruled the army according to his will, and consequently the Balogun was indignant at this usurpation of his rights and the other chiefs sympathized with him. After frittering away their time doing nothing the men became disheartened and began to steal away home. Hence this expedition was termed " Agbamaja," i.e. fully armed but engaging in no fight.

The Baṣọrun at home was kept informed of all that was going on at the seat of war and when they arrived at home a mass meeting was held of all the war-chiefs and men and the whole of

them complained bitterly against Elêpo ; he was accused to his
face of usurping the rights of the Balogun when he had himself
declined the office, but on account of the love and respect they had
for him they were prepared to let bygones be bygones, only he
must prostrate before the Balogun and offer an apology and the
matter would end there. He apologised but would never bemean
himself by prostrating before the Balogun. This last act therefore
set a seal upon his downfall; his humiliation was there and then
decided upon.

The next step taken was to deprive him of his principal subordinate war-chiefs by conferring town titles on each of them, making
them members of the town council with equal votes. Elêpo's
eyes were now open to his own folly, but almost too late. At
the next public meeting, he apologized again but was too proud to
prostrate before any one save the Baṣọrun alone. He was told
all round that his apology was accepted and the pardon granted.
He went home glad at heart, but was soon to be undeceived, for
when he went the following day to the houses of all the principal
chiefs to thank them, not one of them would see him ; at every
house he called he was told " The master is not at home." He
understood the full import of this, and moreover none of his subordinate chiefs called at his house as before, and all matters in his
quarter of the town were taken straight to the Balogun. Thus
Elêpo saw himself isolated.

§ 4. THE OṢOGBO WAR. THE ILỌRINS CHECKMATED

After a short pause that followed the Eleduwẹ war, the aggressive
spirit of the Ilọrins once more impelled them to the accomplishment of their aim, viz., the subversion of the entire Yoruba
country, and hence for the third time they laid siege to Oṣogbo.
The command this time was entrusted to their brave and experienced general Ali, the Hausa Balogun of Ilọrin.

Oṣogbo was closely besieged, and terrible battles were fought
between the assailants and defenders to the advantage of the
former. When the king of Oṣogbo found the Ilọrins too strong for
him he sent to Ibadan for help.

It now devolved upon the Ibadans as defenders of the north
and north-east to meet the coming danger. They sent them some
auxiliaries under the leadership of one Ọbẹ̀le alias Mọbitàn, and
Alade Abinupagún. As this force proved insufficient for the
defence of the town, another contingent was sent under a more
experienced leader. But still the Ilọrins were gaining ground
after every battle until the besieged and their auxiliaries were
confined to the thickets surrounding the town which in all Yoruba

towns were reserved for the purposes of defence. The Ibadan contingent thereupon sent an express report home to the Baṣọrun that they would soon be overpowered and the town taken if timely aid was not forthcoming.

The Baṣọrun unwilling that the Fulanis and Jamâs of Ilọrin should be masters of the forest lands to which they had been driven from their homes in the plain, was resolved to raise the siege at all cost. It was with the Ibadans a matter of now or never and hence the Balogun was instructed to endeavour to deal a decisive blow to the Ilọrins once and for all, for should he fail now the Fulanis would be masters of the whole Yoruba country.

Balogun Ọdẹrinlọ now marched out with the whole of the Ibadan mighty men save Elêpo and the Baṣọrun, the former having been rejected by the war-chiefs for his actions at the late Agbamaja expedition. The Baṣọrun approved of this resolve and therefore Elêpo stayed at home, but he felt himself far too exalted to care for any of them.

When the Ibadan army arrived at the seat of war and saw the situation they had some misgivings as to the probability of success without the aid of Elêpo their champion. They could not show their face in the open field for fear of the Ilọrin horse, and for about 20 days after their arrival at Oṣogbo, they also could not fight outside the town thickets.

The Baṣọrun himself having some doubts as to the hopes of success of his generals in the absence of Elêpo was much depressed in mind on hearing the news from the seat of war, and he was minded to send Elêpo to meet them ; he gave him a cow to worship his god *Ori* and told him to prepare to join his comrades in the field.

The Ibadan war-chiefs hearing this were fired with jealousy lest the honour of the victory might be his and hence were resolved to risk a battle at all cost. Again and again they held councils of war, and at length they fixed a day for the venture. Still they were afraid to attack the Ilọrins during the morning hours, Oṣogbo being practically in a plain, the Ilọrin horse might have the advantage of them with disastrous results : from prudence therefore they resolved to make the attack in the afternoon, as they might be able to hold on until dusk when the Ilọrins would no longer be able to use their horses to advantage, or if defeated, the shades of night would assist them in their retreat.

About 2 p.m. the standard of the Ibadan army left the gate of Oṣogbo for the battlefield. Again, another council of war was held and it was finally resolved that they should not proceed until dark, as it was necessary that their movements be as private as possible. About sunset they were again on the move and the vanguards were instructed to keep a strict watch and arrest anyone suspected as a spy on their movements.

About a mile from the Ilọrin camp they halted and arranged the order of the attack. The Oṣogbo army and the earlier auxiliaries were to maintain the centre of the battle, Chiefs Abitiko and Lajubù to command the right wing, Balogun Ọdẹrinlọ with the rest of the Ibadan war-chiefs to form the left wing of the army. About midnight the Ilọrin camp was attacked on all sides. The watch word was *Elò ni owo odo* ? (The fare of the ferry ?) [The river Ọṣun had to be crossed in entering Oṣogbo from the south. Any one who could not tell was known to be an enemy.] The first camp attacked was that of the Elese, and as soon as they rushed in, they set it on fire. The Elese himself was shot dead as soon as he showed his face at the tent door. A panic seized the whole Ilọrin army thus startled from their beds ; they could not offer the slightest resistance, they simply melted away ! Those who fell by the hands of their own friends to make way for their hasty flight were probably more than those who fell by the hands of their enemies. Several who summed up courage enough to saddle their horses had not the presence of mind to loose them and were caught in the stables digging spurs into the poor beasts and wondering why they would not go, forgetting that they were still tethered by the feet.

But Ali the commander-in-chief was calm and resolute ; he ordered his horse to be saddled, and gathering around him a goodly portion of his cavalry they dashed through the ranks of the Ibadan army : these quickly making a way for them to gallop through without daring to oppose them, especially as numbers of the men were scattered about on plundering bent.

The principal Ilọrin war-chiefs captured in this defeat were :—

1. Jimba the head slave of the Emir of Ilọrin.
2. One of the sons of Ali the commander-in-chief.
3. Chief Latẹju and
4. Ajikobi the Yoruba Balogun of Ilọrin.

The first two were released and sent home privately by the Ibadan war-chiefs, a form of chivalrous etiquette among the war-chiefs. The latter two being Yorubas by birth were regarded rather as traitors to their country, and were sent home to Ibadan as distinguished captives of war.

The Baṣọrun sentenced Latẹju to death alleging that it was in his house that King OLUEWU, the last of the ancient ỌYỌ, was fettered when taken at the Eleduwẹ war, before he was put to death. That was the ostensible charge but the chief reason really was because Oluyọle's wives fell into Latẹju's hands at the collapse of that expedition, and he was not chivalrous enough to release them and send them to him as a brother chief.

Ajikobi being a more distinguished personage was sent to the ALÂFIN of Ọyọ for capital punishment.

The messengers with the illustrious captive met the King engaged in one of his annual festivals, and he ordered that the *feu de joie* his servants were then firing should be directed on Ajikobi. This was accordingly done, and he was roasted to death with gunpowder.

Besides a large number of captives the Ibadans captured numbers of horses but very few of them were brought home. These hardy people cared very little then for the luxury of riding on horseback: what they cared for more was the horses' tails upon which to tie amulets as preventives against bullets in war. These were always a part of their war kits. The only attention bestowed on the hundreds of tailless horses now roaming about the field was for replenishing their larder as occasion required!

This victory at Oṣogbo was a most important one and forms a turning point in Yoruba history. It saved the Yoruba country as such from total absorption by the Fulanis as a tributary state. From this time forth the power of the Ilọrins for an independent aggressive warfare in Yoruba land was for ever broken and the Ibadans gained the ascendancy. The Ilọrins without losing sight of their ultimate objective to "dip the Koran in the sea," i.e. the subjugation of the entire Yoruba land, henceforth contented themselves with allying themselves now with one, and then with the other of the contending tribes with the hope of ultimately weakening the whole, so that eventually the entire country might fall an easy prey into their hands.

That the ALÂFIN did not seize this opportunity to gather all the forces of the kingdom and strike a final blow at the enemy was a matter of surprise to many, but a great dread was still entertained of meeting the cavalry in the plain, in which case it would not be that of Ilọrin alone, but also those of Sokoto and Gando. Hence the return home to the ancient capital was fraught with danger, the probability of their being continually harassed and attacked and taken by surprise being very great.

Other reasons also have been advanced for remaining in their present position, among which was the comparative proximity to the coast and greater facilities for trade. As new generations sprang up who knew little or nothing of the old country they grew less and less disposed to abandon the comparative safety and advantages of the present position for the old cities with all the attendant risks, however fertile and salubrious they might be.

After the siege of Oṣogbo was raised, Ibokun an Ijẹṣa town not far from Oṣogbo was taken by the Ibadans, being one of the tributary towns and allies of Ilọrin.   On the approach of the enemy, having heard of the defeat of the Ilọrins at Oṣogbo, Kuṣì the Ilọrin Resident of the town escaped to Ilọrin leaving Ibokun to its fate.

§ 5.   The Expulsion of Elepo from Ibadan

Chief Elêpo not being allowed by his colleagues to go with them to the Oṣogbo expedition, and having heard of their success marched out with his own troops against Qtẹfan, a Yoruba town in the western province, which he took, and returned home with many captives and much booty by which he satisfied the cravings of his war boys, whose loyalty to him prevented them from going with their comrades to a successful expedition.

After his return from Qtẹfan, Elêpo was told by the Baṣọrun that the other war-chiefs in the field had sent home to say that he should leave the town, alleging that he was heard to have said that they could not achieve any victory without his leadership, and now that the Ilọrins had received a crushing defeat at their hands without his presence, it was evident they could do without him.   Whether this message was actually sent or whether it was an arrangement concocted between the Baṣọrun and the war-chiefs is not certain, but as a matter of fact the whole of them stood in dread of him and he was also an object of envy and jealousy. It is evident that if the Baṣọrun had been as true to him as he was loyal to the Baṣọrun such a question could not have arisen at all. Elêpo was said to have been the greatest general Ibadan ever produced ; before him and after him there has yet been none to be compared to him whose very name strikes terror and confusion in all around.   Even the Baṣọrun himself was secretly afraid of him, as with one breath he could upset him and his government, and yet there has never been a chief at Ibadan so humble, so loyal and devoted to his chief as Elêpo was to the Baṣọrun.   But for him Oluyọle could never have attained to his present position nor could have maintained it for a month, before his murder or expulsion would have ended his career.

Oluyọle was blind to his own interests when he was arranging this plot against Elêpo.   Elêpo on the other hand, unsuspicious of the intrigues of his chief, was negotiating through him with the other chiefs.   He loved and trusted him too well for him to entertain the slightest doubt of his good faith.

As the war-chiefs were on their homeward march, threatening messages were said to have been sent to Elêpo through the Baṣọrun ;

the latter, in order that he might be able to accomplish his design, ill-advised Elêpo to leave his house a while, assuring him that all would be right in the end. He knew quite well that as long as Elêpo was in his own house their plans must fail, for no one would dare to face the lion in his den.

Atipo his brother at once suspected the intriguer by such advice, and asked, " Why should it be deemed necessary for the Mọgaji (i.e. Elêpo) to leave his house when you the chief were employing your good offices for him ? Which of the war-chiefs would be bold enough either to go against your declared wish or to attack Elêpo backed by his chief the Basọrun ? " But the Basọrun evaded the question ; on the contrary he kept pressing the point with great urgency knowing that once Elêpo left his house he would never be allowed to return to it.

Elêpo disheartened by the bad faith of his hitherto trusted lord yielded with pain and disappointment only out of respect to him. He removed all his effects to the Basọrun's house as well as all the captives and booty from the late Ọtẹfan expedition. Thus unmindful of the good Elêpo had done him when he was somewhat similarly situated after the Ọta expedition, Oluyọle requited him with ingratitude out of sheer jealousy ; he desired to wield an absolute power and felt he could not safely do so with such a man under him, and thus he plotted to gain his end at the expense of a faithful and loyal friend and colleague.

When the war-chiefs were nearer home, Oluyọle told Elêpo that he had failed in his negotiations with them and that they threatened a civil war in case he sided with him, and consequently should Elêpo leave the town he, the Basọrun, would arrange matters with them so that he might return home in peace.

By this Elêpo saw plainly the intrigues of his friend and master. Thrice he asked him pointedly " Do you really mean me to leave the town ? " Each time the reply was " Yes for the present but all will be right in the end." Then chief Elêpo uttered the following parable :—" Once upon a time the leopard was king of the beasts, and the god *Orisa* was the only object of his dread. The Orisa's house was built in the open fields, and he was protected with an earthenware pot. The beasts of the field had no respect for Orisa but used to walk and graze around the pot with which he was covered without incurring any harm. But at the yearly festival when king Leopard headed all the beasts to worship the Orisa, to their surprise, he used to prostrate at a distance, and do homage by putting earth on his head, and never allowed any of the beasts to approach too near lest they give offence to the Orisa. The beasts used to say among themselves ' And why all this precaution ? We often grazed around that pot without experiencing any harm, can Oɪiṣa kill at all as king Leopard would have us believe ? ' Now upon one such occasion when the Leopard and all the beasts in his train were prostrating at a distance, the Oriṣa said to the Leopard ' Why not allow these my children to draw near to me ? ' The Leopard replied, ' O most adorable Oriṣa, the beasts you would have to approach your sacred presence are ignorant creatures that know not your worth ; were they allowed to do so they will tread on the mat on which you are seated and will soon after end by treading on yourself.' This parable is for you, O Baṣorun. The war-chiefs you are making so much of do not know your worth, they pay honours to you only on my account, and should I leave the town as you say, they will soon tread upon the mat on which you are seated and finally upon yourself."

After this Elêpo left the town with about 1,000 followers and retired first to Ipara a town in Ijẹbu Rẹmọ and resided there for a while.

CIVIL WAR AT IBADAN

Not long after the departure of Elêpo the truth of his parable became quite evident, the prophecy had all but obtained a terrible fulfilment.

Enriched by the treasures of the expelled chieftain, and his wealth further augmented by the portion allotted to him by his war-chiefs from the successful expedition of Oṣogbo, Oluyọle became much elated, feeling himself now the sole and absolute master of the town of Ibadan without the fear of any possible rival. But it was not long before an insurrection was raised against him ; Chiefs Olubọdun, Akiliyi, Atipo, Lajubu, Akinlabi and Ogidi took up arms against him and the whole town was soon in an uproar. Nothing but the mere chance of their leader Olubọdun being killed before the action really commenced brought the rising to a sudden close.

One of Oluyọle's men from the roof of his house espied Olubọdun hastening to the scene of action and as he must pass by the corner of his house to gain the main street, the man raised the thatch of his roof, levelled his gun at Olubọdun at very close quarters and shot him dead on the spot ! The suddenness and unexpected-ness with which this was accomplished created a panic among his followers and it spread instantly among the other chiefs and their men, and they fled precipitately pursued by Oluyọle's men. Akīliyi and Ogidi were taken but the rest escaped to Ijaye. Akīliyi was executed. Ogidi was pardoned, but was ordered out of his

house and district at Isalẹ Ijẹbu, the former being levelled to the
ground and left in ruins, and he had to occupy a small house at
Isalẹ Ọṣun under strict surveillance.

[The site of the house was subsequently given to the Rev. D.
Hinderer the first missionary of the Church Missionary Society at
Ibadan in 1851 and has since become the C.M.S. station at Oke
Kudẹti.]

IJAYE AND THE IBADAN REFUGEES

Of the three men who escaped to Ijaye after the tragic end of
Olubọdun, Lajubu somehow effected a return home and was
pardoned, but Atipo and Akinlabi did not return but made Ijaye
their home permanently.

They occupied the house of one Akīọla who was put to death
by the Arẹ of Ijaye under the following painful circumstances :—
In one of their expeditions to the Sabẹ provinces Akīọla captured
a young maiden of whom he became enamoured ; he first shared
his bed with her, and on the return home of the expedition this
captive was among others he apportioned to their chief Kurūmi
the Arẹ of Ijaye.   But the Arẹ also was captivated by
the charms of this young woman and he at once included her in
his harem.   And so it happened that on finding afterwards that
she had already been tampered with, he became enraged with
Akīola and constituted this a crime for which he murdered him !

Atipo and Akinlabi retaining the spirit and energy of Ibadan
were restless at Ijaye ; they made two expeditions to the banks
of the Niger on their own account, captured Ogodo in the first
and Gbajigbo in the second expedition, and brought home many
captives and much booty.

After this Atipo went to Ipara to fetch his brother Elệpo to
Ijaye by way of Ilugun. Elệpo's followers had by this time
dwindled to about 70 men, the rest having returned home to
Ibadan weary of the inaction at Ipara.

Oluyọle became very jealous of the success and the popularity
of these men at Ijaye, and Kurūmi ever suspicious of any brave
and distinguished man, readily listened to the insinuations of the
former that these men would one day prove a danger to the state,
that they would sooner or later desert him for Ilọrin (their common
enemy) and that Kurūmi should at once dispose of them.

Kurūmi invited them both to a banquet and there, completely
in his power, he murdered them both and seized all their property.
Thus ended the career of these brave men of Ibadan and Ijaye.

Chapter XVI

A SERIES OF FRATRICIDAL WARS

AFTER the events narrated above, the history of the Yorubas centred largely at Ibadan which, down to the time of the British Protectorate continued to attract to itself ardent spirits from every tribe and family all over the country, who made it their home, so that while the rest of the country was quiet, Ibadan was making history.

An Episode.—The Oṣu War.—After the return of the Ibadans from the Ọta war, and the civil war which placed Oluyọle at the head of the government, Inakoju the Seriki died and was succeeded by one Ladanu. After his promotion, Ladanu led out an expedition to Oṣu which turned out disastrous. He was accompanied by most of Oluyọle's men, e.g., Akinṣọwọn, Abipa, Aijẹnku and Erinlẹ Sànkú.

Oṣu not being far from Ileṣa the capital of the Ijẹṣa country, the Ijẹṣas, hearing of their approach, lay in ambush, and cut the Seriki's army in pieces. The Seriki himself in an attempt to rally his discomfited army was slain. Chiefs Akinṣọwọn and Abipa were also slain leaving Aijẹnku and Erinlẹ Sanku who escaped with difficulty alone to tell the tale.

The Eleduwẹ war which followed soon after, and the Abemọ and Oṣogbo wars subsequently, fully engaged the attention of the Ibadans ; now they were at leisure they were resolved to avenge the loss of their late Seriki. Balogun Ọdẹrinlọ led out the whole Ibadan army. Their route lay through the Ẹdẹ farms and there they were encamped for many days foraging. The Ijẹṣas of the capital joined by the army of Oṣu met them at Ilọba which was 4 hours to Oṣu eastward, and between 6 and 8 hours to Ileṣa, Oṣu itself being about 6 hours to Ileṣa. Here several battles were fought, and when the Ijẹṣas could stand the fire of the Ibadans no longer, they evacuated the town, and the place was taken. The Ibadans followed up the victory to Oṣu their objective, but the town had been deserted ; they made no captives there but carried away booties, and returned home to Ibadan in triumph. After this there arose a series of neighbourly strifes all over the country.

§ 1. Aàye and Ọ̀tun

Whilst the revolutionary wars were raging all over the rest of the Yoruba country, the Fulanis devastating the Metropolitan province, the Ọyọs the Ẹgba province, and the Ifẹs, Ijẹbus and Ọyọs striving for predominance in the south, the Ijẹsa and Ekiti provinces, save for the late Polẹ war, were enjoying the blessings of peace. Entrenched in their mountain fastnesses, they were safe from the Fulani horse and other foes.

But it seems they were not to be exempt from the ban that hung over the rest of the Yoruba nation, and hence they commenced an internal strife among themselves, which led to their inviting outside help and resulted in their final subjugation.

Aàye and Ọ̀tun were two towns in the Ẹfọn and Ekiti districts contiguous to one another ; the people bear the same relationship to each other as the Ẹgba bear towards the Ọyọs or Ijẹbus. They are all included under the term Ekiti.

A feud arose between these two towns about their boundaries which culminated in a war in which Ọtun was worsted, but so determined on revenge was the Ọlọtun (king of Ọtun) that he sought help from abroad ; he sent to Ibadan for that purpose and Balogun Ọdẹrinlọ was sent out with the whole of the Ibadan army, and Aàye was besieged.

Finding that the Ibadans were too strong for them the Alâye (king of Aàye) sought help from Ilọrin, and the Ilọrin horse under their general Afunku appeared in the field in aid of Aàye. The choice fell on the Fulani Balogun as the Hausa and Yoruba Baloguns of the Ilọrins had already failed at Oṣogbo.

The Ilọrins did their best to raise the siege by attacking the Ibadans in the rear, but the Ibadans rounded on them and inflicted on them a severe defeat. Their leader general Afunku fell in the conflict, about 100 Ilọrins were made prisoners, and the rest escaped home, leaving Aàye to its fate.

Such a turn of affairs was least expected at Aàye. The town was now closely invested, and when they were reduced to feeding on roots of trees, reptiles, and other loathsome objects they went about the streets bewailing their misfortunes and endeavouring to move the sympathy of their kinsmen of Ọ̀tun, and sang " Ọlọtùn njẹ otitọ li o yio fi kini yi ṣe ? " (O king of Ọtun, will you then make of this matter a stern reality ?)

But there were some men in the town who were encouraging them to hold out a little longer, saying that great as their distress was in the town, greater still was it in the Ibadan camp where they were reduced to pounding hay for food ; and if their allies could not raise the siege, famine would do it for them.

Thus encouraged, the men of Aàye held out heroically, they built forts upon the town walls from which sharp shooters harassed the Ibadans continually, and among those killed by that means was a notable chief Toki Onibudo[1] the Seriki of Ibadan. But when they could hold out no longer, when men, women, and children were dying in the streets from starvation, Fagbeñro the Alâye with his mother were resolved to risk going in person to the Ibadan camp to sue for peace.

When they entered the camp and were being conducted to the Balogun's quarters, the Alâye was overcome with surprise on finding yam, corn, flour, and other articles of food exposed in the market for sale, " What do I see ? " exclaimed he " What about the famine we were told existed in the Ibadan camp so that men were reduced to feeding on pounded hay ? " He there and then ordered some yam to be purchased for him, even before he got to the presence of the Balogun.

The Balogun received the Alâye in a friendly manner, and terms of peace were agreed upon, the Alâye promising to serve the Ibadans. But he was told that as they could not return home to Ibadan empty-handed, he should give them a small force and a guide to Isàn the next town of importance ; and in order to allay the Alâye's apprehensions the Balogun ordered a chief named Lajubu to return with the Alâye to the town to protect the same against the wild soldiery until the whole army had passed on to Isàn. But this seems to have been a ruse, for Lajubu and the Alâye had scarcely reached the gate of the town when the whole Ibadan army was on the move, Lajubu himself rushed forward not to protect the place, but to be amongst the first in plundering and slave-catching. Very few however were the captives taken, as famine had done its worst with them ; most of the survivors were weak and sickly, with œdematous hands and feet, and only about 100 comparatively able-bodied were found amongst them, and even these nearly all soon perished from the indiscretion of their captors, who in hopes of restoring them speedily to sound health fed them immoderately after a long spell of starvation.

The Ibadan army pushed on and took Oro, Yapa, Isì and Isan. At the last mentioned place all the war-chiefs remained, but the war-boys followed up the conquest as far as to Itagi, where they suffered a disaster and were checked.

The people of Itagi left their town and hid themselves in the bush hard by. The Ibadan war-boys having rushed in, dispersed

---

[1] This chief was succeeded by his nephew, Ibikunle, who became a famous Balogun.

all over the town, intent on plundering ; when the Itagi armed men came out and hunted them down everywhere butchering them to pieces. Chief Lajubu was amongst those caught in the market place and there he ended his career.

This expedition opened the way for the Ibadan raids into the Ekiti country, which continued year by year until the whole of that province was brought under subjugation by them as will be seen hereafter, and they remained a subject people under the Ibadans until, united in one, they struck for freedom, which was won by the aid of the British government many years after.

§ 2.   The Egbas and Egbados

About the same time as the events recorded in the previous section, the Egbas were waging war with some of the Egbado tribes. Ado was besieged, but held out for many years. All the Baloguns of Abeokuta were there present except their chief Sodeke ; but they spent their strength and skill to no purpose.

It was just about this time (A.D. 1843) that the Missionaries of the C.M.S. arrived at Abeokuta for inspection with a view to carrying on mission work in this country. The pioneer was the Rev. Henry Townsend a European missionary, with Mr. Andrew Wilhelm Desalu his interpreter, both from Sierra Leone. They met Chief Sodeke the Balogun of Itoku and leader of the Egbas to Abeokuta who received them with a cordial welcome. Mr. Townsend left Abeokuta after a short stay with a promise to return soon for a permanent stay amongst them for missionary work.

Thus light began to dawn on the Yoruba country from the south, when there was nothing but darkness, idolatry, superstition, blood shedding and slave-hunting all over the rest of the country. There was an old tradition in the country of a prophecy that as ruin and desolation spread from the interior to the coast, so light and restoration will be from the coast interior-wards. This was a tradition of ages. Is not this event the beginning of its fulfilment ? Whilst the Egbas were encamped before Ado, the Dahomians led out an expedition, and were on the march for Ilaro. It was privately reported to the Egbas that the Dahomians would suddenly fall on them and raise the siege. Hearing this the Egbas first sent out spies to ascertain their situation ; they thereupon surprised the Dahomians one morning as they spread themselves about their camp airing and drying their accoutrements that had got wet from a drenching rain after a storm that took place on the previous evening. In the confusion of the flight the Egbas captured the standard of the Dahomian army, which was an umbrella made of the skins of different kinds of animals, and burnt it. It was said that the King of Dahomey negotiated for it, and would have redeemed it at any price, but as it had been destroyed, it could not be restored ; and this was the cause of the mortal enmity and sworn hatred that has existed between successive Kings of Dahomey and the Egbas of Abeokuta unto this day. By the intervention of the Rev. Hy. Townsend, the siege of Ado was raised after a duration of 5 or 6 years, and the Egbas returned home.

§ 3. IBADAN AND IJAYE. THE BATEDO WAR, A.D. 1844

Inflated with the success of his intrigues at home and his arms abroad, the Basorun of Ibadan was aspiring to the throne of Oyo ! That this was so was evident from his style and manner at this time, and the insinuations his drummer was permitted to make when greeting him :—

> " Iba, kuku joba,   (Be the King at once, my lord,
> Mase bi Oba mo."   Cease acting *like* a King).

He, however, had his own misgivings ; he was the King's nephew but by the female line, and no such succession is possible in the Yoruba country. He would however make a venture trying might where he had no right, and in order to effect his purpose he was seeking occasion for a rupture with the ALÂFIN, and at the same time, by entreaty and bribery, endeavouring to secure the connivance if not the alliance of the Are of Ijaye, the only obstacle in his way. The latter refused to listen to him, and even remonstrated with him for his presumption and disloyalty to his lawful sovereign whose first minister he was. But as he would not be dissuaded from his projects, the Are finally sent word to say no one would venture to attack Oyo unless he the Are-ona-Kakanfo be first removed out of the way.

The Are kept the King well informed of all that was passing between himself and the Basorun. His Majesty also was well aware of the Basorun's intentions and of his power, hence he dealt wisely and patiently with him, never evincing any hostile spirit towards him, nor taking any notice of his insults. Thrice did Oluyole the Basorun send word to the King to say he should now fulfil the promise he made before his coronation to lead the people back home and remove the seat of government back to the ancient capital. The King knowing his intentions, thus replied to the messengers on the third and last time : " Tell your master that if he is ready let him come on, I am ready. As the present Oyo is on the high way to the ancient capital, he should start first and meet me here." At the same time the ALÂFIN was fortifying the town against a sudden attack, and employed a fetishman one Latubosun to bury charms at all the gates leading to the city as a preventive. As he was evincing much anxiety for the safety of the town both this fetishman and the Ondasa (the official fetishman) assured him that not a single shot would be fired against this place.

Oluyole on the other hand lost no opportunity of seeking an occasion for a rupture between himself and the King. He sent a body of troops to intercept Abudu Alelo and Kosija the Ilari whom the King sent to Porto Novo for a supply of ammunition. Abudu's teeth were shattered by the fire of one of Oluyole's men, for this the King neither remonstrated with Oluyole nor demanded a redress knowing it to be a deliberate *casus belli* ; he treated the matter as an accident.

With Kurũmi the Are also Oluyole was provoking a rupture as he was the only obstacle in the way of his carrying out of his projects. He demanded that Kurũmi as Kakanfo should acknowledge the seniority of himself as Basorun by coming in person to Ibadan to pay his respects to him, as he goes to Oyo to do homage. Kurũmi was too wide awake to venture his head into the lion's mouth, notwithstanding that Ogun-ko-roju his Balogun urged him to comply for the sake of peace. The Basorun constituted this refusal a *casus belli*.

A circumstance, however, occurred which accelerated the war. One Asu the Areagoro of Ladejo, an Ijaye chief, was expelled the town for treason, and he escaped to Fiditi, a town mid-way between Ijaye and Oyo; he rebuilt the ruins and had the town re-inhabited. The Kakanfo sent a company of 100 men to surprise and disperse this little band, but they found Asu and his men ready, and proving too strong for them, they were defeated and driven back. Fearing therefore the resentment of the Are, Asu sent to Ibadan for help. The Basorun who had long been seeking an opportunity for war against Ijaye hailed the present offer and sent out Balogun Oderinlo and Ibikunle the Seriki with instructions to confine their operations to kidnapping expeditions in Ijaye and Oyo farms, in order to harass them, and render farming both useless and unsafe so that famine might do half the work before a direct attack was made.

This continued for many months and several skirmishes took place on the Aregbe hills in the Ijaye farms with varying results. At length the Ibadans suffered a great disaster at Odogido in the Ijaye farms which put an end to the Fiditi campaign. On that eventful day the Balogun arranged to lead an expedition to the Ọyọ farms and entrusted that to the Ijaye farms to the Seriki. At a place called Odogido the Ijayes lay in ambush and suddenly attacked the Seriki's army on all sides and routed it completely. About 140 masters of compounds "who went to war on horseback" were caught and slain exclusive of private soldiers. It was said that Ibikunle the Seriki himself only escaped by falling into some friendly hands and was quietly let off. The Ijayes pressed hard in pursuit until it was dark and the shadows of night saved the remnant of the defeated. Hence this expedition was sometimes named "Oru gbà mi là." (The night saved me.) One Lampejọ was wounded in about 60 places all over his body, and was left for dead, but at night he revived and found his way home.

The expedition to the Ọyọ farms under the Balogun was also unsuccessful, though not disastrous ; not a single captive was brought back with him for they met nobody in the farms.

The Arẹ of Ijaye put to death all the captives that fell into his hands ; and made a platform on which he piled up the heads of the slain. For three months after this, the Ibadans remained inactive at Fiditi.

Oluyọle received the news with great indignation. He was resolved upon a siege of Ijaye ; and at once declared war and ordered his army at Fidili to meet him on the way thither ; they met him at Ọjọhọ his first encampment about six miles from Ibadan.

Thence they removed to Ika about midway between the two belligerent towns. From this place they began to clear the bush taking a north-easterly direction to the Ijaye farms which they reached on the 5th day and there encamped. Here the Ijayes met them and for two full years hard battles were fought with equal success on both sides ; but the war was very unpopular.

Also an incident reported from home contributed largely to the failure of the expedition on the part of the Ibadans. The war-chiefs were told of the Basọrun's boast when he heard of the disaster of Odogido that if there remained but himself alone and Ọyainu (his favourite wife) he would take Ijaye. Ọyainu herself, a lady of a masculine temperament and very popular was heard to swear by the Egūgun gods (a thing forbidden to women) that if the war was left to herself alone, she would take Ijaye.

The war-chiefs were naturally hurt by this implied slur cast upon them by the Basọrun and his wife. This, added to the un-naturalness of the conflict, rendered them perfectly indifferent to the issue of the war, they followed their chief and his wife half-heartedly, rather as spectators to see how far they could do without them ; it was even asserted that some of the chiefs fired only blank ammunition. Whatever may be the truth of these reports, it was quite certain that the war was unpopular, and that the Basọrun and his wife had to bear the brunt of the battle.

The war at length became a general one. Both sides sought the alliance of the Ẹgbas ; the Ẹgba chiefs were divided, Sodẹkẹ and Anọba declared for Ijaye, but Apati being Oluyọle's friend and relative declared for Ibadan. Sodẹkẹ himself never went beyond Arakanga, 3 miles from home, but sent his eldest son forward to Ijaye.

The alliance of Ogbomọsọ was also sought ; there was also a division here, the Balẹ declared for Ijaye but Ogūrunbi a notable war-chief, for Ibadan. Oluyọle further sought the alliance of the Emir of Ilọrin and the aid of his powerful Balogun Ali. He also sent provisions for the Ilọrin troops on account of the great scarcity of food then at Ilọrin, and asked them to beseige Ogbomọsọ. He also sent a contingent force of infantry in aid of the Ilọrins. The men of Ogbomọsọ defeated this army but could not pursue them far, for fear of the Ilọrin horse.

The Oke Ogun districts also were divided in their allegiance Iṣeyin declared for both Ijaye and Ibadan   [The fact is that that town was practically situated between two fires]. But Ile Bioku Berẹkodo, Igbo Ọra and Pako were for Ibadan.

In the Eastern districts Apomu, Ikire and Oṣogbo were vassals of Ibadan and had no choice, but Iwo and Ẹdẹ revolted. The people of Ẹdẹ were at first the allies of the Ibadans, and Fọlarin their prince was in the Ibadan camp from the beginning of the campaign, but when he received information that his people at home had revolted, he one day went over with all his men to Ijaye and was there received with open arms. The Arẹ sent him home in peace under the escort of Chief Elêpo late of Ibadan.

Lodifi an Iwo chief also went over and was similarly sent home. But Kọlọkọ and Adẹpo two Ibadan war-chiefs were stationed at Ejigbo to raid the Ẹdẹ farms ; when therefore Prince Fọlarin and Chief Elêpo arrived at Ẹdẹ, they went against Ejigbo to drive away these raiders. Elêpo, confident in the terror his very name inspired thought they would not dare await his approach, but alas, that time for Elêpo was past and gone ; Prince Fọlarin fell in an engagement and Elêpo was seriously wounded in the arms. He was thus invalided at Ẹdẹ for about a whole year before he was sufficiently recovered to return to Ijaye.

Thus the war between Ibadan and Ijaye involved nearly the whole country ; it lasted for two full years and during this period, the deadly conflict was chiefly between the Basọrun and the Arẹ, for Ọdẹrinlọ the Balogun of Ibadan and Ogūoroju the Balogun of

Iiaye had free though private communication with each other, and so all the minor chiefs and privates on both sides met each his kinsman and exchanged greetings and presents with one another.

The ALÂFIN of Qyọ held himself quite neutral and rendered no aid to either party and was thus able to come forward as an arbitrator between the contending parties. He sent the emblems of the god Sango with the high priest from Qyọ to Ijaye, and thence to the Ibadan camp saying, "What the king on earth may not be able to effect, surely the King from the other world can do, and this unnatural conflict must now cease."

Sango's intervention was respected by both parties now tired of the war, and peace was immediately concluded. The Ibadans in the camp flocked to Ijaye and *vice versa*, each one to see his friends and relatives and to offer congratulations.

It was during this war that locusts were first seen in the Yoruba country. They swarmed through the land and devoured every blade of green grass, but there was no famine in consequence for providentially it occurred just before cereals were planted, and they did not pass over the same region again ; but there was agricultural depression in some parts of the country for the locusts did not altogether disappear from the land for about two years.

§ 4. ABEOKUT AAND ABÀKÀ. THE ABÀKÀ WAR, A.D. 1846

About a year after their return from the Ado war, and after the death of Sodẹkẹ the Ẹgbas found a pretext for waging war against Abàkà a suburban village. It was at first considered an easy task, but the Abàkà men defended their town so vigorously that they compelled the Ẹgbas to beat a hasty retreat. The war was, however, renewed and the small town closely invested for fully four months and was reduced by famine. The distinguished Egba war-chiefs then were ; Apati the Generalissimo, Anọba, Olufakun, Somoye, Ogunbọna of Ikija and others. On their return from this expedition about 150 captives were allotted to Anọba alone.

The Ẹgbas being now fully settled in their new home, Abẹokuta, deemed it necessary to organize themselves for complete civil duties and have a king over them ; and Okukẹnu one of their war-chiefs who bore the Qyọ title of Sagbua (one of the junior Ẹsọs of Qyọ) was unanimously elected the first king of Abẹokuta.

§ 5. THE ILE BIOKU EXPEDITION AND END OF CHIEF ELEPO

At the same time the Abàkà war was going on, Kurŭmi the Arẹ of Iiaye sent an expedition against Ile Bioku one of the Oke Ogun towns to punish them for having sided with the Ibadans

M

during the late Batẹdo war. This expedition was entrusted to Chief Elêpo late of Ibadan. This chief was for carrying the place by a *coup de main*, but the men of Bioku having heard beforehand of the impending danger were on the alert, and were fully prepared to offer a determined resistance. Elêpo arranged for a night attack and headed his men for the assault. The men of Bioku fought desperately, but so vigorous was the assault that they were compelled to retreat into the town and some captives were made among them.

But Elêpo the leader of the expedition had been wounded with a poisoned arrow at the first onslaught, and as he stepped aside as was his wont, for his troops to rush forward, he expired soon after unknown to them.

But the men of Bioku rallied and repulsed the attack, and when at this moment Elêpo was expected to re-appear on the scene to support his men he was not to be found. The repulsed assembled at the foot of the hill on which Ile Bioku was built waiting for their leader ; his drum was kept up beating and calling him if perchance he had missed his way, but alas he had fallen and they knew it not.

The Bioku men had not the courage to descend from their heights and attack them, nor could the Ijaye invaders venture on another assault without their leader. Thus both parties retired.

At dawn, the men of Bioku in removing their slain observed the corpse of Chief Elêpo, and they called to the Ijaye men from their heights : " Examine among yourselves and see who is missing ; here is the corpse of a fallen soldier with striped trousers." Then the Ijaye men knew that they had lost their leader. Thus the expedition against Ile Bioku failed.

The Late Chief Elêpo.—Chief Elêpo was a native of Iwágbà and was acknowledged to be one of the greatest generals Ibadan ever produced. In no other man was power ever seen so combined with humility, loyalty, and devotion as was characteristic of Elêpo. He was remarkable for simplicity of manners, and could not be distinguished among his common soldiers by dress or any futile accessories. At home or in the field he mingled freely with them all and carried a gun on his shoulders like one of them. He was almost always victorious. Unlike the other generals of the day, he used to march at the head of his troops leading them to the fight, and when on the scene of action he stepped aside with his attendants, for his men to rush forward, and if they were repulsed he would at once re-appear on the scene and repel the enemy.

The following anecdote told of him will serve to illustrate how much was the dread which his very name inspired in people's breasts.

It was once rumoured at Iwo that Elêpo was coming against them at the head of his army. There was a great consternation in the town and a Babalawo (Ifa priest) in consulting his god as to his safety and that of his family was so distracted with fear that he transposed the words of divination, substituting the name of Elêpo for that of the god, and vice versa; said he, " Elêpo nkan kán, Ọrunmila li o gbe ogun de oke odo yi. Ngo ti ṣe kọ ti ọmọ ti ọmọ," i.e. O Elepo the ineffable, heie is Ọrunmila (the god Ifa) with his army at the banks of the river.[1] By what means shall I perish children and all ! Upon his son calling his attention to the mistake saying " Father, you are saying it wrong, it is just the other way," he turned round and dealt him a blow on the head saying, "Bi mo ti nfẹ ẹ ki ñto da iya rẹ nu u" (i.e. that is how I used to be engaged to it, before ever I divined with your mother), intending to say that was how he used to divine with it before he was ever engaged to the lad's mother. Such was the dread Elêpo's name inspired.

He was generally loved and respected by his colleagues, but his oldest friend and chief to whom he was devoted proved false to him and contrived to bring about his ruin. Such is man !

When the corpse was recognised by the Bioku people his head was taken off and sent to the Baṣọrun of Ibadan. What grim pleasure or delight that great intriguer took in it, tradition did not say, but such was the end of that great man.

§ 6. SAGAUN AND IGBO-ỌRÀ

The fires of the Batẹdo war were still smouldering in the embers. The Baṣọrun of Ibadan at the zenith of his glory, but unable to attain the height of his ambition became very oppressive at home. No one escaped the virulence of his tongue; he had no regard for any, least of all for the Balogun who was the next man to him in the town. A general insurrection was therefore raised against him which involved nearly the whole town. The Balogun and Ọtun connived at it, but professed neutrality ; the Seriki and the Aṣipa alone were for restoring order in the town, and through their intervention, by remonstrating with the two senior chiefs, and addressing a strong appeal to the Baṣọrun to check the excesses of his men, the insurrection was quelled. The Ibadans however soon found a vent for their overflowing energies by events transpiring elsewhere, as an outcome of the late Batẹdo war.

---

[1] The River Ọbà near Iwo.

We have seen above how parties were divided in their allegiance in the Oke Ogun districts during the late Batẹdo war, how Sagaun declared for Ijaye, and Berẹkodo, Igbo Ọra, and Pako for Ibadan. Agidi the chief of Sagaun found a pretext for declaring war against Igbo-Ọra, and besieged it, but finding the place too strong for him, he applied to Ijaye for help, and the Arẹ sent out the Balogun to his aid. The Igbo Ọra people on the other hand sent to Ibadan for help as their misfortunes were occasioned by their loyalty to Ibadan. The Baṣọrun at first sent to their aid a war-chief named Akãwo but Akãwo soon sent home for a larger force ; then Ibikanle the Seriki, Opẹagbe the Osi and others were sent as re-inforcement. The principal war-chiefs remained at Berẹkodo, but they sent all the Badas to Igbo-Ọra. But the Ijaye army was still too strong for them and when they could hold out no longer they retreated with the whole of the Igbo-Ọra people to Pako. The Balogun of Ijaye besieged them here also and would have crushed them had not timely aid come from Ibadan. The Baṣọrun hearing of the straits in which his men wẹre, ordered the Balogun to the rescue. But Odẹrinlọ the Balogun of Ibadan and Laṣilọ the Balogun of Ijaye were sworn friends, and rather than prove false to him, Odẹrinlọ from his first rendezvous at Odo Ọna sent to tell his friend that he was coming with an overwhelming force which the Ijayes could not possibly withstand, and therefore he would advise him to retire from Sagaun as soon as possible; nothing could be gained by the enormous loss of lives that must ensue, and the pangs of broken friendship ; and Sagaun must fall. Laṣilọ and his men accordingly ıetired from Sagaun, and on that very day the Ibadan hosts entered and Sagaun was taken.

Chief Agidi who originated the war fell from the heights of Oke Tapa and was killed. Within 13 days of their departure the Balogun of Ibadan with his army returned home but met the Baṣọrun seriously ill. During their absence in the field the Baṣọrun called at the houses of all the principal chiefs and respectable citizens to ask after the welfare of their households ; he was everywhere received with marks of honour. In one of these rounds he unfortunately met with an accident, by being thrown off his horse and he sustained an internal injury from which he was laid up and was unable to see or welcome home his army. Five days after their arrival, he breathed his last.

What the populace could not do during his lifetime they were determined to do now, viz., to pull down and plunder his house on account of the enormities perpetrated by him. But the Balogun prevented this, he posted the Agbakin with his men at the entrance of the palace to prevent any outrage or disorder.

Thus passed away one of the most distinguished figures in the Yoruba country.

The Late Oluyọle Baṣọrun of Ibadan.— Oluyọle was the son of Olokūoye, grandson of Baṣọrun Yamba, and Agbọnrin the daughter of King ABIODUN the ALÂFIN of ỌYỌ. He was born during the period of the Fulani ascendancy and the ravages of the Jamâs, and hence his parents were reduced to absolute poverty. As a lad, he was apprenticed to a metallurgist for whom he carried charcoal. It was during this period that he obtained the friendship of Oyainu (his favourite wife) whom he afterwards married ; but his first wife was Latoñde. When he first asked for her hand she refused him on account of the idle life he was then leading as a dancer ; but his friends Lanọṣẹ and others begged her to accept him, pledging their honour to see her taken care of and properly supported.

When Oluyọle rose to power and eminence he took revenge on her for this circumstance which he never forgot.

Oyainu had no children but Latoñde was the mother of his first born Akīọla whom he loved very much ; so much so that when the lad was seriously ill, at the advice of an Ifa priest he offered a slave in sacrifice as a ransom for the life of his son. Akiọla however died.

Oluyọle joined at Ipara the band of marauders which subsequently settled at Ibadan. Fortune favoured him there and he rose to a position of some distinction in the army, first as an Arẹagoro, then the Osi of Ibadan, and lastly he became the Baṣọrun of the kingdom.

He was the friend of Ologun l'Eko and of Kosọkọ of Lagos whose ally he was during the Ọta war : he survived all his colleagues and after the Eleduwẹ war obtained the title of Baṣọrun from the ALÂFIN ATIBA.

As a ruler he was arbitrary and oppressive and that was the cause of several civil wars at Ibadan. As a commander he was almost always successful although he had many narrow escapes.

As an excuse for him, his was an age of anarchy and lawlessness, and a ruler who showed himself weak would soon be compelled to give place to another. He could endure no rival and was exceedingly ambitious, hence the two inexcusable flaws in his life history, the perfidy to his faithful friend Elêpo, and the disloyalty to the ALÂFIN his uncle and sovereign.

He cannot be properly spoken of as a bloodthirsty tyrant because although sometimes inexorable, yet he was frequently merciful and forbearing. We may note for instance his treatment of those caught in the insurrection against him. In this respect he contrasted most favourably with his contemporary Kurumi of Ijaye.

Ogunmola who subsequently rose to distinction was but a private during his early administration: he had only a single drummer as his attendant whom he used to mount on a tree in front of his house and himself sitting on an empty keg of powder challenging the Basorun to a civil war! His drummer used to beat :—

 " Ogunmola, ija 'gboro ni yio pa a dan, dan, dan !
  O nyi agba gbiri, gbiri, gbiri !
  O mu agbori lowo, o nwo ona Orun yan, yan, yan !."

(Ogunmola, of a civil fight he shall die for sure, sure, sure !
He keeps kegs of powder a rolling, rolling, rolling !
With a jack knife in hand he is looking heavenwards steadily,
 steadily, steadily !)

His Highness, amused at this imp, used to send him some presents, saying " He is hungry hence he is challenging me to a fight."

His contemporary of Ijaye would have made short work of him for this.

Oluyole was fond of husbandry ; he had extensive plantations of okra, beans, vegetables, corn and yams, a separate farm for each, and whenever he had to take any to the market, no farmer was allowed to sell that particular article that day as he had sufficient to supply all the traders in the town, and could undersell any farmer. He made an experiment in yam planting so that a single root should be large enough for a load. The soil was first prepared, and a hole dug about 3 or 4ft. deep, and as many in diameter ; this was filled with weeds and pieces of banana stalks, earth was raised upon it, and the yam planted therein ; as the underlying rubbish decayed room was made for the yam to extend in all directions until the hole was filled and the size of the yam large enough for a load.

The Basorun owned nearly all the kola trees in the town as well as the kola groves, and often offered human sacrifices in them in order to make the trees fruitful One of his wives, the mother of his son Owolabi, was for a trifling offence punished by being sacrificed in one of these groves.

Silk velvet was then very rare and of a high value ; he allowed no one but himself alone to use a velvet robe ; the chiefs might use velvet caps only, but this no common man dared to do. The argument for this was that when poor people begin to aspire to what they could not easily obtain, they neglect the more necessary things of every day life and thereby impoverish those dependent upon them. Moreover, it fosters the spirit of ambition and covetousness which may lead to robbery and other evils. It is better, therefore not to encourage such, and thus they were forbidden altogether.

Oluyọle kept a large harem, for when he had become great his wives used to seize any good-looking maiden found in the street or market place, and bring her to him to become his wife. Hundreds of these he did not even know by sight, his palace being an enormous compound. On his death, the relatives and betrothed husbands of these maidens boldly entered his palace and took them away.

He had many children, the most distinguished among them were : Owolabi who perished in the Ará expedition (to be noticed hereafter), after him Alade who became the head of the house, but he also died not long after, and Aborisade the next eldest who stood for many years the head of the house.

The central market at Ibadan known as " Ọja Iba " was so named after him when he became Ibasọrun ; formerly it was Ọja Labọsinde after the Baba Isalẹ of the early settlers.

By the death of the Basọrun the government of the town devolved upon Ọdẹrinlọ the Balogun, but as some of the important chiefs were then absent from home, he was not disposed to assume a higher title till their return, and a general re-arrangement of titles take place. But he survived his chief only a year, and Lajumọkẹ the Ọtun and next in rank to him having died, the headship devolved upon Ọpẹagbe the Osi, but he survived them only 11 months, and after his death, by a unanimous vote Olugbode an Owu man was elected Balẹ, but he was not properly installed into office until the war-chiefs returned from an expedition now to be noticed.

CHAPTER XVII

SUBJUGATION OF THE IJĘṢAS AND EKITIS BY THE
IBADANS—SOME IMPORTANT EPISODES—SOCIAL
REFORM AT IBADAN

§ 1. THE ỌPIN WAR

AFTER the crushing defeat of the Ilọrins at Oṣogbo and the Ibadan
ascendancy, the Ilọrins ventured no more into the Ọyọ provinces,
except for the little help they endeavoured to give to the Ibadans
during the Batẹdo war, by attempting to besiege Ogbomọṣọ,
which ended disastrously for them. They appeared now to have
recovered somewhat from their military depression, at least
sufficiently to essay an aggressive warfare into the Ẹfọn districts.

A man called Eṣu, a native of Iyé, a town between Ilemọṣọ
and Eluku who had been a slave at Ilọrin was redeemed by one
Lalẹyẹ for 12 heads of cowries; the latter also redeemed one Oni for
25 heads of cowries, and gave her to him to wife. Eṣu, however,
turned out to be a *ne'er do weel* of a roving disposition, unfit for
any trade. He left Ilọrin and settled first at Ẹgbẹ then at Itagi
and finally at Iṣan, leading a predatory life in those regions, kidnapping peaceful traders, sparing none, and was particularly
hard on the Ilọrin traders. In that way he became a person of
some importance in those parts; hence the Ilọrins were now
resolved upon capturing him alive.

Finding himself obnoxious to the Ilọrins he hastily declared
his allegiance to the Ibadans their great antagonist. Through
the assistance of Oluòkun a distinguished Ibadan gentleman
residing at Ila, he received an introduction to the Baṣọrun
of Ibadan (then living) who received him cordially, and in dis-
missing him, gave him a war standard and commended him to
the care of Yemaja his tutelary deity, Oluyọle being a very
religious man in his own way. In his incursions Eṣu never forgot
his patron, for during the Baṣọrun's lifetime, he continually sent
him slaves and booty taken in his raids. After the death of
Oluyọle the Ilọrins were resolved to besiege Eṣu at Ọpin where
he then was.

Ali the braveBalogun of Ilọrin was entrusted with this expedition.
He sought the alliance of the Ibadan chiefs, as the relation between
Eṣu and Ibadan was only a personal one with the late Baọruns;
and besides, the Ibadans were somewhat under an obligation to

Ilọrin for assisting them in the futile siege of Ogbomọṣọ during the late Batẹdo war, but as a matter of fact in order to forestall his opponent. Although any pretext however small was quite sufficient as an excuse for the Ibadans to mobilize, yet in this case only a junior war-chief named Kọlọkọ with a small force was sent to represent the Ibadans.

For three years Ọpin held out heroically and had nearly baffled the prowess of Ali when a sudden accident occurred which extinguished their hopes. Aganga Adọja a noble citizen was the hero of the town ; one night Aganga was inspecting his magazine with a naked lamp in hand, when suddenly a terrific explosion was heard and the hopes of Ọpin with her heroic defender perished together in a moment.

Eṣu escaped to Iṣan, thence to Ọyẹ, and then to Ikọle. These places were taken one after another as Eṣu was being pursued to be taken alive. He escaped finally to Omù Ijẹlu, a place fortified by nature against primitive weapons of warfare. Situated on a high hill, and surrounded for a mile on all sides by a thorny hedge and thickets, it was impenetrable to the Ilọrin horse. Ali died soon after Ọpin was taken and his body was conveyed to Ilọrin for interment. The command of the army now devolved on Hinna-konu the Fulani Balogun, assisted by Alanamu the Yoruba Balogun of Ilọrin.

After the capture of the above named towns the camp was broken up, and the Ilọrin army as well as the Ibadan contingent returned to their respective homes. Kọlọkọ of Ibadan, however, did not reach home, but fell sick by the way and died at Oṣogbo.

§ 2. SUBJUGATION OF THE IJĘṢAS

After the return home of the war-chiefs from the Ọpin expedition and all were now present at home, Chief Olugbode was regularly and formally installed into office as the Balẹ of Ibadan. It was now his turn to confer the principal titles on the war-chiefs. The important titles of Balogun, Ọtun, Osi, i.e., the commander-in-chief, commander of the right and of the left, were vacant. As titles were sometimes given not to the most worthy but to the highest bidder, Ibikunle the Seriki was advised to bid for the title of Balogun ; but he refused to do so with words which have become memorable, showing the character and quality of the man " A ki ifi owo du oye alagbara," i.e. the title of the valiant should never be contested with money. As the most worthy of his compeers, the title of Balogun was conferred upon him without a dissentient voice. The other titles followed in due course.

The Ibadan army as now constituted being the instrument of

raising the reputation of that military state to its highest pitch of fame, which was maintained for many years afterwards and has never been surpassed, the names of the principal leaders and their offices may here be given :—

Bale—Olugbode

Titles.	Names.	Titles.	Names.
Balogun	Ibikunle	Seriki	Ajayi Jegede
Otun	Ogunmola	Asaju	Madarikàn
Osi	Osundina	Otun Bale	Sumala
Asipa	Akere	Osi Bale	Tubòsun
Ekerin	Orowùsi	Ajiya Bale	Abayomi
Ekarun	Oyasawe	Areagoro Balogun	Aijéñku

Of these the first three and last two were exceptionally brave men. There was at this time in the Yoruba country a great increase in the population, a marvellous agricultural prosperity, and an abundant energy not always directed to useful purposes.

It was always the custom after conferring of titles especially that of Balogun to seize the first opportunity that offered to prove one's fitness for the title ; an opportunity was soon afforded for the purpose.

THE IJEBU ERE WAR

The Ijesas of Ilase and Ibokun reinforced from Ilesa were at this time making incursions into the Osogbo farms. Osogbo being under the protection of Ibadan, the Bale of Ibadan therefore sent out his Balogun on his first expedition to punish Ilase for the raids.

On reaching Osogbo, the Ibadan army marched direct to the Ilase farms, clearing the bush, making wide paths and encamped by the Yawo stream.

But the expedition nearly collapsed before ever they came in sight of the enemy. A quarrel broke out between Orowùsì the Ekerin and two of the Bale's war-chiefs Ojo Orôna and Okunlà, which nearly involved the whole camp. There appeared to be an old grudge between them and they clashed with each other when choosing sites for their tents. The Bale's principal war-chiefs the Otun and the Osi took no part in the fight but their men did. Neither the Balogun nor Ogunmola the Otun could interfere without appearing to take sides and then the strife would be general.

Ogunmola who was distinguished for his tact and diplomacy therefore sent to the Balogun that he should give orders for battle as if the Ijesas were coming upon them. This was done. They marched out in order of battle, crossed the Yawo stream and opened fire upon an imaginary foe. They then sent a company of men to the camp to raise an alarm " The Ijẹṣas in sight." When therefore those rival chiefs heard the sound of musketry they left off fighting among themselves. The matter was amicably adjusted on the next day.

The Balẹ at home was informed of everything that transpired by a special messenger Oni by name (afterwards Josiah Oni) and he sent to pacify both parties.

For a whole year Ilasẹ withstood the attacks of the Ibadans. In order to raise the siege, the Ijẹṣas of Ibokun attacked the Ibadan camp from the rear, but the Balogun had provided against this contingency. Ali the powerful Balogun of Iwo was always left in the camp with a reserve force whenever they were engaged in battle. The Ibokuns were routed, driven back, and pursued right home, and the town was taken. The Ibadans were now able to concentrate all their forces on Ilasẹ. When Ilasẹ could no longer hold out, their Ilẹṣa auxiliaries withdrew and the town was taken. The Ibadans now left the camp at Yawo and pitched in a plain having the ruins of Ilasẹ and Ibokun on one side, and on the other Ẹsa Egure and Ẹsa Olusọpọ. Olusọpọ and Mesin Oloja Oke surrendered through Oluokun of Ibadan, a resident in those parts, and peace was concluded with them. From thence they removed to Ijẹbu Ẹrẹ.

A large number of the people of Ilasẹ escaped to Ijẹbu Ẹrẹ. This was a large town, and a large force from Ilẹṣa the capital was sent to defend it. The Ibadan army was met at a considerable distance from the town. Three severe engagements took place; at the third the Ijẹṣas were defeated and 160 of them made prisoners.

Ijẹbu Ẹrẹ was now closely besieged. Being a large town, the Balogun divided the Ibadan army into three parts; he encamped at Iwaye, and placed the Ọtun at the Ẹrinmọ road and the Seriki with all the Badas at the Ẹfọn Aye road. He intentionally left the Ilẹṣa road free as if to suggest a way of escape for them.

The Ijẹṣas made a desperate effort to carry the Iwaye camp, but found the Balogun too strong for them. Next they concentrated their attack on the camp at the Ẹrinmọ road; thrice they attempted to carry it by assault, but they were repulsed. The Balogun thereupon left a few of his war-chiefs in the Iwaye road, took the Seriki's place in the Ẹfọn Aye road, and sent him to reinforce the Ọtun where the fight was now strongest.

The Ibadans were then in the habit of using coloured or variegated umbrellas in the field as banners, and the Ijẹṣa war-chiefs having then no umbrellas raised their broad sun hats upon a pole covering them with a red cloth, to serve the double purpose.

Ọpẹjin the chief of Ibokun, was one of the bravest defenders of this place.

Finding that the defenders continued stubborn, the Ibadans began to kidnap on the only route left them, viz. the road to Ilẹṣa. The Ijẹṣas fearing that this also would be lost to them quietly deserted Ijẹbu Ẹrè and escaped with the people of the town.

After they had clean gone the information was conveyed to the besiegers by a man left in shackles ; not a soul was found in the town when they entered. The principal chiefs remained there, but the juniors went in pursuit : they found many of the smaller towns had likewise been deserted.

At Ẹrinmọ a feeble resistance was made. About 200 men kept up fire from the forts ; this continued for some time, but they escaped, leaving two cripples who were good marksmen to keep up the show. When the town was attacked on all sides and the walls scaled then the Ibadans found to their amazement that the town had been wholly deserted, and that the fire was kept up by only two cripples. They were brutally dragged down from the fort and slain ; the gates were then thrown open for their comrades to rush in. The Ibadans continued their pursuit to Ọmọ Ẹrin where they found a few aged men and women, the able-bodied having fled away ; next to Ẹrinta-dogun where a feeble resistance was made until night-fall when the men had an opportunity of making good their escape. Leaving Ẹrinta-dogun they came to a place where three roads met, one leading to Ipindun, another to Akata, and the third to Ikeji. Those who took the way to Akata met all the women and children of the several towns and villages that were deserted, and they were all taken captives. But the section that took the way to Ikeji (which was four days distant from their base at Ijẹbu Ẹrẹ) met with a disaster by an ambuscade and were nearly annihilated but for the timely aid of Ali of Iwo and Jeñriyin of Ibadan. This disaster was subsequently avenged by the Ọtun whom the Balogun sent to their assistance when the news reached him at the Ijẹbu Ẹrẹ headquarters.

This expedition was termed Ijẹbu Ẹrẹ because of the amount of mud and slush along the way from Ijẹbu to Ikeji the terminus of the present expedition.

The Ijẹṣas of Ilẹṣa the capital here surrendered to the Ibadans bringing them presents of cowries, beads, etc., and also hostages. The people of Ọgọtun put up a white flag at the approach of th pursuers and surrendered to Ọṣundina the Ọsí. Igbara did the same and surrendered to Ajayi Jegede the Seriki. Some of the minor chiefs who were not satisfied with what they got asked leave to make incursions in other directions ; they were allowed to do so.

Some met with good fortune, others with privations and terrible disasters from ambuscades. The wreck of this subsidiary expedition reached the camp at Ijẹbu Ẹrẹ. Nine days after this the standard of the Ibadan army wended its way homeward.

Before starting on this expedition the Ibadans sent presents to the Ilọrins, requesting their co-operation. The Ilorin army marched out, but on reaching Ọtun it was reported to them that their old enemy Eṣu was encamped on a rock about a mile from Ọtun. Knowing that he was sure to be attacked there, the principal war-chiefs of Ọtun, against the protest of the Òwòrè their prince, admitted Eṣu into the town, and the Ilọrins instead of joining their allies thereupon encamped against Ọtun. But Ọtun is a tributary town of Ibadan, the Balogun and Ọtun of Ibadan therefore sent to remonstrate with the Ilọrins for fighting with their friends when they were asked against their enemies. The reply was, " Not Ọtun but Eṣu ; we find our old enemy here, and we must not pass him by." The Ilọrins, however could not take Ọtun till the Ijẹbu Ẹrẹ campaign was over. Ajayi Jegede the Seriki, therefore asked permission to go to the help of his friend Eṣu at Ọtun, and Lisibade the over-lord of Ọtun did the same. Not only was permission granted, but the Balogun, Ọtun, and each of the principal war-chiefs also sent a small detachment with him, about 3,000 strong to re-inforce the town. The rest of the Ibadan army now returned home. Thus the whole of the Ijẹṣas were subdued by the Ibadans.

§ 3. The First Dahomian Invasion of Abẹokuta, a.d. 1851

The first Dahomian invasion of Abẹokuta took place on Monday the 3rd of March, 1851, during the absence of the Ibadans at the Ijẹbu Ẹrẹ expedition. We have seen above Chap. XVI, § 2 what was the cause of their sworn hostility to Abẹokuta.

Commander Forbes a British naval officer, and Mr. Beecroft, Her Britannic Majesty's consul for the Bights of Benin and Biafra were at Abomey (the capital of Dahomey) when preparations were being made for the invasion of Abẹokuta, and they communicated a full account of the same to the English Missionaries there with a view to forewarning the Egba chiefs, while they themselves were exerting their good offices in dissuading the Dahomians from these periodic raids on their neighbours.

It was alleged by an eye-witness that as the troops were assembled in the market square, the leaders pledged themselves to their sovereign not to shrink before the foe, and exhibited what prowess they would display in the coming struggle. The leader of the Amazons demanded for her regiment the honour of leading the attack upon the ground that on previous expeditions they (the Amazons) had always carried the positions when the male regiments failed to do so. The arrangement was accordingly agreed upon.

But the Egba chiefs were rather indifferent to the representations of the missionaries urging them to a vigorous preparation, except Sagbua the Alake and Ogunbọna the Balogun of Ikija, who repaired the walls of the town in the direction of the main gate to Aro : the rest were left in a dilapidated condition.

When the Dahomians reached Iṣaga, a small town about 17 miles from Abẹokuta, the people tendered their submission to them and whilst concluding terms of amity and friendship with them, they despatched private messengers to Abẹokuta to apprise the chiefs of the situation. It was now too late for the Egbas to begin to repair their walls. The whole town was seized with panic and consternation, some fleeing to Oṣiẹlẹ, some to Atadi, others going where they knew not. The women everywhere raised the cry of alarm " Elelè m'elè " (every man to his matchet), and hurried the men to the walls to watch the approach of the enemy. Fortunately for Abẹokuta the Iṣaga people had induced the Dahomians to alter their plan of attack from a night to a noon day assault, and from the north west where the walls were in a dilapidated condition to the western gate where repairs had recently been executed ; and to this circumstance alone Abẹokuta owed her safety ; had they followed their original plan, nothing could have saved the town. Even as it was many eye-witnesses do aver that what contributed most to their safety was confidence in the presence of the missionaries in the town. " The God of the white man " said they " is on our side." From this they derived moral courage.

On that memorable Monday the Dahomians were descried advancing towards the Arò gate. Some of the Egba chiefs went out to arrest their progress, but they could not withstand the force of those brave warriors. They were said to be advancing in the order of battle, marching steadily and solidly onward, ignoring the fire of the Egbas and paying no attention to those among themselves who fell, but kept marching stolidly onward. They never fired, but at the word of command, and when they did, their volleys were demoralizing. By this we can see that the Dahomian soldiers were disciplined troops such as the Egbas had never faced before. Those who went to arrest their progress fled precipitately and would not even stay to man the walls ; some of them never halted till they reached the Abẹtu stream within the town. The general idea that the Dahomians cared more for skulls than for captives and that the drinking cup each soldier carried in his knap-sack was a human skull added greatly to the dread entertained of them. But Ogunbọna the Balogun of Ikija, and Şokẹnu the Seriki of Abẹokuta displayed undaunted courage and bravery, opposing, the enemy with all their might.

The courage and noble deeds of the Egba women on this occasion were beyond all praise, and demand our special notice. But for them some of the men who were cowardly would have fled before the enemy. In the thick of the fight, with bullets flying right and left the Egba women could be seen in the ranks of the fighting men with water, mashed ẹkọ (a cooling drink), refreshments and encouragements, so that they need not fall to the rear for anything but continue the fight. Some of the missionaries were also there encouraging them by their presence, and doing what they could for the wounded.

Notwithstanding all this the trench around the town wall being full of dead bodies, the Dahomians were actually scaling the walls. Some of them with one hand cut off would hold on with the other or with the stump with grim determination in their faces; they kept pressing on, and a few did actually get into the town.

Up to this time the Egbas did not know that they were fighting with women. Following the barbarous custom of the age, it was customary to send as a trophy to the chief ruler of the town, the head and the private parts of the first enemy caught in warfare ; when those who actually entered the town were caught and slain, and the trophy was to be sent, then the Egbas knew that these terrible fighters were the Amazons !

Immediately the news spread among all ranks that they have been fighting with women, and for very shame all the Egba men were exasperated beyond measure and rushed upon them with one accord and compelled them to retreat. The Dahomians left thousands dead behind the walls of Abẹokuta.

The Egbas thought they only retreated to prepare for a more vigorous attack the next day, and they also went to prepare for a more determined resistance; but the Dahomians were already on their homeward march, they were not accustomed to lay siege or repeat an assault ; if an assault failed they retreated altogether to renew it at another time. They were determined to punish the Işaga people for their treacherous conduct towards them. The Egbas, finding that the attack was not renewed the next day, followed in pursuit and met them at Işaga, the chiefs of which were just then apologizing and defending their conduct. The battle fought here was said to have been more fierce than that before the walls of Abẹokuta. The Egbas contemned the idea of being attacked by women hence the furious onslaught they made at them.

The Dahomians left more dead behind them than the captives they succeeded in taking away, including the skulls of the unfortunate victims caught in the farms.

Soon after the invasion, on the 16th of May, 1851, the Rev. D. Hinderer, a German missionary of the C.M.S., who was then labouring at Abẹokuta and witnessed the attack, obtained permission from Ṣokẹnu and the other chiefs to carry the gospel to Ibadan. At this period, none of the surrounding tribes was at peace with Ibadan. The Ijẹbus especially were kidnapping on the roads, and one had to reach the town by a circuitous route of four instead of two days from Abẹokuta. Caravans to Ijaye and Ibadan were under escorts up to a certain point, and the Rev. D. Hinderer was obliged to risk the rest of the journey by himself when the escorts could proceed no further for fear of Ijẹbu kidnappers.

The Rev. D. Hinderer was received kindly by the Balẹ and the other leading chiefs of Ibadan. When he told them the object of his visit, the five leading chiefs, viz., the Balẹ, Balogun, Ọtun, Osi, and an elderly chief Lanọsọ by name, in whose house he was lodged, held consultation whether they should receive the white man and the message he brought or not. Ọsundina the Osi a staunch Moslem raised great objections, evidently on religious grounds; he stoutly opposed his stay amongst them. Said he "Awọn ọbaiye jẹ ni iwọnyi." (These are the world spoilers), "There is no country they enter but misfortune will follow for that place." Ogunmọla the Ọtun said: "But white men are at Lagos, Badagry, and Abẹokuta; why should we refuse him? We are not the first nor shall we be the last to receive them, and whatever be the consequence to others let the same be to us also." Ibikunle the Balogun suggested that the national god Ifa should be consulted, and if Ifa prognosticated evil let the white man be ordered out of the town at once; but if favourable, let him be received. These five chiefs accordingly repaired to the Ogboni house at the Ibasọrun market and consulted the brazen Ifa which is the national god. The omen was favourable and Mr. Hinderer was accorded a cordial welcome and well entertained. A place of residence was assigned to him, the house of the late Chief Ogidi, and he was placed under the special care of chief Abayọmi the Ajiya Balẹ the head chief of that part of the town through whom he could always approach the chiefs in council; and he in turn entrusted him to Olumiloyọ his Balogun whose house was not far from the mission premises.

Mr. Hinderer remained five months at Ibadan on this his first

visit, preaching and teaching and making general observation
on the place as a field of missionary enterprise.   He then returned
to England to recruit his health and to prepare for a permanent
stay there.

§ 4.   The Ará War and Relief of Otun

Ará is a town of considerable importance in the Ekiti country.
This expedition was named after it, although Ará was not the
primary objective when the Ibadan standard left home, but it
was the last important place taken before the Ibadans returned
home.

We have seen above that the Ibadans invited the Ilorins to the
Ijẹbu Ẹrẹ expedition and that the Ilorins instead of joining them
as allies encamped against Otun a tributary state of Ibadan because
of Ẹşu their inveterate enemy ; and at the close of the campaign,
certain Ibadan war-chiefs who were interested in Ẹşu or the
town of Otun obtained leave to go to the assistance of their
friends.

Now, although the Ilorins failed to conquer the defenders,
and they could not drive the Ilorins away, yet by overpowering
numbers, Otun was closely invested and famine began to do its
dreadful work within the town ; therefore the Ibadan contingent
there sent home to ask for a larger relieving force, and " if possible,
let the Balogun himself come."

The Ibadan army was once more on the march to the Ekiti country
for the relief of Otun, but other complications occurred which
diverted their attention from Otun.

Prior to this expedition the Alára (or king of Ará) had been
deposed by his people for stealing and selling their children ; the
poor victims were bound and conveyed out of the town in hampers
of cotton. The Alára appealed to the Ibadan chiefs at Otun for
their kind offices and they composed the difference between king
and people and reinstated the former, the people yielding more
from fear of the consequences a refusal might entail.

But about a year after, he was deposed again for his atrocities
and he escaped again to the Ibadan chiefs at Otun. By this
time the Balogun of Ibadan and his hosts were on the way to the
relief of Otun, the chiefs therefore sent their messengers along with
the Alára to meet the Balogun at Igbajo to tell his own tale   Thence
the Balogun and the principal war-chiefs sent special messengers
with the Alára once more to compose the difference between him
and his people and to reinstate him. He was accepted with very
great reluctance, more from fear of the Ibadans than otherwise.

This ended the first act in the tragedy which sealed the fate of

Ará. Up to this point there was not the slightest intention of destroying the town.

The Ibadan expedition left Igbajọ for the Ilá farms and everything having been eaten up far and near except the farms at Koro, the war chiefs after consultation sent special messengers to the Ajero of Ijero the paramount chief of Koro for permission to forage in the Koro farms. The Ajero replied " The Koros are wild boys: a yam may cost you a human head." The Ibadans felt insulted at this reply and sent back to the Ajero to say " We only applied out of courtesy, and if our peaceful overtures are not complied with, two ' wild boys ' will meet in the field within three days, and, therefore, all Yoruba (Ọyọ) residents at Ijero should leave the town at once."

The Ajero called together the Ọyọ residents in his town and had the message repeated in their ears, then he said to them " You may go now, but you need not go far, you can wait at Ará or Eriwo until the Koros have driven away this Ibadan army, then you can come back." So confident was he of the strength of the Koros. The Ọyọ residents accordingly left the town.

The Ibadans now wended their way to Koro and the Koros about 2,000 strong came out to meet them on their frontier at a place called Ita Oniyan. The Ibadans were marching according to their ranks, the Balogun and Aṣipa being in the rear, and the junior war-chiefs in front, but the Koros had lain in ambush and the Ibadans walked into it ; suddenly they fell upon the Balogun's and the Aṣipa's ranks, but in both places they were utterly defeated with great slaughter. The Ibadans advanced to the river Oyi, the scene of the next fight ; the Koros met them here, and again they were defeated. The Ibadans advanced to Yawo a place not far from the town, and here the Koros made a stand. The Ajero their paramount chief now got alarmed and hastened to their assistance. He applied to the Ilọrins before Ọtun, for help, and the Ilọrins whose sole policy was to help one set of Pagans against another until they had weakened each and both fall a prey to them, lost no time in sending two war-chiefs Adedeji and Magòbọn with horse and men to help the Koros. The Ajero sent also to all the towns in his territory including Ẹfọn and Ará to come to their help and save Koro the strongest town in their district which now seemed doomed to destruction.

Ará alone refused to comply; the Alára said he had just been re-instated by the Ibadans, and he could not take up arms against them. But the men of Ará were angry with their king's decision, they were all for going to the help of their kinsmen against the " Ọyọs "

But there were two rebel chiefs of Ará who had been expelled the town and were living at Ohan; they considered themselves free to join the coalition, and they defiantly came outside the walls of Ará inviting their townsmen to come along to the aid of their kinsmen.   The Alára, unwilling that Ará should be represented in the coalition against his benefactors summoned his people to come out and drive these rebel chiefs back ; but his summons was not obeyed, and he went out himself unaided to intercept them ; there was a brief but sharp fight between them in which fell a stout and well-to-do citizen who exposed himself between them, trying to put an end to the fight, thinking that his person would be respected. So the rebel chiefs went on to the help of Koro.

Ará was not officially represented, as the Alára refused to go, and Lejofi the most powerful man in the town whom the people would rather follow remained sulky and neutral.

But when these rebel chiefs saw that there was little hope for Koro they sent a private message to apprise the Ará people that they would leave Koro at such and such a day and that they were to hold themselves in readiness that together they might fall upon the Alára and murder him before Koro was taken and his friends the Ibadans were free to avenge him.

The Alára having an intimation of this, summoned the Ọyọ residents at Ará, inviting them to be ready at once to leave the town with him, reminding them how on the former occasion Chief Ogunmọla had reprimanded them for not leaving the town when he did, thereby casting their lot as it were with rebels.

The Alára and these Ọyọ residents quitted the town fortunately just a day before the rebel chiefs came, who together with the townsmen gave chase, and pursued after the fugitives and overtook them.   These had to fight their way to Ęfọn Ahàyè; they lost nearly everything.   At a place called Oke Ogbe they made a stand and offered a determined resistance to enable the women and children to escape safely to Ahàyè.   This action sealed the fate of Ará as we shall see.

In the meantime the Ibadans were drawing a cordon round Koro, and the Ilọrin contingent true to their characteristics were prepared to escape and abandon their friends.   Magọbọn one of their leaders conceived the bold idea of marching right through the Ibadan lines, trusting that he would escape undetected.   The Ibadans who never imagined any venture so foolhardy, at first mistook them for a company of their own men, as Magọbọn stood by the standard of chief Sumála the Ọtun Balę while his people were marching past.   But as a chief on horseback rode past, a man eyed him closely and recognized in him an Ilọrin man and at once took his gun and shot him down dead on the spot. Being now discovered, they took to their heels and were pursued and many were caught, but a few swift-footed escaped. Another company which took another route likewise was discovered and captured.

But Adedeji the other leader remained at Koro being afraid to run the risk: the Ibadans therefore offered him protection if he would commit himself unreservedly to their clemency ; he did so (there being no alternative) and was allowed to come to the Ibadan camp. He remained there a few hours ; he and his men were well entertained, and were sent away in peace. Even a hatchet one of them left behind at the Ibadan camp in their haste to get away the chiefs sent to them in the Otun camp.

This noble deed of the Ibadans so put the Ilorin general to shame that he negotiated peace with the Ibadans and raised the siege of Otun.

The siege of Otun being raised, the Ibadan contingent there together with Esu whom they went to defend were now able to join the Ibadan army at Koro ; the " bad boys " were finally beaten and the town fell. Ijero the chief town of the district, and three other towns also which assisted them were taken, Oro surrendered and was placed under tribute but Ará held out for two years, being well defended by the powerful chief Lejofi.

Finding further resistance useless Ará now surrendered and brought presents to the camp, and an armistice was concluded. On account of their past conduct, and the useless waste of life occasioned, the Ibadans while accepting the presents imposed two conditions upon them :—

1. That they should recall their king from Ahàyè.

2. That all the Ará chiefs with Lejofi at their head should come and meet him in the camp so that they might have the opportunity of hearing both sides, and adjust matters between them.

The Ará chiefs thought this was a stratagem to get them all into their power for capital punishment. They sent for the Alára into the camp but the chiefs declined to venture themselves there : they offered to pay whatever fines might be imposed on them.

Then another proposal was made, if they would not come then let them send them their fighting men and a guide to Igèdè in the Ado territory. Neither would they comply with this but they begged to be subjected to whatever fines they pleased and to be placed under tribute, and they would serve them.

The armistice was now declared at an end, and fighting resumed, till the Balogun at length forced his way into the town by an assault, and Ará was taken.

The scene that followed showed how courageous and stout-hearted the Ará people were. A band of about 1,600 young men choosing death rather than slavery put the muzzle of their loaded guns in their mouth, pulled the trigger with their great toe and shattered their brains to pieces.

The great and wealthy Lejofi, in order that the Ibadans might not profit at all by his wealth, destroyed all his valuables, with his store of provisions, cutting the yams into bits and strewing them all over the yard (provisions being so scarce for this great host). Then two of his wives were killed to be his attendants in the other world, and himself with his own jacknife cut his own throat. His eldest son met him weltering in his blood, life not extinct, being unable to complete the deed ; he, therefore put an end to his father's agonies, loaded the gun afresh and shattered his own brains !

A man from Oke Mẹsin, Ladojudé by name, whose brother had been killed by Lejofi came to avenge his brother's death upon the corpse. He kindled a fire from wood obtained in Lejofi's own house, threw his body into it and burnt it.

Thus ended the Ará campaign, as it was called, in 1854 and the Ibadan army returned home triumphantly.

Ẹṣu who was relieved and was the indirect cause of this campaign, did not go home with them, neither stopped in the vicinity any longer, but penetrated further into the Yagba country and there established himself.

§ 5. Raids by the Minor Ibadan Chiefs

The subjugation of the Ekitis, including the Ịjẹṣas, Ẹfọns and others, may now be said to be complete, but the process seems to have reacted to the demoralization of the Ibadan war-chiefs and others. Slave-raiding now became a trade to many who would get rich speedily, and hence those who felt themselves unlucky in one expedition, and others who quickly spent their illgotten gains in debauchery and all excesses would band together for a raiding expedition on those minor places that have hitherto escaped the misfortunes of war. A brief notice will be taken of some of them.

Ayọrinde.—Chief Ayọrinde did not return home with the army after the destruction of Ará, but went on first to Iṣan with Ẹṣu ; thence they went against the Àdés, whom they conquered, and then he returned with his hands full.

Intoxicated with pleasure at his own success, he was lavish in his enjoyments and out-stepped the bounds of moderation. He offered a thanksgiving sacrifice to his Ori (god of good

fortune). About the same time for an alleged offence he flogged one
of his wives to death. For this he was brought under the power
of the civil authorities, and was told to die. It must be remembered
that a private individual would be executed at once for murder,
but a chief must commit suicide by any method he may prefer,
for if executed publicly his house would be demolished and his
family ruined.

But Ayọrinde begged hard for his life. He surrendered nearly
all he had to no purpose ; then Chief Ogunmọla his patron advised
him privately to leave the town speedily and go into voluntary
exile to those regions he lately came from, for even he could not
save him from the penalties of the law.

Ayọrinde left Ibadan secretly with only 12 followers out of all
he brought back with him! When his escape became known
he was hotly pursued and narrowly escaped with his life. He
went back to Eṣu with a tale of woe, and located him in a place
called Irùn, and there he remained and organized a band of
marauders and ravaged all those regions till he encamped against
a place of some importance named Ọgbàgi. He was here for fully
ten years with varied fortune. Adoyan Okorigi a great and
powerful warrior came to the help of Ọgbagi and Ayọrinde was just
on the point of being defeated when by a skilful move he took
Okorigi in the rear and inflicted on him a crushing defeat and slew
him.

Next the Ọgbagis obtained help from Rabbah and Ilọrin. Sinabu
King Masaba's son and Hinakonu the Fulani Balogun of Ilọrin
came against him ; thrice was Ayọrinde routed, and many of his
fighting men speared, but he rallied again and maintained his
ground. Ọgbagi was at length taken. Ayọrinde became lord of
the Akokos and Ido Ani. He opened a caravan way to Ọwọ̀
through which he obtained ammunition from Benin. He was
kind to all Ọyọs, who flocked to his standard ; every one could
enjoy himself to any extent he liked but he absolutely forbade
the introduction of intoxicating liquor into that country. They
might buy whatever they liked with their slaves and booty. He
himself undertook to supply all ammunition required for their
raids. But no one must think of deserting him ; in order to ensure
this, he posted men in all the exits of his territory : any Ọyọ
caught escaping lost all he had and returned home as he came ;
but any Ekitis or Ilas similarly caught were seized with their slaves
and sold to Ọwọ̀.

At last after many years as old age approached Ayọrinde longed
for home. But he knew that he would not be allowed by the
people of Irun, who befriended him all these years, to depart

with all his effects to Ibadan, so he manufactured a quarrel with them, and captured Irun the headquarters of all his expeditions and destroyed the place. In spite of all this precaution not one tenth of his slaves returned with him to Ibadan.

Ayọrinde returned to Ibadan in 1872 after a very long absence. Nearly all the chiefs he left and the whole of his compeers had died out. He met at the head of the government subordinate chiefs, who had risen into power during his absence, and to his mortification he had to submit to them. He was, however, honoured with the title of Osi, but he did not hold it long; he died in the following year.

Abayọmi.—Abayọmi the Ajiya Balẹ with Olumiloyọ his Balogun got up an expedition to relieve Isẹ a tributary town of his in the Ekiti country. He met Ayọrinde at the siege of Ọgbagi but he passed off and encamped against Àgbádó. The town was soon taken and he had an immense number of captives and booty. From hence he was proceeding to the relief of Isẹ. But the captured town Àgbádò being in the territory of Àdó, the Balogun of the king of Àdó was sent to intercept him; an ambush was laid for him, and he was hemmed in on every side. He had to fight his way to Isẹ, and lost all he had taken, and what was more he left behind him some of his best fighting men including two of his powerful slaves and Olumiloyọ his Balogun. He arrived at Isẹ with the wreck of his army and returned to Ibadan in a worse condition than he left. This was in the year 1857. It will be remembered that Olumiloyọ was the chief who had direct supervision of the missionaries at Ibadan. Readers of " Seventeen years in the Yoruba country " (Life of Anna Hinderer) will find frequent mention of the name of this chief and how kind and friendly he was to the missionaries. He gave Mr. and Mrs. Hinderer two of his children a boy and a girl to train, in which he showed himself more enlightened than the superior chiefs. The boy was trained first by these good missionaries themselves: subsequently at the C.M.S. Training Institution at Abẹokuta, then he was employed as a schoolmaster, Mr. Hinderer himself continuing his education. Later he was employed as a catechist in 1885, and finally as an ordained missionary of the C.M.S. at Ogbomọsọ in 1892, where he is still labouring.

Ajọbọ and the Badas.—While the sieges of Ọgbagi and of Agbado were going on, all the Badas of Ibadan headed by Ajọbọ the senior Bada got up an expedition against Pakùnde. All the Ẹfọn, Ijẹsa, and Akoko territories had now become a field for slave hunting for any number of men who could band themselves together for an expedition.

The Badas at first meant to take the place by stratagem, encamping outside the walls, professing friendship and asking for a guide to Ọgbagi to meet Ẹṣu. But the men of Pakunde were too wideawaḳe, and so when strategy failed, hard fighting was resorted to.

But it was reported at Ibadan that these Badas meant to establish themselves there after the capture of Pakùnde and not to return home. This would eventually mean the loss of all the tributary towns tò Ibadan ; consequently Chief Ogunmọla of Ibadan sent to all the surrounding kings and chiefs subject to Ibadan not to let Pakùnde be taken. The town was almost on the eve of falling when tidings reached the camp that all the men sent to procure provisions at Ikọle, Ado, Ọyẹ, Odo Ijẹsa, Ikoyi had been seized and either slain or sold into slavery ! This was a blow to the Badas. In whatever direction they sent to procure food, they could not get any and no farms were near them for foraging. Being in a strait, the camp was broken up in the night and they made for home. Their guide took them by a way between Ikọle on the left and Omwò in the right ; the Ikọles waylaid them and they had to fight their way through. At Omù Ijẹlu whilst they were satisfying the cravings of hunger in the farms, the men of the town fell upon them and killed many with poisoned arrows. At Aiyede, a town built by Ẹṣu they were not allowed to forage in the farms. So by forced marches, and in a starved condition the wreck of Ajọbọ's army arrived at Ibadan.

§ 6. SOCIAL REFORMS.

The Present Condition of Slaves.—Ibadan had by this time been greatly augmented, not only by immigrants from the provinces and elsewhere who repaired there as affording a safer place of abode, but also by the thousands of slaves brought in annually. It had now become necessary to crystallize into law a custom that had gradually grown amongst the chiefs and people generally, who had thousands of them in hand.

Except under especially pressing circumstances the chiefs do not now sell their slaves or rather captives of war excepting the old and infirm and that chiefly to procure arms and ammunition. The able-bodied men are kept and trained as soldiers, and it has become the law and custom that soldier-slaves are never to be sold under any circumstances ; they are to remain permanently as members of the house. The fair young women are added to the harems by the great, and young men save themselves the expenses of a dowry by making wives of any that come into their hands.

Any slave-woman taken as a wife becomes *ipso facto* a free woman. All the rest are sent into the farms, each to be employed in his or her own line of work. The chiefs had large farms and farm houses containing from a hundred to over a thousand souls. The men are engaged in clearing the bush, cultivating the soil, cutting palm nuts and doing other male work ; the women in making palm oil, nut oil, soap, weaving mats, rearing poultry and the smaller cattle, cultivating kitchen vegetables of all kinds for the weekly markets and the fairs ; older women in preparing and spinning cotton, shelling palm nuts, etc. All are engaged as " hands " in time of harvest.

These extensive plantations not only support their huge establishments but also supply the markets, so that a military state though Ibadan was, food was actually cheaper there than in many other towns.

The male slaves had wives given them by their masters from among the slave women, whomsoever they may choose, or if their choice lay elsewhere, the master would redeem any woman for them. Their offspring are home-born slaves, belonging to the master ; their condition is hardly different from that of the freeborn, all grow together as children of the house. Thus by slave-raiding and procreation the great houses are enlarged and the population of the town increased.

Well-to-do women in the town also buy slaves of both sexes, their offspring belong to them in the same way as the parents themselves, but barring exceptional cases of distress occasioning the ruin of the house they are never to be sold.

Of the slaves who are kept as soldiers, some are selected as body-guards or personal attendants; these are provided for in every way by the master. The rest follow their own avocation and provide for themselves ; their services are only required in time of war. If the slave is successful in war and catches several slaves, he is to surrender them to his master ; a kind master will return him one or two fifths for his own purpose and keep the rest. An unkind master will keep all, as the service he has rendered him is his duty. Some masters would give money as consolation from the proceeds of any of the slaves he may sell. Any of these slaves is at liberty to procure his own freedom at any time. A wise one, who has captured one or two slaves in war, gives them back to his master in the presence of witnesses in lieu of himself, and thereby his ransom is paid ; he is free now to go any where he likes. Those who wish to remain permanently with the master nevertheless remove to a friend's house for a short time and in that way publicly make known their freedom;

and then they may return to the master's house, and serve under him in war as freeborn soldiers and in that case give to their master as any other freeborn does one or two captives as the case may be and appropriate the rest. They are protected by the law as any freeborn citizen.

Others who consider themselves free and safe under the protection of a great name, as slaves of a powerful chief, will squander whatever they may have in hope of replenishing their stock at the next opportunity.

Freeborn soldiers who are independent give to their captain a proportion of 1 or 2 out of 5 and appropriate the rest ; but if he is an idle fellow and dependent on his captain for everything, including his war accoutrements and his debts, he has to give up more than a half or nearly all of what he captured.

Highly Placed Servants.—At this period the chiefs were in the habit of installing favourite slaves into a position of trust and responsibility especially if they were brave and energetic and proved themselves worthy of trust. These keep horses of their own, farms and farm-houses, have harems, a drummer and fifer, etc. Young slaves and recruits are placed under them to be trained for war. At the return of every expedition a fourth or a fifth of the captives taken are given to the master; they appropriate the rest. They are generally more richly dressed and make more show than their lord. Whatever the misfortunes of the house these of course are never sold : they remain the guardians of the house and of their master's sons. Their children may be considered as home born slaves, but practically are indistinguishable from freeborn children. These servants are "slaves" only in name for want of a better term. These customs originating at Ibadan have been followed by all the Ọyọ states throughout. The more of these highly placed servants a chief has, the greater he is held to be.

The Law of Inheritance.—Hitherto when a man dies all his effects are inherited by his brother or brothers in succession until the turn of the eldest son comes, then he gets whatever may remain of what was once his father's, but in most cases, he gets nothing at all. It has happened within the experience of the chiefs that whilst one is toiling and saving, some brothers are idle and dissolute, and yet at his death, the idle and dissolute will step in and squander all he has saved, leaving his children to welter in poverty and want.

At a deliberative council held in the year 1858 it was proposed to alter this custom. For whom is a man toiling and saving? The answer comes naturally " For his children." Why then should a brother displace one's children in the succession? If the children are minors the uncle may act for them until they are of age, otherwise the eldest surviving issue of the founder of a house must succeed as the head of the house in rotation until it comes to the turn of the children of the next generation. This is not like the English law of primogeniture in which only the eldest sons succeed, but it is the eldest surviving issue of the founder of a house that succeeds, until the turn of the eldest son of the first successor comes round.

But the members of the family are not totally overlooked. At the time of the succession the personal effects are distributed amongst the nearest relatives, every one having a share of the clothes, slaves, money, etc., but the house, inalienable slaves, principal farms, in a word, the real property, and all that goes to make the house what it is, are never to be alienated. These are assigned to the eldest surviving son and successor.

Every house is under the protection of a chief, a chief's house is under the protection of the paramount chief or the town council and these will see about the installation of the successor. In a great house, the highly placed servants will be in charge to train and direct their young master in the ways of his father.

These resolutions were communicated to the ALÂFIN of ỌYỌ for his approval, and he not only approved but adopted the same for all Ọyọ states, and moreover he adopted the same for the Crown also. He ruled thereupon that the custom that has arisen during the degenerate times of Old Ọyọ that the Arẹmọ (Crown Prince) die with his father should cease and the earlier custom reverted to. He wished his eldest son ADELU to succeed him, and after him the eldest surviving issue of the house as seems fit to the King Makers.

In the year 1858 Ibadan was so thickly populated that it was found necessary to extend the town walls. The new wall was known as Odi Ibikunle (Ibikunle's town wall) after the Balogun, as it was he who suggested, planned and superintended the carrying out of the work. This is the present town wall.

Ogunmọla also suggested that Ibadan should have what is known as " Igbo Ile," i.e. home forest, the thick bush surrounding every town in the Yoruba country, which may be exposed to raids and sieges. But the Ibadans did not care for any such thing and it could not be carried into effect, for they had no one to fear. The annual bush fires were allowed to nullify Ogunmọla's suggestion.

A GLORIOUS END AND THE GORY DAWN OF TWO REIGNS—THE IJAYE WAR.

§ 1. DEATH OF KING ATIBA.

ATIBA the ALÂFIN of Ọyọ lived to a good old age. Of few Kings do we know so much as we do of him ; he was a link with the past, and lived within the days of authentic history. He was the father of several princes and princesses whose names are the following :—

Princes.		Princesses.	
Adelu (The Crown Prince)		Bojẹ	Adewẹni
Adelabu	Adelẹyẹ	Atowurọ	Ogboja III.
Adesiyẹn	Adesetan II.	Adedoja	Ade Oyè
Adeyẹmi	Adedọtun	Durokilu	Adeyimka
Adediran	Afọnja	Ogbọja I.	Ogboja IV.
Adejumọ	Agbọnrin	Ogbọja II.	Siyè
Ọlawọyin	Tẹla Okiti papa	Akere I.	Ogboja V.
Tẹla Agboju l'ogun	Ọgọ	Akere II.	Popoọla
Àlá	Mọmọdu	Twins { Adeduntan { Adewale	Lapemọ Ogboja VI.
Adewusi	Adesọkan	Akere III.	Adetọla
Adesetan I.	Adejọjọ		

Of these the 1st and the 4th succeeded to the throne.

A few remarks on some of the princes :—

Adelu was much older than his brothers or sisters, for he was born when his father was quite a young man, long before he entered into his career of a war-like prince. He was much beloved by his father because he was a very dutiful son and shared with him most of the dangers and privations of war in those turbulent days of his early career. By virtue of his birthright he became the AREMỌ when his father ascended the throne.

Ọgọ was the Arẹmọ Oyè i.e., the first born after the father's accession.

Adewusi was Adelu's brother, of the same mother, and was of a contrary disposition. He was wild, undutiful and cruel. He once quarrelled with his father, and with a cutlass cut off all the mattings that enclosed the Aganju (throne room). He quarrelled with his half brother Àlá by seizing from him a plot of land the latter had obtained for farming, containing many palm and kola trees. Adewusi went and secured the same spot for himself by affixing thereon a symbol of the Egūgun curse on any trespasser. When Àlá went to remonstrate with him, he stabbed him to death with a knife! The father thereupon sentenced him to be executed by strangling !

Alá was of the same mother with Adelabu.

Adeyẹmi who subsequently succeeded his brother on the throne was of the same mother as Olawọyin. He enjoyed the longest reign of modern times ; more of him hereafter.

Agbọnrin, nick-named Allah ni yio bo Aṣiri (God will hide secrets) was also a prince of a most cruel disposition. His favourite (?) wife was once preparing his Okra leaf sauce with strained ash, which was a milder form of the carbonate of potash used in such cases. He thereupon compelled her to drink a calabashful of caustic potash, and she died soon after from inflammation of the stomach and bowels. He once caught a young man in his farm cutting palm nuts. Upon his begging him to spare his life Agbọnrin said he would do so if the young man could climb up again and replace the nuts; this being impossible he clubbed him to death !

The conduct of many of these princes brought great discredit on royalty. Very few of the crimes they committed ever reached the ears of their father for who would undertake to report them. Hence the licence they allowed themselves without the father's knowledge for he never spared them.

King ATIBA was now old and full of years. Early in the year 1858 he was resolved on celebrating the Bẹbẹ (the Bẹbẹ is akin to the Royal Jubilee, and only Kings who have had a long and peaceful reign celebrate it). Yorubaland is now free from the incursions of foreign foes, the Fulanis of Ilọrin permanently checked. All now was peace ; the people were content and prosperous, and therefore the King thought a Bẹbẹ should be celebrated. But inasmuch as the few Kings who celebrated it died soon after doing so, that festival came to to be regarded as celebrating one's funeral rites, hence Bẹbẹ is sometimes termed the " Iku " (death).

The Arẹ of Ijaye and others who were attached to him strongly advised him not to do it, as it might portend his death. His Majesty replied " Well, I am old enough and do not care to live much longer."

Notification of this was sent round everywhere and delegates came from every part of the Yoruba country to observe this festival with the King. From Saki alone came about 200 Egūguns, and so from all other Oke Ogun towns for the ceremonies.

Booths were erected all over the palace street from the Abata (frontage of the palace) to the Akẹsan market for the visitors. The Ọyọ noblemen also lived in tents, in front of their houses, until the ceremonies were over.

The ceremonies partook of the character partly of the coronation and partly of the funeral rites, the principal part of it being done privately, at dead of night.

On the eve of the Bẹbẹ the King paid a visit to the Bàrà to perform certain ceremonies there as a thank-offering sacrifice to his fathers. We have mentioned in Part I. that only on the coronation do the Kings ever enter there, and never afterwards till they are taken there for interment. This festival forms an exception.

Tents made of beautifully woven cloths were set up and enclosed with mattings at the Abata, the Akẹsan, the Apini, and near the Bàrà for the King as on the coronation. Attended by all the noblemen he issued from the palace and entered each of these tents in succession, the noblemen waiting outside and only one woman (probably a priestess) accompanied him into the tent. He remained half an hour or an hour in each performing certain ceremonies, and sent presents of kola nuts to those waiting outside and so on till he reached the Bàrà. On his return, that very evening the general festivities began. All the Egūguns observed a vigil, the voice of the Agán being heard all night. The next day an Egūgun confinement was proclaimed in which all women and children must remain indoors. The Egūguns our readers will remember are the denizens of the other world, and are supposed to be our dead relatives on a visit to us.

For a limited space of time during the day, licence was granted to all the Egūguns' attendants to seize goats, sheep or fowl found in the streets: none was to exceed that fixed time, whoever did was arrested and made to pay a fine of 25 heads of cowries (equiv. to £1 5s. then) for each animal. In the afternoon of this day the King came outside the palace attended again by a woman, the large gate being shut; the whole area between the palace and the Akẹsan was full of Egūguns. He sat on a hide, and reclined on a bolster, the wife sitting by his side was by special permission initiated into the Egūgun mysteries. Then appeared the supposed spirit of his father dressed in the skin of the red monkey; the King prostrated before his father and the " monkey " rubbed him all over with its tail and blessed him.

It was supposed that Ẹru-ifa one of his slaves was under the mask on this occasion. The King's "funeral" expenses on this occasion can only be imagined.

Not long after this celebration, the King's health which had not been very good lately, markedly declined. He was soon reported ill. Whether anything deleterious to health was applied on him with the tail of the red monkey or not, we cannot tell, but His Majesty succumbed under the ailment and was gathered unto his fathers, and the Bàrà was soon again the scene of a great ceremony sombre and sad.

Before the King's death, anticipating trouble for his eldest son Adelu, from sticklers after precedents, he reminded the Ibadans of the new law of succession he had sanctioned and begged them to stand by the Crown Prince and support his claim for he did not wish him to die with his father. And this they promised on oath. Thus passed away ATIBA the first ALÂFIN of the present OYO and ADELU his son was proclaimed King in his stead.

§ 2. CIRCUMSTANCES THAT LED TO THE IJAYE WAR.

ADELU the son and successor of ATIBA was acknowledged King by all, except Kurũmi the Arẹ of Ijaye.

Towards the latter end of Atiba's reign, there was some disaffection between him and the Arẹ ; this breach with the Crown widened by the succession of ADELU whom the Arẹ refused to acknowledge as a lawful successor to his father. "It is contrary to custom" said he, "and the Arẹmọ should die with his father." He never repaired to OYO to do homage according to custom, nor even sent a congratulatory message. He was for seeking for another prince of the older line, of the royal family at Igboho or Kìhìsi to succeed ATIBA, but ADELU having been duly elected and accepted by the denizens of the palace and obtaining the support of the Ibadan chiefs, ascended the throne in due form, and the pretext for an open rupture which the Arẹ had long been seeking was hereby afforded. The common people also catching the spirit of the times sang in their dances:

" ATIBA ma ti ilọ,   (" ATIBA don't go yet awhile,
   Duro de ADELU O ! " Wait for your ADELU pray ! ")

The ALÂFIN was conciliatory towards the Arẹ, who was the comrade of his father in their old warlike days, but the Arẹ remained irreconcilable. Every means of averting war was resorted to, but the Arẹ remained obdurate and insolent. Matters came to a crisis when a rich lady Abu by name, died intestate at Ijanna; she left no heirs, and as such the property reverted to the Crown. But Ijanna being directly under Ijaye, owing to the breach between the King and Kurũmi, the townfolk were divided in their opinions as to the disposal of the property. They feared the power of Ijaye on the one hand and yet loyalty to the Crown dictated a contrary action ; so one party sent to Ọyọ to request that the King should send to take over the property, the other party sent a similar message to Ijaye. The King anticipating danger to those whom he sent for the treasure ordered a well equipped force under Akingbẹhin Alẹyọ the Ọna-aka, and the Arẹmọ's Balogun to escort them. But Kurũmi sent a body of troops to waylay them, and the Ọyọ escorts with the messengers bringing the treasures were attacked by the Ijaye troops at Apata Màbà near Oke 'ho and were dispersed some escaping to Oke'ho others to Isẹyin. Within four days they collected themselves together at Isẹyin and met there with the Ọyọ traders who could not return home for fear of the Ijaye kidnappers but who now availed themselves of the protection of the escorts to return home.

The Ijaye troops under the command of Amọdu intercepted them again between Isẹyin and Ọyọ. The Ijayes encamped on a rock named afterwards Apata Jabata because there the Jabata of Ọyọ fell. When they met, the Ọyọ escorts asked, " And who are ye ? " They replied, " We are from Ọyọ sent by the ALÂFIN to escort you home," allowing them to come very near; when suddenly the Ijaye troops opened fire upon them and so dispersed the Ọyọ troops with the traders and all. About 240 of them were taken captive exclusive of some minor chiefs, e.g. Aridẹde, Alẹyọ̀, Jigin, etc. The head priest of Sango lost 10 of his daughters caught in this raid.

The ALÂFIN sent again and again requesting the Arẹ to release them but he obstinately refused to do so, saying unless they were redeemed for 10 bags of cowries each. [The price of slaves at that period being about half that amount.]

The ALÂFIN sent back to say " I have a claim on you to demand the release of these people, for besides being the King of YORUBA to whom allegiance is due, remember what I did for you in the past. When you sent one Dayiro on an expedition and the people of Saki defeated him and made about 210 of his men prisoners, did I not use my authority and influence and obtain the release of them all and send them to you free of charge ? Why should you now detain my own people ? "

[The above incident relates to one of the acts of the King to conciliate the Arẹ's refractoriness]. Still the Arẹ refused point-blank to release them. And further, in order to avert war with Ijaye, His Majesty sent the Samu (one of the Ọyọ MESI) via Ijaye to Ibadan to ask the Ibadan Chiefs to second his remonstrance and prevail on the Arẹ to release his people. The Arẹ was inexorable, and even chased the Samu on his way to Ibadan ; the Samu escaped the pursuers and returned home via Iwo. The ALÂFIN then gave orders that the Ọyọ people should go to Ijaye and redeem each one his relatives as soon as possible.

The ALÂFIN was now determined to punish Ijaye by the help of the Ibadans; he therefore sent to them 40 slaves, 8 demijohns of beads, with gowns and vests, saying he had declared war against Ijaye.

The matter was taken up warmly at Ibadan; many remembered that the town was placed under a ban by the late Baṣọrun Oluyọle who failed to take it himself. The Balogun of Ibadan alone among the senior chiefs was for peaceful measures. " Kurũmi is an old man " said he, " and will soon die, and the Ijayes are our kinsmen."

The other chiefs imposed a fine on him for thus " betraying cowardice." But they knew well enough his matchless valour and undaunted courage, and the real cause of his reluctance to rush into a war of this kind. Ijaye was a town of equal importance with Ibadan, equal in valour, courage, and skill, and both with vast connections between each other and all over the country ; for them to engage in war would mean deluging the whole of Yorubaland with blood. But when he could not prevail over his generals, and the common soldiers affixed a crow to his house at night implying that he was a coward (as cowardly as a crow is a common expression in this country) ; and also threw stones into his house, he yielded to public opinion and commenced his own preparations for war.

When the Arẹ of Ijaye heard of the movement against him, being self-confident he was loud in his boastings : " On this post will I chain that imp of Ogunmọla," " Ibikunle will have cause to remember the Odogido disaster," and so forth. He gave orders that all the youths of Ijaye should be trained to the use of bow and arrows, the older men superintending the practice. To those who succeeded as good marksmen he awarded prizes. This practice was termed " Ṣẹ ẹ " and was carried out daily without intermission.

Being fond of singing and dancing the Arẹ kept amusing himself with parabolic songs and witty sayings e.g.

> " A ta ọpọlọ ni ipa, o sun ikakà,
> Gbogbo wa ni yio ku bẹrẹ."
>
> (A frog is kicked and lies on its back,
> We shall all die by myriads.)

The common people took up the same against the ALÂFIN and the Ibadans. Against the Ibadans they sang :—

" Ibadan a kò gba Ajẹlẹ   Ibadan we can accept no Resident,
    Orogun li awa iṣe."   For rivals are we.

This meant to say "We cannot serve or yield to you."

N

Against the ALÂFIN they sang :—

> " L'aiye Onalu[1] li a ro okan le okan
> L'aiye Kurūmi li a ro'gba ro'gba
> L'aiye Adelu ni ipele di itele idi."

(In Onalu's time we used changes of dress.
In Kurūmi's time we used cloths of the finest weaving
In Adelu's time our best becomes our every day's.)

This last description of Adelu's time is a well-understood irony. It is a common saying in this country " Ibere otosi bi omo oloro la iri " (When poverty begins, one appears like a rich man's son) which means that when one cannot afford to replace the everyday dress, one resorts to his best for every day use and thus appears like a rich man ; but the real condition soon becomes apparent when this cannot be replaced. This condition is what they would now apply to Adelu's regime.

The tocsin of war was now resounding from one end of the country to another. Kurūmi disallowed the exportation of foodstuffs to Ibadan. The Ibadans sought the alliance or at least the neutrality of Abeokuta and Ilorin and pressed into service the Oyo towns under her protection. Kurūmi sent one Oje to conclude an alliance with the Egbas and to procure ammunition, but Ogunmola of Ibadan, who was entrusted with the negotiations with Abeokuta forestalled him, and they took an oath of friendship and neutrality with Ibadan.

The populace of Ibadan were now singing in their dances :—

> " Akope Ijaye ki o má ko ti Iká mo,
> Onigbo da 'gbo meji."

(Palm cutters of Ijaye do not venture to Ika,
The lord of the forests divides it in two.)

By a transposition of names the Ijayes were singing the same ditty, Ika being just midway between the two towns. Intercommunication now ceased. On all hands were heard "Onile ki o gbe ile ko kan odi yiyàn." (Let every man keep to his own house, that need not imply animosity.) The kidnappers soon began to infest the farms; thus the Ibadans kidnapped two American missionaries who hearing of the rumours of war and incursions of the kidnappers went in search of Mr. J. C. Vaughan at his farm at Ido. Mr. Vaughan had escaped back to Ijaye by another route, and the missionaries were caught and brought to Ibadan

---

[1] Kurūmi's other name.

on the 20th of February 1860.   These war boys, not knowing what to do with white men, brought them with their horses mounted as they were, to the Rev. D. Hinderer, saying " White man, we have brought you your brothers," Mr. Hinderer thanked them and gave them some cowries to procure refreshments.   The gentlemen were sent on to Abẹokuta the next day, communication with that town being then still free and uninterrupted.

All hopes of a pacific settlement were now given up, for private messages, advices, and remonstrances were without number to the Arẹ ; but for all this Kurūmi remained unyielding to the King, and defiant to Ibadan.   War was now formally declared.   When at the next meeting of the town council, the Balogun arose in his place and harangued the assembly ending with " Ẹyin ọmọ Jamâ, Mo fi Ijaye jin o " (Young men, Ijaye is now given up to you) a loud and prolonged huzza of " Muso, Muso," greeted his astonished ears.   He was painfully impressed with the knowledge of how popular the war was.   Ọrañyan was worshipped and the standard of war was borne out once more by the valiant and experienced commander-in-chief Ibikunle on the 10th of April, 1860.   It was known to all that Balogun Ibikunle went forth to this war with great reluctance.   He had seen many battles and known well the horrors of a siege, and of all sieges one against one's own blood relations was particularly horrid and heartrending to him. Inter-marriages and national festivals which they had in common had made them one ;   they were sharers together in times past of weal and woe ;   supply of foodstuffs for overgrown Ibadan came largely from Ijaye where the soil was fertile and the people industrious.   These considerations therefore made the bravest shrink from a war that might possibly be averted.

When starting for the expedition, as soon as his foot was on the stirrup, his Akewi (bard) gave utterance to the following pathetic strains.

> "Baba mi ñre igbo ọdaju o ! o ! o !
> Nibi ti ọlọmọ meji yio ku ọkan,
> Nibi ti ọlọmọ kan yio pòhórá,
> ' Iya mi ni ñma wa'—ki o pada lẹhin Baba mi,
> ' Baba mi ni ñma wa'—ki o pada lẹhin Baba mi,
>   Kiniun Onibudo.
> ' Iyawo mi to igbe "—ki o pada lẹhin Baba mi, i, i,
>   Kiriniun Onibudo."

(My master is going to the field of the heartless ah ! ah ! ah me !
Where the parent of two will be left with but one.
Where the parent of one will be left all forlorn.

Let him whose mother forbids him to come return from following my Lord,

Let him whose father forbids him to come return from following my Lord.

The Lion of the Master of camps,

Let him whose betrothed is of age to be wed return from
following my Lord.

The Lion of the Master of camps).

As the expedition started the drummer struck up the war march
" Kiriniun Onibudo."

[Toki surnamed Onibudo, master of camps, it will be remembered was a formidable war-chief, the Seriki of the Ibadan army
and the uncle of this chief. He succeeded his uncle as Seriki
from which post he rose to be Balogun. He is eulogized as the
lion that rendered chief Toki to be so formidable.]

Ogunmola who had gone to intercept Ojẹ did not return home,
but awaited the Balogun at Orita Elêpo a small resting place
about four miles from Ibadan town, at the junction of the
two roads leading from the Ọyọ gate and Inalende gate of
Ibadan.

§ 3. When Greek meets Greek

The Ijayes were not idle either, and did not wait at home
with folded arms for the Ibadans to come. The first battle
took place at Apata Ika—the Ika rock just midway between the
two towns—and the Arẹ soon found, too late, and to his cost the
truth of the message sent him that he should yield and accept a
compromise and not haughtily compare the Ibadans of the present
day to those of yore. But he was truly a born warrior and never
lost courage, notwithstanding that he had now to contend with a
younger generation of Ibadans who were quite inured to the hardships of the field and whose trade was war.

But the Arẹ's eyes were now open when too late to yet another
folly of his. In order that he might secure for himself a safe and
despotic position, he had killed so many brave men of Ijaye and
had forbidden any chief to accumulate ammunitions of war, that
only three hard battles were fought before he found his magazines
exhausted. The Ijayes now resorted to bows and arrows and
consequently they lost ground rapidly. But for this probably
the war would have ended in a draw as before.

The Egbas were now resolved to take part in this war. The
majority were for assisting Ijaye. Sokẹnu alone was against
their taking this course " after the oath of alliance and friendship

taken with the Ibadans," said he, " it will be a serious breach
of faith, and even the gods will be against us."

This opposition, it was said, was the cause of his early death.
The altercation was sharp, and the other chiefs in going said to him
" We must not meet you alive on our return," and he retorted
" If at all you return alive." Shortly after this Sokenu became
paralysed (from poison it was said) and died.

The expedition was commanded by Anoba the Balogun of Oba
as generalissimo—all the other Baloguns including Somoye
" Basorun " the Balogun of Iporo had to serve under him. They
halted for a long while at Atadi, 12 miles from home, undecided
what course to take : then they proceeded to Olokemeji where,
still of two opinions, they debated the matter afresh, whether to go
to the help of the Ibadans with whom they had formed an alliance
or to the assistance of Ijaye. (Olokemeji is a central and neutral
ground for the Ijaye, Ibadan, and the Oke Ogun hunters). They
finally decided to help the Ijayes, " to raise the siege, and drive
away the Ibadans and dispossess them of those kola groves originally
planted by our fathers and grandfathers." This last idea swayed
them. Thus it was subsequently reported at Ibadan. But there is
an Egba version of the reason why they decided to ally themselves
with the Ijayes. Some one alleged that Ogunmola was reported
to have said that after shaving the crown of the head he would shave
the occiput ! Meaning after taking Ijaye he would also take
Abeokuta ! But there is no proof whatever of this assertion,
especially as there was no occasion for any such thing. And
again Ogunmola the author of the treaty of friendship and alliance
was not the man to utter such a threat, which he certainly was
not in a position to carry out, being a subordinate officer. And if
he did say it, there would not have been such a prolonged
hesitation amongst the Egbas, and such divided counsel as
to what course they should pursue. The former version therefore, is far more probable.

Thus they proceeded from Olokemeji to Ijaye. But the venerable Chief Ogunbona, Balogun of Ikija did not proceed with them;
he remained encamped at Olokemeji to be a protection and guard
to caravans going and coming between that place and Ijaye.

The Ijebus also as kith and kin to a portion of the Egbas seemed
to have entered into an agreement to be one with them for offensive
and defensive purposes. Hence when the Egbas went to Ijaye
against the Ibadans, they also for no other reason entered into a
state of warfare against Ibadan.

Mele the Ibadan state messenger to the Ijebus in the days of
Oluyole the late Basorun was again sent with Kobiowu the

Jagun to conclude a treaty of friendship with the Ijẹbus before their attitude was known. But the Ijẹbus sent a body of troops which attacked them at Odo Ọnà even before they had left the Ibadan farms, on their way to Ijẹbu ! With shield and spear Mele bravely defended himself and retreated with his party home with only slight wounds.

The Emir of Ilọrin also embraced this opportunity for declaring war against Ibadan. The " Kafiris " (infidels) said he, " are at war with one another, and we should combine against this Ibadan which has often baulkèd us of our prey ; we may yet carry the Koran to the sea." He sent some horsemen to Ijaye, who when they observed the starvation and distress that ensued, could not remain long ; however, they kept kidnapping in the Ọyọ farms.

The Ọwa of Ilẹṣa not only revolted against Ibadan, but also took advantage of the coalition to take revenge upon Ẹfon Ahàye and other towns which were allies of the Ibadans during the late Ijẹbu Ẹrẹ and Ará wars.

Thus practically all the principal states in Yorubaland were combined to crush the Ibadans who had rid the country of the great bug-bear of the Fulani subjugation, but in turn became so restless as to be a source of anxiety to them all.

But a section of the Ijẹbus viz. Ijẹbu Rẹmọ with Kẹhẹ́rẹ́ the Balogun of Ipara at their head was friendly to the Ibadans. They held that they were a commercial people, and Ibadan not only their best, but also their only customer, and one time their deliverer in the time of Lakanlẹ ; and they could not see their way to join in a war that did not concern them. The periodic 9 days' market, therefore, was continued between them, and as we shall see hereafter the Ibadans had to fight their way there and back, escorting earavans.

Meanwhile the struggle between the combatants was proceeding. The third and last battle fought before the arrival of the Egbas had exhausted the Arẹ's store of ammunition. The battle was fought in his own farm and was one of the bloodiest ever fought in this campaign. Nothing but the intrepid personal bravery of the Arẹ saved him from being taken alive that day ; had he given ground an inch he would have irretrievably lost the day.

There were only two fierce battles fought afterwards that may be compared to this last ; on the last occasion the Arẹ at the head of his choicest troops charged the Ibadan centre with intrepidity and desperation, with a determination to break through, but the Ibadans remained firm and impregnable. The circumstances will be related below.

The Egbas arrived at Ijaye in the nick of time to replenish

the exhausted stores of the Ijayes. The Aṛẹ who from experience knew the strength of the Ibadans, forewarned them to be very cautious and not to encamp outside the walls of Ijaye. The Ẹgbas fresh from home and buoyant in spirits spurned the idea of " sheltering " themselves within the walls of the town ; however, they encamped without but close by the walls of Ijaye.

The camp of the Ibadans was at this time at Oloriṣa Oko, about 3 hours' walk from Ijaye. The Balogun of Ibadan could not at first be made to believe that the Ẹgbas came as allies to the Ijayes after the oaths they had taken with Ibadan. To those who brought the report he said " Yes, they may have come but it must be to negotiate peace between us." Over and over again he was assured that they have come with a mighty army. " Yes," he replied, " it must be to put an end to the war." But at last, the Balogun was taken quite aback when a band of skirmishers returned and reported that they were driven back by the Ẹgbas who came in overwhelming numbers against them. The Ibadans were alarmed and dismayed at the report. " In Kurũmi," said they, " we have an equal match already, and how to face the combined force with the overwhelming host of the Ẹgbas ? "

But the principal chiefs encouraged one another and were determined to die rather than yield. " Death," said they " was preferable to the shame of a defeat, or the humiliation of being made a prisoner." " Here is his head is better than here is his face" said Ogunmola. " If we cannot resist them here, surely we shall not be able to do so at home if driven from this place." He then took out his jack knife and displaying it before all his colleagues he said " It must be victory or——Death."

A council of war was held, and it was resolved that they should wait until the Ẹgbas came and attacked them, and if they succeeded in repelling the attack then they would have hopes of being able to maintain their ground ; but if they went and offered battle first and were forced to retreat, it was certain the men would be disheartened and really demoralized, and there would be a poor chance for them—it would end for them in a total defeat. One Kujẽñyọ a babalawo or Ifa priest was thereupon commissioned to make charms to provoke the Ẹgbas to come forward to fight.

The Ẹgbas on the other hand fresh from home were eager to offer battle, contrary to the advice of the Aṛẹ of Ijaye. " Let them come first and attack you here," said the Aṛẹ to the Ẹgbas, " but never go after them." But the Ẹgbas replied that when they left home they meant business and were not afraid of the Ibadans. A period of about a fortnight elapsed in which there was inaction on both sides.

At length the day arrived and to the field the Egbas led their troops with flying colours. The Ibadan outposts reported the advance of the Egbas in the order of battle. The Balogun of Ibadan issued orders that no one should fire a gun until the word of command was given. The Egbas came within a few yards of the entrenchments and their fire wounded several persons within the Ibadan camp before the command was given. The Balogun's voice rang out " Ọmọ Ibadan, ẹ gba ẹ fi ti wọn " (Ibadan boys, up and at them). Then the Ibadans rushed out, and the struggle commenced.

At the first onslaught of the Ibadans, the Egbas retreated about a hundred yards and made a stand, and then ensued a most desperate fight on both sides. To the Ibadans it was a matter of life and death, and their one thought was whether they would be able to maintain their ground against the overwhelming odds of the Egbas, the Ijayes being now at a discount ; but it was not long before they became confident that they could certainly maintain their ground.

Ogunmọla being a man of small stature was wont to be mounted on the tallest horse he could possibly obtain, and move from point to point in the field observing the men's behaviour, and singling out individuals for praise or blame. On this occasion, having observed for a while the methods of the Egbas, he rode up joyfully to the Commander-in-Chief saying " Ibikunle, a o ṣe won, a o ṣe wọn, Egba kò mọ ogun jijà " (Ibikunle, we shall win, we shall win. The Egbas have no knowledge of the art of war).

What Ogunmọla observed was as follows :—As the combatants on both sides came company by company to the firing line (what they call Tawusi), Ogunmọla noticed in the first place that the Egba shooting was too high, and that the men under fire were rarely ever hit, whilst the Ibadans had been taught to shoot low, and consequently they scored several hits among their foes. Again the Egbas discharged all their muskets at once and all turned back together before the relieving company came up ; whereas the Ibadans kept a reserved fire with which they accompanied the retiring foe, so that the retiring was more or less a disorderly retreat, and again they kept their place until their own relieving company came up, and more often gained a few yards forward before those of the Egbas came up, and thus gradually were gaining more and more ground. Ogunmọla noticing all this was sure that, according to their own method of fighting, when later on, the Balogun arose to fight, and all men and all arms must push forward in a general engagement, this disorderly retreat of the Egbas would be converted to a general rout. Hence he was confident in assuring the Balogun that they would win.

But long before it was time for that, another officer, viz. Abayọmi the Ajiya Balẹ planned out tactics of his own. As all the Balẹ's fighting men were disposed as strategy requires he seemed to know that the Ẹgbas left their flank unguarded ; he left the main body of his men at their post, and chose out a number of brave fellows to cut through the bush a great way off and suddenly burst upon the Ẹgbas at the rear with a shout, and away fled the whole host panic stricken, and the rout was complete. There was a morass a little way off called Alàbàtà which many of them were driven into, and were either slaughtered or taken alive. Some never halted but fled from the battlefield into the camp and from the camp into the town of Ijaye, others at full speed homewards the Ibadan boys pursuing.

Ijaye would have been taken that day but for the Arẹ. Watching the movements of the Ẹgbas, he noticed their lack of skill in their manœuvring and fighting, and anticipating a disaster he held his men in readiness for eventualities. As soon as the Ẹgbas gave way and the Ibadans were in pursuit, he made a flank movement and intercepted the Ibadans ; and these, seeing there were no chiefs behind them to back them up, hastily retired from the pursuit. The chiefs did not give chase for fear of what the Arẹ might do, but they kept an eye on him ; for he might take them in the rear and convert their victory into a defeat.

From that day the Ibadans were confident of ultimate success and the Ijaye chiefs despaired of driving back the enemy. The Ẹgbas were much enraged and ashamed of this defeat which they attributed to the cowardice of their Generalissimo Anọba, and for this they ordered him to " go to sleep " (a euphemism for suicide). They said that instead of coming up to their assistance with the reserved forces, he himself gave way also !

The Ibadan boys ascribed this victory to Ajiya Abayọmi in their songs and dances :—

" Ajiya nikan l'o le'gun, 'Twas Ajiya singly routed the foe,
Iwi l'a kò gbọdọ wi." But we must not say 'tis so.)

A very large number of captives fell into the hands of Ogunmọla, and as the author of the treaty, which was so perfidiously broken he took vengeance on many of them, by ordering their faces to be branded with broad Tapa marks, and exultingly took a name on it " Emi a sọ Ẹgba di Tapa " (the transformer of Ẹgbas into Tapas). He, moreover, ordered yam peels to be rubbed on the marks in order that the irritant may cause thick scars on them.

In order to show what contempt the Ibadans now had for the
Egbas as fighters, they sang while they danced :—

" Kanakana Ajibade
 Ohan, ohan ni ndun.
 A ri Egba lokankan a ṣe bi ogun ni,
 Ija ṣukẹ ṣukẹ ni ija Egba,
 Ija lile lile n'ija Oyọ."
(The crows of Ajibade
 Ohan ohan they cry.
 Egbas at a distance appear like men,
 Nerveless and feeble Egbas are in fight,.
 Strenuous and brave Oyọs are in fight.)

Emboldened by this success, the Ibadans removed their camp
further to a place called Ajibade (where the Egbas were defeated)
and the battle ground was now at Alabata (where they were
driven to) about two hours' walk from Ijaye.

Several hard battles were fought before they could establish
themselves here, but at every fight the Ibadans gained ground,
and so they again removed their camp from Ajibade to Alabata,
and the battle ground was now at the River Oṣẹ not far from the
walls of Ijaye.

By this time the ammunition of the Ibadans was exhausted,
and but for Kẹhẹrẹ the Balogun of Iparà the expedition would
have ended in failure if not disaster to the Ibadans. Kẹhẹrẹ
was faithful to them to the end.

The unfriendly Ijebus of Ode and Igbo were daily raiding the
Ibadan farms. Flying columns had to be organized to protect
the farmers and chase away the Ijebus. They also kidnapped from
the caravans to Ijebu Rẹmọ (viz. Ipara, Iperu, Ode, Ikorodu) ; the
Ibadans were obliged to send escorts from the camp from time
to time to protect these traders to Ipara and back. The Ijebus
more than once made a regular encampment and erected forts
to block the way after the caravans had passed on to Ipara, the
intention being to prevent their return ; but the Ibadans
always succeeded in routing them, pulling down the forts, and
returning home safe with the caravans. In one of these defeats,
one Kongo a well-known Ijebu, who was formerly a trader and a
resident at Ibadan was caught with several others ; but Chief
Ogunmọla lost two of his most valiant men in this fight, Kukula
and Erin. He showed his resentment by ordering Kongo to be
killed on Kukula's grave, and the rest of the Ijebu captives they
led to the camp at the river Oṣẹ, exhibited them to the Egbas
and Ijayes, and then killed them under their eyes, to show that
they had been victorious over their allies as well.

But there was a memorable battle of this kind fought at the river Ọmi in the Ijẹbu Rẹmọ road which was terrible.   The Ijẹbus exasperated by the former defeats were determined to deal a crushing blow to the Ibadans the next time.   For some weeks the caravans could not proceed, the road had become more unsafe than ever ; all who came from the provinces assembled at Ibadan. Then the chiefs sent powerful escorts from the camp under chiefs Abayọmi, Tubọsun, and Madarikàn.   The name of Abayọmi raised the hopes of the caravans, and an extra large number of them flocked together to take advantage of this opportunity.

After the caravans and escorts had passed on to Rẹmọ, a large Ijẹbu army was sent to prevent their return.   They erected strong stockades right across the path in three places, and placed bodies of troops behind each, the main army and the encampment being behind the strongest stockade towards Ibadan, and there awaited the return of the caravan.   Madarikan the leader of the van first came at them and fighting ensued ; the first stockade was won and they came up to the second.   Madarikan was wounded in half-a-dozen places and driven back towards Rẹmọ, bleeding all over and was *hors de combat*.   When Ajiya Abayọmi came up, he dashed upon the Ijẹbus with great intrepidity and won the second stockade ; he then repelled the enemy until they came to the third and strongest stockade with the encampment behind it of the main Ijẹbu army.   At the sight of the Ibadans, the Ijẹbus raised a great shout of triumph and tauntingly asked " By what way will you get home now ? You had better try flying."   From behind the stockade they wrought havoc among the Ibadans with impunity, being protected from the bullets of the latter by the stockade.

Chief Abayọmi thereupon called some of his most trusty servants, and posted them with their men on the highway with orders not to yield an inch if all had to perish there. He then chose a band of trusty veterans, cut a path through the forest and attacked the Ijẹbus in the rear.   When the Ijẹbus driven to bay, saw the foe before and behind, they were furious and dashed upon the Ibadans with great intrepidity.   At the first onslaught, Abayọmi the Ibadan leader was shot off his horse, and when his veterans saw their master fall and their own fire languishing, they became exasperated, and with drawn swords they rushed upon the Ijẹbus with great fury and madness, broke through their ranks and put to the sword those that could not escape. They immediately pulled down the stockade and rejoined those of their comrades who had been posted in the highway and had come up. They pursued the Ijẹbus a little way and rescued as many as they could of the women and others of the caravans whom the Ijẹbus had captured before the main body of escorts came up. Thus the Ibadans eventually won ; the victory though dearly bought was complete. Abayọmi, however, rallied, and was able to lead the people home. When reports of this victory reached the camp and the cost at which it was achieved the Balogun and other senior chiefs immediately sent congratulations to Abayọmi, Madarikan and others, and allowed them to remain at home until their wounds were healed before rejoining their comrades in the camp before Ijaye.

From this and previous achievements Abayọmi (through his bards) added to his other names " Death to traitors," " Terror to the Ijẹbus," " Maker of safe paths through tangled forests."

There were further skirmishes on this road while the Ijaye war lasted, but none to be compared to the above two remarkable ones.

Meantime the war before Ijaye continued with undiminished vigour the invaders being now replenished with ammunition.

The Ijaye watchman was posted on the top of a tall tree near the River Ọsẹ, from whence he could command the view for several miles around, and announce the approach of the enemy.

For a long time the River Ọsẹ was the scene of action : whichever party arrived first at the stream gained the opposite bank and held it until repulsed. In course of time the Ibadans gained the river permanently, and the action thenceforth was on the Ijaye side of it.

At this time all the farms being in the hands of the Ibadans, the distress, starvation and consequent mortality at Ijaye were indescribable. Hundreds, nay thousands died in the streets from starvation, whole families perished without anyone to bury them. All the livestock had been consumed, the garden, the streets, and the yards were all planted with corn, but the cornstalks were devoured when they could not wait for the corn to develop. The herb Gbọ̀rọ̀ a common creeper in the streets was planted in every available place and used for food.

It was generally said then that the advent of the Ẹgbas replenished their magazines but exhausted their granaries. Now the Ẹgbas procured food for themselves from home, but instead of succouring their allies, they took advantage of their distress to benefit themselves. A child who wandered longingly to an Ẹgba tent and obtained a meal of beans (awujẹ) thereby became his slave ! The Ẹgba man who could procure several loads of Awujẹ beans from home, covered all his expenses by securing so many Ijaye children as slaves for feeding them ! All these were sent home to Abẹokuta.

But the good offices of the missionaries of the C.M.S. and American Baptists at Ijaye at this time were never to be forgotten. Sympathizing friends at home and abroad sent them supplies, and they received and maintained as many Ijaye children as they could. The parents also received some assistance and were glad and thankful to see their children provided for.   The names of the Rev. Adolphus Mann, C.M.S. and Mr. J. T. Bowen, American Baptist, can never be forgotten by any Ijaye born.

Mr. Mann's skill in surgery also was in requisition ; he was of immense service in extracting bullets and binding up wounds. Thus in ministering to the wants of famished children, sheltering orphans and performing surgical operations he had his hands quite full.

The Ijaye people had also to oppose a war behind them from Ọyọ. A small force under Amọdu was sent to Iran, as he alone was quite enough to oppose the Ọyọ army which encamped at Ilọra whence they issued for the fight.

The ALÂFIN whose battle Ibadan was fighting had to supply both the Ibadan and Ilọra camps with gunpowder and bullets and for the latter purpose the services of all Ọyọ smiths were in requisition.

The ALÂFIN also invited the Baribas, but their cavalry on which they solely depended were of little use in forest lands ; the Ijayes at Iran concealing themselves in the thickets surrounding the town had the advantage of them.   Although Iran was a small village yet the men were able to repulse the attacks of the Ọyọs and Baribas.

But if they could not capture Iran these Baribas were a source of great annoyance to the Ijayes by kidnapping in their farms and thereby increasing the amount of distress and starvation in the town.   This gave rise to the pathetic wail:

> " Ibadan mu, Fiditi mu
> Ojojumọ ni ara Agọ ñmu ni l'oko
> Ojojumọ ni ara Agọ ñyan múmùsin lẹhin odi
> Ọran yi jọ bi àlá l'oju mi."

Ibadan kidnaps, Fiditi kidnaps,
Daily the men of Agọ kidnap in our farms,
Daily the men of Agọ capture for service behind our walls,
This matter to me is like a dream ! "

§ 4.   FAMINE AND THE SWORD

As we have already noticed, most of the Oke Ogun towns were under the rule of the Arẹ of Ijaye ; at this crisis they became the source of food supply to Ijaye, and both men and women frequented these regions for procuring provisions.

By this time the people of Ijaye had recovered from the first shock and horror of a siege, and as the town could not be carried by assault, and was now fairly supplied with food from the Oke Ogun regions, and with ammunition from Abeokuta, the hopes of taking the town soon became very small.

The Ibadans now tried to cut off their supplies by sending a small army to Oke Ogun. Iseyin was friendly to Ijaye and Ibadan, and both were admitted within her walls. A man called Ojelabi went to Iseyin and began to seize people's things in the market for " privilege " as an Ibadan man; Majaro the Aseyin ordered him out of the town, but he not only refused to go but was also setting houses on fire with a lighted torch. He was ultimately driven out under a shower of stones. The Ibadans hearing that Ojelabi was driven out and not knowing the cause, sent one Rogun to ask whether it was their intention to rebel, or why had they expelled Ojelabi. But as Rogun and his party were likewise pillaging the town they did not fare any better but were driven out by force of arms. Before this happened however, the Iseyin people showed evident signs of impatience at the language and actions of these men, and sounded in their songs a note of an impending civil fight :—

> " Ibadan ti o kọ̀ ti ko lọ
> Awowo a wò o "

(The Ibadan who sticks and won't go.
A great crash will crush him.)

The Ibadan boys on their part took up the challenge and retorted with

> " A f'adamọ dá 'mọ lẹkun Awówó."

(The shot gun will shut up all crashes and crushings.)

The civil fight soon set in, and Rogun held out till the evening before he was finally expelled the town.

Iwawun, Ẹrin, and Awayè were for Ijaye, but Bẹrẹkodo and other Ibarapa districts were for Ibadan. One Akāwo was sent from the camp to ask the Iwawun people why they were supplying food to Ijaye, the answer returned not being satisfactory the result was a little war here also. The Arẹ hearing this sent Amọdu, Arawọle, Adelakùn, Abẹsẹ and Labudanu to reinforce Iwawun. When Akáwo found them too strong for him, he sent to the camp for re-inforcement, and Latosisa and other petty war-chiefs were sent to his help. Still they found the power of the Ijayes too much for them to withstand, so much so that instead of besieging Iwawun, they were on the defensive, being practically besieged in their camps.

Iwawun and Erin were advantageously situated for defensive purposes, being built on a high hill and surrounded by a mass of huge craggy rocks; the town wall was built at the foot of the hill.

The Ibadan chiefs knowing that as long as Ijaye could draw supplies from these places the town could not be taken, Ogunmola was resolved to go himself and deal a decisive blow to their power here. The Balogun alone with his men and some minor chiefs being left in charge of the camp, Ogunmola his Otun and Osundina the Osi headed the rest of the war-chiefs to Oke Ogun.

Passing by the Ijaye farms to Fiditi, they reached the Oyo camp at Ilora. The ALÂFIN sent one of the eunuchs to welcome them and take them presents of bullocks, sheep, goats, fowls, etc. Ogunmola respectfully declined to accept them now : he sent to tell the King that he would receive them after his return from taking Iwawun within nine days.

Ogunmola spoke that day as an oracle. He ordered Ajayi Ogboriefon the captain of the Ibadan contingent there to march on before him and receive a shot in that well-fed stomach of his.

" You are leading an easy life here with our King under pretence of fighting against this little place," he said to him.

On reaching Iseyin Ogunmola went to pay his compliments to the Aseyin, and prostrated before him in salutation. The Aseyin forgetful of himself received him as a subject, but he had to pay dearly for it some years afterwards when Ogunmola became a Basorun of Ibadan, and consequently his official superior. The army passed on to Iwawun ; rumours of a large reinforcement to the Ibadan force there reached the ears of the Ijayes at Iwawun, and some of those among them suggested that they should withdraw entirely before the break of day, but Arawole and Amodu said " Should we not see what is driving us before we run away ? Or what shall we say to the Are at home ? " Up to this time they had no positive knowledge as to who the leader of the expedition was.

Early next morning the Ibadans took a hasty breakfast, and soon after they filed out for the attack on Iwawun instead of waiting for an attack as usual. Those of the Ijayes who had suspected an access of reinforcement were now positive, for otherwise the small Ibadan force could not have been so bold this morning. In order to keep the expedition as secret as possible, apart from his rapid movements, Ogunmola forbade his drummer to beat and those of the other chiefs likewise, lest his arrival be known to the enemy ; but when the hour for battle was come, he ordered all the drummers including those of the other chiefs to strike up his own battle cry. Consequently the Ijayes were all dismayed and panic stricken when they heard :—

> " A f'okè, afi 'gbo   (But the hills, but the woods,
> Ko s'ẹni ti o le duro."   There's no one to withstand me.)

Now they were forced to credit the report that Ogunmọla himself was the leader of the expedition. It was thought most improbable that in the face of the Ijaye and Ẹgba armies Ogunmọla and staff with the other war-chiefs would venture to leave the camp.

But the Ijayes were men in the true sense of the word ; after the first shock of this discovery, they steeled their hearts and threw themselves on their assailants with great intrepidity but the odds were greatly against them. It is reported that the chief of Awaye was bribed or terrorized into disclosing a secret path by which an enemy might enter Iwawun, but this is very doubtful, because Awaye herself had to share the fate of Iwawun afterwards. Whatever it may be, Iwawun was taken by assault, and within an hour the town was in flames ! The Ijaye heroes had an opportunity of escape but did not avail themselves of it. Amọdu fought and died a hero's death. He had borne a distinguished part all through this war, and in him Ijaye sustained an irreparable loss.

Five of the Arẹ's sons were caught and slain, including Arawọle his eldest surviving son. The death of Arawọle sent a thrill of horror and grief throughout the camp and town of Ibadan. Many were the ill-suppressed murmurs against Ogunmọla for this heartless murder, for, although Kurūmi was now a foe, he was still a name and a venerable figure in the history of Yoruba, a contemporary of the fathers of these Ibadan chiefs and the last surviving link between their past in the old homes desolated by the Fulanis, and these forest lands to which they have escaped. Now he was old and on the verge of the grave, to extinguish his light in his eldest son was an event no reflecting patriot could calmly contemplate. Ibikunle the Balogun was said to have shed a tear when he heard it, and none but that heartless diplomat Ogunmọla could have killed Arawọle thus. Of the Ijaye chiefs, the Abẹsẹ, Labudanu and Adejumọ alone escaped to tell the tale. About ten others perished there.

Ẹrin also was taken very easily the same day, and numbers of the Ijaye caravans who went there to buy provisions fell into their hands but a great many escaped into the bush.

On the return march of the Ibadans Ogunmọla had

recourse to a ruse by which he entrapped hundreds of those
who had escaped into the bush. Instead of his own battle cry,
he ordered the drummers to strike up that of the Arẹ of Ijaye,
and when those who had escaped into the bush heard :—

" Ija Orogun korò, Orogun."
(Bitter is the quarrel of rivals, the rivals.)

they naturally thought their master had come to their help
against Ogunmọla, and as they issued one by one from their
hiding places to flock to his standard, they fell an easy prey
into the hands of the Ibadans.[1]

On the 9th day of his leaving the Ilọra camp, he arrived there
again as he promised to do ; and singularly Ajayi Ogboriẹfọn was
also wounded in his " well-fed " stomach, even as Ogunmọla said.

But during the absence of Ogunmọla and the flower of the
Ibadan army at Iwawun, brave deeds were done behind the walls
of Ijaye. It was now or never with the allies, and the Arẹ was
determined to take the Ibadan camp before their return. Had
Ibikunle not been a particularly brave and experienced general, he
could never have withstood the force of the impact made upon him.
Appraising the Ẹgbas at their true valuation, notwithstanding
numbers, the Balogun opposed to them his Arẹagoro Aijẹnku
but himself withstood the more vigorous attack of the Ijayes.

It was on this occasion that the Arẹ at the head of a choice body
of veterans made a dash on the Ibadan centre with a determination
to break through ; but he might as well have hurled himself upon
an immovable rock ! Again and again he tried and failed, and not
only so, but the young woman, a devotee, who carried before him
into battle his covered calabash of charms for safety and success,
was severely wounded and had to be carried away. An eye-witness
who stood by him all through and who related the events to the
writer, said seeing his non-success, all disconsolate and despairing
he sat under fire in the midst of the battle saying " How can I go
back, how can I ? I cannot, I cannot." His attendants and body-
guard had literally to carry him to the rear. The old general
seemed to have forgotten that he was no longer young, and that
for deeds of might and strength, age must give place to youth.
Aijẹnku acquitted himself against the Ẹgbas so well, that he had
no need to ask for reinforcement from his chief. There can be

---

[1] History repeats itself. It will be seen hereafter how by a
singular act of retributive justice, Ogunmọla lost his only son
and heir in battle by the same trick being practised upon
his son by the Ekitis.

no doubt that the Balogun gained in prestige enormously by this action and fully justified the eulogies of his bard

> " Odunbudẹrẹ Ọkunrin
> A to fi isẹ ogun ran."
>
> (Ọdunbudẹrẹ (an untranslatable word) a mighty man,
> Fit to be entrusted with the onus of war.)

On the return of the Ibadan expedition after the usual welcome the Balogun was said to have expressed himself bitterly to Ogunmọla on the slaughter of the Arẹ's sons especially that of Arawọle. "Arawọle," said he "is our own companion, and the Arẹ, a contemporary of our fathers, how long further has he to live, and who is to uphold his house?" Ogunmọla was said to have justified his acts by saying "If we want the war to be over soon, sentiment must give way to something practical, a crushing blow was needed at Iwawun, and that is what I have dealt."

The cutting off of provisions by the destruction of the Oke Ogun towns gave a death blow to Ijaye. The Arẹ on hearing the sad news was crushed entirely by it. It was as if he had received his death warrant; he saw clearly that all hopes for Ijaye were now gone, and with a dejected spirit he was often seen in his house wandering about abstractedly and muttering to himself "Njẹ emi ni mo jẹbi ọran yi?" (am I then in the wrong in this matter?) He had hitherto been confident of success from the supposed justice of his cause, but now he was sadly disillusioned.

From this time the old general began to languish, and no more great deeds were recorded of him. He died of a broken heart in the month of June, 1861.

Thus passed away one of the most venerable and historic figures in Yoruba history.

Prior to his death occurred that of another notable figure, a friend, colleague, and brother in arms. The Olu-Ọde or chief of the hunters of ancient Ikoyi with Kurūmi were among the bravest defenders of the old country. After the Fulani destruction of their homes he retired hither with Kurūmi and lived the rest of his life at Ijaye. During this war he wrought havoc amongst the Ibadans with his cross bow and arrows. He was never known to miss his aim. In one of their skirmishes he was caught by the Ibadans. When brought into the camp it was said that the Balogun met and saluted him, prostrating before him as to his own father, and there and then gave him his liberty on parole. This was against the wish of Ogunmọla who would have him killed at once, but the Balogun overruled it.

Another chief, a cavalry officer was also caught, one who had successfully crossed spears with the Fulanis in olden days.   He, too, was set free on parole, and he wisely retired to Ibadan where he spent the rest of his days.

But the Olu-ọdẹ broke his parole, he was caught again trying to escape back to Ijaye. This time even the Balogun could not save him, much as he would like to do so; the other war-chiefs threatened to mutiny if the Olu-ọdẹ was again spared, and the Balogun was obliged to give way. " Why are you going back to a doomed city ? " he asked of the old chief. His reply was direct and simple: " My children are there." " Alas sire, you die, but for a cause not unworthy, you are laying down your life on account of your children." Thus did the Balogun address him before he was led away to execution by Ogunmọla's swordbearers.

After Kurūmi's death, Abogunrin his head slave had the honour of burying him. This was done in secret, and the two slaves who dug the grave were slain also to accompany their master so that the spot might not be disclosed ; but the place was found out afterwards, and the skull taken over to the ALÂFIN as the custom was, for all who bore the title of Arẹ-ona-Kakanfo.

The government of the town, and the conduct of the war now devolved upon Abogunrin the Arẹ's head slave, who had been placed in power even before his master's death. His treasures and all his ammunition being under the charge of Abogunrin, implicit obedience was rendered to him by all, in all matters both civil and military.

The only road left to the Ijayes by which they could obtain provisions and ammunition was the Abẹokuta road, and on this the Ibadans began now to kidnap regularly. The caravans had to be under military escort, and the Egba outpost at Olokemeji was an immense service to them at this time.

The old chief Ogunbọna the Balogun of Ikija who was stationed there died of illness, but a small force was still kept there to assist the caravans half way ; the danger lay between Ijaye and Oloke-meji, beyond this it was safe. One Ojẹ was a notable escort, but he was caught in the Ijaye farms, and publicly executed.

Early in 1862 the Ibadans removed their camp once more from Alabata, and crossing the river Ọsẹ they pitched their tents in the battlefield ; three fierce battles were fought to prevent this but as the Ibadans were able to maintain their ground, the fate of Ijaye was sealed.

Leaving the Balogun to face the Ijayes, Ogunmọla now went to the Abẹokuta road and besieged the Egbas in their camp. The Ijayes thereupon left the town and encamped in the field opposite the Ibadan camp. The fighting now was both obstinate and frequent, for besides fighting in the day, a special band of skirmishers was organized to keep it up all night.

On the 15th of March, 1862, Lieut. Dolbein, of H.M.S. Prometheus, accompanied by Mr. Edward Roper, a European missionary of the C.M.S. came up to Ijaye to the relief of Mr. and Mrs. Mann.

A battle was fought on the 16th which he witnessed, and he was said to have expressed his opinion that the Ibadans were superior warriors judging from the manoeuvrings on both sides, and that the town was sure to be taken. But Mr. Mann was unwilling to leave his post, the state of Mrs. Mann's health, however, rendered it imperative that he should take her down to the coast and he promised to return soon to his post. Mr. Edward Roper volunteered to hold the station until his return.

The Rev. A. and Mrs. Mann with Lieut. Dolbein left Ijaye early on the 17th March, 1862, and as soon as it was known that the white man had left the town, it was regarded as an evil omen for that town. The Egbas said that the white man's God had shown them that evil was coming, and would not themselves wait for it either. Before night fall, there was a rush, fugitives overtook them even in the course of the day, and they had to redouble their speed both to avoid the crush of fugitives and also to escape the expected pursuers. Fortunately the Ibadans did not know in time that the town had been deserted or they might have met them by the way; still some of the stragglers were met later on when pursuit was made.

Thus fell Ijaye, a town of ease and plenty, a town compact, and full of brave men, an industrious town, but too despotically governed, a town in which the citizens were marked by restlessness and daring.

Ijaye and Ibadan being sister towns and the people one, many wise heads in the former place made captives (as it were) of their wives and children, putting halters round the necks of their own brothers and led them to Ibadan to the house of their relatives without being detected. Once there, they were free. But knowing each other so well, some were detected and captured. Some lost their bearings and missed their way in the town and were captured, some fell into the hands of acquaintances and were rescued. The Ijaye warriors in the camp with their chiefs escaped with the Egbas to Abeokuta, Abogunrin at their head.

The Egbas assigned them a portion of land where they pitched their tents, and there they subsequently built their houses. The spot is known as Agọ Ijaye to this day.

When the Rev. D. Hinderer of Ibadan heard of the capture of Mr. Edward Roper, he sent to negotiate for his release from Ogunmola in whose possession he was, but this hard-hearted soldier refused to give him up unless he was released for 200 bags of cowries (equivalent then to £200) 200 kegs of powder and 200 guns. Mr. Hinderer then went in person and remonstrated with Ogunmola. The latter grew more stern, refusing to abate any one of his terms, rather than that he would keep him, and if he was incapable of performing any material service for him, still he should be able to tend his poultry yard in his farm. " We have learnt that white men live on eggs and milk I will feed this one with parched corn." And he added " We know that this is not the actual white man of Ijaye, whom we often saw in the battlefield : this one only entered the town a few days ago, hence you have such easy terms, otherwise we should have killed him right out, for he fought us, and we had our eyes on him." Mr. Mann we know did not fight, but relieved the wounded men; however, there were two " Afro American " sharp-shooters,[1] who harassed the Ibadans a good deal with their rifles.

Mr. Hinderer then asked for the interference of the Balogun, of Aijenku and of Ajiya Abayomi ; they all interceded but in vain, he remained obdurate. Mr. Hinderer then sent two of his agents to the ALÂFIN of Oyo to appeal to His Majesty for his interference.

The King then sent the following message to Ogunmola :— " What your Balogun Ibikunle, and your colleagues Aijenku and Abayomi failed to obtain from you, I know you have reserved the honour for me, and now I ask you to give up the white man freely and without any charges." In obedience to the King Ogunmola gave Mr. Roper up to his friends, the latter being too glad to be once more among his countrymen.

Besides the Rev. Mr. and Mrs. Hinderer, Mr. Roper met also at Ibadan, Mr. George Jeffries a friend and college mate of his, and both of them resided together.

A few months after Mr. Roper's arrival at Ibadan, his friend Jeffries was laid up from diarrhœa. Roper's presence here at this time cannot but be regarded otherwise than as providential, to comfort and cheer up his friend's dying hours. Jeffries passed quietly away and Roper undertook the charge of his station at Ogunpa, Ibadan. He remained there till he was able to return to England in 1865.

The good offices of His Majesty the ALÂFIN to the missionaries claim our special notice. This was the second of the kind during this war. Mr. Samuel Cole, a native schoolmaster, was once

---

[1] Messrs. Vaughan and Pettiford.

kidnapped between Ijaye and Iseyin in the early part of the conflict, (1860). Mr. Hinderer hearing this sent Mr. (now Rev.) D. Olubi to the ALÂFIN, who kindly ordered his release and sent him to Ibadan. Mr. Cole returned to Abeokuta by the Remo road.

The Ijaye war was one of the bloodiest fought by the Ibadans, as may be expected " When Greek meets Greek." But the only chief of note that fell was Osundina the Osi (father of the well-known Ibadan chief Apampa). He was shot in the knee, but he kept his post till the battle was over that day. He died a few days after. How many thousands upon thousands of common soldiers died on both sides it is impossible to say, but a faint idea could be had from the only authentic account kept.

At the commencement of the war Ogunmola ordered that a correct account of his soldier slaves who fell in battle should be kept. For that purpose a huge basket 5 or 6ft. high was kept and the cap of every slave of his who fell in battle was thrown into it. When Ijaye was taken Ogunmola counted the caps, they amounted to 1800, representing the soldier slaves of his who fell between April 10, 1860, and March 17, 1862, exclusive of freeborn soldiers ; and that was for only one single chief ; what then of the whole Ibadan army and those of the provinces ; what of the Ijayes, the Egbas, the Oyos, and the Oke Ogun peoples, and Ijebus engaged in this war !

It shows the redoubtable courage of the assailants and the obstinate resistance of the defenders. It justifies Ibikunle's reluctance to declare war upon their kith and kin. But those who knew Ijaye best, and were acquainted with the details of the enormities being committed there in the years before the war, were satisfied that their judgment was from above ; the cup of their iniquities was full and not only the besiegers but also their very allies helped to bring about their ruin. This was evident from the significant song commonly sung in their dances in those days :—

> " Onigbeja li o fo 'gun,
> Iwi l'a kò gbodo wi."
>
> ('Twas our allies caused our rout,
> But we must not say 'tis so.)

The Egbas have always been ashamed of this defeat which did not admit of being explained away, but many regarded it as a just punishment for their perfidy. And singularly, scarcely any of the principal chiefs concerned survived the war, thus recalling Sokenu's retort on them. Henceforth Oyos never have any fear in meeting any Egbas in the field, whatever the odds.

Ijaye was taken, but the war was not over, the bad blood left behind rankled for the next three years.

CHAPTER XIX.

SEQUELS OF THE IJAYE WAR

§ I. THE AWAYE WAR

THE Ibadans being determined to punish Awayè for supplying Ijaye with provisions during the siege, now sent the Aṣipa and subordinate chiefs at the head of the army against it, leaving only the Balogun and the Otun in the Ijaye camp ; and so Awayè was besieged.

Awayè was a small but beautiful town situated on a plateau, the scenery from which is very picturesque, the Ado mount rising in lofty magnificence a few miles off, and the open country for miles around interspersed with the locust and the Iyá trees. The inhabitants were a very peaceful and agricultural people, and were faithful and loyal to Ijaye to the very last. In fact, Ijaye was the only town of importance to which they could sell their agricultural produce.

The men of that town had no guns, but they were very expert in the use of their bow and poisoned arrows, and for full seven months they obstinately defended the town. It was at last reduced by famine, being closely invested on every side, so that they could not get to their farms ; but the able-bodied men cut their way through the Ibadans and made good their escape. In fact the Ibadans hastily made way for these desperate men, when they saw them making a furious charge and were singing the well-known song of desperadoes escaping life in hand :—

> " Oyin ṣù, Oyin lọ o
> Oyin a ṣù, Oyin a pọn roro."

(Bees in a swarm, bees swarming away,
  Bees will swarm, the swarm, o how red.)

Thus these brave defenders deserted the town when famine and the sword rendered it no longer tenable.

The remnant of the Awayè people are now encamped at the foot of the Ado mount.

The Ibadan army returned from this expedition in the month of October, 1862. The latter rains were then incessant and the rivers much swollen ; the Ogun river in particular swept many away, both horses and men.

§ 2. The Iperu War

During the siege of Awayè, the Egbas and the Ijaye refugees at Abeokuta went also to take revenge on the Remo towns that were friendly to the Ibadans during the siege of Ijaye.

On the 19th of June, 1862, the Egbas destroyed Makun, and advanced against Odè, Ogere, aiming specially at Ipara whose Balogun Kehérè was a particularly active ally of Ibadan. The Remos therefore sent to Ibadan for help and Ogunmola went straight from the Ijaye camp to Remo, the Balogun himself although in ill health rejoining him soon after, until the army at Awayè could join them. Ogunmola in the meantime found his way to Ikorodu for a supply of ammunition.

Iperu easily surrendered to the Egbas and there the triple forces of the Egbas, Ijayes and Ijebus were concentrated to repel the Ibadans and overrun Remo.

The Ibadans retook several towns as Ipara, Ogere etc., sweeping all before them until they came up with their old antagonists again, re-inforced by the Ijebus at Iperu.

At home, the Ibadans at first made light of the combination, hence they sang in their dances :—

> " Ijebu ko pe okòwo,
> Nitori erù l'a se nlo."

(The Ijebus are not worth a sou [lit. 20 cowries]
Only for booty are we going).

But the chiefs knew the difficulties that confronted them, especially as the foe blocked the route of their supply of ammunition. Moreover Ajiya Abayomi pointed out that Remo being a non-agricultural country, could not supply an army with food : they must therefore be provisioned from home and would thus be far from their base ; besides Ijebu is proverbially destitute of water ; he therefore, suggested that they should attack them from Ijebu Igbo, which is not far from the Ibadan farms S.E. as opposition from that point would be almost nil, and in that way they would withdraw the coalition against their friends the Remos, and with their own farms as base, they would have a safe and easy task.

The other chiefs saw with him, but, said they, their aim was not to destroy the Ijebus but to protect their friends ; and it would be most ungracious to leave the Remos who had been so loyal to them in their hour of danger,.

Thus the encounter was again renewed between the old antagonists in a different battlefield. The Ibadans were again sweeping all before them, and Iperu was just nearly taken and the confederates crushed when Providence decreed the arrest of   their progress. The tide turned dead against them ; a combination of causes created insurmountable difficulties.

1. The Egbas now introduced superior weapons. They were armed with breach-loading guns and rifles.

2. One Mr. Pettiford an American sharp-shooter was engaged to pick down the chiefs, thus Odunjo the Seriki, Madarikan the Asaju, Chief Adêpo, and others fell. Ogunmola himself was nearly hit, his hat being knocked off his head.

3. The Ibadans having hemmed them up at Iperu were consequently near enough to be within the range of the rifles, and so from within the town walls and surrounding thickets they were constantly harassed in their camps.

4. The Balogun's illness grew worse, he could not leave his bed and several of the leading chiefs were killed.

5. The distance of their base, the difficulty of food supply and the scarcity of water told against them. The whole camp had to depend upon one single well which they dug when water could not be obtained otherwise ; a very deep well it was and the only one.

6. No scope to deploy their troops for manœuvring against superior numbers and superior weapons ; and worst of all they ran short of powder for the old Dane guns they were using, so that instead of taking the offensive they were now on the defensive in their camps; the Egbas could come out and cut down the corn they had planted and offer battle.

The direction of the war devolved upon Ogunmola alone in the absence of the sick Balogun, the Osi killed at Ijaye, the Seriki, Asaju and others shot down at Iperu. Matters came to such a pass one day, when Ogunmola was hard pressed that he sent to call the Balogun from his sick bed " to die if needs be like a soldier in the field."

Once more the " lion of the master of camps " aroused himself and appeared on the scene of action for the last time. He was literally helped and held on horse back, one desperate effort was made, and the Egbas were pushed a little way back. But the Balogun could not continue long, he left some of his men with Ogunmola, to hold the ground they had regained and he was borne back to his tent. His legs had become so œdematous when he was lifted off his horse, that his riding boots had to be ripped open with a knife in order to release his legs ! Thus the war dragged wearily on, Iperu could not be taken by assault or otherwise, nor could the Ibadans be dislodged from their entrenchments.

Towards the latter part of 1864 the ALÂFIN intervened, as his father did in the late Batedo war. His Majesty sent the high priest of Sango with the emblems of the deity, and a eunuch to represent himself, to the belligerents. They came first to the Ibadan camp, and then passed on to Iperu to the Egbas, Ijayes and Ijebus ; in each place, homage was paid to the god and fealty to the representative of the monarch. The " God Sango had enjoined a cessation of arms and the return of each one to his home." Peace was then declared between the belligerents.

Congratulatory messages were sent home by friends and relatives in opposite camps, mutual visitings took place and all went well for three or four days.

But the Ibadan principal chiefs had no great confidence in Egba good faith, having the perfidy of 1860 before their eyes ; they, therefore, took certain precautions.

First, they ordered all the sick and wounded home (except the Balogun), together with the women and children by slow marches. Secondly, the bones of the fallen chiefs were exhumed and sent home for re-interment.

They were apprehensive of treachery from the Egbas immediately they turned their backs, but to prevent a panic they did not disclose their fears or suspicion, but Ogunmola knowing himself to be the most invidious of the lot and a special object of hate hastened away in the night and before daybreak had reached Ipara. In his hurry his slaves on occasion made way for him with the sword, and seeing his only daughter Omosa in the company of women who had been sent on the day before, he lifted her on to his saddle and never halted until he reached Fawe in the Ibadan farms, there to await his comrades.

But the majority of the women lingered by the way, others in the camp, seeing no reason why they should be in a hurry as all was peace. The Balogun who was dropsical and could not ride was borne on a litter.

Now when the day arrived for the breaking up of the camp, and the Ibadans already on the move, the Egba nature asserted itself by justifying the worst apprehensions entertained of it. They had crowded the Ibadan camp in friendly intercourse, and exchanged greetings, but the prey was now eluding their grasp ; they pounced upon the unsuspicious and began to make prisoners and pressed forward in pursuit. Some of the chiefs who did not suspect treachery were caught. The venerable Sumala the Otun Bale who would have been made the Bale of Ibadan on their return home was caught and killed. Chief Abayomi was one of the unsuspicious, the Egbas had begun to make prisoners before he was aware of what was going on. Mounting his horse when it was tethered he forgot to unloose it till one of his slaves severed the cord with his sword.   He had to fight his way out and escaped.

Soderinde, although a native of Iperu but a resident at Ibadan, and a distinguished cavalry officer was then at home among his relatives enjoying himself ; he was there arrested and had to ransom himself by the payment of a heavy fine, and had to remain there at home for the time.   At the stream Afidiwo the Egba pursuers overtook the Balogun and his guards ; these stood fighting whilst those who bore him were hastening on.   But the Egbas were pressing closely endeavouring to take the Balogun alive. When they reached the river Omi the Balogun ordered his carriers to put him down and that the Egbas be driven back from that place Akere the Asipa was the only war-chief who waited to protect the Balogun besides his own men and bodyguards.   Here, when they had rallied and arranged themselves in order of battle, they made a furious charge on the Egba pursuers and drove them clean away with a heavy loss.   These soon finding it unprofitable to pursue armed men when hapless women and children were to be got, quickly gave up the pursuit.

All, as many as escaped, assembled at Fawe from which place they returned home one by one, mostly at night on account of the disastrous ending of the expedition.   More women were lost than men.   Kehere the Balogun of Ipara wisely came to Ibadan until peace had been completely restored.

For weeks and months, people were coming home by degrees, as numbers had escaped into the bush and lost their way ; some strayed to Ijebu farms and were captured, some found their way back to the road or to Ibadans farms and returned home, whilst some perished in the forests.

A small force of armed men was ordered to proceed as far as the river Omi with the hopes of rescuing them, following the directions in which those who had escaped located large bodies of them.   A few were rescued by them, for guns fired to attract their notice unfortunately had the effect of driving them farther into the forests, as reported by the few which escaped.

The view taken of this disaster by the Ibadans was expressed thus in the song and dances of the day :—

> " Sango l'o laja ti o d'obirin nù,
> Ogun ko le wa."

("Twas Sango's mediation that lost us our wives,
We've suffered no defeat.)[1]

---

[1] It is only fair to mention that the Egbas atoned for this action in a very diplomatic way as we shall find in §5 following.

The experience gained from this circumstance was the reason for the caution displayed many years afterwards when peace was being arranged between the Ibadans and Ekitis at Kiriji by various parties. The Ibadans refused to decamp in the face of their foes without a guarantee against a pursuit until the British Government intervened in 1886 and arranged for a simultaneous decampment.

§ 3. The Ikorodu War

The Egbas instead of returning home after this, led the conjoint army against Ikorodu. Ikorodu is a town situated on the Lagoon about 3 hours' steam from Lagos. Whether because as a Remo town she took no part in the late war, or because she was secretly in alliance with Ibadan is not certain. They were here for several months and some good fighting was done on both sides. But Ikorodu was hopelessly outnumbered. When she was nearly taken, the chiefs applied for the protection of the British Government at Lagos. The Lagos traders and merchants also suffering from the closing of the markets approved of the interference of the Governor. His Excellency John Hawley Glover, then governor of Lagos, therefore sent to the Egbas to raise the siege, as Ikorodu was a peaceful town on the Lagoon with a regular trade with Lagos, which was thus being indirectly injured. On their refusing to do so, he sent them an ultimatum which was also disregarded. On the 29th March, 1865, the Governor sent about 100 men of the West Indian regiment then quartered at Lagos with a few shells and rockets.

Within an hour of the engagement the Egbas had taken to their heels, large numbers perished in the flight. It was ascertained afterwards that those who fell from bullets were very few indeed but the majority died from fright and thirst induced by exhaustion in the flight ; for as the rockets flew overhead with hideous noise and streaming fiery tails, a thing unseen before, they were panic-stricken.

As soon as the report reached Iperu of the flight of the Egbas from Ikorodu, Soderinde in order to retrieve his losses and to avenge himself on the Egbas, collected his men and as many Ibadan boys, as he could collect who had come down for trade, and they fell upon those of the Egbas who had escaped from Ikorodu and were recovering their breath. He made many captives, and returning he stayed no longer at Iperu but passed on straight to Ibadan where he domiciled until his death in 1880 full of days and honour having attained to the rank of Balogun in the cavalry. Thus Ikorodu was saved.

§ 4. The Second Dahomian Invasion of Abẹokuta

During the Ipẹru war, the Dahomians taking advantage of the absence of the Egba war-chiefs made a second attack on Abẹokuta on the 15th of March, 1864.

It was alleged by some that this was at the instigation of the Ibadans in order that the Egbas might withdraw from Ipẹru, and also that men were sent to teach them how to encamp and lay siege. How far this is true is not known, but it is certain that the Dahomians required no instigation for raiding Abẹokuta nor did they at any time lay siege against her.

The Egbas had profited by the experience of 1851, the town wall was well repaired, and the trenches dug deep, two or three field guns were mounted on the ramparts and sentinels placed to prevent a surprise.

The Christian community, now a numerous body, formed a corps by themselves under John Okenla their Balogun, encamping apart during intervening Sundays, and having their religious services in the field.

False alarms of the approach of the enemy and the usual cry of the women " Ele lè m'elè " were constant. The Christians gave the people a sign that when they heard the booming of the cannon, then they were to be sure of the approach of the enemy.

Early in the morning of the 15th of March, the booming of cannon in rapid succession, and the rattling of musketry told the town that the enemy was in sight ; the women resumed their cry, and the men hastened to man the walls.

About 7 a.m. the noise of fire-arms was quite deafening and for the space of half-an-hour without intermission, all on the side of the Egbas who were well within the walls having learnt by experience never to attempt to meet them in the open field to arrest their progress.

The Dahomians without returning the fire, or breaking their ranks marched steadily onwards, the Amazons this time bringing up the rear. On they marched stolidly till they began to scale the walls. Cannon and muskets were now of little use, it was a matter of hand-to-hand fighting. The Egbas well within the walls kept lopping off the hands of the Amazons as they attempted to scale the walls, and in that way hundreds of their advanced comrades were left in the trenches.

When they were repulsed, they fell back and took to their guns. The Egbas kept up a steady fire from the holes made in the walls. Finding it useless to renew their efforts of taking the town by assault, the Dahomian army retreated but in good order.

The Ẹgbas now came out, hovering in their rear until they saw them pass Ibara to Isaga. Many captives were made, of whom were Amazons so ferocious, that although chained, many found means of killing their captors, and were of course killed in turn. A male soldier penetrated as far as Igbein, being caught near the C.M.S. station there by the son of an old Ogboni man. He was put in stocks, but great care was bestowed upon him to soften his ferocity. He refused to eat, and was resolved to die. He was heard muttering something in his language, not understood by those around, his intention therefore was not known. But he managed to obtain and conceal a large bit of stone near him, and watching for an opportunity, he dealt a heavy blow with it on the face of the old Ogboni man, who, thereupon fell down and fainted away. The women-folk in the house set up a yell, and as the fellow could not possibly escape he was shot dead on the spot.

The subsequent Dahomian invasions never came up to the walls of Abẹokuta, but almost every year their expedition would come as far as Ibara, 10 miles from the town, the inhabitants deserting the place for Abẹokuta, and sometimes they would encamp on the Ata hills 5 or 6 miles distant, remaining for a couple of months, devastating the farms all around. The Ẹgbas would remain day and night keeping watch by the walls till the beginning of May when the rainy season had fairly set in, and the rivers began to rise. The Ogun river at this time became a wall of protection for them, as the Dahomians could not ford it nor bridge it, and they had no canoes. The Yewa river also flowing between the Yoruba and Idahomian territories had to be forded. The Dahomians therefore invariably raised their sieges and returned home before the rains had fairly set in.

During these periods of what is called siege, there were some desperadoes among the Ẹgbas who would venture across the river to within two miles of the Ata hills to spy out the enemy, and sometimes to scare them by letting off fire arms. In order to capture such men the Dahomians would come down unseen as near as possible to the river, dig trenches at intervals on either side of the path, and conceal men in them, setting scouts to apprise them of the approach of Ẹgba spies. After these had passed on towards the Dahomian camp, they would emerge from their hiding places and cut off their retreat, driving them onwards towards their camp. In this way several were caught, and some of those who escaped capture died of fright, or of exhaustion and thirst.

The panic and distress caused by these yearly raids became very great at Abẹokuta, depression of trade and the arrest of all agricultural pursuits followed. The Ẹgbas, although better armed, yet lacked the courage to leave the security of their walls and meet their enemy in the field. This national disgrace was subsequently wiped off by John Okenla the Christian Balogun, who in 1873 with a company of his men attacked and defeated a body of Dahomian raiders at Ọbà who went scouring the fields and pillaging the farms.

The English Government was now memorialized by the secretaries of the C.M. Society on account of the Christians at Abẹokuta, and, in response to this appeal, the King of Dahomey was warned against meddling with Abẹokuta any more.

The Dahomians now turned their attention to the Yorubas of the western province, and were actually devastating the Egbados and the Oke Ogun districts until a higher power decreed " Thus far shalt thou go, and no further."

§ 5. The Atonement

The Balogun of Ibadan died ten days after their return home, and was given a public funeral with full honours.

The government of Ibadan now devolved upon Ogunmọla the Ọtun Balogun, and the first thing he did was to assemble the other chiefs in council with a view to arranging terms of peace with their neighbours. But the perfidy of the Egbas and the great loss sustained especially of the women must in some way be avenged at any rate.

The secret somehow leaked out that the Egba chiefs gave up Osiẹlẹ to be taken by the Ibadans to satisfy their honour if it could be done by a *coup* before the news of it reached Abẹokuta.

Ogunmọla himself led out the expedition, but remained with the reserved forces in the forests, and entrusted the enterprise into the hands of Ajọbọ the newly made Seriki. He was to surprise Osiẹlẹ, swoop down upon it, make a clean sweep of the place and retire ere help could come from Abẹokuta.

Ajọbọ, however, lacked the courage to take it by an assault and hence the expedition failed. Ogunmọla keenly regretted having stayed behind, but as the attempt could not be repeated without provoking a war with the Egbas he led the Ibadan forces home again. It was a diplomatic offer and should be done in one stroke.

A few weeks after this Ogunmọla again led the Ibadan troops against Atadi another village of Abẹokuta, this time entrusting it to no one, he went in person, and on the 9th of March, 1865, Atadi was taken by assault. The two powers now felt that honour has been satisfied on both sides.

It was said that the news of the Ibadan attempt on Osiẹlẹ met the Abẹokuta chiefs at a public meeting, but in spite of the excitement shown by the people, and the urgent requests for a pursuit, the chiefs gave no heed, but were coolly going on with the business in hand, which was quite an unimportant affair.

To the peoples' importunities they simply returned a derisive answer pointing out the impossibility of the thing, and when they knew the Ibadans must have gone then they bestirred themselves to find Osiele intact.   Hence when the report of Atadi was given they were able to say " False alarm again, so they did in the case of Osiele the Ibadans would not dare to think of it" etc.

This daring attack was not followed by a retaliation or by further kidnapping on either side which was a proof that it was a diplomatic affair secretly arranged by the authorities on both sides.

Ayawo the wife of Somoye the Basorun of Abeokuta, who was taken at Ijaye was now restored to her husband and on the 15th of July, of the same year, the Ibadan messengers arrived at Abeokuta for a formal negotiation about the re-opening of the roads for intercommunication and trade. A month after this peace was proclaimed, and the roads became free and open to all. The Egbas, however, forbade the sale of arms and gunpowder to the Ibadans, and these forbade the sale of horses to the Egbas.

The paths through the forests fields and farms having been overgrown and blocked by large trees falling across during the period they were disused, had now to be cut and cleared on either side right on to the frontier.

This brings to a close the Ijaye war and its consequences.

CHAPTER XX

THE CLOSING AND THE OPENING CAREERS OF
TWO HEROES

§ 1. OGUNMOLA'S ADMINISTRATION

THE attention of the Ibadans was now turned to home affairs, vacancies among the chiefs had to be filled up, and new titles conferred. The first to be conferred was, of course, that of the head of the town as he it is who has to arrange for the others.

It was known that if the Balogun had returned home in good health, he would have negotiated for the title of Kakanfo, as he was the conqueror of the late Kakanfo, and being a native of Ogbomoso, was said to be related to a former Kakanfo of that place. But when his fatal illness supervened it is said that hopes were fixed on the venerable Sumala the Otun Balẹ for the title of Balẹ on their return home, but Sumala was caught and killed at the retreat from Iperu. Ogunmola now found himself the undisputed head of the town. He declined the title of Balẹ alleging it was an effeminate title, for Balẹs do not go to war, and so many brave men having perished at the war, Ibadan would lose her military prestige by his retiring so early from active life. But he might have negotiated for the title of Kakanfo now vacant. That is a military title *par excellence*, but his vaulting ambition aimed higher than that, he usurped the title of Basọrun notwithstanding that Gbenla the first Basọrun of the present Ọyọ was still alive, and there can be but one Basọrun of the kingdom.

The Basọrun is a prince of Ọyọ and the title hereditary, but this impudent upstart who found himself temporarily entrusted with the great force of Ibadan was a native of an Iwo village a provincial of a rough type. He demanded that His Supernal Highness Gbenla should make way for him.

The ALÂFIN, however, was up to the occasion. He agreed to confer on him the title of Basọrun *pro causa honoris* in recognition of his services at the Ijaye war. He was firmly against the demand for the death of his aged Basọrun. The times said he, demand that such should be the case, Gbenla must remain the Basọrun of the kingdom with his official duties to perform at Ọyọ, but Ogunmola may be a provincial Basọrun as a special reward for services done.

Ogunmola having been installed in office demanded His Highness

O

Gbenla's "chain of office" (represented by the beads round his neck), and his Wabi (a specially ornamented hide on which only the Baṣọrun sits). The ALÂFIN sent him both and consoled his chief minister by giving him others and begged him not to mind the insult, nor commit suicide out of grief, as he was inclined to do. He further sent to tell Ogunmọla that he might have all he wanted but he was not to demand the death of the Baṣọrun any more, as he the King willed that there should be two Baṣọruns at this time, one in the city and the other in the province.

It may here be mentioned that 7 years before this event, that is before the Ijaye war, the town of Ibadan was one day startled by the report that Ogunmọla (then Ọtun Balogun) whilst divining with his Ifa, was told by the priest that he would attain to the title of Baṣọrun before his death ! What seemed then to be an utter improbability now became a realized fact.

The Baṣọrun's next duty was to confer titles on his chiefs, the more important of them were the following :—

Akere the Aṣipa became the Balogun.

Tubọsun the Osi Bàlẹ his old colleague and supporter, the Ọtun-Balogun.

Abayọmi the Ajiya Balẹ, who distinguished himself so much before Ijaye and at the Ijẹbu road, the Osi.

Orówùsi, who afterwards became better known, the Aṣipa.

Ali Laluwoye, brother of the late Ọṣundina, the Ẹkẹrin.

Ajọbọ, the head of the Badas, the Seriki.

Latosisà, who afterwards became famous, the Ọtun Seriki.

Tahájò, was made the Sarumi.

Sodẹrinde, a distinguished horseman, the Balogun Sarumi.

These names were given and we shall come across every one of them again in the course of this history.

Some Ọyọ titles were now introduced to satisfy distinguished men who were for some reason or other passed over, but who could not accept subordinate titles, in the same way as the Aṣipa had been introduced for one who failed to get the Ọtun or Osi. Aijẹnku negotiated for and obtained the title of Fòwọ̀kọ̀.

Ọmọteji took the Ẹsọ title of Gbọnkâ.

Ojokofo that of Òwòta. These purely Ọyọ titles were for the first time introduced into Ibadan.

According to merit the man who by far was probably the fittest person for the title of Balogun was the redoubtable Aijẹnku the Arẹagoro or *alter ego* of the late Balogun Ibikunle—the man who alone withstood the whole force of the Ẹgbas at Ijaye when he was left with the Balogun in charge of the camp at the

storming of Iwawun by Ogunmola and subordinate chiefs. But
Aijenku failed in his duty to protect his chief at the retreat from
Iperu. · Akere on that occasion performed the duty that was his
and, therefore, obtained his reward. Ibikunle before his death
was said to have bequeathed the title to him.

This offence might probably have been pardoned and an
opportunity given him to retrieve his good name by prowess
in the field for the public benefit ; but the secret underlying this
treatment of him was, that after the death of Oluyole the first
Basorun of Ibadan, who tyrannized over his chiefs so mercilessly,
subjecting them to his cutting wit, the Ibadans were resolved
never to give the higher titles to any Oyos of the pure type, i.e.
one born in the ancient capital or in the Metropolitan province.
They far excel the southerners in astuteness and diplomacy and
rather look down on them, Ibolos and Epos being preferred.
Aijenku moreover, was one of Oluyole's household officers and
was said to be of an irritable disposition and inflammable temper.
There was every probability of his emulating his old master.

And besides this, he was one of the original settlers ; he was
one of those who " entered the town on horseback " showing that
unlike most of the present chiefs he was never at any time a
common soldier, and he never ceased to rebuke or educate the men
of another generation in the light of former day experience, which
goes the wrong way with them. Having been passed over he
negotiated for and obtained the title of Fòwòkò a lieutenant
of the Kakanfo.

After enjoying a short period of rest, attending to home affairs,
Ogunmola now turned his attention abroad. In communication
with the Governor (Glover) of Lagos, he effected the opening of the
road to Lagos *via* Remo for intercourse with the interior.

He now thought of avenging all the insults offered to the
Ibadans, by some of the provincial kings, which could not have
been done before this without unnecessarily multiplying enemies
against themselves. Foremost amongst them was the Aseyin who
was fond of extemporising epigrams and ditties directed against
Ibadan in parabolic songs and dances, and who received him
as a subject on his way to Iwawun. Now, as a Basorun takes
precedence of all provincial kings, Ogunmola summoned the Aseyin
to Ibadan. He came attended by his principal chiefs and Prince
Okanlawon. On their arrival they met all the Ibadan chiefs at
the Basorun's in full council. It was now the Basorun's turn
to lord it over him. He at once ordered him to do homage ; this he
did by running backwards and forwards to the street three times,
putting earth on his head, and prostrating each time before the

Baṣọrun, performing acts of humiliation. His life being also threatened, he had to beg hard for it, and some of the chiefs who were friendly to him interposed on his behalf and he was pardoned.

Ogunmọla having thus satisfied his vanity afterwards treated him kindly, and sent him away loaded with presents. Being in part friendly to Kurũmi of Ijaye, he could not have been sincere in his loyalty to the ALÂFIN his liege lord during the war, but he would sooner entrust himself into the hands of the rough Ibadans, who would at any rate have some regard for the person of a king, than into the hands of his Suzerain at Ọyọ ; he, therefore, took a bush path to Ibadan and back, and on his return home he extemporized a ditty in his dances, congratulating himself on his safe return thus :—

> " Kàkà ki Arẹmu ba ti Ọyọ lọ si Ibadan,
>   Bi o jẹ ọdun mẹta Arẹmu a sun igbẹ."

Rather than to go by Ọyọ to Ibadan,
If it takes Arẹmu three years, he will sleep in the bush.

§ 2. THE IGBAJO CAMPAIGN

About this time there was a civil commotion at Ileṣa ; the then Ọdọle, one of the ministers of the Ọwa being a man of power and influence was in great favour with his master, practically holding the reins of government; without his fiat nothing could be done at Ileṣa.

The Ijẹṣa chiefs about this time were resolved to declare war against Igbajọ, a frontier town of a composite nationality (as its name implies) not far from Ikirun, because of their sympathies with Ibadan; but the Ọdọle, a wise and far-seeing man, was opposed to that measure, fearing the consequences it may entail. The other chiefs said they were not going to stoop to him any longer, and in spite of him they declared war against Igbajọ.

The Ijẹṣa standard of war left the town with all their mighty men under the leadership of the Lokiràn, Lejọka, Isihikin with the Loro at their head ; thus they laid siege against Igbajọ.

The Ijẹṣas of Ileṣa were never on good terms with the Ibadans since the late Ijẹbu Ẹrẹ and the Ará expeditions and their movements at this time were being closely watched at Ibadan. But several wild Ijẹṣa boys had come of their own accord to reside at Ibadan being driven out of the town by chief Ọdọle for their wild and lawless habits ; these preferring the unrestrainèd life at Ibadan, distributed themselves under the principal chiefs Ibikunle, Ogunmọla, Ọṣundina and others, and fought for them in all their expeditions. The most notable amongst them were Ọmọle, Ayibiowu, Fayiṣe, Ọdọ́ Edidi, Jege, Oṣogbo, and Ogedemgbe.[1] Ọmọle was the chief of them all and knew the Ijẹṣa farms and all the secret paths quite well. He often led the Ibadan kidnappers to kidnap his own people and bring them captive to Ibadan; for this he acquired the nickname " A ni ọbara ojulumọ̀ l'apò " (one who has in his sack a cord for binding an acquaintance). It was the services of these Ijẹṣas driven out of the town that were successfully utilized by the Ibadans in the Ijẹbu Ẹrẹ and the Ará expeditions. In this way they resented their expulsion from Ilẹṣa by betraying their countrymen, and their exploits served but to increase the disaffection of the Ijẹṣa chiefs against the Ọdọle.

Just about this time (1866) Mr. Phillip Jose Meffre a well-known Ijẹṣa at Lagos with some other Ijẹṣas, taking advantage of the opening of the roads went up for a short visit to their native land. On their returning to Lagos, they bought as curios several native mats, fans, etc., with other articles of merchandise for presents. On both journeys they stayed at the C.M.S. compound and premises at Kudẹti, Ibadan.

But the Ijẹṣas of Lagos being at variance with one another, sent secret intelligence to Ibadan, and a hint was given to the Baṣọrun to watch the clandestine movements of Mr. Meffre against the interests of Ibadan.

In the afternoon of the 2nd of March, 1866, the Baṣọrun sent for Mr. Meffre and all his countrymen who were with him and charged them with working secretly against the interests of Ibadan.

They, of course, denied it and declared their innocence. Most of them had been carried away as slaves to Brazil and other parts and having effected their ransom and returned to Lagos they now simply took advantage of the opening of the roads to revisit their native land; with political matters they had no concern whatever. But the Baṣọrun detained them and cast them all into prison, and sent to the mission premises to confiscate all their goods. The Rev. J. T. Smith, missionary in charge of the station during the absence of Mr. Hinderer, interposed on their behalf, because they were all Christians from Lagos. In vain did he plead their cause, invoking the aid of some of the friendly chiefs. They were all put in chains, and there was no peace or rest at the mission compound on their account. Thus matters stood for nearly a fortnight.

On the morning of the 14th of March all at the Mission were glad to see Mr. Meffre and his countrymen released and sent back free

---

[1] The youngest and destined to be the most famous.

unconditionally ! What had happened ? On the previous night, there was a terrible conflagration in which the house of the Baṣọrun had a very narrow escape. All the houses around that part of the building in which these men were chained were burnt to the ground but their prison house was intact ! The Baṣọrun was so struck with this miraculous escape that he exclaimed " Surely these men are innocent persons, and this is naught else but the interposition of their God, and I am not the man to defy the white man's God." So he hastily released them and sent them back to the mission.

In the meantime the siege of Igbajọ was being vigorously prosecuted by the Ijẹṣas, and Igbajọ was nearly hemmed in on every side. In their extremity they sent to Ibadan for help. The Baṣọrun sent to them Ọṣuntoki the Mayẹ with some minor war chiefs, but the Ijẹṣas were too strong for them. The town was well nigh taken when the Ibadan contingents there sent home to the Baṣọrun for the Balogun to come to their rescue as mere reinforcements were of no avail.

On the 16th of December, 1866, the war staff was propitiated, and on the 17th the standard was out under the command of the new Balogun Akere on its way to Igbajọ. They arrived at Igbajọ about the 14th of January, and they obtained a victory as easy as it was complete.

On the first day the fight was to take place, while they were holding a council of war, the Ijẹṣas marched out to give battle. Abayọmi the Osi impatient of much talk left them all at the council, by a private arrangement he entered the forest, and through a secret path was led to the rear of the Ijẹṣa army. All of a sudden he burst upon the principal chiefs where they were lounging without guards and without protection : the younger men were all in the battle field. Escape was impossible, he fell upon them and butchered them all to pieces, carrying the camp by assault. The Ijẹṣas who had marched out to give battle were filled with consternation when they saw the camp in flames behind them, and the Ibadan army before and behind ! Panic stricken they were simply pounced upon as does a cat on a mouse. It was a matter of " veni, vidi, vici," the battle did not last an hour. The Ijẹṣa camp was at the foot of a hill, neither chiefs nor men went on horseback, all were on foot and in the chase up the hill not a single chief escaped to tell the tale ! Those who escaped the sword died of exhaustion and thirst, many of them corpulent men. Here the power of the Ijẹṣas was completely broken. Ilẹṣa was partly deserted as they expected an immediate siege. Esa was taken on the 26th of January.

The news of this tragedy travelled swiftly to Lagos, and the Ijẹṣas of Lagos approached the Governor (J. H. Glover) beseeching him to interpose on their behalf, that their capital city be not destroyed by war.

The Governor sent a messenger to the Baṣọrun of Ibadan, deprecating the capture of Ilesa, and accordingly repeated messages one after another from the Baṣọrun were sent to recall the Balogun who had advanced towards Ilẹṣa.

At the same time also, the Ọwa had sent demijohns of beads and heavy presents to the Baṣọrun at home tendering his submission. Thus Ilẹṣa was spared. The Ibadan army returned home in triumph on the 17th of February, 1867.

§ 3. THE LATE OGUNMOLA BASORUN OF IBADAN

The Ibadan war-chiefs after their arrival at home paid the customary tribute in slaves to the ALÂFIN. The senior war-chiefs also contributed their share to the Baṣọrun Ogunmọla and the minor chiefs received their share from the subordinate chiefs according to custom.

After this the Baṣọrun paid a visit of congratulation to each of the principal war-chiefs on their safe return. Each of them received him with every mark of honour and offered presents of a slave and some heads of cowries. They also paid a return visit according to custom.

A few days afterwards it was rumoured that the Baṣọrun was sick: the rumour soon gained ground, and from the abundance of the sacrifices being offered the malady was known to be serious. It was said to be an attack of small pox, and the Babalawos (priests of Ifa) advised that a gun loaded with bullets be fired in the direction of the Isalẹ Oṣun district ; this was done and more besides, but all to no purpose. On the morning of the 28th February, 1867, repeated rattling of musketry announced to the public that the august patient had passed away.

Not two months after, on the 12th of April, 1867, Abayọmi the Osi died after a few days' illness. On the 30th of the same month died Tubọsun the Ọtun Balogun also suddenly.

These important deaths in quick succession struck one as very remarkable, as if to atone for the wholesale butchery of the Ijẹṣa chiefs at Igbajọ. Thus of the five principal chiefs who held the council of war for the relief of Igbajọ within four months only the Balogun and Seriki remained alive.

The Cause of the Baṣọrun's Death.—From the nature of the malady it was generally held that the death was not due to natural causes. During the absence of the war-chiefs at Igbajọ, the

Baṣọrun in the height of his glory was so elated that he sent to the
ALÂFIN to send him Aháyán posts and bẹrẹ grass for his Kọbi.
As a nobleman he was entitled to a kọbi (a bay projecting from the
house with a conical top higher than the roof of the house).
Aháyán is a rare tree found in certain parts of the country, and
used by the great alone.   It is neither affected by weather, termites,
or ordinary fire.   The bẹrẹ is a grass used for thatching that grows
only in the plain.   Annual contribution of this grass is made
by subordinates to their chiefs between December and January
in the country of the plain, so that a gift of bẹrẹ has come to be
regarded in the light of paying tribute ; it has thus passed into
a proverb to illustrate anything most incongruous " Odi ori odì
ki ara Qyọ ki o pa bẹrẹ fun ara Oko " (the height of incongruity
for citizens of Qyọ to contribute bẹrẹ to country folks).   This time-
honoured maxim Ogunmọla was bent on violating out of sheer
vanity, not caring for the fact of its being an insult and great offence
to his sovereign.   The King ordered both to be sent to him, but
it was noticed that the posts were wrapped in mats, and tied
precisely the same way corpses are wrapped in this country for
interment.   Ogunmọla did not enjoy his acquisition for two
months.   This can only be regarded as a paternal imprecation
on an undutiful and disloyal son.

The more probable and direct cause of his death alleged by
those who had access to his presence was the following :—

It was reported to him by one of his roaming followers that he
had seen a cloth with one of the Ekiti Kings, the like of which
could be found in the possession of his superiors.   The cloth
was so finely-woven that it could be folded up into so small a
compass that it could be stowed away by stuffing it into a moderate
sized conch shell, and yet unfolded was an ample covering for a
man.   [The cloth probably was silk, as the best kind of Samayan
or rough silk, comes from that part of the country.]

Ogunmọla did not adopt a course which one would have
expected from so astute a man, viz. to ask the said Ekiti king to
send him the weaver to weave one like it for him, or even one of a
superior quality, and also to teach the art to his people.   On the
contrary he sent to take possession of the cloth.   Here again we
see the operation of that vanity that demanded the title of Baṣọrun,
that required Aháyán and Bẹrẹ for his kọbi, and which displayed
a show of triumph over the Asẹyin.   The cloth was sent him.   It
was noticed that from the moment he unfolded the cloth and
wrapped it around his body, he began to feel some inconvenience,
this grew to a feverish heat which baffled every effort to cool
down, nay not even when they resorted to pouring buckets of

cold water upon him ; it went on increasing in intensity, and in this agony of heat he writhed until he passed away. This gave colour to the bulletin issued that His Highness died of the fever of small pox.

Ogunmọla as a private man has been brought to our notice first during the time of Bạsọrun Oluyọle. He was as a soldier bold, hardy, fearless, and very astute. He rose rapidly to distinction by the aid of some of his colleagues who saw in him qualities of a great leader, viz., Awanibaku, who became his Balogun, Tubọsun, who became the Ọtun Balogun, Arunà, who afterwards became a distinguished cavalry officer, Kukoni who afterwards became a Christian and retired from their company, Ọdunjọ the Seriki of Ibadan during the Ijaye war, and others. He led them on several slave-hunting expeditions, and, as their captain received a lion's share of the booty, so as to be able to fill his position with credit and provide them with arms and ammunition for another expedition. His fame brought him many more followers, and he soon obtained a title and a voice in the government, and thus rose from one post of distinction to another until he attained the head chieftaincy of Ibadan.

We may note here that this is the precise way most of the war-chiefs of Ibadan rose to distinction.

As a general he was unsurpassed for boldness and courage, he knew not how to give his back to the enemy, and these qualities often saved him from many a critical position. Being a man of small stature, he always rode on the tallest horses he could find, with his eyes on all around, to single out the brave by name for praise and encouragement, and the coward for disgrace. His fame eclipsed that of Ibikunle his chief, who was his superior in every respect, so much so that those who knew little of Ibadan took him for the head of the town even when he was only the Ọtun Balogun. But he knew how to obey commands and yield implicit obedience to his superior officer. Of the three senior war-chiefs in the early sixties, Ibikunle, Ogunmọla and Ọṣundina, he was their bull dog, hence his name was universally known and his fame grew.

As an administrator he was very just, and was never influenced by bribes. On the contrary if money was brought to him to prejudice his mind in a case to be heard, after patiently hearing the case if it went against the man who attempted to bribe him, he would disgrace him openly for what he had attempted to do, bring out the bribe in public and the fine would be more than the bribe. The following story will serve to illustrate a case of this kind showing also his practical common sense :—A disagreeable man's goat broke through the fence of his neighbour and destroyed several stalks

of his standing corn ; the latter in driving it away inadvertently
hit the goat on the head with a stone and killed it. The owner of
the goat demanded redress, and charged an exorbitant price for
his goat, refusing all entreaties, and when the money was not
forthcoming, he summoned the poor man the next day before the
Baṣọrun.

The Baṣọrun saw at once that the act was merely an accident
and that the plaintiff was altogether spiteful; he was, therefore
determined to teach him a lesson.

The case having been stated in open court, the next day the
Baṣọrun acted as if he were all in favour of the plaintiff. He rated
the man, who killed the goat soundly for his clumsiness and want of
caution etc.; it served him right, he was to pay the price demanded
by the owner of the goat, 10 heads of cowries ; but as the man
could not afford the money (on account of which the case came to
court at all) he offered to lend him the amount, and the amount of
10 heads was brought out. Both parties now began to get confused
before this extraordinary judge. As the poor man thanked the
Baṣọrun and was going away (the plaintiff being afraid to take
the money) the Baṣọrun called him back saying " Where are you
going, you duffer? Why don't you bring a counter-charge for the
destruction of your corn? I suppose about 30 or 40 stalks were
destroyed. As he has received 10 heads of cowries for *one* goat,
supposing you demand 10 heads for each stalk of your corn
destroyed? That would be fair according to his own code, won't
it ? " And there in open court he told how this disagreeable
neighbour had come the previous evening with three heads of
cowries to bribe him on this case. He had kept the money on one
side and now ordered it to be brought out in open court saying,
"After carelessly leaving your goat to stray out and destroy
another man's property you have the heart to come here and
charge about double the market price for the loss of it, when this
was due to a pure accident." (The utmost amount for goats then
was about 6 heads.) It was now the plaintiff's turn to beg trembling
where he lay prostrate before the Baṣọrun. Thus His Highness
dealt with the case, the plaintiff not only losing his bribe, but
also had to pay about 30 or 40 bags for the corn destroyed. It
was generally known that it was of no use bribing the Baṣọrun,
that would not affect the decision of the case.

Previously to Ogunmọla's regime, no young man or youth could
be seen out of doors unarmed with some weapon or other ; it was
considered effeminate to go about without any. Firearms of course
were absolutely forbidden by the fundamental laws of the town
but a young man did not consider himself fully dressed without

a short sword or knife girded to his side, a jack knife buckled to his left wrist, and wielding in his right hand a large-headed club or cudgel ringed or pegged with iron ; consequently street fighting was a common affair. To spend a good day out without wounds and bruises to show for it was not considered manly. Ogunmọla put a stop to all that because thereby the innocent often suffered at the hands of brute strength.

To prevent fire accidents those whose occupation demands large fires like brewers and those who cook ẹkọ or yam for sale were ordered to do so during the dry season in open spaces, preferably near wells or streams, and not under a shed, much less under a roof. The master of the compound was made answerable for every case of fire. In order not to escape justice the rough and ready method pursued was to seize some of the members of the house and the head of the house would be compelled to effect their redemption. When everyone in the compound is liable to suffer, every one will be concerned to see that no mischief arises from carelessness.

Warriors are honoured by him far more than farmers or traders. If, for instance, a warrior's wife is outraged by a farmer or a trader (which was considered one of the most serious offences) he usually imposed the heaviest fines, i.e. a dog, a goat, and 10 bags of cowries which in those days was equivalent to £10. But if the case was vice versa the fine is lighter, perhaps only 5 heads of cowries (one-twentieth of the above) and a goat ; but he was usually reminded that the rest of the fine would have to be paid with interest on the battlefield ; i.e. by showing courage and bravery. He was loved and trusted as a leader because he knew how to appreciate and reward valour. As an instance of this the following story may be told :—During the year 1866, one Samuel Peeler, alias Biorán, a Sierra Leone emigrant, who had distinguished himself in many a battlefield was summoned before him by certain hunters and charged with appropriating a deer they had shot, the blood and footprints of which they traced to his farm ; he did not give it up to them, on the contrary when it was demanded he offered them a share ! According to the customary laws of the country that was a serious offence (hunters are a privileged class of men, they are the national foresters, scouts, and bush detectives) and heavy fines were usually imposed on such offenders.

When Biorán was asked what he had to say, he replied, " Kabiyesi " (may your highness live long) " When the Ibadan army was before Ijaye between the years 1860 and 1862 on several occasions when such and such (naming them) important personages fell in the thick of the fight and a deadly struggle ensued with the enemy for the appropriation of the body, when none could do it, it was I Biorán, who went forward, lifted the body on my shoulders, and brought it to the camp. Again before Iperu when certain important chiefs fell it was I Biorán with bullets flying about my ears who went to the midline of battle and rescued the body from the enemy. Now, in walking over my farm 2 days ago, I saw a dead deer in the border of my farm, so I said to myself. If Biorân can shoulder a dead man *between two fires* (lit Àlà ijà) why should he be unable to shoulder a dead animal between two farms (lit Àlà oko) that was why I shouldered it. Kabiyesi."

The Basọrun who remembered the occasions very well laughed outright and exclaimed "Bẹhẹ na ni wayi Biorán, bẹhẹ ni tirẹ ri " (and exactly so it was old Biorán, and that is just like you). The skilful way in which he touched the Basọrun's sensitive parts and his witty play on the words " Àlá ijà àlà oko," between two fires, between two farms, amused the whole court, and there before the assembly the Basọrun praised and honoured him for his valour, and calling for a head of cowries and a bottle of gin (instead of fining him), he said, "Take these Biorán, you can go home and enjoy your venison and wash it down with this bottle of gin. I see no reason why a valiant man should not enjoy a bit of venison." Turning round to the hunters he said " That is not the sort of man to be fined, he is a valiant man." He then satisfied the hunters with some presents to console them and dismissed the case.

Ogunmọla had only two sons Ọsun and Ilọri and one daughter Ọmọsa. He kept a large harem ; his wives could be numbered by hundreds and having but three children by all these, the Ijayes during the war often taunted him in their songs :—

" Ogunmọla kò bi'mọ (Ogunmọla without children
Ọmọ Ibadan li o warun." Ibadan lads he would destroy.)

but he left several grandchildren to mourn his loss.

Ibadan lost in him a wise and just Administrator, and a veteran leader and successful soldier. He was a liberal minded man, who, instead of crushing delighted in lifting up the hands of a weaker comrade. For example, Ọsundina the Osi, his junior colleague was a powerful warrior but a poorer man than either himself or the Balogun. Thus in one of their expeditions one of his tributary towns gave up more than 200 refugees to him. As these were not captives of war, but refugees (termed Ẹyọ́) they should be distributed among the senior chiefs ; but Ogunmọla suggested to the Balogun that they should let Ọsundina keep all in order to increase his means of keeping up his position with credit ; the

Balogun accordingly agreed. Ogunmọla would never address him by name or title, always " Ekeji mi " my comrade.

§ 4. Ogedemgbe and the Fall of Ilesa

Ogedemgbe a young Ijẹṣa warrior as we have noticed under §2 was one of those restless spirits of Ilẹṣa who came to domicile at Ibadan, where they could find for their energies the scope which was denied them at home.   He was placed under Bada Aki ikọ o a distinguished warrior, under whom he learnt the art of war. When the Ijẹṣas rebelled against Ibadan, he was one of those who returned home to rejoin his compatriots to lay siege against Igbajọ.   When they were defeated he was caught and brought back to Ibadan and handed over to Ogunmọla.

The fact of his having been at Ibadan before and then joined the rebels against the country of his adoption rendered his crime to be regarded as treason for which he should suffer the extreme penalty.   He was ordered by Ogunmọla to be executed. He was being led to the altar of Ogun (the god of war) for execution when his old colleagues Ayibiọwu, Ọmọle, and Ọdọ ran to the Baṣọrun to plead for his life ; they went through Latòsisa then the head of Ogunmọla's war boys and a favourite at court.   Had Latòsisa delayed a minute he would have been too late: the Baṣọrun granted his release, but to mark the gravity of his crime he disfigured his face with the À Bunu marks which he carried to his grave as a lesson for the future, and handed him over to Ayibiọwu[1].

After this was done, Ogunmọla as his custom was to divine daily with his Ifa, was told by the priest that the young man so disfigured was destined to become a great man hereafter, and that he would cause the Ibadans any amount of trouble.   Immediately His Highness ordered a propitiation to be made on the spot where the blood from his face was spilt ; and this was done accordingly. He was the man destined by Providence to be the deliverer of his country from bondage as we shall see hereafter.

A short time after this, Ogedemgbe escaped back to Ilesa, and other young men also who had escaped at the defeat at Igbajọ to Odo, Iperindo, and other places returned home one by one. Ogedemgbe now headed a conspiracy against the Ọdọle who had warned them against the siege of Igbajọ, and who by his repressive

---

[1]This act of deliverance Ogedemgbe never forgot until the day of his death.   Many Ibadan young men in after years that fell into his hands he spared and was often heard to say " They did not kill me when they might have done so, we must spare them ! "

measures caused many young men to flee from the city of Ileṣa. A civil war ensued ; for seven days the Odọle kept them at bay, but at last, overpowered by numbers, he was shut up in his house for three days, and when his boys grew weary and disheartened and began to disappear, the Odọle fell by his own hands.

Immediately the news of the death of the Baṣọrun of Ibadan reached them, Ileṣa again rebelled openly against Ibadan and war was declared against them.

Balogun Akere was now the senior chief after the death of the Baṣọrun, but he declined to assume the Baleship till after their return from the Ileṣa war. It was alleged by some that the Baṣọrun before his death left a charge that Ileṣa should not be spared. Whether it was so or not, yet the Ibadan chiefs were not all unanimous about this expedition, not from any love for Ileṣa or fear of its almost impregnable forts, but rather that titles should be re-arranged so that they might have promotions. The Balogun could obtain the assent and co-operation of Obembe alone, the son of the late Balogun Ibikunle ; having secured the confidence of this powerful chief he declared war in spite of the others.

The war-staff was propitiated on the 20th December, 1867 ; it had to be done at night on account of the disaffection among the chiefs. The Balogun left the town on the 22nd of December and as in duty bound, the rest of the chiefs joined him on the 23rd. They marched straight via Oshogbo and encamped first at Ilaṣè and marched thence to Ibala. Here the Ijẹṣas began to oppose their advance, and the first battle fought.

Hitherto the war chiefs followed the Balogun just mechanically but would not fight for him ; but with the help of Obembe he felt he could dispense with their services and so he took no notice of them. But now a formal measure was adopted to put an end to the disaffection, the matter was talked over, the Balogun pacified them with large presents, and being satisfied they fought with a will, and dislodged the Ijẹṣas from Ibala, forcing them to fall back on Afara Jegede. This was a trench about 30 or 40 feet deep with drawbridges, carried almost round Ileṣa. Here the Ijẹṣas made a long stand, but it was taken at last and the camp was removed forwards.

There was another entrenchment with foᵣts beyond a stream which the Ibadans named Fẹjẹboju (washing the face with blood), so named from the bloody battles fought there which caused the stream to flow with blood constantly from the wounded and the dying. In an attempt to take this second entrenchment an ambuscade headed by Ayibiowu went to the Oke Esa road, but they were discovered and waylaid : they were dispersed and

Ayibiowu their leader was taken alive by his countrymen, and butchered to pieces.

The Ibadans were over a year in this place fighting but could not take it, and without that there was no hope of taking Ilesa. Notwithstanding this the Ijesas considered it prudent to surrender, as sooner or later Ilesa would surely be taken; hence they began to negotiate for peace. There was an armistice; during the negotiation, they brought over 400 bags of cowries into the Ibadan camp as submission money, but the chiefs feared to touch the gift, for it might have been poisoned ! But Ogboriefon who about this time began to make a name being a poor man, was willing to take all. " Let me die if poisoned," said he, " I do not mind." With this he entertained the fighting men, and made fresh preparations for the conflict. At this crisis Akere the commander-in-chief died. A council of war was held to consider the decision to be made under present circumstances. It was resolved to continue the war " lest the Ijesas would say we agreed to peace because we had lost our leader." So the next day they forestalled the Ijesas by telling them that they had killed their Balogun because he was inclined to peace, the armistice therefore was now at an end. A terrible battle ensued that day, they fought till sunset. This was done chiefly to inspire courage into those that might be faint-hearted amongst themselves and lose courage on account of the death of the Balogun. This battle was fought on February 15th, 1869.

The command of the army now devolved upon Orowùsi the Asipa. Orowùsi was a powerful chief but very unpopular. He was disliked by all the senior war-chiefs of the day, he had no influence even with the men; however, by virtue of his office as senior chief all agreed to submit to him.

What was denied him, however, was accorded to his eldest son Akeredolu. This young man had several friends among his companions, several left their masters and made him their captain, and at last the honour was his to capture this entrenchment which had baffled the whole army for over a year. The trench which continued as far as they could extend their lines to the right as well as to the left, they thought was carried right round the town but it was disclosed to Akeredolu that it terminated at the foot of a mighty rock several miles distant and that the terminus was concealed by a dense forest. Excepting on the day of battle very few men were generally left to guard the entrenchment and the fort which was considered impregnable, the majority being left at home for rest and enjoyment.

Akeredolu kept the secret to himself, he told not even his father. One afternoon he and his companions put on their arms, and it was reported to his father that he was going to the battlefield. Not being the day of battle the father was alarmed that he was going single-handed to attempt what had baffled the whole army for more than one year ! He sent peremptory messages to call him back, failing in that, he sent a pathetic remonstrance "Come back, oh, come back, for so was I bereaved of your elder brother at the Iperu war, when he was attempting a feat of valour." Akeredolu heeded nothing, but went off in another direction. When out of sight of camp he dismounted and carried a gun on his shoulder like the rest of his companions, and was led to the foot of the rock where the trench terminated. They climbed it to the other side and made for the battlefield, nothing preventing them.

The Ibadan chief being anxious about his son and not knowing his whereabouts, armed himself and went out to the battlefield, the whole army, of course, following him. Then all of a sudden Akeredolu and his companions appeared on the other side of the moat, fell upon the small guard left there and dispersed them ; the drawbridges were thrown over to admit his father with the whole Ibadan army, the walls of the fort were quickly beaten down. In a few minutes the trench was filled up to a considerable distance, every one throwing in something, and with hoe and digger it was soon levelled up enough for a passage for the whole army. Thus Akeredolu won for his father and for himself a great reputation. The Ibadans were now able to remove to a third encampment by the walls of Ileṣa.

Before Ileṣa was taken two other chiefs signalized themselves, viz. Latosisa the Otun Seriki and Ajayi Ogboriẹfọn. The latter rose into prominence by heading a band of young men for exploits, as most of the Ibadan chiefs did. He was always poor, because he spent lavishly, but he was a brave leader and smooth tongued, knowing well how to encourage soldiers and inspire courage into the faint-hearted. Thus in the thick of the fight with men falling right and left, he used to produce beans from his satchel showing them to the men saying, "See, this is what they are firing now, they have no bullets, come let us get at them." Then he used to remind them of home and all its pleasures, telling them that it is the bravest that will be honoured, who can break the laws with impunity. "Remember the bazaars, the Iba market, what pleasures you often enjoy there, pleasures bordering on crime. Now is the time to atone for them if you will enjoy yourself again with impunity." With such words he often spurred them on to the fight.

The Ibadans now discovered that the Ijeṣas were well supplied with food and ammunition from Òdò, and it was evident that unless this road was taken there was little hope of taking the town. The arduous task of doing this devolved upon these two war-chiefs Latosisa and Ajayi Ogboriẹfọn.   This road being the life of Ilẹṣa was heroically defended by two armies.   A more desperate battle was never fought in this campaign than what took place here. Latosisa opposed the Ijẹṣa army from the country, and Ogboriẹfọn that from the city.

An Ijẹṣa eye-witness reported that in the first day's fight a heap of 140 corpses was made, the corpses not being allowed to be removed home or lie about for fear of causing a panic! The wounded were more in number, and these on the side of the Ijẹṣas from the city alone.   For five days the contest continued, fighting went on day and night till in the end the road was taken and the Ibadans under Latosisa and Ogboriẹfọn made an encampment there.   Ajọbọ the Seriki encamped in the Oke Ẹsa road, and the body of the army with the head war-chief at Ita Ogbogi in the main road.   The walls of Ilẹṣa were very thick, high and slippery, the moat very deep, and as long as Ogedemgbe was there to defend it, there was no telling how long the town could hold out. But the end was inevitable.

Added to the distress in the city were the ravages of the band of ruffians called Ipaiyẹ.   These were Ogedemgbe's war boys organized like the Jamâs of the days of Afọnja.   They would enter houses and help themselves to food and whatever they could lay hands upon.

When the Òdò road was taken and food supplies cut off, people died of starvation in the streets by hundreds ; the ravages of the Ipaiyẹs became more intolerable.   Whole families left the town and entered the Ibadan camp giving themselves up as slaves in order to save their lives.   Ajọbọ the Seriki was largely benefited by these, for hearing of his unparalleled liberality, they entered the Ibadan camp and named him as the chief they gave themselves up to, and were conducted to his tent.

Ogedemgbe at length sent word to Ogboriẹfọn to grant him an interview.   This interview took place on the battlefield, the two generals leaving their armies in the rear met at the centre of the battlefield.

At the second interview they made a covenant of friendship and Ajayi promised to allow him a safe retreat.   The fate of Ilẹṣa being now a foregone conclusion, in order to prevent further unnecessary loss of lives by the sword and by famine, they arranged that the Ibadan army should make a way for Ogedemgbe and his followers to go in peace leaving the town a prey to the besiegers.

On the appointed day Ogedemgbe brought valuable presents in beads and cloths to Ajayi, and the covenant was ratified.

Early in the morning of the 4th of June, 1870, Ogedemgbe with his Ipaiyẹs left Ilesạ and threw the gates open. According to arrangement the Ibadans opened their ranks for them to pass, and closed them against stragglers, and then the town was taken.

The Ọwa came into the camp. The Ibadan chief gave him 10 of his wives and as many of his children as could be found, also 10 bags of cowries and a basket of kola nuts. They then left him in charge of the king of Ibokun (a neighbouring Ijẹsạ tributary town) to be reinstated when the fugitives and all who escaped capture could have returned to their desolate homes.

The Ibadans pursuing their conquest as far as Òdò and Iperindo, both places were taken. The army now divided into two parts, one part went against Igángán, the other to Ipetu ; the former made a long resistance but was at length taken.

The Ibadan army returned home in triumph on the 10th of July 1870.

All the war-chiefs in procession escorted home the coffined bones of the late Balogun Akere. Before this coffin when fixed in state the leading chief prostrated and in a formal way told the result of the war as to the living Balogun, and then wept over his remains lamenting his loss !

The whole of them now accompanied Orowùsi home, thereby acknowledging him their head, then they dispersed to their homes.

Ogedemgbe whose opening career we have now related disappeared from view for a time. We shall hear of him again.

CHAPTER XXI.

TWO ADMINISTRATIONS OF OPPOSITE POLICIES

§ 1. Orowùsi's Administration

IBADAN was the one place that loomed largely in people's eyes at this period (1870). To have taken Ilesa was regarded as a feat of extraordinary magnitude it being a town of great strength, both in its fortifications and in its able-bodied citizens ; and consequently the eyes of all surrounding tribes were fixed on the town situated on the hills.

The first duty of the Ibadans now was to fill up the vacancies among the ruling chiefs and to settle home affairs.

They had only been at home for less than two months when on the 1st of September the town had to lament the death of Osun, the first-born son of Ogunmola the late Basorun. It was a great loss to the community, as the late Basorun had only two sons and a daughter. The town went into mourning for a month, and then arrangements were made to confer the title of Bale on Orowùsi. On the 30th September Agbarò the Ilari sent by the ALâFIN for the purpose conferred the title on him in the presence of all the chiefs and a large assemblage of people.

On the 5th day after, the Bale began to confer the principal titles by batches ; the most important of which we need mention are :—Ajobo who became the Balogun, Latosisà the Otun, Ajayi Ogboriefon the Osi, Ali Laluwoye the Asipa, Lawoyin the Seriki, Ojo Oroñna the Otun Seriki, Tajo the Otun Bale.

All these men played some important part more or less in the history of the country. By the end of October the affairs of the town had been settled.

On the 5th of November the old Chief Mele was again despatched to Ijebu to negotiate for an Agurin (consul) in order that peace and amity might once more be established between them. The last Agurin was recalled when Ijebu declared war against Ibadan during the Ijaye war. Now peace and tranquility reigned over all the land.

This Bale encouraged agriculture himself setting the example. Under such peaceful rule the Christians of Ibadan numbering about 400 with their teachers thought it right to do honour to the Bale, who was well disposed to Christianity. They went in a body with the school children to his house, and he came out to receive them in

the square in front of the house and a short service was held
including the prayers for the King and all rulers. The Bale was
immensely pleased and the Christian body enjoyed a pleasant day.

Civil commotion.—The next trouble started where the last
ended. The Qwa of Ilesa being dead, it devolved upon Ibadan
as the Suzerain power to appoint another Qwa. There were,
however, two claimants, each with his rival party, and both parties
were seeking for help among the Ibadan chiefs to promote their
cause.

Prince Odigbadigba, backed by Ogedemgbe, sent about 50
slaves and a quantity of beads to Balogun Ajobo to promote his
cause. Ajobo instead of bringing the matter before the council,
with whatever backing he could bestow on his client, appropriated
all the presents and gave orders that Odigbadigba be crowned.

When the Ibadan chiefs came to know about all this they were
fired with rage and ordeied both claimants to Ibadan. In the
meantime Ogedemgbe's nominee had been crowned at Ilesa, but
on their arrival he was set aside as being irregularly crowned, and
the rival was crowned at Ibadan on the 22nd of May, 1871, and
sent home in state. Prince Odigbadigba was detained at Ibadan,
and lodged with Ogundepo the Bale's brother.

This action of Balogun Ajobo hurt not only the Bale whose rights
he had often usurped, but also his brother chiefs, especially
his principal lieutenants Latosisà and Ajayi, on whom fell the
brunt of the task of taking Ilesa at the final stage.

Ajobo's popularity lay in his largess to the people, which
gained him fame at home and abroad. and secured for him a large
following among whom were some brave men that could not be
overlooked; this popularity turned his head, leading him to act
as he did. As a leader he was much lacking in courage and ability
as the fiasco at Osiele showed, and therefore he carried no weight
or respect among the body of the people. He arrived at his post
more by order of seniority than by merit and by the large number
of men behind him which must be taken into account. But for such
a grave political blunder his deposition was resolved upon.

Chief Ogedemgbe was very anxious about the safety of Prince
Odigbadigba hence he was sending some slaves and presents to
the Ibadan chiefs to effect his release. On this being known, the
Ibadan chiefs sent to intercept the messengers out of spite to the
Balogun to whom they were sent direct.

On the 23rd of June, the war-staff was demanded from him,
—a sign that he was deprived of his title: there was consequently
a great commotion in the town, the people apprehending a civil
war, but Ajobo had not the courage to attempt one; on the

contrary he spent largely to purchase his pardon. This pardon was granted on the 29th and all was quiet again, and he attended the weekly town council as before.

But the disaffection against him among some of the chiefs was as great as ever, and the desire to encompass his fall very strong, especially with Ajayi the Osi, and Lawọyin the Seriki, who were under great obligation to him for the means of attaining their present position. To them his fall would mean one lift upwards in their titles, and an obliteration of their feeling of obligation to him, the shame and remorse of conscience for their ingratitude to him in his distress, being intolerable when he was pardoned. Consequently there was another explosion engineered by these two chiefs ; he was deprived of all his tributary towns, was forbidden to attend Council, and was rejected by the chiefs in council.

Ajọbọ now resolved to die, and ordered his coffin to be made and the grave to be dug. On the evening of the 5th of July, he returned the war-staff to the Balẹ. But early on the 6th when everybody was expecting to hear of Ajọbọ's death, and his lying in state, he escaped from the town ; passing by the C.M.S. station at Kudẹti he took a by-path by which he regained the main road to Ijẹbu and escaped to the town of Ipara in the Rẹmọ district. Some of his ill-wishers actually gave chase when the news of his escape was heard but failed to overtake him.

Now his principal opponents Latosisa and Ajayi Ogboriẹfọn came to congratulate the Balẹ on having got rid of the Balogun. But the Balẹ's reception of the news disappointed their expectations. The Balẹ's wish was that his pride be humbled for such a gross public offence, but that he be finally pardoned. With surprise and alarm he asked " Gone away? Who drove him away ? What message did you send him which obliged him to leave the town? " Latosisa and Ajayi replied "Who drove him away but yourself?   Did you not send a messenger to us to say we should accept no terms of reconciliation ? " " What " replied the Balẹ " What is the name of the messenger I sent ? " In great anger the Balẹ retired within and shut the door against them leaving them where they prostrated before him.

He saw at once through the scheming of the war-chiefs who would get rid of a chicken-hearted Balogun ; but he the Balẹ had no need of a fire-eater for one, and hence he apprehended trouble from these younger war-chiefs.

That was the last time the Balẹ was seen in public, he never showed his face after this till his corpse was exposed in state before interment. The rumour of the Balẹ's death began on the 15th of August, but there was no public announcement. On the 19th

Prince Odigbadigba, who was the cause of all these troubles was sent away to his country, but private orders were given to his escorts, that as soon as they were a good way off from the town he should be murdered.　On the 30th of August, Ijẹbu ambassadors arrived at Ibadan to plead for the restoration of Ajọbọ, but they were sent away with a negative reply.　On the evening of the 19th September it was publicly announced that Orowùsi the Balẹ was dead.　The expulsion of Ajọbọ being the cause of his death his people went that same evening and set Ajọbọ's house on fire.

Ibadan was once more without a head.　Tãjo the oldest among the war-chiefs declined the honour.　When the other chiefs were going to assemble in his house, as the Qtun Balẹ, he met them at the central market and there declined the offer.　No elderly chief agreed to accept the title from the unsettled state of the town due mainly to Latosisa and Ajayi.　For some time their meetings were held in the central market till at last Latosisa agreed to undertake the responsibility though not as a Balẹ but as a Kakanfo. He alleged that he was a Moslem and none of his creed had been Balẹ before, but Ojo Amepo who was a Moslem was a Kakanfo and he took his precedent from him.

The Ibadan chiefs did not like the idea, and the ALÂFIN of ỌYỌ was reluctant to grant it knowing the national troubles usually caused by strong Kakanfos, but in the end Latosisa won all parties over and obtained the title.

The Late Balẹ Orowùsi.—The late Balẹ was a native of Ogbágbá a town about 6 miles from Iwo.　He was originally an elephant hunter hence his name Orowùsi, super-deadly poison (from his poisoned arrows in hunting big game).　He rose into power by his own merits, but he was unpopular among the other war-chiefs who were his seniors in the days of Ibikunle and Ogunmọla.　Notwithstanding instances of slights and indignities he endured in the earlier days, he lived to be the head of the town of Ibadan.　His rule was short but was marked by a wise administration and by peace with the surrounding tribes.

He was a far-seeing man, of sound judgment and strong determination.　He once summoned a meeting of the chiefs and after addressing them on matters political and inter-tribal, he laid down the following advice which he wished them to treasure up and act upon for the present and future.

" 1. That on no account should Ibadan wage any aggressive warfare with any of their principal neighbours the Ẹgbas, Ijebus and Ilọrins.

2. That high and responsible positions should not be given to the Mọgajis (heirs to large estates) because of the men and means at

their command, on account of their inexperience, but rather to older men who were the companions of their fathers for the country will be the gainer by their experience.

3. That they should rely more on the children of the soil than on their slaves, as it has now become the fashion to make of their slaves high stewards and confidants ; for how can these who are slaves after all seek the permanent interests of the country that enslaved them and made their own country desolate ? The seed of bitterness towards ' Oyos ' must have sunk deep in their hearts. Their women also should not be made their principal or choice wives.

4. Never should the slaves be entrusted with messages of importance to the interior, for having nothing to lose, their conduct will not be marked by moderation or discretion."

These words were well received by the assembly and he set the example by refusing to grant the title of Seriki to Iyapo the son of the late Balogun Ibikunle, although for wealth, power, and the highest war-like qualities he was unsurpassed by none at Ibadan, but his youth was against him. Hence the title was given to Lawoyin an old and experienced veteran who had seen many wars.

How these precepts were reversed by the succeeding administration and with what consequences to the country we shall see hereafter.

§ 2. Ibadan Under a Kakanfo

Latosisa usurped the title of Kakanfo by might over right, by displacing Ojo Aburumaku the Kakanfo at Ogbomoso, as Ogunmola attempted to do in the case of Gbenla the aged Basorun of Oyo. He sent to Ojo for all the insignia of the office, which he was obliged to resign to him, and on the 3rd of October, 1871, he was publicly installed. On the 9th he gave titles to his chiefs the most principal of which were to Ajayi Ogboriefon, Balogun the title he intrigued so much for, and to Ali Laluwoye the Otun. They were barely a year at home when the Ilesa complications cropped up again, but this time they appeared as defenders of that city.

We have seen in the preceding section that Odigbadigba was the man Ogedemgbe desired to be crowned as Owa, so when he heard that Odigbadigba was murdered at Ibadan he came with an army from his place of exile, captured Ilesa and drove away the Owa placed there by the Ibadans. Thus Ilesa was destroyed a second time within a short period. Ogedemgbe remained at Ilesa in defiance of Ibadan.

The Ogedemgbe Campaign.—The Ibadans accepted the

challenge by espousing the cause of the expelled Qwa. The standard of war was propitiated on the 28th of December, 1872, and on the 30th Ajayi Ogboriẹfọn as commander-in-chief marched out. His orders were simply to capture or drive away Ogedemgbe and restore the Qwa.

But Ogedemgbe would not risk another war with the Ibadans so shortly within the walls of Ileṣa, so he left the town at the approach of the Ibadan army.

These encamped near the walls of Ijẹbu Ẹrẹ, and although their orders did not include seizures at Ilesa, yet, as individuals among them entered the city with the intention of buying provisions one and another among them seeing their run-away slaves of the previous campaign, seized them, others following their examples seized under false pretences, and in order not to go away empty handed, seizures became general, and so Ileṣa was taken again as the people were just settling down.

The Arẹ of Ibadan on hearing this was much displeased with the Balogun, and, although he pleaded his innocence in the matter, yet the fact remained a stigma on his character. He was sent to relieve Ileṣa not to plunder it.

Passing from Ileṣa in pursuit of Ogedemgbe, Òdò was again taken. The commander-in-chief being somewhat in a state of destitution before he left home, did not abide by his orders, but was only intent upon slave catching and was always ready with excuses. Ogedemgbe was pursued from place to place until he lured them to a great forest called Igbo Alawun east of Ikẹrẹ where he made a stand. Ogedemgbe encamped at Ita Ogbolu and the Ibadans at Qgotun with the forest between them ; there they fought several battles. Ogedemgbe inflicting disasters upon them checked the restless ambitions of the Ibadans.

If the Ijẹsa and Ẹfọn towns in the rear had had the courage to rebel, the Ibadans would have been cut off to a man.

The third battle fought here was simply disastrous to the Ibadans. Ogedemgbe and his allies lay in ambush while a small body of men was sent forward to draw the Ibadans ; this was soon defeated and in the pursuit the flower of the Ibadan army was hemmed in and cut off from the main body at the base. Most of the young Mọgajis were there such as Akeredolu heir of the late Balẹ Orowùsi, Aderibigbe, heir of the late Balẹ Olugbode, also the Aṣaju with all the Badas, the Seriki with his Qtun and Osi Seriki. These last sat on the very spot the ambuscade was laid their men all scattered in the pursuit for slave catching when all of a sudden the Ijẹsas opened fire upon them ! The Seriki was shot off his horse, seriously wounded, his Otun and Osi were killed on the spot and their heads taken off (the Osi Seriki alone had 2,000 followers in this campaign not one of them being with him when this disaster occurred) When the pursuers knew that they were hemmed in, they began to fight their way back, and the pursued now became the pursuers. It was " save himself who can " with the Ibadans, the chiefs had only with them their bodyguards who must always be by their sides in weal or woe.

It was now that Balogun Ajayi began to redeem his honour. He was a man for any emergency. Unrespected hitherto because he was inferior in men and means to any of the Mọgajis, but for presence of mind, courage and resources, he was unequalled by any. He came up at once with the reserve forces, bore down on the Ijẹṣas, and in one tremendous charge he dispersed them and in that way he saved those who had been cut off. The news of this disaster was received with great mourning at Ibadan.

To military skill, Ogedemgbe now added state craftiness ; he sent large presents to the Arẹ at home and tendered his submission. The Arẹ sent one messenger after another to recall the Balogun, but from shame the Balogun would not return till the third messenger reached him. A great deal is attached to a Balogun's first expedition, and to go home empty handed with nothing but tales of disaster was enough to make him afraid of falling into disrepute, especially as there were murmurings against him already among the war boys.

He turned his steps homeward with a heavy heart. He spent a few days at Ikẹrẹ. It was in his mind to surprise the town and capture it, but when it was privately intimated to him that they would be hemmed in, he left quite unexpectedly.

The army arrived home on the 1st September, 1873.

The Arẹ reprimanded the Balogun sharply for disobeying orders, and he wept in the public meeting like a little child. He would have been deposed from his high office, but the Arẹ knew his worth as a soldier, and that his misfortune lay in not having the wherewithal to command respect and that for that reason he was bent at all hazards on risking everything in order to secure the necessary means.

The war-chiefs now began to disrespect their commander-in-chief but conscious of his own capabilities he took no notice of slights and insults knowing that occasions will arise when he was sure to command their respect. In order to quiet the restlessness and general dissatisfaction the Arẹ promised to lead the next expedition in person when they would have an opportunity of retrieving their losses.

The Arẹ however, deposed the Seriki Lawọyin alleging that he was too unlucky as a general to lose his two principal lieutenants in his very first campaign. But the underlying reason was that the principal chiefs felt he was a disgrace to them for the glaringly base ingratitude he displayed towards the deposed Ajǫbǫ who had helped him to defray the expenses incidental to his taking office by giving him 800 bags of cowries, a horse, a sword, gowns, etc., and this liberality he requited by pursuing the fallen chief with the very horse he had given him !

Lawǫyin submitted calmly, relinquished public life altogether and retired to his farm.

The title was given to Iyapǫ the Mǫgaji of the late Balogun Ibikunle who commanded all his late father's resources, and for men and means was unapproached by any of the other chiefs in the town. And Akeredolu son of the late Balę Orowùsi the Ǫtun Seriki. Thus the Arę began to reverse the policy of the late Balę Orowùsi in the advice not to exalt inexperienced young men over elderly men of ripe judgment although comparatively poor. His idea was that these young men should be advanced to responsible position in order that they might use the means at their command for the public benefit which they would otherwise not do. Subsequent events will prove which of these two policies was the right one.

§ 3. An Unprovoked War.—Ado

The Ibadans were not long at home before they found another pretext for marching out. for slave raiding. The Ifęs, seeking an occasion against Modakękę, but mindful of the past were afraid to attack them direct, and secretly invited the Arę and gave up the town to him. So the Ibadan army left home again, under the Arę, on the 8th December, 1873.

He rendezvoused between Ile Igbo and Kuta, villages of Iwǫ, and was just preparing to cross the Ǫsun river and march against Modakękę when the Ifęs thought better of their offer and regretted their rashness. They now prayed the Arę to leave Modakękę alone ; for it occurred to them that there was no wall separating the two towns, and what would prevent the wild soldiery of Ibadan from rushing from one to the other ? They would just be bringing disaster on their own heads.

So the Arę desisted. The Ibadan army then marched to the Ekiti country with no express object in view. The Arę now remembered that he had lost a brother in the Agbado war, when they were waylaid by the Balogun of Ado ! He now made up his mind to destroy the Ado country.

The Ados met them at Iyin a frontier town of theirs, and were routed in a single pitched battle on or about the 16th of January 1874. They could not rally, so the Ibadans made an easy conquest of the whole district. Men, women, and children were captured without the slightest attempt at resistance. So many were the captives and so much the booty, that the campaign appeared more like a promenade.

The king of Ado entered the Ibadan camp in full regal attire attended by a few followers who had nearly all stolen behind him ere he could get to the Arẹ's tent.

The Arẹ received him with every mark of honour and respect; he now remembered that his second wife was a native of Ado and so he would do honour to her king. He obtained for him 41 of his wives, 21 of his children, 30 of his chiefs, and bought him a horse and caparison for 3 slaves, and re-instated him. The Ibadan army arrived behind their town wall on the 21st February and entered in a triumphant procession on the 22nd.

The conquest of Ado was so easy that not a chief was missing, but Akeredolu, the Ọtun Seriki, who signalized himself in the Ilẹṣa and Ogedemgbe wars was taken ill, and remained two months at Ila but growing worse was brought home to die on the 5th April, 1874. His brother Ajayi Oṣungbẹkun succeeded him both as head of their father's house, and in his office of Ọtun Seriki.

§ 4. THE ARE'S ADMINISTRATION

Latosisa the Arẹ-ọna-kakanfo at the commencement of his administration ruled with great clemency, but after this successful expedition be began to show himself *a Kakanfo* with all the characteristics of a Kakanfo—obstinacy, recklessness, blood thirstiness.

The Arẹ's first act after his return from Ado was directed against Ẹfūṣetan the Iyalode or Ladies' Queen. The charges against her were :—1. That she did not accompany him to the war. 2. That she never sent him supplies during the campaign. 3. That she did not come in person to meet him outside the town wall to congratulate him on his safe return.

He was, therefore, resolved to depose her and this was done on the 1st of May, 1874, and Iya Ọla her Ọtun (first lieutenant) was promoted to the office.

Iya Ọla was very reluctant to accept the office, but the Arẹ sent a peremptory message to her to say, if she refused, she was to take a single cloth and a head tie, and leave the town immediately. She was obliged to accept the title. We may mention in passing that Ẹfūṣetan herself took the title from her chief a former Iyalode, who, from adverse circumstances lost her wealth, whilst fortune smiled on Efúṣetan. She lived to see Efúṣetan deprived both of the title and of her life.

When men or women of high rank and great social position are deposed, it means that their death is determined upon ; but if they have fallen into poverty and insignificance and so have lost influence before deposition, their death is not insisted upon.

In order to save her life, Efúṣetan with lavish gifts sought the aid and interposition of all the influential chiefs, paid the fines imposed upon her, but all to no purpose.

It must be remarked that many of the chiefs were against this treatment of the Iyalode, but the Arẹ at this time was haughty and unapproachable. She was summoned to the meeting of the Town Council on the 22nd of June and was publicly disgraced, after which she was told that she was pardoned ; but when a few days after the voice of the Agán was heard in the night (i.e. the Egúgun that executes women) it was known that her death was resolved upon.

But the Iyalode could not be openly attacked. It has been made one of the constitutional laws of the town that there was to be no civil war, that if any chief ventured on one, whether his case be right or wrong the whole town was to rise against him and crush him. All that could now be done was to effect her death by some means or other, either by poison, or by direct violence when unguarded.

Kumuyilọ the Iyalode's adopted son and her relatives were heavily bribed by the Arẹ and his abettors, to murder her in cold blood ! The Iyalode spent miserable days and nights suspicious of every sound and movement. She changed her sleeping place from night to night as she could not trust any of her domestics. She prepared her food herself, could not go out of doors, received no visitors, as she did not know from what quarter the fatal blow would fall. At length on the night of June 30th, 1874 knowing where she slept, two slaves instructed by Kumuyilọ entered the room from the ceiling and dashed out her brains. The next morning, when her death was reported, she was accorded a public funeral befitting her rank and having no son of her own the Arẹ installed Kumuyilọ her adopted son as head of the house.

The late Madam Efúṣetan was an Egba by birth but made Ibadan her home, where she grew to be very rich. The Egbas hearing of her death sent to ask the cause of it. This made the Ibadan chiefs, who were against the cruel deed, declare their innocence leaving the onus of it upon the Arẹ. To show their displeasure in the matter they demanded of the Arẹ at the public

meeting to prove his innocence by producing the murderers.   He
tried by one way or another to evade the question : they rejected
his excuses, the meeting became stormy and they adjourned in a
rage.   The Arȩ was ill at ease, fearing a general sedition against
himself; hence he summoned a meeting daily to settle this matter,
and to have a reply for the Ȩgba messengers.

On the 8th of July the town was in a feverish excitement, for
the chiefs demanded that Kumuyilǫ be summoned to the meeting.

Kumuyilǫ although the son of a notable citizen was brought
to the meeting bound with cords, and compelled to name his
accomplices.   He named the Oluwo, the Balogun, and the Sȩbaloju.
This last was the Arȩ's spokesman at public meetings.   Of course,
all present knew that he meant this for the Arȩ himself whom he
was afraid to name.   Consequently it became clear that the first two
chiefs of the town, the Arȩ and the Balogun, were the doers of the
deed, and if due justice were to be done, it was they who should
atone for the crime with their lives ; but such a course would mean
the destruction of the town.   The rest of the chiefs, finding that
Kumuyilǫ only carried out the orders of the rulers had not the
conscience to order him to execution or rather to clamour for
his life, they were content therefore to have him publicly
disgraced, ordered out of the great lady's house to his own humble
dwelling, and appointed a distant relative as head of the house.

In this way the chiefs signified their displeasure at the action
of their leaders, and these, conscious of guilt, could not oppose the
verdict,

But as life must go for life, they further demanded the actual
perpetrators of the deed to be produced.   On the 10th of July,
1874 these two slaves were brought to the public meeting and the
writer who saw them prostrating there before the chiefs saw them
a few minutes later impaled at the Baṣǫrun market.   Thus ended
the matter.

The Late Madam Ȩfuṣetan as we have said was an Ȩgba by
birth- but made her home at Ibadan.   [There were several Ȩgbas
of note residing at Ibadan at this time, Chief Lisibade being the
head of them and Lânisà an Ȩgba was the Balogun of Lawǫyin
the Seriki].   She was very rich owning some 2,000 slaves in her
farms alone exclusive of those at home.   She had also her own
captains of war and warboys.   She had an only daughter who died
in childbirth in 1860 and since that sad event took place she
became strangely cruel to all her female slaves found in an interesting condition, using all cruel means to cause forcible abortion, most
of which ended in death.   And these things were known to the chiefs.
Her property at her death was regarded as belonging to the state.

Ọmọkọ a distant relative was placed over the estate as the responsible man but her sister was the chief manager.

§ 5. THE ẸMURẸ WAR.

Chief Ogedemgbe being driven out' of Ileṣa gathered around himself a band of marauders infesting the Ẹfọn district. He also made himself obnoxious to the Ibadans by attacking their tributary towns being bent upon harassing them in every way possible. For that 'purpose he encamped against Isẹ an Ibadan tributary town, and it had to apply to Ibadan for help. On the 7th of December, 1874, the Arẹ sent two of his powerful generals Iyapọ the Seriki and Ilọri the Osi to relieve Isẹ.

The Arẹ himself knowing the imprudence of such an appointment sent an elderly chief called Olupòyi to go with them as Baba Isàlẹ (chief adviser). The council of war was to be held in his tent, and he had to order the battle. He was their senior in age, but far inferior to the least of Iyapo's or Ilọri's captains.

A wise policy this as these young men refused to submit to each other, although they agreed to submit to this old chief. Iyapọ was the heir of the late Balogun Ibikunle, and was possessed of all his father's men and his means. Moreover a brave Seriki considers himself second to the Balogun alone as he could leap from the one title to the other as his late father did, occupying as he did the same relative position to the young warriors, as the Balogun to the veterans.

Ilọri was the heir of the late Baṣọrun Ogunmọla, he also was possessed of his father's men and his prestige, and considered himself the senior in rank being the general commanding the commander-in-chief's left, and generally taken as senior in rank. What they would not yield to each other they agreed to concede to this old chief out of deference to his age. The wisdom of the advice of Balẹ Orowùsi may be indirectly noticed here also.

But the fame and prestige of Iyapọ far eclipsed that of Ilọri, and he was virtually the leader of the expedition ; where he encamped there all encamped, and when he struck his tent all were bound to be on the move.

Ogedemgbe hearing of their approach-raised the siege of Isẹ and escaped again to his stronghold at Ita Ogbolu. The Ibadan army not willing to return home empty-handed went against Ẹmurẹ which was giving supplies to Ogedemgbe at Isẹ. The town was taken the next day but all the fighting men escaped in a body.

The Seriki became ill after this, and it was with difficulty he could reach Ila the sanatorium of the Ibadans in all their

Ekiti and other wars in those parts : there he remained until
he was well enough to come home.

As it would not be wise for all the army to remain at Ila until
his recovery, they returned home on the 15th of February, 1875.

The Seriki was well enough to leave Ila about six weeks later ;
he arrived outside the town wall of Ibadan on the 28th of March,
and there most of the members of the expedition who had returned
home joined him to grace his triumphal entry the next day.
The joy, the excitement, and the enthusiasm attending the
pageantry of this young man so moved the whole town that the
like of it had scarcely ever been seen.   Whilst it stirred the envy
of some to its very depth, it excited the admiration of others.
Thus a young man was heard to say " If I enjoy such a glory for
only one day and I die the next, I shall be content."

On the 7th of April following died that distinguished veteran
and commander-in-chief Ali a former Balogun of Iwo who was
expelled by a civil fight from Iwo to Ibadan.

CHAPTER XXII

A NEW REIGN AND EVIL PROGNOSTICATIONS

§ 1. The End of Adelu the Alâfin of Oyo and Accession of Adeyemi

King Adelu did not attain to the age of his father. His accession was marked by confusion, wars, and rumours of war all over the country for about four years, due chiefly to the Ijaye war and its sequels; but after this peace and tranquility prevailed, except for the Ibadan raids and the subjugation of the Ijẹṣa and Ekiti provinces.

Towards the end of his reign he met with an accident by being thrown off his horse, and as a consequence a prolonged illness ensued. After his convalescence he had an attack of paralysis which was probably due to internal injury sustained by the fall, but it was generally attributed to poison administered by the Crown Prince, who was impatient to come to the throne ; it was also said that his accomplice and agent was the King's favourite wife Alayọayọ. Among all the denizens of the royal harem she was the only one who could be termed Queen, for she had the whole village of Âwẹ and half the city of Qyọ serving her, and the whole of the King's treasures were at her disposal, so that one could scarcely imagine what could have so alienated her affections as to make her an accessory to such a crime. It was subsequently discovered, however, that the Crown Prince had an illicit intercourse with her, and that she was *enceinte* by him ! It was in order to cover her shame and disgrace, therefore, that she lent herself to the accomplishment of this double crime, and the more readily as the Crown Prince promised her the same position and influence when he came to the throne, as he fully expected he would.

As the King grew worse day by day and had to keep his bed for about a month, the rumour of his death began to gain ground. Thereupon the Qyọ Mesi repaired to the palace and requested to see his majesty even in his sick bed, in order to be assured of his condition. Accordingly, he was bolstered up in one of his apartments, and the curtain was drawn in order that the noblemen might see him and thus he held his reception for the last time. A few days after, the beating of the Koso drum and the blowing of the ivory trumpet at midnight announced to the public the death of their King.

Such an occasion was a time of dire distress in the palace, for apart from those who were bound by their special office to die with the King immolation was more or less indiscriminate in order to furnish the monarch with a large retinue in the other world. Hence every one tried to hide himself or herself in every nook and corner imaginable and in the ceilings of their apartments.

As an instance of the indiscriminate slaughter which occurred on this occasion we may mention the following :—

Kudẹfu the King's favourite Ilari and head of all his slaves on the morning of the death before it was officially announced went to know of his master's condition, and learning he was dead he was going home sad at heart to die of his own accord.

· Alega the keeper of the gate seeing him coming from the inner apartments, being inquisitive, approached him to learn of their august master's condition. Kudẹfu at once unsheathed his sword saying " You go before, I am coming at your heels to be attendants on our master in the other world " and in one stroke he cut off his head and then coolly went home to die. Several who were too inquisitive lost their lives in this way. In that vast compound those in one corner of it may not know what was taking place in another.

It was also a time of mourning for the relatives of those who have received the " death cloth " knowing that they must have to bury in the evening a relative strong and healthy in the morning and up to the time the fatal cup is taken.

Alayọayọ was very reluctant to die, and begged hard that her life should be spared, relying probably on the Crown Prince's promise to her. But in this she was sadly disappointed ; for this reason she stayed much longer in the palace than she was expected to do, for according to custom she must die at home among her own people. When at last she knew that death was inevitable, she issued from the palace well-dressed in her " death cloth " with her drummer before and her maidens carrying large calabashes full of kola nuts, she trod her way homewards to the measures of the drum scattering kola nuts with a lavish hand right and left to the crowd of spectators thronging her way from the palace gates to her home, to have a last glance at her.

In the meantime a great feast had been made at her home for all friends and relatives to partake with her for the last, during which time the grave was in digging and the coffin made. She distributed her property among her relatives and her only son. When the hour was come she bade all farewell and repaired to her

P

chamber and the fatal cup was placed in her hands. But owing to
the preventives she had fortified her system with, the effects
were neutralized ; this was repeated again and again, with the
same result. So towards sunset the disappointed relatives in
order to prevent an indelible disgrace to the family had to strangle
her, and then gave her a decent funeral. The same may be said
more or less of all those who had received the " death cloth."

The Aremọ (Crown Prince) also was told to die, but not only
did he refuse point blank to do so but was also determined to ascend
the throne. His grandfather had abolished the custom of the
Aremọ dying with the father, his own father the monarch now
deceased was his father's Aremọ and he succeeded him on the
throne, and why then should he die ? But the Ọyọ Mesi were
not in favour of his ascending the throne because of his surpassing
cruelties. One instance among many to illustrate this :—

A young man Fọlarin by name had a mistress of whom he was
deprived by the Aremọ. One day, seeing Fọlarin pass along
the street he sent for him and with a heavy blacksmith's hammer
smashed his knees and ankles rendering him a cripple for life,
and then nicknamed himself " Alagbẹdẹ Akẹsan ti itun Fọlarin
l'ẹsẹ rọ " (the Akẹsan blacksmith who can recast Fọlarin's limbs).
By such deeds he forfeited his rights to the throne, which would have
been indisputably his had he been as kind and humble as his
father.

In the meantime he was bidding high for it, he secured the
support of the King's slaves by feasting them on a bullock and
a donkey slaughtered every day. But the Ọyọ Mesi who rejected
him put forward the Asipa (son of the founder of the town) to
oppose him, and both parties were in arms. Not aware of the
actual facts of the situation he distributed arms and ammunition
to all the men of the Apara, Ajagba, and Sẹkẹ wards and was
determined to expel the Asipa from the city that day and demolish
his house. The war drum was beating, and the Famifami trumpet
calling to arms and he was just ready to mount his horse when the
Basọrun appeared on the scene with about 400 men behind him
all unarmed like himself. Said he to him " Your royal highness,
will you pull down the fabric your fathers have set up ? Will you
destroy the city your father and grandfather helped to raise ? Be
quiet, all will be right."

With such soothing words he dissuaded him from going forward.
By this time the King's slaves had been won over. The Basọrun
had scarcely finished when the Apeka (the head slave) came
on horseback with his men all unarmed. He began with " My
lord, what is it ? Why is this ?" The Aremọ in a rage retorted with

" Away with you. Are you not my club who ought to have been striking hard for me by this time ? Is it now to ask such a question when you ought to be acting ? "

The slaves took exception to this language of their master to their chief. We have noticed in Part I what influence these so-called " slaves," especially the titled ones, wield, as their good-will and assent with those of the members of the harem must be obtained before any election can be considered valid. They now professed to be offended because their chief was metaphorically styled "kumọ" i.e. a club, and they declared openly that they would have nothing more to do with the Arẹmọ. They refused to enter his house from that day ; the cow and the ass were slaughtered as usual and the feast prepared but no one came to partake of it.

The Prince again sent for the men in the Apara, Ajagba, Ṣẹkẹ and Akeitan wards, who were loyal to him ; their chiefs came as in duty bound but their men had been disbanded, and not a single armed man came with them !

The Prince was now at his wits' end, and greatly mortified by seeing himself deserted by all those who had promised him their support. At last Prince Iyajin his father's uncle sent for him, and undeceived him of his hopes. " The Ọyọ MESI have not elected you and there is the end of it. I would advise you to leave the city quietly or build a house at the outskirts, and live there in dignified retirement."

The Prince returned home much depressed and made preparation to leave the city. He entered the palace and denuded it of all its treasures. He sent several loads to the Bara to be kept there until sent for ; and whatsoever he did not or could not take away he smashed and made a bonfire of them in the palace courtyard, and the wells he filled with kegs of gunpowder and broken pieces of crockery. Some wives of his who had offended him he confined in a closed room with ceilings, and had the entrance walled up. He then proceeded to his farm at Agodomgbo and unfettered a few hundreds of the slaves put in stocks there, and ordered them to carry all those loads with him to Ibadan. The Arẹ of Ibadan received him with open arms and assigned him a portion of land to build on in the Yemẹtu quarter.

The late King ADELU was the first born son of his father ATIBA. He was born when his father was but a youth. He became a companion to his father in all his turmoils, especially when as a private man ATIBA chose the career of a soldier of fortune.

ADELU was much older than his brothers, as they were born a very long time afterwards when their father was in better circumstances. As a son, he was very obedient and dutiful, always ready to answer his father's calls whatever he may be doing, and many a time whilst at his meals. He was an absolutely just man, strict to a fault. He so abhorred stealing that with him robbers had no alternative but instantaneous execution. The following stories told of him will illustrate his strictness.

1. A certain young woman sold beads on credit to a buyer, but when the money was not forthcoming in time the creditor went to demand it. Not finding the debtor at home but seeing her beads hanging on a peg in her apartment being determined to have either the money or the beads, she went in and took her beads away until they should be paid for.

An imperfect report of this came to the hearing of the King representing her as having entered the rooms of another woman when she was out, and taken her beads away ! The King without further enquiries and proper investigation of the case ordered her execution at once ! He keenly regretted this afterwards, when the whole facts were brought to his knowledge.

2. He sent a few of his slaves for tall poles to build his Ko̩bi. On their return he saw a yam tied to the load of one of them. He questioned the headman how he came by it, but not being satisfied with the plea that it was a gift of a farmer, and surmising that they had been taking undue advantage of poor farmers out of privilege , he was determined to put a stop to that custom.

The executioner was immediately at his service and he was instantly decapitated. This incident had the desired effect. All through his reign stealing or taking by violence out of sheer privilege, so common with the King's slaves, was utterly unknown, everybody's property was safe.

His public executioner was called Kòlohó. A call at his name Kòlohó was usually sufficient. He was at his duty at a moment's notice.

He loved his people and would never allow any of the princes to distress the poor with impunity. An instance was given of a prince who fought with a commoner and cut off one of his fingers. This being reported to his father he severely reprimanded the prince, and was determined to exact a full retaliation of the deed. But the constitution of the country forbade him to disfigure a prince so he ordered someone to be brought from the family of his mother as a substitute. A young virgin was met in the house beating corn and she was summoned to the palace. The King ordered Kòlohó to lop off the same finger of the young woman as that which the prince cut off from the man's hand. This was done instantly. Then said the King to her " It is not my fault it is your cousin who deprived you of your finger."

That was his rude idea of justice.   As that young woman and all the relations of the prince's mother enjoy great advantages under his auspices, so they should be ready to suffer for his crimes. And again, the training of children devolves greatly on the mothers, therefore both herself and her relatives would learn to train their children to good behaviour.   A misguided notion of doing what was right.

With his children he was very strict and scarcely any one of them escaped punishment from him, and whoever among them he had occasion to lay his hands on, carried sore sides for weeks or months and would have to lie on cotton wool or banana leaves.

He was particular to see them all engaged in some industry, either weaving or farming.   Even the Crown Prince, who has official duties to perform, must employ his spare moments in weaving or tailoring.   The King was particularly strict with him for his many cruel acts ; and although above law many a time would the father surprise him in his house, and ere he could escape would lay heavily on him with a stick or the flat of a cutlass.

His Majesty encouraged agriculture in every possible way. As he could not visit his farm by daylight he often did so on moonlight nights to examine the crops and advise the head farmer, who was often taken by surprise at his visits.   His crops were usually stocked in huge barns until food was becoming dear, which was usually just before the next harvest ; then he would open his barns and flood the markets with food at a little below the market price, " My children must not starve," he used to say.   Notice was usually given and farmers warned before the King's stores came into the market, so that they might not run the risk of a loss by being undersold.

He was exceptionally kind to the thrifty and to those farmers and their wives who showed themselves industrious.

It is customary in this country to give goats to the womenfolk to rear for their own keep, the kids being shared with the owner. But in his case, he would demand none from those who kept theirs well except a young billy occasionally.   He would rather add to their store.   But careless owners would get no encouragement from him.

He was a perfect organizer, a man of taste, he appreciated and rewarded excellencies wherever found.

If any man was accused before him and he understood the individual was then in his farm, he would never allow him to be sent for, and whenever the case was heard the defendant would have every consideration from the King : but if actually guilty he was let off with a light fine.   " If a man is not idle " he used to say, "he must be a good man." He loved and respected the C.M.S. and American Baptist Missionaries at Ọyọ in his days. He was kind and liberal to them during the Ijaye war when they were in straitened circumstances. He was universally mourned by his people.

THE ACCESSION OF ADEYẸMI.

Prince ADEYẸMI the fourth son of ATIBA was elected to the throne in succession to his eldest brother the late King ADELU. He at first declined it in favour of an elder brother Adeṣiyẹn who had a prior right, the eldest surviving Adelabu being at that time an exile at Ibadan, and from his character was on no account eligible. Adeṣiyen, however, urged his younger brother to accept it as he was in bad health, and for him to have to go through all the ceremonies and wear the crown perhaps for only a few days would be inconvenient for all concerned, and for himself also. He was on a decline from phthisis. He promised however to aid ADEYEMI as much as he could with his advice and counsel, wishing him a long and prosperous reign. Then ADEYEMI accepted the offer.

ADEYEMI'S accession was acclaimed by the populace without a dissentient voice, he being very popular with all the people especially with foreigners and provincials. All the traders from Ibadan, Abẹokuta, Ijẹbu and elsewhere used to lodge in his house, and all used to partake of his hospitality. As a prince, his weakness was drink ; not that he did it to excess, but he was in the habit of visiting the brewers of native malt liquor every day with numerous followers and would satisfy them all at his own expense. Hence his popularity and universal acceptance. High hopes were, therefore, entertained of a happy and prosperous reign for one who was a friend to all.

But no sooner had he ascended the throne than an evil reign was prognosticated for him. As usual the divination was sent from the sacred city Ile Ifẹ. The " IGBA IWA " consisting of two covered calabashes identical in shape and size, similarly draped but the contents of which were different were brought before him. The one contained money (cowries), cloth, beads, etc., indicating a happy and prosperous reign, the other gunpowder, bullets, razor, knife, miniature spears and arrows, indicating wars and turmoils. He was to choose one and by his choice determine the fate of the Yoruba kingdom. Unfortunately he chose the latter and from that time evil days were held to be in store for the country. This was fulfilled by the troubles initiated by the Arẹ of Ibadan, which culminated in the protracted 16 years' war which involved the whole of the

Yoruba country and ended by the British protectorate and the loss
of the Yoruba People of their absolute independence.

The " sword of state " or rather of justice was also sent from
Ile Ifẹ which every sovereign must have before he can order an
execution.

The following were the sons born to ADEYEMI before he ascended
the throne :—Adelakun (the Arẹ̀mọ) Ajùan, Akère I, Akère II,
Tẹla Kundukẹ, Tẹla Kankanṣi, and Origade.   Adelakun, however,
was his natural son and consequently it was Ajuan's mother that
was created an Ilari and raised to the title of Iyalagbọn.

§ 2.   IBADAN RAIDS ON THE CONFINES OF THE KINGDOM
THE WỌKUTI EXPEDITION

At this time there was peace all over the Yoruba country, trade between the coast and interior was brisk, caravans went to Abẹokuta
from the interior every day, and to Ijẹbu via Ibadan once a month.
These littoral tribes however, would not allow those from the interior
to pass on to the coast, but traders from the coast can travel in
safety right on to the Niger and Bida.   The Ibadans were now at
the zenith of their glory.   All the Ijẹsa and Ekiti tribes and some
Oké Ogun towns paid their tributes regularly, and from the easy
victory of the Arẹ's first expedition all the tribes dreaded the power
of the Ibadans, and gave no cause of offence, and the Arẹ himself
was very much elated, being almost idolized by the war boys.

In the midst of this profound peace the Arẹ and his chiefs on
the 26th of November, 1875, started on his second expedition
for slave-hunting.   They proceeded to the Ekiti country direct
via Ila and encamped at Yahapa.   Seeing such a large hostile
force menacing, a large number of the Ekitis concentrated their
forces at Ijẹsa Ahayè for self protection.   The place was taken without much opposition.   But the expedition was intended against
Aiyede the capital city of Eṣu the Ata, lord of the Yagba and Akoko
tribes in the confines of the Yoruba country North-eastwards.
But ere this large army reached Aiyede that city and its environs
had been deserted.   It is said that the Ata was rather their friend
and not a foe, and nothing but plunder hunger took them there.
Some of the Ibadan chiefs, therefore, had privately sent and
apprized the Ata of the coming danger which he would never
be able to oppose, and therefore he should at once seek safety in
flight.   Some escaped to a distance of five days' journey knowing
the ferocious way the Ibadans have of pursuing their prey.   The
Àta himself escaped to Omù Ijèlu, a town supposed then to be
impregnable.   Built on a high hill, strongly walled, and surrounded

by a thorny thicket, the pathway for entering the town being narrow and well guarded. It had successfully repulsed three attacks before and therefore was considered safe. Finding Aiyede deserted, the Ibadan Seriki who led the way tracked the fugitives to this place. He had a preliminary skirmish that evening and he encamped at the foot of the hill awaiting his chiefs. In course of the night, the Balogun, and afterwards the Arẹ arrived, and next morning the Seriki went to pay his respects to them awaiting orders. But as he was returning to his tent and his drum was rolling " Kiriniun Onibudo " before him, the warboys thought he was going to the battlefield. " The Seriki is going, the Seriki is going " flew from mouth to mouth and immediately the great host not waiting any longer for orders from the leaders rushed after this young and intrepid general, himself being borne along with them, unable to reach his tent to put on his war-dress; these were brought to him in the field. In one assault the thorny thickets were crumbled like matchwood under the feet of myriads, Ọmù was taken and Ẹṣu the Àta brought a prisoner before the Arẹ.

The illustrious captive was kindly treated by the Ibadan chiefs, but the Ilọrin army (which accompanied them) requested the Arẹ to hand him over to them as their mortal foe. This the Ibadans positively refused to do. " It is not our custom," said they " to put to death a fallen leader or hero." This refusal created a disaffection between the Ibadans and Ilọrins which the latter were determined to avenge whenever an opportunity offered.

Ọmù was after all a very small town and the Ibadan host a large and insatiable one, the Arẹ and the Balogun therefore returned to their base at Yahapa and allowed the Seriki to lead the young men further on in search of prey.

The next place attacked was Ikọle. They had a preliminary skirmish in the evening of their arrival before retiring to prepare for a regular pitched battle the next day; but at moonlight the Ikọle people deserted the town and sought refuge by flight to various places. The Ilọrins who were well acquainted with their haunts did very well for themselves in the pursuit, but the others who did not fare so well scattered themselves throughout the length and breadth of the Akoko country like hungry wolves seeking for prey. The people hid themselves in caves, ravines, and in dens, some escaped as far as to Ẹgbẹ. The Ibadans pursued on and on until they reached the border of the Emir of Bida's territory. There they came up with some of the Bida cavalry who questioned the leading chiefs as to their authority for trespassing in King Imoru's territory. They apologized, and after an exchange of presents and kola nuts, they parted as friends.   These cavaliers were described as seated erect on powerful horses, their spears were of burnished brass which glittered in the noon-day sun.

Having reached the utmost limits possible the Seriki now retraced his steps to meet the Are at their base. But a great disaster befel a part of the Ibadan host on their way back. Some who lingered behind were hastening on to join the Seriki and took a shorter route to the left with a steep descent. The mass behind pressing on those before, hundreds were hurled down and trampled underfoot ; the clouds of dust raised by myriads suffocated many and left them no power of resistance, and so within the space of half-an-hour hundreds had lost their lives !

There the survivors, in order to find the bodies of relatives and friends to perform the last offices for them, piled corpses in heaps, presenting a gruesome sight ! A man on horseback rode up, and seeing he had lost there all his brothers and friends who came with him to the expedition groaned out " and what shall I say at home?" He drew out his pistol and discharged it in the ear of his horse. Reloading, he blew out his own brains ! So that not one out of that family returned home to tell the tale.   This tragedy gave the name to that expedition, " Wokuti," piling of corpses.

At Yahapa before the camp was broken up for the homeward march, the Ilorins once more made a strenuous effort to get the Ata, but Chiefs Aijenku and Iyapo the Seriki confronted them saying " If you were the leaders of this expedition and we followed you, you would have had a claim ; but as we are the leaders and you follow us, we have told you it is not our custom to kill a fallen king or general and that is the end of the matter." The Ilorin troops parted here in no pleasant mood.

The Ibadans returned home on the 19th of February, 1876. This was the last of the Ibadan raiding expeditions in the Ekiti, and was, perhaps, the most powerful force that ever marched out of their gates.   They were now confronted with the task of statesmanship, of consolidation and organization which turned out to be a more difficult affair.

§ 3. The New Policy

The power of the Ibadans being dreaded by all the interior tribes, their messengers to the provinces under them took undue advantage of the subject states and that to such an extent as to drive them to rebellion. The very name Ibadan stank in the nostrils of all the Ijesa and Ekiti tribes, so that they were only seeking for an opportunity for throwing off their yoke. And strange to say these messengers who were doing all the mischief were not the Ibadan born, but the Ijẹsa and Ekiti slaves who were sent with messages to their own native towns !

As soon as each one gets outside the Ibadan town walls he secures to himself the services of a drummer and fifer and a bard to sing the praises of his master as if the latter were coming : he collects behind him idle fellows who follow no regular employment and he moves as a little chief aping the master who sent him. When he enters a town he asks for the Ibadan Ajẹlẹ there and introduces himself as the messenger of such and such a chief, the Ajẹlẹ is to introduce him to the authorities of the town who will assign him quarters for lodging. The landlord has to defray all expenses of the keep of this messenger and his followers who will remain there as long as they like, time being no object to them. The best local dishes with chicken or mutton must be provided every day with pots of local beer or palm wine. The master of the house has to levy on all the inmates for the contribution of their share, even to the old women who lived on spinning cotton for their keep, none is exempted, all are to contribute their quota. Nor is this all : cruelty, vanity, debauchery were more common with them than otherwise. A landlord would be compelled to wait on them at meals, at times holding the lamp in his hand for them and sometimes the lamp is placed on his head making him as it were a lamp post whilst they are partaking of his hospitality ! Forcing their women, raping their girls, rifling their valuables, are common causes of complaints, and they generally return to Ibadan with booty as from a raid. Who dares touch the messenger of a great Ibadan chief ? Thus all the Ibọlọs under their protection, the Ijẹsas, Ekitis, Yagbas, and Akokos were groaning under the yoke of Ibadan, not from paying tribute which was only nominal, but from the excesses of these messengers who weie their own sons.

Thoughtful men at Ibadan hearing this, recalled the advice of the late Balẹ Orowùsi and his policy now reversed by the Arẹ.

It was found that the messengers of the Arẹ and of the Balogun were the greatest offenders in this business leading the country into the vortex of a revolution. The other chiefs foreseeing the evil, remonstrated with their leading chiefs, but these, from what they profited by these messengers would not check them. Matters came to a crisis in October and November 1876 when the minor chiefs made matters too hot for the leading chiefs and compelled them to put a stop to these enormities. Three of these messengers were caught decoying people from the provinces to Ibadan to be sold. Being brought before the council and convicted, two were executed at the Basọrun market (the usual place of execution) and the third outside the north eastern (or Iwo) gate, the highway to their hunting grounds as a warning to other messengers. The effect however was only slight and transient, the feelings in the provinces were by no means allayed.

§ 4. THE CIVIL MURDER OF CHIEF AIJENKU THE FỌHỌKỌ.

The Arẹ now began to evince more and more the characteristics of a Kakanfo. Experience has shown us that a Kakanfo always caused trouble at home and abroad. Their paths were always marked with blood. We have only to recall the history of Afọnja of Ilọrin, Ẹdun of Gbogun and Ojo Amepo who were rivals, of Kurũmi of Ijaye among others ; and now Latosisa of Ibadan was on the same track. His primary object was to suppress all the leading chiefs who were his equals or superiors, and the first man to feel his power was Çhief Aijẹnku that old and experienced war-chief, who had made a name in the field when the Arẹ was nowhere. He was the only check on him at the commencement of his administration. Aijẹnku was amongst the first settlers of Ibadan. He entered the town on horseback being then a little chief. He was a powerful man as we saw that he alone opposed the whole forces of the Ẹgbas before Ijaye, when Ogunmọla and the other chiefs were absent at Iwawun (vide Chap. xviii) and, although fortune did not set him at the head of affairs yet he was, as he had always been, one who could not be overlooked. He was never a private man at Ibadan. He was the Aṣaju for Oluyọle the first Baṣọrun when the Arẹ was only a palm tree dresser ! And, although fortune had now raised Latosisa the Arẹ above him, yet Aijẹnku was like a king in his own quarter of the town, where he was acknowledged, loved, and venerated by all the Okè Àsà people, a tribe in the Ẹkun Osi province now resident at Ibadan. Aijẹnku at the public meetings in course of debate often told the chiefs of the administrations of former distinguished rulers that made Ibadan what it was to-day. This the Arẹ and others of grasping propensities like him never liked to hear, and the Arẹ in particular was ever on the look out for an opportunity of putting an end to this " historian."

Aijẹnku on the other hand whenever he spoke did so boldly as one who by age, experience, and past services in many a bloody field was competent to give them advice. He had little sympathy even amongst the junior chiefs, who were all affected with the prevailing avarice ; for he was said to be of an irritable temper, too bold and pointed in his remarks, and when he reproved, did so without respect of person or rank ; and being so capable a warrior there was a latent fear that if this man was backed up and eventually placed at the head of the government he would rule with rigour and become oppressive.

At length an opportunity afforded itself for taking revenge on this chief, and the Arẹ and the other chiefs were not slow to make use of it. Igbajọ was one of the tributary towns under him. The people of that town being dissatisfied with their ruling chief deposed him and appointed another Aregbajọ. The deposed came to Ibadan to ask the aid of the Ibadan government to reinstate him. The Arẹ and the other chiefs were for reinstating him, but Aijẹnku was opposed to that measure and gave his reasons. He spoke in his usual authoritative way which offended his brother chiefs and hence on the 13th of January, 1877, he was rejected by all the chiefs in the public meeting, and that declaration was confirmed by his being deprived of all the towns hitherto tributary to him, including this very Igbajọ. He bore his humiliation patiently and the next day (14th) went to the adjourned meeting with a few slaves to offer to the assembly in payment of fines, and to ask to be pardoned. The chiefs refused to pardon him, they further disgraced him ; he had to return home disappointed and with a heavy heart. But what roused the old Lion to desperation was the attempt to deprive him of the tolls of the Abẹokuta gate. This was on the 20th of January, when the chiefs sent other gatemen there, and drove his men away. He was exasperated beyond measure, and was resolved upon civil war, come what may. Said he :—" The Abeokuta road was opened at the peril of my life. The scars in my body and my disfigured hands were the result of that special conflict when none of the present chiefs was in existence, and while I am living no one will deprive me of this." He drove away those who had displaced his men and resorted to arms, defying anyone who would oppose him. He roused the town to action by permitting the women in his district to sing :—" O di ori òdi, àṣa ko le wọle ko gbe ẹiyẹle " (next to an impossibility, the hawk cannot enter into the house to take away a pigeon). Meaning that no one would dare face their chief in his own house.

The town was in commotion, the excitement in that part of the town was very great, but no one came forward to oppose him. The C.M.S. agents waited on the Arẹ to express their regrets for the events of the day. The Arẹ made only a cursory remark on the subject. He said " It is the public that is against him, not I, and we were surprised to hear that he was in arms, against whom, we know not."

Knowing his might, the chiefs moved cautiously to undermine his great power. Nothing was done till the following Monday the

22nd at the general meeting of the town council. There they won over all the chiefs who were his personal friends, and to his subordinate chiefs they offered titles and ranks and tributary towns, and then decided to attack him in a body.

Having thus deprived him of all his mainstays, word was sent to him to quit the town, or die, or to prepare for the worst. His slaves seeing their master in such a plight, and the impossibility of their being able to resist the whole town opposed to him sought each one his own safety by flight, some to one chief, some to another.

A private message was sent to him to seek refuge in old Tajo's house, who had received permission to shelter him, for if he resisted it would mean not only his own life, but also the lives of his wives and children.

As soon as it was known that he had left his house, the whole town in arms swooped down upon his quarter of the town, and sacked every house, removing everything, even to grinding stones, earthenware pots and dishes, doors, firewood, etc., leaving the whole place in desolation and ruin as a conquered town. The writer could not suppress his emotion when he saw the sight the next morning. It was heartrending, especially when on reaching Chief Tajo's house he met the chief quite besieged by scores of mothers wailing the loss of their children. Several interested friends called on him in Chief Tajo's house and even the Arẹ himself called in the evening, disclaiming all responsibility. It was the doing of the town, said he, and not the work of an individual. He was said to have offered him the following cold comfort : " Take comfort and be thankful your life is spared you. Remember how many towns subverted by your arms have been made desolate, and how many kings have suffered as you now do. Be of good courage, be not cast down, all will be right."

At the public meeting of the town council of the 25th January, 1877, at the Arẹ's, it was decided that he should return to his house, and hence, each of the principal chiefs sent his sword bearer to accompany him home from Tajo's. Two days later the chiefs having heard that Tajo's people were taking advantage of the fallen chief's condition to pillage his farm, sent to warn the old chief to check his people ; the main object of the chiefs was to humiliate Aijẹnku and not to ruin him altogether.

On the 30th of January, 1877, the C.M.S. agents, by the permission of the Arẹ, paid the fallen chief a visit in grateful recognition of his kindness and the protection he extended to the agent and the body of Christians in his quarter. After some expressions of sympathy and a few words of comfort addressed to him, he said

" I did not at first expect that matters would come to this crisis, but having come up to such a pass, I restrained my people from fighting as I was unwilling to shed a drop of blood in a town of which I was among the foremost of the settlers, and where I built houses, and where I was blessed with wives and children. This is the third compound I have built at Ibadan. If I had chosen to go, I have friends at Abẹokuta who might receive me with open arms ; and who will dare pursue me if I leave the town ? But I prefer to die here, and to have an honourable burial."

But alas, the chief's troubles were not over. The matter was revived again by some of the ill-disposed. At one of the public meetings of the council it was insinuated by some that, " if he is not finished up with, such a man like that, a turn of the wheel of fortune may one day place him at the top, and woe betide any one of us or our offspring then living."

His slaves who had sought the protection of other masters, seeing their master now at home, began to return one by one to him. So it was resolved by the chiefs in council that he should not receive them again but that each should return permanently to their temporary masters. The fallen chief submitted to this also. Yet still at a meeting of the 12th February, 1877, word was sent to him that it was resolved that he should die ! " What else have I done ? " asked he of the messengers. They replied, " We do not know, we are only sent to tell you to die." Aijẹnku went again to Tajo's house where he had taken refuge before, to ask for his interference again ; but this chief had been forewarned not to meddle in this matter again, and therefore he did not show his face to his doomed friend. " The Master is not at home " is a well understood phrase, and the veteran soldier, overpowered with grief went home, gave his last orders to his children 'and retired finally to rest, by blowing out his own brains. This was the second cold-blooded murder perpetrated by the Arẹ.

§ 5. Plot Against the Seriki Iyapọ

Strange as it may seem, yet so it was that the young and intrepid Seriki Iyapọ was one of the principal agents in hounding the late chief to death. One would have supposed that the chief being the Arẹagoro or *Alter Ego* of his own father in his days, he would have looked up to him as a second father. But it seems Iyapọ felt that his own glory would not be complete while this old chief was alive, and that the house of Aijẹnku should look up to him as supreme in that quarter of the town as it did in the days of his father which could hardly be the case while the old chief was alive. But retributive justice soon overtook him also. The

main object of the Arẹ being to suppress all who could successfully
oppose his designs, the Seriki Iyapọ was not exempt from his
ban and he readily raked up charges and accusations against him.

Iyapọ was one of those engaged in the plunder of the house
of the late Aijẹnku. He was now accused of having in his possession
a basket of beads which had belonged to the late chief ; and,
although it was given up on demand, yet the chiefs were resolved
upon his overthrow, for his independent and defiant attitude.

It would seem as if the virtue of gratitude was at a discount at
Ibadan in those days, for the Arẹ himself was much beholden
to this young and valorous chief, when there was an insurrection
against him for his overthrow, on account of his atrocities ; but
for Iyapọ he certainly would have put an end to his own life.
Instead of succouring him now, he joined the others and turned
against him.

Just a fortnight after the death of Aijẹnku, Iyapọ was impeached
at the meeting of the chiefs, and was told either to quit the town
or die. The young and brave general was determined not to
pay any fines, but if needs be to fight it out.   Fines only whet their
appetites for greater demands, and they are never satisfied
until they have seen the last of their victims.   He had the cases of
Ajọbọ, the Lady Ẹfūṣẹtan, and the late Aijẹnku before him,
he therefore "stood by his guns" and defied them all.
Unfortunately for him, his own brothers joined in the plot
against him, and on threatening them they fled to the Arẹ for
protection !

But the elders of the Arẹ's house waited on him and reminded
him of the good and loyal services Iyapọ had rendered him in the
past, and they prevailed upon him to relent, and not to proceed
to the extremity with him, for really he had done nothing unpardonable. He listened favourably to them, and the Iyapọ
affair was lulled for a while.

But the intention was not given up, for within two months it
was revived again, and again suppressed, each of the chiefs disclaiming any responsibility for the rumour. But still, they were
only feeling their way, for Iyapọ was too influential a man to be
overpowered suddenly. The Arẹ's chief grievance against him
was that Iyapọ had usurped his rights, because he would allow no
confiscation of houses in his quarter.   Whoever offended he
punished himself, for which purpose he always kept a bundle of
atori whips in his house. Those great chiefs who enriched themselves
by plundering and confiscating people's houses as a punishment for
slight offences found they could not do so in Iyapọ's quarter.
" The whole of my quarter consists of but one compound and I

am the head of it," he used to say. No outside interference was allowed, and any head of a compound convicted of any offence he punished himself. The Arẹ had cause to hate him for this.

The Balogun also eyed him suspiciously as potentially a usurper of his title, for the Arẹ more than once threatened to depose him and transfer the title to Iyapọ. The Ọtun was not even taken to account, he was regarded as "white-feathered." The Osi and the Seriki were rivals, both equal in age, each the head of their father's house, and commanded their means and men ; the Osi's title was higher, but Iyapọ's influence was greater, and so it was that he was positively hated by the principal leading chiefs, but none had the courage to face him.

CHAPTER XXIII

THE COMMENCEMENT OF THE 16 YEARS' WAR

§ 1. THE BOKOFI EXPEDITION

SINCE the Ijaye war (1860-62) the Ijebus and the Egbas had strictly forbidden ammunition to be sold to any of the interior tribes, notably Ibadan. On the restoration of peace in 1865 the trade between them consisted of foreign clothes, salt, rum and gin from the coast in exchange for produce, chiefly palm oil, kernels, cotton, etc., from the interior. In order to obtain ammunition, the late Basorun Ogunmola opened the Oke Igbo road via Ifẹ to Benin solely for that purpose.

The late King ADELU, however, had purchased a large quantity of gunpowder at Porto Novo which was sent half way to Bokofi but no further for fear of the Egbas kidnapping the whole. On hearing this, the Arẹ was resolved to send the youngest Mọgajis for it, secretly wishing they might encounter the Egbas or the Dahomians who might probably help him to get rid of one or other of them. Ilọri the Osi, and Iyapọ the Seriki were sent on this expedition under the elderly chief Olupoyi as Baba Isàlẹ.

The name of Iyapọ drew the whole of the young men of Ibadan to this expedition leaving only the Arẹ, the Balogun and the Otun at home. Their simple instructions were :—" Molest no one, steer clear of Egba territory, go straight by Oke'ho, Igãna to Mẹkọ ; but if any one molest or interfere with you, follow the party home, and we shall come and meet you outside their gates." The Arẹ hurried the Seriki out of home the same day he gave him the order, the less prepared the better the chances of his fall in the Arẹ's opinion.

The expedition left Ibadan on the 26th April, 1877, and returned safely on the 21st June, without encountering either Egbas or Dahomians. They brought with them about 800 kegs of gunpowder, a few Dane guns, and casks of rum, etc. On the next day the whole of the powder was forwarded to the ALÂFIN who took a few kegs and made a present of the rest to the Ibadan chiefs. During this expedition there was a great stir among the Egbas. They charged the Ibadans with seeking an occasion of quarrel with them by sending an army into their " backyard " as they styled it, but as the Ibadan government had sent formally to

413

apprise the Ẹgba chiefs of their movement and object before the expedition left, the responsible chiefs of Abẹokuta like Ogundipẹ, and others paid no heed to the hue and cry that was being made. But the great majority of them at a meeting at Sodẹkẹ street decided to close the roads against Ibadan and forbid especially the exportation of salt and foreign goods.

Ajagunjẹun the Balogun of Itoko took the lead and went to the caravan town gate to turn the Ibadan traders back home and to see that those already in the town leave empty handed.

This was really the first hostile act that led up eventually to the 16 years' war, which involved practically the whole Yoruba country, and caused so much loss of lives, and much distress and misery, and destruction of towns, subjugation of the Ijẹbus by the British Government, reduction of the military power of Ibadan, the placing of a British Resident in that town, and of District Commissioners in the principal towns of the Yoruba country.

§ 2.   The First Act of War

The Arẹ's avarice and ambition at this time were unbounded. His ambition was to eclipse the fame of the two greatest chiefs of undying memory at Ibadan viz Ibikunle and Ogunmọla (his late master) who both left a name behind them, and sons who upheld the fame and greatness of their father.   To this end he sought occasion first against Ilọri Ogunmọla's son, and then against Seriki Iyapọ, Ibikunle's son.   If he could reduce these men who eclipsed himself in all that made for feudal greatness and glory, his own star would then shine undimmed.

Further, he now undertook to organize a military band for his own house, raising some of the principal slaves to power and greatness, some of them commanding from 400 to 1,000 soldiers each, horse and foot ; and accumulated also a vast store of ammunition in his own house.   Also he put up his eldest son as a rival to the other Mọgajis in the town, and organized a military band for him, and a guard consisting of the sons of the well-to-do men in the town.

These doings of the Arẹ did not escape the observation of the chiefs.   It seemed to them that the Arẹ wanted to perpetuate the administration of Ibadan in his own family, and they were determined to resist this with all their might.   The Arẹ on the other hand was much elated with his military organization, and he made it clear that he was bent on an enterprise which he was determined to prosecute to a successful issue with or without the help of his chiefs.

On the 25th of June, 1877, the Arẹ declared at the meeting of the Town Council that as the Ẹgbas first shut their gates against Ibadan since the 3rd of June they must now shut theirs against the Ẹgbas, and 17 days hence commence hostilities.

The chiefs one and all remonstrated with him against this enterprise, but he was obdurate. Messengers were despatched to their neighbours the Ijẹbus, Ilọrins, the Ijẹsas, Ekitis and Ifẹs telling them of the impending struggle and requesting their co-operation. The *casus belli* were stated as follows :—

1.   That they only performed an act of loyalty towards the King by sending to Porto Novo to bring home ammunition he had bought there, when the Ẹgbas refused to sell to them.

2.   They never trespassed on Ẹgba territọry, nor gave any cause of offence to any, and yet the Ẹgbas resented their action by closing their roads against Ọyọs forbidding all trade and intercourse with them.

3.   Hundreds of their people who went to Abẹokuta for trade had been stolen and sold into slavery which alone gave them the right to demand redress.

But before the return of the messengers the Ẹgba chiefs sent their ambassadors headed by one Leasu to negotiate peace and on the 12th of July, 1877, a full meeting was convened to hear them. But Leasu proved himself most unfit to play the part entrusted to him ; he spoke disrespectfully and in an impertinent manner, addressing the Arẹ by name, but his own head chief by his title Alatiṣe. The chiefs were indignant at this and the Seriki Iyapọ at once confronted him with " You ought rather be gone as you are most unfit to discharge the duties of a messenger. Why did you not call your own chief Ogũdipẹ by name but by his title Alatiṣe, but our own chief you keep calling by name Latosisa ? That is his name true, but he has a title and he is the ruler of this town. If you cannot do him respect we will show you the gate."

Leasu had to leave the town the next day without a reply to his message.

Whilst the chiefs were for negotiation, the Arẹ was bent on hostilities. He found in this affair a plausible pretext for a thing he had long premeditated to carry out, viz., the subjugation of Abẹo-kuta as the first step towards bringing the whole country again under one head.

Seeing the storm brewing the native missionaries in a body interviewed him and endeavoured to dissuade him from prosecuting his mad project. They pointed out to him that the thing could not be done, as the Ẹgbas were well supplied with breach-loading guns which are terrible weapons of precision, whilst he had none. He

laughingly replied " And with muzzle-loading ones will I break
them." They further remonstrated with him saying " Ọtẹ
aladugbo ko dara " (warfare between neighbours is a great evil).
He received them hitherto with his usual smiles and affability,
extenuating his actions, etc., but now, all of a sudden (probably
thinking they were moved thereto by the chiefs) he grew stern and
resolute, not to say fierce (his Kakanfo blood seemingly flying
into his head) and he said " I am going to perform a task which
God has allotted to me to do, and those who say they shall see that
I do not accomplish it will not live to see it done, as done it shall
be, and when I have finished there shall be no more wars for
ever in the Yoruba country." How truly prophetic his words
turned out to be, but how differently from what he intended
them to be.

Kidnapping Expedition to the Egba farms.—The Arẹ was as
determined to commence hostilities as the chiefs were against
it. Hence at the meeting of the Town Council on the 31st July,
he said to the chiefs, " There is no subject for discussion to-day
but you should all go home and prepare for a kidnapping expedition
to the Ẹgba farms to-morrow morning." The Balogun and the
other chiefs were against the proposal, they said they were not
prepared for such a big undertaking. But the Arẹ coolly returned
this ironical answer, " Very well, as you are not prepared you can
have as much time at home as you wish, meantime I go, and perhaps
by the time I return you may then be ready." This sarcastic
reply was felt, and each one went home for a hasty preparation
for the morrow.

The Arẹ led out the Ibadan host to the Ẹgba farms on the
1st August, and captured Atadi, and Alagbara, and pushed on as
far as Arakanga behind the gates of Abẹokuta, and captured a
young bride there. The Ẹgbas were not prepared for this. At
the instance of Chief Ogundipẹ they were about to send another
ambassador to undo the mischief done by Leasu, but this attack
on their farms and villages put an end to their pacific intentions.

As it was now evident that war was inevitable, the Ijẹbus to
show on which side their sympathy lay, recalled their Agurin at
Ibadan, a sign of declaration of war.

The Arẹ with reference to Abẹokuta said " Too large for a close
siege but for that reason the more vulnerable to famine." His
plan was to swoop down on the farms now and again, cut off
supplies, prevent cultivation, and thus reduce the place by
famine. Hence in his expeditions, the main object was to destroy
foodstuffs, fire the barns, cut down standing corn, chop in pieces
yam and other tuberous foodstuffs.

The second expedition was known as "Igbẹ Igbin" (the Igbin expedition), because some of the Ibadan soldiers encountered Igbin an Ẹgba war chief. But the Ibadan war-chiefs had made a compact among themselves not to fight, but leave the brunt of everything to the Arẹ alone ; therefore when they reached the farms they located themselves at short distances from one another, leaving Aturu the Balogun's head slave to lead the men in search of prey. There was no chief with them when Igbin attacked them vigorously and pursued them a great distance until they reached the vicinity of the Seriki's location when he sent a body of men to drive back the pursuers. Aturu also rallied those within his reach, and led them back safe.

This second expedition was less beneficial to them than the first.

§ 3. Insurrection Against the Arẹ, and the Death of Seriki Iyapọ

The aversion of the chiefs to this war grew stronger every day, and so also did the obstinacy of the Arẹ.

Being bound by a sense of duty to follow him wherever he went, the plot they had made, viz : to take advantage of whatever chance may bring within their reach, but to leave all the fighting to be done by the Arẹ and his slaves, did not prevent the latter from prosecuting his mad resolve. So then the chiefs in order to put an end to this undesirable war were determined to rise against the Arẹ, and make an end of him and with him of the war. For this purpose they met at a given signal in the dead of night on the 1st October, 1877, in the Ogboni house at the Baṣọrun's market. There they took a solemn oath of secrecy and mutual confidence and ratified the same by splitting of kola nuts and the slaughter of a ram, each of them taking his portion home. But they were not all faithful to one another. Solalu the Osi Seriki a notorious tale-bearer went that very night and divulged the whole secret to the Arẹ. Ilọri the Osi also who but lately had incurred the Arẹ's displeasure had not the courage to go the whole length with them, fearing the consequences to himself in case of failure ; he also went secretly and exposed the plot. The majority of the rest of them, knowing this, followed suit, each one to save himself, but the Balogun and the Seriki considered it *infra dig.*, so to betray themselves.

At a general meeting on the 2nd of October, the Arẹ told them what he had heard : they all denied it one after another. But the Arẹ told them that he trusted none of them not even those who professed loyalty to him, he was sure that with a better prospect they would all kick against him.

The matter was suppressed for the time being, but in less than a month it broke out again. The insurrection was fixed for the 1st of November but the secret was divulged again by the notorious Solalu.

The Arẹ was terribly ill at ease. Before the morning of the 1st November he had left home for his farm with his slaves armed. Some surmised that it was his intention to escape from Ibadan, but where to go to? He had offended all their great neighbours. Restless in the farm, he returned to town. He made little account of all the chiefs except the Balogun and the Seriki each of whom was a match for him. In his perplexity he resorted to Chief Mosaderin the brother of the Balogun, with two slaves and valuable presents, begging him to use his influence with the Balogun for good on his behalf. He succeeded. Chief Mosaderin called his brother and remonstrated with him. " What have you as compared with the Arẹ in slaves or wealth to satisfy the greedy appetite of Ibadan chiefs? If he is overthrown to-day it will devolve upon you to-morrow to assume the reins of government, and it will not be long before the same measure is meted out to you. And the Seriki with whom you are in league, have you forgotten that he was the one aspiring to your title when the Arẹ threatened lately to depose you? Will you be able to manage him if you become the Balẹ and he the Balogun? Remember that his father was a native of Ogbomọsọ and descended from an Ẹsọ. He will soon aspire to become a Kakanfo as by right, and what is to become of you then? "

In this way Mosaderin won the Balogun over to the Arẹ and on the latter's return from his farm the Balogun called on him in the evening.

The Arẹ, almost beside himself with joy, greeted him with " Aye my brother and companion in arms, you have almost done for me ! " Having won over the Balogun he was determined not to spare the Seriki. The latter hearing that the Balogun called on the Arẹ called also himself the next day, but the Arẹ refused to see him. He returned home under a shower of stones from the Arẹ's slaves.

Seeing that evil was determined against the Seriki the other chiefs tried to interpose on his behalf, but the Arẹ was resolute. He was determined to rid himself of one whose power and influence had always made him uneasy.

On the 4th of November the Arẹ declared that he pardoned him, but this was a ruse to get him into his power, for he instructed his slaves to shoot him down, when he least expected danger. The Seriki who had friends amongst the Arẹ's slaves heard of it and never committed himself into his hands. The Arẹ could not treat him, however, as he treated the late Aijẹnku, and all measures adopted to get at him and kill him suddenly, failed. So he had recourse to depriving him of his brave men. He deposed him from his title conferring the same on Ajayi Ọsungbẹkun his Ọtun. The notorious Solalu the Osi Seriki he made the Ọtun. Amọwo one of Iyapọ's brave men he made the Osi Seriki, Iyapọ's Bada he made his own, and so of all his principal fighting men, thereby weakening his hands if he meant to fight, and having done this he sent to him to die.

Ajayi, however, was reluctant to supersede his chief, so the Arẹ sent to him to take with him *One wife, one horse and one groom* and leave the town.

On Iyapọ hearing this he sent at once to Ajayi advising him to accept the title. " I know that I am a doomed man," said he " and I must not involve you in my ruin ; as for me, my father was an Eso and I was born an Eso, and like an Eso I will die." He summoned his brothers together, and gave them his last charge, all being present excepting Akintọla the next to him. He distributed his property to his sons and daughters, left directions about the family property (to which he added something) and how to keep up the glory of the house and their father's name, etc. In the meantime he ordered his grave and his coffin to be prepared, and having inspected and approved of both, and having thus set his house in order, on the evening of the 17th November, 1877, this young and brave general entered his bedroom, and put an end to his life !

When the news got abroad, the consternation and agitation in the town were indescribable. All the young Mọgajis Iyapọ's comrades quaked and trembled. They combined and took a solemn oath of mortal hatred of the Arẹ for the death of Iyapọ and a determination to avenge it. They agreed never to win for him a battle, or conquer a hamlet until he was dead and gone. Thus the Arẹ by putting an end to the life of such brave men as Aijẹnku and Iyapọ started the decadence of Ibadan military power. His chief motive was a selfish one, to immortalize his own name and exalt his family never taking into account what providence may have decreed for him.

THE SUCCESSION OF AKINTỌLA

After the death of Iyapọ, Akintọla his brother succeeded him as the head of the house but of course not to his title nor to any public title at all, as the Arẹ was determined to diminish if not extinguish the glory of Ibikunle's house. That quarter of the town of which that house was the centre was broken up, all the strong chiefs therein being assigned to several petty chiefs so that Akintola was left with no following and had none to depend upon but his father's slaves. But all the same he felt that none was equal to him among all the chiefs in that quarter and that the prestige of his father's house was in no way obliterated, he knew that the " Lion of the Master of Camps " will one day arise and shake up himself in all his former power ; but for the present he had to bow to the inevitable.

§ 4. FURTHER RAIDING EXPEDITION ON EGBA FARMS.

On the 19th November, 1877, the Balogun was sent out to raid the Egba farms and he ravaged those that lay near the Ijebus. On the 28th December, he went northwards against those that lay in the direction of Iberekodo and an attempt was even made to capture a village called Ogatedo at the confluence of the Oyan and Ofiki rivers. But the rivers were swollen and the Ibadans having waded waist deep were compelled to retreat before the steady fire of the men of the place, who posted themselves behind the large trees growing along the side of the river, and prevented their gaining the opposite bank. The Balogun being ill in the camp they could not renew their efforts. The expedition returned home on the 17th of January, 1878, the Balogun being borne on a litter.

A NINE DAYS' RAIDING EXPEDITION

On the Balogun's recovery from his illness the Are proposed another expedition and was determined to make a longer stay in the Egba farms this time and thus draw them out to a fight. Hitherto the raids lasted only three days each time and only the Ibadan war-chiefs were concerned, but now he proposed inviting outside help as well. For that purpose he sent the Otun to clear the road leading to Arawo, that is a place midway between Ibadan and Abeokuta on the caravan route. He also invited the war-chiefs of Ife, Modakeke and other subject towns. He could not count upon the complete loyalty of the Ibadan war-chiefs because of their opposition to this enterprise, and because he knew how deeply he had offended most of them ; but he knew the courage and intrepidity of the Ifes and relied more on them. The expedition left Ibadan on the 24th of March, 1878 and encamped next day at Alakisa a few miles beyond Arawo. Having this for their base they ravaged the farms on the right as far as Iberekodo, and on the left as far as they could go. They lived on the spoils of the farm and destroyed the rest, setting the barns on fire. The Egbas however, did not show their faces, but contented themselves with bravely manning their walls against any attack. The Ifẹ army arrived on the 28th and joined them in the field.

At the end of nine days the Arẹ summoned a council and announced that as the Egbas did not take up the challenge and come out for a fight, they should take a roundabout course and capture Oṣiẹlẹ before they returned home. He was opposed by the whole of the Ibadan war-chiefs without exception. They alleged:

1. That they were already exhausted by this 9 days useless exposure.

2. That Oṣiẹlẹ not being taken into account before they left home, they had not first consulted the gods nor offered propitiatory sacrifices as they usually did before attacking a town.

3. That to go to Oṣiẹlẹ from where they were was too risky and inadvisable, because they would leave rear and base exposed to attack by the Egbas should they undertake to attack them by way of Atadi. If Oṣiẹlẹ is to be taken why not go home first and make a direct attack from home by a route shorter and safer ? The Arẹ replied " You had better go and reconsider what you intend to do, as for me, my mind is made up. I am decided, and if there remain only my slaves and Ayikiti the Ifẹ General and the Modakẹkẹ people with me, I shall take Oṣiẹlẹ."

The chiefs retired, but to strengthen the plot against him. They agreed to follow but only to witness how he and his slaves with the Ife and Modakẹkẹ people would take Oṣiẹlẹ. In the meantime private messages had gone to apprise the Egbas of the impending assault on Oṣiẹlẹ. The Ibadan war-chiefs also let their men know that they were not obliged to stand by their masters, nor to stay and fight in case of an attack, but as for themselves they were bound by their office not to desert the Arẹ. Before daybreak on the 1st of April they had started for Oṣiẹlẹ.

The Oṣiẹlẹ army met them at a great distance from their home, and without firing a shot those who led the van of the Ibadan army melted away, bringing the Arẹ himself and his principal war-chiefs face to face with the enemy. Only their bodyguards remained with the chiefs, their fighting men had all gone. The Arẹ and his slaves threw themselves into the attack vigorously, and in the first attack, about 300 of them became *hors de combat* in dead and wounded. Nothing daunted, a second onslaught was made and about 200 became *hors de combat*. The Arẹ's slaves now perceived that the brunt of the fighting was left for them alone to bear, and suspected it was a plot to annihilate them, therefore they also gave way. The Ifẹ and Modakẹkẹ people quickly took in the situation and they themselves gave way, leaving only the Arẹ and his principal war-chiefs with their bodyguards. None of the war-chiefs deserted the Arẹ so that no one could be accused of cowardice. The chiefs knew the risks they were running by thus exposing themselves to be enveloped and taken but they could not have done otherwise; that was the only way to accomplish their plot and bring the Arẹ to reason.

It is now evident the day was lost, and as the Arẹ began to retreat the rush became general and the Ẹgbas pressed hard in pursuit. The camp was a long way off, nearly a day's journey, and hundreds died of thirst. The Arẹ and the veterans about him retreated in good order, or let us rather say were allowed to retreat in good order, for if Ogundipẹ and the Ẹgba war-chiefs had determined to press hard in pursuit the Ibadan army would have been annihilated, but the war-chiefs on either side knew secretly the game they were playing. About 2 p.m. the Arẹ expressed a desire to say his afternoon prayers. "By all means," said the Balogun "you can do so." The Balogun then dismounted and expanding his arms in the direction of the pursuers he said to them "Fire all your shots here." But Sanusi the Arẹ's eldest son and Idagana one of his principal slaves threw themselves forward and kept· the Ẹgba pursuers at bay until the Arẹ had said his prayers ; and once on the saddle again they retreated hastily. The casualties on the whole were slight. Sanusi was wounded in the lip, the Balogun lost a favourite servant in this campaign, and the Mọgaji of the late Chief Bioku was captured by the Ẹgbas. The wreck of the expedition returned home on the 2nd of April, 1878.

The Arẹ was greatly disappointed, especially in his own slaves. He said he had thought that come what might he could always count upon a thousand at least to stand by him for weal or woe, but alas he was deserted. However, he comforted himself with this reflection : "There is no one who may not suffer a defeat, for even the prophet of God (Mahomet) suffered a defeat."

After this all the interior war-chiefs returned to their homes but Ayikiti and the Ifẹ war-chiefs. Several offices had to be filled among them. Also the office of the Ọwọni of Ifẹ was vacant by the death of Ayikiti's father, and he was desirous of succeeding him. The Ifẹs, however, were for another prince and not Ayikiti, but he so pressed his claims that the Arẹ had to give in, and so on the 8th April after titles had been arranged for all vacancies in the Ifẹ chieftaincies, messengers from the Ibadan chiefs followed Ayikiti home to crown him the Ọwọni of Ifẹ.

Another Raid.—The Arẹ, however, was not dispirited by the defeat and failure to capture Ọsiẹlẹ, he sent the Ọtun out again to clear the direct route *via* the Agangan hill. In the meantime he was carrying on a private negotiation with the Ijẹbus for

a treaty of friendship and commerce working chiefly through
the Ijẹbus resident at Ibadan and the Ijẹbu Rẹmọs. But the
answer of the Awujalẹ of the Ijẹbus was insolent, bidding the Arẹ
first to be on friendly terms with the Ẹgbas, the ALÂFIN, the Ijẹsas
and the Ifẹs, and when he saw the messengers of the heads of these
states he would reconsider his relations with Ibadan.   The Ibadan
chiefs hearing this reply were so enraged at its insolence that they
were willing to yield to the Arẹ's determination that the reply to
the Awujalẹ should take a practical form by sending the Balogun
to ravage the Ẹgba farms.   Although they held a different view
from their chief in this matter of Abẹokuta yet they could not
brook any insults to him from outside.   They marched out on
the 20th of May, 1878.

§ 5. THE REVOLT OF THE EKITI TRIBES

The Ekiti tribes who had long been groaning under the yoke
of the Ibadans, seized the opportunity of the latter being involved
in complications with the Ẹgbas and Ijẹbus to rebel against them.
Adeyàlá, prince of Ila, Fabunmi and Odẹyale both of Mẹsin-
Olọja-Oke, allied themselves together to commence hostilities
against the Ibadans.

Their first act of rebellion was to seize all Oyọs (Yorubas proper)
residing peacefully amongst them with their families.   They killed
some, and the rest they sold into slavery.   Then they collected
together a large number of hen coups, and skulls of cattle, set them
up as fetish, and offered to them sacrifices of human beings, the
victims being (1) The Ibadan messengers that oppressed them so
much ; (2) and the Ajẹlẹs (political residents) of the Ibadan chiefs
among them ; fowls and cattle being the chief articles of diet these
messengers generally demanded from them.   The massacre at
Ila alone was estimated at about 1,000 human beings !

The Ijẹsas of Ilesa who had more than once come into collision
with the Ibadans before, were rather wary and felt very reluctant
to join this coalition ; indeed they were frequently seized with
panic from false rumours of the approach of the Ibadans, so that
Ilesa itself was more than once deserted from this cause.   There
were good reasons for this however.   One was the transport of
ammunition from Ibadan to Mẹsin Ipole, a town which had not
then thrown off its allegiance, but this was in order to settle between
two brothers a dispute which had risen to undue proportions and
in which an armed intervention had become necessary.

The other was that Ayikiti the Owọni lately crowned by the
Arẹ for the Ifẹs captured some Ijẹsa towns, viz., Ipindun, Ifẹ
wàrà, and Osu in order to possess himself of the wherewith to

defray the expenses of his coronation.   All these gave rise to the
panic at Ilesa.

On the 16th June news reached Ibadan that the Ilorins had
joined the coalition against them, and the King of Ilorin was
said to have sent the following message to the Are of Ibadan.
" If a man's wife deserted him, and afterwards repented and
came back to him, is not the husband justified in receiving her
back " The Are's reply was " Yes he is, but let the husband
beware of what he may contract from the whore." The key to the
parable is this :—When the Fulanis overran the northern Yoruba
territories, the Ilorins became masters of the Ekiti provinces also ;
but when the Ibadans rose to power the Ekitis transferred their
allegiance to them. But now they are disposed to return to their
" first love " and thus are compared to an erring wife returning to
her former husband. The meaning of the Ibadan reply is obvious,
the Ilorins may thereby involve themselves in a war of which they
may have cause to regret. The Are took no heed of the rebellion,
but was prosecuting his desultory warfare with the Egbas.

On the 23rd of June, there was a terrible conflagration at Ibadan;
the Balogun and Seriki in whose quarters the fire broke out went
to arrest its progress, but unfortunately, before they reached home,
sparks from the flames had set their own houses on fire. Every
preparation having been made for an expedition to the Egba
farms, it was thought that it would be postponed, but early next
morning (June 24th) whilst the embers were still smouldering,
the Balogun's drum was heard on its way to the Egba farms.
This expedition returned on the evening of the 26th June bringing
about 40 captives.

On the 14th of July another expedition went out under Ali the
Otun, the Are sending Kupolu with him, but they were not as
successful as the last.

The people of Ila afterwards got alarmed at their own acts, and
began to be afraid of the consequences. They therefore sent on the
16th July ambassadors to Ibadan to make amends, and to sue
for peace ; but these were roughly received and were sent back
home to prepare for the worst. Upon this the Ekitis sent no
more to Ibadan but took further steps to strengthen their alliances
and put their defences in order.

The confederates now aimed at wresting from the Ibadans
all their subject towns including Oyo towns under their protection
from Ikirun to Iwo, and limit the Ibadan territories to the river
Oba, that is the natural limits of their farms in that direction.
It soon became evident that the Ifes had joined them, because
their only safe route to Benin for ammunition via Oke Igbo became

unsafe from kidnappers ; but the people of Modakẹkẹ being Ọyọs and not Ifẹs refused to join the coalition knowing that the destruction of Ibadan would be their own ruin, as the Ifẹs were ever hostile to them, but remained quiet for fear of the Ibadans.

On the 19th August news reached Ibadan that the Ekiti allies had marched against Igbajọ. Igbajọ is a border town and as its name implies contains a mixed population of Ọyọs, Ijẹsas, Ekitis and other clans. In its physical aspect it is like the rest of the Ekiti towns but the rulers and principal inhabitants were Ọyọs and all were Ọyọs in sympathy. They maintained their allegiance to Ibadan refusing to join the coalition. Hence the resolve to remove them out of the way before marching on the nearest genuine Ọyọ town—Ikirun.

Not even did this news move the Arẹ. He sent the Balogun to ravage the Ẹgba farms on the other side of the Ogun river, not only because those on this side had been utterly despoiled, but also because he meant further to straighten Abẹokuta, and more especially to be in touch with Porto Novo in order to procure ammunition. He took Ọgatẹdo by an assault, and from Mẹko he sent on the caravans that accompanied him to Porto Novo for ammunition and salt, and the Seriki to escort them beyond the danger zone, and there to await their return.

On hearing that the army of the Ẹgbas was out to waylay his caravans, the Balogun formed links from his base at Mẹko right on to the Seriki's post for mutual defence ; the Ọtun and Osi being placed within easy reach of the Seriki, and then his own division under Aderibigbe the Mọgaji of the late Balẹ Olugbode, and a part under his own brother Mosaderin, and his eldest son Babalọla and his head slave Jato.

This last division considered themselves practically secure ; hence they neglected all precautions, placed no sentinels and were completely off their guard. It was this division the Ẹgbas surprised and attacked. They were dispersed, and Kurakura the Hausa slave of Chief Ogundeyi of Abẹokuta hotly pursued after Aderibigbe and would have caught him, but that the latter was a splendid rider and was well mounted on a powerful steed. It was late in the afternoon when the Ọtun and his companions hearing the continuous report of musketry at their rear contrary to expectation came up with their forces, and drove the Ẹgbas away and once more cleared the road.

The Balogun before leaving Mẹko sent a kidnapping expedition to the Ketu farms, a part of which was successful ; but the Ketus, being well acquainted with their country, took by-paths, attacked the kidnappers and rescued their people. Several Ibadans were caught, but most of them escaped to Mẹkọ and Ibadan.

But whilst all this was going on in the South-west the scene in the North-east was one of dreadful carnage. The Igbajọs defended themselves heroically and repelled the enemy more than once ; at the second instance the Egũgun Chief Priest of Ila was caught and slain. But the allies were reinforced and returned to the attack.

On appeal to Ibadan for help Ọsuntoki the Mayẹ of Ibadan was sent with a small force to assist Igbajọ, but it was found that the Arẹ underrated the strength of the coalition. Igbajọ could hold out no longer, Mayẹ was obliged to retreat with the Igbajos to Ikirun, with the allies at their heels, laying siege to Ikirun.

The King of Ilọrin now sent out his forces under the command of Ajia to join the allies at the siege of Ikirun with instructions to sweep all Ọyọ towns, right on to the river Ọba at the confines of the Ibadan farms, that is to say, to take Ikirun, Oṣogbo, Ẹdẹ and Iwo with their villages.

The Ilọrins commenced operations at Ọtan a village near Ikirun, and at the onset met with an ominous disaster. The people of this village hearing of their approach deserted the place and hid themselves among the craggy rocks surrounding the village. The Ilọrins finding no one to oppose them flew to the spoils, and thus engaged, the men of Ọtan came in and set on them slaying many ; only a few of those who entered the town made good their escape, and that with great difficulty. The Ilọrins receiving reinforcement from home laid siege also against Ikirun. Thus was Ikirun hemmed in nearly on all sides by the Ilọrins, the Ekitis and Ila, with the Ijẹsas, and the inhabitants were obliged to defend themselves within their walls, and the thickets surrounding the town.

The small Ibadan contingent at Ikirun reported matters at home but no help was speedily forthcoming, as the Balogun, with the flower of the Ibadan army had not yet returned from Mẹkọ. On the 14th of October, 1878 the Ibadan expedition returned home. The Balogun was ordered to make a hasty preparation and march out in five days.

CHAPTER XXIV

CONFLICTS IN THE NORTH

§ 1. THE CELEBRATED BATTLE OF IKIRUN OTHERWISE CALLED— "THE JALUMI WAR"

THE Aṛẹ of Ibadan at this crisis hastily filled up one or two gaps in the ranks of the chiefs. Ọranyan was worshipped on the 20th October and the standard of war immediately marched northwards to the seat of carnage. It was a most unfavourable time for the army to march out, as it was the time of the latter rains. The rivers were unusually full, and unhappily many of the soldiers found a watery grave in the overswollen Ọba and Ọṣun rivers before ever they came in sight of the enemy.

The expedition was altogether a trying one for the Balogun, for the Aṛẹ even in this hour of danger recklessly continued to practise those short-sighted, suicidal policies of his which tended to weaken the power of Ibadan, thus showing a great lack of statesmanship. He slyly tried to handicap the Balogun by making the Osi his rival. To this young man already of considerable importance he assigned most of his own war-chiefs and his fighting slaves, and also all the fighting men of the late Seriki Iyapọ his old rival. Intoxicated with such honours conferred upon him, the Osi looked down upon the Balogun ; he not only refused to obey orders, but often dictated his wish to the Balogun. Happily the latter was a man of great experience, of consummate tact, and marvellous resources ; he would readily yield in minor points as of no great importance in order to maintain peace and harmony at this crisis. Twice before they reached Ikirun he claimed in advance from the Balogun a reward for the victory that he would achieve, for he was confident that the honour of the victory would be his. At each time the Balogun sent him 10 heads of cowries. It must be added, however, that he was scarcely ever sober during the expedition. The free use of spirituous liquors was considered at this time the acme of pleasure and mark of greatness ; spirits being at this period beyond the reach of poor men.

At Oṣogbo the Osi deeply offended the principal slaves that formed his body guard, and on whom he depended at the supreme hour of danger, by disfiguring two of them with facial marks for an offence of seizing things from people in the market by way of privilege. The big slaves interceded in vain. They pleaded for any other punishment but that, but he gave them no heed, the culprits were marked with two gashes on either cheek from the top of the head to the chin. This action they were determined to revenge whenever opportunity offered.

At Oṣogbo, he also related to those about him a dream he had in which he saw his late father Ogunmọla and his brother Oṣun. He felt rather uncomfortable thereat, and was advised to offer sacrifices to them. This he did with a horse and a cow.

Meanwhile at Ikirun matters were growing from bad to worse. The last battle fought before the arrival of the Ibadans was on the 30th October, 1878, in which the Ikiruns were hemmed in on all sides, and they had to fight within the town walls. Balogun Ogboriefọn with the Ibadan forces at last entered Ikirun on Thursday the 31st October. It was said that the Akirun, Oyebode the chief ruler of Ikirun, when he saw the Ibadan forces marching into the town for his succour was so overcome with joy that he could only say to the Balogun " Ajayi, are you come ? I am almost done for." The Balogun replied, " Take courage, take courage, we are come, your deliverance is at hand."

The Balogun of Ibadan now learnt from the Ikiruns the situation of affairs. The allies were in three different camps. The Ilọrins under the command of Ajia were encamped by themselves North-eastwards, near the Ikirun farms ; the Ilas and Ekitis together not very far off from the Ilọrins under Prince Adeyala of Ila, and Fabunmi of Oke Mẹsin respectively, and the Ijẹṣas under their generals Ayimọrọ and Ogunmọdẹde eastwards. These last had in the meantime captured the small town of Iba near Ikirun and were encamped within its walls. Iba we may mention was the paternal town of Oṣuntoki the Mayẹ of Ibadan (afterwards Balẹ) who headed the contingent for the relief of Igbajọ.

From these three points the foes marched in the day of battle, and attacked Ikirun on all sides.

At a council of war held the very day of their arrival the Balogun of Ibadan proposed to give the men one or two days' rest, the journey from Ibadan being tedious on account of the incessant rains and the privations they endured, and then to march against the confederates. The Osi again opposed the Balogun. He was to march at once the next day " before the allies are aware of our arrival ; " and if the Balogun will not go, he will. " To-morrow," said the Balogun " will be Friday, and Fridays being unlucky days it is not likely the allies will attack us, and the men may as well have some rest."

The Osi again objected, and the Balogun yielded the point. Then again the Balogun in ordering the battle proposed to divide the Ibadan army into two parts, one led by himself against the armies of the Ilọrins and the Ekitis encamping not very far off from each other, especially as he had been told that was the strongest part ; and the other under the Osi to go against the Ijẹsas encamping eastwards at Iba. Again the Osi objected. "The Ilọrins and the Ekitis lie to the left of us," said he, " and I am the commander of the left, to the left therefore I go." "Very good," replied the Balogun " You can have your own way."

As the Osi commanded nearly the half of the whole Ibadan forces, there was no reason why he should not accomplish successfully what he proposed to do, provided he acted with reason and judgment.

Those about him reported that he was restless and sleepless all night, he ate little but drank much, and it had been so since their arrival at Oṣogbo. He emptied ·a bottle of gin before ordering his horse to be saddled long before daybreak. He marched out of the town by the Northern (Ọfa) gate, long before his war-chiefs including Akintọla were ready. He dismounted and halted a while before dawn behind the town wall until some of his men came and then he proceeded ; the others had to hurry after him one after another as each was ready.

The Balogun at dawn with the Ọtun marched out by the eastern or Oba'gun gate leading past the ancient village of that name, along the fine road that leads to the town of Iba where the Ijẹsas were then encamped.

The Osi's route lay for about three miles along the highway to the north, then it verged towards the right nearly at right angles along a farm road, a high range of mountains parallel to this separating the forces of the Osi from those of the Balogun. About three miles along this farm road the Ilorin camp could be descried on the left hand side, situated on a hill on the other side of a morass, but approachable by a ford which lay about a mile further on, which point was more directly near the Ekiti camp. Those of Osi's men who had gone before went straight along to this ford, but the Osi wishing to take a short cut to the Ilọrin camp left the road and went by a bush path and through farms with the intention of attacking the Ilọrins on both sides at once. This after-thought he never communicated to those before. Many of his war-chiefs coming on after him went straight on along the road not knowing that he had left it for a bush path straight for the Ilọrin camp.

The Ekitis were surprised to see the Ikiruns out against them but the reason soon became evident, they had been reinforced. Those who went early to the stream were driven back at the sight

Q

of the Ikiruns, and they reported to the camp the advance of the enemy.

Fabūmi and his colleagues attacked them vigorously and over-powered them ; they were surprised at not seeing their chief and no reinforcement coming up to their aid, so they were driven back and dispersed. Fabūmi pursued them till he came to the spot where Ilori the Osi took to the bush path, and this was pointed out to him. By that time Ilori had attacked the Ilorins and had repelled those out against him, and was pressing hard to capture the camp when he heard the sound of Akintola's drum coming up behind him " *Kiriniun Onibudo*," " *Kiriniun Onibudo*." He sent a mounted messenger to greet Akintola and to say " You are rather late in coming, I had almost entered the Ilorin camp, however, you are welcome."

But the messenger never returned, and Ilori's men noticed that the rolling of the drum was not perfect in style, they therefore suspected treachery and communicated their fears to their master. But he replied " Who else can it be ? Is not that Akintola's war-cry Ki-ri-ni-un Oni-budo ? " When too late, he discovered the treachery. Fabūmi of Oke Mesin it was who was counterfeiting the war-cry of Akintola, who had been left behind.

It was at such a crisis like this that his guards would have stood by him to a man and kept the enemy at bay until relief should come from those he left behind ; but he had insulted those trusty servants and this was their time of revenge. He was helped to his horse, but at best he was not a good rider, and his head had become muddled by drink. The horse soon got entangled in a yam field and fell down, and the illustrious Ilori was taken alive and conducted to the Ilorin camp ! At the camp he was stripped of everything he had on, a rag being given him to wrap across himself and was kept in a room under close supervision. One Koiditan a renegade from Ibadan betrayed his personality to the Ilorins, and they in ecstasies of joy at the capture of so illustrious a prisoner gave themselves up to feasting and enjoyment for the day, appre-hending no further trouble. The Ikiruns sadly disappointed at this turn of events were ready to stone the Ibadans, they insulted them to their face saying to them " We could not drive them away indeed, but we never suffered so ignominious a defeat as this, and what is the good of you ? "

So the Osi's men were scattered, many of them fleeing back to the town met those just coming out, and together they fled back to Ikirun.

But some of them instead of retracing their steps to Ikirun went across the mountain range to the other side and told the Balogun

what had happened.   They met him in the thick of the fight with
the Ijẹsas, company after company on both sides marching to the
fighting line, attacking each other furiously.   As soon as the
escaped arrived and reported " The Osi has been captured alive
and his army dispersed ! " The Balogun was startled ; but he
was a man full of resources, and endued with remarkable presence
of mind " Sh——" said he to the men, " say nothing of this to
any one as you value your lives."   He quickly called about half-a-
dozen of his slaves, and bade them roll themselves in the dust
—they did so.   He then bade one of his servants " bind them hand
to neck as men captured in battle and take them to the Ọtun
with my compliments, and say Ilọri has entered the Ilọrin camp,
here are captives that he sent us.   What are we doing ? " He then
sent a message to Babalọla his eldest son saying " I can see what
your younger brother is doing but goodness alone knows what
you are doing ; be careful, lest I disinherit you in favour of him."
Just then a company of Ijẹsas were coming to the attack, but
instead of another company of Ibadans meeting them in the
fighting line, he threw his whole force suddenly upon them and
overwhelmed them.   He ordered that everyone be put to the
sword, and they were all massacred.   They had scarcely done this
when another company was coming gaily on to relieve these.
The Balogun ordered a feint retreat so as to allow the company
to advance further before firing, so his men hastily retreated, and
this retreat encouraged the Ijẹsas to advance forward. The Balogun
meanwhile had his eyes on them to see the effect of the massacre.
As soon as the Ijẹsa company came up suddenly on their
massacred comrades, finding them wallowing in their blood,
they stood stock still, panic stricken.   The Balogun noting this
at once ordered a general charge " Ọmọ Ibadan, ẹ gba ẹfi ti wọn."
(Ibadan boys, up and at them).   " Ẹ ma jẹ wọn o lọ—" (let not
one escape) at once rang throughout the whole army, and the
panic stricken Ijẹsas gave way, the panic spread throughout their
army, and the Balogun followed them up foot to foot into the town
of Iba where they were encamped, and Iba was retaken.   The
bulk of the Ijẹsas fell into his hands.   He then issued that heartrending, never to be forgotten order " Let no one stay for booty
or captive, all prisoners must be slain at once, both will hamper us,
the latter may prove treacherous."   And so all the Ijẹsas captured
were put to the sword.   It was a heartrending sight, for many of
them were formerly slaves at Ibadan who ran away to enlist
under the flag of rebellion or of liberty (from whatever point we
view it).   Old comrades, calling each other by name craved for
mercy.   But the Balogun's orders rang out " Whosoever will not

kill his captive, let him be killed with his captive." So all were massacred! And then the Balogun immediately turned his face northwards towards the Ilọrin camp without delay. As they marched along a body of Ekitis about 1,000 strong appeared on their right flank to attack them, but the Balogun neither noticed nor regarded them, notwithstanding all their efforts at firing ; they had to cease firing of their own accord, amazed at such a spectacle. There was but one thought uppermost in the Balogun's mind, and in that of every Ibadan soldier, viz., how to rescue Ilori the Osi.

It was about 2 p.m., when the Ilọrins heard the drum of the Balogun coming. " And who is that again ? " they asked, and were told " The Balogun." " Any other Balogun besides the one we captured this morning ? " they asked. They went out to meet the Ibadans, and within a short time, they were repulsed. The fine river that flowed by the town of Iba, flowed also along the foot of the hill where the Ekiti camp was situated, and from which they obtained water. That river loses itself in a morass here below the Ilọrin camp, and the only spot where a ford was possible was along a winding stream breast deep at this season. The Ilọrins having retreated to the other side held the Ibadans in check for a while on the other side of the morass. There they stood face to face, the attackers and the defenders.

Chief Akintọla, who we may remember was attached to the Osi's army, was left behind as we saw when that unfortunate chief rushed on before daybreak to his own fate. By the time he came up to his chief, the tragedy had taken place, and he was met by the fugitives defeated by Fabũmi. He therefore retraced his steps back to Ikirun, and took the other route to join the Balogun. By the time he reached Iba, the Balogun had finished with the Ijẹṣas and had cleared out of the place, and he had to follow in his track to where the battle was now raging. The Ibadan boys all but exhausted after the morning's fight and the day's march, encouraged at the sight of fresh troops were exhilarated by the in-spiriting air of Akintọla's war cry, which the whole army took up with a swing " Kiriniun Onibudo Kiriniun Onibudo." Thus came up Akintọla ; and stretching forth his hand across to the enemy, half turned on his saddle to his men he said " Awọn ta nu ? Awọn ta l'ẹmba ṣe ta nta ? " (and who are those ? Who are they with whom you are exchanging shots?) Immediately the Ibadan boys dashed into the morass, treading on one another they struggled across the quagmire and hurled themselves upon their foes. The Ilọrins taken aback by this unexpected, this mad rush became completely demoralized and gave way. The Ibadans

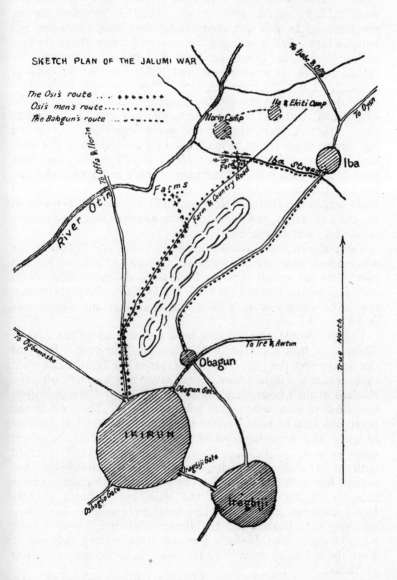

SKETCH PLAN OF THE JALUMI WAR

The Osi's route .... ++++++++
Osi's men's route..............
The Balogun's route ...- - - - -

entered the Ilọrin camp, captured a large number, put some to the sword and demolished the camp. All those who were captured in the morning with the Osi, speedily rejoined their comrades and made captives among their captors. The Osi's men were among the foremost to seek out their master, but alas, the worst had befallen him. When he heard the noise and tramp of the Ibadans within the Ilọrin camp, he tried to make his escape ; he rushed out of his confinement and hid himself in a clump of fignut trees not far from the tent. The Ilọrins in their hasty flight did not forget the illustrious captive, but he could not be found until betrayed by a woman who saw him in his hiding place ; then a man with drawn sword rushed upon him and put him to death before he made good his own escape. The same fate befel several of the minor chiefs, Ilọri's fighting men who were caught with him that morning. Ijẹsas and Ekitis who had lived at Ibadan and knew all these chiefs at sight easily pointed them out to the Ilọrins. Koiditan the renegade and betrayer of the Osi was caught, and taken to Ikirun where he was subsequently tried and publicly executed.

The Balogun then turned towards the Ekiti and Ila camp. It was evident that they had no longer any spirit of resistance left in them. By one assault that was taken also, and so the three camps were smashed on one and the same day by Balogun Ajayi Ogboriẹfọn. The victory was decisive and complete, and Ikirun was saved.

The Ọfa people who had long been groaning under the yoke of Ilọrin took this opportunity to throw off their yoke. They cut the bridge over the Ọtin river at the rear of the Ilọrins, and when these in their flight came to the river now swollen, with the Ibadans at their heels, they rushed into it. Here thousands upon thousands of men, women and horses perished. The river at one point was said to be so choked with human bodies and carcases of horses that some fugitives who came later were able to escape upon corpses. Ajia the Ilọrin commander-in-chief escaped with great difficulty with one of his favourite wives, but several Ilọrin chiefs and well-to-do people were caught. Prince Adeyala of Ila fell among the slain but Fabũmi of Oke Mẹsin managed to escape. The roads were said to be strewn all along with loads which the Ilọrins could not carry in their hasty flight. The Ibadans pursued their victory right up to Ẹrin about 8 miles from Ọfà ; the head chiefs however remained at Ikirun.

This event gave the name to this expedition " Ogun Jalumi," i.e. the rush-into-the-river war.

NOTABLE EVENTS OF THE DAY

1. Roti, Ilọri's head slave and a very great favourite, with whom he was as a most intimate friend, eating out of the same dish and drinking out of the same cup, and from whom he was never parted, was in another part of the field that fatal morning when the disaster overtook his master. When he observed that something was wrong, he rode up hastily asking " Ilọri da ? Ilọri da ? " (And where is Ilọri ?) The reply was " Ogun mu u lọ " (taken by the enemy). He uttered one deep groan " O—h " He then bade his comrades farewell " Good-bye to you all, no home for me again." He drew his sword, put spurs to his horse and dashed into the midst of the Ilọrins, slashing on the right and on the left, killing many before he fell among the slain.

2. Akintọla's drum played a most notable part in the day's business ; it won and lost for the Ilọrins, it lost and won for the Ibadans. And here let us note a most remarkable instance of retributive justice. The trick now played upon Ilọri by Fabũmi by which Ilọri was captured was the same played by Ilọri's father the famous Ogunmọla upon the Ijayes after the Iwawun war. It will be remembered how on his return march he counterfeited the war cry of Kurũmi of Ijaye, and in that way all Ijayes who had escaped into the mountains thinking their master was come to their rescue came down from their hiding places and fell a prey into his hands (vide Chap. xviii, page 349). The same trick was now played by Fabũmi on his son with fatal results.

3. The Ifẹ and Modakẹkẹ people who always joined the Ibadans in every expedition of theirs came up late this time after everything was over. The Ibadan boys taunted them to their face and accused them of intentional delay because of the formidable appearance of the war ; but said they " we have already shown that we can do without you."

The Ifẹs never uttered a word of excuse, nor resented the remarks but followed up the chase and took Ilọfa. (The fact was that the Ifẹs had secretly wished the issue to be otherwise in order to cast off their own yoke also ; and the Modakẹkẹs having their eyes on them would not leave them behind). They also joined in taking Omù, Ẹrinmope, Gogo, etc., and the conquest was pursued up to Ẹkan. This was a small town but the men of that place were mostly hunters and sharp-shooters. They manned their walls so that the Ibadan boys failed to take it by assault. The Balogun hearing this sent Ali Laluwoye the Ọtun to their help. He was nearly a month in this small place and was content to reduce it by famine. They negotiated peace, sending valuable presents by Aturu who was sent to conclude a treaty with them. The Balẹ and Balogun of the place were sent by Ali to Ikirun to the Balogun of Ibadan to ratify the treaty.   The Otun was thereupon recalled from the siege, to the great disgust of the Ibadan warboys who grumbled much against their unlucky and inefficient chief.

The victory and its cost were reported at Ibadan simultaneously on the 5th of November, so that the joy was greatly tempered with the painful loss they had sustained by the death of Ilori and his brave comrades.

The Balogun received orders not to waste time to retaliate on the Ijesas or Ekitis as they would soon tender their submission.   He was not to go beyond Ila, but rather to turn his face against Ilorin towns.

On the 18th November the Ilorins sent ambassadors to Ibadan to sue for peace.   The Are took occasion to remind them of the parable of the whorish wife returning to her husband and what he predicted would likely be the result.   Knowing that their overtures were only for the purpose of redeeming their chiefs who were captured in the war, and kept as state prisoners, and still smarting under the loss of Ilori the Osi and his brave comrades, the Are and chiefs sent them back home without an answer.

Whilst the Ibadans were rejoicing and mourning at the same time over the affairs in the north, the Egbas came to kidnap in their farms on the 22nd of December, and some farmers were carried off to Abeokuta.

The Balogun was at length recalled and the Ibadans returned home on the 23rd December, 1878, with the Balogun in an indifferent state of health.

§ 2. THE RESULTS OF THE JALUMI WAR.

The results that followed this crushing defeat of the allies were totally different from what the Are of Ibadan had expected. In his opinion the disastrous results to the Ilorins were quite sufficient to make them hold aloof from the rebel states, and these he expected would tender unreserved submission, and that things would henceforth move as smoothly as before ; but, as we shall see matters took a totally different turn everywhere.   The Are now saw the necessity of being on friendly terms with at least one of the neighbouring states.   The Ijesas and Ekitis were subject states, he could never treat with them on terms of equality.   The Ilorins lately defeated were characteristically untrustworthy, Ibadan could have nothing to gain from that quarter.   The Egbas the Are was determined to subjugate so as to open a free route to the coast to all Oyos through the river Ogun.   There remained only the Ijebus with whom Ibadans could possibly treat, and therefore the Arẹ sent large presents with some slaves to the Awujalẹ of Ijẹbu and craved for friendly relations, as there had never been any cause of quarrel between them. But the Ijẹbus refused a *rapprochement* and declined the presents. They openly declared themselves allies of the Ẹgbas and Ekitis, surmising that all this pretence of friendship was mainly for the purpose of procuring war materials from the coast through the Ijẹbus themselves.

The Arẹ resented this rebuff by sending another raiding expedition to the Ẹgba farms. The Balogun who returned home from Ikirun ill, was getting worse and worse every day, so he sent the Ọtun and the Seriki, but they returned on the 4th of January, without a single captive.

Meanwhile the storm was gathering thick in the north and north-east. The effect of the late defeat was to exasperate rather than dishearten the allies, and they were determined more than ever not only to wipe off the disgrace but also to crush the Ibadan power if not destroy that town altogether.

Although the Ilọrin refugees were well treated at Ọfa yet they were determined to take vengeance by destroying that town for their conduct in destroying the bridge over the river Ọtin which occasioned such tremendous losses to them.

Karàrà the Hausa Balogun of Ilọrin, who, on account of his marked disloyalty to his King was denied the honour of conducting the battle which ended so disastrously, came out to succour the escaped. He came as far as Ẹlẹhinjare, but when he heard of the Ibadans pursuing as far as Ẹrin, he retreated to Ganmọ as he was not then prepared to fight. Here he remained until he received orders to destroy the town of Ọfa. This he meant to do by stratagem, and to make quick work of it. He asked leave of the Ọlọfa to allow him to pass through his town to Ẹrin in order to punish that small town for intrigue. But the Ọlọfa was wide awake ; he knew who the prime intriguer was, therefore, the reply he gave was " Not until I am removed out of the way." Karàrà now threw off the mask and openly declared war against Ọfa ; leaving Ganmọ he went forward and pitched his first camp.

This expedition was not popular at Ilọrin, because King Alihu wished to be on good terms with the Ibadans, at least for the present, in order to ransom all the Ilọrin chiefs caught in the last war. But Karàrà it was said threatened to convert his camp into a town, and set up Mọ́mọ́ the heir apparent to be king over it, in opposition to Ilọrin, and so Alihu was obliged to let him have his own way.

The Ọfas sent to Ibadan for help on the 20th of February, 1879 ; the Arẹ sent Ali the Ọtun with all his forces, also Kanike one of his own head slaves with some of his men, and the Ǫtun, Osi, and Ękęrin of the Seriki ; later on he sent Akintǫla.

This on the whole was a very weak force, for, although there were some very strong men in it, yet the leader of the expedition was held to be both unlucky and incompetent.

But King Alihu did not despair ; in order to conciliate the Ibadans he declared all the roads in his territory open for trade so that all Ǫyǫs immured in Bida and in Hausa towns were able to come down in safety. He then sent an embassy again to Ibadan to negotiate for peace between them, and to arrange for the ransom of the Ilǫrins captured in war, but the Arę declared he could not entertain the idea unless the siege of Ǫfa was raised.

The Arę now endeavoured to fill up the gaps made in the late war by making some indispensable appointments. Akintaro the heir of the late Balogun Akere he made the Osi Balogun in place of the late Ilǫri. For the great house of Ogunmǫla there was none but the youthful Kongi son of the late Ǫsun, Ilǫri's elder brother. He was now advanced to be the head of the house with the title of Aręagoro. These two were the most important.

Death of the Balogun of Ibadan.—In the midst of this crisis the Ibadans suffered an irreparable loss by the death of their Balogun. On the 7th of April, 1879, the firing of musketry, volleys upon volleys announced to the public that Ajayi nick-named Ogborięfǫn had passed away! The town went into deep mourning, as he was the last of those veteran generals of Ibadan, who had seen great fights and made a name, with the sole exception of the Arę. Those who were now to the fore were not the old and experienced but the young and untried heirs of great houses according to the policy favoured by the Arę. He was buried at about 10 p.m., with full pagan and military rites. An eye-witness thus described the interment. The grave was dug in his bedroom, the large coffin was first lowered, and the body wound up as usual was placed in it, and then nailed up. Four flint-lock guns, a naked sword, and strings of cowries were placed upon the coffin, and a kid was immolated, the blood being poured on the lid of the coffin, and prayers offered to the gods for his soul.

Ajayi was a native of Ejigbo, he came to Ibadan for the love of a military career. He was nick-named Ogborięfǫn from the following circumstance :—At a battle in the Ęfǫn country, he noticed a man who posted himself behind a large tree doing havoc to the Ibadans. The man was using two guns giving an assistant the one he had discharged to be reloaded for him while he took his deadly aim with the loaded gun. Ajayi then a common soldier quietly crept into the bush behind him, going on all fours till he came near enough to this marksman, and then suddenly shot him down dead. The assistant bolted clean away. Ajayi then cut off the Ẹfọn's head held it by the ear between his teeth being besmeared all over with blood, and with the man's guns on his shoulders came again to his comrades who raised for him a shout of triumph and acclaimed him " Ogboriẹfọn " i.e. a carrier of the Efọn's head.

He was always a poor man, for he spent too lavishly, but he was a brave and hardy soldier. This characteristic cleaved to him all through life from a private to the post of commander-in-chief and was the cause of many errors in his procedure which all but marred his career. For a long time his favourite companions were his only slave Jato, a man with a fair complexion, and his horse ; then some friends associated together and made him their leader, and thus by degrees he rose to a responsible position. His first military appointment was when he ·was created an Abẹsẹ and sent to Ilọra during the Ijaye war to reinforce the Ọyọ army against Iran. He was marched off with Ogunmọla to Iwawun where he received a wound which nearly proved fatal to him.

The next period where he made a name was the Ilesạ war, when he and Latosisa were stationed at the Òdò road where he had to oppose Ogedemgbe and the army from the city, and Latosisa that from the country ; and Ogedemgbe capitulated to him.

The blot on his character was serious. He intrigued to get rid of Ajọbọ who had helped him to bear the expenses incidental to his taking office on filling the post of Osi Balogun which was bestowed upon him after the Ilesạ war. Also his withdrawal from the coalition in the insurrection against the Arẹ and the betrayal of Iyapọ. Added to these was the wholesale massacre of the Ijẹsạ .captives in the taking of the camp at Iba, for which however, he pleaded military necessity.

But there were pleasing traits in his character. His liberality and humility gained him the respect of the soldiers and made his memory lasting. He will always be remembered as the hero of the Jalumi war. His eldest son Babalọla was his heir, and became the head of his house.

§ 3. THE EKITIPARAPỌS

Instead of tendering their submission as the Arẹ thought they would do, the Ijẹsạs, Ekitis, Ẹfọns and other tribes hitherto subjected to the Ibadans formed an alliance which they termed Ekiti parapọ i.e. the Ekiti confederation. They raised a formidable army and were determined not only to liberate themselves but also to overrun the Ọyọ tribes right on to the Ibadan farms at the river Ọba.

They invited Ogedemgbe to come over to lead them ; but this hardy warrior, having crossed swords more than once with the Ibadans was loth to do so again, but rather tried to see what might be done by entreaties and remonstrance in order to ameliorate the condition of his people. The arrogance of the Arẹ made him deaf to reason ; he simply snubbed Ogedemgbe for his pains ; but this simple hearted soldier regarding his oaths to the Ibadans kept to his promise and for a long time never moved from his retreat. Meanwhile Fabūmi of Oke Mẹsin headed the confederates and was on the march again for Ikirun ; the news of the death of the Balogun of Ibadan seemed to put more spirit and courage into them.

When the news of this reached Ibadan the Arẹ ordered the Seriki to arrest their progress. The Seriki was very reluctant to go for two reasons. Firstly, he wished to be present at the funeral obsequies of the late Balogun his chief, but the urgency of the affairs in the north-eastern frontier brooked no delay. Secondly, he had been clipt of his wings as it were, for his Ọtun, Osi, and Ẹkẹrin had been ordered to Ọfa and he was left single-handed.

But he must obey orders, and thus he started for Ikirun. On reaching Iwo, he was detained by the venerable King of Iwo. " What do you intend to do," asked he, " with such a small handful of men ? The Arẹ could never have had the slightest idea of the nature and strength of the confederacy." His Highness thereupon sent to Ibadan and acquainted the Arẹ with the formidable nature of the task before him.

The Arẹ with enemies all around him was trying to behave cautiously and with prudence : he did not know what the Ẹgbas and Ijẹbus might do if the town were denuded of men ; however, he sent a small force to reinforce the Seriki at Iwo. The allies at this time were using all their endeavours to isolate Ibadan by cutting off all communications from it. At this crisis the Lisa of Ode Ondo sent messengers to Ibadan to inform the Arẹ how the allies had offered him large presents to induce him to join the alliance, and close against the Ibadans the only route by which they could now communicate with the coast, viz, that by Oke Igbo, but he wished to be neutral. He might send if he liked to verify his statements, and let his messengers see the presents for themselves. The Arẹ replied by sending the Lisa large presents and begged him to keep strictly neutral, and to keep that road open.

The Ijẹbu Rẹmọs in the South who are simple traders were much annoyed by this closure of the roads, which put a dead stop to their occupation. Ibadan is their only customer, but their Suzerain the Awujale of Ode having joined the alliance, they were helpless. They however conceived an idea of sending to their countryman resident at Ibadan, Chief Soderinde the Balogun of the cavalry, to induce the Are to send another embassy to the Awujale and that they would act as a go-between. The Are was glad to comply with this request, but the Awujale took the presents and the slaves sent, but rejected the Remos as intermediaries.

The fact of his accepting the presents sent a ray of hope into the Are to make one more effort. He therefore summoned to him all the natives of Ijebu Ode resident at Ibadan with Abinusawa, an Ijebu Prince, at their head, one who had some influence at home and begged them to act as plenipotentiaries for him in arranging terms of friendship with the Ijebus. These were glad to be of some service to their hosts, and were confident of success. But they were not even allowed to reach the town of Ode, they were stopped at Aha by an Agurin and sent back with the following message :—

" Why should the Ibadans now desire our friendship? Let them remember the scant courtesy with which they have treated us in the past. When they were going to the Ijaye war we remonstrated with them but to no purpose. When we entreated them to receive back Ajobo expelled, they utterly refused even to take home his dead body. When they had differences with Efusetan, Aijenku, Iyapo we interfered and offered our good offices but were not listened to. If they are tired of the war and want peace, let them first arrange with the Egbas, recall their troops from Ofa and from Ikirun, and let the Are go to sleep."

This was the end of all negotiations with the Ijebus, but the Ijebu residents still continued to make efforts to negotiate, but the Are would not expose himself to another rebuff.

Once more the Lisa of Ondo sent messengers to Ibadan on hearing of the Balogun's death ; they brought the Are some presents and performed funeral obsequies for the late Balogun, killing a ram and pouring its blood on his grave.

§ 4. The Beginning of the Actual Conflict

The Seriki's forces met the confederates near Ikirun, and once more the clash of arms resounded between Oyos and Ekitis. After several battles, the Ekitis began to retreat before the Ibadans towards Mesin Ipole via Igbajo ; this town was deserted at the approach of the allies. The Seriki drove them beyond Igbajo and pitched his camp about a mile beyond, and from thence cleared

the undergrowth in the forest for miles in the direction of Mẹsin
Ipole.   Another reinforcement from Ibadan met him here in the
person of Akintaro the newly-made Osi, and chief Aderibigbe.
Here was enough force now to crush those opposed to them. The
Arẹ's young Chiefs could fight, but they lacked the wisdom gotten
by experience.

The Ibadans were surprised to see the allies advancing to attack
them in their camp through the openings they had made in
the forest, and concluded that they must have received
reinforcement from Ogedemgbe, the rumour of whose approach
then filled the country. They therefore took the precaution of
guarding the camp and the rear by the Osi whilst the Seriki
advanced to the attack. The Seriki had his father's veterans
about him who instructed him in all his movements, where he was
to sit, and when he was to charge.   There was a dreadful carnage
that day on both sides. When at the right moment the Seriki
(through his advisers) ordered a general charge, they found the
Ekitis immovably firm as a rock ! From repeated conflicts, and
from their former slaves, the Ekitis had grown accustomed to the
methods of the Ibadans, and were prepared against them.   There
was then no help for it but to maintain their ground *vis à vis* whilst
a desperate struggle ensued. At length, the Ibadans a little
while after made a sudden dash and secured a prisoner. From the
obstinate resistance offered, the Ibadans thought they were
opposing Ogedemgbe, but the prisoner told them it was Fabūmi
of Oke Mẹsin. " Where is Ogedemgbe then ? " they asked, and
were told, " Not yet come." And further : " Who lay in ambush
at our rear ? " " No one." " Where is the remnant of your
army ? " " This is all." With this assurance the Seriki now sent
to the camp for reinforcements. It was about 4 p.m. that the
drum of Akintaro the Osi was heard coming, and when the Ekitis
saw fresh troops coming they gave way and fled. But it was too
late to pursue them far. The Osi's men claimed the honour of
the victory as theirs, as the enemy did not dare to await their
approach. Those who bore the brunt of the fight since morning
were naturally hurt at this, and trifling as this circumstance
might appear, it altered the character of the whole campaign, and
the larger issues that depended upon it. Jealousy and rivalry now
take the place of judgment and discretion.

Disaster upon disaster followed on both sides in subsequent
battles ; the allies again and again sent repeated messages to call
Ogedemgbe to their help. " We will fight now," said they, " to the
best advantage, the Ibadan army is divided into three parts, one
part at home to guard the town against the Egbas and Ijẹbus,

one part at Ọfa against the Ilọrins, and it is but a third part we have to oppose."

Ogedemgbe was a very straight-forward man, he was always true to his word. Although a sworn enemy to the Ibadans, yet he wished to be faithful to his covenant with them, for he had sworn never to oppose them. On making Ita Ogbolu his headquarters for excursion into the Igbo Ani country, he sent to Ibadan, and the Arẹ gave him a war standard, and also sent him a contingent consisting of his slaves and volunteers among the restless and warlike youths of Ibadan. Hence Ogedemgbe was reluctant to enter upon this war rashly. But he received invitations from all the allies, as well as from the Egbas and Ijẹbus, Ibadan being con-considered a formidable neighbour whose power they all dreaded and were resolved to see it crushed this time.

Ogedemgbe at last issued from Ita Ogbolu his retreat, and took the field at the head of the Ekiti parapọs against the Ibadans.

On hearing this, the Ibadan war chiefs sent home again for more reinforcements, and on the 3rd November, 1879, the Arẹ sent the following chiefs, viz., Babalọla the son and heir of the late Balogun Ogboriẹfọn, Ojo late Balẹ Ọpẹagbe's son, and Ogundepo the uncle of the Seriki.

It was the belief of the war chiefs that the Arẹ deliberately planned to weaken them all one by one, so as to make room for his own son to be supreme over them, for instead of sending an adequate force which could deal with the whole affair in one blow he kept sending them by dribblets, promising each batch that which-ever came out victorious would take the lead of the others, thus creating a spirit of jealousy among them. Hence every newcomer had to fight singlehanded, and never received support from those already in the field.

Babalọla had to oppose Ogedemgbe at Kiriji as his father opposed him many years ago at Ilesa. The combatants met about three miles from Mẹsin Ipole, and Babalọla fresh from home and probably in order to make a name, fought three successive battles which established his fame as a worthy heir of the hero of the Jalumi war. He bore the brunt of the battle with the Ekitis alone, the Seriki and all he met before him just sat in the battlefield sur-rounded by their men, all looking on, ready to retrieve a disaster should any occur.

A custom initiated by the late Balogun Ibikunle and Ogunmọla at the time of the Ijaye war was still kept up for the war chiefs to have about them pages in training called " Baba ni ñma sa " (the Master says I must not run away). They were all dressed in red uniforms and were to sit around their master whatever may be the condition of the fight : they may be beyond gunshot, or equally exposed with their master in a close fight. Babalola had about 400 of these ; at the first fight he lost 140 in killed and wounded. At the second fight he lost more, at the third fight they were wiped out !

Thus the Arẹ began by wasting their strength, and those in the field, out of jealousy of each other, played his game until experience brought about a better judgment when too late.

§ 5. The Arẹ to the Front

Such was the state of affairs at the seat of war whilst the Arẹ's son and his slaves and household war-boys were enjoying themselves at home, till they became surfeit with pleasure and all excesses, the report of which reached the war chiefs from time to time at the seat of war. Whenever the Ijẹbus or Ẹgbas were descried kidnapping in Ibadan farms, the war chiefs at home would be sent after these, but the Arẹ's sons and slaves would march out leisurely after these in blazing costumes, and instead of pursuing after the enemy would contentedly encamp in the Ibadan farms, feeding on the crops and cutting down standing corn as fodder for their horses !

The war chiefs in the field having wasted their strength in the manner indicated above, and finding themselves as it were being over-ridden by the Arẹ's sons and slaves, were resolved to invite himself to the war, to take command of the army in person, and when there they were determined to take revenge on him and his menials for all their insolent acts at home. By virtue of his title as Kakanfo he was bound to respond to his people's call, and consequently he sent to the King at Ọyọ to ask leave to take the field, and to return home within 17 days. The King granted his consent reluctantly, knowing that he was determined to go.

The Arẹ at this time exhibited some of the worst phases of human nature. At such a pitch of glory his word being law to all Ibadan and its dependencies, he became the dupe of his flatterers ; he considered himself a god and that nothing was impossible for him to effect. He certainly thought he would make a short and easy work of the task before him, but the chiefs who invited him to the war had a different plan in their head. Their resolve was to humble his pride, and to avenge the death of Aijẹnku and that of Iyapọ, the late Seriki in particular, both of whom he ordered to " go to sleep."

Sanusi, the Arẹ's eldest son, further exasperated the war-chiefs

by the impudent songs he permitted his bards to indulge in at
their expense ; thus :

The expedition that occupied Akere's son[1] three years,
The war over which Awarun's son[2] has spent six months in
    vain,
But one day will it take Alabi[3], son of Iyanda Arọ[4],
With silver-studded hands he'll extricate and bring them home.

Again they sang :

    A club is thrown at a lime,
    Both lime and club got entangled,
    And the stick and the lime,
    Iyanda's son will disentangle and bring home.

But there were those even among his followers at home who
disliked these proceedings. Many were the followers of Sumọnu,
the Arẹ's nephew, who was a more affable and good-natured fellow
and much preferred to Sanusi. The followers of the latter,
noticing this, permitted his drummer to beat :

    "Sanusi jọba na a gbọ ni Kanu,
      Irọ, irọ, Arẹmọ ko pe meji."

(That Sanusi is supreme is known up to Kanu,
    Nay, nay, two heirs there cannot be.)

The retort to this came from the populace in their dances :

    " To prostrate to father, and then to the son,
    I cannot stoop to two at once.
    And where is such a thing ever done ?
    On the hilltop is such a thing done."

The Arẹ's house at Ibadan is on the top of a hill.   All these
sayings and doings were duly reported in the camp, and the war
chiefs there were resolved to have these high-flown talkers in the
camp, where only valour counts.

The Arẹ, in order to strike a blow with effect, recalled Ali the
Ọtun Balogun and Akintọla the late Iyapọ's brother from Ọfa
to join him at the camp. Akintọla preceded Ali to the camp
and, as a young Mọgaji he also was allowed to fight a battle
singlehanded as each of his predecessors had done. He distinguished himself above them all ; by a flank movement he bore down
on Ogedemgbe suddenly with a vigorous onslaught, surprised and
captured him, but he was let off.   It was not the intention of these

---

[1] The Osi.   [2] The Seriki.   [3] His own attributive.   [4] His
father's attributive and totem.

war-chiefs to defeat their enemy to the Arẹ's advantage, but each of them wished to show what he can do.

Ogedemgbe fell into the hands of one of Akintọla's slaves who said to him, " Ologun, yara, Ọyọ nbọ̀ " (Captain be quick, Ọyọs are coming.) The hide on which he was sitting, the kegs of gunpowder all about him, his charms and amulets were all taken, the Ijẹsas were utterly discomfited, but Akintọla withdrew and there was no further fighting that day.

But the result of this fight was to drive the allies to a vigorous preparation for a more desperate resistance, especially as they heard that the Arẹ was coming. It was reported that Ogedemgbe, on hearing the rumour of the Arẹ's coming, sent a messenger to ask him whether the report was true, and if so, in regard to the oath he had taken, and for past favours he had received from him, he was loth to meet in the field a chief who had given him the war standard he was using. He would therefore retire with half the Ekiti forces, leaving the rest for an easy conquest ; only he prayed for his clemency towards his countrymen. So faithful and honest was Ogedemgbe. But the Arẹ, instead of returning courtesy for courtesy, proudly dared him to remain if he would share the fate of those he would soon crush under his heels !

But Ogedemgbe, out of deference to the Arẹ, sent another private messenger to meet him at Oṣogbo on the same errand. The Arẹ's answer was, " Is he still there and not gone away yet ? Well, he will have himself to thank for the consequences." Ogedemgbe and his countrymen were fighting for freedom ; courtesy and generosity he was prepared to yield to, but threats and defiance he was determined to meet with obstinate resistance.

The Arẹ, on reaching Irèhé went by Ọtan and intended to take the Ekitiparapọs in the rear, thus placing them between two fires. But the Ibadan chiefs lest their plans should be defeated grew excited, sent urgent messages after messages entreating him to come to them to the camp and take no other course. Said they : " The veterans and the flower of your army are here in the camp, who are those about you with whom you would risk your safety by taking another course ? They are but slaves who will desert you at the sound of the first gun. Not so did Lakanlẹ of old when our fathers called him to their help at Ipẹru in olden days. As he went straight to them so do you come to us now and lead us to victory."

In the meantime the Ijẹsas, hearing the Arẹ was contemplating another route, were determined to checkmate him. Ogedemgbe left the command with one Olubayọde, a great war-chief, and took with him his well-trained veterans to waylay the Arẹ. and if

possible to take him alive. He was rather disappointed at the
Arẹ's being dissuaded from carrying out his plan. He missed his
game.

The war-chiefs' estimate of the value and fighting qualities of
the Arẹ's slaves and household officers was not from spite but from
actual fact ; they had learnt to appraise them at their true valuation in the Ado and Aiyede wars and in the raids on Ẹgba farms
especially before Oṣiẹlẹ. They were no longer the hardy and trusty
veterans of the Ilẹsa and other wars when there was keen rivalry
between them and the late Ajayi Ogboriẹfọn. A life of ease and
debauchery had since brought about degeneracy ; they were more
distinguished for displaying red and showy uniforms, sitting round
their master and boasting of past deeds.

The Ibadan war-chiefs entered into a secret compact before the
Arẹ's arrival never to achieve a conquest or capture a town while
he was living, for, said they, "What is the use ? The lion's share of
our achievements will go to him, and we shall only help to increase
the number of his slaves who are now lording it over us."

The Arẹ again on arriving at the camp did not call them all
together and harangue them or praise them for what they had done.
On the contrary his son Sanusi marched straight on through the
camp and pitched his tent in a field of standing corn which the
Ibadans had planted outside the camp. " Cut all down," said he
" we do not need it, how long are we going to stay here ? "
He had cause to regret this afterwards.

The Arẹ led the host to the field the next day, the 4th of May,
1880. The war-chiefs fought with their accustomed bravery to
show him what they could do, but no more. At the first onslaught
the Ijẹsa chief Olubayọde was caught and slain, the Ijẹsa army
became demoralized, and gave way ; the Ibadan warboys pursued
them right into the gates of Mẹsin Ipole. The Ibadan war-chiefs
seeing this passed the word round from mouth to mouth, " Afaro,
afaro," i.e., " Refrain, refrain " (or " halt, halt.")

The Ajero saved the situation for the Ekitis that day, for seeing
all in full retreat he stood by the gate of the town, and the first
Ibadan boy that entered he shot down dead ; the others, seeing no
war-chief or leader of any kind behind them, retreated hastily.
The Ibadan war-chiefs sat in groups, each under a tree here and
there in the battlefield surrounded by their men as if resting for
a while, but the Arẹ could not get them to do anything more than
skirmishing that day. He took in the situation at a glance, and
was determined to sleep on the battlefield that day, and offer
battle the next day, although it was pouring with rain, and there
was no shelter. Cold and wet he was advised to return to the camp,

but he at first refused to do so ; then the chiefs and elders of his house approached him and remonstrated with him, saying, " It is folly to remain on the battlefield ; we are all wet, and it is still raining. Suppose the Ekitis were to fall upon us in the night, it will be all to their advantage, because they will come from home quite fresh, with ammunition dry." The Arẹ was sore at heart, recalling the achievements of his old rival and comrade the hero of the Jalumi war. That he, the Kakanfo, should not be able to achieve as much and a great deal more was a mixture of shame, pain and grief to him. With great difficulty he was prevailed upon to return to the camp for the night, and the fight was resumed the next day.

The secret combination against the Arẹ was divulged to him by Chief Aderibigbe, probably with the hope of his making amends to the war-chiefs, but the Arẹ, instead of calling these young men together and pacifying them, answered with some asperity, " I have fought in front of their fathers and it is now their turn to fight for me and they will not ; as we are all equally concerned, let us agree to remain indifferent."

The Ekitiparapọs, on the other hand, fighting as they were for their independence, went on strengthening their forces by drawing recruits from the utmost bounds of the country behind them, throughout the Ijẹsa, Ekiti, Ẹfọn, Yagba and Akoko countries right on to Ẹgbẹ. They further strengthened their alliance with the Ilọrins by an exchange of troops. One Ogunmọdẹde with a strong force of Ijẹsas, was sent to the Ilọrin camp, and the Ilọrins sent one Lasẹbikan with his men to the Ekiti camp. This arrangement, we should rather say, was an astute measure of the Ilọrins by which they retained a firm hold on the Ekitis, so that they could not withdraw from the alliance even if they wished to do so, and this proved to be the case many years afterwards as we shall see in due course.

The allies had also the great advantage over the Ibadans, in that they had free access to Benin for ammunition whilst nearly all the roads were closed to the Ibadans. Long flintlock guns with large muzzles were imported from Benin ; these, when fully loaded and fired, gave a report which reverberating from hill to hill all around sounded like Ki-ri-ji-i, from which this war was named the Kiriji Campaign.

Famine soon broke out among the Ibadans, the provisions they brought from home were exhausted, and the standing corn around the camp had been cut down by Sanusi to make room for his tents. The common soldiers had now to live on palm nuts, certain edible roots, and whatever they could procure from the forests to sustain life, whilst there was plenty in the town for the allies.

The Are, to emphasize his determination to see that this business should at once come to a finish, removed the camp to the spot where he sat at his first battle, called Elebolo, from the abundance of the herb Ebolo in the place. The Ekitis, to show their determination to resist him, left the town of Mesin Ipole and encamped on the spot where Babalola fought his three celebrated battles ; and so both camps stood face to face to each other surrounded on all sides by high mountains, deep ravines and craggy rocks. It seemed Providence had brought both armies into this defile, to teach them a lesson. In the day of battle there was no room for them to deploy, the situation being worse for the Ibadans than for the Ekiti mountaineers in their native mountains. The battles now became more frequent and bloody, and at every fight the Ibadans lost one or more distinguished war-chiefs.

At a battle on the 18th May Kupolu, the Commander of the infantry of the Are's bodyguard, was killed, and Akintaro the Osi Balogun was mortally wounded.

On the 1st of June died Opehinde, one of the chiefs left in charge of the town.

On the 11th of June Ajenigbe the Ekerin was mortally wounded. He died the next day.

Chief Oluferegbe, Kongi's stepfather, also fell in battle.

On the 31st August a sanguinary battle was fought at Kiriji with heavy losses on both sides.

Thus for a long period of time a serious battle or a skirmish took place nearly every other day with heavy losses on both sides.

Chapter XXV

IBADAN AT ITS EXTREMITY—BLOODY STRIFES.

§ 1.   Home Defences

THE preceding section has given us an idea of how matters were for the Ibadans at Kiriji.   Now, whilst all this was going on at the seat of war, the Ijẹbu and Ẹgba kidnappers were not inactive at home, raiding the Ibadan farms, sometimes successfully, but sometimes repulsed, but making farming risky and unsafe until a scheme was evolved of a complete organization for home defence.

There are three main points from which the attacks may be expected (a) the farms contiguous to those of the Ẹgbas ; (b) the route leading to Ijẹbu Igbo ; and (c) that leading to Ijẹbu Ode. Arrangements were perfected by building forts in a central point in each of these main routes, for the better protection of the farmers.   Whilst the hunters were in the forests, hunting for game and on the look-out for kidnappers, the farmers could work in their farms with composure and confidence.   They were instructed to hasten to the forts with their women and children at a given signal by the hunters.   The men went to their farms well armed, and were ready for any emergency.

The fort in the direction of the Ẹgbas was left in charge of some hunters, and a few old warriors left at home.   But the Ẹgbas once surprised the fort at Itosi and carried away much people ; some of them, however, were rescued by the hunters who pursued after the kidnappers.

In the direction of Ijẹbu Igbo, where the forest was thickest, the forts were in charge of the principal hunters, the chief of these were Ajiya, Obisẹsan, Ọdẹyale.   These kept the fort while the younger hunters were dispersed about in the forests.   The fort was the rendezvous of the women and children.   By this arrangement the defeat of the Ijẹbus became such a constant and regular thing that the vulgar people put it into a song :

Are de, are de,	For the flight, for the flight,
Igbayi l'are ma de o,	Now is the time to flee,
Oni yọyọ-gọ̀.	Ye clothed in Yọyọgọ̀.

Yọyọgọ̀ is a coarse and loosely woven sort of cloth which the Ijẹbus were accustomed to wear at this period.

The fort in the direction of Ijẹbu Ode was built at the point of divergence of the roads leading to Ijębu Ode and Ijębu Rẹmọ, the convergence of the roads being at the middle of the fort, enclosed with a wall all round. This was in charge of certain cavalrymen left in town, there being no scope for their services among the crags of Kiriji. Associated with these were the Sango chief priest and one Ogungbẹsan.

The only fight which took place in this direction was on Palm Sunday, the 10th of April, 1881, and was far-reaching in its results. When the alarm was given, a mounted messenger was sent post haste to the town to call up those in charge of this direction. Ṣolaja and Ṣonikàn, sons of Ṣodẹrinde the Balogun of the Cavalry, performed feats of valour that day, and distinguished themselves. In the thick of the fight, Ṣolaja with his horse dashed into the Ijębus, knocking down two or three, and returned with a captive on his horse. Seeing this, Ṣonikan the elder brother, not to be outdone by his younger brother, performed the like feat, and also returned with a captive. This was a signal for a general rout. The Ijębus, who scarcely ever saw a horse in their country and could not face a cavalry charge, gave way and were pursued as far as Odo Ọna kekere in the Ijębu Ode route, and about 20 captives were taken among them. At Odo Ọna kekere, the Ijębus met reinforcements and there they made a stand. The struggle here was fierce and obstinate, and the brave captain of the Ijębus, whilst leading and encouraging his men, was shot down dead : a general rout was the consequence, and in the pursuit, among other captives made, was Omitogun, the brother of the old Balogun of the Ijębus.

This distinguished captive was well treated at Ibadan. When the report of what had taken place reached the camp, the war chiefs sent back to say that Omitogun was to be allowed to go back home to arrange for his own ransom and on his own terms ; but that he was to exert his influence at home with the authorities there so that the roads may be opened for trade, remembering that they never had any quarrel with the Ijębus, and never attacked their farms, and that the Egbas, whose cause they said they were espousing, had slyly opened a roundabout road for themselves *via* Eruwa to trade with the interior Yorubas.

Omitogun himself had another tale to tell. He bought and took home with him some corn, beans, etc., to show his people at home. Ibadan, which was reported to be on its last leg and on the verge of starvation, was actually revelling in plenty such as they never enjoyed at home ! The farmers had no outlet for their produce whilst the Ijębus, who are nearly all traders were sorely in need of foodstuffs.

This circumstance made a deep impression on the Ijẹbus, there was no more raiding in this direction. Its further development had a far-reaching effect which bore fruit in the following year, as we shall see.

§ 2.   CLOSURE OF ROADS AND THE RESULTS

The greatest needs of the Ibadans now were ammunition and salt, and the only route by which they could obtain them even in small quantities was· the roundabout way *via* Oke Igbo to Ondo and thus to the coast. Hence they endeavoured to keep on friendly terms with Derin Ọlọgbẹnla, the Balẹ of Oke Igbo, and humoured him every now and then by sending him presents of slaves.

Derin was an Ifẹ prince, and as to the Ifẹs themselves, although their army was in the Ibadan camp, yet their sympathies were all on the other side.

But it happened in March, 1881, that the Ibadans suspecting treachery in a town named Oṣu, situated between Ile Ifẹ and Ilẹṣa, sent a small force secretly by Awo, son of the late Labọsinde, against the place, to capture it by surprise in order to keep their rear clear of any trouble But all the towns in the neighbourhood were in the secret of the expedition and in sympathy with the Ekitis as men striking for freedom, therefore it leaked out. Oṣu was prepared and reinforced against a surprise, and hence the expedition failed.

The town of Oṣu not being far from the city of Ifẹ, to suspect Oṣu is to suspect Ifẹ itself, and Derin of Oke Igbo, taking this as a cause of offence, openly declared for the Ekitis and endeavoured to close even this road to all Ọyọs by allowing the Ijẹsas to kidnap caravans on the road. But the Ogunsua or Balẹ of Modakẹkẹ, knowing that the safety of his town is linked with that of Ibadan, by protecting caravans and attacking kidnappers did not allow the road to be altogether closed.   In vain the Ifẹs tried to win the Ogunsua over : the position of Modakẹkẹ to Ifẹ is analogous to that of Belfast to the south of Ireland ; the Modakẹkẹs are Ọyọs and of the same tribal affinity with Ibadan with which their own safety is linked.

The price of salt rose so high that a pound of salt could not be had for less than ten shillings wh.ʌ it could be obtained at all. Poor people therefore could not even think of preparing their meals with salt ; those who could obtain a few grains of it, ate their meals insipid, and then qualified the tastelessness in their mouths with the few grains of salt afterwards !

But the distress in the country was not all on one side.   The Egbas also were indirectly affected by this closure of the roads against the interior tribes. They were free to trade with Lagos indeed, but they wanted produce from the interior and slaves to work their farms. They therefore managed to open a circuitous route to Ketu and Ejio, where they and the Porto Novians established a market to trade with all Ọyọs from different parts of the country, but they still rigidly excluded the sale of ammunition, only cloth and salt were the articles of merchandise, and even this was considered a godsend by the interior folks, for their distress from want of salt was by this greatly alleviated. ⌐

An anecdote from an actual occurrence will forcibly illustrate the point of desperation to which these people were driven at this time :

A man with his wife and daughter—a marriageable young woman—went to Ejio to trade. At the close of the fair, the woman was being taken away by an Egba man ; a hue and cry was immediately raised, and the Egba was arrested as a man-stealer. He denied the charge and told his tale. The woman had been bartered to him for salt and cloth, he only claimed what was his by right. Upon investigation it was found that he was quite right, the seller was the woman's own daughter ! She had bartered away her own mother for salt ! But the man could not allow his wife to be taken away, a compromise must be made. So after he and the woman had consulted together they agreed that this undutiful daughter was to be given to the Egba in exchange : they showed him that the mother was old and would be of little service to him, whereas the young woman might be taken by him for a wife and that they, the parents, would regard the cloths and salt as an adequate dowry given by him. The Egba man was highly pleased with the offer and went home delighted with having had the best of the bargain, and the parents on the other hand were satisfied that to all intents and purposes their daughter had been comfortably settled. This was by no means a solitary instance of desperate acts such as this.

The distress at the seat of war at this time was indescribable : the Oke Igbo road being closed there was a great dearth of ammunition. The Ekitis knowing this from escaped slaves often came as near as possible to the gate of the camp and assaulted them. The Ibadan army would be drawn up but they could not return the fire of the enemy. They could hardly muster 100 kegs of powder throughout the whole army, and this they reserved for an extreme case of emergency. The writer was present in the camp on one such occasion, when Chief Babalọla sent a slave wife of his round to all the traders present in the camp for even a handful of powder if possible. From private soldiers who had not exhausted their allowance, and others who did not use theirs in previous fights she collected a small quantity in exchange for food ! The writer being a friend of the Seriki's brother, asked him confidentially on that occasion, " Supposing the Ijẹṣas and Ekitis were to come upon you suddenly one day to rush the camp, what will you do ? " He replied, " 'Tis true we have no ammunition, but there are not wanting among us about 5,000 accomplished swordsmen who will be more than a match for the Ekitis with their guns at close quarters, and they know it or they would have attempted to do so."

Further, the Ekitis often taunted them by appearing on top of a rock where they could well be seen by the Ibadans, and tantalized them by emptying kegs of gunpowder on the rock, throwing a lighted torch on the pile, and blazing all away.

The muster for battle at this time took place almost every day. The Ekitis came as near as possible to the camp, firing into it. The method adopted by the Ibadans to meet the present crisis was to assemble near the gate of the camp, and thence make a sudden and vigorous dash on the Ekitis driving them back to the battlefield : then the swordsmen would spread themselves in the valley and trenches awaiting those who would venture near ; the Ekitis being on higher ground could be seen by them much sooner. Now and then as opportunity offered they would pounce upon them sword in hand, and often come back with captives. Thus they would hold out till about five or six in the evening before the main Ibadan army marched out, when they could not all fire more than one round before nightfall.

For months and months affairs dragged on in this way, each party being afraid of the other. The sentries at the camp gate were doubled for fear of a night attack.

On one occasion a few kegs of powder were obtained at Ejio at a very high price ; when these reached the camp such a shout of joy was raised as if they had won a victory ; a *Feu de joie* was fired that evening. The shout was heard at the Ekiti camp. But this joy was short lived, for a grave danger threatened the Yoruba country from another direction.

§ 3. DISTRESSING EPISODES

A. *Dahomian Invasion.*—The Dahomians, who had hitherto confined their depredations to the Egba and Egbado districts, now for the first time advanced into the western districts of Yoruba proper. The Ibadans, since the destruction of Ijaye, on whom it would have devolved to meet this threatened danger, heard this news with chagrin ; they could only chafe but could

render no help in that quarter.   In fact it was their pre-occupation
that rendered such unprovoked invasion possible.   It was said
that the Dahomian guide and counsellor in this enterprise was
Afin the Chief of Ketu, and in May, 1881, the following towns were
taken : Ejio, Ọbaniñsunwa, Ilaji, Àtasá, Oke'le, Iwere, Aiyetorò
and Igãna.

Lawore the Asẹyin marched out in defence of the district but
he narrowly escaped with his life ; at Igãna a young man who,
kneeling before him, was shooting arrows on the enemy was
suddenly approached by the Dahomians and his head taken off !
The Asẹyin himself had to escape on horseback.

This conduct of Afin in introducing the Dahomians into this
part of the country gave pain to all, but retributive justice soon
overtook him, for at the next campaign of the Dahomians, his
own town Ketu was taken and himself slain.   The other towns
taken with Ketu were Idikumọ, Isẹlu, Dain, etc.

Ketu is an ancient town bordering on the Sabẹ and Ọyọ
countries.   It is a place badly watered, their drinking water being
miles away from the town.   They used deep underground tanks
for storing rain water.   The scarcity of water in Ketu has passed
into a proverb.   " Omi d'oyin ni Ketu " (" Water becomes honey
in Ketu ").   The destruction of Ketu was about the 17th of July,
1886.

In order to record all the ravages of the Dahomians together we
shall have to anticipate the dates of events in the history.

Their third campaign was again in the western districts of
Yoruba Proper—Ilesàn, Ibisẹ̀, Oke Amù, Agọ, Iluku, Gbagba,
Agọ Sabẹ, Irawọ, Ọwọ, and for the second time Ilaji, were all
destroyed.   This was in 1887.

Their fourth campaign was against the towns bordering on
Egba districts, and also on the western districts.   Berẹkodo,
Oke Tapa, Aiyetẹ, Bakọ, Gangan, Igbo Ọsa, Idọfin, Idire, Papa,
Gbunginu were all taken.   Eruwa was deserted.   This was about
the year 1890.

Thus far they went, when a higher Power decreed their fall ;
they were themselves subjugated by the French.

Travellers in the western districts will find all the towns enclosed
in double walls.   The city of Ọyọ was connected with the village
of Awẹ by a wall.   This outer wall was called " Odi Amọlà," or
by some, " Odi Amọnù."   The former term indicates " The Wall
of Safety," used by those to whom it has proved a source of safety
and the latter term, " The Wall of Loss," used by those to whom
it has proved unavailing for security.

B. *Destruction of Ile Bioku.*—Ile Bioku was one of the Yoruba

towns in the Oke Ogun district between Eruwa and Iseyin, and
consequently under the protection of the Ibadans.

The following is a short history of its foundation and destruction.

Ile Bioku was quite a modern town built by two friends, Bioku
and Lebebi, Bioku being the Chief. It was one of the towns
beautifully situated on a hill and easily defended against a hostile
attack, and consequently, for the safety it afforded, it got peopled
rapidly and soon became a prosperous town.

There were several men of note in this town besides the founders,
e.g., Oguntaiye the Areagoro, Odunmbaku the Ikolaba, Aremu
the Jagun, Alawo and his son Ladipo (both being men of note),
also Oje, Adebawonpe, and Maborisaje.

Bioku lived to a good old age, and the town prospered under him.
At his death he was succeeded by Lebebi the co-founder. Oyedokun, son of Bioku, was the head of his house. But Lebebi
did not outlive Bioku long, he also died and was succeeded by
Ajadi as the head of his house. Oyedokun, son of Bioku, now
became the head chief of the town, and so the succession would
have continued in the two families alternately had all continued
well.

Alawo also died about the same time and was succeeded by
his son Ladipo. Oyedokun, son of Bioku, however, was a bad
ruler ; he soon disgusted all the chief men in the town. When
he could no longer be endured Ajadi, the next man to him as ruler,
left the town with a large following and founded a settlement at
the foot of the hill, leaving Ile Bioku to Oyedokun and his party.

In order to avenge himself for this defection Oyedokun sent to
Ibadan to invite an army to destroy the new settlement ; but the
Are Latosisa, then at the head of Ibadan, sent one Aiyeleru to
reconcile the two parties, but he failed in his efforts and returned
to Ibadan.

Now, with the Ibadans away from home, Oyedokun sent a
similar message to Chief Ogundipe at Abeokuta to come and
destroy the new settlement. Ogundipe responded to the call
with alacrity and came with an Egba army, as he had been seeking
occasion to go against Itabo, a small suburb town of Ile Bioku.

The alleged cause of offence to Ogundipe was that when the
Egbas fled from Ijaye in March, 1862, one of his wives (then in
delicate state) fell into the hands of an Itabo man. Chief Ogundipe
offered to redeem her, but the man refused to part with her. After
the child was born Ogundipe sent two slaves to the man in exchange
for mother and child, but the man still declined the offer. For this
reason Ogundipe now embraced this opportunity of going against
the settlement of Ile Bioku hoping to recover his wife and

child at the suburb. His route lay through Eruwa, he invited the Balẹ of this town to join him, but he declined. But Ogundipẹ having gone forward, the Balẹ went with an army by a shorter route to assist the doomed town, their kith and kin.

The Ẹgbas were actually repulsed by this handful of men of the new settlement, and were in full retreat when Omiṣina, Oyedokun's brother sent to tell Ogundipẹ not to lose such a splendid chance of victory by retreating so hastily as the ammunition of his foes was all but exhausted and the Ẹgbas had victory close at hand. Ogundipẹ, hearing this, returned to the attack, and ammunition failing the men of the new settlement, the town was taken. Of the chiefs who escaped were :—Ajadi, Ladipọ, Adewọgba. Omiṣina the traitor was hunted down by the remnant of the people and was discovered in a cave at Itabọ, thence he was brought back, slain, and his family sold into slavery.

In order to avenge themselves on Oyedokun the remnant that escaped sent to him a message of submission and offer of reconciliation. Negotiations followed and all the terms of peace settled, it only remained for him to come down from the hill to perfect the terms which could not be conveniently carried out by messengers. He did so, and as the men lay prostrate before him and *pourparlers* were going on, all of a sudden they rushed upon him and butchered him to pieces ; and in order to show their abhorrence of him they roasted his flesh in the fire and had a taste of it all round.

Thus the remnant that escaped gathered themselves together and formed another settlement in the plain opposite Ile Bioku, and they called it Lanlatẹ̀ and had Ajadi as their Balẹ.

The remnant of the old town of Ile Bioku soon joined them here. Like all other Oke Ogun towns, the people of this place are industrious, food is plentiful and they seem quite contented.

§ 4. New Developments, Clouds and Sunshine

After the Dahomian invasion and the destruction of the market towns of Ejio and Ketu distress prevailed again in the country. At this crisis the ALÂFIN of Ọyọ sent a special deputation to Abẹokuta to negotiate through Chief Ogundipẹ foi the opening of the roads for salt. It was an open secret that the ALÂFIN connived at the combination against the Ibadans and the consequent closure of the roads ; but the want of salt touched even His Majesty himself as well as his people ; hence his action.

At this period the ruling chiefs of Abẹokuta were four, *viz.*, Ogundipẹ the Balogun of Ikija, Onlado of Kemta, Ogundeyi of Iporo, and the Jaguna of Igbein. Ogundipẹ was the leading chief,

Onlado was at the head of all the Ogbonis, and Ogundeyi of the war party, the Alake being a nonentity. It was said that Ogundipẹ and Onlado were more in consort, the public meetings were generally convened either at Ogundipẹ's gate or in the front of Ṣodẹkẹ's house. Ogundipẹ was always the spokesman, queer in his ways but shrewd in his methods. He generally spoke in his own name. Public acts were said to be done by his order, but he was only carrying out the conclusions which himself and his colleagues had arrived at. Thus it was given out that the Eruwa road to Ọyọ had been opened under the auspices of Chief Ogundipẹ. Eruwa now became the market town for the exchange of commodities with the further interior.

It was also shrewdly suspected that Ogundipẹ, as the friend of the Arẹ of Ibadan, was doing his utmost to relieve the Ibadans at this time. He had always been against the closure of the roads, but he could not get his colleagues to see with him. Cloth, salt and spirits were the articles sent to the Eruwa market in exchange for slaves and produce from the interior, but all but one of the so-called demijohns of rum, and cases of gin sent up by Ogundipẹ, were gunpowder secretly being sent to the Arẹ. The gatemen at the tall gates were supposed to know nothing about them, a glass of rum or of gin was poured out of the genuine package for them and the whole passed free, especially as it was known to be Ogundipẹ's, and this particular road was under the charge of the Egba Oke Ọna, of whom Ogundipẹ was the head, as the river route was under the immediate charge of the Egba Agbẹyin. This favour of Ogundipẹ's was highly appreciated by the Ibadans.

This Eruwa market was called the Erẹbẹ market, only guns and gunpowder were prohibited as articles of trade.

But the road to Eruwa was now and again infested by two notable highway robbers, Kurakura, a Gambari slave of Chief Ogundeyi, and Gata, an Ilọrin outcast, a notorious robber. Both of them were sharing the spoils with their masters, of whom Ogũmẹfun was one. One-fourth of the booties went to them, the remaining three-fourths to the robbers themselves.

In spite of this, the Eruwa market and the secret supply of Ogundipẹ were a great boon to the Ibadans but for the supply of a whole army something more was required, hence all their efforts were bent on keeping the Oke Igbo route open.

Derin the Chief of Oke Igbo now the Ọni elect of Ifẹ, seemed at this time to have the key of the whole situation in his hands, and his favour and goodwill were sought by all. The Ibadans sent him slaves, and excellent native cloths and other valuables as presents that he might keep the road open. The Ilorins sent him horses, the Ekiti kings sent him baskets of kola nuts and other valuable presents, and other costly presents came also from Ijẹbu and from Abẹokuta that he might keep the road closed.

The Ogunsua of Modakẹkẹ refused to ally himself with the Ifẹs, and a well-to-do Ọfa man resident at Oke Igbo was as a bone in Derin's throat, as the safety of their respective towns depended upon the safety of the Ibadans. So this road could not be altogether closed.

About this time the rumour spread that Derin of Oke Igbo with the confederates sent to tell the Ibadan chiefs that if they wished for peace they should send to beg the King for he also had his grievance. There was his nephew Lawani harboured at Ibadan, who, on leaving Ọyọ, emptied the palace of all the royal treasures so that he, the ALÂFIN, was practically a poor King. To this the Ibadans replied, " He is our prince, what can we do to him ? We cannot eject him out of the town, and we cannot touch his property, since he was allowed to leave Ọyọ with all he brought with him we cannot question his right to them." However, they sent accredited messengers to Oyọ to beg the King to arrange matters for them, pledging their devotion and loyalty to him.

His Majesty, as was his wont, returned them a fair answer, and sent them a few Ọyọ fighting men and a Babalawo (Ifa priest) ostensibly to make charms for their success : but the Ibadans, having reason to believe that the action of the priest was just to the contrary, drove him out of the camp.

About this time Sneider rifles were introduced by the Ijẹsas. The Ijẹsas at Lagos purchased a large quantity with cartridges for their country people " for the defence of the fatherland." At first the Ibadans did not know what they were nor their deadly character ; they made a mock of them for the Ijẹsas did not know how to use them properly. Being short compared with their long Dane guns, and making but little noise when fired, they called out to the Ijẹsas in jest, " Are you reduced to using tobacco pipes now ? Do send me one " (O ku tèmi o). But the scene was soon changed when certain Ijẹsa young men who had learnt the use of these weapons at Abẹokuta during the Dahomian invasions there came over to teach and to help their people in the use of them, Labirinjọ of Lagos, Gureje and Apara of Abẹokuta being the principal leaders. Moreover they formed a rifle corps which they carefully instructed.

These new weapons of precision now struck terror into the Ibadans. " What is this ? " " What is this ? " they began to say when they saw their effects upon the body of the slain. To quote an instance :—In the battle fought on the 15th May, 1881,

Chief Akintọla was shot through the leg as he sat on horseback, the same bullet killed the horse and a page standing by ! To make matters worse for the Ibadans, their precarious supply of the coarse gunpowder for their Dane guns was exhausted. They were greatly perturbed by this new development, thinking that the British Government at Lagos must be supplying the Ekitis with new weapons, especially when they saw the rifle corps in uniform. From a great distance in the battlefield men, women and children were shot dead within the Ibadan camp, some mortally wounded, others crippled for life !

Ogedemgbe accorded these rifles a doubtful welcome. "Sooner or later," said he, "the Ọyọs will get possessed of similar weapons, and what is to become of us then, unless we can finish them up before they do, which is very doubtful ? "

It became a matter of great difficulty for the Ibadans to muster together and troop into the battlefield on the day of battle. When they assembled at the gate of exit the rifles wrought havoc amongst them, every man had to try and find his way through nooks and corners, crawling along valleys, picking out shelters till they could approach near enough within the range of their Dane guns, to return the fire : others, sword or cutlass in hand, would crawl still nearer to pounce upon them. In this way some Ijẹsas were caught with rifles and cartridges which were examined with great curiosity. They were so perplexed in mind that they sent home for a native missionary—one of their sons—and laid this matter before him. "Why should the Lagos Government supply the Ekitis with such weapons to fight us ?" It was then explained to them that the Lagos Government had nothing to do with it ; the Ijẹsas at Lagos formed a committee which purchased these weapons, and sent them up *via* Aiyesan, Itebu, to Ondo, and thence to Ilesa to assist their countrymen.

" Can any of you chiefs be held responsible for whatever a man may buy at the Ibadan markets and bazaars for their friends at Ọyọ and Ogbomọsọ ?—No.—So then this matter stands."

Still, they were hardly satisfied, feeling that such strange weapons and men to teach the use of them could not have left Lagos without the Governor's knowledge.

At this crisis they sent again to the Awujalẹ of Ijẹbu on the 28th June, 1881, craving either for the opening of the roads or for his arbitration : but the Ijẹbus did not even allow the messengers to enter the town of Ijẹbu Ode ; they were refused a hearing.

Now, about the month of August, 1881, Derin of Oke Igbo as the Ọwọni elect of Ifẹ came forward, professing to arrange terms of peace for the belligerents. His messengers met those of the

Ibadans and the Ekitis on the battlefield and everything was arranged for the restoration of peace, but the whole thing broke down when it came to the last point, who was to decamp first. The Ijẹsas said, " We are in our country and you came from afar, how can you say we should leave our country ? " The Ibadans replied, " Nobody said you were to leave your country, you are only asked to retire from the camp into the town of Mẹsin Ipole behind you, so as to give us the chance to extricate ourselves from the defile through which we must pass. Bitter experience has taught us never to decamp in the face of an enemy for thus it was in 1865 when decamping from Ipẹru after peace had been made between us and the Ẹgbas and Ijẹbus, the Ẹgbas pursued after us, and we bought our retreat dearly. Should we repeat the same thing here under the very eyes of the Ekitis it will mean annihilation for us in these ravines and precipices. Retire to the town and so put some distance between us, and we will then decamp."

As neither party would agree to decamp first the negotiations failed and the war was resumed.

At this failure of the negotiations the people began to murmur against the Arẹ for bringing all these troubles upon them ; matters came to such a pass that the Arẹ, on the 1st September, was going to take poison and put an end to his life, but his family and the chiefs begged him not to do so. " It is God's will that things should be so," said they. " Such a thing has never happened to us before, but God wills it so."

On the 18th September, 1881, they sent again to the Awujalẹ, and again he would neither arbitrate nor open the roads, but sent them a taunting reply, " If you are tired of the war, come home." They returned the reply, " How can we come ? We are in a defile."

The Ijẹsa rifle corps still continued to do havoc amongst the Ibadans. On the 26th December the Ibadans received a terrible blow by the death of Belo, the brave son of the late Ọsundina (whose younger brother became afterwards so well known as Chief Apampa). He was a born soldier, and second to none in the whole camp. The death produced such a shock that his body could not be taken to the camp for fear of causing a panic ; from the battlefield it was conveyed outside the camp walls to Ikirun for interment. The mourning for this chief was deep and universal, for he was a very good man. On the news reaching home, all markets and bazaars were broken up for the whole day and the town went into mourning. Thus bloody strife continued on both sides for months and years.

R

Chapter XXVI

FAILURES AT RECONCILIATION

§ 1. The Alâfin's Efforts for Peace

After the failure of Derin's efforts, circumstances compelled the Alâfin to make a genuine effort for the restoration of peace.

(*a*) The Dahomian ravages of the western district, and the threats to " visit Qyọ this coming dry season."

(*b*) The men of the frontier towns sent to him to say that they will all desert their towns if the King could not send an army to protect them.

But the King's most effective army are the Ibadans, and those with them and they are pre-occupied.

On the 9th of October, 1881, he sent for the Rev. D. Olubi of Ibadan as head of the missionaries in the interior at the time, and with him " any two of *his* sensible colleagues." The order was obeyed on the 12th and the interview took place on the 13th.

There were present at the interview :

Two Qyọ officials, *viz.*, The Olosi, who is the King's *vade mecum* as it were, and the Apeka, who is the white men's intermediary with the court.

Also Mr. Jonathan Ojẹlabi, the foremost Christian gentleman at Qyọ at the time. These are of Qyọ. The Rev. D. Olubi, Mr. J. Okusẹhinde, and the writer, both Catechists under Mr. Olubi at Ibadan. Also Mr. A. F. Foster, by whom the letter to Mr. Olubi was written for the King, being the C.M.S. Scripture Reader at Isẹyin, and also the Asẹyin's messenger.

He consulted Mr. Olubi in particular as to the best way to reach the British Government to crave their assistance (1) to put an end to the fruitless war ravaging the country ; and (2) to offer a check to the Dahomian inroads into the Yoruba country.

He said that he was led to take this step as all his efforts to stop the war at its commencement failed, and also recently he fared no better. Also because the Egbas would intercept any messages of his to the coast.

It had happened more than once that when his messengers were at Abẹokuta on peaceful errands then the Egbas would start an expedition against the Ibadans as if he egged them on to it. So it was at the time of the expedition against Ile Bioku, and also at a raiding expedition to the Ibadan farms, and twice in the

Oke Ogun districts. The Egbas would seize any letter that he wrote to the British Government, and he would be glad if Mr. Olubi could reach the British Government for him.

After some discussion it was finally arranged that a letter be written to the Lieut.-Governor W. Brandford Griffiths at Lagos, and another to the Rev. J. B. Wood, Secretary of the C.M.S., requesting him to second his efforts ; and as he knows the country very well, to explain matters to the Governor of Lagos on any point His Excellency may require further elucidation.

The Palace, Ọyọ.
October 15th, 1881.

To His Excellency,

Lieut.-Governor W. B. Griffiths,

Sir—I hereby approach your Excellency and through you to the Imperial Government of England with this humble request : (1) My country has long been disturbed by a desultory war, which your Excellency well knows and which has put a stop to all trade and impoverished the country, and thousands of lives have perished by death or hopeless slavery.

I have several times undertaken to bring about the long-desired peace, but my efforts have from time to time been frustrated. Instead of terminating the war is extending, to threaten the utter extinction of the Yoruba race.

The Dahomians have taken advantage of this to ruin my kingdom. A few months ago seven towns have fallen a victim to their rapacities and Iseyin is now threatened. The next turn might be to my own royal city.

With all possible speed I beg that the Imperial Government —for which I have always a great respect—to come to my help. I crave your assistance both to come to settle this unfortunate war between the belligerent powers, and to stop the Dahomians who have made an inroad into my kingdom.

To assure your Excellency of my great anxiety I pledge myself to undergo any expenses if only peace be effected as the issue.

All my frontier towns are in great panic now, and if I make no stir to protect them they will all scatter and so I will undertake this in the coming dry season.

I mention this lest you may say after asking your help I make a movement.

I beg to remain,

Adeyemi, King of the Yorubas.

The second letter, addressed to the Secretary of the C.M.S

The Palace, Ọyọ.

October 15th, 1881.

THE REV. J. B. WOOD—

DEAR SIR,—I beg to approach you with my humble request : You might have heard of the desultory war in my kingdom which has been wasting its thousands. I have undertaken several times to effect peace, but my authority was not respected by the belligerent powers. And seeing that if this is not done in time, the extinction of the Yoruba race is inevitable I sent specially on the 9th inst. to call your representative here at Ibadan to consult with him how the Imperial Government might be reached that I might crave assistance to bring about the peace speedily.

Now, I humbly beg you to assist me in urging the Government to attend to this my request speedily. The letter addressed to the Government will be forwarded by you and please use your influence in this important matter for the sake of humanity to save my kingdom from extinction.

I am, etc., etc.,

ADEYEMI, KING OF THE YORUBAS.

§ 2. THE ALÂFIN'S MESSENGER

The writer was the bearer of these letters *via* Oke Igbo, Ode Ondo, and the Mawẹn country to Lagos.

Simultaneous with the invitation by the ALÂFIN to Ọyọ the Rev. D. Olubi received also a strange oral message from Derin of Oke Igbo by Solomon Ọlọrunfũmi the C.M.S. mailman to Lagos to the effect that as all the belligerents had applied to him to settle their differences for them, he wished Mr. Olubi to give him authority to do so, and if he was backed by him, he would have the confidence to act.

The fact was, that Derin was over-elated with the regard paid to him by all the principal states in Yoruba-land. Mr. Olubi being then the head of the missionaries in the interior came to be regarded as the representative of the white man, and Derin, in his vanity, wished for the recognition also of the white man hence the message.

In sending the writer with the ALÂFIN's letter to Lagos Mr. Olubi asked him to say to Derin that he had no power to authorize him but that he was sending down to Lagos and that the messenge would have an interview with the Governor of Lagos on the subject and would bring him word on his return.

The message was delivered to Derin and he said, " Yes, I might settle their differences but for the presumptions of the Ibadans, who wished the confederates who are in their own country to decamp first, which thing is impossible."

At this time the Mawẹn a piratical tribe in the eastern waters of Lagos, and the people of Ẹpẹ—an Ijẹbu town on the Lagoon—were fighting with each other, thus rendering the passage to Lagos from Ondo most difficult. The Ẹpẹs had rashly declared war against the Mahins on account of their piratical habits; they fitted out their large war canoes, and scoured the lagoon to the Mahin districts. The Mahins in their small canoes easily escaped into the jungles and had no difficulty in shouldering their canoes into places of safety. The Ẹpẹs, not meeting with any Mahin, wished also to scour the Ọfara River on the other side. They dragged their war canoes over the bit of land separating the lagoon from the Ọfara River about a mile distant ; this gave opportunity to the Mahins who lay hid in the jungles and behind large trees to shoot down the Ẹpẹs without being seen, and so the latter were utterly defeated, and those who survived escaped to Itebu, and burnt some of their war canoes with their own hands while the rest fell into the hands of their enemies. Itebu is in the Lagos protectorate and consequently Manuwa the head chief, himself a Mahin, held himself neutral. But the Mahins besieged them at Itebu for three months and they had to ransom their lives for a large sum of money before they were allowed to return home to Ẹpẹ. But the Ẹpẹs commanded the lagoon and would allow no Mahin canoe to proceed to Lagos.

Several Lagos traders in this district suffered by this war, and the Governor of Lagos had to come to these waters to restore order and rescue some of the Lagos traders from the Mahins.

Such was the disturbed state of things when the bearer of the ALÂFIN's letter to Lagos reached Ode Ondo. He was twelve days at Ondo before he found it possible to proceed to Aiyesan, where he had to embark for Lagos, and eight days at Aiyesan before he could get a passage at all to Lagos.

His Excellency the Governor had several interviews with the ALÂFIN's messenger in order to learn from him particulars about the country, and the state of things there at present political and otherwise. He also interviewed the representative Ọyọs and Ijẹsas at Lagos separately, but these being ignorant of the real state of things in the interior at the time could do no more than display tribal jealousies of each other without conveying any useful information. The Ijesas thought that the opportunity of their countrymen had come, and that they should not be interfered with. The Oyos were indignant with the ALÂFIN's messenger and discredited his mission, alleging that the Oyos being the leading tribe should never be the first to ask for the Governor's interference. They questioned the genuineness of the letter, and asked where was the King's Ilari (state messenger) and where his staff as the messenger's credential.

Under the circumstances the Governor asked the messenger to put down in writing his opinion of the situation, the exact state of things, and his reasons for believing that the people wanted peace and that the Lagos Government's interference would be acceptable. And this he did in a letter addressed to His Excellency on the 28th of November, 1881.

In the letter he showed that all parties would welcome peace but could not arrange it between themselves, being jealous and distrustful of one another. That the Ibadans and Ekitis wished for peace was evident from the fact that the messengers of both met those of Derin (the Owoni elect of Ife) in the battlefield for the purpose, the only hitch being who was to decamp first. Distrustful of each other, either party feared a treacherous pursuit by the other of the one to decamp first, hence the negotiations failed. With the representatives of a power respected by both between them there was no doubt that the war would at once come to an end.

As to the Egbas, he showed that they were never unanimous about the closing of the roads, one party being for it, the other against, hence they managed to find a circuitous route to Eruwa for trade. They also would welcome peace but would not take the initiative for fear of losing prestige. The same thing might be said of the Ijebus. In fact, it was well known that the Awujale, their King, was the only one for hostilities, the Ijebus themselves would rather have peace, hence the strained relations existing between the people and their king. That at the time of his leaving Ibadan for Lagos, steps were being taken to renew their attempts at negotiation, the chances this time being more favourable from the fact of the capture by the Ibadans of the brother of the Balogun of Ijebu in a raiding expedition which he undertook to their farms, and his being sent home to arrange for his own ransom.

From these facts it seemed evident that they would gladly accept from a higher and neutral power what all wished for but could not effect themselves.

§ 3. The Governor's Delegates

The Governor after due deliberation decided to send accredited messengers to sound the feelings of the chiefs of the tribes most concerned as to how far they desired peace, and also to ascertain whether the ALÂFIN's letter was genuine and if so that he should send an Ilari down with his staff.   The delegates entrusted with this business were : For the Ọyọs—Messrs. Simeon D. Kester and Ọderinlọ Wilson ; for the Ijẹsas—Messrs. Phillippe Jose Meffre and Joseph Haastrup.   These delegates with the ALÂFIN's messenger left Lagos on their mission on the 5th January, 1882, bearing letters to the ALÂFIN, the Ibadan war chiefs, and to the Ekitiparapọ from the Governor.   A copy of the ALÂFIN's letter was sent back for confirmation if genuine or otherwise.   The Governor himself, visiting the eastern waters of the Colony at the same time, conveyed them in his yacht to the landing place at Atijẹrẹ.

In order to secure greater importance for the mission, his Excellency arranged that those interior chiefs who occupied a neutral position, such as the Chiefs of Ondo and Derin of Oke Igbo, should send their own messengers also to accompany either party. Accordingly the parties from Lagos proceeded first to Ode Ondo and then to Oke Igbo before directing their footsteps each to his destination with messengers from these two places.   At Oke Igbo, when all from Lagos were being introduced, Derin flew into a rage with the ALÂFIN's messenger for not telling him the purport of his message to Lagos.   He was inclined to doubt the genuineness of it.   He said that the ALÂFIN could not have sent him without first consulting him ; that it was his cause they were defending, that blockading ammunition from the Ibadans was done by his instructions, etc., etc.   The messenger in reply reminded him of the message he brought him from the Rev. Mr. Olubi, which he admitted, and further said it was the same Olubi that sent him. He would not hear the messenger defend himself any further. Then Mr. Joseph Haastrup one of the delegates who was for fair play, and one Akitonde one of Derin's own men, interposed on his behalf, the former said the messenger was a man of God who was not likely to bear a false message.   The latter said—He was but a messenger and is not supposed to know the contents of a sealed letter, how then was he to communicate the same to you ?

The fact was that Derin was elated by the honour and respect accorded him by all the powers, and also by the recognition of the Governor.   He thought it was because he was an Ifẹ, a city which tradition says was the cradle of mankind, and not because he happened to hold the key of the situation to lock against or to open for the Ibadans to obtain ammunition from the coast.

The delegates separated at Oke Igbo, those for Ọyọ proceeded to Isọya, Modakẹkẹ and Ibadan, those for the Ekitis returned to Ode Ondo, and went by Iperindo and Odo to Ilesa.

The Ọyọ delegates were well received at Ibadan, in fact they received such welcome as would be accorded to the actual peace messengers ; and also at Ijaye they were met at a distance of four miles from the town by the Balogun and about 100 followers drumming, fifing, and the firing of a *feu de joie* showing with what eagerness they were seeking after peace.

They arrived at the capital on the 10th. His Majesty the ALÂFIN had two interviews with the delegates, he confirmed his letter to the Governor as genuine, briefly recounted the history of the war, adding : " Humanity forbids me to be indifferent to the hundreds of lives perishing daily. The whole Yoruba race is a gift from God to me, and hence every loss of life even to an untimely birth is a loss to the ALÂFIN of Ọyọ.

The antagonists are formidable, and without the intervention of a power stronger than both, peace will not be effected, hence I applied to the English Government for their intervention.

If I call upon the whole Yoruba country at large, they might respond to my call for enforced peace, but the issue will not be good, peace will be too dearly bought. What I desire is an intervention without any further loss of life."

The ALÂFIN also wrote, thanking the Governor for his letter, confirmed his former letter as genuine, and sent an Ilari, Ọbakọsetan by name, with his staff, which was a fan embroidered with red and green, as his credential.

From Ọyọ the delegates proceeded to the Ibadan camp. By this time those to the Ekiti camp having a shorter route to traverse had come to those of their own side and gone back.

The Ibadan war chiefs received the delegates well. According to custom they offered them cold water, and afterwards suitable presents, and lodged them.

At the interview Chief Mayẹ was the spokesman. He recounted the history of the war and laid great stress on the desirability of having a safe route to the coast for trade which should not be subject to the whims of their littoral neighbours ; and of the different possible routes, they preferred the Ikorodu route to Lagos which was freely opened for their use in the time of Governor Glover, and said they were ready to subscribe any amount that may be required for opening the road on their side, provided the Lagos Government would guarantee its security from the molestations of the Ẹgbas and Ijẹbus.

The delegates were the bearers of a letter also from the Ibadan war chiefs to the Governor of Lagos. In their letter they pointed out strongly that they were there not as aggressors, but as defenders of their frontier towns. That the commencement of hostilities was not on their side but on the side of the Ekitis, who perpetrated a most horrible massacre at Ila of all Ọyọs on peaceful avocation in their midst. The reason alleged for this was the cruel and oppressive measures of our messengers among them but of which they never made any formal complaint.

And this brutal massacre the Ekitis followed up by the invasion of their frontier towns. They have been defeated before but they renewed the invasion of Ikirun, and that was what brought them where they now are.

With the Egbas they had their complications : the Egbas kidnapped Ọyọs and they retaliated. They expelled all their people trading at Abẹokuta, and they (the Ibadans) remonstrated ; the Egbas sent an impertinent messenger to them whose conduct was openly outrageous, and they replied by raiding the Egba farms. All this they admitted, but with the Ijẹbus and Ilọrins they had no case whatever, nor could they understand why these should join any hostile coalition against them. They remonstrated with the Ilorin King but in vain. The Ibadan war chiefs sent two messengers down, the one Ojẹniran representing the Arẹ with his staff, and the other Ọdẹrinde representing the rest of the war chiefs. The writer, who was formerly the ALÂFIN's messenger, had again to accompany them with the Ilari Ọbakọsetan to Lagos.

By the hands of their messengers the Ibadan war chiefs sent specimens of the cartridges taken from the Ijẹsas to the Governor of Lagos, and asked whether it was the Lagos Government that supplied the Ekitis with such ammunition to fight them.

By a strange coincidence the messengers of the different kings and war chiefs each with his staff met at Ode Ondo, with them Derin of Oke Igbo sent his son to represent him, and the Oṣimowe and chiefs of Ondo appointed their own messengers to accompany them to Lagos. They were also fortunate enough to meet his Excellency the Governor of Lagos in the eastern waters, who, when he heard of their arrival at Aiyesan, steamed up and conveyed them all in his yacht to Lagos on the 10th February, 1882.

The Governor had several interviews with the messengers, and at the same time communicated with the Governor-General, Sir Samuel Rowe at the Gold Coast. The latter ordered that the messengers should wait for him. They were two months at Lagos waiting for the Governor-General, who when he arrived in his gun-boat, summoned the messengers to an interview the next day. He heard them all round and reserved his decision until further deliberation.

The failure of the mission was evident from what transpired at the meeting. At the Governor's instance the messengers related their messages in turn :

Qba-ko-ṣetan the ALÂFIN'S Ilari said, " My Master presents his compliments to your Excellency. He has sent me to invite your kind interference in the protracted war that has been going on these several years in the interior, in which thousands of lives are being sacrificed yearly. His own effort for the purpose proving abortive he has been constrained to apply to you as representing a higher power, to enable us to effect peace throughout the land."

The messenger of the Are of Ibadan had nothing else to say, " The ALÂFIN," said he, " is our King, and where his representative speaks the Ibadans cannot say otherwise. We abide by what he says."

Apẹ-ni-di-agba the Qwa's messenger said, " We have the Ibadans in our clutches now, and they should not be plucked off." The Governor replied, " Why then did you not eat them up before this time ? And why come here to ask this Government for their interference ? "

The Ijẹsa messenger further stipulated as their condition that unless the Ibadans would give a guarantee that they will never make war in future with either the Ijẹbus, Egbas, Ilọrins, Ijẹsas and Ekitis, they would not agree to peace.

The Seriki Ogedemgbe's messenger agreed with what the Qwa's messenger said.

The Ondo messengers wished for peace all round.

The Governor-General a fortnight later dismissed the messengers with a copy of an identical letter to each of the different kings and chiefs that sent them. The letter reads as follows :

" I have carefully thought over the message you gave to me a fortnight ago, and I have heard from the Lieut.-Governor all that passed in this matter before I came to Lagos.

I appreciate the action of the King of Qyọ in sending to the Governor of Lagos to ask him to send an officer to make peace between the Ibadans and Ijẹsas.

I thank the King of Qyọ for the compliment he has paid to the English Government in doing this, showing that he believes in the honour of the English Government, and that he feels confident that an officer from the English Government will deal justly in this matter.

The great Queen whom I serve, Her Most Gracious Majesty the Queen of England and Empress of India, has no other wishes than good wishes towards the entire African people. Her Majesty's instructions to her officers whom she sends to govern this colony are to promote by all proper means friendly intercourse between the people under their rule and the native tribes living near them.

In doing this from time to time her Majesty has approved the visits of her officers to many of the tribes neighbouring Lagos.

But Her Majesty has no desire to bring the inland tribes neighbouring Lagos under British rule, and though wicked people have said that if the white man comes to the interior he will take the country, I tell you publicly that my Queen has no wish to take your country.

As to sending the messenger asked for by the King of Ọyọ, I am quite aware that in sending to ask the Governor to send a messenger to the Ibadan and Ijẹsa camps to make peace, the King of Ọyọ has done a great thing. He has made a request that is not to be lightly answered.

I have thought over it patiently and very anxiously and what I have to say is this : the message given by the Ijẹsas was not a clear message. They said they wanted the Ibadans to go away and they would agree to make peace on certain conditions, and a part of this condition was—that the Ibadans should sign a promise that they would never again make war on any of the allied tribes whether Egba, Ijẹbu, Ijẹsa, Ekiti, or Ilọrin.

I cannot send an officer to your camp to dictate to you what you shall do there, but I will report all the circumstances to Her Majesty's principal officer, and if hereafter the Ibadans and Ijẹsas should wish to cease from fighting, and to agree to such a condition as one of the Queen's officers may think right, and if Her Majesty should direct that one of her officers should visit you to try to find out their conditions, then I will do all in my power to carry out your wishes ; and although I have found fault with the difficulties in the road, I would even come willingly myself if I were directed to do so.

The Queen is very much interested in your welfare and she wishes her officers to use every right endeavour to increase your prosperity."

Government House, Lagos.
  April 14th, 1882.

Each of the messengers was sent back with presents for themselves and for their respective masters. To the Ibadans the Governor sent two specimens of the cartridges used for the regulation

Martini-Henry rifle which were quite different from those of the
Sneider, showing that what the Ijẹṣas were using were not Government property.

In the meantime, news had come to Lagos of the unsafety of
the road between Oke Igbo and Modakẹkẹ. It was given out that
a body of Ijẹbu kidnappers were stationed at Isọya to blockade
the traffic in ammunition only, but what proved to be the fact
was that at the instance of Derin the Ijẹbus were concentrating
their forces at Isọya with the object of attacking Modakẹkẹ in the
rear, whilst the Ifẹs attacked them in front. The Ogunsua (Balẹ of
Modakẹkẹ) and a distinguished Modakẹkẹ Chief Ajarawa by name,
died suddenly and rather mysteriously, it was said by poison, and
further that Derin distributed arms and ammunition to the
neighbouring towns of Ikire Gbangan, Ipetumodu and Oduabọn
to join in the attack on Modakẹkẹ, which being removed out of the
way Ẹdẹ would be besieged and thus the Ibadans in the camp
would be taken in front and in the rear. But these towns not only
refused to take part in such coalition, but also forwarded all the
ammunition to the Arẹ in the camp.

This news meant a great peril for the Ibadan and Ọyọ messengers.
The Governor-General, hearing this, sent a special message to
Derin by his son that he should see to it that no harm came to
the messengers between his town and Modakẹkẹ. But notwithstanding this Derin arranged with the Ijẹbus to meet his own men
halfway in the forest, and that the ALÁFIN's first messenger with
the letter (*i.e.*, the writer) should be killed. It was in the presence
of the writer that Derin's men were sharpening their matchets ;
they went out early before dawn to waylay the messengers but it
happened that for want of carriers they could not go that day:
and when the kidnappers saw some traders coming with their
loads wrapped with tarpaulin they mistook them for the messengers
from Lagos and fell on them. The news of this disaster reached
the messengers in the afternoon of that day and it caused great
consternation at Oke Igbo. Derin was approached again, and
reminded of the Governor's orders and an escort was demanded from
him. After much trouble he sent one Aṣaju with five men, three with
old and useless Dane guns, one with a revolver, and the fifth carried
a native bell ! That was all. The escort demanded presents from
them at once before leaving home for the services he was about to
render. In mid forest he demanded more or he would leave
them at the mercy of the Ijẹbus. Much trouble was experienced
so that they could not reach Isọya that day ; they were soaked
by a drenching rain, but this rain proved the providential means
of clearing the road of kidnappers who betook themselves to shelter

when we passed. On reaching Iṣọya there was another detention. The Ijẹbus were loth to let them all go safe, the ALÂFIN'S first messenger being the principal person they wished to kill; but Aṣaju the escort interposed with, " If that had been done in the forest, it could not have been helped, but you cannot do that here now, my master will put the blame on me." So with much reluctance they were all let off. At Iṣọya they heard of the party that went to waylay them the previous day, about a hundred men armed with muskets ! It was a merciful deliverance.

At the gate of exit from Iṣọya, and at the Ile Ifẹ gate they experienced further troubles before reaching Modakẹkẹ.

On the arrival of the messengers at Ọyọ the ALÂFIN was much disappointed at the failure of the mission. When the Governor's letter was read to him he said, " Let us say in a word the whole thing has collapsed ! "

At the camp the war chiefs were very glad to see back their men of whom they had heard nothing for over two months. The failure of the mission did not seem to move them much, as they had expected it.

On hearing the letter read they said—"We expected as much. Such has been the action of the Ijẹsas on a previous occasion when attempts at peace-making were undertaken by the ALÂFIN and by Derin of Oke Igbo." Thus ended the mission in a total failure.

§ 4. THE LION AT BAY

Resumption of Hostilities.—On the morrow of the return of the Ibadan messengers, the Ibadan war chiefs announced to the Ekiti confederation the end of the truce which they had observed while negotiation was going on, and gave notice of battle.

The war was resumed and vigorously prosecuted in all its horrors and with desperation. During the stay of the ALÂFIN's messenger (the writer) in the camp, fighting went on almost every day with varied success on either side. The Ibadans often scored over their opponents, but from the lack of ammunition on their side, and owing to the arms of precision on the other side, they could not dislodge the Ekitis from their strongholds.

The Ijẹsas dug trenches in the battlefield in which they sheltered themselves from the Ibadan fire; two of the Ibadan war chiefs *viz.*, Fijabi and Sumọnu Apampa, and one of the Arẹ's big slaves, Idagana by name, intrepid horsemen all, distinguished themselves at this time by plunging into these trenches and dislodging the Ijẹsas and Ekitis from them. This daring act they styled "Tengba," or "Ajapa," *i.e.*, a speedily accomplished job: it was always done at a tremendous risk of their lives, for whilst they were exposed to the steady fire of their foes, their own men behind them could not return the fire for fear of wounding them and those who accompanied them on horseback, until all had jumped into the trenches and dispersed the foes.

The Ibadans were now determined to possess themselves of breach-loading guns and cartridges at whatever cost. Letters were written to the Ọyọs of Lagos, individually to distinguished men among them and collectively to the whole, stating their own case for the war, and calling for help as those on the other side had been helped by their own people, but for political reasons they received no response, as we shall see hereafter.

Hostilities by the Ẹgbas.—Not only at Kiriji was the war being vigorously prosecuted, but the Ẹgbas also resumed activities in kidnapping in the Ibadan farms at home. About the 15th of June, 1882, the Ẹgbas closed the Bẹrẹkodo and Eruwa roads ; the Arẹ had not ceased carrying on some negotiations with them all this time, for it was by his goodwill and connivance markets were opened formerly at Ketu and Ejio, and afterwards at Eruwa and Bẹrẹkodo for trade, to the mutual advantage of both sides. Now they professed at this time to be displeased with the message brought by Okò the Arẹ's principal messenger, hence they recalled all their traders who were as far as Bẹrẹkodo and Isẹyin and expelled all Ọyọs from Abẹokuta before closing the roads.

Lawore the Asẹyin did his best to pacify the Ẹgbas, and bring about a good understanding to keep the roads open, but all in vain. At a public meeting held at Iseyin on the 19th he took from a certain man an Ẹgba slave who had escaped to Isẹyin and sent him back to Abẹokuta as a mark of goodwill ; but his messenger was not even allowed to enter the town. This act was repaid on the 31st by another raiding expedition on the Ibadan farms, but the Ibadan hunters gave chase, overtook them and rescued all the captives.

The Dahomians again.—On the 18th August, about 200 Mẹkọ refugees arrived at Isẹyin who escaped the second invasion by the Dahomians. They were well received, and a portion of land allotted to them to build on, with ample room for more of their friends who might escape to this place.

A Bogus Peace Negotiation.—About this time the Ilorins sent some messengers to the Ibadan camp to negotiate for peace between them. The Ibadans had good reasons for suspecting their sincerity and therefore they sent them back with the message that if they are sincere in their overtures for peace, let them raise the siege of Ọfa and return home, and if they are loth to return home empty they may take the town of Ọtùn. This place was offered to the Ilọrins to be taken because of the mortal hatred they knew the Ilọrins had harboured against it. It had hitherto been secure under the protection of Ibadan, but now Ọtùn had joined the confederates against them. She, however, had already submitted to Ilọrin and accepted an Ilọrin political Resident. As this overture was only a ruse to lead the Ibadans to withdraw their contingent at Ọfa so that they might capture that city and advance to their rear, the negotiation fell through.

About the 14th September, 1882, a comet appeared in the heavens, which to the Yorubas is a very ominous sign. They are always on the look out for the demise of a great king or a mighty chief or the destruction of a great city ; consequently at such a time every important king or chief in the country usually consults his Ifa and offers a propitiatory sacrifice for the preservation of his life. The last seen before this was in 1859, when King Atiba of Ọyọ died.

The Revolt of the Ifẹs.—Although the Ifẹ auxiliary army was with the Ibadans in the camp at Kiriji, yet it was known that the Ifẹs at home sympathized rather with the Ekitis than with their overlords and would long ago have attacked the Ibadans from the rear but for the presence of the Modakẹkẹs near them. There might be other reasons for their hostility against the Ibadans but the chief one alleged was the forcing on them of Ayikiti, the son of a tyrant, as their Ọwọni (or king) in 1877.

It will be remembered that the Arẹ engaged the services of the Ifẹs and Modakẹkẹs in his raids on the Ẹgba farms in 1877, and after the retreat from Osiẹlẹ Ayikiti the Ifẹ general requested as the greatest favour he could show him that he should place him on his father's throne in order to preserve his seed from utter destruction, which he was sure would happen in revenge for the great mischief his father had done during his reign.

The Arẹ demurred, being unwilling to force upon the Ifẹs a king not in consonance with their desire, but Ayikiti brought great pressure to bear, and the Arẹ felt bound not only to reward his services, but to secure at least the loyalty and friendship of one leading provincial king. But he very soon after turned against the Ibadans. Ayikiti however did not survive long but the Ifẹs all the same harboured a feeling of spite and resentment against the Ibadans on that account, and *that* they were seeking an opportunity to give effect to. The Modakẹkẹs at their doors rendered this impossible, they refused to join in any coalition against Ibadan and hence the Ifẹ hostility was directed in the first instance to the Modakẹkẹs themselves ; they began kidnapping in their farms at first. Living in such contiguity to each other intermarriages of course were frequent and social intercourse unrestricted, but at this time several Modakękes who went to their relatives at Ile Ifę were heard of no more, some the Modakękes had to redeem back.

A distinguished Ifę chief, Akingbade by name, and the Aşaju of Derin of Oke Igbo went and joined the Ijębu camp at Isọya to kidnap Yoruba caravans, and they made no exception of Moda-kękes their neighbours.

The Arę hearing this sent over and again to conciliate them, and urged on Derin rather to come over to Ile Ifę and be crowned the Qwọni and restore peace to at least that part of the country ; but Derin refused to comply unless the Ibadans would first cede to him the following towns which once may have belonged to Ifę but had ceased to be so for at least 50 years, viz., Ipetumodu, Qdũabọn, Gbangan, Ikire, Apomu, and the villages in their vicinity. Other-wise (said he) he would not go until the close of the war which he thought could only end in one way, which would indubitably place these towns in his hands.

To conciliate the Ifęs the Arę sent one Tõki to mediate between the two parties, which done, they were to take a mutual oath of amity and to ratify the same with the blood of a sheep he took with him.

But matters in the meantime had come to a crisis. The Ifęs raided the Modakękę farms, caught and maltreated a woman by cutting off her breasts, the Modakękes in turn resented the affront, they retaliated by raiding Ifę farms, caught four persons and also sent to the camp at Kiriji to recall Oyebade their Balogun, for it was evident that war has now become inevitable.

The Arę did not like the look of things. In permitting Oyebade to go home he sent also an influential Ifę chief, charging each of them to go and quell the faction, put the ringleaders to death on either side and restore peace at home.

These chiefs went by forced marches and took the precaution that the news of their coming should not precede them. They reached home together. Oyebade and Adepọju, his second in command, marched straight to the house of one Qbalaiye, a known intriguer who was carrying on secret correspondence with the Ilọrins and had obtained a horse from them, and stood before his gate. Hearing that the war chiefs were come, he came out to welcome them ; whilst these war chiefs lay prostrate to receive the greetings of this venerable man, a swordsman who had been instructed walked round to his back and, ere he was aware, by one sweep of the sword his head fell off from his shoulders ! His house was immediately confiscated and levelled with the ground. The war chiefs saw this accomplished before they went to their own homes.

But the Ifẹs not only did not punish but condoned the action of the ringleaders on their side, and were prepared to give battle the following morning. Oyebade nearly lost his life by trusting himself too far among the Ifẹs trying to explain that they were not sent home to fight but to punish the ringleaders and respect the oaths ; he was luckily pulled back in time. On account of the oath the first shot fired by the Ifẹs was by a man who climbed up a tree to do so ; the idea being that to break the oath standing on the earth on which the oath was taken would surely result in disaster. But notwithstanding this, when they joined battle the Ifẹs were defeated and driven away out of the city and many of them were taken captives.

Ile Ifẹ and Modakẹkẹ being practically one town with only a small stream separating the two, they had not to go outside their walls to fight, the battle took place at the Akọgun market. It was practically a civil war.

The Arẹ and Ibadan chiefs hearing this ordered that the Ifẹ captives be released, and Toki was sent again with a sheep and a cat to worship at the tomb of Ọrañyan, and to bring both parties together again into a covenant ratifying the same with an oath on the blood of these victims.

But ere this could be done the Ifẹ young men had collected another force and made a determined attack on Modakẹkẹ. This was on the 1st December, 1882. Victory was again on the side of Modakẹkẹ, but the victory was dearly bought ; Oyebade their commander-in-chief was mortally wounded and he died a short time afterwards leaving the command of the army to Adepọju.

While all this was going on at home the Ifẹ war chiefs were in the Ibadan camp at Kiriji fighting against the Ekitiparapọs but one night before daybreak they left the camp in a body with their wives and children and went over through the battlefield to the Ekitis. They were received with open arms and sent home to join their comrades to make efforts to destroy Modakẹkẹ.

Modakẹkẹ now became the third seat of war.

Reinforcements came to the Ifẹs from the Ijẹsas and Ijẹbus. An Ijẹsa force under their war chief Ayimọrọ encamped on the north-east and the Ijẹbus under their Seriki Ogunṣigun of Igbo crossed the Ọsun river and encamped in the south. The Ifẹs themselves were encamped in a village eastward of Modakẹkẹ. From these three points Modakẹkẹ was attacked at one and the same time. The fall of Modakẹkẹ would mean an attack in the rear for the Ibadans at Kiriji and consequently they were obliged to send as reinforcement the following chiefs on the 4th December, viz., Akintọla, Sanusi, Bamgbegbin and Aturu.

At this new development the Ekitis redoubled their energies to overwhelm the Ibadans in the camp the battle raged at Kiriji with unabated fury and many valuable lives were lost on both sides.   Of the men of note on the Ibadan side were : Ali Laluwoye the Ọtun (from illness) Aderibigbe son of the late Balẹ Olugbode (from wounds previously received) Awo the son of the late Labọsinde, the Baba Isalẹ, Ogunrinde son of the late Agbakiu.

Some of the reinforcement at Modakẹkẹ had to be recalled when the fighting at Kiriji was becoming too strong leaving Akintọla alone and subsequently Sumọnu Apampa was sent to join him.

Thus stood the Ibadan lion at bay facing five fronts, with ammunition spent, yet flinching from none, at Ọfa, at Kiriji, at Modakẹkẹ and against the Ẹgbas as well as the Ijẹbus at home.

Chapter XXVII

A RIFT IN THE CLOUDS

§ 1. A Turning Point

When everything was thus dark and gloomy for the Ibadans, quite unexpectedly, on the 17th December, 1882, Ijẹbu messengers arrived in the town to negotiate for peace between the two countries !

The messengers were received at the Arẹ's gate at Ibadan. They were hooted at in the streets and called all sorts of names, being taken for spies. Their message was however conveyed to the war chiefs in the camp and the home authorities were instructed to send a messenger back along with them to ascertain the truth of their statements.

The hearts of all were made glad on the return of the messengers when they heard that the Ijẹbus were sincere in their overtures for peace. Ajako the messenger sent reported that about 800 of the Ogbonis met at Orù and without a dissentient voice all agreed to make peace. Ten kegs of powder and ten bags of salt were the presents sent to the Arẹ and war chiefs as a token of their goodwill. These sent as return presents slaves, gowns, and sheep. Thus peace was concluded with the Ijẹbus and trading relations resumed. Provisions which were scarce at Ijẹbu were taken down and bartered for salt, and cheap foreign made cloths and cutlery, the Ijẹbus for the present forbidding the exportation of powder and firearms. What led to this negotiation for peace has been told in a previous chapter (vide p. 451). And again, the Ijẹbus, being essentially a commercial people, their only market for interior products and for disposing of their wares from the coast was closed to them since the commencement of the war, and scarcity of foodstuffs caused much distress among them also, and yet the Egbas, whose cause they were espousing—having no grievance of their own—had managed to open markets for themselves, first at Ketu and Ejio, subsequently nearer home at Eruwa by which their own wants were relieved. The Ijẹbus had no such outlet ; they were therefore inclined towards peace with Ibadan, but the Awujalẹ their king was for prosecuting the war vigorously for which purpose he ordered the Balogun out to encamp at Orù, from whence he might send raiding expeditions out to the Ibadan farms. We have seen the disaster that befel them on the 10th of April, 1881, and the capture of the Balogun of Ijẹbu's brother, who was sent back by the Ibadans to effect a good understanding between them and the Ijẹbus. That episode made a deep impression on the Ijẹbus, and ever since they had been working for peace against the wish of the Awujalẹ, and a small clique about him ; but a quiet revolution had been going on towards this end. The people were now determined to have the road open in spite of the Awujalẹ, and this led to something like a civil war as will be seen below.

Another Ilọrin Episode.—Simultaneously with this event was the arrival of a peace embassy from the Sultan of Gando to the Ilọrin and Ibadan camps. The Ibadan chiefs, who would not listen to any overtures from the Ilọrins, knowing their treachery, paid more regard to these messengers, gave them a cordial welcome, treated them respectfully, believing them to be sincere. To show their willingness to accept peace with Ilọrin the Arẹ sent home for about 60 of the Ilọrin captives at Ibadan, who were men of influence, and sent them all home on horseback. Moreover they accepted all the terms offered by the Ilọrins. Peace was so far concluded that the opposing armies at Ọfa exchanged visits with each other. Several Ibadan and Ọfa people even passed on to Ilọrin and traders on both sides who had been shut up in other towns hailed the opportunity of returning home, and others did a good trade as far as Bida in potash and salt while the opportunity lasted.

But still the Ilọrins refused to raise the siege of Ọfa, on the contrary they insisted on the Ibadan contingent going away. The Ibadans on the other hand promised that not only would they leave Ọfa, but also that they would not claim the overlordship of that city, they would hand it over to Ilọrin, but only on one condition, namely, that the town be not destroyed ; but as they were there to defend that town they could not retire except the siege was first raised. This test of the sincerity of motives of the Ilọrins being insisted on, the negotiations failed and hostilities were resumed.

§ 2. Rambling Talks of Peace

The Rev. David Hinderer, a retired missionary of the C.M.S., who for many years had laboured in Yoruba land and who continued to take a lively interest in the country and its people, addressed a letter to the representatives of the tribes residing at Lagos on the difficulties present in the interior, well knowing the tribal feelings and jealousies existing at Lagos which were fanning the flames of the hostilities in the hinterland. He invoked them as patriots and especially as Christians to see that all tribal feelings and jealousies be set aside in the interests of peace to their father-

land, and that they should act in concert in order to restore good
understanding among their fellowmen, and prosperity to their
unhappy country.

This led to a representative gathering at Lagos of the elders of
the different tribes, in which it was resolved that a deputation
should wait upon the Lieut.-Governor Alfred Moloney, on the
subject of peace between the interior tribes. Those appointed for
the purpose were : The Rev. Jas. Johnson, Pastor of St. Paul's
Breadfruit, Messrs. Henry Robbin and I. H. Willoughby, native
merchants. They waited on the Governor on the 8th of December,
1882, and presented the following resolution :

"At a meeting of the representative elders of the different
tribes, Yorubas, Egbas, Ijebus, Ijesas Ifes and Ondos, held at the
Breadfruit parsonage on the 7th of December, 1882, in reference
to the long-standing warfare in the interior, from which both the
interior countries and Lagos have suffered, the following resolution
was after a full consideration of the subject unanimously
adopted :

'That this meeting, convinced of the ex-king Dosumu's
influence with the kings and chiefs of the interior, though he no
more exercise regal power in Lagos, and this is known everywhere in the interior, decides that a deputation composed of
nominated representatives of the different tribes be appointed
to wait upon him, and respectfully solicit his interference with
the King of Jebu and the other kings and chiefs in the interior
for the peaceable settlement of the interior difficulty, His
Excellency the Governor of Lagos having been first respectfully
informed of it, and the countenance and support of his influence
had.' (Sgd.) JAS. JOHNSON."

His Excellency the Governor replied that no one was more
desirous than Her Majesty to see peace restored among the people
of the interior, and with such an object so far as counsel, advice
and moral influence went, he would not hesitate to do all he could
in Lagos. Giving the deputation distinctly to understand that
neither Dosumu nor his chiefs were allowed to exercise any rule
in the settlement ; yet the Governor considered that he would
best suit the interest of the Government and meet the aim of the
community by having a meeting of the ex-king and his chiefs, at
which he would allow to be introduced the members of the deputation who could then repeat the resolution on which he would then
for himself hear the views of Dosumu and his chiefs.

The meeting accordingly took place on the 11th, at which, after
some introductory remarks by the Governor, the Rev. Mr. Johnson

repeated the resolution, explained the desire of the community and advanced his hopes.

King Dosumu next spoke but said nothing of importance.

He was followed by the Apena, who acted as spokesman for the king and the remaining chiefs, conveying that they would like the matter reported to the Queen, and if they were then asked to exercise their influence with the king and chiefs of Ijẹbu they would willingly do so.

One and all they expressed their desire for peace. In support of the aim of the community Messrs. Robbin and Willoughby also spoke forcibly.

We may remark that the Apena evinced such caution and reluctance in the matter of action as desired because of the trouble he fell into in 1875 during the administration of Governor Dumaresq when he was personally forbidden by the Lieut.-Governor Lees to interfere in Ijẹbu matters.

The Governor said that if Dosumu and the chiefs would put to loyal advantage their influence in the matter of the restoration of peace to the country he was confident that Her Majesty's Government would be appreciative of any such effort ; and that a general move for good in the way of an honest endeavour to restore peace was very different to direct and meddlesome interference in the interior economy of a government such as Ijẹbu.

This movement was the first of a series of fruitless meetings held at Lagos between the years 1882 and 1892 which had for their object the restoration of peace in the hinterland by the exercise of " influence." The subsequent meetings however were not under the ægis of the Government but among the tribal representatives themselves.

The ALÂFIN's letter to Lieut.-Governor Griffiths in 1881 made it clear that it required a higher power which commanded the respect of the combatants on both sides to make them lay down their arms.

The ALÂFIN's messenger emphasised the fact over and over that *nothing less than an armed intervention could prevail upon the belligerents to decamp.*

But then the interior at that time was so little known that people living at ease and security at Lagos had no idea of those arduous circumstances of life that moved men resolute and brave to protect their interests by the sinews of their own right arms. Probably there were not half a dozen men in all Lagos, certainly not among the " influential " personages—so-called—who knew the exact state of things prevailing in the interior, or we would have heard less of the " influence " which the ex-king of Lagos or the Awujalẹ of Ijẹbu Ode was able to exert with the heroes of a Homeric struggle, incapable as they were to intervene with a force or to guarantee safety for an hour ; nor was it apparent by what means they could sheath the sword of men who meant business.

What was happening at Ijẹbu at that very moment furnishes an amusing commentary on the resolution read before the Governor, and affords incontestible proofs of how little Lagosians knew about up country affairs, not even of what was going on, so to speak, at their very doors and also of what value the Awujalẹ would be in the matter of peace.

The tribal parties at Lagos evidently missed the point of Mr. Hinderer's letter. The idea expressed in their resolution and their procedure seemed rather far-fetched, and roundabout, except the object had been to show that the Awujalẹ of Ijẹbu was an important personage.

The remarks of Apẹlidiagba to the Governor General, Sir Samuel Rowe, which served to wreck the peace embassy initiated by the ALÂFIN were dictated at Lagos ; the same expression had been used before by the Ijẹṣa representatives to the Lieut.-Governor W. B. Griffiths. As the tribal antagonism of compatriots at Lagos served to inflame and excite the belligerents, so unanimity amongst them might serve to soothe their feelings and dispose them to yield even at a mere message—say—of the Governor, behind whom there was known to be a force of incalculable weight. Such was the intention of Mr. Hinderer.

On the 26th of December, 1882, the Apena waited on the Governor to intimate to His Excellency that he was the person deputed by the ex-king and council to proceed to Ijẹbu on the above mission.

THE APENA'S REPORT

The Report makes long and tedious reading, but the following extract is the gist of the same.

The Apena of Lagos who was sent up on a mission to the Awujalẹ of Ijẹbu with the object of adopting measures for putting an end to the war in the interior, left Lagos on the 28th December, 1882, and landing at the first Ijẹbu port at Itọ Ike, he learnt of the civil commotion at Ijẹbu Ode the chief town, and instead of sleeping there for the night he left at midnight, went through bush paths with lighted torches and by forced march reached Ijẹbu Ode by daybreak. He lost no time, but was announced by the Apena of Ijẹbu Ode to the Awujalẹ, who granted him an audience at once.

The Apena told in few words the object of his visit and what gave rise to it, *viz.*, a letter written by a retired missionary to the representatives of all the interior tribes at Lagos in the interest of peace ; and that his mission was at the instance of the ex-King Dosumu and his council, with the approval of the Governor of Lagos.

The Awujalẹ, after hearing the Apena's mission, requested him to proceed to the Ijẹbu camp at Orù to deliver the same to the war chiefs there. But the Apena would like to know the King's mind, as it was most likely the war chiefs would ask, " What did he say to your message ? " The King then said he could not give an authoritative reply to a political message without the advice of his councillors, and that they were all disaffected now, and were deserting the town. The Apena might be able to find out why they were leaving the town. But he might mention that the object of the Apena's mission, strange to say, bears strongly on the present condition of things at Ijẹbu, viz., the restoration of peace in the interior. That it was with the advice of all his councillors, the Oṣugbos, Ipampas, Ilamurins, and the Ogboni Odis, that he embarked on hostilities against Ibadan, and that he sent messengers to the sixteen kings of the Ekiti confederates, also to the king of Ilọrin, to the ALÂFIN of Ọyọ and others before he commenced hostilities, and he promised the Ijẹsas and Ekitis his support in breaking off the Ibadan yoke ; and now after entering into an agreement with all these kings his own people turned round and said they desired peace with Ibadan, and he was to break his word to the other kings !

The war chiefs by his commands are at Orù as a base of operation against the Ibadan farms, but why were the civil chiefs deserting the town for the village of Imọwo? The Apena might be able to ascertain the reason when he got there. The Apena of Ijẹbu Ode told him that the civil chiefs were having a meeting that day at Imọwo and that he was to be quick so that he might meet them all together.

Accordingly, the Apena on his way to the Ijẹbu camp at Orù passed through the village of Imọwo, where he met about 320 of the Ogbonis and others. He told them his mission and three times they asked him, " Is it customary with you at Lagos to settle a quarrel or not ? " He replied in the affirmative. " Then," said they, " we are of the same mind." They said, moreover, that they had been there seven days since, under great personal discomforts, to interpose between the Awujalẹ and the war chiefs at Orù who were bent on a civil fight, as the Awujalẹ would not listen to any arrangement to terminate hostilities and bring peace and prosperity to the country. He was to hasten at once to Orù as the war chiefs were holding a council there " to-day " and the result might be some strenuous measures. He did so, and met them just dispersing from the meeting, but they resumed their seats when they saw him. He related to them the object of his mission and the Balogun asked him, " Is it customary with you at Lagos to settle a quarrel or not ? " He replied in the affirmative ; the Balogun then turned to the chiefs and people asking them what they thought of the message of the community of Lagos by the Apena about the restoration of peace in the interior and resumption of friendly relations ? The answer was one loud shout of joy.

The Balogun thereupon told his own story. For the last seven years (said he) they had been stationed at Orù to carry on hostilities against the Ibadans, they had spent their all, their money and their goods gone, and they were now impoverished. " You may have heard of the fame of Ibadan," said he. " Do you think anyone in his senses can go against such a people with a pouchful of parched corn ? "—No.—Then as the King has made his statements, by the leave of the war chiefs the Apena should patiently hear their own verison.

The Balogun then proceeded to say that they had no cause of quarrel with the Ibadans but were drawn to one by the Ẹgbas. That the same thing was done in 1860-62 during the Ijaye war, the Ẹgbas sent to them to say two Ọyọs were fighting, and they were going to flog them both ; but on the contrary it was the Ibadans that flogged both the Ẹgbas and Ijayes. The scene of battle was changed from Ijaye to Oke kere in the Rẹmọ district, and there was an appalling amount of bloodshed before they succeeded in driving the Ibadans home : but that they, the Ijẹbus, were then impressed with the irony of the whole situation : the Ibadans were there to defend Ijẹbu towns against the Ẹgbas, " and we joined the Ẹgbas in fighting them ! After all, we were the losers because the result was the destruction of so many towns in the Rẹmọ districts. And with all their pretensions the Ẹgbas were no men. Akodudu was the only brave man we saw amongst them in those days."

Then the Ẹgbas needlessly went and interfered with the Ibadans in their new road to Porto Novo which was the origin of the present imbroglio, and sold 1,460 persons of those who went to trade amongst them, and they had involved them (the Ijẹbus) in the quarrel. Some distinguished and influential Ijẹbu chiefs who disapproved of the war had been ruined by the Awujalẹ and would have been killed but that they escaped from the country.

" We attacked the Ibadan farms and caught three men, but the home garrison chased us and caught 143 of us ! The Arẹ of Ibadan not only released them, but sent them back by one Dawodu, with emblematic messages, *viz.*, a ¹fan, Ọsin feather, and a white sash. But the Awujalẹ kept listening to the advice of ill-disposed persons who were against peace, representing the message from the Arẹ as a false message, originating from the Balogun, who, knowing salt to be dear at Ibadan, wished to drive a lucrative trade therefrom ! After a while Oluguna the Awujalẹ's own slave, who was caught by the Ibadans in our raids, was sent back with a present of twelve slaves to the Balogun with a message that he should assist him to beg the Awujalẹ. The Awujalẹ approved of his receiving the presents, but arranged that future messengers should come to himself direct by a new road, and not by the old route through Orù where the Balogun was stationed. This of course they did not mind, thinking he might thereby be amenable to peace.

" After this, the Arẹ of Ibadan sent messengers to the Awujalẹ several times, and each time with presents, 72 slaves in all, valuable cloths, a demijohn of sẹgi beads and a crown ! All which he appropriated but still would not declare the roads open for commerce so that we here might return home. On the contrary, he sent an army to Isọya to aid the Ifẹs in destroying Modakẹkẹ. We are suffering, and the Ẹgbas on whose account we embarked on this suicidal policy are trading on their own account at Ẹrẹbu. But the Awujalẹ entered into all sorts of intrigues with the men of Iwo, Ẹdẹ, Modakẹkẹ, Ifẹ, and the Ijẹsas, and all Ijẹbus were scandalized at this after receiving so much from the Ibadans ! " They attributed it to the fact that since his accession he never removed to the palace of the kings but remained in his mother's house, where he was accessible to everybody, and he followed other advices than those of the official councillors. Hence they were determined he should reside in the palace if needs be with their guns, or he must be deposed. They told the Apena he was free to inform the Awujalẹ of their determination, nobody else would tell him. He promised them he would.

He thereupon went back to the king and remonstrated with him. The determination of his people was that he should remove to the palace, demolish his present residence, send away his sons from him, as by custom they were to visit him only once a year, and that he was to execute all his bad advisers.

The King demurred. He said that kings should reside in the

---

¹ A fan in Yoruba is Abẹ̀bẹ̀ the root bẹ̀ means to beg.
Ọsin is a water bird. Sin in Yoruba means to serve
A white sash—white is an emblem of peace.
The message means, we beg you, we will serve you, let there be peace between us.

palace true, but he declined to receive orders from the people, and he could not be compelled to do so.

After much remonstrance, showing him the evils of life in exile, reminding him of Akitoye's case at Lagos, etc., he prevailed upon him to yield. He asked him to take a retrospective view of his life and try to meet the wants of his people : that there was a time when he commanded and his people obeyed ; now they command and he must obey. He had been fed by God hitherto with honey but now He gave him a taste of bitter herbs : the King would not refuse that.

After much difficulty he obtained for the Awujalẹ five days' grace in which to carry out the demands of the people, *viz.*, to demolish his present residence, send his sons away, and execute his bad advisers. (These marked victims, however, escaped to Ẹpẹ, an Ijẹbu town in the Lagos protectorate.)

There was a great deal more of complications attending this business, but he (the Apena) should not meddle with Ijẹbu internal affairs.

The King reluctantly took leave of him and wished there were many like him for the sake of affairs of the country : he gave him two bags of cowries, and he left Ijẹbu Ode on the 9th inst. via Ẹpẹ for Lagos. On the 10th the King's " ill advisers " who were marked for destruction met him at Ẹpẹ, he advised Agbaje, the chief ruler of Ẹpẹ, not to deliver them up for death but rather refer the case to the Governor of Lagos through Dosumu. The mat whereon he sat at Ẹpẹ, valued about 20 heads of cowries, was given him as a present, and they expressed high appreciation of his services in bringing the affairs in Ijẹbu to such a peaceful issue. He arrived at Lagos early on the 12th of January, 1883.

The following letters marked A, B and C from Agbaje, the Balogun of Ẹpẹ (an Ijẹbu port subject to Lagos), to the Governor of Lagos, will show us the condition of the Ijẹbus at that time and the sequel to the Apena's visit.

Letter A.

SIR,—I have the honour of informing your Excellency that I have had the mind of laying before your Excellency's information the other day when here in H.M.S. *Gertrude* the quarrel between the King of Ijẹbu and His Majesty's subjects who compose His Majesty's war camp at a place called Orù in the Ijẹbu territory.

The King's subjects said that they would not fight against the Ibadans any more : they having made three subsequent raids on the Ibadan's farms but were not successful, therefore they are tired of fighting ; they are threfore desirous of making peace with the Ibadans and then resume trade.

The King not agreeing to peace-making but determined to carry his purpose in fighting with the Ibadans. He does not want any thing else but war. His Majesty's subjects said in charges against him that since he has been proclaimed the King of Ijẹbu he was never seen to sit on the king's throne, he resides in his mother's house. He was requested by his subjects to sit on the throne as were his predecessors and to yield to the peace-making with the Ibadans. These the King refused to accept but determines to fight with the Ibadans and no peace. His Majesty's subjects are being prepared to fight a civil war with their king and to have him dethroned while the King is being prepared also to resist their purpose !

The King and the subjects are now ready to fight the civil war. I have however, sent three messengers to the King at different times towards peace-making, but he would not permit me and my chiefs. Notwithstanding my further effort in sending the fourth message to the camp at Orù, but I am afraid they will not accept my offer. In a plain word, war is imminent. Your Excellency may say I have not given you a due notice. If I am successful all right otherwise I could not help.

I have the honour, etc.,

AGBAJE, Balogun of Ẹpẹ.

December 25th, 1882.

[NOTE that this letter was written three days before the Apena left Lagos, but the news it contained was not known before he left.]

Letter B.　The Balogun of Ẹpẹ's second letter to the Governor of Lagos.

January 12th, 1883.

SIR,—I have the honour to asknowledge the receipt of your Excellency's letter of the 27th December and noted its contents.

As per my promise in my last letter that I have sent message to the Ijẹbus at Orù in the way of mediation—mediation between them and their King—and as I also promised to you the result of such message, the messenger has returned saying that it is a quarrel between a father and his son, we have no hand in it and that in a few days after that I heard that the Apena from Lagos has arrived in the camp thinking that he would settle the matter, but sorry he could not do it, it is still continued.

Since the Apena has left the camp and Ijẹbu Ode to this

place and proceeded to Lagos, the King's sons have been driven away together with four of his notable slaves with their men. When they left the country (? town) Ode they did not stop in any of the Ijẹbu districts but came right off to Ẹpẹ.   I am hearing that the fugitives will be pursued by their opponents, and that wherever they are met with the country (? town) will be destroyed.   And now, acting to the advice of your Excellency's, *viz.*, that I should be neutral in the matter, so I do but in considerating I am determined not to give up the fugitives to their pursuers.   I will not do it to please anyone.

Your Excellency's obedient servant,

AGBAJE, Balogun of Ẹpẹ.

[NOTE this letter was written on the very day the Apena reached Lagos.]

Letter C.   The Balogun of Ẹpẹ's third letter to the Governor of Lagos.

January 15th, 1883.

SIR,—Since mine of four days ago, things here have continued in the zigzag manner.   To-day the King of Ijẹbu Awujalẹ has left his town Ijẹbu Ode and has arrived at this place (Ẹpẹ). His Majesty's complaints are that he was requested by his subjects to reside in his father's house, he has done so.   To drive away his sons, and to accept the opening of the roads to Ibadan, and these he has yielded to.   Not satisfying with these, they further requested him to go to sleep—meaning that he should die.   This he will not do as he is not ready to leave the world when it does not please God to take him away yet from the world he will not force it.   Seeing that Ẹpẹ is his country and he had had a house there before, therefore he returned to his home.

I remain your obedient servant,

AGBAJE, Balogun of Ẹpẹ.

[NOTE that the above was written only three days after the return of the Apena to Lagos, when he was supposed to have settled everything.]

Thus ended the movement at Lagos which had for its object the termination of the deadly struggle going on at Kiriji by means of the " influence " of Dosumu the ex-King of Lagos, and Afidipòte, now the ex-King of the Ijẹbus.

§ 3. DESPERATE MOVEMENTS

The following letter, addressed to some gentlemen at Lagos, will show how straitened the Ibadans now were, from the use of the rifles against them.

To I. H. WILLOUGHBY, Esq.,
    D. C. TAIWO, Esq.,
    SUMONU ANIMASAWUN, Esq.,
    SHITTA, Esq.,
    And all LAGOS OYOS or YORUBAS,

SIRS,—We, the Are and Chiefs of Ibadan, send you our greetings.

We have written and sent a special messenger to you and that letter was our first to you, on the subject of the present war. We there mentioned that the Ijesas of Lagos have supplied their brethren with superior weapons of war, and that we believe the Lagos Government had no hands in it. Our grounds for believing so was this. We have sent a specimen of the rifle shots that they have been fighting us with to the Lieut.-Governor W. B. Griffiths by the hands of his messengers, Messrs. Kester and Wilson, asking at the same time whether it was the Government who was supplying them with the same. Our messengers who accompanied them down returned with two different kinds of cartridges, one for the Henry Martini, and the other for the Government rifles, and word was sent by our messengers that their ammunitions of war were quite different from the specimens sent. We believe them so far and have agreed that they should act the part of a peace-maker.

But soon after our letter was written we were informed from good authority that influential people of Lagos, who could not have left the colony without the Government's notice, have actually left Lagos, and have been fighting with us with superior weapons of war, *viz.*, with the Gattling gun, and with plenty Sneiders.

We undertake to mention the names given to us, *viz.*, T. F. Cole, Esq., Labirinjo, Esq., F. Astrope, Esq., Messrs. Campbell and Osifila, and that Mr. Vaughan was hired as the artillery man. How is it that such eminent men should leave the colony without the Governor's notice?

The Ijesas may truly plead that they are fighting for their country, but we have written to the Lagos Government telling them the cause of this war. It was they who first originated the war by encamping against Ikirun and their watchword was "Odo Obà ni Àlà." The Obà river will be the boundary;

that is to say Iwo at a day's journey from us will be annexed to their own territory ! They were once defeated and this is a second confederation ; and we have said, and do say now, that we are in our frontier protecting the Ọyọ provinces from their inroads.

Trusting you would give the matter your serious consideration for the interest of your country and people. We submit the matter to you, our kinsmen, that you bring the matter before the Government, that an enquiry be made if the above-mentioned persons could be found in the settlement.

We have the honour, etc.,

LATOSISA, A.O.K.
and the IBADAN CHIEFS.

The above letter was read by the Yorubas of Lagos and was published anonymously. Mr. F. Astrope was at that time farming at Aiyesan, although all the same he and the other Lagos Ijẹṣas were there in the interest of trade, or rather for easy transport to their country, but did not actually go to Ilesa, much less to the Ekiti camp to fight. He now brought pressure to bear upon the editor of the newspaper which published the letter, and I. H. Willoughby was disclosed as responsible for its publication.

Mr. Astrope then took legal proceedings against Mr. Willoughby for libel and was awarded damages of £50.

The Ibadan war chiefs did not content themselves with the letter to the Ọyọ descendants at Lagos alone in general but wrote also two other letters, one to Mr. D. C. Taiwo, on May 26th, 1884, by one Joseph Ọṣunrinde, and the other to Sumọnu Animaṣawun on the 6th of June, 1884, by one Ọtẹṣile. Both letters bearing the same contents, viz. :

" As the Ijẹṣas are determined to spoil the Yoruba country, and their countrymen at Lagos are supplying them with European weapons of war, we send (here the messenger's name) to you for a supply of Sneider rifles with cartridges, and we promise to pay in palm oil and palm kernels which we are collecting for the purpose. We wish you to arrange with the Balogun of Ijẹbu in order that our produce might reach you," etc., etc.

" We are,
" LATOSISA, A.O.K.," Etc., etc.

Warned by what happened to Mr. Willoughby, great caution was displayed. The following was the reply sent by one who styles himself—A Yoruba.

Shitta Street, Lagos.
June 16th, 1884.

THE ARE-ỌNA-KAKANFO,

DEAR GENTLEMEN,

I hope this to meet you in a good health as I am at present. Your message has been delivered to us and we note your saying. Doubtless whatever thing you are wanting, if you give Ijẹbu goods they will supply it to you. May God let this war settle sooner.

If you want to send here again, you must send to Government directly with · King's token, either walking-stick, or other instrument, but if you want to send to Yorubas, you can send it separately. You must believe all what your messenger will tell, and receive from them advice, for they have seen here and yonder. You must not send such person as foolish as Apara, for he is thoughtless person. If you want to send here again, you must elect clever and wise person in order that your wishes may be attended to ; and you must not send verbal message, all that you have to do must be written in letters.

With kind regards and best wishes.

Yours very faithfully and affectionately,

A YORUBA.

Thus the Ibadans received no help whatever from their compatriots at Lagos. However, with the deposition and expulsion of the Awujalẹ from his capital, the strain between Ibadan and the Ijẹbus became relaxed. Through Chief Kuku of Ijẹbu Ode, who had resided at Ibadan for many years, as well as through the Balogun of Ijẹbu, and from private traders through the Ijẹbu country, the Ibadans were now able to obtain at very high prices some rifles and ammunition, just sufficient to render their position more secure at Kiriji. The guns were sold to them at the rate of £10 to £15 a piece, and the cartridges at 6d. each—prices which (considering the scarcity of money and the general impoverishment induced by this prolonged war) only men in desperate condition would care to pay. Sanusi, the Arẹ's eldest son, was the first to purchase a few, then Lady Ọmọsa, the daughter of the late Baṣọrun Ogunmọla, procured a few for her nephew Kongi, who was now the head of the house. After this the possession of a rifle became a general thing, every war chief trying to get a few for himself. For this purpose many had to sell their slaves and slave wives, a matter of pain and grief to them, as altogether contrary to their custom, but the body politic must be preserved at all costs.

Now and then contributions had to be made at home from those in easier circumstances. To assist those at the seat of war the chiefs in council ordered that those who are well-to-do, and every large compound, should give an equivalent of a slave each, and smaller compounds should combine and do the same. But the messengers often exacted much more than they were authorised to receive, and were rather indiscriminate in their exactions : the distress in the country in consequence can well be imagined, with practically the closure of the roads for trade and the restriction of farming through the kidnappers.

Bad as things were on the Ibadan side latterly it was almost worse on the Ekiti side where Ogedemgbe's Ipayes (war-boys) helped to impoverish the country by a sort of licensed robbery. The town of Ilesa was all but deserted through their rapacities before a peremptory stop was put to their excesses. Even the more important Ekiti kings, *e.g.*, the Ajero of Ijero, the Owòrè of Otùn and the Olojudo of Ido had to be present at the seat of war ; not however in the camp, but in the town of Mesin Ipole. The Owa of Ilesa did not actually go to the field, but he had to leave home to reside at Ijebu Ere halfway to the town of Mesin Ipole.

Notwithstanding his expulsion, the ex-Awujale of Ijebu was not quiet in his place of exile, he kept moving those favourable to him to start a revolution in his favour : but as all were tired of the war nothing of consequence was done. He however sent his big slaves to Isoya to help Ogunsigun against the town of Modakeke.

CHAPTER XXVIII

THE REV. J. B. WOOD AND THE A.O.K.

§ 1. The Visits of the Rev. J. B. Wood to the Camps

Such was the condition of the country as related above when the Rev. J. B. Wood, then the oldest missionary of the C.M.S. in the Yoruba country residing at Abẹokuta, obtained permission from the Egbas to go on his round of visits to the Mission stations in the interior, chiefly Isẹyin, Ọyọ and Ibadan. He arrived at Ibadan on the 24th August, 1884. The Ibadan war chiefs, hearing of the arrival at Ibadan of the white man through whom the ALÂFIN lately communicated with the Lagos Government, sent to him a special messenger with a letter written in the Yoruba language, once more asking for his kind interference in the interest of peace. They thought that, as a white man, and one who knew the country well, he could so represent matters to the British Government who alone could interpose with effect.

The reverend gentleman was highly desirous of doing something in that direction, but he felt that nothing could be done without fuller knowledge of all the facts obtainable only from the spot. He was therefore determined to proceed to the seat of war, taking with him the Rev. D. Olubi of Ibadan, Mr. Abraham F. Foster, C.M.S. Catechist at Isẹyin who accompanied him from Isẹyin to Ibadan, and the writer, then C.M.S. Catechist at Ibadan.

They left Ibadan on the 16th of September and got to the camp on the 24th. It was the period of the latter rains when it poured incessantly, the roads were in their worst condition, and the rivers much swollen.

That a white man should brave it all and visit them in the craggy heights of Mẹsin, at such a distance and under such conditions filled the Ibadan chiefs with surprise and gratitude.

The first interview with the chiefs was held on the following morning, when the principal war chiefs met the Rev. Mr. Wood and his colleagues in the Arẹ's reception room. He opened by telling them the object of his visit to the camp, that he was moved to do so by their letter to him, and that his wish was to visit both camps if possible in order to know how to proceed about the matter.

Chief Mayẹ was the Ibadan spokesman. He gave a full history of the origin of the relations between themselves and the Ekitis, and how they became masters of the Ijẹṣa and Ekiti countries. That in most cases they were invited over by the Ekitis themselves, who placed themselves under their protection after throwing off the yoke of the Ilọrins ; and that they never had any war with any of the Ekiti towns unless invited by one or other of themselves. He ended his statements by telling briefly the cause of quarrel between themselves and the Ẹgbas, and how while thus engaged there followed the rebellion and aggression of the Ekiti confederates into the Ọyọ territory. He concluded by saying, " We are here now in the interests of the Ọyọ tribes fighting their battles and safe-guarding our frontiers from aggression, and the country from being overrun by the enemy as they seem determined to do."

The Rev. J. B. Wood offered no remarks or comments but asked to be allowed to visit the other side, and thus alternately going and coming till he could bring both parties to understand each other.

The Ibadans at first demurred to this proposal saying that the Ijẹṣas will publish it far and wide that they were so hard pressed that they were obliged to sue for help from the white man. But after some talk over the matter they agreed only out of deference to Mr. Wood, that he should pass from their camp to that of the other side. But how to reach the other side ? It was agreed that Mr. Foster and the writer should go to the Ekiti side with a flag of truce, bearing a message from Mr. Wood to Chief Ogedemgbe, asking for an interview. They proceeded therefore unarmed, each with his boy, Mr. Foster's boy carrying the flag of truce before them. The Ibadan skirmishers in the field were withdrawn in order to disarm suspicion, thus they crossed the Eleriko or Fẹjẹbọju stream. The events which followed were thus described :

" The Ekiti soldiers seeing us coming towards them advanced to meet us, levelling their guns at us ; the flag of truce was waved vigorously and we shouted, ' Do not fire, do not fire, we are peaceful messengers sent to your Commander-in-Chief.' With that they desisted, but walked on towards us, and we towards them, when all of a sudden one of them levelled his gun at Mr. Johnson, saying, ' Ma ṣi yin eyi na ' (I must first discharge this anyhow). With that he let off ! The flag of truce was thrown away and we all fled precipitately back : Messrs. Johnson and Foster, who had their boots on, fell down at the top of Fẹjẹbọju hill and rolled down the stream. The Ibadan skirmishers who were watching from the Elebolo hill hastened to our rescue and drove back the Ijẹṣas, recovering the flag and personal articles dropped in the flight. The whole camp was astir at this incident, and sympathizers poured in on all sides, congratulating Mr. Wood on our providential escape. We offered our thanksgiving to God for this merciful deliverance."

But the Ekitis reported this incident at home, describing what sort of men they fired on, thereupon Messrs. Gureje and Apara, Ijẹṣa Christians from Abẹokuta who formed and led the rifle corps, came to the field the next day and desired the sentinel to ask those men fired at yesterday to come again. As they came unarmed, we also approached them unarmed, and when we met we recognised old faces well known years ago at Abẹokuta. They were surprised to hear that Mr. Wood was in the camp.

These men reported the matter to the Ekiti kings and leaders and a deputation was sent to meet Mr. Wood on the battlefield to hear what he wanted. There Mr. Wood repeated the same words as to the Ibadan chiefs. The Ijẹṣas demurred to any proposal of peace, they said their determination was " to fight it out to the last drop of blood." But Labirinjọ of Lagos, who was amongst them, spoke most sensibly till he won them over ; he dilated on the vicissitudes and uncertainties of war, and the desirability of peace. He begged Mr. Wood to do all in his power to bring about the desired peace ; but they could not ask him over to their camp without first obtaining the consent of their kings and leaders.

The object was gained at last on the 29th September, 1884, when Mr. Wood and his colleagues passed over to the Ekiti camp and stated his mission of peace. There was a good deal of high-flown talk, and a show of fierce determination not to yield ; at the end there was an adjournment till the next day.

That day, September 30th, happened to be the Moslem festival of Beiram, no meeting was held in the morning. The Moslems on both sides had to repair to the battlefield for their prayers and sacrifice. On such days on previous occasions the most sanguinary battle used to be fought the Ekitis being determined that Ọyọs should not worship on their soil : great preparations for the strife was usually made, and human blood often mingled with that of rams offered in sacrifice ! But on this occasion, out of respect to Mr. Wood's presence in the camp, there was no battle. Mr. A. F. Foster and the writer were sent with the flag of truce to post themselves between the two parties and. thus their worship was performed in peace, each party returning quietly to the camp.

In the afternoon of the same day there was another meeting of the chiefs, after which an elaborately written document was placed in Mr. Wood's hands, stating the terms on which they would agree to make peace. This was with some difficulty deciphered to read thus :

1. That they claimed their independence and would no longer serve the Ibadans.

2. That the Owa, being the ALÂFIN's younger brother, would still acknowledge him by a yearly gift, which is not to be taken for tribute but as a token of respect.

3. That they would not carry war into Oyo territories provided their own territories were respected.

4. That they would claim Igbajo, Ada, Otan and Iresi for the Owa of Ilesa, those places being his originally.

5. That the Ibadans should withdraw from Ofa, handing Ofa over to the Ilorins.

6. That the Modakekes, being Oyos, should remove from Ife soil. That it had been their purpose after defeating and driving away the Ibadans from their territory to fall upon Modakeke and destroy it, selling the captives to defray the expenses of the war, but out of respect for Mr. Wood they would give up the idea, but Modakeke must be removed.

7. That the exile Awujale be re-instated.

8. That there be a general and lasting peace throughout the country.

The Rev. Mr. Wood and party returned to the Ibadan camp the next day with these conditions of peace, and delivered them verbatim to the Ibadan chiefs in council without any comment. After a private consultation among themselves they gave the following replies to each :

1. That out of deference to the white man, and in order to peace, they agreed to grant the Ekitis their independence.

2. That the brotherly relationship between the ALÂFIN and the Owa should by all means be revived; they could have no objection whatever to that, as the ALÂFIN is their own lord and master.

3. That they agreed to respect Ijesa territories provided the Ijesas respected theirs.

4. As to Otan, Ada, Iresi, Igbajo, the Owa's claim to these places belongs to a remote antiquity, and that by tradition only, at present they are not subject to the Owa if even they ever were ; and note that the inhabitants are not generally Ijesas, but Oyos. It should be left to the people themselves to decide under whom they would be.

5. They objected to remove Modakeke now, being the key to their own situation, but when the war was over they would require at least two years respite for preparation to remove the town to another site.

6. That if the King of Ofa choose to return to his former allegiance to the Ilorins, that is his own affair, they were protecting

him only as a friend, he had never been nor is he now under their allegiance. They are defending Ọfa because they would not like to see an Ọyọ city so historic to be destroyed.

7. As to the King of Ijẹbu, they had no hands in his dethronement. They only heard the report of it in their camp : they were for years begging the Ijẹbus to open the road for trade and they refused : they were only too glad to accept their offer for trade now : how it came about they are not supposed to know, but they could not hold themselves responsible for the Awujalẹ's reinstatement.

On the next day Mr. Wood and party returned again to the Ekiti camp with the Ibadan replies. This the Ekiti chiefs met to consider on that and the following day, and then they formulated their resolutions :

1. That the four above-mentioned towns be removed at once and go with the Ibadans, the Ọwa desiring them no longer as his subjects.

2. That Ọfa should be evacuated at once and go with the Ibadans.

3. The same with Modakẹkẹ.

The Rev. Mr. Wood for once broke through his reserve and put in a kind word for Modakẹkẹ in consideration of the sick, the infirm, women and children. On account of these time ought necessarily to be allowed for their removal, Modakẹkẹ being a large town.

The Ekiti chiefs then said they would grant them 18 days and no longer, after which they should fall a prey.

With these demands Mr. Wood and party returned to the Ibadan camp in the afternoon, and reported to the Ibadan chiefs. The chiefs were rather indignant at the Ekitis dictating terms to them as to a conquered people, they only submitted to these indignities out of deference to Mr. Wood : but they refused point blank to remove any of these towns until they had returned home to Ibadan.

Mr. Wood returned the next day to the Ekitis and reported to them the resolution of the Ibadans. The Ekitis now agreed to extend the 18 days to 120 days, " after which they should fall a prey if not removed."

This ultimatum was conveyed to the Ibadans the next day by the Rev. Mr. Wood. It aroused a great deal of indignation among the Ibadan chiefs that the Ijẹsas should be dictating terms of peace to them ! Some hard words were used which threw a damper on Mr. Wood's spirit. Finally the chiefs met the next day to speak out their own minds. They said to Mr. Wood, " Hitherto the Ekitis have been dictating to us, and we have practically

accepted all their terms ; but now we have only one request to
make : as nothing can be done until we reach home, in order to
expedité matters let the Ekitis retire from their camp into the town
of Mẹsin behind them—only a mile distant—on that same evening
we shall be ready to leave.

And again, why stipulate about the removal of these towns
when they said they wanted universal peace ? Is it an essential
of peace to bring such distress upon thousands ? However, if such
be necessary to a lasting peace all over the country, we require
15 months at least in which to remove Modakẹkẹ, Igbajọ, Ọtan,
Irẹsi, and Adà.

On the 8th of October Mr. Wood returned again to the Ekiti
camp with the requests of the Ibadans, which were duly considered.

Whilst the Ekitis would be prepared to grant the 15 months
respite they would on no account remove from their camp into the
town. They assured Mr. Wood they would never pursue after
the Ibadans. Their Commander-in-Chief Ogedemgbe exclaimed,
" Aja ki ilepa Ẹkun, Ẹkun ni wọn, Aja l'awa, Oyinbo maha mu
wọn lọ " (" The dog cannot pursue after a leopard, they are
leopards, and we but dogs. White man, do take them away.")

As an assurance of their sincerity the Ekiti chiefs said they
were ready to build a temporary house for Mr. Wood and his
party on the battlefield and leave with him all the Ijẹsa Christians
to stay there as a witness until the Ibadans were clean gone.

Mr. Wood returned to the Ibadans on the next day with these
proposals.

To these the Ibadan chiefs replied, " We have no objection to
the temporary house being built, and the Ijẹsa Christians remaining
there with the white man (though what effectual guarantee that
will prove we fail to see), but we do certainly object to entrap
ourselves in a defile under their very eyes. What the chiefs may
desire is one thing ; what the uncontrollable war-boys may do is
another. If they are sincere let them put a mile between us and
themselves, Mẹsin Ipole is not far. We have accepted all their
terms, that is the only stipulation we have to make, and that is
reasonable enough."

No argument could prevail upon the Ibadan chiefs to yield this
one point, and they asked Mr. Wood to try his utmost to get the
Ekitis to agree to this, then all would be right, and the honour
of putting an end to this war would be his. With a trembling
heart Mr. Wood made this last effort, and the result justified his
fears. The Ekitis would not hear of it. They grew wild at the
very idea.

Thus ended in failure Mr. Wood's effort at peace negotiation.

On that very night the Ijẹṣas came to the battlefield and fired three rockets into the Ibadan camp which, however, did no harm. Before Mr. Wood left the Ibadans wrote him a letter of thanks for his efforts, and addressed letters also to Chief Ogundipẹ of Abẹokuta, who had shown much interest in their affairs, and also to the Governor of Lagos, lauding Mr. Wood's efforts.

The Rev. Mr. Wood and party left the Ibadan camp on the 17th October, 1884, and hostilities were resumed with much vigour during the remaining months and during the whole of the following year.

Early in 1885 Mr. Wood, in order to complete his tour of inspection, left Lagos to visit the C.M.S. stations at Ondo and Ilesa via Leke, Itebu and Aiyesan. On reaching Ondo the Rev. C. Phillips, the pastor of those parts, accompanied him to Ilẹṣa, and thence to the seat of war again, from the Ijẹṣa side, and he repeated his efforts of the preceding year between the two camps, asking the same questions whether it was not time for a cessation of hostilities. He had to face the same objections as before : and this second effort also, like the first, ended in failure.

§ 2.   Death of Latosisa the Are-Ọna-Kakanfo

In the year 1885, not long after the Rev. J. B. Wood left the camp the second time, Latosisa, the Generalissimo of the Ibadan army, died. His death being wholly unexpected, various reasons have been assigned as the cause of it : (1) That he had forfeited his title as A.O.K., having exceeded the traditional 60 days in the campaign. But this could hardly have weighed much with him considering that times had greatly changed and many ancient customs with them. (2) That he had lost his influence among the war chiefs, and therefore he committed suicide.

There is not the slightest doubt about this loss of influence. It was he himself who, by reversing the policy of his immediate predecessor, and advancing to high position many of the young men heirs to great houses in preference to older and more experienced men but with less means at their command, brought it about. The few older chiefs formerly his companions in arms having died out, he now found himself surrounded by much younger folks, the companions of his son. There is a certain *camaraderie* amongst these young men, nearly all of the same age, and sons of distinguished bygone chiefs bred in the same atmosphere, and naturally of a common sympathy with one another. These young men have never ceased to lament those of their number whose deaths were due directly or indirectly to the intrigues of the Arẹ, especially of Iyapọ the Seriki, son of the late Balogun Ibikunle,

whom he sent " to sleep," of Aderibigbe, son of the late Balẹ
Olugbode, Belo, son of the late Osi Ọsundina, and Awo, son of
the late Baba Isalẹ Labọsinde, all of whom perished in this war
which the Arẹ had brought about.   And even of Ilọri, son of the
late Baṣọrun Ogunmọla, who met his death at the Jalumi war by
the Arẹ's bad statesmanship ; not to speak of men of lesser note.
They felt sure that his object in bringing about these deaths was
to make room for his own son to outshine the rest, so that
he might perpetuate the headship of Ibadan in his own family.
But the proximate cause of his death seemed to be due to the
action of one of his slaves towards Ajayi Ọsungbẹkun, the senior
chief among the young men, and next to himself in command.

The actions of the Arẹ's slaves at this time beggar description,
both at the seat of war, especially in the provinces, and at
home, they carried on their excesses regardless of age, rank or sex.
Robbery, seizing by violence, rape, etc., were of daily practice.
The knowledge that these slaves were captives led to the town by
the very people of whom they had now become masters through
the indulgence of the Master, made their crime less pardonable.

The Seriki having sent home for a ram and other things to offer
sacrifice, the time for which was drawing near, his mother sent
him also some Ẹkọ, home-made, with her love.   The messenger
came all the way quite safely with his charge.   Leaving Irèhe, he
was making for Igbajọ and was within a few hours from the camp
when he came up with some of the Arẹ's slaves who had gone out
looting !   One of them in particular wrested the ram from him,
and seized the Ẹkọ, devouring the latter there in the messenger's
presence, who kept crying out, " It is the Seriki's ! It is the
Seriki's ! "   " And who is the Seriki ? " retorted the slave.   Both
of them got into the camp together, and the messenger related to
his master all that happened to him and his charge all within
sight, as it were, of the camp.   The Seriki called together his
comrades and poured his tale into sympathetic ears.   They were
mad with rage.   They assured him of their support in whatever
measure he might adopt, but the slave must never go with impunity
(for they knew that as usual the Arẹ would never deal condignly
with him), for the same thing might occur to any one of
themselves to-morrow.

Together they accompanied him to the Arẹ to complain of the
action of his slave and to demand redress. Unfortunately the
Arẹ took the matter lightly : instead of dealing out sharp punishment to the slave he left him to dispute the matter with the Seriki.
He even attempted to shield him, before the culprit was forcibly
brought forward.   The Seriki then asked him, " Did not the

messenger tell you the things were mine ? " He answered, " Yes, he did, but how am I to know that he was speaking the truth when he said, ' It is the Seriki's ' ? I thought he was deceiving me." There was no apology made, his master looked on amused. The Seriki thereupon arose, unsheathed his sword, and with one sweep severed his head from his shoulders in the very presence of his master !

All the war chiefs present neither moved nor said a word. The Arẹ, imperturbable as usual, but comprehending at once what it all meant, said nothing. The meeting was immediately adjourned.

It was said that the Arẹ afterwards sent the Seriki 11 heads of cowries. (This being the amount usually paid to the head chief for unsheathing his sword.) This the Seriki was said to have accepted without any apology. It is a metaphorical way of asking, " Are you prepared to take the headship ? " His acceptance of the money was an answer in the affirmative.

Not one of the chiefs called on the Arẹ or sympathized with him on this direct affront offered him, and this grieved him most, being a clear evidence that their sympathy was all on the other side. He then knew that this was but the beginning of the end, and it became him to die an honourable death. He was not laid up for long, the fact of his ailment was not known throughout the camp before the rumour of his death followed. Just before the end he sent for Sanusi, his eldest son, and gave him his last charge. Sanusi left him smoking his pipe, his courtiers sitting all around him. He was heard to cough gently as if suffocated by the fumes of his pipe, and putting down the pipe he lay quietly on his mat and adjusted his cloth over himself and thus passed away gently. Those sitting about him and looking on scarcely believed he was dead !

Thus passed away one whose name will ever be remembered in Yoruba history as the man who raised the fame of Ibadan to its highest pitch of glory and by his bad statesmanship brought it down to its lowest level, and there left it.

The late Latosisa was the son of a private man, a native of Ilọra, a suburb of Ọyọ. He joined the marauders at Ibadan as a private soldier, and in early life he was a very unfortunate man ; although he never missed any predatory excursions, he never did well for himself in any. He lived to be an old bachelor because he could not afford the means of marrying a wife. He was a palm dresser and from his own statement he could tell the nature of all the palm trees for miles around Ibadan. His turn of fortune began when in a civil war at Ibadan he was fortunate enough to have caught a woman with some children. It was then he had a wife ! And he sold the children to start life with.

Being inured and accustomed to poverty he continued to the end of his days to be thrifty, to feed sparingly and mostly on dry food, as in early life when he could afford nothing else.

He was one of the faithful followers of Ogunmọla, the late Baṣọrun of Ibadan, the captain of whose guards he was when Ogunmọla was the Ọtun Balogun of Ibadan. He was a man of a genial disposition and of winning manners.

His first military command as a captain was when he was sent to take over charge of the army under Akāwo before Iwawun, but both were hard-pressed and even besieged in their camp by the Ijayes that came to the succour of Iwawun, before Ogunmọla and Ọṣundina came to their aid and defeated the Ijayes (*vide* Chap. XVIII, p. 346).

He was originally a pagan, and thrice was he taken to an Ifa grove for purification in order to have children (for he had none for many years after the firstborn, who was killed at the Ijaye war), but to no purpose. He then embraced the Moslem faith, and became confirmed in the faith by the birth of a son whom he named Sanusi. This was during the Ijẹbu Ẹrẹ war. He signalized himself at the late Ilesa war when, in taking the last road to the city, he had to oppose the army from the country whilst Ajayi Ogboriẹfọn opposed that from the city. Together with his colleague he rose rapidly; owing to political changes at Ibadan he soon found himself at the head of affairs. He wrested from Ojo Aburu-maku of Ogbomọṣọ the title of A.O.K. He obtained the Ojiko (*vide* p. 74) from the King with two slaves; he never wore it himself but his favourite slave Idagana used to wear it in front of him as Abogunrin that of the late Arẹ Kurunmi of Ijaye.

He was the hero of the Ado and Aiyede wars when he took the field in person. The wars were unprovoked, they were simply for the love of slave hunting. Elated by the easy victories won, he declared war against the Ẹgbas, against the expressed wishes of the King and his own war chiefs; this complication with the Ẹgbas gave room for the rebellion of the Ijẹṣa and Ekiti provinces which culminated in this war.

He was undoubtedly an ambitious man, and envied the glory of the two foremost houses at Ibadan, *viz.*, those of Ibikunle and of Ogunmọla. He strove to efface the fame and glory of both houses and to exalt his own over all, but in this he failed. His death was rather inglorious. His bones were preserved and taken home to Ibadan for interment.

§ 3. THE VICISSITUDES OF WAR

After the death of the Arẹ, Ajayi Ọṣungbẹkun, the Seriki, became the leading General of the Ibadan army. In fact he was the only titled war chief, the older men having all died, and the Arẹ did not fill up several important vacancies before this war began.

But the Ibadans were loth to retain a Seriki as their leader, they had always been led to victory (said they) by a Balogun and not by a Seriki. It was unanimously agreed that he should assume the title of Balogun.

As the leading chief the title that really devolved upon him was that of Balẹ, but that is a non-combatant title, and for him to take it would mean that he should retire from the seat of war and go home—which was impracticable at this crisis.

And again, after the death of the late Balogun Ajayi Ogboriẹfọn, when the national god Ifa was consulted as to his successor the oracle declared for Akintọla, son of the late Balogun Ibikunle, and brother of Seriki Iyapo. Akintọla then was an untitled chief, only an Arẹ-agorò, and the Arẹ was not prepared to grant so high a title to the head of a house he was then determined to see degraded, consequently he left the title open, and was not going to fill up this and other vacancies till after the war. In conferring the title on Ọṣungbẹkun now, it was understood that he was merely to hold it in trust for Akintọla, as Akintọla could not rightly be placed over him, but after the close of the war, when he entered upon his rightful title of Balẹ, Akintọla would then come to his own.

But there are many amongst the Ibadans who attributed their failure in this war to disobedience to the voice of the oracle in not making Akintọla the Balogun, and that they were not likely to win under any other against the voice of the oracle. And again it is to be noted that when Akintọla first arrived at Kiriji and had to fight single-handed, then Ogedemgbe was caught and let off, because of the secret combination against the Arẹ, which pointed to the fact that the oracle divined correctly. But his advancement now would be most inexpedient, and the present arrangement seemed fair enough.

The War under the Leadership of Ajayi.—The young war chiefs who had resolved to win no victories which would redound to the praise and glory of the Arẹ, had been greatly seconded in their resolve by circumstances they never dreamt of, and now that they would wish to do so, events which had transpired were too much for them. Very few battles were fought during the years 1885 and 1886, as the Ibadans had now been able to secure some rifles, and were not slow to learn the use of them (though nothing to be compared to those of the Ekitis in point of number). The Ekitis could no longer approach the Ibadan camp to shoot into it with impunity and to offer battle. But still they had the advantage of position. While the Ibadans were filing out of camp in the day of battle their rifle corps could always make a target of them, but when they had all spread themselves on the battlefield the chances were somewhat even, both sides had to seek cover and shelter from the sharpshooters. They then did more of skirmishing than of real battle.

The War at Ofa.—But the war at Ofa was raging with unabated fury. The men of Ofa and the Ibadan contingent there encamped outside the city, and erected double walls connecting the city with the camp. Behind the outermost wall they engaged the enemy. The Ilorins, trusting more to their cavalry, had but few infantry men, besides those supplied them by the Ekitis, and they were armed with swords. The method of the cavalry men was to gallop round and round beyond the range of bullets, and then watch the opportunity for seizing a weak point or take their enemies unawares and endeavour to pull down the walls or spear the foe. When they were pressing too hard upon the defenders, the Balogun of Ibadan sent over one of his slaves, Babare by name, a sharpshooter, with a rifle and a good supply of cartridges. His presence was always in demand at whatever point the battle was hottest, and by dropping two or three horsemen he always caused the Ilorins to decamp.

The War at Modakeke.—Here the battle was fiercest, as the Ifes, Ekitis and Ijebus who were pressing hard to destroy the town, were better supplied with arms of precision. Akintola, who was sent to reinforce the place twice, suffered disasters by ambuscade which nearly proved fatal to his life. At the first instance the Ifes came to provoke a fight after having placed ambuscades in several places in the ruins of the city. As the Modakeke war chiefs and the Ibadan contingent joined battle with them at the Akogun market, the Ifes retreated as if defeated, and they were being pursued until the pursuers were drawn off to a considerable distance from the town, then the ambuscades opened fire behind them. They were completely hemmed in on every side, and had to fight their way back. In the rush, Akintola's horse slipped and fell, and he was fortunate enough to escape being trodden to death as many others were, horse and foot ! As soon as they had fought their way through one set of ambush men, and were walking slowly to take breath, another set would open fire upon them ; thus they went from one to the other, the Ifes and Ijesas pressing hard in pursuit, determined to take Modakeke that day. But Adepoju, the Balogun of Modakeke, at the expense of his life saved the situation : with a band of a faithful few he barred the way against the pursuers and fought desperately like a hero, against great odds until he fell among the slain. It was instantly reported in the town that both Akintola and the Balogun had fallen, and many had already begun to pack up to flee when Akintola's drum was heard approaching. He himself by this time was completely exhausted, panting and thirsty. He owed his safety to his cousin Latunji, an intrepid horseman. Latunji it was said, woke up, that morning feeling sad and depressed, and on consulting his Ifa he was advised not to go out that day, and consequently he kept at home ; but when he heard of the disaster he immediately saddled his war horse and went to the succour of his cousin. He met him at the Akogun market, being hotly pursued and almost taken alive. He dashed upon the pursuers, spearing them right and left, then cantering round and round his cousin said " Arẹ agorò maha rin pẹlẹ pẹlẹ " (Arẹ agorò, do walk on gently, gently) and kept the pursuers at bay until they reached the town of Modakẹkẹ.

In this disaster Akintola lost his favourite charger, his Dane guns were thrown away in the flight, and what he prized most of all, his father's war dress, an heirloom in the family. It had descended in due order through his elder brothers Ko-ẹjo, Babayẹmi, Obembe, and Iyapọ to himself; being a garment studded with charms, it was too heavy for him to carry in the flight so he entrusted it to one of his men who in the rush fell down and lost the garment. It was picked up by the Ifẹs and carried away in triumph, together with his horse as a trophy of war.

The second disaster was at an engagement with the Ijẹbus at Isọya. The Ibadans and Modakẹkẹs were enticed into a distance in the forest in the direction of Isọya, and there the ambush attacked them on every side. Akintola had to fight his way back and lost several of his guns, his men throwing them away in their flight. The brave son of Chief Olubọde fell in this disaster.

Having failed to dislodge the Ibadans from Kiriji, the confederates were determined to take Modakẹkẹ at all costs, so that Kiriji might be taken at the rear. They now reinforced the Ifẹs strongly from the Ijẹsas and Ekitis, Prince Fabūmi at their head. He was determined to take Modakẹkẹ at his first fight, but in this he failed. In the same way he had determined to defeat the Ibadan army at Kiriji before Ogedemgbe can.e to take over the command, but in a fair fight he met with intrepid warriors like himself in Akintola and Apampa. He left several of his veterans dead on the battlefield, and many more—like himself—wounded in several places. Ogunsigun the leader of the Ijẹbus was also reinforced by the ex-Awujalẹ's party from Ẹpẹ.

The Modakẹkẹs now took great pains to fortify their town.

They repaired the walls thoroughly and built forts upon them in several places, placing in them sharp shooters with rifles. But they never shielded themselves behind these walls, they always engaged the enemy outside.

Akintọla also replaced his lost Dane guns with rifles, mainly at the expense of his tributary town of Ipetumodu ; Apampa also acquired some rifles but was far more lenient with his tributary town of Ẹdūabọn. (Edun-j'abọn.)

The houses of the two most powerful war-chiefs at Modakẹkẹ in the 'sixties, Ojo Akitikori thẹ Balogun and Ajombadi the Ọtun, were duly upheld by their worthy sons and successors, Oyebade and Adepọju respectively, both of whom fell in the defence of their town.   They were duly succeeded by their brothers, Detomi of the the latter and Ọkẹ (nicknamed pupa, i.e., yellow, from his light complexion) of the former.   Ọkẹ also fell in an engagement and was succeeded by his half-brother Ọkẹ, surnamed Dudu (the dark) from his complexion.

Detomi became lame in both his feet, but still directed the battle on horseback.

With the command of a few rifles by the Ibadans the ardour of their foes cooled, and the war here, as at Kiriji, became less frequent than formerly and might practically be said to be at a standstill.

CHAPTER XXIX

THE INTERVENTION OF THE BRITISH GOVERNMENT

§ 1. MEASURES BY GOVERNOR MOLONEY

ABOUT the end of January, 1886, the Government of Lagos was severed from that of the Gold Coast, and Lagos was constituted a separate colony with Capt. A. C. Moloney as its first Governor. One of his first public acts was to feel his way towards the settlement of the interior difficulties.

In an interview the writer (who happened to be at Lagos at the time) had with his Excellency on the 23rd of January the topic of conversation turned mainly on the state of things in the interior and he asked the writer to put down in writing an account of the interview, stating all he knew about the complications from the commencement, and what prospect there was of peace ; also to give the names of the principal chiefs of Ijẹbu, Abẹokuta, Ibadan, Ekiti, and Ilọrin concerned in this war, and an account of the visits of the Rev. J. B. Wood to both camps in 1884, and also to state his opinion as to how they might receive some one like himself coming among them to settle their difference for them. This the writer did in a long letter to H. E. the Governor.

The Governor was then resolved to make use of the writer as a messenger to the Ibadan camp, and of the Rev. C. Phillips to the Ekiti camp.

Having obtained the consent of the local secretary of the C.M.S. for making use of their services (both being C.M.S. agents) the Governor issued the following instructions :

Government House,
March 1st, 1886.

SIR,—The Venble. Archdeacon Hamilton has most considerately placed your services at my disposal in connection with satisfying to the latest date on the feeling in the direction of peace that obtains between the Ibadans and the Ekiti parapos. You have in a most praiseworthy and philanthropic manner come forward to carry out on the subject of my wishes. They are embodied in the accompanying letter addressed to the Baloguns, chiefs, elders and people of Ibadan with whom you say you are on the most intimate and friendly terms.

You will be good enough accordingly to consider the contents of such letter as your instructions, and in view of the interviews I have had with you I will hope to find success as far as it can will attend your endeavours to act as my instructions dictated.

I have, etc.,

ALFRED MOLONEY, *Governor*.

The instructions to Rev. Phillips are the same, only substituting for " Balogun, chiefs, elders and people of Ibadan, with whom you say you are on the most intimate," etc., to " Owa, Balogun, elders, chiefs and people of Ijẹsa whom you at times visited."

The following is a copy of the letter addressed to the chiefs by Governor Moloney :

Government House.

February 27th, 1886.

GOVERNOR MOLONEY TO THE BALOGUNS, CHIEFS, ELDERS AND PEOPLE OF IBADAN,

GENTLEMEN,—I have the honour to convey that I take this opportunity to announce to you my return on the 8th ult., and my assumption as Governor of the administration of the Government of the Queen's Colony of Lagos.

2. It is a pleasure for me to come again amongst people whom I know and who know me, and it is almost needless for me to assure you that, as it has been in the past so it will be in the future, my aim and object to promote in every legitimate way I can, the general interest and development of West Africa and the peace of the country.

3. I attach, as I am informed you do, much importance to the restoration of peace between you and the countries with which you have unfortunate differences.

4. Entertaining as I have always such a feeling and a due appreciation of the value of a general good understanding and friendly relationship in our surroundings, I sincerely invite the entertainment by our neighbours of like sentiment.

5. I am pained to learn that the unfortunate differences which have fruitlessly, as regards the country's good, struggled on for years between you and the Ijẹsas, and others still continue. The country and people are, I gather, tired generally of the miserable and obstructive state of things, which has done so much mischief, and has been productive of no general benefit ; on the contrary, there have followed bloodshed, loss of life, devastation, desolation, and other miseries.

6. Good kindly feelings have always existed between you and

this colony, may they long continue so ; knowing this, I feel it due to inform you of my return.

7. As regards restoration of tranquility once more to the country, and the desire of the contending parties for mediation to be undertaken by this Government, it may be convenient I should remark that, as a matter of course, distinct and unconditional overtures for peace must be made to this Government by all the parties concerned ; then I may feel myself in a position of being enabled to send an officer into the interior with a view to attempt to effect a peace based upon conditions which are likely to render it a lasting one.   Each side should but know what conditions as far as he is concerned he has to offer, and would be most likely to prove of duration.   On this part I should like to be clearly informed.

8. Then it would be well I should be clearly enlightened by each on the nature of the terms of responsibility, as such must rest entirely with the parties craving peace, for the fulfilment of their engagements, if peace be restored each is prepared to offer and accept.

9. What are the guarantees each will give for his sincerity and earnestness in his appeal for peace.

10. Each side may, for instance, suggest or voluntarily offer that he will enter into an agreement binding on him to suspend hostilities for, say, six months or any other duration deemed advisable, then there should be no need for fresh supplies of guns and ammunitions for such a time.   Such an agreement as to cessation of hostilities, and of armament should be entered into not only at the camps but also at all other places concerned within the territories of the opposing parties.

11. Each side may, for all I know to the contrary, be prepared to give as hostages influential persons to any arbitrator, appointed by the Government, against treachery during period of withdrawal of encampment to home, so that neither side may have cause to continue the entertainment of any doubt as to security of retreat.   Each side may be ready to engage to withdraw his army at a given time, to subsequently disembody it, and to allow component parts to return to their respective towns, homes, and families, and to the resumption once more of peaceful avocations.

12. From past experience there must be prominent in the minds of contending parties a desire of the Government to befriend them, and to bring about a reconciliation amongst them if they will only place themselves to abide by the settlement the Governor may make.

13. I shall be glad to hear from you soon, and to receive any representative messengers you may be pleased to send to me, who can faithfully give me your mind on your interior troubles, and satisfy me on the sincerity of your desire for the restoration of peace.

14. It should not any longer be viewed or allowed that the present disordered state of things in the interior should be subservient merely as I fear has been the case to the advantage of the few.   Peace should be established for the common good of all.

15. The bearer of this letter, the Rev. Samuel Johnson is well known to you all, let me commend him to your kind care and consideration.

16. I have sent a like communication to the other side.

17. Both of my messengers may, with the desire and concurrence of parties concerned, meet on the encamping ground.

Wishing you and your people peace, and to your country an early resumption of peaceful occupation on the part of its inhabitants.

> I have the honour, etc.,
>
> ALFRED MOLONEY, *Governor.*

The Rev. C. Phillips is the bearer of a similar letter to the Ekiti chiefs, with the exception that "the Rev. C. Phillips" is the messenger named in paragraph 15.

The writer left Lagos on the 2nd March, 1886, via Ijẹbu, with an oral message from the Governor to the Balogun of Ijẹbu to the effect that the Governor being his old friend, desired to announce to him his return to administer the government of Lagos, and that during his administration he wanted peace all over the country. That the bearer of this message was a messenger from him to the interior kings and chiefs for that purpose and that he wished him to convey this to the Awujalẹ.

This message was delivered to the Balogun in his camp at Orù on the 6th, when the messenger got there.   He was so pleased to hear that the Governor saw his way to interfere in the interior difficulties that he at once sent for the other war chiefs to hear the joyful news from the mouth of the Governor's own messenger.

He at once despatched a messenger to the new Awujalẹ asking him to send one of his trusty Agũrins to come and hear the good news delivered to him.

The Awujalẹ felt rather hurt that he was ignored by not hearing the message first before the Balogun.   He said that it was for him to inform the Balogun, and not the Balogun him.   However, he would not let his feelings stand in the way of so important a message. He sent an Agūrin as desired, who spoke out the King's mind on this (what he considered) breach of order ; but he was immediately pacified when told that it was just otherwise, but that the Governor only wished to approach his highness through his old friend the Balogun. The Agūrin then said, " The Governor and the Awujalẹ are of the same mind, wishing nothing else but peace."

The Ibadan home authorities were much pleased at the prospect of peace, and Tahajo, the senior chief, assured the messenger that the war chiefs would not hesitate to accept the terms of peace with the Governor as arbitrator.

From Ibadan, the Governor's messenger proceeded to Ọyọ. The Rev. D. Olubi of Ibadan, then the Superintendent of the C.M.S. Missions of that district, and who was equally interested in the subject of peace, embraced this opportunity of going with the Governor's messenger, to pay his usual pastoral visits to Ọyọ, Isẹyin and Ogbomọsọ, and to see what influence he could exert with the King to induce him to send one of his Ilaris and His Majesty's staff, with the Governor's messenger.

On the 19th March they had an audience with the King and the following letter from the Governor of Lagos to His Majesty was read to him :

GOVERNOR MOLONEY, C.M.G., TO HIS MAJESTY KING ADEYEMI OF ỌYỌ.

Government House, Lagos,
February 27th, 1886.

KING,—I have the honour to convey that I take this oppor- tunity to announce to you my return to Lagos on the 8th ult. and my assumption as Governor of the administration of the Queen's Colony under that name.

2. It is a pleasure for me to come among people whom I know, and who know me, and it is almost needless for me to assure you that as it has been in the past so it will be in the future, my aim and object to promote in every legitimate and peaceful way I can the general interest and development of West Africans.

3. I attach as I am confident you do, knowing how long you have longed for the restoration of peace to the Yoruba and other interior countries, much importance to the promotion of good relationship, between this colony and our interesting and friendly neighbours, among whom stands prominently yourself.

4. Entertaining as I have always such a feeling and a due appreciation of the value of general good understanding and

friendly relationship in our surroundings, I sincerely invite the entertainment of our neighbours of like sentiment.

5. I am pained to learn that the unfortunate differences which have fruitlessly as regards the country's good struggled on for years between the Ibadans and the Ijẹṣas still continue. The country and people are generally tired of the miserable and obstructive state of things which has done so much mischief and been productive of no general good. On the contrary there have followed desolation, bloodshed, and other miseries.

6. I shall be glad to hear from you soon and to receive any representative messengers you may be pleased to send to me, who can give me your mind on the interior troubles, an end to which should be brought about as soon as possible ; such is the cry and desire of every right-minded African having at heart his country's interest.

7. I hear both sides are tired of the war. I should be glad to be satisfied that such was the case.

8. Wishing you and your people every good wish.

I have the honour, etc.,

ALFRED MOLONEY, *Governor.*

His Majesty King Adeyẹmi,
    The ALÂFIN of Ọyọ.

After hearing the letter read he said that he was glad that the Governor after all saw his way to interfere and that he was prepared to bear the expenses of whatever it would cost to restore peace to his dominions. He further said that the news was too good to be true, however, he would let the Ọyọ MESI know about it.

The last sentence cast a damper on the enthusiasm of the messengers. The control of foreign relations is vested in the King and for him to say he would consult the Ọyọ MESI in this matter made it evident that he had ceased to take active interest in the matter. And so it turned out to be. Having sent twice to Lagos (in 1881 and 1882, Mr. A. F. Foster being sent by the Abẹokuta road) on the same subject, one would have expected his active interest and co-operation on this occasion, but it turned out to be otherwise ; the failure of the measures initiated by him must have pained His Majesty, and he did not care to compromise his dignity any more by furthering measures doomed to failure. He did not take into consideration the difference in the personality of the new Governor of Lagos.

After repeated messages to the palace on the following day, the King at last sent two private gentlemen, and without his staff, as his messengers to Lagos ! Taught by the experience of 1881, the Governor's messenger declined to proceed with these men except with an Ilari and the King's staff. Three times he was waited upon the third day, before he at last granted an Ilari, with his staff, and the Ilari was none other but the same Ọba-ko-ṣe-tan as before !

The Governor's messenger with the King's Ilari and his staff left Ọyọ on the 22nd March and reached the Ibadan camp on the 26th.

The war chiefs were glad to see the former but the presence of the latter—with his significant name—cast a damper on their spirits. After hearing the Governor's letter read they were very reluctant to accede to the Governor's request of sending down a messenger, saying, " It will all end in failure as before," thinking that an embassy headed by an Ilari, " The King is not ready," can scarcely ever be successful. Consequently they raised one objection after another, alleging the absence of the messenger of the King and the Balogun of Ijẹbu, that they could not afford to ignore those to whom they were indebted for being able to keep their position at Kiriji to that day, etc. However, after further deliberation better counsel prevailed, and they agreed to send their messengers down with the Governor's messenger.

By a happy coincidence, the Governor's messenger to the other side reached the Ekiti camp on the same day, and almost at the same hour, and on the following morning both messengers met on the battlefield with their flags of truce and each had good news to tell of the pacific tone of the respective chiefs they were sent to. On the following day they exchanged visits to the opposite camps and both were well received, and were much pleased to know that the chiefs of the opposite camp agreed to the Governor's interference.

A proposal emanating from the Ekiti chiefs pleased the Ibadans very much as showing the sincerity of their motives, *viz.*, that both the messengers of the Governor should visit the Ilọrin camp and induce the Ilọrins to agree to the truce, as the hostilities going on at Ọfa were part and parcel of those at Kiriji and Modakẹkẹ, only that they had no control over the independent Ilọrin chiefs.

The Ibadan chiefs also proposed that both flags of truce should be set up, and kept flying at the battlefield until the terms of peace were definitely signed. This also was accepted by the Ekitis, and it was accordingly done the next day.

Both messengers read to the chiefs of the opposite camps the letters with which they were entrusted, in order to show that they were identical, the better to secure their confidence.

The messengers then took leave of each other to meet again at the Ọfa and the Ilọrin camps, each by his own route.

§ 2. The Ilọrins and the Peace Proposals

The Ijẹṣa chiefs were not willing to allow the messenger of their side (the Rev. C. Phillips) to pass through the Ibadan and Ọfa camps to that of Ilọrin, although a shorter route of a day and a half's journey, lest it prejudice the minds of the Ilọrin chiefs at the outset; he had therefore to take a circuitous route of five days with the messengers of the Ọwa and the Owòrè through the Ekiti and Igbomina provinces to Kàràrà's camp near Ọfa.

The Governor's Ibadan messenger, who went by the direct route, arrived at Ọfa on the 1st of April and met the belligerents on the battlefield fighting, and was not lodged till the battle was over. Similarly the Governor's Ekiti messenger who arrived at the Ilọrin camp on the 3rd met them on the battlefield, but as Kàràrà, their Generalissimo, did not take the field in person that day, he had the opportunity of a preliminary talk with him on the subject of his mission. The battle lasted till 3 p.m. and he lost no time in obtaining permission from the Ilọrin chiefs to come over to the battlefield to meet his colleague who he was sure would have reached Ọfa. The messenger at Ọfa had instructed the sentinels that as soon as they saw a white flag coming towards them they should send for him, and this they accordingly did, by despatching two men on horseback to apprize him of the same.

Both messengers welcomed each other on the Ọfa battlefield as they did at Kiriji; they arranged to rest the next day (being the Lord's day) and to commence work on the Monday as they did at Kiriji.

Although Chief Kàràrà received the Rev. C. Phillips well, yet he showed plainly by his conduct that he was not agreeable to the mission; he appeared rather indifferent and his replies were evasive. When he heard the Governor's letter read, he said, " The Ibadans are so treacherous that we cannot agree to an armistice, and again I cannot act without the orders of my King and therefore I cannot say anything good or bad."

At a second interview the Rev. Phillips had with him he repeated the same thing and laid so much stress on " the King's orders " that the messenger asked whether he wished him to go to Ilọrin to obtain the King's consent. The General was glad of the proposal, which he said he could not have made, but he wished that he should be accompanied by his colleague of the other side, and that they together visit the King at Ilọrin.

This was perhaps to test the sincerity of the Governor's messenger. The latter objected, but the General insisted upon it that he should not go to Ilọrin alone without his colleague at Ọfa, adding that as the Governor did not send to them direct, and that this visit to his camp was an afterthought, it was but giving King Alihu the respect due to him that both messengers should go together to deliver the Governor's message to him.

The Rev. C. Phillips came over the next day to inform his colleague of Kàràrà's proposal. Although they were not sent as far as to Ilorin yet they were resolved to leave no stone unturned in order to bring about the desired peace, even at their own risk.

Accordingly both of them went, accompanied by Adu the General's swordbearer, and the messengers of the Qwa, Owòrè and Ogedemgbe. It was but a day's journey, Ilorin was reached the same evening. The King did not lodge them, but sent them back with Kàràrà's messengers to Kàràrà's house, which augured ill for their mission.

At Kàràrà's house the accommodation given them was a room in which the smallpox epidemic had destroyed all the inmates thereof, the rags and rubbish of the deceased being still left in it uncleared away ; they had therefore to sleep in the open air and fortunately for them the weather was fair during the few days they spent at Ilorin.

The next thing which augured the failure of the mission was the reception the King gave the messengers. He had no private interview with them, they were sent for to deliver their message in open court amid the assembly of men, women and children, with a few of the chiefs. After reading to them the Governor's letter to the belligerents, King Alihu asked whether the Ibadan and Ekiti kings had heard it read, and whether it was acceptable to them. We replied in the affirmative. He then asked, " Why then did the Ibadans give battle to the Ekitis after the arrival of the Governor's messenger among them ? " He was told that the last battle fought took place five days before the arrival of the messengers to the camps. After a pause he asked, " When are you returning ? " " As soon as Your Majesty sends us back, even if it be to-morrow," was the reply. " You shall wait three days more," continued he, " and I believe the Governor will not take it ill when he knows that it was I who detained you."

With this reply the messengers were sent back to their lodgings, amid the jeers and scorn of these Mohammedan fanatics who were calling them names, styling them " Anasaras " (i.e., Nazarenes) etc. There was no doubt but that communications passed between Ilorin and the camp in the meantime.

The King dismissed the messengers the third day with these words :

" I have not much to say. Who should be entreated to give up a struggle, the assailant or the assailed ? I want peace myself

therefore my words will be few.   The stronger should be entreated
to let go the weaker."   Turning to the Governor's Ibadan
messenger he asked, " How many days it took you from Ibadan
to the camp ? "   " Five days."   " And from the Ibadan camp to
Qfa ? "   " One day."   " And how many from Qfa to Ilọrin ? "
" Only one day."   " Well," continued His Majesty, " the fact that
the distance from Ibadan to our camp being six days and from the
camp to Ilọrin but one day shows that I am not the aggressor ;
we are the weaker party and are only on the defensive.   Our camp
may be described as a shield raised to defend our country against
reckless invaders.   I am thankful to the Governor for his message
and I will instruct my Balogun to send you back with a good
message."

On asking the King if he would send a messenger to accompany
us back to the Governor he replied, " If the Governor had sent to
me direct I might do so."   Being asked further whether he would
comply with the Governor's wish in suspending hostilities for six
months and accept him as an Arbitrator, he replied, " That is not
my business, that is the Balogun's business."   Then turning to
the Balogun's messenger the King said, " Tell your master to agree
to whatever the Governor's messengers tell him."   With these
words the Governor's messengers left Ilọrin for Kàràrà's camp,
where they arrived on the morning of April 10th, 1886.

Kàràrà congratulated them on their safe return and told the
Governor's Ibadan messenger to send his boys over to Qfa at once
in order to allay their apprehensions, but that he should himself
wait till the afternoon when he would convene a meeting of the
war chiefs to hear the Governor's message and to reply to the
same.   Soon after the Governor's messenger returned from the
battlefield whither he had accompanied his boys on their way to
Qfa, the Balogun Kàràrà sent for him and his colleague and told
them that one of his slaves had just escaped to Qfa, and that if
he had not suspended hostilities since their arrival the slave
would not have had the chance of doing so ; and that was one
reason why he could not agree to the armistice of six months
according to the Governor's wish.

The messengers replied that they had nothing to do with the
escaping of slaves, and objected to his connecting it with the
suspension of hostilities, for slaves could always manage to escape
at any time.

He then began to brag and boast of his prowess, detailing the
number of successful battles he had fought with the Ibadans in
this place.   He gave an account of the origin and progress of this
war from the time of the defeat of the Ilọrins before Ikirun at the

Jalumi war. This, he said, was his third camp before Ọfa, and from here that city would be taken. He stated how he had fought with and killed in one day the Balogun and Ọtun of Ogbomọsọ, and had tried conclusions with every one of the Ibadan chiefs except the Arẹ himself. They the Ilọrins had been masters of several towns in the Ọyọ and Ekiti provinces and had their Ajẹlẹs (political Residents) in them ; but the Ibadans had ousted them from every one of them and would like to oust them from Ọfa also ! That he would agree to the armistice of six months only on condition that the Ibadans withdrew their contingents from Ọfa. He said, moreover, that the Ibadans were remarkable for their treachery " but could they equal the Fulanis for wiliness and cunning ? The Fulanis have seven different tricks, they have only used one as yet against Ọfa and Ibadan, before they have made use of the remaining six Ọfa will be taken."

" Two years ago the Sultan of Gando sent his envoy here to mediate between us. We observed the armistice for five months. Not only did we suspend hostilities, but also allowed traders on both sides to carry on between Ọfa and Ilọrin and even beyond. Unexpectedly the Ibadans shut their gates upon our traders, they refused to release them though we sent back their people to them."

He went on to say that the Ibadans were the common enemy of all, for even the ALÂFIN their King was on friendly terms with Ilọrin and had exchanged presents with the King of Ilọrin. " If the Governor would interfere at all let him bid the Ibadans retire from the Ekiti and Ilọrin territories."

He went on further to dilate on his own prowess, and what his horses could do, and as a proof thereof he sent for the son of the King of Ẹrin, captured a few days before the arrival of the messengers, heavily-laden with a couple of chains, for them to see him and hear from his own mouth. " Whose son are you ? " " The son of the King of Ẹrin." " How came you to be here ? " " I was captured by the Ilọrin horse." " Go back to your prison."

After all this talk the messengers were dismissed to prepare for the afternoon meeting.

About 3 p.m. a full meeting was convened in Kàràrà's reception room, all the war chiefs being present before he sent for the Governor's messengers. The General opened the meeting by introducing to them those who were present thus :

" Sitting on my left are the Balogun of the Fulanis, Ajikobi the Balogun of the Yorubas, and the last in order the Balogun of the 4th Standard of the Ilọrin army, I myself being the Balogun of the Gambaris. Sitting before me are Agidiako the Balogun of Ọfa who deserted to me at the rebellion of the King of Ọfa ; next to him is Ogunmọdẹde the head of the Ijẹsa contingents here.   Sitting on my right are the Princes, the King's brothers.   Now go on to deliver your message."

The Rev. C. Phillips read to them the Governor's letter to the belligerents, after which Kàràrà threw the subject open for discussion.   The Balogun of the Fulanis began and was followed by each of the others, giving vent to their feelings in bitter invectives. One of them exclaimed, " A new era is come for us and Alinu's Jehad has had a fresh start, we shall carry the koran to the sea."

Kàràrà himself spoke last in the same strain.   One and all of them evinced bitter feelings against the Governor's Ibadan messenger in particular, now and then calling him " You Ọfa man," and further, " If you choose to remain at Ọfa you shall see what we can do."   Another said, " In a few days we shall take Ọfa, and you, if you remain there, will be taken."   And another, " If you loiter on your way back to Ọfa the horsemen will be upon you." and so on to that effect.

The Governor's messenger replied, " I am not an Ọfa man, but the Governor's messenger."   " Yes, we know that," replied one of them.   " Did you not go three days ago when at Ilọrin to see your grandmother's grave ?   But you have come to us through Ọfa and anyone who did we call an Ọfa man and is our enemy and worthy of death."

The messengers were thereupon dismissed.   Seeing the excited feelings of the mob, a kind-hearted man standing by suggested to the Governor's Ibadan messenger, " Had you not better ask Kàràrà for some one to escort you across, otherwise the mob will have torn your dress from your body ere you get to the gate of the camp.   This friendly advice was followed, and the General told off his sword-bearer to escort the Governor's messenger as far as the locust tree in the battlefield where he used to take his seat on the day of battle.   His colleague also was permitted to accompany him as far, and they stood there till they saw the messenger safely at Ọfa.

The Ọfa people were quite prepared for the failure of the mission ; they said they expected as much, and would never have allowed the effort to be made, but that they thought that probably the respect due to messengers from the Governor of Lagos might carry some weight with the Ilọrins.

The Ilọrins, true to their word and to show to both messengers that they were determined to take Ọfa, attacked the city furiously on the next day.   The battle raged from the morning till the afternoon when both sides returned to their respective camps.

The Ọlọfa's Statements.—Before the Governor's messenger left Ọfa, he had an interview with the Ọlọfa, who made the following statements as to the true cause of the war :

" We are pure Yorubas by descent, and as such the subjects of the ALÂFIN of Ọyọ. It was after the fall of the ancient capital and the ascendancy of the Fulanis at Ilọrin that we became subjected to the conquerors. We have been loyal to them ever since, we paid our tributes regularly, performed every menial work for them and submitted to all indignities without any complaints. We built their houses, worked their farms, and at every confinement in the King's harem we are to give tributes in money called ' soap money ' meaning soap to wash the babies with. Such was the menial servitude to which we were compelled to submit. Besides all these we served in all their wars. To all these we submitted in order to avoid such a crisis as this.

"But nine years ago the King of Ilọrin sent to inform my late father, the then Ọlọfa, of his intentions to wage war with the Ibadans. My father warned him against embarking on such an enterprise, so unnecessary and so risky, the Ibadans having given no cause of offence ; on the contrary their influence on the whole had been for good, for the whole of the Yoruba country in general, and the Ilọrins also, had derived much benefit from the same.

" This advice offended the Ilọrin king and chiefs and they had ever since regarded us as traitors and rebels. My father had to pay heavy fines for his advice, so heavy that all Ọfa and her dependent towns had to subscribe to it, and yet they were not appeased. Again and again my father sent to assure the King of our loyalty and each time he used to utter smooth words and evasive replies.

" In spite of the warnings the Ilọrins joined the Ekiti confederates and besieged Igbajọ which they destroyed, and proceeded to Ikirun, and there the Ibadans dealt them a crushing blow in the Jalumi war. Those of them who escaped here naked and destitute we clothed and fed, the well-to-do we sent home on horseback. All this we did to please our masters, but all in vain. Three days later they intended to resent the shame and disgrace of their defeat upon us by taking Ọfa by stratagem. A large army was collected and war was ostensibly declared against Ẹrin, a suburb town of ours, my father being apprized of this so-called expedition replied that Ẹrin could not be taken except Ọfa be removed out of the way. Then war was openly declared against Ọfa.

" Such was the cause of the present war. We had done nothing really to provoke it

" Three years ago the Sultan of Gando sent Pọtun one of his officers to mediate between us and to effect peace ; for four months there was an armistice after which the war was resumed. The Ilọrins accused us of breaking the truce, which was a false charge, for while the negotiation was going on, instead of breaking up the camp they were removing it nearer and nearer, swelling their numbers by fresh recruits from home, and strengthening their position. Secret intelligence reached us from the Ilọrin camp that we should be taken by surprise. The Arẹ of Ibadan hearing this sent at once to put a stop to communications. This order was given not a minute too soon, for the report came on that very day that the Ilọrins had seized all the Ibadan and Ọfa people at Ilọrin and in the camp. All the Ilọrin people shut up at Ọfa I collected and sent home, and Karara released also those of ours they had seized in their camp. If anything is said to the contrary it is absolutely false, we neither broke the truce nor was the initiative in releasing captives theirs. We shall be thankful if the Governor will interfere and save us and our people from undeserved ruin."

The Governor's messenger left Ọfa on the 12th of April and arrived next day at the Kiriji camp to await his colleague.

§ 3. The Messengers and Preliminary Arrangements at Kiriji and Modakeke

On the third day (April 15th) after the arrival of the Governor's messenger at the Ibadan camp, an incident worth recording occurred which nearly marred the success of this mission entirely.

A young man in the Ibadan camp who was out of his mind went to the Elebolo camp, where an advanced column of the Ibadan army was stationed under Chief Ẹnimowu. He had in his hand a bow without an arrow and roaming all over the camp at night, he kept shouting, " In heaven it was decreed that the war should come to an end, but you Elebolo soldiers are obstinate. The Balogun, the Mayẹ, Agbakin, Timi of Ẹdẹ, Atawọja of Oṣogbo, and the Olobu of Ilobu have all agreed that peace should be restored, but ye refuse, and yet at the day of battle, you prove yourselves cowards and cannot fight. I am just from the rock in the battlefield where I found this arrowless bow, a sure sign of the decree of heaven that hostilities should cease."

The man was taken to Ẹnimowu that night, to whom he repeated the same words. Early next morning Ẹnimowu went to the Balogun to report the incident, and it was surmised that the Governor's messenger must have sent one of his boys to proclaim these words ! The Balogun then sent for the messenger to come with his boy, he then questioned them as to the message the boy was sent to proclaim at the Elebolo camp last night.

Of course they denied all knowledge of any such thing. Enimowù thereupon confronted them, describing how the boy came with a bow in his hand, and how clad, and what he said. But the messenger's boy said he went nowhere last night, whilst Enimowu insisted that he did for he saw him himself. At this stage it dawned on Ọgọ, one of the Balogun's young men, that there is a lunatic abroad, answering to the description of Enimowu, and who was accustomed to roam about the camp at night. It was suggested therefore that he should be sent for. Ogungbeñro, the master of the lunatic, was reluctant to allow him out by day, but as the Balogun insisted that he should be brought, the lunatic himself sent a message to the Balogun to say if he wanted to see him he should come himself to him, as inferiors must always go to their superiors. Then the whole incident became a matter of laughter as a huge joke. Ogungbeñro was, however, ordered to remove him from the camp at once, lest he might one day take it into his head to set the camp on fire.

The Governor's Ekiti messenger arrived on the other side on the 16th and hastened early on the 17th to his colleague at the Ibadan camp to announce his arrival.

The Ijẹsa chieftains were much disappointed at the failure of the negotiation with the Ilọrins ; but the Ibadans did not expect otherwise. Ogedemgbe, the Ekiti Generalissimo, however, said " If the Ilọrins would not agree to peace there was no reason why he should not on his part accept it." The Ibadan chiefs hearing this urged on Ogedemgbe to act the part of a plenipotentiary to the Ilọrins and to do his best to bring them to reason, and this he did by sending a special messenger at once, but the Ilọrins would not yield. The astute Ilọrins, as we have mentioned above (vide p. 448), had taken the precaution of holding the Ekitis fast to the alliance by placing a contingent force among them, whilst retaining an Ekiti auxiliary force among themselves which they held more or less as a hostage.

The belligerents at Kiriji now proceeded with preliminary arrangements between themselves, through the Governor's messengers of both sides. Chief Ogedemgbe sent to the Ibadan chiefs to say, that whilst both parties had agreed to an armistice, and that hostilities should cease between them for at least six months until the Governor or his deputy should arrive among them they should not avail themselves of the opportunity for reinforcing their contingents at Ọfa and at Modakẹkẹ. The Ibadans could not promise that because the safety of their position here depended upon defensive measures in both places, unless the Ekitis would pledge themselves not to reinforce both places against them ; for if they heard that the fighting was getting unusually strong, and that their men were likely to be overpowered, they could not help sending reinforcement. Next, the Ibadan chiefs considering that the interval of six months' truce being so long, and the possibility of some misunderstanding arising which in the absence of the Governor's messengers, might undo the work now begun proposed that a special messenger on either side be appointed to meet in the battlefield every morning with the compliments of their respective masters, and if any untoward incident should occur, that they should have the power of arranging matters amicably. This proposal pleased the Ekitis so well that at their suggestion two were appointed on either side as a provision against illness or any disability, and a third from the Ibadan Elebolo camp who was to report on the approach of the messengers on either side. The principal messenger appointed by the Balogun was Ọṣun and the Agbakin appointed another to represent the other war chiefs. The principal messenger appointed by Ogedemgbe was Lupọn, and another was appointed to represent the rest of the Ekiti war chiefs, and all met with the Governor's messengers at the battlefield under the flags of truce, first on one side, and then on the other side, a little ceremony being performed by this small party. The hands of the special messengers of both sides were joined by the Governor's messengers in friendship, and by the ALÂFIN's Ilari and the Ọwa's messenger in the name of their respective masters. They were enjoined to have a friendly intercourse with each other to help to preserve peace until the arrival of the Governor or his Deputy. The ceremony was concluded by a ratification of the promises made, by the splitting of kola nuts.

The Governor's messengers, and those of the King and the Ọwa thereupon bade each other adieu to meet again at the Ifẹ and Modakẹkẹ battlefield each by his own route.

The war chiefs on either side were grateful to the Governor for his disinterested interposition, and this they showed by sending some valuable presents to him by the hands of the accredited messengers of either side. The Ibadan chiefs sent him a horse and an alari cloth, the Balogun an ivory tusk, the Ọwa and Ekiti kings also sent valuable presents. Certain messengers whose names will be found below were deputed to accompany the Governor's messengers to Lagos according to his wishes expressed in Clause 13 of the " Instructions."

At Modakẹkẹ.—The Governor's Ekiti messenger had this time a shorter route than his Ibadan colleague, who did not reach Modakẹkẹ till the 24th of April. The latter, however, lost no time in setting up his flag, and going to the battlefield to meet his colleague who he was sure must have arrived at the Ifẹ camp some days previously ; but he had to wait till 6 p.m. before the colleague made his appearance, and explained the difficulties in their way. The Ifẹs would not listen to any pourparlers whatever until the Modakẹkẹs should explain the reason for their being in arms and prepared for a battle the previous day ; they regarded that action as a challenge they must take up. But the explanation was soon made, for the Governor's Ibadan messenger had heard the story as soon as he arrived. The Modakẹkẹs having heard a shout in the Ifẹ camp on the night previous, similar to what usually took place when the Ifẹs were worshipping the god of war previously to a battle, consequently put themselves in readiness against a sudden attack ; it is this precaution of theirs the Ifẹs construed into a challenge. This explanation satisfied the Ifẹs who came with the Governor's Ekiti messenger ; the latter had had great difficulty with the Ifẹs in preventing them from giving battle that day under the plea of taking up the "challenge."

The Ifẹ chiefs being satisfied with the explanation of the so-called challenge agreed to confer with the Governor's Ekiti messenger, and subsequently allowed him to visit his colleague at Modakẹkẹ, the same methods being pursued in this place as at Kiriji. The meetings took place on the 25th and 26th, after which interchange of visits were allowed the Governor's messengers both at Modakẹkẹ and at the Ifẹ camp.

During the conference at Modakẹkẹ the report of a gun was heard which startled them all ; upon enquiry, however, it was found to have been fired at the Ijẹbu camp at Isọya.

The Modakẹkẹ chiefs readily assented to the armistice as their overlords at the Kiriji camp had done ; they however stipulated that the Ifẹs should refrain from kidnapping them in their farms.

Both the Governor's messengers then went over to the Ifẹs with the result of the conference on this side, and the requests of the Modakẹkẹ chiefs. Before listening to what they had to say, the Ifẹs first wanted to know the meaning of the firing of a gun on the previous day. That was explained to them. It was done at Isọya. On hearing of the requests of the Modakẹkẹs they replied that they themselves had one request to make, viz., that they should be allowed to go and rebuild their city. But the Governor's messenger pointed out that that was too advanced a step to take, which would surely bring about a collision. The Ifẹs moreover objected not to the armistice but to the hoisting of the flag of truce on their soil, which was "sacred to Oduduwa, who was a

King." But they agreed that two " heaps of witness " be raised on either side, and that two messengers on either side be appointed to meet each other in the battlefield every morning as was arranged at Kiriji. This being done, both the messengers of the Governor and the ALÂFIN's Ilari and the Ọwa's messenger joined the hands of the appointed deputies of both sides as was done at Kiriji. Both parties now shook hands and parted, each by his own route, to meet again at Lagos.

The Apology of Modakẹkẹ.—Before the Governor's messenger left Modakẹkẹ, the principal chiefs had a meeting to state for the benefit of the Governor their own version of the present war between themselves and the Ifẹs. An old man of probably about 100 years of age was sent for, and he came, leaning upon a staff ; he was a boy when Modakẹkẹ was settled. The main object in giving the history of the foundation of Modakẹkẹ was to rebut the oft-repeated story that they were slaves to the Ifẹs. He stated (as we have learnt above) that they were originally refugees from the Ancient Ọyọ Provinces, who escaped south when the Fulanis became masters of the country. They were well received at first at Ifẹ, and treated with much sympathy and cordiality, but the turning point of the cordial relations came when Mayẹ the Ifẹ general was expelled from Ibadan, and the Ọyọs gained the ascendancy in that town. Then a systematic method of cruelty began to be practised on the Ọyọs of the city of Ifẹ, they were treated more as slaves than as freemen till a favourable Ọwọni (or king of Ifẹ) assigned them this settlement of Modakẹkẹ.

Ọdunlẹ was the Ọwọni they met who treated them well, the disaffection began towards the close of his reign.

Gbanlare succeeded him. He was more friendly disposed.

Gbegbaaje, who succeeded, revived the animosity ; some of them were even sold into slavery, no one questioning.

Winmọlaje, who succeeded, was kind to them as he appreciated their services in assisting to suppress Ijẹsa kidnappers who were committing depredations in Ifẹ territory.

Ab'eweila, who succeeded, made the Ifẹs swear, before he accepted office, that they would not find a pretext to murder him as they did so many of his predecessors. By this time the Ọyọs had become very important in the state, having one Wingbolu as their chief. The Ifẹs soon broke their faith and wanted to kill the Ọwọni. A civil war ensued but the Ọwọni was too strong for them ; he defeated them. The Ọyọs were neutral. The Ọwọni then questioned Wingbolu why the Ọyọs were neutral. He boldly replied that if the Ọyọs had been invited by his enemies he could not have thus gained the upper hand, or if the Ọwọni himself had

T

invited them, his victory would have been more complete. This
answer the Ọwọni pondered over, and as a result assigned them
this settlement so that all Ọyọs should remove from the City of Ifẹ
to this place, and he had a strong guard of Ọyọs in his palace.
Soon their numbers rapidly increased in the settlement. This
favouring of Ọyọs irritated the Ifẹs the more against him.

After his death, which was due to poison by the Ifẹs, the Modakẹkẹs met and repelled two attacks of the Ifẹs on their settlement ;
at the first of which they captured 12,070 of them but subsequently
released them because they had not the heart to enslave their
quondam benefactors.

But thirty days after when one Chief Ogūmakin received reinforcement from Oke Igbo the Ifes attacked them again, and were
defeated again. At this second time they followed up the victory,
captured the City of Ifẹ and ventured to sell the Ifẹs caught.

The city was however rebuilt in 1854 by the advice of Ognumọla,
the Ibadan general. Under the Ibadans they had lived amicably
together until the present war, which had largely divided the
interests of the country, the Ifẹs sympathizing with the Ekitis,
and the Modakẹkẹs whose safety and interests were intertwined
with those of Ibadan cast their lots with the Ibadans. He further
related all that took place between them during the war up to
the present time.

Chief Tahajo of Ibadan, who was twice sent to reconcile the
Ifẹs and Modakẹkẹs together, also made his own statement showing
the efforts at reconciliation that were put forth and the implacability of the Ifẹs, who broke faith and fired the first shot from a tree.

All these statements, as they have been noted in full above,
were duly recorded to be placed before the Governor.

The Governor's messenger left Modakẹkẹ on the 28th of April, and
after a short stay at Ibadan proceeded to Lagos via Ijẹbu.

The new Awujalẹ of Ijẹbu, who was all for peace, was very glad
to hear of the armistice at the seat of war. He assembled his
chiefs to hear the report from the mouth of the messenger himself,
and at their advice he willingly sent his messengers down with the
Governor's messenger to show that he was at one with those who
wished for peace.

The following is the list of messengers who accompanied those
of the Governor down :—

In the Ọyọ and Ibadan district :—

The Rev. S. Johnson, the Governor's messenger to the Ọyọs.

Ọyọ { Ọbakọsetan, envoy of the ALÂFIN, Feudal head of the
           Yoruba country.
       Belewu, representing the Ọyọ nobility.

Ibadan
- Arinde, messenger of the Balogun of Ibadan.
- Atẹrẹ, from the Mayẹ, representing the Ibadan war chiefs.
- Elegbede, from Tahajo, representing the Ibadan home authorities.

Ijẹbu
- Awonimẹsin, messenger of the Awujalẹ of Ijẹbu.
- Ogundẹkọ, also messenger of the Awujalẹ of Ijẹbu.
- Odusajo, confidential messenger of the Balogun of Ijẹbu.

Those of the other side :—

Rev. C. Phillips, the Governor's messenger to the Ekiti parapọs

Ijẹsa
- Apẹlidiagba, messenger of the Ọwa of Ilesạ.
- Olukọni, also messenger of the Ọwa of Ilesạ.

Ekiti
- Fatiye, messenger of the Owòre of Ọtun.
- Orisalusi, messenger of the Ajero of Ijero.
- Obasạ, messenger of the Olojudo of Ido.
- Dawudu, messenger of Ogedemgbe, Ekiti Commander-in-Chief.

Itebu   Lomi, messenger of King Manuwa of Itebu.

Ondo
- Akinlamu, messenger of the Osimowe of Ondo.
- Saba, messenger of the Elders of Ondo.

§ 4. THE TREATY OF PEACE

The Governor of Lagos had several interviews with the different envoys and messengers from the interior kings and chiefs, from which he gathered much information ; His Excellency thereupon drew up a treaty which was read and interpreted to them and which obtained their assent on the whole.

Ọbakọsetan, the ALÂFIN's envoy, however objected to Clause 5 of the treaty which refers to the removal of Modakẹkẹ from its present site, but he was told that as he had already agreed to the Governor's arbitration he could not object to any article of the treaty. The treaty was accordingly signed by all the envoys and messengers on behalf of their masters.

The following is the text of the treaty :

Treaty of peace, friendship and commerce between the ALÂFIN of Ọyọ, the Balogun, the Mayẹ, the Abẹsẹ, the Agbakin, the Ọtun Balẹ of Ibadan; the Ọwa of Ilesa, the Owòre of Ọtùn, the Ajero of Ijero, the Olojudo of Ido, the Seriki of Ilesạ, the Ọwọni of Ifẹ, the Ọbalufẹ, the Ọbajiwo, the Ọbalọran, the Ajaruwa, the Arodẹ, the Arisanre, the Balogun of Ifẹ ; the Ogunsuwa of Modakẹkẹ, the Balogun and Ọtun of Modakẹkẹ, the Awujalẹ of Ijẹbu and the Balogun of Ijẹbu.

Whereas the Kings, Chiefs, Baloguns and Chiefs above enumerated, parties to this Treaty, and to the conditions and articles of agreement hereinafter set forth, profess to be earnestly desirous to put a stop to the devastating war which has for years been waged in their own and adjoining countries, and to secure the blessings of lasting peace to themselves and their peoples, and have appealed by their envoys and messengers duly accredited to His Excellency the Governor of the Colony of Lagos as representing Her Most Gracious Majesty the Queen to mediate between them, and to arbitrate, and determine such terms and conditions as shall secure a just and honourable peace to the contending parties, and have each and all of them agreed to abide by such arbitration and determination, and to do his and their utmost endeavour to carry into effect the terms and conditions so arranged and determined. And whereas the envoys and messengers duly accredited by the aforesaid Kings, Baleṣ, Baloguns and Chiefs have been received in audience by His Excellency the Governor, and have themselves assented both verbally and in writing to the terms and conditions of peace hereinafter specified, and have agreed to be bound thereby, and faithfully to observe the same.

Now this is to testify that the Kings, Baleṣ, Baloguns and Chiefs aforesaid hereby ratify and confirm the said agreement made and entered into by their envoys and messengers for them and on their behalf and solemnly pledge themselves faithfully, loyally and strictly to observe and carry out the following terms and conditions so far as they are individually or collectively concerned :—

1. There shall be peace and friendship between the Kings, Baleṣ, Baloguns and Chiefs, the signatories to this Treaty and their peoples respectively and the Kings, Baleṣ, Baloguns and Chiefs aforesaid hereby engage for themselves and their peoples that they will cease from fighting and will remain within or retire to their own territories as herein provided, and will in all things submit themselves to such directions as may seem necessary or expedient to the Governor of Lagos for better and more effectually securing the object of this Treaty.

2. The Kings, Chiefs and peoples comprising the Ekitiparapọ alliance or confederation on the one hand, and the Baleṣ, Balogun, Chiefs and people of Ibadan on the other shall respectively retain their independence.

3. The ALÂFIN and Ọwa shall stand to each other in the relationship of the elder brother to the younger as before when the Ekiti countries were independent.

4. The towns of Otan, Iresi, Ada, and Igbajo shall form part of the territories of Ibadan, and be subject to the Bale, Balogun and Chiefs of Ibadan. Such of the inhabitants of the towns aforesaid as desire to leave shall be permitted to do so at such time and in such manner as the Governor, his envoy, or messenger shall direct after conference with the governments of the parties principally concerned, and such people shall not be molested by the signatories their peoples or allies.

5. In order to preserve peace the town of Modakeke shall be reconstructed on the land lying between the Osun and the Oba rivers to the north of its present situation, and such of the people of Modakeke as desire to live under the rule of the Bale and Balogun of Ibadan shall withdraw from the present town to the land mentioned, at such times and in such manner as the Governor his envoy or messenger shall direct after conference with the governments of the parties principally concerned, and such of the people as desire to live with the Ifes shall be permitted to do so but shall not remain in the present town of Modakeke, which shall remain the territory and under the rule of the king and chiefs of Ife, who may deal with the same as they may think expedient.

6. Except as herein provided the boundaries of the territories of the respective parties and signatories shall remain as at present and shall not be interfered with.

7. The Kiriji camp shall be broken up and the contending parties agree quietly and peaceably and without any demonstration to withdraw their armies and their peoples at such time or times in such manner, and by such routes as shall be directed by the Governor, his envoy or messenger after conference with the governments of the parties principally concerned.

8. The signatories engage themselves at or immediately after the signature of this treaty or at such times as may be directed by the Governor, his envoy or messenger after conference with the parties principally concerned, to withdraw their peoples and warriors and allies employed or associated with the contending peoples or armies at Modakeke, Isoya, or elsewhere, and wherever such allies or people or warriors may be employed in war, or likely to foster or promote war, and further when their peoples, warriors, and allies have been withdrawn, and the camp of Kiriji broken up and dispersed to do their utmost by peaceful and friendly means to bring about peace at Ofa.

9. The signatories bind themselves to endeavour in every legitimate way to promote trade and commerce, and to abstain from dissension and acts likely to promote strife.

10. The signatories agree if any cause of strife or dissension should still exist after the ratification and carrying out of these conditions which is not dealt with herein, to refer such cause or matter unreservedly to the arbitration of the Governor of the Lagos Colony and peaceably and without resorting to strife or provocation to await his determination thereof and abide by it, testifying their gratitude to Her Majesty's Government for efforts already made and undertaken in their interest and their sincerity and earnestness in the cause of general peace and goodwill.

11. The armistice now existing between the hostile forces in the camps of Kiriji and Isoya shall be promoted, and the signatories bind themselves to cease from all warlike operations or acts of provocation, and to do their utmost to promote friendly relations until the Governor, his envoy or messenger shall be able to, and shall communicate with the signatories hereto.

12. As a guarantee of good faith, and for the further and better securing the objects of this treaty and the faithful and strict observance of the terms and conditions thereof, the signatories agree to place in the hands of the Governor his envoy or messenger as and when he may determine, such of their leading chiefs as he may require as hostages, who will continue and remain with him on the battlefield of Kiriji, whilst the armies and peoples of the respective signatories are dispersing therefrom, and for and during such time or period as the circumstances or necessities of the case may require, or to give such other or further guarantees as may seem just or expedient to the Governor, his envoy or messenger.

In witness thereof we have hereunto put our hands and seals the days and dates specified.

Name.	Title.	Country.	Mk.	Seal.	Date.
1. Adeyemi..	The Alafin	of Oyo ..	×	LS	June 25th, 1886.
2. Ajayi ..	Balogun ..	Ibadan ..	×	LS	July 1st, 1886.
3. Osuntoki	Maye ..	Ibadan ..	×	LS	July 1st, 1886.
4. Fijabi ..	Abese ..	Ibadan ..	×	LS	July 1st, 1886.
5. Fajinmi ..	Agbakin ..	Ibadan ..	×	LS	July 1st, 1886.
6. Tahajo ..	Otun Bale ..	Ibadan ..	×	LS	June 14th, 1886.
7. Agunloye	Owa ..	Ilesa ..	×	LS	July 7th, 1886.
8. Okinbaloye	Owore ..	Otun ..	×	LS	July 3rd, 1886.
9. Oyiyosoye	Ajero ..	Ijero ..	×	LS	July 3rd, 1886.
10. Odundun	Olojudo ..	Ido ..	×	LS	July 3rd, 1886.
11. Ogedemgbe	Seriki ..	Ilesa ..	×	LS	July 2nd, 1886.
12. Derin ..	Owoni-elect	Ife ..	×	LS	July 18th, 1886.
13. Awotionde	Obalufe ..	Ife ..	×	LS	July 14th, 1886.
14. Oramuyiwa	Obajiwo ..	Ife ..	×	LS	July 14th, 1886.
15. Akintola ..	Obaloran ..	Ife ..	×	LS	July 16th, 1886.

	Name.	Title.	Country.	Mk.	Seal.	Date.
16.	Osundulu	Ajaruwa ..	Ife ..	×	LS	July 14th, 1886.
17.	Jojo ..	Arode ..	Ife ..	×	LS	July 14th, 1886.
18.	Aworinlo	Arisaure ..	Ife ..	×	LS	July 14th, 1886.
19.	Oga ..	Balogun ..	Ife ..	×	LS	July 14th, 1886.
20.	Ogunwole	Ogunsua ..	Modakeke	×	LS	July 14th, 1886.
21.	Sowo ..	For Balogun	Modakeke	×	LS	July 14th, 1886.
22.	Ayanleye	For Otun ..	Modakeke	×	LS	July 14th, 1886.
23.	Aboki ..	Awujale ..	Ijebu ..	×	LS	June 9th, 1886.
24.	Nofowokan	Balogun ..	Ijebu ..	×	LS	June 10th, 1886

Signed, sealed, and delivered in the presence of the under-signed after the terms and condition therein contained had been interpreted and explained by us, or one of us to the respective signatories.

(Signed) SAMUEL JOHNSON, *Clerk in Holy Orders,*
Messenger and Interpreter for the Governor.

(Signed) CHARLES PHILLIPS, *Clerk in Holy Orders,*
Messenger and Interpreter for the Governor.

Affix to Treaty, dated 4th day of June, 1886.

The undersigned envoys and messengers duly accredited to His Excellency the Governor of Lagos to convey to the Governor the terms and conditions which they and the Kings, Baleş, Baloguns and Chiefs who have despatched them duly accredited as aforesaid are willing to observe, abide by, and carry into effect in order to secure peace to their respective peoples and countries, having heard the foregoing treaty and the terms and conditions thereof read over and the same having been inter-preted, and fully explained to them, solemnly agree themselves to abide thereby and faithfully and loyally to observe the same on testimony whereof they have hereunto set their hands and seals this 4th day of June, 1886.

Their marks.

Obakoşetan   × accredited by the ALÂFIN of Oyo.
Belewu   ×   ,,   ,, ,,   ,,   ,,
Arinde   ×   ,,   ,, ,, Balogun of Ibadan
Atere   ×   ,,   ,, ,, Maye of Ibadan
Elegbede   ×   ,,   ,, ,, Otun Bale of Ibadan.
Apelidiagba ×   ,,   ,, ,, Owa of Ileşa.
Olukoni   ×   ,,   ,, ,, Owa of Ileşa.
Fatuye   ×   ,,   ,, ,, Owore of Otun
Orişalusi ×   ,,   ,, ,, Ajero of Ijero.
Obasa   ×   ,,   ,, ,, Olojudo of Ido.

Their Marks.

Dawudu	×	accredited by the Ogedemgbe, Seriki of Ileṣa.
Apẹlidiagba	×	,,	,,	,,	the Ọwọni of Ifẹ.
Olukọni	×	,,	,,	,,	,,	,,
Arinde	×	,,	,,	,,	Ogunsua of Modakẹkẹ.
Awonimẹsin	×	,,	,,	,,	Awujalẹ of Ijẹbu Ode.
Ogundẹkọ	×	,,	,,	,,	,,	,,	,,
Odusajo	×	,,	,,	,,	Balogun of Ijẹbu Ode.

Signed, sealed, and delivered in the presence of

ALFRED MOLONEY, *the Governor*.

SMALMAN SMITH, *Judge*.

H. HIGGINS, *Asst. Col. Secy. and Private Secretary*.

CHAS. PHILLIPS, ⎫ *Governor's messengers to the Interior*
S. JOHNSON, ⎭ *and Interpreters on this occasion*.

§ 5. THE RECEPTION OF THE TREATY BY THE INTERIOR KINGS AND CHIEFS

His Excellency, A. C. Moloney, the Governor took the envoys and messengers with him in the colonial steamer on his visit to the eastern waters of Lagos on the 7th of June, 1886. Instructions were also given to his special messengers to have the Treaty read and interpreted to the different kings and chiefs concerned, and to obtain their signatures to it, and then to forward it down to Lagos ; and then, not till then, would he see his way clear to go personally or to send to complete the arbitration.

The Ọyọ messengers with the Governor's special messenger were landed at Ejirin, and the Ekiti messengers with the Governor's special messenger to the Ekitis were landed at Atijẹrẹ.

The Treaty in the Ọyọ Division.—On the 9th of June the Awujalẹ signed the Treaty in the presence of his chiefs. Nọfọwọkan, the Balogun, also signed it the next day at Orù in the presence of all the war chiefs, not being concerned they had nothing to say against it. The messenger passed on to Ibadan, and Tahajo, the head chief at home, who was represented at Lagos by his messenger Elegbede, also heard the Treaty read and interpreted ; after some consideration he subscribed to it in the presence of the Home authorities. The Governor's messenger with the rest of the messengers passed on to Ọyọ.

At Ọyọ the ALÂFIN expressed his surprise at the way matters were hurrying on to a crisis in the following parable :—

" The Governor is like an Egũgun enchanter who is about

to perform a transformation trick. The mortar is ready, the drummers already at their posts drumming with all their might and the eyes of the whole world are now fixed upon the enchanter to see what he would become before they shout hurrah, hurrah ! If success attends his efforts the Governor will then know that there are humble Africans here who know how to appreciate kindness." He also signed the Treaty on the 25th of June, 1886. As soon as the Governor's messenger got him to sign the Treaty, he lost no time, but with the rest of the messengers left the next day for the Ibadan camp which they reached on the 30th of June.

The interview with the Ibadan chiefs was on the 1st of July when the Treaty was read to them and fully interpreted. Of course they are the ones who were most concerned in this division. They brooded a bit over clause 5 of the Treaty ; but the leading chiefs whose names were affixed to the Treaty signed it without raising any objection. They said that they had no alternative since the Awujalẹ and the Balogun of Ijẹbu had signed it, as well as the ALÂFIN : and on the whole they considered the Treaty just and fair.

The Treaty in the Ekiti Division.—The Ekiti kings and chiefs did not sign the Treaty so readily, having a strong objection to paragraph 4 of the Treaty which left Ọtan, Irẹsi, Ada, and Igbajọ in the hands of the Ibadans.

The report of the Rev. C. Phillips the Governor's messenger relative to it, will show the difficulty he met with in getting them to sign the Treaty.

Extract from the Report of the Rev. C. Phillips.

2. THE IJẸSAS AND EKITIS.

" I reached Èsa where the Ọwa was stationed on the 28th June. After the Ọwa had called his chiefs together I read the Treaty to them and gave them an oral account of our interviews with the Governor of Lagos. The Ọwa hesitated a little to set his hands to his seal on account of some objections he made with respect to the fourth article. But after I had made some remarks, showing him the impartiality of the Governor's decision, he set his hands to the seal. From Èsa I proceeded on the 29th with all the messengers to the camp. At Oke Mẹsin I met a messenger telling me that it is the Seriki's wish that I should not stop to see the kings, but that I should come straight on to him in the camp. I did so. The Seriki seemed to have the chief authority in these matters, but I cannot say whether it is an authority delegated to him by the gratitude of the kings,

who regarded him as their deliverer, or whether it is arrogated
on the principle of 'might over right.' However, as this may be,
the fact stands that the Seriki is invested with much authority,
and all state business must be done with him. Therefore I gave
him a full account of our interviews with the Governor of Lagos
and read to him the Treaty in the presence of his comrades.
He said he would not sign the Treaty on account of the
fourth article which transfers (? retains) Igbajọ, Irẹsi, Ada,
and Ọtan to the Ibadans wholesale. I was sorry to find that the
Seriki was instigated to this obstinacy by the Ijẹsa emigrants
from Lagos and Abẹokuta who seemed to have gained much
influence over him. There is a section of them in the camp under
the leadership of one James Thompson Gureje who came from
Abẹokuta, and I also found that a special messenger from the
' Lagos Ekitiparapo Society ' had preceded me to the camp.
He is a Brazillian Creole, a carpenter by trade, his name is Abek.
The opposition which I had from these emigrants was greater
than that of the Seriki himself. They were very clamorous.
Not only did they set up the Seriki but they also tried to influence
the Ekiti kings not to sign the Treaty. Their objections to the
fourth article were principally two. First, that the cession of
those towns to Ibadan was an infringement upon Ijẹsa territory ;
secondly, that the position of those places was too contiguous
for the Ijẹsa and Ekiti people to be safe in future from Ibadan
invasions or surprises. In vain did I advise the Seriki to confer
with the Balogun of Ibadan on the subject. In vain did I
represent the impartiality of the Governor's decisions. In
vain did I remind them of his former promise of unconditional
submission to the Governor's arbitration. Still the Seriki continued refractory until Thursday afternoon, July 1st.

" On that morning Mr. Johnson wrote to me to announce his
arrival at the Ibadan camp, and I went out immediately to have
a interview with him on the battlefield. At this interview he
informed me that the Ibadan chiefs had signed the Treaty
though the fifth article was galling to them, and that they would
not yield any further upon the Igbajọ question. However, I
asked him to tell the Balogun of the difficulty I met with.
When I returned to the Ekiti camp, I told the Seriki that the
Ibadans had signed the Treaty, and he would be responsible
for the continuation of the war if he persisted in his refusal.
I should state that nobody stood by me except Mr. G. A. Vincent[1]
the C.M.S. agent at Ilesa. The Ekiti war chiefs were entirely

---

[1]Latterly known as " Daddy Agbebi."

silent. Apelidiagba and his comrades with Mr. G. W. Johnson the Lagos book-binder, hid themselves.

" When I found that remonstrances were of no avail I retired to my lodgings, and was on the point of leaving the camp to appeal to the Kings Owòrè, Ajero, and Olojudo, when the Seriki sent for me and signed the treaty.

" Whether he shrank from the responsibility of the continuation of the war or whether his former violence and stubbornness was only a ruse to disconcert the Ijesa emigrants whom he was unwilling to displease (because he had been much indebted to them for the supplies of breech-loading guns and cartridges) I could not tell. But since he signed the Treaty I was astonished to find that his language was changed and he openly avowed his indifference about the Igbajo question, even in Mr. Johnson and the Ibadan messengers' presence. This could not be a mere capriciousness, it seemed to me a deeply contrived artifice. He told me afterwards that if he had signed the Treaty at once his countrymen would afterwards reproach him and his children with having handed a portion of their land to the Yorubas. . . .

" Lugbosun, the head Ekiti war chief, in the Mesin camp, told Mr. Johnson and me afterwards that the Ijesa emigrants who made much gain by importing the breech-loading guns and cartridges desired the prolongation of the war, but he and his colleagues who had nearly spent all their possessions did not approve of the opposition to the Treaty. They were anxious to decamp, and were impatiently expecting the Governor.

" The Ajero asked Mr. G. A. Vincent to tell me in confidence that they (the Ekitis) do not make much of the Igbajo question.

" When I returned to Èsa the Owa thanked me very much for the patience with which I endured the opposition I met with, and begged me not to make much of it, for it was only unruly people who resort to the camp. He gave me some historical account of the defection of Igbajo, in which he acknowledged that it was due to the ill-treatment that the Igbajo people suffered from some Ijesa head chiefs (who then tried to keep the Owa in the dark as to the real state of matters) that they were obliged to surrender themselves to the Ibadans. He begged me to urge the Governor to come or send at once to put an end to the war."

The Ibadan chiefs commenting upon the objection of the Ekitis to paragraph 4 of the Treaty remarked that " their request for the removal of Igbajo was unreasonable, not to say dictatorial and presumptuous. For if, according to the terms of the Treaty, we are to live in peace and amity, why should Igbajo be left a desolate wilderness and a rendezvous for highway robbers and men-stealers ?   And again, Igbajo is not nearer their town of Oke Mẹsin than their towns of Ibokun, Ilasẹ, Oke Bode are to our towns of Ikirun and Oṣogbo. Should we then ask that these places be removed from our vicinity ?   This seems to us to be promoting unnecessary complications and difficulties."

After the signing of the Treaty at both camps at Kiriji the messengers left by their respective routes to meet again at Modakẹkẹ.

At Modakẹkẹ the state of affairs was different from that at Kiriji.   The latter place is a battlefield, and no personal animosity existed between the Balogun of the Ibadans and the Seriki of the Ijẹsas, only that they were unwilling to sacrifice public good for their own private interests, hence the efforts made to obtain as much as they could. Not so, however, at Modakẹkẹ. But for Fabūmi the Ekiti General who was the mollifier, hostilities would have been resumed. No sooner had the Governor's messengers left them on the former occasion when the truce was arranged, than the road between Modakẹkẹ and the Ifẹ camp was thrown open, and not only the messengers of both parties met, but also parents, children and friends and relatives long separated rushed into each other's arms, the Ifẹs flocked to Modakẹkẹ, some spending three to five days there, and the Ifẹ women and children who were captured at the fall of Ile Ifẹ were allowed to go and see their kindred at the Ifẹ camp. Some of them never returned again and the Ifẹs refused to give them up, thus abusing the privileges granted them   Therefore the Modakẹkẹs resolved never to allow any of the rest to go over to the Ifẹ camp any more till peace was actually restored, but they allowed the Ifẹ women to come into the town to buy pots and utensils or whatever necessaries they were in need of.

As to the signing of the Treaty, the Ifẹs were of course very glad to do so, because their wishes had been gratified in the matter of Modakẹkẹ ; they would now get rid of them altogether. The Modakẹkẹ chiefs on their part, pained though they were by the terms of Clause 5 which stipulates for their leaving a spot sacred to them as containing the graves of their ancestors, yet signed without demur, hoping to ask the Governor when the time comes, for an amendment providing for the separation of the two towns by a wall as there is none existing hitherto.

The Awujalẹ of Ijẹbu in complying with the articles of the Treaty, sent his Agūrins (state messengers) to accompany the Governor's messenger to tell Ogunṣigun the Seriki of Ijẹbu Igbo at the Isọya camp to return home in peace with the forces under him. Scarcely did the messengers expect any opposition from that

·quarter. When Chief Ogedemgbe, during the negotiations at Kiriji, asked the Ijẹbu messengers whether the Ẹpẹ refugees and the Isọya band were reconciled to their new Awujalẹ, he was told that the latter had sent a friendly message to the Ẹpẹ refugees, inviting them to return home, with nothing to fear from him ; and to Ogunṣigun and the forces under him at Isọya he was favourably disposed, and was sending a friendly message to them.

The Rev. C. Phillips and his party who went by a shorter route, had seen the Ijẹbu Seriki before the arrival of his colleagues on the other side, and was good enough to prepare their minds against the reception they might likely meet with : it was as much as he could do to prevail upon Ogunṣigun to receive the messengers at all, and he finally agreed to see them not in his camp but in the battlefield. The interview was a hot one. But for Fabūmi there would at least have been a damper cast on the whole affair, if not a collapse of the embassy. He and the Governor's messengers had great difficulty in restraining the Seriki and his war chiefs from doing violence to the person of the Chief Agūrin sent by the Awujalẹ : they vented their feelings in bitter invectives and curses on their countrymen the Ijẹbu messengers.

The Seriki said that the Ijẹbus having been bribed to take up arms causelessly against the Ibadans who had done them no wrong, the late Awujalẹ was prevailed upon to declare war against them, and so was himself forced to engage in it. For full seven months he hid himself in his farm to avoid it, and five times was his house confiscated till he was obliged to come forward to this war. Their king having been led to this, why was he driven away to die at Ẹpẹ ? (Turning to the Agūrin, he said) " And you, Awonimẹṣin, have you the audacity to come on an errand to me ? Were you not sent with us to this war ? Were you not encamped with us at the river Ọṣun ? Who made you an Agūrin ? Was it not the late king whom you helped to dethrone ? deserting us here and going home for that foul purpose, you put your own master to death and raised up another ! You are the wrong man for this peace embassy, and this will be your last."

At last, turning to the messengers the Ijẹbu Seriki said, " I agree to all the terms of the Treaty, but I cannot acknowledge the present Awujalẹ as king, because he was installed not by the general consent of all the Ijẹbus : and besides, the funeral obsequies of the late king have not yet been performed."

CHAPTER XXX

DISPERSAL OF THE COMBATANTS BY SPECIAL COMMISSIONERS

§ 1. SPECIAL COMMISSIONERS SENT UP.

THE Treaty duly signed was forwarded to the Governor of Lagos by his special messengers, themselves awaiting further orders at their respective posts at Ode Ondo and Ibadan.

By this time the Governor's furlough was due, but, with the sanction of the Secretary of State for the Colonies, he had arranged everything for the accomplishment of this work, and matters were left in the hands of the Acting-Governor, F. Evans, Esq., the Colonial Secretary, to carry out. Mr. Henry Higgins, the Asst. Col. Secretary and Mr. Oliver Smith, Queen's Advocate, were appointed Special Commissioners for this business. They were to be attended by an escort of 50 Hausa soldiers, each provided with 50 rounds of ball cartridges for their Martini Henry rifles. They had also with them a 7-pounder gun, and a rocket trough with necessary ammunition.

Capt. W. Speeding, the Harbour Master, also accompanied the expedition, with instructions to make geographical observations all along the route from Ejirin on the lagoon—the point of disembarkation—through Ijẹbu Ode, Ibadan, to Oṣogbo and Kiriji, to return to Lagos if possible via Ileṣa, Ode Ondo, Aiyesan, Itebu, and Atijẹrẹ. He was also to make as far as possible a survey map of the route and to fix the positions of the principal towns, the number of houses and inhabitants in each village, names of chiefs, depth, width, and courses of rivers crossed, heights of hills, nature of roads, and all other useful and statistical information to be carefully obtained and recorded. The Commissioners were the bearers of the following letter :—

Government House, Lagos,

August 14th, 1886.

TO KINGS, BALẸS, BALOGUNS AND CHIEFS,

I send you greeting.

2. Your good friend, Governor Moloney, has been obliged to go to England for health and rest. But before leaving Lagos he put you all in my hands ; he told me how you had all said you were tired of war and wanted peace. He told me how you

had all sent your most trusted messengers, to beg him to assist you, and how you had signed treaties promising to be faithful. He told me all he had done for you, and how sorry he was he could not be present when you broke up your armies and camps according to your promises.

3. If I could have come to you myself I would have done so.

4. You would, I am sure, have received me with welcome, but my people in Lagos wanted me, and I regret to say I cannot arrange to leave them.

5. I send you, however, two of my officers in whom I have much confidence ; they are next in rank to myself.

6. I ask you to receive them as my envoys and to accord to them the same cordial welcome you would have given to me.

7. They have my full powers to act for me in helping you to fulfil the engagements you made in your Treaty, and I ask you to treat with them as if they were myself.

8. You have promised to place hostages in the hands of my envoys while your camps are being dispersed and while you are settling the difficulties between yourselves.

9. I rely upon you to fulfil your promises and now call upon you to do so.

10. It is hardly necessary for me to remind you of the advantages to be derived from a lasting peace, you who have been unfortunately so long at strife must know the troubles a war entails ; you must feel when you see your people decreasing in numbers, your children fatherless, your women without husbands, your trade declining, and your villages decaying, that the time has arrived when you should fight no more.

11. Let that time be now, as you have promised it shall be ; let there be peace and friendship among you all ; go home to your villages, and make your women glad, and see your children grow around you, and let me have the pleasure of telling my Queen, the great and good Queen of England, that your troubles are now at an end.

I am, Kings, Bales, Baloguns and Chiefs,

Your good friend and well wisher,

FRED EVANS, *Acting-Governor.*

[Governor Evans' letter seems very remarkable in its own way. To us it reads like an admonition to a number of truant schoolboys rather than an address to commanders of about half a million men who for over ten years had been engaged in a death struggle with one another, pouring out their life blood unflinchingly for honour, power and freedom—worthier objects than those which often

The expedition left Lagos on the 16th August via Itọ Ike the first Ijẹbu port. Great difficulties were experienced with regard to the transmission of their loads ; the Ijẹbus are by nature averse to carrying loads, they depend more on their slaves for such purposes. Besides they also considered it derogatory to the dignity of a free people to " ru asingba," i.e., transmitting state loads from point to point which in this country is a compulsory duty and regarded as a sort of taxpaying.

The Commissioners arrived at Ijẹbu Ode on the 19th and were well received. The Lisa (prime minister) called on them immediately after their arrival with a message of welcome and presents from the Awujale, and conducted them to the quarters prepared for them. On the same day the Governor's Ibadan messenger arrived at Orù where he was ordered to meet the Commissioners.

A public interview took place on the 21st at which about 3,000 people were present.

What was uppermost in the Awujalẹ's mind was the case of Ogunṣigun the Seriki of Igbo who had been sent to Isọya and his refractory behaviour in refusing to decamp. This the Awujalẹ considered a difficulty in the way ; the Commissioners, however, treated the matter lightly, saying they did not anticipate any difficulty in his case.

The Awujalẹ, not satisfied with this reply, sent word to the Governor's Ibadan messenger (the writer) at Orù to this effect. " When you reach Modakẹkẹ, if the Commissioners could not prevail upon Ogunṣigun to decamp at once, tell them to kill him, he

---

stained the swords of mightier nations—ambition, jealousy and greed ! " Go home to your villages," says the Governor, " and make your women glad," etc. Those " villages " are towns with 50,000 to 250,000 souls ! And is there any reason why their " women " should be denied the right and dignity of being termed their wives ?

Men who can control such huge masses of humanity, capacities which can guide, control, and direct all the intricacies of municipal and political machineries of a government, and can wage honourable wars for years without external aid or a national debt bequeathed to posterity might at least be considered as possessing some serious qualities beyond those of children, as they appear to be regarded, and deserving some honourable consideration due to men although they be Negroes. But happily the patronizing language of the letter which discloses so much thinly-veiled contempt, will be lost in the translation, and in other respects interpreters may be trusted to make up in tone and expression for what is wanting in style and diction.—Ed.]

is my slave, and let his followers return home in peace." Such was the autocracy and the rude form of government that prevailed in the Ijẹbu state. The Awujalẹ being ignorant of British methods, thought this order would be carried out as a most ordinary and insignificant matter ; its non-execution nearly cost the writer his life subsequently, the Awujalẹ noting him down as a personal enemy in league with Ogunṣigun, and gave orders that he should be hunted down and murdered should he be seen in any of the Ijẹbu provinces !

Carriers were supplied the Commissioners from Ijẹbu Ode to Orù at the border of the forests a few hours distant, beyond which the Ijẹbus refused to go, unless carriers came down from Ibadan ! But the Ibadans were very reluctant to adopt this unusual course ; the custom was for the Ijẹbus to transmit to Ibadan, and they to the next town on the route, and so on to the terminus, hence a considerable delay ensued until the Balogun of Ijẹbu sent word to the Ibadan Home authorities, and the Governor's Ibadan messenger also sent to the Rev. D. Olubi to move the chiefs to send down the needed carriers. In consequence of this delay the carriers never turned up till the 27th of August, and the Commissioners left for Ibadan on the 28th, leaving 17 loads behind for want of a sufficient number of carriers.

The Ibadan carriers did not wait, but went forward with great speed with the bed and bedding as well as the provisions, so that at their sleeping place at Olọwa the Commissioners had to pass the night in their hammocks suspended on trees ! The carriers were overtaken the next morning at Odo Ọna nla in the Ibadan farms where they halted and there the Commissioners breakfasted before proceeding to Ibadan, where they arrived in the afternoon and were lodged with the Ọtun Balẹ, who received them very kindly.

From Ibadan, the Commissioners would have proceeded direct *via* Iwo, Ede, Oṣogbo to the Kiriji camp, but the Governor's Ibadan messenger made them to understand that the Ibadan chiefs would never act without their King having a voice in the matter, as they were not constitutionally competent to treat with a foreign power without the King, whose prerogative it was. They were only his army. Consequently the expedition started for Ọyọ on the 2nd of September, 1886.

This affair the Commissioners remarked in a letter to the Acting-Governor thus : " We have been induced to visit Ọyọ on the representation of the Rev. S. Johnson that we should be unable to carry out our mission without having an interview with the ALÂFIN previous to visiting the Kiriji camp."

Hearing of their approach, the ALÂFIN sent an escort consisting of a few of his big Ilaris to meet them at the village of Fiditi, a distance of about 14 miles from the city.   As soon as they appeared the escorts ordered their men to fire a *feu de joie*, which they kept up till they reached the city of Ọyọ.   The leader of the expedition was rather unsettled by these demonstrations, he immediately ordered his Hausas to form around him and to fix bayonets, and told the Ilaris to go on before with their men.

At Ọyọ they were lodged at the house of the Apeka, one of the chief Ilaris, who lodges white men.

On the 4th September the ALÂFIN accorded them a formal state reception as a special honour due to them.   He was enthroned full-robed at the Kọbi Aganju with all the princes and the Ọyọ nobles about him, and the usual state umbrellas and all the paraphernalia of royalty displayed on the right and on the left, the trumpeters also sounding lustily the praises of the King and the welcome to the white men.[1]

The usual ceremonies over, the King presented them with two bullocks, ten sheep, four goats, 20 bags of cowries, and eighty baskets of yams.

On the next day they had a private interview in which the ALÂFIN sat with them and discussed affairs in a friendly and familiar manner.   His Majesty advised them not to visit Ilọrin, as Karara the Ilọrin Generalissimo at Ọfa was both obstinate and treacherous.   He gave them a horse and two bags of cowries and wished them God-speed.

On the 6th of September the King having supplied the necessary number of carriers, the Commissioners left Ọyọ with the King's Ilari, *en route* for the Ibadan camp *via* Ifẹ Ọdan, Masifa, Ejigbo, Ilobu, Ikirun.   They arrived at Kiriji on the 10th of September, 1886.

---

[1] The ceremonies on this occasion were nearly marred by the leader of the expedition who, against the remonstrance of the writer of the untimeliness of such a course insisted on going straight to the throne to " shake hands," saying, that as he represented the Governor of Lagos who is the representative of the Queen, he considered himself superior to any African Monarch—which may or may not be true of such a delegated superior rank, but the writer fails to see how it confers the right to commit a gross breach of etiquette at the moment special honours were being done to him. But ere he was half way along the avenue formed by the princes on the one side and the courtiers on the other, two or three big Ilaris rushed forward, and with expanded arms barred the way saying " Oyinbo, maṣe, maṣe " (white man please don't, please don't).   Then he desisted and was shown to the seat prepared for him.

The Ibadan chiefs wished to detain the Commissioners as their guests for a day or two before they passed on to the tents built for them on the battlefield by both belligerents, but they rightly declined, and marched on straight to the neutral ground.

Soon after their arrival, Ogedemgbe called on the Commissioners, the Balogun of Ibadan did the same later on at dusk : presents in cowries and provisions flowed in from both camps day by day, and from the Kings Ajero, Owòre, and the Olojudo at Mẹsin town.

The Commissioners returned the visits to both camps on the 11th at 10 a.m. to the Ibadan camp and to the Ekiti's at 4 p.m.

§ 2. THE COMMISSIONERS AT KIRIJI

The interviews to arrange matters began on the 13th, the Ibadan chiefs coming to the Commissioners' camp for the purpose at 10 a.m. No difficulties lay in their way except in the case of Ọfa, for whilst the Ibadan chiefs lay no claim to Ọfa, yet they were loth to see the town destroyed, because it is one of the principal Yoruba towns, and the birthplace of some of their chiefs.

When asked when it will be convenient for them to decamp they replied, as soon as they had informed their contingents at Modakẹkẹ and at Ọfa, lest the news coming upon them suddenly and probably in a distorted form, there may be a rush in both places with disastrous results. Seven days may be allowed for this, but they cannot send as yet until they shall have known the result of the Commissioners' interview with the belligerents of the other side.

The interview with the Ekitis took place at 4 p.m. of the same day but the results were not so satisfactory ; the Ekitis insisted on the Ibadans decamping first, but the Commissioners were for both camps to be broken up together on the same day and hour. As they could not arrive at an understanding also in the matter of the Ilọrins, whom they were supporting at Ọfa, the meeting was adjourned till the next day.

At the next interview after much talk the Ekitis agreed to the Commissioners' proposals.

On the 15th the Commissioners proceeded to the town of Mẹsin Ipole to see the Ekiti kings, the Ajero, the Owòre and the Olojudo. The Owòre was prolix and pointless in his remarks but the Ajero was more sensible ; his statements were few and to the point. The Olojudo said but little; his words were, " We want our independence, and not to be molested any more in future."

On the 16th the question of the boundaries engaged the attention of the Commissioners : the elders of Mẹsin and Igbajọ said it was the stream Eleriko that divided them. On the 17th at another interview defining the boundaries between Mẹsin, Ọtan, Ada,

Esùwú and Ipetu, they all agreed that the boundaries of each of these towns met at a place called Ata where also was a river called Omi Adà. The last interview was on the 18th September, when the elders of these towns were to sign the document defining the boundaries. On this day the Ifẹ chiefs arrived at the Ekiti camp about their own part of the Treaty. On the 19th the Ibadans sent to build the house for their hostage, the Ijẹsas and Ekitis having done their own two days before.

The interview between the Commissioners and the Ifẹ chiefs took place on the 20th. The latter with Ogedemgbe previously in council had agreed to allow the Modakẹkẹs ten months' respite in which they were to remove to a new spot on the other side of the Ọsun river, but meantime they might be allowed to remain in the small towns of Ipetumodu, Ọdũabọn, Moro, etc.

The interview between the Commissioners and the Modakẹkẹ chiefs took place on the 21st. In vain did they plead that peace and reconciliation be made between the Ifẹs and themselves. In vain did they plead that there should be a town wall separating the two towns from each other. The Commissioners were for carrying out the letter of the Treaty, which was also the resolution arrived at by the Ifẹs and Ekitis. The Modakẹkẹs thought it strange indeed that as a result of peace the vanquished should dictate terms to the victors, and worse still for those terms to include the evacuation of their hearths and homes, and spots sacred to them by a thousand ties and considerations. If that must be, then they prayed that the time be extended to the following dry season which would allow sufficient time to build a new town, and cultivate new fields so that they might not perish from starvation and exposure. Even this was not allowed them, they were to evacuate the present town of Modakẹkẹ at once, and in ten months' time build a new town and destroy the old ! To this the messengers were obliged to yield.

Hitherto the Commissioners interviewed the Chiefs of each of the camps by themselves, but on this day September 21st they were asked to meet each other in the Commissioners' camp in the afternoon. The whole of the fighting men of either side were drawn up on the battlefield but they were not allowed to come near except the leading chief of both sides. The fifty Hausa soldiers accompanying the expedition were drawn up in two rows at the two ends of the Commissioners' camp facing those of both belligerents, and only the leading chiefs were allowed to pass through to the Commissioners' tents, and there the Balogun of Ibadan, the Mayẹ, Agbakin, Adejumọ and others met and shook hands with Ogedemgbe, Lugbọsun and other leading chiefs of the

Ekiti army. Chief Mayę opened conversation, asking after several persons, some still living and some dead, all of them being acquainted with one another. Ogedemgbe was silent, and never uttered a word, probably overcome with emotion : he was finally prevailed upon to speak, but his words were very few. Being late in the day the meeting was adjourned again till Thursday, the 23rd, for the purpose of taking the oaths that there would be peace between them.

The Commissioners also proposed Tuesday the 28th for the evacuation of both camps. But both Generalissimos proposed ten days from date (*i.e.*, October 2nd). This the Commissioners refused ; they also refused the proposal of eight days (September 30th) and the chiefs were obliged finally to agree to the 28th.

[We may remark that the Commissioners did not believe that the Ibadans would really decamp, the assurance of the Governor's Ibadan messenger notwithstanding ; because, said they, the Ibadan camp consisted of substantially built swish houses, which they would be loth to desert, whereas the Ekiti's were only frail huts of bamboo and brushwood, but the events proved that the messenger was right.]

At length Thursday the 23rd arrived, a very memorable day. The Commissioners in their respective uniforms received the leading chiefs of both sides under the canopy of heaven in the space between the two houses built for them by the belligerents.

The final interview can best be told in the words of the Commissioners :—

Extract from the Report of the Commissioners published in the Blue Book :

". . . Thursday, 23rd September.—Early in the morning, although there was drizzling rain, and a mist, yet people began to come from the camps and took up their places at a short distance from either end of our camp, the Ibadans remaining on their side of the Eleriko stream. By nine o'clock there was a crowd of several thousand persons on horseback and foot collected on either side, and the variegated dresses, turbans and umbrellas of the sable warriors, and the showy horse trappings presented a picturesque mass of colouring. We had a line of sentries posted at each end of our camp, to keep off the crowd in case the multitude should endeavour to follow the chiefs to the meeting, as it was not deemed advisable that a large force from either side should be present or come in contact with each other.

" A marquee was pitched in the centre of the camp under which our chair was placed, and a guard of Hausas being placed

on either side of it.   Chairs, stools, and mats were placed for
the accommodation of the chiefs and representatives of signatories of the Treaty in lines from either side of the marquee so
as ·to form a semicircle with it, leaving an open space in
front.

" About ten o'clock the Balogun of Ibadan arrived accompanied by the principal chiefs in the Ibadan camp, and the
Ijẹbu, Ọyọ and Modakẹkẹ signatories of the Treaty or their
representatives, in all some 200 people.   They took their seats
on the chairs to the right of the marquee.   A few minutes later
the Seriki of Ijẹsa (Ogedemgbe) with the principal chiefs of the
Ekitiparapọ army, and the Ijẹsa, Ifẹ and Ekiti signatories of
the Treaty or their representatives arrived.   The Seriki and his
party, about the same number as the Ibadans, took their seats
on the left of the marquee.   All being ready we came out of our
hut and accompanied by Capt. Speeding, the Rev. C. Phillips,
Rev. S. Johnson and Mr. Willoughby proceeded to our seats
under the marquee.

" It was then discovered that the Modakẹkẹ representatives
were not present, and a mounted messenger was despatched to
fetch them.   They arrived shortly afterwards and were present
when the Treaty, and the ratification of it, were read and
translated.

" We expressed our pleasure at seeing all those present and
said, ' After the Balogun of Ibadan and Seriki of Ijẹsa had sworn
friendship to each other, as we understood they wished to do,
we would say what we had to say.'

" The Balogun and the Seriki then swore eternal friendship
to each other by their respective fetishes.

" The Governor's proclamation was then read and interpreted.
The Treaty was next read and interpreted ; and after a few
remarks from us, the ratification of the Treaty was read and
interpreted.   Each signatory then came to the table as his name
was called and affixed his mark and seal to the document.
We then congratulated all in the name of the Queen of England,
and the Governor of Lagos, upon the peace which they had
concluded and ratified and said we sincerely trusted that they
would observe the peace as faithfully as they had observed
the Armistice.

" The proclamation of peace was then read and interpreted
after which the bugles played and a salute of seven guns was
fired (first gun 12.20 p.m.).   The Balogun, Seriki and others
came and shook hands with us heartily thanking us for what
we had done for them.   Even the Ijẹbu representatives,

generally undemonstrative and even supercilious in manner, were effusive in their thanks and congratulations.

" The rains ceased before the meeting took place and the mist clearing away the sun shone brilliantly on the scene. Thousands of people were to be seen posted on the huge boulders of rock which were scattered through the Kiriji Camp, and crowned the summit of the mountain (the Oke Mẹsin Camp was not visible from the place of meeting there being a slight rising in the ground between) and as we learned afterwards the sound of the gun which was to announce that peace had been concluded, and that people could go to their homes, was most anxiously awaited in both camps, and received when heard with cheers and hurrahs."

§ 3. The Proclamation of Peace and Firing of the Camps

The following is the Proclamation of Peace between the Ibadans and the Ekitiparapọs at Kiriji-Mẹsin battlefield on the 23rd September, 1886.

Whereas through the friendly mediation of His Excellency the Governor of Lagos an understanding has been brought about, and a treaty of peace, friendship, and commerce concluded between the ALÂFIN of Ọyọ, the Balogun, the Abẹsẹ, the Mayẹ, the Agbakin, and the Ọtun Balẹ of Ibadan ; the Ọwa of Ilẹṣa, the Òwòre of Ọtun, the Ajero of Ijero, the Olojudo of Ido, the Seriki of Ijẹṣa, the Ọwọni, the Balogun, the Ọbalufẹ, the Ọbalọran, the Obajio, the Ajaruwa, the Arodẹ, and the Oriṣanire of Ifẹ ; the Ogunsua, the Balogun, and the Ọtun of Modakẹkẹ, and the Awujalẹ and Balogun of Ijẹbu.

And whereas due provision has been made by us after conference with the heads of the governments principally concerned, or their representatives duly accredited to us, for the complete fulfilment of the conditions of the said treaty.

Now therefore we, Special Commissioners appointed by His Excellency the Governor of Lagos for the purpose of executing the said treaty in accordance with the provisions thereof, do hereby proclaim, in the name of the signatories of the said treaty, that peace has this day been established and shall henceforth continue for ever between the signatories of the said treaty and between their respective peoples.

Dated at Kiriji-Mẹsin battlefield this 23rd day of September, 1886.

(Signed) HENRY HIGGINS) *Special Commissioners.*
OLIVER SMITH }

Ratification of the Treaty of Peace, Friendship, and Commerce between the Ibadans and Ekitiparapọs.

We, the undersigned signatories, and duly authorised representatives of signatories of the Treaty of Peace, Friendship, and Commerce signed in the months of June and July in the current year, by the ALÂFIN of Ọyọ, the Balogun, the Abẹsẹ, the Mayẹ, the Agbakin, and the Ọtun Balẹ of Ibadan, the Ọwa of Ilẹṣa, the Ọwòre of Otun, the Ajero of Ijero, the Olojudo of Ido, the Seriki of Ijẹṣa, the Ọwọni, the Balogun, the Ọbalufẹ, the Ọbalọran, the· Obajio, the Ajaruwa, the Arodẹ, and the Orisanire of Itẹ, the Ogunsua, the Balogun, and the Ọtun of Modakẹkẹ, and the Awujalẹ and Balogun of Ijẹbu, and having for its object the termination of the war between the Ibadans and their allies, on the one hand, and the Ekitiparapọ confederacy on the other hand, hereby ratify and confirm the said treaty, and all and singular the conditions and stipulations thereof, and do further agree to, and approve of the following provisions, for the more perfect fulfilment of the same, made after conference with the governments of the parties principally concerned or their representatives by the Special Commissioners appointed by the Governor of Lagos as representing Her Most Gracious Majesty the Queen of Great Britain and Ireland to carry the said treaty into effect.

1. Peace between the signatories of the treaty and their peoples shall be proclaimed by the Commissioners immediately after the signing hereof.

2. Immediately after the proclamation of peace the breaking up of the camps at Kiriji and Oke Mẹsin respectively shall begin, and upon the signal being given by gunfire in the Commissioners' camp the Ibadans encamped in the Kiriji camp and the Ekitiparapọs encamped in the Oke Mẹsin camp shall simultaneously begin quietly and peacefully and without any demonstration to withdraw from their said respective camps.

3. The Ibadans encamped in the Kiriji camp shall return to their homes by way of Ikirun, Oṣogbo, Ẹdẹ, and Iwo, and by Ikirun, Ilobu, Ejigbo, and Ọyọ, and the Ekitiparapọs encamped in the Oke Mẹsin camp shall return to their homes by way of Mẹsin Ipóle, and Mẹsin Igbo Odo, and Ẹsa Oke, and Ẹsa Egure.

4. The evacuation of the said Kiriji and Oke Mẹsin camps shall be completed by 12 o'clock noon on Tuesday next the 28th inst. when a signal gun shall be fired in the Commissioners'

camp after which, without further warning, the said Kiriji
and Oke Mẹsin camps shall be destroyed by fire, at such time
and in such manner as the Commissioners shall deem
expedient.

5. The camps at Modakẹkẹ, Isọya, and elsewhere shall be
broken up on such day, and in such manner as the Commissioners
after their arrival at the quarters prepared for them by the
Modakẹkẹs and the Ifẹs, on their battlefield shall determine, and
thereupon the Ifẹs shall be re-instated in their town of Ile Ifẹ,
and the Modakẹkẹs shall forthwith withdraw provisionally to
the towns of Ipetumodu, Moro and Ọdũabọn to the land between
the Ọsun and Ọba rivers, and north of the present town of
Modakẹkẹ, before the end of the month of March in the year
1888, and for their faithful compliance with the provisions of
this article the authorities of Ibadan undertake to be
responsible.

6. During the time that the Modakẹkẹs shall inhabit the said
towns of Ipetumodu, Moro, and Ọdũabọn, they shall be at
liberty to cultivate and carry away the produce of their present
farm of Modakẹkẹ, without molestation from the Ifẹs. They on
their part shall not in any way molest the Ifẹs.

7. Such of the Modakẹkẹs as shall desire to live with the Ifẹs
shall give notice of such desire to the Commissioners for the
breaking up of the said camps at Modakẹkẹ, Isọya, and elsewhere, and any Modakẹkẹ who shall not have given such notice
shall be conclusively deemed to have elected not to live with
the Ifẹs.

8. Those of the inhabitants of the towns of Ọtan, Irẹsè, Ada,
and Igbajọ, who shall desire to remove from those towns, shall
be permitted to do so with all their movable property and without
molestation at any time before the end of the month of January
1887.

Any inhabitant of any of the said towns who shall not have
left such towns before the expiration of the said term shall be
conclusively deemed to have elected to become a subject of the
authorities of Ibadan.

9. The hostages given to the Commissioners by way of
security for the due observance of the article of the said treaty
relating to the breaking up of the Kiriji and Oke Mẹsin camps
shall remain with the Commissioners so long as the Commissioners
shall deem expedient.

In witness whereof we have hereunto affixed our hands and
seals the 23rd day of September, 1886.

		Their marks	Seal
Ọbakoṣetan	} representing the ALÂFIN of Ọyọ	×	O
Belewu		×	O
Ajayi	.. Balogun of Ibadan	×	O
Adejumọ	.. representing the Abẹṣẹ of Ibadan ..	×	O
Ọsuntoki	.. The Mayẹ of Ibadan	×	O
Fajinmi	.. The Agbakin of Ibadan	×	O
Elẹgbede	.. representing the Ọtun Balẹ of Ibadan	×	O
Apẹlidiagba	.. ,, ,, Ọwa of Ilẹsa ..	×	O
Fatuye	.. ,, ,, Ọwore of Ọtun ..	×	O
Oriṣalusi	.. ,, ,, Ajero of Ijero ..	×	O
Ọbasa	.. ,, ,, Olojudo of Ido ..	×	O
Ogedemgbe	.. Seriki of Ijẹṣa	×	O
Ọsundulu	.. (the Ajaruwa) for the Ifẹ Signatories	×	O
Tojo	.. (the Arodẹ of Ifẹ) ,, ,,	×	O
Akinpẹ	.. representing the Ogunsua of Modakẹkẹ	×	O
Sowọ̀	.. Acting Balogun of Modakẹkẹ ..		
Ayanlẹyẹ	.. Acting Ọtun for Modakẹkẹ ..	×	O
Awonimẹsin	} representing the Awujalẹ of Ijẹbu	×	O
Ogundẹkẹ		×	O
Okunlaja	.. ,, ,, Balogun of Ijẹbu	×	O

Signed, sealed, and delivered in the presence of

(Signed) HENRY HIGGINS,
    Acting Col. Secretary
(Signed) OLIVER SMITH,
    Queen's Advocate
        Special Commissioners.

(Signed) CHARLES PHILLIPS,
    Clerk in Holy Orders
(Signed) SAMUEL JOHNSON,
    Clerk in Holy Orders
        Interpreters on this occasion.

As it was evident that the camps must be evacuated, all the women with their movable effects and live stock cleared off to Ikirun within three days.

The Ibadan slaves who did not wish to return home with their masters took this opportunity to escape to their country. In order to effect this with safety, without drawing attention, they set fire to some houses, and during the confusion and bustle attending the conflagration hundreds of them made good their escape to the Ekiti camp which overlooked the Ibadan camp. The houses of the Mayẹ of Ibadan, and the Timi of Ẹdẹ and those of several men of lesser note, were consumed in this conflagration.

This was on Friday, the 24th September.   One chief alone (Sanusi the son of the Are) lost about 400 slaves.[1]

The Ibadan chiefs, fearing they would lose all their slaves in this manner, thought they ought rather to go at once and wait no longer for the 28th or they might have to do so with grief and gloom.   By the 25th the camp was all but deserted.   On the 26th the Balogun with the rest of the war chiefs left for Ikirun.   Ogedemgbe hearing that the Ibadan chiefs had gone, left also with his men for Mẹsin Ipole.   The Commissioners, however, were determined to keep to the letter of the treaty and to fire both camps on the 28th.   The hostages, Chief Mosaderin and Fakẹyẹ of the Ibadans, and Aṣipa of the Ekitiparapọs, were detained still by the Commissioners until the camps were fired.

The following extract from the Commissioners' report will describe the proceedings of the 28th when the camps were fired :—

' . . . Tuesday, September 28th.—There was heavy rain during the night, and the thermometer registered 66 degrees, the lowest temperature we had experienced.   The morning was fine though cloudy, and there was a slight breeze.

Mr. Johnson left for Ikirun with presents from us to the kings and chiefs whose sudden departure from Kiriji had not allowed us the opportunity of giving them prior to their leaving the camp.

We sent 50 of our carriers to either camp to be in readiness to fire them on the signal gun being fired from our camp.   Two guns were fired at 12 o'clock, and three minutes later both camps were in flames.

The breeze being slight the smoke did not clear away but hung in dense clouds over the camps.

By half-past one o'clock both camps were almost completely burned, but the fire smouldered during the day and night. The houses in the Ibadan camps were not so completely destroyed, as those in the Oke Mẹsin camp, the former being mud with thatch roofs, while the latter were chiefly constructed of bamboo with leaf roofs.

Immediately the camps were fired, Chief Mosaderin and the Ọyọ hostage came to say good-bye to us. . . . He was a fine old man, with very courteous manners, and he was in a desperate hurry to get away, always fearing that something had happened

---

[1] Many of them finding their old homes quite different from what they had expected, and conditions of life more arduous, returned to their former masters at Ibadan.

to his wives and belongings at Ikirun, or that we might take him to Lagos.

The Ijẹṣa and Ekiti hostage also came to say good-bye, and to express their gratification at the sight of the burning camps. The Aṣipa was very anxious for us to allow him and his party to walk to the gates of the Ibadan camp. For obvious reasons we would not grant his request."

We may remark· that Ogedemgbe, the Seriki of the Ijẹṣas, showed much anxiety about the camps at Ọfa, wishing this offshoot of the war to come to an end also ; but the Ilọrin Generalissimo would not give in as we shall see later on, nor allow the Ijẹṣa contingent with him to come away.

§ 4. THE COMMISSIONERS AT MODAKEKE : FAILURE.

The Commissioners left their camp on the 29th September, 1886. They thus described the ruins of both camps in their report :—

" The rain which fell heavily during the night turned into a drizzle in the early morning, and the mountains and country enveloped in a thick cloudy mist for some hours after sunrise, when the weather cleared up somewhat.

About 150 carriers all Ekitis furnished by Chief Ogedemgbe had come to our camp the preceding evening, and so facilitated our making an early start. However, notwithstanding the fact of these carriers being on the spot, it was a quarter past ten o'clock before they could all be got off and we ourselves able to start. . . .

As the dense mist cleared under the rays of the sun we could discern the still smoking ruins of the Kiriji (Ibadan) camp, the downpour of rain during the night not having completely put out the conflagration.

Passing through the Oke Mẹsin camp (Ekitiparapọ) a complete ruin, the leaf roofs and bamboo sides of the huts having burned more rapidly than the mud walls and thatch roof of the huts in the Ibadan camp, we reached the town of Mẹsin Ipole at ten minutes past eleven o'clock."

The Commissioners halted here awhile to have an interview with the kings for the signing of the enactment for the abolition of human sacrifice. The Seriki's speech on the occasion shows the amount of power and influence he had over the Ekiti kings. His speech to the Òwòre embodied in the Commissioners' report of the occasion is as follows : " I command you to sign it, in the name of the white man, and when I command no king dare disobey. I will send word to all the Ekiti kings."

Leaving Mẹsin Ipole at one o'clock the Commissioners had to travel through a difficult path under a heavy shower of rain which drenched them to the skin. The path in some places was steep and rugged, and in consequence of the rain quite overflooded. Ilare was reached at 3.30, and Ẹsa Egure at 6 p.m. where they passed the night.

Here they had an opportunity of an interview with the Ọwa of Ilesa who also signed the enactment for the abolition of human sacrifice.

At 11.30 the next morning the Commissioners started on their onward march, reached Ijẹbu Ẹrẹ at 2 p.m. and passing through a very bad and slippery road where most of the carriers had numerous falls, and the horses floundered, and had occasional falls with the rider, all which rendered the journey an unpleasant one, they at length arrived at Ilesa about 6 p.m.

The accident at Ilesa was that of a fierce bull which attacked the chief Commissioner's horse, but was driven away by the sentry. The bull went next to the Queen's Advocate's horse when it was tied up, and gored it so badly that next morning it had to be shot.

Leaving Ilesa on Saturday, October 2nd, Ibodi was reached at 11.20, Gunmodi at 2 p.m., and after resting here one hour the Ifẹ-Modakẹkẹ battlefield was reached quite late on the same day. On the next morning the following Ijẹsa, Ekiti, and Ifẹ chiefs came to welcome the Commissioners: Fabūmi (Ekiti), Lodifi (Ijẹsa), Oluyọ, the Balogun, and Bambẹ, the Seriki of Ifẹ. Also the civil chiefs Ọbalufẹ, Ọbalọran, Ọbajio, Ajaruwa, Arodẹ, and the Orisanire.

In the afternoon the chiefs of the Ibadan contingent defending Modakẹkẹ, viz:—Akintọla, Sumọnu Apampa, Ojo Wanwanmasi the Ẹkarun paid them also a friendly visit of welcome. Of the Moda- kẹkẹ chiefs Sowọ the Ogunsua's respresentative, the Agbakin, Oyelẹyẹ the Ọtun Agbakin, Detomi and Ọkẹ the two powerful war chiefs also came to pay their respects. The conference at the Ifẹ-Modakẹkẹ battlefield lasted about 30 days without any result till the Commissioners left them. It was thus summarized in the Commissioners' report :—

We arrived at Ifẹ-Modakẹkẹ on the evening of the 2nd of October, and on the 5th inst we had an interview with the Ibadan chiefs, and impressed upon them the necessity for the Modakẹkẹs removing from their town as soon as possible.

The Ibadan chiefs promised to see the Modakẹkẹ authorities and return on the following morning.

On the 6th the Ibadan chiefs' messengers and one Modakẹkẹ chief's messenger came to say their masters could not come as it was an unlucky day. We said we should expect to see their masters on the following day.

On the 7th the Ibadan and Modekẹkẹ chiefs came together and the latter asked for five months in which to remove to Ipetumodu, etc.

In the afternoon of the same day we saw the Ifẹ chiefs and their allies and informed them of the Modakẹkẹs' request. The Ifẹs would not hear of five months being granted, saying it was only a ruse to get rid of us, and that the Modakẹkẹs would never leave if they did not remove in our presence from their town.

On the 8th inst. we saw the Ibadan and Modakẹkẹ chiefs, and told them that we had decided upon careful consideration that the Modakẹkẹs must remove from their town to Ipetumodu within ten days from that day, and that the Ibadans on the one side and the allies of the Ifẹs on their side should decamp also within that time. The Agbakin said he would tell the Ogunsua what we had decided.

In the afternoon we informed the Ifẹs and their allies of our decision. On the 9th the Ijẹbu, Ibadan, and Ọyọ representatives came to tell us that the previous afternoon, on our decision becoming known, there was an uproar at Modakẹkẹ, the people saying they would die rather than leave their town. The representatives considered matters serious and therefore came to ask us if some other arrangement could be made as the Modakẹkẹs seemed very determined.

We told the representatives that they had better go and see the Ibadan chiefs and Modakẹkẹ authorities and try to learn from them the true state of affairs and let us know.

In the afternoon the representatives returned and said the Ibadan chiefs told them that the uproar had been directed against them the previous day, the Modakẹkẹs alleging that the Ibadan chiefs had betrayed them and saying they would not leave their town. The representatives said the Ibadan chiefs had sent a messenger to the Balogun at Ikirun asking for instructions as to how to act and expected an answer in about five days' time.

On the 11th the Agbakin and representatives of the Ogunsua and Ọtun Agbakin and the Ibadan chiefs came to see us : they said they wished us to reconcile the Modakẹkẹs and Ifẹs, that the former never had intended to leave their present town, and that their proposition of five months' grace being granted meant nothing. We told them that the Agbakin was the only chief present, and that if the chiefs had any proposals to make they must make them in person.

On the 12th the junior commissioner had an interview with the Ibadan and Modakẹkẹ chiefs, and impressed upon them that if the Modakẹkẹs persisted in their refusal to quit their present town within the time given, the Ifẹs and their allies would not be bound to break up their camps, while the Ibadans would have to retire from Modakẹkẹ if we so ordered them, they having made peace with the Ifẹs and their allies.

The Ibadans appeared to side with the Modakẹkẹs at this interview, and two of the chiefs were somewhat insolent.[1]

No progress with affairs under consideration was made. We had subsequent interviews with the Ifẹs on the 13th and with the Modakẹkẹs on the 14th, and at the request of both parties agreed to the chiefs on either side meeting in a shed by our house with a view to their possibly being able to come to an understanding.

We gave them distinctly to understand, however, that any scheme they might agree upon must be submitted to us by noon on Monday the 18th of October.

Several meetings of the Ifẹ and Modakẹkẹ chiefs were held, and at one time it almost seemed that they might be able to come to an understanding ; the Ifẹs offering to allow all the Modakẹkẹs to live with them in Ile Ifẹ[2] provided the present town of Modakẹkẹ was destroyed.

On Monday the 18th both parties appeared before us and asked for an extension of 24 hours which was granted to them.

---

[1] These were Akintọla and Sumọnu Apampa the latter being the spokesman. The chief commissioner being indisposed on this occasion, the Queen's Advocate conducted the negotiations in his own way. Foiled and silenced at every turn by his dialectic skill, the young war-chief fiercely broke out " You were sent here to make peace not to destroy lives. When you ordered a population like that of Modakẹkẹ to remove *at once* and go and live in a forest what is to become of the women and children, the aged and infirm, how and where are they to live ? How to be sheltered and how fed ? If anything should happen to them, at your hands will God enquire their lives. They and the Ifẹs had lived in peace between themselves before, and they can do so again if only you would reconcile them together."—Ed.

[2] Modakẹkẹ contained a far larger population than Ile Ifẹ and more powerful war-chiefs.—Ed.

The chiefs then resumed their meetings, which shortly afterwards became very stormy and ended by both parties leaving without having come to any agreement. No proposal was submitted to us by the authorities on either side at all.

On the 18th we had an interview with the Ibadan chiefs and pointed out to them that we might have to call upon them to retire from Modakẹkẹ if the Modakẹkẹs did not abide by the treaty. They begged us not to send them away before the allies on the Ifẹ side, but gave no hint that they would not obey our orders.

On the 20th we saw the Ibadan chiefs and told them that the Modakẹkẹs having broken the treaty, we called upon the Ibadans to retire from the town of Modakẹkẹ they being at peace with the Ifẹs and their allies.

The Ibadan chiefs replied that they had sent all their things away, but would not leave Modakẹkẹ unless the Ifẹs' allies also decamped, without orders from the Balogun.

We warned them that in remaining in Modakẹkẹ after we had ordered them to leave, they were breaking the treaty. They said they had not signed the treaty and therefore were not responsible. We said we should send direct to the Balogun.

On the 21st October we despatched the Rev. S. Johnson to Ikirun with a letter to the Balogun of Ibadan informing him of the state of affairs, and requesting him to withdraw the Ibadan contingent in Modakẹkẹ without delay, and also to let us know what measures he intended taking to carry into effect the obligations undertaken by him and the other Ibadan authorities in clause 5 of the ratification of the treaty.

On the same day we despatched the Rev. C. Phillips to Mẹsin Ipole with a letter to Chief Ogedemgbe and with orders to proceed on and meet Mr. Johnson at Ikirun. Mr. Phillips returned to us on the 26th bringing a letter from Chief Ogedemgbe asking us not to allow the Modakẹkẹs to remain in their present town.

Mr. Phillips reported that the news he took to Mẹsin Ipole about the Modakẹkẹs caused much indignation.

On the 27th Mr. Johnson arrived with a messenger from the Balogun of Ibadan who delivered the following message to us :

Ọdẹjayi [the messenger] : " The Balogun salutes you. He had heard of all your trouble with his people who are here. He begs you to pass it over. He has sent them word that they are all to clear out at once. He salutes you for being hungry on his account. He least expected that the Modakẹkẹ people would be so obstinate. He thought it would be a thread but it has passed a twine. He thought with one word he would tell the Modakẹkẹs to clear out, and they would obey him ; but now they are so obstinate, and disobedient. He would beg the Ifẹs to come home, and the Modakẹkẹs as many of them as are his friends or relations or belong to him he will tell them to clear out to Ipetumodu, and those who remain will have their choice whether to clear out or live with the Ifẹs.

" He says as to the Ọfa case, they are negotiating with the Ilọrins therefore the Modakẹkẹ case will take time. Now you are settling things here there will be no firing of guns ; he will try to settle everything peaceably. He will never break the treaty in any way."

The Commissioners : " Are you charged with any message to the Modakẹkẹs ? "

Ọdẹjayi : " No."

The Commissioners : " Is there any other messenger going to them ? "

Ọdẹjayi : " The only message I have for the Modakẹkẹs is that the Balogun is withdrawing his army in compliance with the treaty. I am sent with a message to Fabūmi."

The Commissioners : " What is that message ? "

Ọdẹjayi : " That the Balogun has sent to the Seriki as well as the Ọwa to beg the Ifẹs, and he asks Fabūmi also to beg the Ifẹs, and that he will put matters straight. All their forefathers came from Ifẹ and so Ifẹ must not be a desolate place."

The messenger said he would deliver his message to the Ibadan chiefs that afternoon, and let us know their intentions as soon as possible.

The next morning the messenger came to tell us that he had delivered the message to the Ibadan chiefs at a meeting the previous evening, and they had said they were ready to go when the allies on the other side went, but not before.

The messenger said he had seen one of the Ibadan chiefs that morning who had said they were going to have another meeting to consider again the Balogun's message.

On the 29th a messenger arrived from Chief Ogedemgbe with a letter in which he said, if the Modakẹkẹs did not leave their town he would attack the Ibadans at Ikirun.

It seems Chief Ogdemgbe sent the messenger whom the Balogun had sent to him back to Ikirun, with a message that he could not agree to the Balogun's proposal to reconcile the Ifẹs and Modakẹkẹs and let the latter remain in their town, and asking the Balogun to send any answer he might have to make direct to us so as to save time.

U

On the 30th we sent for the Balogun's messenger who came with Mr. Johnson, and learnt from him that the Ibadan Chiefs said they could not leave until matters were settled, or in other words, that they had decided to disobey the Balogun's order to quit Modakẹkẹ at once.

We now came to the conclusion that it was useless our wasting any more time in endeavouring to see the treaty carried out, and accordingly addressed a letter to the Modakẹkẹ authorities which was read to them by Mr. Johnson on the 1st of November charging them with having broken the treaty and holding them primarily responsible for any complication which might arise through their default.

We had twice since our arrival at Ifẹ-Modakẹkẹ sent word to the Ogunsua through Mr. Johnson that we proposed to visit him, but each time he had begged to be excused from receiving us.[1]

We had a final interview with the Ifẹs on the 1st November and impressed upon them that neither they nor their allies should do anything to provoke a renewal of hostilities but await the action of the Balogun of Ibadan to whom and also to Chief Ogedemgbe, we were sending particulars of the situation.

They all said they had no wish to recommence the war, and would do what they could to keep the peace.

Mr. Johnson told us that the Modakẹkẹs and Ibadans had also expressed themselves as most strongly averse to more fighting.

We addressed letters to Chief Ogedemgbe and the Ọwa, and the Ekiti kings, telling them of our intention to return to Lagos, and pointing out to them that every effort should yet be made to have matters settled peaceably, and that they should afford the Ibadan authorities every opportunity of carrying out their part of the treaty. We also addressed a letter to the Balogun of Ibadan impressing upon him that if the Ibadan authorities did not at once actually withdraw their contingents from Modakẹkẹ, and fulfil their obligations under the 5th clause of the ratification of the treaty, they would be equally guilty with the Modakẹkẹs of a breach of faith with the Governor of Lagos, and all the signatories of the treaty, and be held responsible

---

[1] Which is a great pity; for had the commissioners done so, they would possibly have been impressed with the size of Modakẹkẹ, a town of over 60,000 inhabitants and the practical difficulties in the carrying out of their proposals. Ipetumodu did not contain more than 10,000; and how can 10,000 accommodate 60,000?—Ed.

should war ensue in consequence of their failure to abide by their pledges.

This letter we entrusted to the Rev. S. Johnson to take to Ikirun, and he was to leave Modakẹkẹ on the 3rd November, and should reach the Balogun at latest in four days after.

We left Ifẹ-Modakẹkẹ on the morning of the 2nd November for Ode Ondo.

While we were at Ifẹ-Modakẹkẹ, and especially towards the end of the time, there were constant communications between the opposite camps, and we were asked by Akintọla the leading Ibadan chief, and by Fabũmi to allow them to meet in our presence with a view to the withdrawal of the respective allies of the Ifẹs and Modakẹkẹs.

This we declined to do, as we did not consider it consistent with the object of our mission : but we informed Fabũmi that if he and Akintọla choose to meet, we had no objection to their doing so, and if they came to an arrangement between themselves, that was their concern.

> H. HIGGINS ⎱ *Special Commissioners.*
> OLIVER SMITH ⎰

After the Commissioners had gone, Fabũmi said to the envoys from the ALÂFIN of Ọyọ, the Awujalẹ of Ijẹbu, and the Balogun of Ibadan, that if the white men could not wait to settle their differences, they should wait to accomplish what they had begun, and to bring matters to a final issue. He asked them to summon the Ibadan chiefs with Akintọla at their head for a conference. This was done, and all the Ibadan chiefs went out but had not the confidence to go unarmed as far as the Commissioners' camp, where they used to meet the Ifẹ chiefs when the Commissioners were there. They went half-way and sent word to Fabũmi to say they had come. Fabũmi however could not prevail upon the Ifẹ chiefs to meet them for a conference, hence he sent word to say that he would meet with the Ifẹ chiefs at a conference and would let them know the result.

On the 3rd November Fabũmi went to Ayimọrọ's camp and brought pressure to bear upon him that under no circumstance should they provoke a fight and recommence hostilities with the Ibadans and Modakẹkẹs. On his return, he told Ọba-kosetan that he had secured the promise of Ayimọrọ upon good faith that the Modakẹkẹs should not be kidnapped or provoked to a fight and that the armistice should continue.

The Ibadan chiefs sent a message to Fabũmi that a sensible messenger should be sent from each of the three camps to them, *viz.*, the Ifẹ's, Ayimọrọ's and Ogunṣigun's camps, and they would tell them their minds.

Fabūmi alone took the initiative, and he sent back to say that unless he visited each of these camps in person and prevailed upon the chiefs to send each a messenger, they would never do so. He also suggested that the free intercommunication between them should continue, for if communication be interrupted there would soon be another difficulty.

The envoys were not allowed to leave Modakẹkẹ for about a month after the Commissioners had gone, and as the result of their negotiations, the Ibadan contingent at Modakẹkẹ, as well as Fabūmi and the Ijẹṣa contingents with the exception of Ayimọrọ (Ijẹṣa) and Ogunṣigun (Ijẹbu) left their respective allies the same day ; the Ibadan contingent leaving for Ikirun to join their brethren and Fabūmi for Mẹsin Ipole to join Ogedemgbe, and subsequently for Mẹsin-Ọlọja-Oke his home.

The Ifẹs however remained in their camp, refusing to go home (as yet) and rebuild their city, but there was no resumption of hostilities.

CHAPTER XXXI

DISTURBANCE IN EVERY PART OF THE COUNTRY

§ 1. ILORIN INTRIGUES AND THE FALL OF OFA

We have seen above how anxious Ogedemgbe was about the war going on at Ofa, how he wished the Commissioners to include this in their efforts, being as it were a part of the same war. He tried to induce them to send a messenger with his own, and one from the Balogun of Ibadan to prevail upon Kàràrà the Ilorin Generalissimo to accept terms of peace ; but the Commissioners declined to do so. They however approved of their sending their own messengers if they so wished. Seriki Ogedemgbe and the Balogun of Ibadan agreed to ask Lasebikan the head of the Ilorin contingent with the Ekitis to send also with them, but he backed out of this obligation. It appeared that Seriki Ogedemgbe had some communications with Kàràrà, urging him to the acceptance of peace, and had not succeeded. He was also very anxious about the Ijesa contingent in the Ilorin camp. He sent to tell Kàràrà that matters had been settled at Kiriji, and that if he would let the Ekitis with him leave his camp, he would let the Ilorins with him leave Oke Mesin. The following was the reply returned by the wily Kàràrà : " Let my men perish with you, and let your men perish with me." Showing that the astute Gambari knew what he was about when he made the arrangement. The fact was that the Ilorins had no grievance which could be settled like that of the Ekitis, they were simply on conquest bent.

Kàràrà had good reasons to be so haughty and implacable. He was on bad terms with his king at home, and embarked on this war against his strong behest, and to return to Ilorin otherwise than as a victor might cost him his life. Hence all negotiations with him proved abortive ; he was determined to take Ofa either by force of arms or by stratagem.

Shortly after the firing of the camp at Kiriji, the Seriki Ogedemgbe sent to assure the Balogun of Ibadan that they wished peace to be made at Ofa also, so that they might withdraw their contingent from the Ilorin camp, and that the Ibadans should do nothing to prevent this being done. The Balogun sent back to say he also wished for peace there so that he might recall his men, Ofa would be restored to the Ilorins provided they might promise not to sack the city. They (the Ibadans) would await the result of the efforts of the Ijẹṣa and Ekiti kings' mediation with the Ilọrins, and should Kàràrà refuse to let the men quit his camp, the Ibadans would be quite ready to let them pass safely through their ranks to Ọfa, and thence safely to their homes without a calabash or a pot being broken. Having sworn friendship to him he would never go back on his word. As the result of the messages sent to him by Seriki Ogedemgbe Kàràrà sent to the Ibadan war chiefs to say that the Ibadans should withdraw their contingent from Ọfa, and must not fear any molestation from the Ilọrins.

The messengers arrived at Ikirun on the 9th of November, 1886. The Ibadans considered it puerile to demand that the defensive should withdraw from a beleaguered city before the offensive, and therefore replied as follows : " Before we remove a single man Kàràrà should decamp first, and if he refuse to do so, let him await us. And why should he ask us to withdraw our forces when he is still encamped against Ọfa ? When Ali his father encamped against Ọtùn, and we sent Ajayi Jegede to defend that city some years ago and peace was made between us, was it not Ali his father that decamped first ? So it should be in this case also."

The messengers however were well treated ; the Balogun entertained them with two large calabashes full of Iyán (pounded yam), a potful of meat, and also gave them ten heads of cowries and a goat.

When this strong message was delivered to Kàràrà he opened a secret communication with one Lagbẹja, one of the powerful chiefs who re-inforced Ọfa. Lagbẹja was carrying on this communication without informing his brother chiefs in the camp, and when this was found out they all set against him, and the quarrel was so hot that Lagbẹja had to escape from the camp over the walls and took refuge in the town of Ọfa.

The news of this disunion among the re-inforcement alarmed the Balogun and the other war chiefs at Ikirun ; they immediately despatched one Oyesunle to reconcile them, and Lagbẹja returned to his post.

On the very night of his return, two messengers from the Ilọrin camp came to ask for an interview with him. He declined the interview for obvious reasons, but the other chiefs hearing this, advised him to grant the interview, and let them hear what the envoys had to say. He was invited to the Ilọrin camp for peace negotiation.

Oyesunle the Balogun's messenger was deputed to conduct the negotiation. He was the chief envoy, and each of the principal war chiefs sent a man with him. Thus he visited the Ilọrin camp, and proceeded to Ilọrin city for an interview with the Emir.

The Emir of Ilọrin received the messengers graciously, and before granting an interview he treated them with *cold water, bananas, honey,* and *sugar* ; saying " As sweet and refreshing as these are, so I wish the country to be."

The following was the message sent by the Emir to the Ibadan chiefs : " Ọfa has always been mine, the royal gift of my father to me, and hence I do not wish it to be destroyed. My request is that the Ibadans should treat me as a King, and to let my words come to pass. They should recall their army first, and I shall recall mine." He presented the messengers with 13 gowns (one to each man), fed them sumptuously, and gave them some cowries.

The Ilọrin Emir also sent his own messengers to the Balogun, about 17 of them, all on horseback : and he also treated them with similar generosity ; they were sent back with a similar message as the one they brought, asking the Emir to withdraw his attacking force, and they would withdraw the defending one.

The Ibadans were quite alive to the Ilọrin intrigues.

Kàràrà in the meantime never ceased to breathe out vengeance against Ọfa, and to speak disparagingly of the Balogun of Ibadan : he was often heard to say, " And who else is called Balogun besides myself ? " However, there was an armistice till the month of June, 1887, when the ALÂFIN as a part of his engagement in the Treaty, and at the request of his subjects, took the negotiation in hand. His Majesty sent Ọbajuwọn, one of his chief Ilaris, who went to the Ilọrin camp in a style befitting his rank. A tumult arose in the Ilọrin camp when he entered there with his drum. He was set upon by the Gambari faction, and his drum was ripped with a knife ! The Yoruba element in the camp immediately rushed around him to prevent violence being done to his person, and effected his safe return to Ọfa. Ọbajuwọn arrived home on the 30th June, 1887. Thus failed the negotiation of peace at Ọfa, and hostilities were recommenced afresh.

All prospects of peace appeared very dark and cloudy once more, the war being vigorously prosecuted at Ọfa, and it was under consideration at Ikirun whether the army at Ọfa should be re-inforced or not. The Ibadan senior chiefs were reluctant to do so, lest the conflict between themselves and Ogedemgbe be renewed, and the scene of war be but changed from Kiriji to Ọfa and Ikirun, for Ogedemgbe had not disbanded his forces.

The war chiefs had once a stormy meeting at Ikirun on this subject, when Chief Ẹnimowu (son-in-law to the famous Basọrun Ogunmọla) in the heat of passion volunteered to go to the relief of Ọfa if the leaders would not move. Without obtaining any sanction he left the meeting in a rage to prepare for Ọfa.   Kongi his nephew and heir to the house of Ogunmọla being then but a youth volunteered to go with him, as all the members of the house must go.   Ẹnimowu encamped at Ẹrin, a small town a few miles from Ọfa where he was of great help in provisioning the beleaguered city.

Unfortunately this new re-inforcement suffered a disaster so great as to be compared to none but that in which his brother-in-law the late Ilọri the Osi was taken alive at the Jalumi war.

The Ilọrin horsemen were in the habit of kidnapping the caravans between Ọfa and Ẹrin bringing in provisions.   On this occasion Ẹnimowu attacked the kidnappers, and in a short time put them to flight, and pursued them rather too far.   One notable Ilọrin horseman, Nasamu by name, but surnamed " Gata-ikoko " (*i.e.*, a devouring wolf, from his great fondness for meat) in the chase easily out-distanced his pursuers, and with a few choice horsemen he made a wide detour and re-appeared at the rear of their pursuers !   The alarm was soon given at the rear.   The pursued had now become the pursuers.   Great was the havoc wrought by the Ilọrins with their spears on the panic-stricken pursuers now taken in the rear.   Ẹnimowu, the leader of the expedition, was found sitting on a keg of powder fanning himself after the chase, his horse led to be watered, and he congratulating himself that he had given a good account of the enemy, when suddenly the enemy burst upon him from the rear, and there he was taken alive with other illustrious war chiefs, *viz.*, Salakọ, the heir and successor of the late Aijẹnku, Winkunle, late Tubọsun's son, Malade, son of the late Seriki Ọdunjọ, and others of lesser note.   Salakọ refused to to go with them as a prisoner of war, and was killed on the spot ; the rest were taken to Ilọrin and were there treated as respectable prisoners of war.

Young Kongi was so terrified at the news of this disaster that he waited no longer at Ẹrin but fled precipitately back to Ikirun. For this abject cowardice he was cold-shouldered by everyone of the chiefs and forbidden to attend their councils.   He was fined heavily for this before he was allowed to re-occupy his former position, but all the same he subsequently lost the title that would have been his on their return home.

No sympathy was expressed for Ẹnimowu because of the arrogant manner he volunteered for the war, as if all the rest were cowards.

Whilst all this was going on, reports from time to time reached the Ibadans of the disaffection existing at Ọfa itself, a portion of the people were in league with the Ilọrins, and their messengers had several times been caught.   These belonged to the party who would not have Adegboye the present Ọlọfa as their king, for the only reason that he was the son of the last king.   They held that the son should not succeed the father at once, an uncle or elderly cousin should come between.   Adegboye did not insist on his right, but was determined to retire from the scene with all his belongings.   The case was reported to the Ibadan chiefs and the Are—then living—said to the opposing party, " With an enemy at your gates can you afford to ignore this young prince?   Whose are the guns, the kegs of powder, and other ammunition you are using to fight the foe ?   If he should retire with arms and ammunition belonging to him what will be your prospects ? "   Then they reluctantly yielded to Adegboye succeeding his father.   They were now unremitting in their intrigues against him.

The Ibadan chiefs being apprehensive of a great act of treachery which might overwhelm their men were, for this reason, no longer disposed to sacrifice the lives of any more of their men after the loss of Ẹnimowu.   They were determined therefore to withdraw their army from Ọfa.

Apparently going to re-inforce Ọfa in strength and avenge Ẹnimowu, the whole of the war chiefs except the Balogun marched out for Ọfa with orders secretly to withdraw the Ibadan contingent, the Ọlọfa, and those in sympathy with the Ibadans.   They halted near Ẹrin and sent for those to be rescued at dead of night.

The Ọlọfa on leaving home, in order to ward off suspicion, and prevent a panic, ordered his horse to be saddled and left in charge of a page outside in front of the palace, some of his wives also were left sitting there and there was a bright light burning, while he escaped by a back door with the rest of his wives, children, and favourite servants.   Till he was clean gone none but his body-guard knew of it.   He joined the Ibadan relief party and all arrived safely at Ikirun.

The Ọlọfa was the head of all the provincial kings of the Ibọlọ district between Ilọrin and Iwo.   He was assigned a portion of land between Osogbo and Ẹdẹ, where he founded a new town called Ọfa-tẹdo, and there he resided till the end of the war.

Next morning when it was known all over the city that the Ibadans had gone and the Ọlọfa with them, those hitherto in favour of the Ilọrins put leaves on their heads, and went dancing to the Ilọrin camp and singing :

> " Awa kò ṣe ti Ibadan mọ o,
>   T'onirugbọn l'a o ṣe."

> (" No more are we for the Ibadans,
>   With the long-bearded our lot we've cast.")

Thus they came and prostrated before Kàràrà. It was said that he asked them, " Have the Ibadans gone ? "—" Yes, they have gone." He then added, " Very well, you can go home, I will pay you a visit shortly."

After breakfast Kàràrà rode up to Ọfa with his army, and took his seat at the palace gates. His first act was to despatch a body of horsemen to occupy each of the gates of the city so as to allow no exit from any. He next summoned him all the remaining Ọfa chiefs and the influential men of the city to be brought before him ; they came with leaves on their heads as a token of sub- mission. He then said to them, " You now say you are all on my side, if that be so, why is it you held out so long against me, and did not open your gates secretly for my troops to enter ? You know now that the Ibadans have gone then you say you declare yourselves for me." And when they lay prostrate before him he coolly gave the order, " Ẹ maha dumbu[1] wọn " (" Slaughter them away.") Thereupon followed the process; a man appeared with a butcher's knife in hand, and another with a basin of water. Seizing these prostrate forms one by one, they were forcibly held down, with head and neck raised and the throat coolly cut, and the blood thoroughly drained and the corpse thrown down. This done, the knife was washed in the basin of water—after the manner of slaughtering animals, and then they proceeded to the second, and third, and so on till they had slaughtered the whole of them ! Then he ordered the shade trees of the market place to be cut down as a sign of victory, and the city to be sacked, the inhabitants (such as were left) to be made prisoners. Thus Ọfa was taken.

The Consequences of the Fall of Ọfa.—When all the towns in the vicinity heard that the Ibadans were gone, and a part of Ọfa with them, knowing what the consequences would be, they all were deserted, and the people went with the Ibadans to Ikirun, *viz.*, Ẹrin, Ijabẹ, Okuku, Igbayi, Ọyán, Iba, Ekusa, Okuwà, Agboyè, Ori, and Asi.

Inisa alone was not deserted, not being far from Ikirun but within a short time the Ilọrin horse was at its gates.

The Ilọrins, who promised so faithfully that if the Ibadan contingent were withdrawn from Ọfa they would decamp, now sent word to the Ibadans to say, " Ọru yin nmu wa ni Ikirun " (" We are feeling the inconvenience of your body-heat at Ikirun "). Meaning that they should withdraw from Ikirun also. Inisa had to be strongly re-inforced, and for a long time a desultory warfare between the Ibadans and Ilọrins was carried on there. The

---

[1] *Dumbu* is the word used for slaughtering animals for sacrifice.

Ilọrins could not leave their camp at Yanayo to encamp against Inisa or Ikirun as before, and the Ibadans did not consider it safe to go against them at Yanayo, where they would be exposed on all sides to the cavalry attack. The strength of the Ilọrins lay in their horses, and they could come from a day's journey to attack Inisa or Ikirun, usually by breaking their journey half-way overnight and give battle next morning. If defeated, they were able to retreat in good order : taught by former experience, the Ibadans did not venture to pursue horsemen far from their base. This continued for a good while.

In course of time the Ilọrin horse kept hovering constantly between Ikirun and Inisa as if to cut off communication between the two places, about six or eight miles apart ; the war chiefs therefore considered it more prudent to concentrate their forces at Ikirun in order to prevent a surprise, and therefore they with-drew Babalọla who was stationed there. Ikirun once more became the scene of conflict, the Ilọrins with their horses paying surprise visits now and then. The Ibadan scouts and outposts being ever on the alert to report their approach the so-called battles now dwindled into occasional skirmishes for half a day, and these few and far between. Taught by Jalumi, the Ilọrins would not encamp against Ikirun, and from the experience of Ẹnimowu the Ibadans would not go after them in the plain at Yanayo.

§ 2. Revolutionary Movements at Ijẹbu

The Ijẹbus at this time were alarmed at the quiet changes going on in the country. Traders and others from the interior were finding their way down to the coast through their country and *vice versa.* The traditional saying, " Ijẹbu Ode, Ajeji ko wọ " (Ijẹbu Ode, no alien to enter) was in danger of being abolished, and they were determined to put a stop to it. The blame for this was laid upon the Awujalẹ and on Nọfọwọkan the Balogun for entering into friendship with the white men and befriending Ọyọs (that is for the part they had taken hitherto towards the restoration of peace in the interior). They begrudged the Balogun his influence with the Ọyọs, and therefore recalled him home from Orù and a civil title was given him. They forced the king to pass a law forbidding Ọyọs to reach Ijẹbu Ode, much less to pass through it to Lagos; all intercourse for merchandise was to be carried on at Orù.

The younger Ijẹbus were instigated to take the enforcement of the law in hand, and some of them went further and even clamoured for the death of the king.

Their King exonerated himself from their charges by arguing with them thus : " Since we have had a closer intercourse with the Ọyọs during the late negotiations for peace—a peace clamoured for and desired by yourselves—you Ijẹbus have had many of their daughters to be your wives, and they have had children for you. Is it not natural for the parents of these women to visit their daughters and grandchildren ? How can you sever the ties of relationship by preventing brothers from visiting their sisters, and parents their children ? If you will be just and fair, send these women back home with the children born to you, then there will be no occasion for any outsiders to enter your country." The law was made so stringent that Prince Adekọya, the Awujalẹ's eldest son went to the Rẹmọ district which had hitherto been free to caravans both ways and took up his station at Ode seizing all Lagos traders passing up or going down. The writer, together with the Rev. D. Olubi of Ibadan, on their way to Lagos met him there on Easter Tuesday, 1887, but just escaped him on their return, having visited other villages for the same purpose.

Previously to their passing down, a son of the reverend gentleman on his way from Lagos to Ibadan had no end of trouble with him ; he had in his custody a goodly number of traders from the interior and from the coast whose goods had been seized and forwarded to Ijẹbu Ode and themselves loaded with chains ! This young man was needlessly detained by the prince, and when he grew desperate he got into a rage and frightened the prince by firing a walking-stick gun into the air, just to show what he could do. This novel sight disposed the prince to let him pass on homewards.

His father when passing down took the opportunity to speak to Prince Adekọya, explaining to him the difference between missionaries and traders, and thus paved a way for the mission's mail-man between Lagos and Ibadan by that route.

Soon after their return home from Lagos, news reached the writer at Ọyọ by one of Balogun Nọfọwọkan's sons that the writer had been declared by the Awujalẹ an outlaw in any of the Ijẹbu provinces, whether of Ode, Igbo, or Rẹmọ. He could be killed by anyone if found in any of these provinces. The crimes alleged against him were these :—

1. That he was no longer on the side of peace, but for the continuation of the war.

2. That he was building a house for the ALÂFIN, whom he knew to be not favourable to peace.

3. That he was supplying the ALÂFIN with arms of precision and ammunition for the Ilọrins in order to enable them to wage a successful war against the Ibadans.

The apparent foundation of these baseless charges was the appointment of the writer by the C.M.S. to take charge of their mission at Ọyọ and of his building a church and a vicarage there.

The Awujalẹ gave a ready credence to this report because of the malicious feeling existing in him already against the writer because the Commissioners of 1886 were not prevailed upon by him to kill Ogunṣigun the Seriki of Ijẹbu Igbo, and to disperse his troops at Isọya according to his order.

The writer seized the first opportunity that presented itself of the Rev. W. B. George, Wesleyan minister going down to Lagos *via* Ijẹbu to request him to deny these reports both to the Balogun and to the Awujalẹ as utterly false and unfounded.

Early in March, 1888, having another occasion to visit Lagos instead of avoiding the Awujalẹ by finding another route, he thought it best to face the difficulty at once and clear himself of these false charges. Accordingly on his arrival at Orù, by the advice of Tunubi, son of the Balogun and grandson of the Awujalẹ by his eldest daughter, the writer sent to apprise the Balogun of his arrival at Orù, and of his intention to proceed forward. The Balogun sent to say he could come on to Ijẹbu Ode, but not until dusk.

Meanwhile the Balogun was pleading his cause with the Awujalẹ, after sending to him about six times to no good effect he had to go in person and urge the claims of the writer, reminding him of all he had undergone as the Governor's messenger on behalf of peace since 1886, and begged the King to see him and hear from his own mouth a true explanation of the charges alleged against him. After two days the Awujalẹ relented and agreed to see him. The interview however was not in the day but about 8 p.m. " Ajọṣẹ " (*i.e.*, Johnson) said the Awujalẹ, " Is that you ? I heard that you are no more for peace but have joined the ALÂFIN in his intrigues." " No, sir," was the reply. " My going to Ọyọ to reside was not of my own choice, but as an obedient servant I went where I was sent. I am like a rod in the hands of my masters, and wherever I am flung there I must be. Who am I to have a voice of my own in these great political matters ? My calling is of a different kind and not political." The King replied, " Don't you say so ; your words have gained the ears of kings and mighty warriors lately, so you cannot think so meanly of yourself. I was so angry with you that I never intended to see your face any more, but thanks to the Balogun who vigorously pleaded your cause." The writer was allowed to proceed to Lagos, but he had to be accompanied by two escorts from the Balogun.

That the King was not quite satisfied with the above explanation was evident by his remonstrance with the writer on his returning from Lagos on the 26th of May following. " Ajose," said he, " the whole Ijebu nation love and respect you, but you will lose that love and respect if you do not reconsider your appointment to Oyo."

Prince Adekoya continued his blockade of the Remo district for a long time, and many valuable lives perished and much property was confiscated in that district ; both persons and effects were transferred to Ijebu Ode and nothing more heard of them, most of the persons being killed or sold far away. A Brazilian freedman who had acquired some substance in his land of exile was returning to his native town of Iwo. He happened to meet with Adekoya here, and was seized by him with all his goods and personal belongings, and sent to Ijebu Ode. The goods were said to be worth over £800, including cash : among them was a large red silk damask umbrella with tassels all round intended for his King, the Oluiwo. The Ijebu King in council in consideration of his heavy losses, granted the man his freedom. · They told him he could go. But the unfortunate man, overcome with grief and despair groaned and said, " What is life worth to me now ? I have committed no crime, I have been utterly ruined. No prospect before me now but utter destitution and beggary ! Death is preferable." "All right," said the Awujale, " we will oblige you in this." He then gave the order " E lo ipo o " (Go and kill him). In a few minutes his head was off his shoulders !

Not content with watching his own country the Awujale also sent an Agurin to the Ibadans with strict orders to arrest anyone in European dress, white or black, and if he is such as cannot be dealt with they should at any rate send him back to Lagos. An attempt was made thus to turn the writer back to Lagos from the very gate of Ibadan, but he left his luggage with them at the town gate and galloped into the town to Awonimesin, the Chief Agurin, his former colleague in his travelling up and down on the peace negotiations in 1886 : he on seeing him sent orders that he should be allowed to enter the town in peace. The Rev. T. Harding, the European Superintendent of the C.M.S. Missions, had to pass through Ijebu to the interior, and was compelled to pay the sum of £4 before he was allowed to pass in 1889, and that was only because he at that time had his home in the interior.

Thus the Ijebus were trying to prevent the opening up of the country.

It should be made clear, however, that the motives actuating the Ijebus to these proceedings, mistaken though they be, were not only the determination of being the middle men between the coast and the interior, but also (as they thought) in order to prevent the country from being taken by white men. A report of what was called, " The scramble for Africa," then going on reached them in one form or another, and they were but safe-guarding the national interests.

§ 2. "A MILD TREATY"

About the month of May, 1888, all Lagos was startled by the report that the emissaries of the French from Porto Novo had reached Abẹokuta, and that they concluded a treaty with the three leading chiefs, Ogundeyi, Onlado, and the Jaguna of Igbein (Ogundipẹ being dead) giving them large presents, and promising them a profitable trade, and the construction of a line of railway from Porto Novo to Abẹokuta. Advantage was taken of the constant misunderstandings and frictions between the Lagos Government and the Ẹgbas shown by the frequent blockading of the river and land route by the Ẹgbas, and the stopping of all trade with Lagos.

The situation was saved for the British Government by the Ẹgba educated natives (*i.e.* Sierra Leoneans whose fathers were of Ẹgba origin) of Lagos, who, as soon as they heard the report, held a meeting among themselves without delay, and sent a deputation to Abẹokuta to enquire from the chiefs how far the report was true. The deputation returned to Lagos on Whit Tuesday, May 22nd, 1888, with a confirmation of the rumour; however, the chiefs were said to have denied signing any treaty. Their language, which was regarded as not quite satisfactory, was to this effect :—

" We thank you for the solicitations you have manifested for your fatherland. You have done well in that, though living out of home, you have not forgotten the homeland and its interests. You call yourselves our children, but what have we, your parents, ever received from you ? But immediately you heard that others have made us a few presents, you hastened to show us the danger lurking in their gifts. Some of you were born abroad and never made our acquaintance until now, very singular way indeed of showing love and interest towards one's fatherland.

" Have you not observed the short weights and the short lengths in the folded cloths ? Have you not noticed that the English cloths contain increasingly more chalk than cotton fibres, the liquor diluted, the price of our produce always falling and never rising ? What have you done to help us in these things to make our labour more remunerative ?   Nothing.   It strikes us that you only concerned yourselves in competing with the white men to make your own profits out of us.   We have been trading with the English for years, and the result is like an operation on the tread-mill, always on the move but remaining where we were with a tendency to a backward motion in spite of efforts continually put forth.   But no sooner we attempt to try for a profitable trade with another people than you hasten to warn us of the danger that lies therein.   We thank you for your anxious care, but neither to the French nor to the English are we giving our country."

Not satisfied with the character of the report of the deputation, the leading members of the educated Ẹgbas of Lagos themselves went up to interview the chiefs, and warned them of the danger they were running of placing themselves between the upper and nether millstones of two European powers.   What really passed between them in this interview was not made known, but the chiefs were said to have received them well, and assured them that they were not giving the country to anyone.   Nothing further was heard of the movement, and thus the situation was saved.

When it was known that the Ẹgbas claimed as far as Ebute Mẹta as their territory, surely no British officer at Lagos could view this movement with indifference.   The very existence of Lagos would be at the mercy of the power predominant at Abẹokuta.

Baulked at Abẹokuta, rumour had it that the French emissaries were proceeding to Ọyọ to establish friendly relations with the ALÂFIN.

As it was about this time the overlapping of interests in the scrambling had begun, and it was said to be laid down by the French that he who possessed the capital had the right to the rest of the country, the Governor of Lagos thereupon sent the writer—who happened to be at Lagos at the time—with a letter and a Treaty to the ALÂFIN of Ọyọ as the Suzerain of Yoruba-land, which he termed " A Mild Treaty."

Government House, Lagos,
May 23rd, 1888.

No. 115/77.

KING,—I received with much pleasure your letter of the 20th February last, and beg to thank you for the present of two cloths of the country, any manufacture of which interests me indeed.

2. To show my esteem to you and my appreciation of the position you occupy I have asked the Rev. S. Johnson, who

returns to his ministerial duties, to salute you and your people with my compliments and respect ; and to wish well to you and yours.

3. As you know, and every Yoruba knows, people to the west and to the north are not Yoruba ; they differ in feelings and object from Yorubas. You will have doubtless learnt I always aim at making all Yoruba-speaking peoples one in heart as they are in tongue. Towards such unity I attach much importance to a definite and permanent understanding between these Yoruba-speaking peoples, and this colony which is mainly inhabited by Yorubas. And where should I look first for sympathy and support but to Adeyẹmi, the ALÂFIN of Ọyọ the titular King of all Yoruba ?

4. Between you and the Governor of the Queen's Colony of Lagos there should be ever friendship, goodwill which no foreign interference should be allowed to influence or disturb.

5. Yoruba-land was comprised traditionally as regards its corners a few years ago of Yoruba proper, Ẹgba, Ketu and Ijẹbu. Where is Ketu now ? And from what direction was it destroyed ?

6. Without the entertainment of the least desire to meddle with the government of such kingdoms as Yoruba, Ẹgba, or Ijẹbu, and with the assurance that not one yard of land is coveted by me, in feeling and sympathy for Yoruba union I desire that Lagos take the place of Ketu as the fourth corner.

7. If the accompanying document be agreeable to you, and embodies your wishes, sign it and return it to me. If your relations with the country to the north of yours be such as to admit of your persuading them what is to their interest, I would be glad to find you can get its people to sign a paper similar to the one I propose to yourself.

8. Look what has been done with considerable expense already by Her Majesty's Government for the Yoruba-speaking countries in connection with the settlement among them in 1886 of what had been known as the Interior War, in which you took such action as should when you look back upon it swell your heart with pride, and your country with gratitude.

9. I am anxious to hear of large markets re-established between Ọyọ Ogbomọsọ, Ilọrin, Abẹokuta and Ijẹbu as they existed in the past, and safe roads. How this can best be done I will be glad to hear from you.

10. You will be at liberty to send your accredited messengers to me should you desire to have a longer conversation than can well be put within the compass of an ordinary letter.

11. I venture to send you five pounds as a small present. Wishing you and all your people every good wish.

I am, King,

Your good friend,

ALFRED C. MOLONEY, <i>Governor.</i></div>

The Treaty.

Treaty between Adeyẹmi, ALÁFIN of Ọyọ, and Head of Yoruba-land, and Her Majesty, Queen of Great Britain and Ireland.

I, ADẸYEMI, ALÁFIN of Ọyọ, and Head of Yoruba-land, the four corners of which are and have been from time immemorial known as Ẹgba, Ketu, Jẹbu, and Ọyọ, embracing within its area that inhabited by all Yoruba-speaking peoples, being desirous of entering into, and maintaining for ever, friendly relations with the subjects of Her Majesty, the Queen of Great Britain and Ireland, and of developing the resources of Yoruba by means of legitimate trade with the subjects of Her Majesty and those under her protection or who may hereafter come under her protection, and in gratitude for what the Queen has at so much expense and risk to life done from time to time for my country, have this day at the city of Ọyọ in the presence of those who have hereunto subscribed their names as witnesses declared my intention of abiding by the following articles :—

1. From henceforth there should be peace and friendship between the subjects of Her Majesty the Queen, and those under her protection, and the ALÁFIN of Ọyọ and King of Yoruba-land and his people, and all other peoples over whom he has authority and influence.

2. The subjects of the Queen may always trade freely with the people of Ọyọ, and the Yoruba-speaking countries in every article they may wish to buy and sell, in all towns, rivers, creeks, waters, markets and places within territories known as Yoruba : and I, Adeyẹmi, pledge myself to show no favour and to give no privilege to the traders or people of other countries which I do not give or show to those of the Queen.

3. British subjects and others under the Queen's protection

are to have the first consideration in all trade transactions with my peoples.

4. No tolls, duties, fees, imposts, or charges shall be charged or levied upon the person or property of any British subject or other person under Her Majesty's protection other than and beyond that or those which are customary and reasonable, or may from time to time be agreed upon to be so levied or charged by the Governor of Lagos and myself.

5. I will not allow any disputes that may arise between people frequenting or visiting the markets in my territory to interfere with or stop the markets ; and all differences or disputes that may arise other than trade disputes between my peoples and those of other nations and tribes visiting the markets shall be adjusted by me or referred for adjustment and settlement to the decision of an arbitrator appointed by the Governor of Lagos, and the decision and award of such arbitrator shall be finally conclusive.

6. I engage as far as in me lies to bring about new markets between the Ọyọs and the other Yoruba-speaking peoples, to promote the enlargement of existing ones, and to keep open all the roads through my kingdom to the Niger, and towards the coast.

7. It is hereby further agreed that no cession of territory and no other Treaty or Agreement shall be made by me other than the one I have now made without the full understanding and consent of the Governor for the time being of the said Colony of Lagos.

8. In consideration of the faithful observance of the foregoing Articles of the Agreement the Government of Lagos will make unto me a yearly dash to the value of 200 (two hundred) bags of cowries, but such dash may upon breach or neglect of all or any one or more of the provisions of the Agreement and at the discretion of the Governor of the Colony of Lagos be altogether withdrawn or suspended.

9. Provided always that the terms of this Agreement be subject to the approval of Her Majesty.

Signed and sealed at Ọyọ this 23rd day of July, 1888.

ADẸYEMI, ALÂFIN OF ỌYỌ ✕ (his mark).

In the presence of
SAMUEL JOHNSON, *Clerk in Holy Orders.*
WILLIAM MỌSẸRI, *Scripture Reader.*

Ratification of the above Treaty.

Government House, Lagos,
June 16th, 1890.

No. 255/142.

KING,—I have the pleasure of informing you that Her Majesty the Queen of England has been graciously pleased to ratify and confirm the Treaty between yourself and Her Majesty which you signed on the 23rd July, 1888, and which subject to Her Majesty's approval I subsequently signed on Her Majesty's behalf.

2. I am glad to think that the Treaty will tend to draw the people of this Colony and your subjects closer together. Both belong to the Yoruba race, and it is but natural that there should be peace, friendship and commerce between them.

3. It will be my duty in future under the Treaty to continue to pay to you as opportunities offer an annual present of 200 bags of cowries, subject always to the performance by you of your own obligations under the Treaty.

4. I forward to you £31 5s. in cash which represents what will become due to you by the 23rd prox.

5. I write to you in the full hope and expectation that you will not only remember, but faithfully and zealously fulfil all your engagements under the Treaty, and especially those relating to the increasing of the markets and the opening of new roads.

I am, King,
Your friend,
ALFRED MOLONEY,
Governor and Commander-in-Chief
of the Colony of Lagos.

§4. THE EXPLOITS OF ẸSAN AND THE CONTROVERSY THEREUPON.

In the year 1888 negotiation was set on foot through the instrumentality of the Oluiwo, one of the oldest and most venerable of the provincial kings in the Epo division, who was very much anxious for the restoration of peace in the country.

He prevailed upon the ALÂFIN to appoint a messenger to head those of the principal provincial kings of Yoruba forming a deputation to negotiate peace with Ilọrin. The ALÂFIN did not object but his appointee was a private man and not an Ilari which augured ill for the embassy, and betrayed the actual feelings of His Majesty on the subject.

These messengers went by Ogbomọsọ. On reaching Ọbaniñsunwa, the last tollgate to Ilọrin, they were met by the

Emir of Ilọrin's messenger who bade them halt there till further orders.

They were detained there for a week whilst private messages passed between Ilọrin and the Ilọrin camp.

Counting much upon the floating report of an august embassy like this, hundreds of traders went with them, seizing the opportunity of trading with Ilọrin, owing to the distress which this protracted war had caused all over the country.

A few days after their arrival at Ilọrin some mischievous persons in Kàràrà's camp went privately and kidnapped on the road between the camp and the city of Ilọrin, and a report was manufactured and circulated, attributing this deed to the Ibadans while negotiation of peace was going on ! This so exasperated the Emir of Ilọrin that when he was returning from the mosque on the Friday he rode direct to the Dongari's house where these messengers were lodged and ordered them to leave the town before sunset ! The truth, however, was soon found out, and the order was countermanded.

The negotiation however proved a failure as was anticipated, and when the messengers were returning home they were detained at Ọbaniñsunwa for three days until the Emir sent an escort of horsemen to conduct them to the Ogbomọsọ farms, it having been known that a party of kidnappers from Kàràrà's camp lay in wait for them.

The Ibadans it need hardly be said, were exceedingly annoyed, by these repeated disappointments. It had become evident now to all fair-minded persons that the protraction of this war was due entirely to the ALÂFIN and the Ilọrins, the Ibadans therefore were resolved to renew hostilities with Ilọrin in right earnest.

It may here be remarked that at this time traders from all parts of the country were finding their way to Ilọrin, and the Ogbomọsọ route was utilized to a large extent. This the Ibadans knew and hitherto connived at, but now they took measures to stop it at once. Another trade route was *via* Iseyin, Papa, Saki, Igboho and Igbẹti to Ilọrin and from Iseyin on the other side to Abẹokuta. Practically therefore peaceful intercourse was going on in one part of the country, whilst war was going on in another, and it was known to the Ibadans that the Ilọrins were importing rifles by this route to fight them at Ọfa ; they were therefore resolved to put a stop to this also. For this purpose they utilized the services of one Ẹsan, an expert in organizing kidnapping expeditions, and sent him to the Oke Ogun districts with a free hand against Ilọrin traders. Twice did Ẹsan kidnap caravans along this route ; several Ẹgba traders were kidnapped, and they suffered an immense loss of their merchandise. This exasperated the Ẹgbas and they complained of it both to the ALÂFIN OF ỌYỌ and to the Governor of Lagos whilst at the same time they themselves kidnapped in the Ibadan farms, as well as the caravans to Ijẹbu.

The letter to the ALÂFIN on the subject:

> Iporo Abẹokuta,
> *February 8th*, 1889.

HIS MAJESTY ADẸYEMI, KING OF ỌYỌ.
YOUR MAJESTY,

We, the undersigned and authorities of Abẹokuta, have the opportunity of writing to you on a subject we have lately heard from your territories. We learnt that the Ibadan people came to stop or blockade the peaceable traffic road at the town Lanlatẹ, which was freely opened to all free traders, even from interior to Lagos, by catching the Ilọrin and Ẹgba peaceful traders. They even proceeded their attempts to Eruwa close to our country simply on account of the war they are still fighting. We beg to request and show you that if this bad practice is just and right? for we know certainly that it will soon create an uneasiness betwixt us and the neighbouring tribes which will cause a great war. Kindly try and put a stop to this bad practice at once, for the road to Ilọrin was freely opened for the Ẹgbas,ʼ Ọyọs, Ilọrins, Baribas, and all these peaceable traders, and even the Ibadan people themselves are trading all along our surrounding countries, even · to our countries. We beg you to drive out from your neighbouring countries these rascals, and vagabonds riot Ibadan people.

We await your favourable reply to the succession of our request. Wishing you health and prosperity.

> We are your true friends,
> ONLADO   X (their marks)
> JAGUNA   X
> OGUNDEYI   X
> ALI BALOGUN   X

The following is a copy of the reply to the above letter from the ALÂFIN.

> The Palace, Ọyọ,
> *February 19th*, 1889.

TO THE ONLADO, JAGUNA, OGUNDEYI AND ALI BALOGUN.
MY GOOD FRIENDS,

I have the pleasure to convey that I have received your kind letter of the 4th inst. and have perused its contents with the diligence it requires and I beg to return my sincere thanks to you for the honour and good faith conferred on me by referring the matter of the raid committed in my territory to me.

I beg to express my regret for the action done by the Ibadan ruffians, and you are worthy of thanks for making this known to me, and I shall take a prompt and decisive step in redressing this evil. I will lose no time in sending to my subjects about the matter. It is well that the peace of the country be preserved that trade should flourish and war to cease, and all my efforts will be to this end. Will you bear with me until matters are rectified?

> I have the honour to remain,
> Your true friend,
> ADEYEMI × (his mark)
> *King of Yoruba.*

The following letter from the Acting-Governor of Lagos, G. C. Denton, to the Ibadan chiefs on the same subject.

> Government House, Lagos,
> *October 9th*, 1889.

No. 310/167.

GENTLEMEN,—In connection with my letter No. 273/145 of the 30th August last, to which I have as yet received no reply, I have the honour to inform you that in a communication which I have received from the Abeokuta authorities, it is alleged that some four months ago the Ibadan soldiers attacked and plundered by night caravans of traders belonging to Abeokuta, and amongst the people killed were Egbas, Ilorins, Hausas and Baribas. Horses, cattle, asses, kola nuts and cotton goods were carried off by your countrymen, and a number of people were captured. Some of the persons seized and a portion of the plunder were sent to you, to the ALÂFIN of Oyo and to the Aseyin, the remainder you conveyed to your camp at Ikirun.

2. On hearing of this raid on your part the Egbas at once sent messengers to the ALÂFIN and the Aseyin to enquire into the truth of the report which had reached them. They discovered the rumour to be well-founded and they therefore recalled their people and the caravans pending the adjustment of the disturbances.

3. Again a few weeks after the occurrence to which I refer it is stated by the Egbas that you suddenly descended on their farms and plundered them.

The Ẹgbas admit that in revenge for what you had done to them they after this attacked the Ibadan farms.

4. It is further alleged that you carried your depredations into the Ijẹbu country and plundered some farms at Ipara.

5. I am very reluctant to believe that the acts with which you are charged have been committed by you ; but in the face of the statement which I now convey to you it is hard for me to exonerate you from blame.

6. When I remember too the part which you took in the Treaty of 23rd September, 1886, and the protestation of the desire for peace which have been made by your messengers in my presence, I am at a loss to understand your action, unless there be some explanation for it, which I am not in possession of and it is to give you an opportunity of exculpating yourselves from blame in this matter that I now address this letter to you.

7. In the letter to which I refer in the first part of this communication, I endeavoured to remind you of the sad and bitter disasters which attend on war, and to impress on you that the prosperity of your country is best served by your peaceful intercourse with your neighbours.

Let me again put this before you and with the assurance of my goodwill, and of the great interest which I take in the affairs of Yoruba-land. Allow me to be,

Your good friend,

G. C. DENTON, *Acting-Governor*.

The reply of the Ibadans to the above letter.

Ikirun,
November 20th, 1889.

To HIS EXCELLENCY, CAPT. G. C. DENTON.

YOUR EXCELLENCY,

We hereby acknowledge the receipt of your kind letter which is a sort of supplement to that of the 30th August. It got to our hands yesterday and it has received our due consideration.

2. We thank Your Excellency for requiring a clear statement from us after the receipt of the communication from the Ẹgbas. We trust that ere this reaches you our reply to Your Excellency's former letter will have got into your hands, wherein you will find but a part of the reply to their charges.

3. It was true we kidnapped the caravans to and from Ilọrin but allow us to say that they were no Ẹgba traders but Hausas

and Ilọrin people, and we are glad Your Excellency has given us an opportunity of explaining ourselves.

4. Your Excellency knew very well that the difference between us and the Ẹgbas and the Ilọrins has not yet been adjusted and yet the road has been opened through our territory, and that we have long permitted this undisturbed. It was for the interest of trade with a view to the final settlement of the war that we have permitted this. But when we found that it will eventually end in our ruin we put a stop to it.

5. Since the late Ijaye war of 1860 the Ẹgbas would not allow any ammunition to pass from their town to us, but those so-called traders were returning with Sneiders and cartridges from Abẹokuta to strengthen the hands of the Ilọrins against us, and having a timely intimation of it we took steps to prevent the ruin of our country, and could we be blamed for preventing our own ruin especially when the ammunitions are to pass through our own territory?

Ẹgba traders were at Iseyin, Ọyọ and in all our Oke Ogun towns and they are not wanting till to-day. Did we touch any of them? If the traders we kidnapped had not traded in ammunition we would not have troubled them.

6. From our last letter Your Excellency will find that it was the Ẹgbas who were the aggressors, having first kidnapped on the Ipara and Orù roads and have committed raids in our farms before we retaliated. We had ceased escorting caravans to Ijẹbu but we were obliged to do so since they were kidnapping on the roads. This was even before the Oke Ogun affair.

7. Why should the Ẹgbas complain of our raids in the Ijẹbu farms? They should let the Ijẹbus complain themselves. The fact of the case is this—The Ijẹbus and the Ẹgbas were not on terms and the Ẹgbas have succeeded in stopping the trade between Ipara and Ibadan by kidnapping and blockading that road. In retaliation the Ijẹbu Remọ at Ipara have obtained re-inforcement in the idle ones at home to harass them in their farms, and why should they saddle this on us here at Ikirun?

Your Excellency must take our word. We beg to affirm once more that if the Ẹgbas cease kidnappping in our farms and the Ijẹbu roads we will not kidnap in their farms. Your Excellency must not doubt our sincerity in whatever we say, and if anything happens to the contrary it must have a reason and we are ready to explain ourselves.

8. It is our wish to be sending our messengers down frequently to keep the Governor well-informed of all the incidents which may be occurring here, but we beg to say we have not the oppor-

tunity of a free communication with Lagos. We say this in confidence to the Governor as we do not mean to complain of the Ijẹbus who have done so much for us. If this get to their hearing they will take it as a complaint against them and we shall smart for it. Hence we say this is private and in confidence. We had to buy the road as it were before our messenger went down also even this we do not mind.

But they are still never pleased and they must know why we send down. We beg to suggest to the Governor that whenever the Governor wishes to see our messenger to let the Awujalẹ know of it, as we are ready to send at any time.

Wishing Your Excellency good health.

Your good friends *their marks.*

AJAYI, *Balogun of Ibadan*	×
OṢUNTOKI, *Maye of Ibadan*	×
FIJABI, *Abẹsẹ of Ibadan*	×
FAJINMI, *Agbakin of Ibadan*	×

In consequence of the remonstrance of the Ẹgba chiefs, the Isẹyin chiefs, with the exception of the Asẹyin himself, were against further raids being committed at least within their territory, but they could not prevent it.

Towards the end of June, 1889, hearing of caravans going again to Ilọrin, Ẹsan came and met them at Isẹyin. It was generally believed that he was invited by Lawore the Asẹyin, but the chiefs insisted that Ẹsan *shall not* capture these Hausa and Ẹgba traders in their town of Isẹyin. Ẹsan with his small body of troops therefore left the town and encamped at a place called Boiboi over against Isẹyin spoiling their farms. The ALÂFIN hearing this sent kegs of powder and bowls of bullets to Ẹsan, not because he favoured Ẹsan's raids, but because he felt that the Asẹyin's authority should be upheld against his chiefs.

The Isẹyin people dared not attack Ẹsan, because that would amount to attacking an Ibadan army, and consequently there was nothing to be done but to have a conference on the subject. Ẹsan would not agree to any terms but the expulsion of the Hausa traders from the town. This was done on the 29th of June, 1889.

Ẹsan hearing of this expulsion, gave chase and overtook them at the brook Odò Ọñkọ́ and plundered them, carrying away much booty.

This was the last of Ẹsan's successful exploits, for early in the following year he led an expedition to the Ṣabẹ country, and besieged Danikan, their chief town. Here he was attacked by the Ṣabẹs in overwhelming numbers, and hemmed in on every side, his little band of troops was dispersed, and he was taken alive and slain.

The late Ẹsan was a native of Modakẹkẹ; he came suddenly into notice in the years 1887 to 1889. He was a first-rate swordsman, and specially skilful in the use of the cutlass called Ọya. He led several kidnapping expeditions to the Ẹgba farms, attacked and defeated several Ẹgba kidnapping expeditions to the Ibadan farms. We have noticed above his exploits in the Oke Ogun districts, three times in succession did he attack and plunder Ilọrin, Hausa and Ẹgba traders. He now lost his life in attempting with a handful of men to take Danikan in the Ṣabẹ country on the 5th of February, 1890.

CHAPTER XXXII

ABORTIVE MEASURES TO TERMINATE THE WAR

§ 1. The Mission of Alvan Millson

WE have seen that by the terms of the Kiriji Treaty, the ALÂFIN was made responsible for the settlement of the Ibadan-Ilọrin war, and that Chief Ogedemgbe failed in 1886 to induce the Commissioners to send messengers to the Ilọrin camp, because they were not commissioned thither.

The ALÂFIN however was suspected of duplicity by his people, for several of his private messengers to Kàràrà had been caught, and instead of making a move, he had to be moved by the Awujalẹ of Ijẹbu, and the Oluiwo of Iwo to undertake measures towards the restoration of peace. Whenever he was as it were forced to send a peace embassy to Ilọrin, he would send a private man for that purpose instead of an Ilari ; if pressed for an Ilari, he sent Ọba-ko-ṣe-tan ! Showing he was not ready. It became evident that although he wanted peace in the abstract, yet he wished to keep the Ibadans fully engaged at a distance from home.

The Governor received several communications from the interior kings and chiefs, notably the Oluiwo of Iwo, praying His Excellency to bring to a finish the good work commenced in 1886, by sending up again special Commissioners for the purpose, as it has proved to be that the seat of war had but changed from Kiriji-Mẹsin to Yanayo-Ikirun.

Unfortunately His Excellency did not consider the matter of so much importance as to send up a strong embassy direct to Ọyọ and Ilọrin. He sent a single European officer, Mr. Alvan Millson, the Asst. Col. Secretary, and a native officer, Mr. F. Colley-Green, a subintendant of police with instructions to gather representatives from both the Ilọrin and Ibadan camps for a " palaver " and to endeavour to mediate between them and get them to decamp and return to their homes !

The Commissioners left Lagos on the 14th January, 1890, arrived at Ijẹbu Ode on the 15th, left on the 17th and arrived at Ibadan on the 19th. Leaving Ibadan on the 24th, they arrived at Ọyọ on the 25th. They had an interview with the ALÂFIN on the 26th when His Majesty was informed of the object of their mission.

Obtaining two messengers from him they left Ọyọ on the 29th

January and arrived at Ikirun on the 3rd February.   It must be remarked that the messengers sent by the ALÂFIN for this important business were both private men, and no Ilari, which is very significant.

The interview between the Commissioners and the authorities of Ibadan took place on the 4th of February, the Commissioners delivered to them the compliments of His Excellency the Governor, and their message and instructions were to this effect :—

That the authorities of Ibadan should assist or second the Governor's effort in obtaining a permanent peace in the Yoruba country.   In order to do this they should facilitate their proceeding to Ilọrin for an interview with the Emir, and negotiate with him terms of peace and the withdrawal of his troops under his Commander-in-Chief Kàràrà, now at Ọfa.   They were also to gather representative people from both powers for a " palaver " and to disperse both camps.

This seemed to the war chiefs like trifling with the affair, as if a fierce race of warriors like the Ilọrins bent on conquest could be induced to leave their camps on such conditions !

The Commissioners found it impracticable to proceed either to the Ilọrin camp or to Ilọrin ; the direct route was the scene of the conflict.   Not only so, but the Commissioners also witnessed two attacks on Ikirun by the Ilọrin army from Ọfa, and were convinced of the risk of venturing to the Ilọrin camp with an escort of only eight Hausa soldiers ! The Ibadan chiefs would not even allow it.

The Commissioners were resolved to try the Ijẹsa route.   The way to Mẹsin Ipole by the old Kiriji route had been closed when the Ijẹsas kidnapped about 150 Ọyọ traders, who, taking advantage of the peace now existing between them after the breaking up of the Kiriji-Mẹsin camps were utilising that way for trade with the Ekiti countries.[1]   This serious breach of the Treaty by the Ijẹsas excited no comment at Lagos at the time, because it was not followed by a retaliation :   the Ibadans simply protested against such actions, and closed the road.

The Commissioners were resolved to try the Ilesa route *via* Osọgbo and Oke Bode.   At the latter place armed men barred the way, preventing further progress.   For three hours they were under the blazing mid-day sun, after which better counsel pre-

---

[1] The Commissioner had occasion afterwards to question Ogedemgbe about this action.   He confirmed the report but justified himself by saying that they were considerate enough to sell the parties to Modakẹkẹ so that their friends might have the chance of ransoming them.   But why do it at all ?   He replied— Because the Ibadans remained still at Ikirun.

vailed, and they were allowed to go under shelter but not to proceed an inch further on their journey; in the meantime they were communicating with the authorities at headquarters. The Commissioners had to write to the Qwa and the Seriki of their detention, and the reply they received was from one G. W. Johnson, a bookbinder of Lagos, acting as secretary and writing in the name of the Kings of the Ekiti parapos. . . . " Who are you ? We do not know you ; are you a Missionary ? Why do you trespass on Ijesa soil without first notifying the 16 kings of the Ekitiparapos ? " The Commissioners wrote back to say who they were and requested permission to visit the Qwa. The reply came that the Oke Bode people should allow them to proceed ; this they did, but refused to supply them with a guide ; they had to write again to the Qwa for a guide which they obtained before they could proceed, after full ten days' detention. The Qwa and Ogedemgbe subsequently apologised to them for this action of the Oke Bode people.

They spent three days at Ilesa before proceeding to Esa Egure where they met with the Qwa of the Ijesas, and spent four days with him, discussing with him the object of their mission.

At Mesin Ipole they interviewed the Seriki and the three principal Ekiti kings : but Ogedemgbe the Seriki objected to their going to Ilorin by way of Mesin. " No road," said he, " the path is full of ditches." On Mr. Millson persisting and offering to go with only his cook if possible he told him plainly he could not be allowed to go as it would involve the loss of their lives. He even declined to take a letter from him to Kàràrà the Ilorin Generalissimo, telling him that it would get him in hot water with the Ilorins as was the case when the former Commissioners came in 1886 to disperse the camps at Kiriji.

The Commissioners had to go back to Ikirun by the way they came, and told the Ibadan chiefs of the failure of their mission.

Thus ended in failure this ill-conceived, unstatesmanlike mission which sought to intervene between two fierce armies in a conflict that had lasted 14 years by means which could scarcely have separated two excited parties in a village riot.

§ 2. SUBSIDIARY EFFORTS OF THE REV. S. JOHNSON

Whilst the above episode was being enacted, the writer who was then at Lagos was invited to an interview with the Governor. His Excellency wishing him to join the above mission, obtained permission from the local C.M.S. Secretary to send him up. He was to be the bearer of letters to the Awujale, the ALÂFIN, the Aseyin and to receive accredited messengers from the first two as well as from the Oluiwo of Iwo and the Balẹ of Ogbomọsọ, and with these, as representatives of their masters join the Commissioners at Ikirun for a conference which was to put an end to the war ! The writer was also to render assistance to the Commissioners as he did in 1886.

Whilst the Governor was interesting himself in the affairs of the interior, and doing his best to restore peace to the country, some ill-informed persons at Lagos, under the plea of patriotism, were trying to undermine his efforts. After the Commissioners had gone up, private messages were sent to the Awujalẹ of Ijẹbu that they should not let the white man terminate this war for them, lest they rob them of their country, deprive them of their wives, give freedom to their slaves, and that eventually they would be reduced to the condition of having to hoe their own farms for themselves, and to perform other menial work.

This was speedily communicated to all the kings and chiefs of the interior. The Ijẹbu authorities went one step further, resolving not to allow any Lagos trader or any foreigner to pass through their country to the interior and *vice versa*. The law was so stringently enforced that the writer, although so well known at Ijẹbu during the peace negotiations of 1886, found it hard to proceed up country ; he had to leave his luggage at the port Itọ Ike and to enter Ijẹbu Ode in the night to obtain permission from the king to pass through his country.   His being also the bearer of a letter from the Governor of Lagos to the Awujalẹ emboldened him to proceed to that capital.

Even the Awujalẹ himself was careful not to infringe the law. He refused to see the writer when he was announced to him ; he sent word to say that whatever message he brought for him from the Governor, should be delivered to the Balogun Nọfọwọkan who would deliver the same to him.   It was in the dead of night at last, that the Awujalẹ arranged for a private interview with the writer, and that was owing to the influence of the Balogun.   He was very careful to have this nocturnal visit in order that he might not offend the Ijẹbus, although personally he did not approve of these measures.

The writer was detained at Ijẹbu Ode for another day.   At the suggestion of the Balogun, with the approval of the Awujalẹ, all the Ijẹbu authorities were summoned together to hear the Governor's message from the mouth of the messenger himself. After hearing the letter read, and after consultation with one another, their spokesman came forward and said : '' We have already sent our messengers to the interior for peace negotiations with Ilọrin, the King his Agūrin, the Oṣugbos, the Lamurins, and the Ipampas their messengers, they are probably now at Ibadan, and we are decided not to send up fresh messengers ; those already sent, the Governor's messenger will meet there, and they will go with him together with the messengers of the Aseyin and of Oluiwo to the ALÂFIN who will appoint his messenger with them to meet the Commissioner.

The Awujale, as one interested in the peace of the country, moreover told the writer in confidence that he had been in communication with the Alâfin, and that His Majesty complained bitterly of the Ibadans, but he had begged him to overlook his grievances at present in the interest of peace to the country at large, and after this he would exert his influence with the Ibadans, and that His Majesty would find in the end that the Ibadans would be more loyal to him.

But, as the sequel will show, it was evident that the insinuations of the so-called patriots of Lagos had poisoned the minds not only of the Awujale, but of all the interior kings and chiefs also, and the Governor's messenger was duped throughout whereever he went.

Arriving at Ibadan on the 21st March, he lost no time in looking up the Ijebu messengers, and informed them of the resolution arrived at by the Awujale in council, and asked when they would be ready to proceed to Oyo. They excused themselves by saying that they had a special message for the war chiefs at Ikirun from home, and that they were expecting the answer on Monday, the 24th, after which they would be ready to proceed ; if the 26th suited him they might start together on that date. To this he readily consented.

On the 25th the Governor's messenger sent to ascertain from these Ijebus whether they would be ready to start on the morrow according to arrangement : they told his messenger he should wait for them at the town gate early in the morning, and there they would join him. But this they never meant to do. The Governor's messenger waited for hours at the gate, but they never turned up. He had to proceed alone.

These Ijebu messengers subsequently arrived at Oyo after the Governor's messenger had proceeded to Iseyin on his errand ; it was after his return from Iseyin that he learnt indirectly from them, that they had not the intention of going with him to join the Commissioner, that was not part of their instructions from home, they were instructed to remain at Oyo and from thence conduct all negotiations with the messengers from the important chiefs of every part of the country, and never to return home until the war should end. The Governor's messenger had no alternative but to leave them, but before going away he suggested to them that they should send a special messenger home to ascertain whether the information he conveyed to them from the Awujalẹ in council was true or not, promising to call again to hear the result.

The Governor's messenger proceeded to Ogbomọsọ on his errand on the 5th April, 1890. The authorities of Ogbomọsọ felt flattered that they should have been so recognized by the Governor as to be required to take part in the peace negotiations; they readily sent two messengers, one from the Balẹ the other from the Ompetu on Easter Tuesday, April 8th, 1890. These repaired to Ọyọ with the Governor's messenger.

The Ijẹbu messengers were again interviewed to learn whether they had heard from home. The Governor's messenger was taken aback to hear them giving vent to their pent-up feelings in these words :

" Why should the Governor of Lagos request the Ijẹbu king to send messengers along with his own ? A year ago did not the Awujalẹ send to the Governor to solicit his aid to bring to a successful issue the good work the English Government had so kindly begun, and was not the Acting Governor indignant at the Ibadans, calling them thieves and robbers, and asking why they remained still at Ikirun, and whether that was their home ? And were not the Ilọrins in their farms ? ' Leave me alone,' said he, " I will only interest myself in the affairs of the Colony. Let the Awujalẹ and the ALÂFIN, who are rulers in the interior, settle their interior difficulties themselves.'.'

" Hereupon "—they continued—" the Awujalẹ at the instance, of the Oluiwo, sent an embassy through Iwo to Ọyọ to negotiate peace. Although the ALÂFIN was prevailed upon to send his messenger, yet he felt the proceedings irregular and his dignity affronted, hence everything promised failure at the start. The messengers had to wait nine days at Ogbomọsọ before proceeding to Ilọrin, and the result proved a failure. Profiting by past experience, we are now instructed to come straight to the ALÂFIN, and to act according to his orders, to go backwards and forwards as he should direct. And why should the Governor now require our king to send delegates with his own after his *locum tenens* had told us to see after the interior difficulties ourselves ? "

This ended the efforts of the Governor's messenger with the Ijẹbus. It was plain now that he could not get them to go with him.

His Majesty the ALÂFIN was waited upon by the Governor's messenger on his arrival from Lagos, and he delivered the Governor's letter and message to him.

X

The Governor's letter to the ALÂFIN.

Government House, Lagos,

No. 3/51.   *March* 13*th*, 1890.

TO THE ALÂFIN OF ỌYỌ.

KING,—I have the pleasure of announcing to you my return in good health to my Government.

2. Since my departure to my country last year, many things have happened, some of which have caused me joy and others regret.

3. It is a source of gratification to me to reflect that my own colony remains prosperous.

4. Unfortunately the war between the Ilọrins and Ibadans continues, and the Ibadans are still at Ikirun.

5. Happily, however, both sides appear to be tired of hostilities[1] and I hope that my Commissioner, who is charged with mediating between them, will induce them to make a lasting peace.

6. You have seen my Commissioner, and been courteous and hospitable towards him. I thank you, and I remember that my Commissioners who made a settlement between the Ibadans and the Ekitiparapọs four years ago retain a pleasant recollection of their intercourse with you.

7. My Commissioner is about to proceed by way of Ikirun to Oke Mẹsin or some more northerly or easterly spot where the final negotiations can most conveniently take place.

8. I think it due to Yoruba-land and desirable that he be accompanied thither, or joined there by accredited representatives of the parties principally interested in the restoration of peace ; and I therefore invite you to send with him or after him messengers who will possess your mind and who will have full authority to enter into engagements on behalf of yourself and your people.

9. My sorrow and astonishment were not small when I heard that the Ibadans had stopped the trade route which leads through your province of Isẹyin.

10. The prosperity of Yoruba-land which I have at heart depends largely as it seems to me upon its trade routes being kept open ; and I shall be glad to consider any suggestions or proposals that you may be prepared to make, with a view to the opening and keeping open of the trade routes of all Yoruba, or at any rate of as many of them as possible.

I am, King, Your true friend,

ALFRED MOLONEY,

Governor and Commander-in-Chief of the Colony of Lagos.

---

[1] Here the governor was mistaken. The Ilọrins were not.—Ed.

§ 3.   THE ALÂFIN'S DIPLOMACY

The above letter being read and interpreted to the King, he expressed his willingness to second the Governor's proposals.

On hearing afterwards what the Ijẹbu messengers said, he was not surprised, but simply said, " I fully expected they would act thus, but being most concerned in the matter, I shall appoint my own delegates. But the Asẹyin's messenger should not be left out, the Asẹyin being equally interested in the matter." The Governor's messenger replied that although his instructions did not include the Asẹyin, he did not think that the Governor would have any objection if the ALÂFIN saw fit to include a messenger from the Asẹyin. Who could have doubted His Majesty's sincerity in such a reply ? But the sequel shows that he was a past master in diplomacy: he resented the Governor's treating with his subordinate chiefs as on an equality with himself and was determined to show it.

He actually appointed his Ọba-kò-sẹtan to go with the Governor's messenger, and sent to the Basọrun to appoint another to accompany his own : but as the Governor's messenger was on the point of starting (Friday, 11th April) he told him that Friday was an inauspicious day when they should never send messages abroad, but that the messengers would join him the next day at Iwo.

The Oluiwo appointed his own man on the Saturday against the arrival of the ALÂFIN's messenger who was to bring with him those from Ogbomọsọ and Isẹyin. But they waited in vain ! On the evening of Sunday the 13th a private messenger came from the ALÂFIN to the Oluiwo and the Governor's messenger to say that since the departure of the latter from Ọyọ he had been informed that the Ibadans had sent an expedition to Ilero, and as a goodly number of Ọyọ princes and princesses reside there, and the Ibadans were going to enslave them, he must wait to redeem them all, before he thought of helping them ! This of course was a made-up story purely invented as an excuse for not sending anyone ; moreover, the Ogbomọsọ messengers he sent back home.

The disappointment of the Governor's messenger can well be imagined. He had to return at once at his call, but to tell the ALÂFIN that if he could not carry out that part of his instructions, he must at all events proceed to meet the Commissioners. He returned for this purpose the next day *via* Iwo again, and met the Commissioners at Ẹdẹ on their return journey after the failure of their mission. Together with them he returned to Ọyọ.

A few days after the happening of the above events, the writer in conversation with a highly respectable Ọyọ gentleman, complained bitterly of the disappointments and rebuffs he lately met

with, not only from the Ijẹbus but also by the action of the
ALÂFIN, to which also the action of the Ijẹbus could be traced. The
ALÂFIN was always fair, courteous, and polite, but no reliance
could be placed upon his words. The writer recalled the incident
of the messengers, how he would send private gentlemen instead
of an Ilari on important state business when he knew the matter
would thereby end in failure, etc. The following dialogue
which passed between them will show the Ọyọ official view of
the matter. To the messenger's complaints the citizen
replied :—

Cit. : Ah yes, but see what treatment the Governor has offered
our Master !

Mess. : What treatment ?

Cit. : Suppose the Queen of the Gẹ̀hẹ́si (the English) is at war
with the King of the Agùda (the Portugese) and the King of
Fransé (the French) offered to mediate between them, and suppose
he sent his messenger to the Queen, and to the Balẹs (Mayors) of
those great English towns we have heard of such as the ship-
building town (Liverpool) the cloth-weaving town (Manchester),
and the town where iron goods come from (Birmingham), asking
them to send their own messengers with that of the Queen for a
conference, putting them as it were on an equality with the Queen,
how would she like it ? Although a woman I believe she would
resent it. Yet that is precisely what the Governor has done,
sending to the Balẹ of Ogbomọsọ, and the Oluiwo to send their
messengers along with that of the ALÂFIN with you to meet the
Commissioner for a conference !

Mess. : Did not the ALÂFIN himself suggest the Asẹyin, how
could it have displeased him when he himself suggested a
messenger from the Asẹyin ?

Cit. (laughing he said) : But can't you see that that is ironical ?
Did you not come with a letter from the Governor to the Asẹyin ?
And yet in the matter of delegates you left him out. The ALÂFIN
simply meant to point out to you your inconsistency in leaving
him out, for he is higher in rank than either the Balẹ of Ogbomọsọ
or the Oluiwo. But don't you see that no messenger from any of
them joined you after all ?

Mess. : Well, if we made a mistake we are quite willing to be
corrected but why did he not tell us so ? Why adopt measures
which will serve to wreck the whole scheme ?

Cit. : That is not Ọyọ etiquette. You know it is never considered polite with Yorubas to tell one to whom respect is due
that he is wrong in his methods, but when he meets with failure
then he will reconsider his methods. It is not for the ALÂFIN

bluntly to correct the Governor, but when he fails in his movements then he must know that his measures were wrong.

Mess.: But the Governor cannot be expected to know these tortuous Yoruba methods, the Englishman prefers straight dealing.

Cit.: But he ought at any rate to know what is due to a Sovereign or he would not have been selected to represent one. You are just looking at the matter from the standpoint of the Governor's messenger that you are, but the ALÂFIN must consider how your message affects him with his chiefs.

Before the Commissioners left Ikirun, they got the Ibadans to sign a declaration that they would in future be more loyal to the ALÂFIN and that the Governor in consultation with the ALÂFIN should delimit the boundaries of the territories immediately under them and that any such delimitation which has the ALÂFIN's signature they would accept.

On the Commissioners reaching Ọyọ they induced the ALÂFIN to agree to this proposal, and further that His Majesty should pledge himself and subjects not to disturb the peace of the country ; should any disturbance arise, before any hostile action is resorted to, that he would communicate at once with the Governor as to what measures would be taken and how the offender would be dealt with.   The Commissioners scarcely saw that in this they were asking the ALÂFIN to surrender his sovereign rights to the Governor. This latter declaration was to be signed also by the Oluiwo, the Timi of Ẹdẹ, the Balẹ of Ogbomọsọ and the Asẹyin of Isẹyin.

On the 10th of May the writer accompanied by Ọba-ko-ṣe-tan, started with a copy of this declaration.   The Oluiwo signed it on the same day, the Ibadan chiefs at Ikirun signed it on the 16th, the Timi of Ẹdẹ's signature the Ibadan chiefs thought was not necessary, being a subordinate chief to Ibadan, and what the Balogun of Ibadan signed was enough for him ; but that the Balẹ of Ogbomọsọ may.   For this purpose, and to expedite matters, they sent a messenger along with the Governor's messenger to assure him of their conclusions.

But the Balẹ of Ogbomọsọ in consultation with his chiefs refused to sign the paper although they agreed with everything it contained.   No argument could shake them from their determination.   " What His Majesty the ALÂFIN signed," said they, " as well as the Ibadan chiefs, was good enough for us, we are their subjects."   This was no doubt due to the rebuff they met with at Ọyọ when sending their messenger to go with the Governor's.

The Asẹyin, amidst the excitement of the Dahomian invasion, signed the declaration on the 2nd of June, 1890.

§ 4. CORRESPONDENCE AND A TREATY

The following letter was sent to the ALÂFIN with a copy of a Treaty by Taniafisara, the ALÂFIN'S messenger, who returned to Lagos with Mr. Alvan Millson, M.A. :—

> Government House, Lagos,
> *May 19th,* 1890.

No. 214/115.

SIR,—On the 13th March last I had the honour to inform you of my return, and I express my sorrow and astonishment to find that the Ibadans had stopped the trade route through Isẹyin.

2. I now hasten to thank you for sending me your messenger Taniafisara. He was accompanied by representatives of the Balogun of Ibadan, of the Abẹsẹ of Ibadan, and the Oluiwo of Iwo.

3. It pained me much, I must admit, to find closed on my return one of the commercial roads to the interior *viz.,* by Eruwa, by which this Colony, the Ẹgbas and Yorubas are benefited ; and another to Rẹmọ, Ipara-Ibadan route rendered insecure from raids. Here you have an example of cause and effect ; because Eruwa road was plundered, the Ipara route was raided.

4. The Ibadan action was a breach by them unwillingly, perhaps, of the provisions of the Treaty of peace, friendship and commerce existing between this colony and your kingdom ; further, it was an unfriendly act towards this Government which has done so much for them and the country.

5. I must disapprove of the Ibadan raids upon the Abẹokuta, Eruwa, Isẹyin road, and as I feel bound to hold the Ibadans responsible for the cessation of communication between Abẹokuta and Isẹyin I must look to the Ibadans to effect promptly by negotiation the opening of the Abẹokuta-Isẹyin road and also the opening up of the Abẹokuta-Ibadan road which has been closed since 1877.

6. Draft of a Treaty in furtherance of the object I enclose. A copy has been furnished to the Ibadans and to the Ẹgbas. The Ijẹbus will also be supplied.

7. Such closures and raids cannot be viewed with unconcern, and from such hindrances to trade, there can only result a block to the general prosperity of the country and universal discontent.

8. At an interview I have had with your representative and those of the Ijẹbus and Ẹgbas, I have advised mutual forbearance and compromise and the substitution instead of the jealous suspicion and hatred of the past, of healthy and friendly emulation and intercourse.

9. The importance of completing the Treaty now forwarded and the necessity for promptitude should be manifest to you, and I venture to urge that you open up communication without delay with Iseyin, Ogbomoso, Iwo, Ibadan, and Abeokuta. The Egbas have been similarly advised.

10. To help you to bring about a better understanding and to secure with all the despatch I can recommend for an end so generally desired, I have taken the liberty to send you the draft Treaty which practically embodies in a formal shape all the Yorubas, Egbas, and Ijebus professed they desire.

11. In any further way I can help you pray let me know. My advice and assistance in promoting your interests and those of the country generally are at your service.

12. It remains for me to convey to you my sincere thanks for your courteous and hospitable treatment of Mr. Millson during his stay in your kingdom.

13. This letter and those addressed to the Balogun and authorities of Ibadan to the Oluiwo of Iwo and to the Aseyin are entrusted to the Egba messengers who have kindly undertaken their delivery.

14. I wish you and your people every good wish, and an early restoration of friendly intercourse between Yorubas and Egbas.

I am, sir, your good friend,

ALFRED MOLONEY,

Governor and Commander-in-Chief.

Draft copy of the Treaty accompanying the above letter. Treaty of Peace, Friendship and Commerce between the Egbas, the Ibadans, and the Ijebus.

Whereas the relations of the Egbas, the Ibadans, and the Ijebus have in the past been frequently disturbed by misunderstandings which have only too often resulted in raids upon one another's territory and other hostile acts.

And whereas the said peoples are desirous of living for the future in peace and amity with each other

Now therefore we, the undersigned authorities of the said peoples, having power to bind our respective peoples solemnly and sincerely promise each other and declare as follows :—

1. The Egbas, the Ibadans, and the Ijebus (hereinafter called the signatories) shall henceforth wholly desist from making raids each upon the territory of either of the others.

2. The signatories will respectively within three months from these presents coming into force restore to each other or make

compensation for or in respect of all captives whom they may respectively have made during any such raid as aforesaid, within the two years immediately preceding the first day of January, 1890.

3. There shall henceforth be peace, friendship and commerce between the signatories.

4. The signatories shall henceforth keep open their roads each to and for the benefit of the others.

5. In particular the Egbas shall keep open so far as in them lies the road from Abẹokuta to Isẹyin by way of Eruwa, and the Ibadans and the Ijẹbus shall so far as in them respectively lies keep open the road from Ibadan to Ikorodu by way of Ipara and Sagamu, and the road from Ibadan to Itọ Ike by way of Orù and Ijẹbu Ode.

6. The last preceding article hereof shall in no way be construed as limiting the provisions of the fourth article hereof.

7. The Egbas and the Ibadans will forthwith open the direct road between Abẹokuta and Ibadan which was closed in the year 1877.

8. The signatories will henceforth only levy and allow to be levied reasonable duties and tolls upon goods imported into or conveyed through their respective territories and will in no case levy or allow to be levied upon any such goods any duties and tolls amounting in the aggregate to more than double the duties and tolls to which similar goods shall be for the time being liable in the territory of either of the others of the signatories or to more than one-tenth of the value of the goods so imported or conveyed, provided that none of the signatories shall be bound to their tariffs of duties and tolls more than once in every year.

9. These presents shall come into force when executed by the Ijẹbus.

10. In case any question shall arise upon the construction of any of the provisions hereof or otherwise in relation hereto, or in connection herewith, such question may be referred by any of the signatories to the arbitrament of the Governor for the time being of Her Britannic Majesty's Colony of Lagos whose decision thereon shall be binding and conclusive upon all the signatories.

In witness thereof we have hereunto set our hands and seals on the days below set opposite to our respective names and titles.

The following is from the Governor to the Ibadan authorities :—

Government House, Lagos.

No. 217/115.   *May* 19th, 1890.

GENTLEMEN,—My Commissioner to Ijẹbu, Yoruba, and Ekiti Mr. Millson, has returned to Lagos, and has informed me fully on the affairs of the interior.   During his absence I collected important facts.

2. During his presence among you he conveyed that I have returned from England and how pained I was to find closed one of the commercial roads *via* Eruwa which connects this Colony with Yoruba-land and another the Rẹmọ-Ipara route raided, and confidence withdrawn therefrom in consequence.

3. I have looked carefully into the situation and find myself unable to approve of the Ibadan raids upon the Eruwa-Isẹyin road of communication between Abẹokuta and Isẹyin.   I must look to the Ibadans to effect promptly by negotiation the opening of that route as also *now* the opening of the Abẹokuta-Ibadan road which has been closed since 1877.

4. In the difficulties that have arisen since I left the Colony you have an example of " cause and effect."   First the owner of a house is responsible for its order.   And whether Ẹsan acted with or without your authority you are responsible : and further I find that the Ibadans, Isẹyins, Ọyọs and Ogbomọṣọs shared the unfortunate captives and plunder, and should now be ready to make good the losses they inflicted.

5. The action was a breach of the Treaty of peace, friendship and commerce existing between this colony and the Yoruba kingdom, and as it interrupted the trade, it was an unfriendly act towards this Government which has done so much for you and the country.

6. Such closures and raids cannot be viewed with unconcern, and from such hindrances to trade there can only result a block to the general prosperity of the country and universal discontent.

7. Again, Ẹsan's outrageous conduct was openly defiant and hostile to Ilọrin at the very time when in your interest and in those of Yoruba generally and on your representations Her Majesty's Government had allowed peace negotiations to be opened through Major Macdonald with that city.   This is a very serious aspect of that affair.

8. At the interviews I have had with your representatives and those of Ijẹbu and Ẹgba, I have advised mutual forbearance and compromise and the substitution instead of the jealous suspicion and hatred of the past, of healthy emulation and intercourse.

9. A copy of a Draft Treaty in furtherance of objects desired in paragraph 3 of this letter I append.

The Draft Treaty has been sent to the ALÂFIN OF ỌYỌ.

10. I have explained to the ALÂFIN the importance of completing this Treaty and the necessity for promptitude and I must look much to the Ibadans for the success of the undertaking.

11. I now turn to another act in the interior drama. Taking up the negotiations for peace between you and the Ilọrins where they were left by Major Macdonald I have addressed a letter to the Emir of Ilọrin. I wish you to know this and to exhort you to avoid adding to the difficulties of the situation as between you and them.

12. In the restoration of freedom to the roads between the Ẹgbas and yourselves you must in no way forget your obligations to Jẹbu in the past. With the Ijẹbus also, remember I desire you to continue to maintain the best relations.

13. It remains for me to convey my appreciative acknowledgment of the courtesy and hospitality you were good enough to extend to Mr. Millson during his stay in your country.

14. Finally, let me wish you and your people every good wish and the early resumption between you and the Ẹgbas of friendly and commercial intercourse, and the continuance of like relations with the Ijẹbus.

I am, gentlemen, your good friend,

A. C. MOLONEY.

To the Balogun and Ibadan Authorities.

The tone of the Governor's letter did not please the Ibadan chiefs ; they complained that it showed a want of sympathy with them in their trying position. They were struggling for existence as it were, but he was only concerned about trade with Lagos at whatever cost to others.

What they took exception to were the charges brought against them of breaking the Treaty, and of ingratitude to the Government "which has done so much for them." Whatever their character may be, they were certainly not an ungrateful people, and no one had paid more deference to the wishes of the Governor of Lagos than they had done.

A Treaty (said they) was made between them and the Ekitis, but none whatever with the Ẹgbas, and when the Ekitis broke the Treaty by kidnapping their traders the Governor said nothing. They yielded to none in their desire for peace and commerce. If proofs of this were required, it might be found in the patience with which they were enduring their sufferings and trials at the hands of the Ijẹbus at that moment, with the same Ẹgbas kid-napping on the route. Again the very fact of the existence of the trade by Eruwa the interruption of which was now the subject of complaint, was another proof in their favour, for although this war commenced with the Ẹgbas, and no formal peace had been arranged between them, yet they (the Ibadans) had hitherto allowed this trade, but certainly not to make it operate to their detriment.

That for twenty years the Ẹgbas had refused to sell them ammunition, but they would sell to the Ilorins and utilise their territory to convey the same ; would it not be folly and suicidal on their part to carry the pretence of a desire for trade so far as to allow that, at a time the Ilorins were laying siege against their frontier towns ?

One of them remarked, " We cannot blame the Governor, the Ẹgbas have gained his ears, and it depends upon how they repre-sented matters to him. It is all the fault of the Ẹgbas. They are like spoilt children who in a fit of temper will hurl a knife at you, but if you in turn flourish a whip at them they will yell out before ever they are touched."

They concluded that as they agreed with the Governor's senti-ments in the main they would only protest to the one objectionable point, viz., *the trade with Ilorin through their territory before the establishment of peace.*

The following letter was then addressed to the Governor in reply.

Ikirun,
July 16*th*, 1890.

To His Excellency, Sir A. C. Moloney, K.C.M.G.

Your Excellency,

We were glad to receive Your Excellency's letter on the arrival of our messengers from you and have given it deep consideration.

2. We have noticed the expression of Your Excellency's feelings respecting the closed roads.

Our reason for cutting off communication or trade with the Ilorins we have given to the Acting-Governor in your absence in a letter under date November 20th, 1889.

We regret the Governor did not see with us in the reasons we have given to the Acting-Governor for kidnapping the Gambaris off Isẹyin, and *not* the *Egba traders*, which the Ẹgbas retaliated in closing of the Eruwa-Isẹyin road and kidnapping on the Ipara road.

However, that has passed ; and now that Your Excellency is come, we feel assured that there will be nothing to fear in what you undertake to do or see carried out. We are ready for the opening of the Eruwa road to Abẹokuta and of the Ibadan road to Abẹokuta and will see to it.

3. The appended copy of draft of a Treaty has been read to us, and we have considered it duly.

4. We are glad to learn that negotiations for peace between us and the Ilọrins have been resumed by Your Excellᵒncy and have no inclination to add to the difficulties of it.

5. Although we agree with the letter of the Treaty in the main, yet we wish to give our protest against the Ilọrin traders utilizing that road as long as we are at war with each other. We are here on the defensive and earnestly wish to return to our homes as soon as possible. If the Ilọrins are allowed to utilize that road is there any possibility of their agreeing to any terms of peace and cessation of hostilities since they have free trade ? Hence we feel ourselves bound to open our minds to the Governor in sending our protest *until peace is made*.

We have no personal ill-will against their trading with us, but there must be cessation of hostilities. " Ọta diẹ, Orẹ diẹ ni ipani " (" A little enmity and a little friendship is always fatal to life "), says a Yoruba proverb.

6. We are thankful for Your Excellency reminding us of our obligation to the Ijẹbus.

Since Ogunṣigun has commenced his troubles the Awujalẹ has sent to inform us, and we feel it our duty to help him in case he should be distressed, but we trust Your Excellency will do your best to avert the impending war there.

7. We have to thank Your Excellency for the kind reception of our messengers, the kind present of money sent, and of the valuable seeds sent to us. They will receive our best care and attention.

8. Wishing Your Excellency good health and prosperity, and hope before long you shall hear that the Abẹokuta roads are opened.

We remain to be,

Your Excellency's faithful friends,

their Marks

AJAYI	×	*Balogun of Ibadan.*
OṢUNTOKI	×	*The Mayẹ of Ibadan.*
FIJABI	×	*The Abẹṣẹ of Ibadan.*
FAJINMI	×	*The Agbakin of Ibadan.*

§ 5. The Alâfin's Measures for Peace and the Issues

We have mentioned above that the Ijẹbu messengers were at Ọyọ waiting the pleasure of the ALÂFIN for making a move towards the negotiations for peace with the Ilọrins, in which they were to take a part. But as His Majesty would not make any move, they were obliged to return home from disappointment ; but after the invasion of Bẹrẹkodo by the Dahomians, and both Isẹyin and Ọyọ lay exposed to their inroads, the whole country began to murmur against their King as the author of all their troubles, by keeping the national force tied down at Ikirun. His Majesty now saw sufficient cause to make a move. He collected messengers again from Ibadan, Iwo, Isẹyin and Ogbomọṣọ and sent them on peace embassy to Ilọrin. This he did in accordance with the wishes of the Governor, and to make a demonstration of his desire for peace ; otherwise provincial embassies are wholly unnecessary. It was an open secret that the ALÂFIN always had a regular correspondence with Ilọrin all through these wars, but his private messenger Alebiọṣu by name, usually went by the bush paths escorted by hunters. The present effort being apparently sincere, everything seemed favourable this time, the Emir of Ilọrin (perhaps playing the same game of duplicity as the ALÂFIN) received the messengers cordially, saying to the ALÂFIN's messenger that his master was rather too long in making this move towards peace, and why so ? For his part (said he) he quite agreed to peace-making but he would wish the messengers to go back to their master and let him ascertain assuredly from the Ibadans whether they were really prepared this time to make peace, and when were they prepared to go home ? Then if the answer was favourable the messengers should come again and encamp between the two armies, and let both decamp on the same day, the ALÂFIN's messengers accompanying each home.

[This stipulation of the Ibadans " going home " throws a doubt on his sincerity as the Ibadans were there to defend Ikirun against his forces.]

The messengers returned to Ọyọ on the 20th July, 1890. There was a universal rejoicing at the bright prospects of peace, the eyes of all being turned to Ọyọ for the next move.

After some delay of over a month the ALÂFIN sent to tell the Ibadan chiefs at Ikirun the result of the embassy, and meanwhile addressed the following letter to the Governor of Lagos.

From the ALÂFIN of Ọyọ to the Governor of Lagos.

The Palace, Ọyọ, *July 23rd*, 1890.

To HIS EXCELLENCY, SIR A. C. MOLONEY, K.C.M.G.

GOVERNOR,

Your Excellency's letters of the 19th May and 16th June have been duly received with the amount of money forwarded with the letter for which please receive my sincere thanks.

2. I hope my last of the 18th June has reached Your Excellency.

3. In that letter I told the Governor that we were about sending our messengers to Ilọrin to negotiate peace, and promised to let him know the result.

4. I am happy to say that my messenger with messengers from Oluiwo of Iwo, Asẹyin of Isẹyin and the messenger of the Balẹ of Ogbomọsọ left Ọyọ on the 25th of June, and they arrived here again on the 20th inst. I am glad to say with favourable results. Both parties have placed themselves in my hands, agreeing to decamp when I send my messengers again.

5. Considering the great interest and kind assistance Your Excellency has rendered us in this matter it would be very disrespectful and a base ingratitude on my part to send to disperse them without Your Excellency's knowledge and approval. I therefore earnestly beg that Your Excellency lose no time in forwarding me a letter of approval so that my messengers should go in time, as both parties are eager to return to their respective homes.

My messenger is also leaving for Ijẹbu to-morrow, the 24th inst., to inform the Awujalẹ of the same as he also has great interest in the peace negotiation.

6. I am expecting Your Excellency's reply within a fortnight from date. I feel I ought not to make a final move without your knowledge as we have a proverb which says, " He that planteth should reap the harvest."

7. When the Ibadans are returned home then the Treaty, a copy of which is affixed to Your Excellency's letter to me of the 19th May will be enforced.

Wishing Your Excellency a good health.

I have the honour to remain,

Your Excellency's good friend,

ADEYẸMI × (his mark),

RECEIPT.　　　　　　　　　　　　*The Alâfin of Ọyọ.*

Received per bearer Taniafisara the sum of £31 5s. by order of the Governor of Lagos on the 21st June, 1890.

ADEYẸMI × (his mark), *The Alâfin of Ọyọ.*

Before the return of these messengers from Ikirun, the Ilọrin horse raided the Ikirun farms and kidnapped some people. A party of horsemen raided the Ilobu farms also and were equally successful as no one expected a raid whilst peace negotiation was going on ; but a third party which raided the Ogbomọsọ farms were worsted, four horsemen being killed, their horses taken and the raiders dispersed.

After this the Ilọrins sent again to the Ibadan camp to negotiate peace independent of the ALÂFIN : the Emir of Ilọrin went so far as to send presents to the Balogun of Ibadan ; but since their last perfidy the Ibadan chiefs would never trust them. Terms of peace were being arranged when a fire broke out at Ikirun. The people took advantage of the peace negotiation which was going on to go out far (to the Ila farms) for sticks and leaves for roofing, all unarmed : suddenly a party of Ilọrin horsemen appeared but, suspecting no mischief, the Ibadans allowed them to pass on Ikirun-wards ; but the horsemen later on wheeled round and captured every one of them, and among the captured were two of the Balogun of Ibadan's nephews, the sons of his late brother Akīrimisa.

This put an end to the negotiation, and although the Ilọrins sent twice afterwards to renew the negotiation, and repudiated the charge of sending a kidnapping expedition while they were negotiating peace, yet as they did not send back the captives, especially the Balogun's nephews, they did not obtain a hearing : the second set of messengers were even forbidden to see the Balogun's face lest they lose their heads.

Failing to negotiate with the Ibadans the Ilọrins opened communication with the Oluiwo of Iwo, but when the Ibadans heard of it, knowing it to be an intrigue they sent to put a stop to it at once.

Thus ended all negotiations with Ilọrin.

§ 6. THE ILORINS AT ILOBU

We have related above that after the taking of Ọfa and the desertion of several towns in the neighbourhood, including Inisa near Ikirun, the Ilọrins still kept to their camp at Yanayo, a full day's journey from Ikirun. Depending on their horses they could come all the way to give battle to the Ibadans at Ikirun, but the Ibadans, without the skill or means to meet a vigorous cavalry charge, were unable to go after them in the plain in which Ọfa is situated. After one or two stiff battles the Ilọrins were convinced that they could not dislodge the Ibadans by direct attack except by stratagem. They therefore left their women and the infirm at the Yanayo camp and came forward to make a new camp at a place called Toribọlà between Ẹrin and Ijabẹ, from which they may carry on surprise attacks on the small towns between Ikirun and Ilobu, cut off supplies, threaten the rear of Ikirun and thus induce the Ibadans to retreat from their present position. The Ibadans therefore appointed Chief Akintọla to Ilobu to guard these strategic points.

A small town behind Ilobu called Ile Aro was surprised and taken by the Ilọrins. When the news reached Akintọla at Ilobu he quickly marched out, gave chase, and intercepted them as they were returning with captives and booty. It was on this occasion that a single combat was fought between the champion lancers of the two armies which recalled similar warfare of ancient times. The two famous horsemen of both armies here met for the first time. Nasamu, nick-named " Gata-Ikoko " of whom we have heard as the captor of Ẹnimowu at Ẹrin, the most famous of the Ilọrin horsemen on his famous war steed named from its colour " Arasi," here met with Latunji, surnamed " Okiti kan," of whom we have heard as the rescuer of his cousin Chief Akintọla at Ile Ifẹ when entrapped in an ambuscade, on his favourite war steed named " Nasañkọrè." Both of them had heard of each other's fame and exploits on various battlefields, and had been longing to meet each other in a trial of valour. They now accosted each other, " Is that you? " " Is that you ? " and then the single combat began according to their accepted rules, with spear on either side, and the hosts on both sides stood holding their breath, and watching these two chiefs of strength. The combat lasted for some time, which shows they were equally matched ; but by a skilful turn Nasamu with his spear knocked Latunji's spear off his hand, and then went about to throw him off his horse and spear him on the ground, when Latunji hastily whipped out his revolver from his side and wounded Nasamu in the right hand, causing his spear to fall off his hand. With the left Nasamu gathered up his reins, put spurs to his horse and escaped : the Ilọrins with one accord gave way and were hotly pursued and badly beaten, all their captives and booty being recovered.

Nasamu's spear was picked up and carried as a trophy before Akintọla ; he returned with great triumph to Ilobu, waiting outside the gate with the spear stuck on the ground before him, the war boys drumming and dancing around it till the pursuers had all come, and so he entered Ilobu in triumph.

The victory was so decisive, the Ilọrins lost so many in dead, wounded and captives, that they waited no longer in their new camp at Toribọla, but retreated to the former camp at Yanayo.

The Ilọrin plan, if successful at Ile Aro, was to attack Ọfa-tẹdo and Ẹdẹ next, and thereby dislodge the Ibadans from Ikirun.

For a considerable time after this the Ilọrins neither attacked the Ibadans at Ikirun, nor at Ilobu, but contented themselves with kidnapping expeditions in the Ogbomọsọ farms.

§ 7. THE CONDUCT OF THE CHIEFS AT IKIRUN

As it had become evident that under present conditions the Ibadans and Ilọrins were not likely to come into closer contact so that the issue might be decided one way or another, and the temper of both remained the same, the Ibadan war chiefs were content to make a home of Ikirun at least for the present, whilst the Ilorins made a home of their camp at Yanayo.

The Balogun of Ibadan gave himself up to a reckless life of wantonness and cruelty, and the other leading chiefs were no better. Moreover the Balogun took to drinking to excess, and his slaves overran the country to an extent hitherto unknown, not even in the days of the late Arẹ with his numerous slaves. The people were literally groaning under fines and confiscations from trumped-up charges ; the Balogun appropriated whatever his slaves brought him, asking no questions as to how they came by it. Cases brought before him were never investigated before he ordered the confiscation of defendants' houses, seizing the women and children to be shared by the three leading chiefs, himself, the Mayẹ and the Agbakin; these were sold to the Ijẹbus if not speedily redeemed. Knowing this to be the case, old grievances were raked up by some men who wished to take revenge upon others, and inflict unjust punishment upon them. Slaves who had redeemed themselves with wives and family were seized, their family shared by the leading chiefs and sold unless speedily redeemed.

Freemen invited to Ibadan by their fathers or grandfathers were seized as slaves, but cases of this sort the other chiefs would have nothing to do with, because nearly all of them came that way to live at Ibadan.

Latterly a house to be confiscated was surrounded very early in the morning before the inmates were up from their beds, but the master of the house was never caught so that he might arrange for the ransom of his household.

Bad as things were at Ibadan they were worse in the provinces.

Chief Akintọla practised the same at Ilobu. Sumọnu Apampa alone, to his praise be it said, was exempt from such practices, and he would not allow anyone in his quarter of the town to be accused or distressed in this way.

The Balogun was determined to enrich himself before they returned home, whenever that might be.

Such was life at Ikirun latterly.

CHAPTER XXXIII

THE DARK BEFORE THE DAWN

§ I. LIBERATION OF THE EGBADOS

WE have related in previous chapters how the Egbados were
among the most peaceful tribes and most loyal to the ALÂFIN of
Qyǫ, from the earliest times down to the period when the provinces
became disorganized by the rebellion of the nobles ; and how the
revolution fomented by the Fulanis spreading south involved the
Egbas who in their turn conquered the Egbados at the battle of
Owiwi ; and how up to 1888 they were under a succession of Egba
rulers to whom they paid tribute. Ilaro the chief town was about
this time under Chief Ogundeyi of Iporo Abeokuta. They were
now to change masters.

The Egbados were groaning under the oppression of the Egbas
on the one hand, and were much harassed by the Dahomians on
the other, their masters being unable to free them from the annual
raids of the latter. They were therefore determined to place
themselves under the protection of the British Government.
Chief Falǫla of Oke Ǫdan, who at this time appeared to be the
greatest of the Egbado chiefs, went to Lagos in person and
represented their case to the British Government, whereby the
various branches of the Egbado tribes should come under the
British protectorate. Prince Tẹla of Ilaro, son-in-law of Falǫla,
was deputed by the combined Egbado chiefs to carry out the
Treaty at Lagos. The British flag, however, was not hoisted at
once in those places, but subsequently when to the oppression of
the Egbas was added the encroachment of the French Government
from Porto Novo, the flag was hoisted at once at Ilaro in 1891
and at Oke Ǫdan.

The following towns which had suffered more or less from the
Dahomians, were included in the Egbado protectorate :—

Ilaro, Oke Ǫdan, Ǫwǫ̀, Ijakǫ̀, Isagbo, Ajilete, Isalu, Onfǒ,
Ipokia Sàhàsà Ilagbẹ, Itakete, Isiyan, Iyakóto, Iwoyè, Idǫgo,
Igbeji, Isoto, Itolu, Pahayi, Pokoto, Ijado, Ibese, Ilobi, Ẹrinja, etc.

The annexation of Ilaro caused great consternation and indignation at Abeokuta ; several indignation meetings were held to
protest against it. They went so far as to threaten Ilaro with
war if the flag was not hauled down. On an appeal to Lagos a

small force of Hausas was sent to protect the place. But the Ẹgbas did not attempt to carry out their threat.

The Ẹgbas at length wrote to the Governor of Lagos attesting their rights and protesting against the taking of Ilaro without their consent.

The Governor of Lagos replied to their letter of protest and sent Mr. F. Colley Green a native subintendant of police up, who induced the Ẹgba authorities to send with him a deputation down to Lagos. The Ẹgbas not satisfied with the explanation of the Governor of Lagos, blockaded the land and river route to Lagos.

With the Ijẹbus and Ẹgbas hostile, Lagos at this time appeared like a deserted village. Canoes were drawn up, markets were extremely poor, shop-keepers sat gazing on their goods, there being no buyers, and the streets seemed to have put on a mournful appearance. Lagos then was but a small town. But it would appear that the Ẹgbas suffered equally with Lagos, having nowhere else to dispose of their produce. Moreover the Ẹgba authorities had not the means of making their blockade effective either by land or by the river, the blockade only benefited certain enterprising individuals at the expense of the community ; the object of it was not gained, therefore the matter ended in negotiation.

§ 2. TROUBLES AT IJEBU

Whilst the interior and the Ẹgbados were in an unsettled condition fresh troubles broke out at Ijẹbu. Ogunṣigun the Seriki-of Ijẹbu Igbo, who was sent by the exiled King Afidipọtẹ to reinforce the Ifẹs against the Modakẹkẹs and who refused to decamp when the camps were broken up in 1886, now returned home to Igbo. Being declared an outlaw by the present Awujalẹ for refusing to acknowledge him as his sovereign he returned at the head of an army composed of Ijẹbus, Ifẹs and Ijẹsas to fight and dethrone the present Awujalẹ. The Balogun of Ijẹbu having been recalled home (vide p. 567) Kukù the Seriki of Ijẹbu Ode alone remained at Orù as an outpost and he was attacked by Ogunṣigun's army. Kukù received a gashing wound in the abdomen, the scar of which he bore to his grave ; but he was well repaid for his liberality and largess to the Ibadan boys, many of whom were with him at this time. Many came down for the markets at Orù where, in the absence of the Balogun, Kukù dispensed justice to them and fair treatment against the grasping and greedy Ijẹbus taking undue advantage. He furnished them with arms and ammunition, and they promised to repay his kindness, and with the rifles he possessed in abundance they were able to repulse Ogunṣigun and his army from Orù.

The Ijẹbus were for asking for re-inforcement from Ibadan to prosecute the war with Ogunṣigun and crush him, but the elderly Ijẹbus counselled otherwise, lest the Ọyọs (*i.e.*, the Ibadan boys) gained an insight into their country. The matter ended in negotiation. Ogunṣigun was said to be fined 300 bags of cowries and 11 slaves. Of these slaves, the Awujalẹ took five, the Ijẹbu authorities five, and one, if report be true, was executed in lieu of Ogunṣigun the outlaw, and peace was restored with the Igbo division of the Ijẹbus.

§ 3. STRAINED RELATIONS WITH THE IBADANS

No sooner was the internecine war of the Ijẹbus over than they picked up a quarrel with the Ibadans. The first thing they did was to prohibit the sale of arms and ammunition to the Ibadans, because (as they alleged) they heard that the Ibadans had written to the Governor of Lagos to say that the Ijẹbus were snags by the way, and that the Governor should assist them to remove these snags in order that they might be able to supply the Lagos markets with produce of every description.

But the truth of the matter was because they heard that on the 22nd of August, 1890, the Ibadans rebuilt their toll-gate leading to Abẹokuta with the intention of opening the Abẹokuta road. But this was in accordance with the wish of the Governor of Lagos in his letter to them of the 19th May on the subject.

The friendly relations of Kuku the Seriki of Ijẹbu Ode with the Ibadans at this crisis led to his expulsion from Ijẹbu; there was a great disaffection between the younger Ijẹbus and their King because he and Kuku were not pleased with their attitude towards the Ibadans. The charge against Kuku was that he was befriending the Ibadans and the white men. On his expulsion he came to reside at Ibadan and built a splendid house in Madam Ẹfūduñkẹ's compound near the Arẹ ẹgbẹ ọmọ market.

Strict Blockade.—The Ijẹbus at this time were more resolved than ever to keep their position as middlemen between the interior and the Lagos traders. The Governor of Lagos on the other hand was continually receiving communications both from the ALÂFIN of ỌYỌ and from the Ibadan chiefs relative to a road to the coast independent of the Ẹgbas and Ijẹbus, preferably the Rẹmọ route opened for them in the 'sixties by the late Sir John Hawley Glover, then Governor of Lagos; especially as the Rẹmọs were never in a hostile attitude towards the interior tribes even when there was war between them and the Ijẹbus.

The Governor of Lagos had from time to time communicated with the Awujalẹ of Ijẹbu on the subject, reporting the same to the authorities in Downing Street. It was decided at last to give an open road to the interior tribes at all cost and this was communicated to Her Majesty's Representative at Lagos.

The Ijẹbu authorities, knowing the mind of the British Government, were equally determined on their part to keep their country closed to all " foreigners " to or from the interior.

The Governor of Lagos, Sir Alfred Moloney, having come to the end of his term of service on the coast, was reluctant to close his career with a war among those with whom he had been on terms of friendship since the time of Governor Glover. He therefore sent a warning to the Egbas and the Ijẹbus through their sons at Lagos, advising them to change their attitude towards the interior tribes ; that Her Majesty's Government had resolved upon an open road from the interior to the coast, that his long residence among them on friendly relations made him feel reluctant to close his career with war, but that another administration would not be bound by such consideration. But this communication was not accepted in the spirit in which it was tendered, but rather in a hostile way ; a strict blockade was resolved upon both by the Ijẹbus and the Egbas.

§ 4. Death of Alihu, the Emir of Ilọrin

About the end of November, 1891, the report of the death of Alihu, the Emir of Ilọrin, gained ground, and spread all over the country ; the precise date of his demise was not known, probably it was in the earlier part of the month. Prince Mọ́mọ́ the rightful successor, whom Kàràrà had regarded as his rightful sovereign, was unanimously chosen by all to the throne of Ilọrin. It was said that about 20,000 horsemen and 20,000 footmen escorted him home from the camp to take possession of the throne of his fathers.

As soon as Mọ́mọ́ ascended the throne the scene was changed altogether. Being partly of Yoruba descent, his mother being a native of Ipapo a town near Isẹyin, he was for peace with the Yorubas. Communications between him and the ALÁFIN OF ỌYỌ were open and frequent, the latter sending him some heavy presents for his coronation : the return presents from the Emir were beautiful horses richly caparisoned. He also sent a horse to the Balẹ of Ipapo, his mother's town. Some of the princes of ỌYỌ also exchanged presents with Ilọrin princes.

Not long after the accession of Mọ́mọ́ the renowned Kàràrà, the Hausa Balogun of Ilọrin, died in the camp and was succeeded by his son Adamu who inherited not only his father's property but also his warlike spirit and his office.

The road to Ilọrin was now partially and informally open to enterprising traders. No active measures were taken any longer on either side, each remaining in his camp, Adamu only barking as a chained dog.

Madam Ọmọsa of Ibadan, whose husband Ẹnimowu had been captured since 1887, and who had been spending largely for his release but all in vain, now sent again to the ALÂFIN praying His Majesty to renew his efforts on her behalf at the present favourable turn of affairs. Success attended their efforts this time, and not only Ẹnimowu but also Malade and the two nephews of the Balogun of Ibadan were released, Winkunle, Tubọsun's son, having died in captivity at Ilọrin. The released arrived at Ọyọ on the 2nd of June, 1892, and after paying their respects to the ALÂFIN rejoined the war chiefs at Ikirun.

§ 5. Ijẹbu Excesses and Infatuation between the Years 1884 and 1892

As middlemen, between Lagos and the interior of Yoruba, the Ijẹbus enjoyed great advantages which were as greatly abused. Ibadan especially was at their mercy for supplying them with arms and ammunition, in which Ijẹbus themselves profited enormously ; and on this account they held themselves practically as their masters, knowing that the Ibadans depended upon them in order to be able to defend their frontiers against the Ilọrins, and must perforce submit to any affront offered them.

An Ijẹbu, whatever his social standing—only because he is an Ijẹbu—considers himself superior to any Ọyọ man. The following will suffice for an illustration :—

The son of the Balogun of Ijẹbu once said in conversation with the writer : " Afi Oyinbo afi Ijẹbu, dede aiye dede ẹru ni wọn. Ko si ọja ti a ita Oyinbo, ko si ọja ti a ita Ijẹbu " (i.e., " Except the white man and the Ijẹbus the whole world besides are slaves : there is no market in which a white man may be sold and none where Ijẹbus may be sold.") Can conceit go any further ?

An educated African, an Ọyọ by birth, resident at Lagos, had occasion to reside at Ijẹbu for some time, where he made some friends. On one occasion he was about to pay a flying visit to the interior and one of his young Ijẹbu friends, trying to dissuade him from going, said to him : " Are you going Ibadan way ? Mark you there are no Ijẹbus there for you to associate with, they are all Ọyọs there ! " This innocent effort at persuasion but provoked a smile, but it showed what the Ijẹbus thought of themselves.

As the only market for trade at this time, thousands of Ọyọs came down once a month from the eastern and western provinces, assembled at Ibadan, and proceeded under escort to Ijẹbu, for salt especially and other necessaries. The market was held at Orù, an Ijẹbu frontier town. The treatment they generally received at the hands of the Ijẹbus beggars description, and can hardly be credited at this distance of time and change of circumstances. For a load of produce worth thirty shillings an Ijẹbu once offered a bag of something tied up. "And wha. is in your bag?" asked the Ọyọ man. The Ijẹbu replied, "A jo d'alẹ" ("Something to make one dance till eventide"). As he was about to examine the contents of the bag offered him in lieu of his produce, the Ijẹbu went away with the produce, and the unhappy man found nothing but snail-shells left in lieu of his merchandise, and redress could not be obtained!

Another offering a bag of something for a load of produce was similarly asked what the contents were, and replied, "Ki ẹiyẹ luwẹ," a newly-coined word—To make birds swim. As their dialects differed the seller would look at the contents of the bag offered him to know what went by that name, and the Ijẹbu immediately went off with the produce. The contents were wooden emblems of Sango! No redress. The Ijẹbu insisted that once the man had taken the bag, he had accepted his offer!

If an Ọyọ man or woman was selling his wares for 7s. 6d. and the Ijẹbu offered 5s. the former dared not refuse. If he attempted to take back his merchandise from the intending purchaser, there was sure to be a scuffle in which the seller would be overpowered by other Ijẹbus coming to the aid of the buyer, some beating him, others pricking him with their hairpins and so forth.

The caravan route at that time was notoriously unsafe from brigands and Ẹgba kidnappers; any Ọyọ carrier for an Ijẹbu who suffered any losses of his package in part or in whole was made to pay double the price or become the slave of the Ijẹbu. Accidents from slippery paths, highway robbers, thorns and thickets of the bush paths were of frequent occurrence; whatever the losses an Ọyọ carrier for an Ijẹbu might suffer from any of these causes, must be made good at double the price by the carrier and members of his compound or he was claimed as slave by the Ijẹbu.

The action of Ijẹbu men towards Ọyọ maidens need not be referred to: rapes and seizures for trumped-up charges were of revolting frequency. A shocking instance occurred of an Ijẹbu who alleged he had contracted venereal disease from a woman he had ravished, and thereupon claimed heavy damages from her husband!

Whatever the price the Ijẹbus are pleased to offer for any article, the Ọyọ man is obliged to accept as it may end in a total loss of his merchandise and what was offered.

As to flogging at the toll gates—that was so common and indiscriminate that Ijẹbu youths were frequently found to come up to the gates on market days with whips, ready to find exercise for their arms with or without any cause.

The only court to which appeal lay was to the Balogun Nọfọwọkan when he was stationed at Orù, and latterly to Chief Kukù. About a dozen applicants would be found before him at once; hundreds had no chance to approach him before the return of the caravan was due.

The sufferings of these people impressed these chiefs who were dealing out justice to them, and hence they were charged with befriending Ọyọs. This is but a poor description of the kind of treatment Ọyọs had at the hands of the Ijẹbus during this period.

Deference and respect to age and station is a marked characteristic of Yorubas everywhere ; but at this period an Ijẹbu man even on Ọyọ soil would pay no respect to any chief or elderly person. Their indignities and impertinences had to be borne.

There were not wanting venturesome and enterprising persons who would risk the way down the coast with an Ijẹbu friend ; several of these were discovered between Ijẹbu Ode and the coast, and were sold into hopeless slavery.

Chief Kukù the Seriki of Ijẹbu Ode had done much for the Ọyọ war chiefs and for his own pocket, by selling them rifles and cartridges at very high prices. Scores of Ọyọ beauties of whatever town they may be, were seized by him for debts alleged to be owing him by an Ọyọ, it might be by a man of another town unknown to her, as long as the maiden seized was an Ọyọ by birth as the supposed debtor was ! Once in his harem he would never consent to their parents coming to redeem them ! This example was followed by several other well-to-do traders.

These are the causes that led the Ibadan chiefs in their letters to the Governor of Lagos, as mentioned above, to ask for a road to the coast which should not be disturbed and preferably the Rẹmọ route.

Added to all this was the unsafety of the road from Ẹgba kidnappers. The caravans had to be protected by armed escorts every month as they trooped down and back. The first station was ODO-ỌNA-NLA in the Ibadan farms. Here Adio the head priest of the Sango worshippers, was stationed with some elderly warriors. Next at ONIPE. Here was the camp named Budo-Ọdẹ (hunters' camp). Here were stationed the hunters and reserved forces. Next at ỌLỌWA. Here lay the main body of the army,

" Iya Ogun " as it was called. Here such brave men like Solaja and Bada Agidi were posted. Further on at ALABATA and at MAMU were the advanced forces consisting of men from the Ibadan town districts of Ọja Igbo, Ọfa, and Oje.

There were frequent brushes with the Ẹgbas at one point or another, but the most serious engagement in this route occurred in November, 1884, when the Ẹgbas came with a large army and attacked the caravans at ALABATA, overwhelming the guards and sweeping away a large number of traders. The report soon reached Ọlọwa and a strong body of men pursued after and overtook them. A sanguinary engagement took place in which the leaders Solaja and Bada Agidi signalized themselves. The Ẹgbas were defeated with heavy losses. They rescued many of those captured, and captured also many of the Ẹgbas. Among the captured were several Christians who formed the rifle corps of Abẹokuta, with Moses Sasegbọn, the Seriki of the Christians, their captain. Luckily for him he fell into friendly hands. He was caught by one of the boys of his old friend Solaja, who seeing him bleeding from wounds he had received, peremptorily ordered his captor to go for some water for the captive lest he lose him altogether. With a wink he then indicated to Sasegbọn a way of escape, and then turned his back on him, pretending not to see him as he slipped into the bush and escaped. He reached home on the 19th of November, 1884, a wiser man, never more to engage in any kidnapping expedition. He was for months on a sick bed from his wounds.

Moses Sasegbọn was well known at Ibadan, especially at the Ijẹbu quarters in the early seventies. He spent a long time there ; he had a factory with several hands ginning cotton till the war broke out in 1877. He was one of the sufferers when Ẹgba properties and slaves were confiscated at the beginning of the war. This was the second time he had a brush with the Ibadans. In an affray the Ẹgbas had with Ogboriẹfọn the Balogun of Ibadan in the Ogun district he took an active part. When the Ẹgbas were routed he was three days in the bush ere he could find his way home to Abẹokuta.

When the Commissioners went up in 1886 to disperse the camps at Kiriji they met the Ibadan warriors as above described.

§ 6. Causes That Led to the Ijẹbu War

(a) Affront to the Acting Governor

Governor Moloney was not a man of action. It was said that he was too fond of writing letters to and drafting treaties for men who hardly appreciated the one or comprehended the other or knew the force or value of their marks of signature.

During his five years of administration he never once visited the people and the scene of which he writes so much : a single visit from him would have cleared up many difficulties in his way and enabled him to understand much, and he would have acted more to the purpose.   No wonder then that matters remained *in statu quo*.

After his departure the Colonial Secretary, Capt. George Chardin Denton, now Acting Governor, in pursuance of the peaceful policy of the Governor proposed to visit the Awujale of Ijẹbu, talk matters over with him in a friendly way, and point out the advantages that would accrue to the Ijẹbu nation by a free intercourse throughout the country under the auspices of Her Majesty's Government of Lagos.   He received permission from Downing Street to carry out his object.

Having communicated his intentions to the Awujale and obtained his assent, the Acting Governor started for Ijẹbu Ode accompanied by Oliver Smith, Queen's Advocate, Thomas Welsh, Esq., a member of the Legislative Council, and a mercantile representative, Dr. J. W. Rowland, the Colonial Surgeon, Capt. A. F. Tarbet and Mr. F. Colley-Green of the Hausa force, Mr. Jacob Alẹsinlọyẹ, an Ijẹbu merchant resident at Lagos, and Mr. A. L. Hethersett, Government Interpreter, with a guard of honour including the Hausa band to give *eclat* to the occasion.   He took with him also large presents for the Awujale and his chiefs.

The Ijẹbus hearing of the Governor's approach sent to stop him at the landing at Itọ Ike ; he was wilfully misrepresented as coming with hostile intentions.   The Governor, however, sent to remind the Awujale that the visit had been agreed upon between them, and that it had received the sanction of Her Majesty's Government, and the travelling expenses granted : what explanaation was he now to give for not being able to reach him ?   He was quite ready to dispense with his guard of honour and visit Ijẹbu with his attendants only if they conceived any fears and apprehensions.

It was not without much trouble and annoyance that the Governor's messengers with the above errand could reach Ijẹbu Ode being stopped repeatedly by the way.   On reaching the town none of the Ijẹbu Authorities would lodge them ; they were sent from one chief to another till at length they had to return to the town-gate to await the morrow.   They managed to get audience of the king the next day and they returned with a message approving of the Governor's visiting Ijẹbu Ode but not with a military escort.

The Governor, who was all the time in the Colonial steamer, the *Margaret*, now proceeded to Ijẹbu Ode with his civil attendants only. At Ode they were kept under strict surveillance, none of the party being allowed to leave the compound. They had audience of the Awujaḷẹ on the fourth day of their arrival when the Governor impressed upon them the determination of the British Government that the interior peoples should have free access to the coast like themselves. The Governor reasoned with the Ijẹbu authorities, showing them the advantages of opening up the country for trade, and that the result would be a general increase in trade which would bring more money into the country and that the Ijẹbus themselves would enjoy a large share of the same.

He also promised them that the Lagos Government would pay to them a sum equivalent to what they were receiving in tolls.

The Ijẹbu chiefs received the Governor's words with displeasure and with every sign of anger against him and against their own king, putting the blame of the Governor coming up to " dictate " to them (as they call it) upon the Awujaḷẹ who granted him the permission to come. They would listen to nothing else but that the interior Yorubas should meet them at Orù for trade, and that the white man's people (*i.e.*, Lagos traders) meet the Ijẹbus at Ejirin.

The Governor proceeded to give the presents he brought for them. The king accepted his own, but the chiefs unceremoniously refused theirs. This of course the Governor considered an insult, and he therefore told them he would return what had been given him. As they made no objection to this he returned their presents of sheep and cowries he had received, and left Ijẹbu Ode the next morning. Thus the Lagos Government received an unceremonious rebuff in the person of its Chief of the Executive.

The Home Government being informed of the attitude of the Ijẹbus and their action towards the Acting-Governor, the Secretary of State for the Colonies, after consulting with the late Governor, Sir Alfred Moloney, resolved upon coercive measures, and hence gave full power to the new Governor to deal with the Ijẹbus.

§ 7. CAUSES THAT LED TO THE IJẸBU WAR

(b) TREATY MADE AND BROKEN

On the arrival of Governor GILBERT THOMAS CARTER in the latter part of 1891, communication was re-opened with the Ijẹbus. Special messengers were sent down to greet the new Governor. He received them in state in the presence of the principal Government officials and heads of departments, members of councils, and principal merchants.

The first thing the Governor required of them was to apologise for their conduct to Acting Governor Denton. This they had to do. Then they were required to sign a treaty, which among other provisions, abolished human sacrifices and enjoined the free opening of the road through their country between Lagos and the interior for all, the Governor of Lagos stipulating to pay the Awujalẹ £500 annually in lieu of tolls hitherto received from caravans. The delegates objected and required authority from home to sign a treaty. They were detained at Lagos until they received authority to do so or, if needs be, men capable of signing the treaty should be sent down. This was duly effected.

After this, there was a small measure of freedom to and from the interior for a few months, to enlightened people who knew of the treaty, but caravans were still not allowed a foot beyond Orù. But the Ijẹbus were incensed with their king and were determined on a revolution. They showed their resentment in moving the Awujalẹ to several intolerant acts. They picked up a quarrel with the Ibadans, threatened to stop all arms and ammunition if Kukù was not expelled out of Ibadan. Kukù was accordingly expelled, and his fine house at Ibadan was demolished by the Ijẹbus there. Kukù returned to Ijẹbu, but was obliged to take refuge at Ijẹbu Ifẹ which to all Ijẹbus is a city of refuge, by which he escaped death. Kukù remained there till after the taking of Ijẹbu in May, 1892.

Next the Awujalẹ also raked up a quarrel against Ṣolaja that intrepid Ijẹbu horseman at Ibadan. A beautiful cushion he had presented to the king a few years before was sent back : that meant heavy fines which had to be paid or he would demand his life. Ṣolaja certainly was not expected to keep the returned article which had been in the possession of his king. Along with this, frivolous charges were brought against the Rev. D. Olubi, the C.M.S. agent at Ibadan, by the Awujalẹ.

(1) That one of his sons took up some corrugated iron sheets for the C.M.S. house at Ibadan through Ijẹbu when they had forbidden all intercourse with white men.

(2) That he was instrumental in bringing Europeans up country. He sent to the Ibadans that he should be expelled the town. The Ibadan chiefs were reluctant to do so as they had no fault to find with him since he had been amongst them over 40 years. Mr. Olubi hearing this sent Mr. W. S. Allen a colleague to ascertain what the real cause of offence was, and that he was to pass on to Lagos and to procure some presents to appease him. This was done and the C.M.S. granted £5 for the presents in the interest of their interior agents, that route being the only one available to

the interior at present. The presents were accepted but unfortunately they seemed but to serve to whet the appetite of the
Ijẹbu king for more.

The Awujalẹ next sent to demand his head, and that of the
white man (the Rev. T. Harding) at Ibadan. Mr. Olubi then
opened negotiation for his life with the Awujalẹ. He demanded
more presents, and the reverend gentleman sent 12 sheep by Mr.
(now Rev.) F. L. Akīyẹlẹ, a C.M.S. Catechist under him. These
were accepted but the ban was not removed, only matters were
quiet for some time.

After a while, the Awujalẹ sent to the Ibadan war chiefs
threatening to stop trade, with all arms and ammunition if his
orders were not carried out. The Ibadans commissioned one
Fade, an Ijẹbu long resident at Ibadan to negotiate with him,
and point out the unfairness of this order against one who came
amongst them as a youth, grew to manhood, married and begat
children and not once offending against their laws. On Fade's
return he reported that the Awujalẹ was inexorable that he
demanded not the head of Mr. Olubi alone but also that of the
European Mr. Harding, and that the houses and property
of all the Christians should be confiscated and that 200 young
men and women should be sent to appease his wrath.

The war chiefs saw no alternative but to yield to this extraordinary demand. A deputation of Christians was sent to the
camp to remonstrate with the war chiefs but all in vain. They
said "rather sacrifice the head of one man than risk the safety
of the whole country." The home authorities sent back to the
camp to ask whether the order was really meant to be carried out.
A peremptory message was sent back to say if the order was
not carried out the heads of the home authorities themselves
should be taken off !

The messengers with this order arrived at Ibadan on Saturday
the 21st May and the home authorities felt extremely reluctant
to carry it out. Action was postponed till after the assembling of
the town council on Monday and the matter discussed afresh.
But on the Sunday, the sound of cannon was said to be heard
at a distance, a conflagration was descried as that of
the burning of a town. Towards the afternoon the rumour grew
stronger and stronger that the phenomenon descried was at Ijẹbu,
and at last the rumour was confirmed that Ijẹbu was taken by the
British forces from Lagos ! The Home authorities withheld their
hand on the Monday and reported matters to the camp. The
war chiefs were so alarmed that they sent special messengers
from Ikirun to ask pardon of Revs. Olubi and Harding and

expressed their regret that they ever yielded so as to issue such an order against the lives of men with whom they had hitherto lived in the closest bond of fellowship from childhood. In this there is no doubt that we can see the interposition of divine Providence.

The treaty signed by the Ijẹbu plenipotentiaries was accepted with bad grace by the young Ijẹbus at home who kept goading the king to such intolerant acts as the one related above. To see people passing up and down through their country was galling to them. A treaty so badly received evidently could not last long. It was soon broken. Now and then it became known at Lagos that individuals going up or coming down were sent back. The caravans were not allowed to proceed to the Ejirin markets. The Rev. T. E. Williams a Wesleyan minister who had gone to Lagos for the annual Synod of that denomination returning to his post was driven back to Lagos. That the Ijẹbus never meant to observe the spirit or letter of the treaty was evident from the events related above towards Revs. Olubi and Harding, the while unknown at Lagos.

What stirred their hostility most deeply was said to be the action of a foreign missionary going up country, who was received with hostile demonstrations by the Ijẹbus. Whilst waiting to pay his call on the Awujalẹ, a crowd assembled and he, it was said, was going to preach to them against their wish : they would hear nothing from him ; on his persisting this inflamed them and both he and his party were literally driven back to Lagos. This matter was duly reported to the Governor. An ultimatum was sent to the Ijẹbus which they ignoied. The Ẹgbas especially since the Ilaro affair were in sympathy with them, and both began to prepare for the fight. The Governor of Lagos sent a letter to the Ẹgba Government by the Inspector of police, Mr. Adolphus Pratt, which they refused to receive and ordered the bearer to leave the town before sunset that very day with his letter. A council was held the same day at Abẹokuta and it was known that emissaries of the Ijẹbus were in the town to take part in it. It was reported that the Ẹgbas offered their services to the Ijẹbus, but that the Ijẹbus averred they could hold their own, and that if they could not drive back the white man in three months, then the Ẹgbas may come to their aid. Meanwhile the Ẹgbas strictly enforced the blockade of both land and river routes to Lagos. War was now declared against the Ijẹbus.

§ 8. THE IJẸBU CAMPAIGN

The officers and men who took part in the Ijẹbu campaign were :

Colonel Francis C. Scott, C.B. Inspector-General of the Gold
Coast Forces, the Commander of the Expedition.

Officers from England, 20. 4. 92 :

Capt. The Hon. A. S. Hardinge, 1st Battalion Scots Fusiliers.
Capt. E. R. Owen, 1st Batt. Lancashire Fusiliers.
Capt. A. V. Ussher, 1st Batt. Scottish Rifles.
Capt. R. L. Bower, 7th Batt. King's Royal Rifles.
Capt. J. R. V. Gordon, 15th Hussars.
Lieut. C. E. Laurie, Royal Artillery.
Lieut. J. F. Davies, 1st Batt. Grenadier Guards.

From the Gold Coast, 20. 4. 92.

Capt. F. M. Bayley, Asst.-Inspector, Gold Coast Colony.
Capt. H. D. Larymore, Asst.-Inspector, Gold Coast Colony.
Native Officer Ali, Gold Coast Colony.
Native Officer Akero, Gold Coast Colony.
Mr. Henry Plange, Quartermaster (Acting), Gold Coast Colony.
2 Sergt.-Majors, 4 Sergts., 146 N.C.O.'s and men Hausas.

From Sierra Leone, 9. 5. 92.

Major G. C. Madden.
Lieut. C. V. R. Wright.
Lieut. E. L. Cowrie.
Surgeon Capt. R. Croft.
99 N.C.O.s and men, 2nd Batt., W.I. Regiment.

Lagos Hausas.

Capt. A. F. Tarbet, Asst.-Inspector, Lagos Constabulary.
Capt. G. B. Haddon-Smith, Asst.-Inspector, Lagos Constabu-
    lary.
Capt. R. E. D. Campbell, Asst.-Inspector, Lagos Constabulary.
Sergt.-Majors Dangana and Dankafi.
Asst.-Supdts. F. Colley-Green, A. Claud Willoughby.
Pay and Quartermaster W. R. Harding.
158 men, rank and file.
With 100 Ibadan Irregulars under their own Captain Toyan.

The expedition left Lagos on the 13th of May, 1892, and arrived
at Epẹ early on the 14th.

The Ijẹbus had expected the expedition to come by Itọ Ike, the
shortest route to the capital, and had therefore spread their army
ready at the Ẹluju grassfields not far from the town of Ibẹfun.
Previously, they had offered in sacrifice a man and a woman,
goats, fowls and pigeons at Itọ Ike, and charms of imprecation for
which they were famous were uttered over the creek that the vessels
might founder and the expedition might end in failure. But they

heard to their surprise that the transports had proceeded to Ẹpẹ
and the troops landed there ! They hastily broke up the camp
and proceeded to the Ẹpẹ road. Of the three routes generally
taken, Itọ Ike, Ejirin, and Ẹpẹ, the last is the longest but the best.
It has the best and easiest landing, and a village of some considerable size to be used as the base, one-half of the population of which
consists of Lagos people. The way to the capital from here was
mostly through farms. The other routes had no such advantages,
they were for the greater part through bush paths: that through
Ejirin especially at that time of the year was worse, the road for
the most part v-shaped paths. The forward march from Ẹpẹ after
every preparation had been made was on the 16th May. Arriving
at Pobo after a short march, an Ijẹbu ambuscade opened fire about
10.30 a.m., and a smart brush took place, the Ijẹbus hastily retreating. The village and hamlets surrounding were immediately
burnt down. In this engagement one of the Ibadan Irregulars
was wounded and died from the wound at Ijẹbu Ode a few days
after. Leaving Pobo on the 17th a larger force was encountered
at Erebo ; here the Ijẹbus made a furious attack but were repulsed
with heavy losses, and here fell A. Claud Willoughby of the Lagos
force, venturing too far in pursuit. The engagement lasted from
8 a.m. till 11 a.m., when the village of Majọda was taken.

No traces of the Ijẹbus were found on the 18th except the
deserted camp. On the morning of the 19th the order of march
was—the Ibadan Irregulars first under their captain Toyan, then
the Lagos Hausas led by Capt. Bower, then the W. I. Regiment
under their Major, the Gold Coast Hausas bringing up the rear
under Capts. Campbell, and Haddon Smith of the English Militia
Force.

The report of the day's event given by an officer who took an
active part in the fight was as follows :—

" As we marched along a few men from the hills at the left
fired at us, but soon ran away ; probably this was intended as
a signal to the main force. We continued our march and all
of a sudden, the Ibadan Irregulars halted, and began drumming
and fixing on their war charms ; Capt. Bower ordered them to
move on, but their Captain replied, ' The Ijẹbus are near, we
have smelt them.' They had not advanced twenty paces when
at a bend in the road the Ijẹbus opened fire at us. Here their
main army was concentrated. They chose their spot well.
The River Yemọji flowed across the path at this time overflowing
its banks breast deep for the tallest man. The river flowed
through marshes except at the ford through which we must
pass and this the Ijẹbus rendered dangerous by snags thrown

into it. As they opened fire the Ibadans were first at them,
then Capt. Bower rushed forward with the Lagos Hausas, and
the engagement began. It lasted full three hours. The Ijẹbus
retreated to the other bank and raised a shout, as much as to
say, ' We will see how you will cross,' but the Maxim gun soon
cleared the opposite bank. The Lagos Hausas were ordered
forward into the river, but they wavered and hesitated. In a
moment· the Colonel thundered out, ' 2nd West, advance ! '
The West Indian Regiment at once rushed into the stream,
stumbling on the snags but kept going at the enemy, the Colonel
himself amid stream giving his orders. The Hausas now came
rushing in whilst Capt. Owen with the 7-pounder fired over
their heads and quite cleared the landing for our men. Inspector
F. C. Green shouldered the 7-pounder across the stream, shells
and shrapnel doing their deadly work. At the right bank of
the river Capt. Owen was wounded in the head and leg. The
Ijẹbus fled in confusion. Their camp was at the village of
Magbọn but they never stayed to defend it. Rockets were
fired into the forest and thick bush surrounding the place,
and thousands of Ijẹbus hidden therein were dislodged and fled
away in terror. The Ibadan Irregulars seeing the rockets for
the first time with their horrid noises and streaming fiery tails,
bursting into the forest, dislodging ambuscades and others
concealing themselves, fancied the whole forest on fire, they
thereupon shouted and acclaimed Colonel Scott, 'Adana sun
igbo '[1] (one who set the forest on fire). The village of Magbọn
was occupied that afternoon and there the expedition passed
the night."

He went on to say :—

" Next morning, thinking the Ijẹbus would make their last
stand to defend the capital at all cost, the Colonel arranged his
troops accordingly with every precaution. The Imperial troops
being more steady led the way under Capt. Bower to his great
delight. From Magbọn right on to Ijẹbu Ode the capital was
one broad path, the bush on either side the road was trodden down,
and articles strewn about the whole way. The Ijẹbus after their
defeat at Màgbọn thought they were being pursued, so they
fled precipitately home. The town was entered on the 20th of
May.

" On reaching Ijẹbu Ode we found that the town had been
deserted, the poor old King was left with only two or three
men, and a few of the chiefs trembling. He came forward to

---

[1] That is the origin of the word, now commonly applied at Lagos
to all raw up-countrymen as the irregulars then were.

Y

Col. Scott and said he thanked him for teaching a sharp lesson
to those disobedient young fellows whom he had warned, and
warned in vain, not to venture to fight the white man.   The
Colonel replied, ' I see you cannot manage your disobedient
boys, so I have come to help you to do so.'   The King was
kept as a State prisoner in his own house, and only allowed to
take a stroll about in the evenings with orderlies behind him.
He felt himself safer with the conquerors than with his own
refractory subjects.

" Less than an hour after we entered the town, we saw an
old man staggering on towards us, saying, ' I want my skin ;
he has taken my skin ; I want it.'   It was the aged Balogun
Nofowokan.   The Hausas looting, one of them entered the
Balogun's house and saw him sitting on a large leopard skin ; he
drove him off from it and took the skin, and this he came to
the Colonel about.   Enquiry was made, his skin was restored to
him, and a strict order was given that the old man was not to
be molested."

The Governor of Lagos went up immediately after.   The Queen's
birthday was celebrated on the 24th with imposing military
ceremonies.   Chief Kukù came from his place of exile and
welcomed the Governor.

It appeared that the Governor had written to the Ibadans to
attack the Ijẹbus on the north at the same time that the troops
from Lagos attacked them on the south.   Nothing was seen of
the Ibadans, and the Governor was inclined to doubt their good
faith ; but when Ijẹbu was taken, a large batch of letters was
found in the King's quarters, letters that had been sent some up
country and some to Lagos, the bearers of which had disappeared ;
among them was found the Governor's letter to the Ibadans.
The bearer had been made away with by the Ijẹbus !   The postal
work of distributing these letters to their respective owners was
the first duty of civilization performed at Ijẹbu.

The expedition left Ijẹbu Ode on the 30th May, leaving Capt.
Campbell as head of the district and Capt. Bower with 100 Hausas
to keep order.   The Ipebi or the king's private residence was
converted into a fort and there all were quartered, the king
occupying a separate quarter within the compound.   The disused
royal palace at Iporogun, and the famous Ogboni house wherein
were several men kept in stocks and tortured, were levelled with
the ground, the victims being released.   The king was allowed
£200 a year and Chief Kukù £100 p.a. to assist the king in the
management of purely native affairs, and the aged Balogun £50
p.a. out of regard to his age and position.

§ 9. EFFECTS OF THE CAMPAIGN

The taking of Ijẹbu Ode sent a shock of surprise and alarm throughout the whole land. The people felt instinctively that a new era was about to dawn on them. A new and foreign power had entered into the arena of active politics in the country, and everyone was exercised in mind as to how the country would be affected by it. Combatants suspended hostilities and all of them together turned their faces coastwards.

At the Seat of War.—The belligerents felt that their operations must soon come to an end, engagements therefore ceased.

In the Country at Large.—To the vast majority of the common people it was like the opening of a prison door : and no one who witnessed the patient, long-suffering, and toiling mass of humanity that week by week streamed to and from the coast with their produce, their manufactures and other articles of trade and returned with their purchases, could refrain from heaving a sigh of gratification on the magnitude of the beneficial results of the short and sharp conflict.

The first night in which, after the fall of Ijẹbu Ode, the troop of the first set of caravans slept at the Kanakana toll gate beyond Aka, large fires were lighted, and all the men and women sitting round, spent the hours in recounting their sufferings and losses for years, in this very place, and the great change that has taken place. They continued thus far into the night, and occasionally raised loud huzzahs for the merciful deliverance, and the prospect of freedom of trade, and the discharge of their debts which the long period of 16 years' war had imposed upon every individual in the interior countries, giving thanks to God and invoking blessings on the head of the good Queen of England.

They brought cloths of native manufacture, cotton, indigo, palm oil, palm kernels, beads, cattle, poultry, yam flour, pots and plates of native manufacture, calabashes in large quantities, turkeys and pigeons, rubber, etc., etc., and took back mostly salt, cloths and other articles of European manufacture, trade rum, gin, matchets, etc., etc.

On the Ijẹbus.—Even among the Ijẹbus themselves, very few if any outside the high officials of the capital who had hitherto maintained the iron system of inexorable exclusiveness and rigour suffered much from the change: the Ijẹbus were exclusively traders and they benefited by the increased trade. But the escape of slaves which was inevitable was their greatest cry. Slavery as an institution, however, was doomed to disappear.

The door was open to the preaching of the gospel. There was

already a small congregation of Christians, the work of Ijẹbu citizens who had been converted at Lagos and Abẹokuta, and who had learnt to read the Scriptures in their own tongue. These, who hitherto dared not show their faces or profess their religion openly were now released from fear, and when a few months later delegates from Lagos were sent formally to introduce Christianity amongst them—in an assembly of the King and his chiefs—these Christians came in a body, and in a humble but fervent address assured the King and chiefs of their loyalty and patriotic devotion, that the religion they professed enjoined both, and that they would never be found wanting in every duty appertaining to loyal citizens.

Permission was then given for the teaching of Christianity publicly, and grants of land were made for churches, schools, and mission stations.

On the Ẹgbas.—It was generally known that a large section of the Ẹgbas was disposed to render the Ijẹbus assistance, but as the community of Abẹokuta included a large number of intelligent citizens mostly Christians, who knew the magnitude of the power they had to deal with, their hands were held back by them. But there is no doubt that if the Ijẹbus had succeeded in repelling the invasion even but temporarily, there would not be wanting a large force of Ẹgbas which would have volunteered to lend their aid and might even attack Ilaro.

As it was, a few months after this event, when it appeared probable that Abẹokuta might also come in for a share of attention from the Lagos Government, a diplomatic move was made by the chiefs through one of their intelligent citizens, and overtures were made to the Lagos Government, accompanied by carefully-worded apologies for their late actions, especially towards the messenger of the Government whom they drove away without even accepting the letter he brought. He apologized for the Ẹgbas in these terms. The letter was addressed "To the Chief of Abẹokuta." Now there was no one to lay claim to that title. The Alake was but a figurehead and had no authority. Ogundeyi of Iparo, Onlado of Kunta and the Jaguna of Igbein, who together managed the affairs of the town, were co-partners, so that not one of the three could by himself lay claim to that title, and the Ogbonis whose voices are supreme in important political crises could not claim the title either. And again, for aught they could tell the letter may have contained certain orders they were not in a position to carry out. It was better therefore that they did not know the contents thereof, than to know and not be able to carry them out. Consequently their action in not accepting the letter was dictated by the high esteem they had for the British Government.

And that the messenger might not linger when he was unable to fulfil the object of his mission—for the letter might have contained urgent matters—they therefore respectfully asked him not to stay or loiter, but to proceed to Lagos at once.

Such was the tenor of the apologies they made, and thus they endeavoured to explain away what was a gross insult to be but a cautious deference. Their explanation was accepted, and the result was a free and uninterrupted opening of the roads by land as well as by the river.

On Lagos.—An abundant supply of produce, a large and steadily increasing volume of trade was the result, not unaccompanied by some disappointment due entirely to over-exaggerated hopes and keen competition, and glutting of the markets. But as the old condition of things was for ever gone, men soon adapted themselves to the new.

Chapter XXXIV

THE END OF THE WAR

§1. Governor Carter's Progress up Country

Governor Carter was not the man to leave his work half done. The refractory and irreconcilable Ijẹbus had been subjugated; the Ẹgbas had submitted and their apologies accepted. He now proceeded to the further interior to put an end to the protracted war, fraught with so much evil to the country. The measure adopted for this purpose was the only one capable of dispersing such fierce combatants, *viz.*, an armed intervention advocated for by the writer all through these wearisome years. Although it might not be necessary to pull a trigger, yet a display of force offered a far more convincing weight of argument than volumes of treaties, faultless though these may be in aim and purpose. The presence of the Governor himself gave additional weight and importance to the Mission.

Governor Carter left Lagos on the 3rd January, 1893, for his tour. He was accompanied by a *posse* of Hausa soldiers, with Captain Bower, one of the officers who came out for the Ijẹbu war. The Maxim gun was *en évidence* throughout the whole way.

The Governor went *via* Abẹokuta. He there had a long conference with the Ẹgba chiefs and a treaty was signed on the 18th of January, 1893 (*vide* App. A). Face to face with the conqueror of Ijẹbu, and knowing the unsatisfactory relations that had always existed between Abẹokuta and Lagos since the time of Governor Glover in 1867, and the part they played recently in conjunction with the Ijẹbus, they were certainly apprehensive of subjugation or annexation: and when the Governor assured them that he would do neither provided they mend their manners in future, they respectfully requested that that assurance should be specifically stated in the treaty; hence the clause.

[Clause 5. . . . So long as the provisions of this treaty are strictly kept, no annexation of any portion of the Ẹgba country shall be made by Her Majesty's Government without the consent of the lawful authorities of the country. No aggressive action shall be taken against the said country and its independence shall be fully recognized.]

This should be particularly noted because in after years other

626

parts of the country, whose independence was never even threatened (*e.g.*, Oyo and IBADAN) there being no need for any such thing, were held by some to occupy less favourable positions because a specific guarantee of their independence was not stated in the treaties signed with them. They were taken to be open to annexation.

The expedition leaving Abẹokuta proceeded to Oyo, the capital of YORUBA *via* Isẹyin.

The Governor was well received by the ALÂFIN of Oyo and His Excellency's tent was pitched in the Asipa's market, hard by the King's garden. This was a concession due to the owner of the town, the Asipa being the son of the late Oja the founder of Ago d'Oyo. His Majesty had several private interviews with His Excellency besides the public reception accorded him, and a treaty was concluded between the ALÂFIN and the Governor. (*Vide*, App. A.) From Oyo the Governor was now about to proceed to Ikirun *via* Ilọrin. The ALÂFIN was asked for an Ilari to go with him to the former place for the dispersal of the Ibadan camp by authority. He once more told off the Ilari Oba-kò-ṣe-tan to go with His Excellency; but the Governor would have nothing to do with that name of evil omen, "The King is not ready." His Majesty was told plainly that it was time the King was ready, for this war must now come to an end. Seeing the Governor was not a man to be shuffled or trifled with the King at once yielded, and ordered Oba l'olu (The King is the Chief) to go instead. The short and sharp lesson taught the Ijẹbus made an impression on the whole country not soon to be effaced.

From Oyo the Governor proceeded to Ilọrin *via* Ogbomọṣọ. He was cordially received by the Balẹ of Ogbomọṣọ, who ever afterwards often referred to the pleasant and pleasurable time he spent with the Governor. He was apprehensive about his proposed visit to Ilọrin, and he did all he could to dissuade him from going there as he greatly feared the perfidy of the Ilọrins and their hostility to Christians generally.

From all accounts the Governor on the other hand unfortunately left with the impression that the Balẹ's seeming anxiety on his account was not due to disinterested motives but to the sight of the large amount of presents he saw going forward to Ilọrin ! The reflective reader of these pages, however, will see that the Balẹ had good and ample reasons for distrusting the good faith of the Ilọrins.

At Ilọrin the Governor had several interviews with the Emir and they parted with an assurance of mutual friendship. But it was generally reported that from the moment the Governor's proposed visit to Ilọrin was known, the Mullahs and others waited upon the Emir and requested him to give them bullocks and money·to make charms in order that the Anasaras (Christians) might not enter their town. The Emir, although not in accord with them in this purpose, nevertheless granted them their request.

He had occasion to throw this in their face and reproach them for it afterwards. He was reported to have said that he knew the futility of their attempts, and that they would have been more candid if they had averred that they wanted something to feast upon. For why should not the Governor visit him ? He liked to see the Governor. The Governor is a European, and himself a Foulah by descent, and they know that the European and the Foulah were brothers, and why should the Mullahs interpose between the meeting of two cousins ? Had he not granted their requests, they would have charged him with niggardliness and would have made the world believe that their charms would have kept the Governor back if the Emir had granted their requests. He concluded in this way, "But the Governor has come and is gone and what about the charms now ? You may now ˈretire and be more honest in future." One thing that struck all the visitors to Ilọrin forcibly at this period was the almost total absence of the fair complexion and straight hair of the original Foulahs. By intermarriages and miscegenation the Negro element had absorbed the Semitic. The Emir himself was of a purely dark complexion, being partly of Yoruba descent, which accounted for his disposition to peace with the rest of the Yoruba country.

From Ilọrin the Governor proceeded to a station between the two camps near the River Ọtin ; there he had several meetings with the war chiefs on both sides. The case for the Ibadans was easy enough, they were there to defend the country against the Ilọrins, as soon then as they decamp they (the Ibadans) would go home. The Ilọrins averred that they were in their own farms and should not be asked to go home. The Ibadans came from full four days' journey, it is they who should be asked to go home.

But the Governor replied that he knew all that, he knew how the Ilọrins came to be there, he even knew how Fulanis and Gambaris came at all to be in Ilọrin, but he did not come there to discuss ancient history. He fixed a day in which both camps should be broken up together ; he appointed those who were to see the Ilọrins home, and those who were to see the Ibadans home. The Awẹrẹ stream near Ẹrin was appointed as a boundary between the two States. And so the camps were broken up on the same day. The Ibadans had wanted to stop a day or two at Ẹdẹ to compose the difference between the people and the Timi Lagunju, who had been deposed by them, but they were hurried homewards so that they could not do so.   Thus ended the sixteen years' war.

We might call attention to the fact that all the towns serving the Ibadans in the Ibolo district asked the Governor for a flag each as a protection against Ibadan oppression.   The Governor did not accede to their wish but promised to give attention to their request. The Ibadan army arrived behind their town wall on the 22nd March, 1893.

§ 2. THE RETURN HOME OF THE IBADANS

The usual mode of a triumphal entry into the town after every successful campaign was followed on this occasion also, because whatever it was, they had not suffered a defeat, their army was still intact.   Hence they slept one night outside the town wall, preparatory to a triumphal procession into the town the next day.   Here friends and relatives visited them, and every preparation made for a grand procession.

Very early, at the dawn of the 23rd, Sanusi, the late Are's eldest son, first entered the town with the bones of his late father in a coffin borne before him. · He set it up in state at the gate of his house awaiting the war chiefs.

Before entering the town the majority of the senior chiefs thought of having a private meeting among themselves to settle their own differences, or they might find it difficult to govern the town peaceably.   Enormous wrongs had been perpetrated upon individuals, houses had been wrongfully confiscated, properties and people stolen and sold and any amount of mischief had been done whilst they were at war, so that most of them thought that those at home would be justified if they should close the gates against them so that they might not enter, and if they did, there was sure to be a civil war.   No one committed greater wrongs than the Balogun's slaves, and the Agbakin his chief adviser. Moreover, the war chiefs had long been ashamed of the Balogun as their commander-in-chief, because he was so given up to liquor and was scarcely ever found sober all the time they were at Ikirun. They once approached him there to remonstrate with him for it, and his reply to them was, " Does my drink cost you anything ? Am I not buying it with my own money ? "   At the seat of war the Balogun was supreme and absolute, nothing therefore could be done ; but at home it was otherwise.

Approaching him therefore to talk matters of so great importance over before entering the town, they found him as usual in his inebriate condition. He answered them roughly ; and he said that

he had no time for a council, and that if any one had anything to
say to him, let him come to him in his father's house.   Thus did
the Balogun stifle all overtures intended for his own benefit.
The chiefs were all stung by this remark, and there and then
agreed to reject him as head of the town.   They however suppressed
their feelings and followed the order of proceeding.   The Balogun
led the way and the others in the strict order of their ranks
followed ; every man as soon as he entered the town gate fired a
gun, and there was a regular *feu de joie* the whole time as the
procession wended its way to the Arę's house on the hill, and
before his gate to give account of the war as they would have done
if he had been alive.   Thousands upon thousands of spectators lined
the route the whole way, shouting welcome to some of the chiefs
and hooting others.   The Balogun was received with a rigid
silence by the crowd, whom his slaves had wronged.   Thus they
came to the front of the Arę's house.   The Balogun in front, the
other war chiefs behind him prostrated before the coffin and wept ;
then he began to give his account :—

"'Twas ye who sent us to the war.   We met the enemy on our
soil and we repelled them, and carried the war into their own
country.   We fought to the utmost of our powers, and finding the
battle too strong for us, we invited you to come to our aid.   Ye
will remember how ye led us to the fight and how many hard battles
we fought in your presence.   Then ye took ill..and..then..it
came to pass..ye were transformed [Ẹ paradà].   And after that
we fought several hard battles, and did all we could to keep up
the Ibadan prestige : we were not able to conquer the enemy,
and they were unable to drive us back, till the white men came
and separated us.

We have since then been at Ikirun defending our frontier against
the Ilọrins.   They were unable to come near to encamp against
Ikirun, and we were unable to go and meet them at Yanayó, until
the Governor of Lagos came and ordered both of us to decamp."

They wept once more, and thereupon Sanusi brought out the
customary presents his father would have given them had he
been alive.   The ceremonies over, the next thing was for the whole
of them to accompany the Balogun home, and thus to acknowledge
him the head, but they had rejected him.   Akintọla was the first
to mount his horse and say to the others, "Haven't ye your
father's house to go to?   I am going to mine."   Each of the
younger war chiefs took it up, "I am going to mine," "I am going
to mine," and mounting his horse each of them went home
direct, leaving the Balogun and his own people to go home by
themselves !

It needed no prophetic eye to see that a storm was gathering which would burst at no distant date.

The usual presents and refreshments the Balogun had ordered to entertain the chiefs with were all ready, but no one came to partake of them. The Balogun at first treated the matter lightly, affecting to care nothing for their plots ; but when he received no message of congratulation from any of them, and no secret message from any to disclose the nature of the plot, then he began to realize the danger of his position. He was severely isolated.

At dusk the next day he went to the Agbakin to ask him to beg for him. But the Agbakin was his chief adviser, aider and abettor all the while at Ikirun ; he was by many considered as guilty if not more so and should be dealt with along with the Balogun ; therefore the Agbakin for the sake of self-preservation, speedily dissociated himself entirely from the Balogun, trying his utmost to secure himself whilst receiving from the Balogun large presents intended to mollify his brother chiefs. But as the Balogun's fate was already sealed what he had thus received he kept for himself.

Governor Carter, following slowly behind, arrived at Ibadan on the 26th of March, 1893, and encamped at the Basọrun market where booths and enclosures had been prepared against the arrival of His Excellency and his party.

The Ibadans in the meantime suppressed their feelings against the Balogun, and His Excellency, not knowing what was going on underneath, had dealings with none else but the Balogun, taking him for the head of the town.

The Governor unfortunately left Ibadan highly disappointed with the conduct of the chiefs because they declined to sign an agreement he drew up for them, and the idea of a European Resident he broached was repugnant to them.

They objected that they had been absent from home about seventeen years ; they had only just arrived, the town was as yet without a head; they were not yet settled down for civil administration and hence there was no one authorized to act in an official position. These essentials must first be seen to before they could consider any treaty or agreement. The Balogun then said to him, " You have said you were sent from home to separate us, then you go home again and tell your masters you have carried out your mission." The Governor's last words to them were, whether they were willing or unwilling they would have to do it.

At a banquet given at Lagos in honour of the Governor's successful mission, His Excellency in his after-dinner speech referred bitterly to this incident. He said that he met with success all along his tour in his going and coming, till he got to the last stage where it was least expected; there he met with a rebuff and he believed they were instigated to it by one in his own train but he hoped all would be right in the end.

To anyone with an open mind the Governor's words sounded very strange indeed; it could only be attributed to an imperfect knowledge of the people. His Excellency might have allowed to such men as could govern a town like Ibadan and all its dependencies some credit of knowing their own minds and not be swayed by a mere clerk in his office.

But what people anywhere in Africa, nay, in the whole world, would readily and speedily fall in with the view of a foreign garrison in their midst if they could help it? Besides, the argument advanced by the chiefs seemed reasonable enough.

As soon as the Governor left Ibadan the Balogun's troubles began afresh. He paid heavily in slaves, cowries and goods to beg for his life. After all had been received the chiefs sent for Ọgọ, the chief officer of Orowusi's house, to come and represent his master's house in the council held at the big market (always the place of meeting when there was no head of the town). The Balogun was charged with all the enormities perpetrated by his slaves, the confiscation of so many houses for little or no cause, rapes and robberies all unpunished, etc., etc., they ended by saying that they had rejected him, and that he should honourably go to sleep.

We may remark that all these charges are such as would have been condoned but for his personal unfitness, which in the eyes of the Ibadans were unpardonable, viz., (1) His great indulgence in liquor (2) his failure to lead them to victory as a Balogun.

A Balogun who has won no victory has a small chance with the Ibadans. The Balogun received the message with much indignation; he was determined not to die but to fight it out. When his determination was known, the people were also determined to meet him; already his quarter of the town was being deserted, for they had begun to seize people about his quarters. Private messages were sent quickly to his brothers. " You know the consequences: will you allow your father's house to be wiped off at Ibadan? " They knew very well that when the people assailed a house, it is to level it with the ground, and make it a dunghill, and the family—such as remain alive—dispersed for ever: no member thereof ever to hold a public position in the town, for fear of his rising to power hereafter and taking revenge on the children of the perpetrators.

The Balogun's brothers stayed their hands and held a consultation in the family, the elders thus addressing the Balogun's sons :

" We must all die sooner or later, and the death of a man advanced in life, with numerous grown-up children, is no early death. Which is better, for such a man who has already made his name and has nothing more to achieve to anticipate the inevitable by a short period at most, and the house remain, or for the said man with his house, family and posterity to be wiped off at once and for ever ? Your father was not the first heir to our father's house, let him not be the last : and so it will be if the citizens lay violent hands on him, and ye yourselves will not escape. It is left for you his children to save your own lives and the honour, dignity and fame of your father's house."

The rest was left with his sons. No one could be accused of parricide for no one could say positively who did it, or how it was done. The Balogun himself scarcely knew what was going on, for he had now a plausible excuse for drowning his grief in liquor ! Rumour says his sons persuaded him to take the fatal cup himself. Others say they took advantage of a time he was the worse for liquor and discharged fire-arms on him, which threw him off his seat but otherwise had no effect on him, and in his inebriate condition he muttered, " Who is throwing stones at me ? "

Warriors like him with system fortified against bullets can hardly be hurt by a musket. Then, it is said that they had recourse to clubs with which he was clubbed to death.

However it be, he was dead, and report was conveyed to the infuriated mob assembled at the market ready for action. Some one was sent to verify the fact, and when it was confirmed, information was conveyed to the principal war chiefs that the Balogun was dead. The mob dispersed. Lamentations were duly set up, funeral dirges sung, and he was buried with full military honours as befits a Balogun of Ibadan, and his next brother Ola was appointed head of the house of Orowùsi.

§ 3. The Return of Governor Carter to Lagos

The Governor's mission to the interior was a complete success from every point of view, and he deserved all the ovation given him with one accord by the Colony.

He had a right royal progress through the town from one end to another. The whole of the streets along which he was to pass from Ebute Ero, the northern landing place to Government House, were decorated with flags and bunting, with palms and triumphal arches ; they were also lined with troops—Hausas and the Constabulary—the mass of the crowd was like a moving sea of humanity shouting welcome at the top of their voices.

Mr. Ademuyiwa Haastrup, a prominent citizen, on a markedly big and powerful horse and in a gorgeous native robe, kept on cantering backwards and forwards round the Governor all the way along. The Governor was visibly affected at the sight of these signs of joyful appreciation of his efforts, and the success attending what he had accomplished.

The work was so thoroughly well done that from that time to this the roads have been completely opened from one end to the other, and never has there been any obstruction to trade, and all this without firing a shot !

As a matter of course (as things were at Lagos in those days) a banquet by the " elite of Lagos " followed a few days after at which His Excellency was the principal guest ; and he recounted amidst plaudits the principal incidents of his mission from beginning to end.

If Governor Carter did nothing more for the Colony, his name will be entitled to an undying fame in the Yoruba country. But we have to place also to his credit the initiation of the system of good roads which now stretches all over the country, being much developed by Governor Egerton. Carter's first road was from Ijẹbu Ode to Ejirin where the weekly caravan was the thickest, next the Ẹpẹ road, then the Ibadan Ijẹbu road. These were the roads most used for the principal markets.

He built a proper Government House at Lagos. Then he started the railway between Lagos and Ibadan, which, under Governor Egerton, was continued to Káno.[1] All this with the small revenue of Lagos at the time.

Two traits in Governor Carter impressed the chiefs and people of this country. One was the unfailing deference usually paid to native rulers, and the non-encroachment upon their rights. The result of this was the almost entire absence of bullying and belittling by subordinate officers which generally brought about disorganization of Native Governments, and other evils consequent thereupon. The other was the Governor's intuitive and almost unerring judgment of character and his sense of justice. The country was

---

[1] Carter's successor was Governor M'Callum whose term was only 12 months spent chiefly over the question of our northern boundary with the French. He secured to the Yoruba country the ancient Yoruba cities to the N.W. of ancient Ọyọ. Next to him was Governor MacGregor under whom the system of sanitation was perfected. Under Egerton his successor the work of his predecessors was far advanced in roads and bridges, and filling swamps by dredgers, and further started on his own initiative the opening of the bar by which ocean liners might enter Lagos harbour.

prosperous in those days. Several causes might have contributed to this but the mass of the people set it down to the fair rule and government of Governor Carter.

§ 4. LOCAL OPINIONS ABOUT THE WAR

As was inevitable, opinions were freely exchanged and conjectures made in those days as to what would have happened had the British Government not interfered in the interior wars, but had left the native states to fight out their own battles. Naturally opinion was divided. Some thought the Ibadans would have been driven from Kiriji, for the Ekitiparapos were all animated with a determination to break their yoke for ever ; they were fighting for life, home and liberty.

Against this the Ibadans maintained that the force which could dislodge them from Kiriji would also be able to conquer Ibadan itself, for if they were unable to hold their ground where they were with all the provincial towns on their side, neither would they be able to do so at home with these towns hostile or neutral, and all their Ekiti fighting slaves escaped ; therefore in holding their own there they were not merely fighting to maintain honour and prestige, but also they were doing it with all the desperation of men guarding hearth and home. As to determination therefore, both sides were even.

But to the unbiassed observer the prospects of the Ibadans seemed much better for the following reasons :—

(1) If the Ekitis could have driven them, they had the best chance of doing so when they were furnished with thousands of rifles, and the roads being closed, the Ibadans had not even ammunition for their old flint-lock guns. When they used to fire into the Ibadan camp with fatal results and these could not reply : when the Ibadans had to go against them in the battle-field crawling on the ground, seeking cover till they were near enough to spring upon them with swords, cutlasses, and the butt end of their Dane guns, capturing men and rifles. But latterly when the Ijebus were compelled by circumstances to open their roads for traffic and the Ibadans were able to acquire a few scores of rifles, their chances became more even, and the Ekitis were no longer able to assume the offensive. It was only a matter of time ; the Ibadans would eventually have increased their stock of rifles, and then the Ekitis would have had no chance against them.

(2) The Ibadans moreover were inspired with hopes of a future success by the following circumstance derived from experience. In all their previous wars, whenever in a difficult campaign, while holding their foes in check they were able to send out a

detachment for a subsidiary punitive expedition which proved successful, victory ultimately rested with them. So it was in the case of Iwawun during the Ijayè war, of Ibokun during the Ilesa war, etc. The victory at Ile Ifẹ showed it would be the same in the Kiriji campaign.

(3) The next ground of hope was of a more solid nature. Ogedemgbe was the only leader in whom the Ekitiparapọs relied to hold their different sections together ; he had to expose himself in every battle as any of the meanest soldiers in order to get his countrymen to follow him. His body was covered with scars from wounds. It was not unlikely that the Ibadans, having acquired rifles, a stray bullet might one day put him out of action, and with him the hopes of the Ekitis would be extinguished.

The Ibadans on the other hand could count upon scores of men willing and able to take the lead. In fact they attributed their non-success to the disobedience to the voice of their national oracle which bestowed the office of Balogun on Akintọla, but which the Arẹ was not inclined to follow, consequently the fall of their own leader was not likely to have a bad effect upon them but probably just the contrary ; and the Ekitiparapọs driven from the field, the Ilọrins were not likely to remain any longer to continue the struggle, as they were unable to take the field against a strong army without an infantry support.

§ 5. Constitution of the Ibadan Town Council

We consider it important to note how the titles were distributed at this time at Ibadan, because these men formed the Town Council and were officially responsible for the Agreement which practically made not only Ibadan but also all Yoruba country a British Protectorate.

Balẹ.—There were two aspirants to the title of Balẹ, and each was backed by the two most powerful junior war chiefs, *viz.* :

(1) Ọsuntoki the Mayẹ, backed by Akintọla, and (2) Fijabi, the Abẹsẹ, backed by Sumọnu Apampa. The latter was determined to carry out his wish at all cost : he eventually succeeded, and Fijabi was elected Balẹ. A special messenger was thereupon sent to Ọyọ to place his name before the King. An Ilari was sent by His Majesty to confer the title of Balẹ on him. The act was known as placing the leaves of title upon his head because it is the plum leaves (Ewe Iyeyè) that are used on these occasions, " Iyeyè " from the root yè, to live, which rendered the act to mean, " May you live long."

Balẹ Fijabi now appointed his rival to the post of honour. The title of Ọtun Balẹ was conferred on Ọsuntoki the Mayẹ, and that of Osi Balẹ on Fajinmi the Agbakin.

The titles of the war chiefs are the most important at Ibadan. That of Balogun happily was indisputable, the National Oracle had declared it for Akintola after the death of Ogboriefon : the late Balogun it was generally understood held it in trust for him while the late war continued. Akintola now by common consent came to his own as the Balogun of Ibadan. There were two aspirants to the next position of Otun Balogun, *viz.*, Kongi the grandson of Ogunmola, and the brave Babalola the son of the late Ajayi Ogboriefon.

Kongi based his claim upon the fact that his grandfather was the Otun to Akintola's father when Balogun, and so it was right that he be the Otun to Akintola as Balogun. But the bravery of Babalola could not be overlooked ; he too was the son of the hero of the Jalumi war and was second to none. Babalola therefore obtained the title of Otun.

That of Osi was offered to Kongi, but he sulkily declined to have it ; he was told either to accept it or receive none at all and was reminded of the cowardice displayed by him at Erin when Enimowu was captured by the Ilorins. Moreover, Sumonu Apampa laid claim to the very title of Osi. His father was the Osi of Akintola's father as Balogun, and so also he would be the Osi to Balogun Akintola. Although in every respect he was deserving of it, yet to accede to Apampa's request would mean to degrade the house of Ogunmola further, which they did not think it right to do, for the heroes of that house were equal to any albeit the head of the house was a cowardly youth. And to Apampa they said that they sympathized with him, he was worthy of it, but as he had been yielded to and had obtained his wish in the matter of the Bale Fijabi, he must not press his claim in this instance. So Kongi was made the Osi Balogun and to Apampa was given the title of Asipa.

The principal titles were as follows, civil and military :—

Name.	Title.	Name.	Title.
Fijabi	Bale	Akintola	Balogun
Osuntoki	Otun Bale	Babalola	Otun Balogun
Fajinmi	Osi Bale	Kongi	Osi Balogun
Mosaderin	Ekerin Bale	Sumonu Apampa	Asipa
Bamgbegbin	Areagoro Bale	Suberu	Ekerin Balogun
Salako	Are Alasa	Ogungbesan	Ekarun Balogun
Lanlatu	Iyalode	Akintunde	Ekefa Balogun
		Olaifa	Asaju
Ogundepo	Seriki	Obisesan	Agbakin
Mosanya	Otun Seriki	Tanpe	Maye
Aina Fagbemi	Osi Seriki	Enimowu	Abese
Dada Ojo	Ekerin Seriki	Eweje	Sarumi

THE ESTABLISHMENT OF THE BRITISH
PROTECTORATE

After the titles and offices had been distributed, and the town settled down once more to the duties of civil life, the chiefs held a consultation about the Agreement Governor Carter had called upon them to sign, and which they were not then in a position to consider. After the *pros* and *cons* had been duly weighed it was agreed that with proper safeguards they might agree to it, provided the Governor gave due consideration to their objections.

A letter was then addressed to the Governor asking him to send up the document for them to reconsider in a regularly constituted assembly.

Governor Carter having in the meantime left for England, on his furlough, this request was cabled to Downing Street and the Acting-Governor, G. C. Denton, Colonial Secretary, was ordered in reply to visit Ibadan in person and present the Agreement. Accordingly in August, 1893, the Acting-Governor visited Ibadan for that purpose.

The document was again read and interpreted to them, and after due consideration the following letter was addressed to the Acting-Governor stating clearly the objections in their way to signing the Agreement.

Ibadan,

August 14th, 1893.

Your Excellency,—We are not unmindful of all the kindness done to us by Her Majesty the Queen, nor are we unappreciative of it : and, in order to be frank we desire to state to you our fears in objecting to a Resident European which we trust Your Excellency will see to.

First, we fear the authority and respect of the Balẹ and chiefs will suffer deterioration, as there may be two courts of appeal.

2. We fear our slaves will assert their freedom by running to the Resident.

3. We fear our wives will be taken by the soldiers which will be a source of great offence to us.

4. We consider our land as our inalienable property inherited from our forefathers, and never subject to sale. We consider it also our greatest wealth bestowed upon us by the Almighty and we do not desire it to go out of our hands.

If the Governor will see that our rights are not trespassed we make no scruple to sign all the terms of the Treaty.

We are your good friends,

FIJABI THE BALẸ × (his mark).

AND OTHER IBADAN AUTHORITIES.

G. C. DENTON, *Acting Governor.*

The following was the reply to the above letter by the Acting-Governor :—

Ibadan,

August 14th, 1893.

GENTLEMEN,—In reply to the letter of this date which was handed to me by you this morning, I have the honour to inform you that the conditions of the Agreement you tell me you are prepared to sign, do not contemplate interference with the Native Government of Ibadan in any way.

2. I may also say that the officer in charge will not as at present proposed hold any court or take any action opposed to local customs and observances so long as they do not conflict with the ordinary principles of humanity.

3. The officer placed in charge at Ibadan will be instructed that it is not the intention of the Lagos Government to interfere with the domestic slavery so long as it is conducted on humane principles, as the country will still remain vested in the Ibadan authorities.

I fail to see that slaves will obtain their freedom by running to the Resident.

4. Any Hausa who takes a woman of the country away from her home, against her will, will be severely punished.

5. With regard to the question of land, the Agreement only deals with a place for the erection of quarters for an officer and men, and sufficient grounds for a construction of a line of railway should it be deemed advisable to undertake such a work.

6. In neither case can it be said that alienation of the land is contemplated. And that there may be no mistake on this point, I am quite prepared to guarantee that in recognition of your right, rent be paid to you for what land is utilized under the Agreement.

7. I can with safety promise you that your rights will not be infringed by the Lagos Government, the only object aimed at being to preserve peace, to secure open roads and reasonable freedom of action to the inhabitants generally.

I am, gentlemen,

Your good friend,

G. C. DENTON, Acting-Governor.

After the receipt of this letter and after further consideration the Agreement was signed the next day by the Chiefs. (<i>vide</i> App. A). But before signing the Agreement, and in consideration of the Treaty signed by them at Kiriji in which the removal of Modakẹkẹ was made binding on them, and in order to speak their minds with regard to the same, they submitted the following document to His Excellency, the Acting-Governor.

A brief statement of the Modakẹkẹ affair.

Ibadan,
August 15th, 1893.

YOUR EXCELLENCY,—We beg to say that the real intent of the article respecting the Modakẹkẹ affair in the former treaty was not understood before signature : but when the first Commissioners (headed by Mr. Higgins) came up and were at Modakẹkẹ and insisted upon the removal, then the late Agbakin of Modakẹkẹ who was one of the signatories was surprised and said, that he did not understand it so, and our contingents there then, <i>viz.</i>, the present Balogun and Asipa, sent to us and we expressed our concurrence with the then Agbakin of Modakẹkẹ as to our understanding of the article. It obliged the Rev. S. Johnson to come to us at Ikirun and we told him the same thing.

When the Commissioners still insisted then the late Agbakin told them that it was one of the late Ifẹ kings, Degunle by name, also known as Abi-ewe-ila, who gave their fathers the land out of pity, as the Ifẹs illtreated them by making sacrifices with them : and since then they lived and flourished there, and served them as landowners ; and the several times they fell out the Ifẹs were the aggressors, or were the first to fire at them, but God usually gave them the victory. They know no other home.

When the Commissioners still insisted on their removal then the Agbakin said that the place beyond the river Ọṣun mentioned by the Commissioners was a forest without a house to accommodate them and no cultivation to supply them with food, he then asked them to look at the town and think of the probable number of old and infirm men and women, with the infants and sucklings that may perish by exposure to the weather and then asked whether they would be able to stand responsible before God for the loss of their lives. This made them desist to press further the point, and matters remain as they are.

2. By right of conquest we have had our Ajẹlẹs in the Ijẹsa, Ekiti, Yagba and Ẹfọn countries right up to Ọtùn and now that the Ijẹsas, etc., have rebelled, Your Excellency, is it right for any one of the rebellious towns to dictate to us as the Ijẹsas have done in asking us to remove our Ajẹlẹ from a town which does not rebel as they have done ?   It is because we are conscious of the Queen's power and goodwill that we have accepted a Resident, paying Her Majesty due deference. Ought not the Ijẹsas to pay us some deference ?· In the first article of the Treaty the whole of the Ẹkun Ọtun and Ẹkun Osi are put under us, the Ifẹ and Modakẹkẹ people form a part of the Ẹkun Osi. We think they and the Ijẹsas need being informed of this.

We leave the subject to Your Excellency's wise consideration.

We are, Your Excellency's,

FIJABI, *the Balẹ*, × (his mark).

With the other Authorities of Ibadan.

After Governor Carter's return from England, Capt. R. L. Bower, with a force of about 100 Hausas, was sent up to be the first Resident and Travelling Commissioner of the Interior Yoruba having his headquarters at Ibadan. The Ibadan authorities were prepared to assign him a place in the town for residence, but he marched through and took up his quarters outside the town walls, in the space between the town and the ancient city of Owu.

With the establishment of the British Protectorate a new era dawned upon the country. It marked the close of the fourth and the beginning of the fifth period.

What the distinguishing feature of this new era will be, and how long it will last, are questions which only the future can answer.

When we have allowed for all the difficulties of a transition stage, the disadvantages that must of necessity arise by the application of rules and ideas of a highly civilized people to one of another race, degree of civilization, and of different ideas, we should hope the net result will be a distinct gain to the country. But that peace should reign universally, with prosperity and advancement, and that the disjointed units should all be once more welded into one under one head from the Niger to the coast as in the happy days of ABIODUN, so dear to our fathers, that clannish spirit disappear, and above all that Christianity should be the principal religion in the land—paganism and Mohammedanism having had their full trial—should be the wish and prayer of every true son of Yoruba.

THE SEQUEL.

THE Protectorate has been established and everything has settled down : but this end has not been easily attained as may very well be imagined. The country had to be convinced that a new regime had dawned upon it, and that the people must conform to it. This was not unaccompanied at first by a method high-handed and somewhat violent under successive Residents, but that was not unexpected.

We shall here but briefly indicate how the new order of things affects each unit, and incidentally we shall discover who were the real disturbers of the peace of the country.

§ 1. ABEOKUTA

The Egbas rigidly kept to the Treaty, so that the Lagos Government could find no fault with them. The intelligent portion of the community was admitted to a share in the Government, and they strove to conduct everything after the model of a civilized state. In fact it was the general opinion that in many things they ignored the rule, " Make haste slowly." The early career of the Alake and the new Government Secretary was highly beneficial to the well-being and progress of the Egba community.

§ 2. IBADAN

It took the Ibadan rank and file some time to realize the fact that intertribal wars are for ever at an end in this country. It was customary with them, after the conferring of new titles that they should go to a war, for each chief and especially for the Balogun to recommend himself thereby to the people as fit for the title he holds. The Ilorins remained the only power they had not come to any definite terms with, so we were not surprised to hear on all hands, " Nje Bower kòni si ogun Ilorin yi fun wa " (" Will not Capt. Bower then open for us an Ilorin campaign ? ") To be at home with nothing definite to do was rather irksome to those whose trade was war. Happily most of the important chiefs had huge farms wherein were engaged many of their domestics, and the majority of the men also were farmers, but a good many were warriors pure and simple. No wonder then that for some time burglaries, arson, etc., were rife in the community.

Again, there soon followed a series of blunders which startled
the community not only of Ibadan but also all the Yoruba country,
e.g., the threat to arrest the Baḷẹ of Ibadan upon the ground of
a supposed intrigue with Ilọrin ! But this charge which had no
foundation in fact, was easily disposed of : all the same it seemed
necessary in high quarters to do something which would strike
terror into the whole country " in order to keep order " ! The
Osi Baḷẹ therefore offered himself to be arrested instead, for the
Baḷẹ's person he said was sacred, and that to arrest him would
mean the break up of the town.

This was followed by the arrest of the Balogun of Ibadan
" until the man was found who had insulted Captain ——". But
there was no such man. The salutation usually accorded to a
gentleman on horseback by shaking the fist towards him was
mistaken for a threat ; and how was the Balogun to know who
thus saluted the Captain out of doors some days after the event,
in a huge town like Ibadan some miles away from his residence ?
But this was speedily atoned for, and the Balogun honourably
returned to his house. Then came the clash with Ọyọ over the
case of Lagunju the ex-Timi of Ẹdẹ, who appealed to his Suzerain
to exert his good offices to restore him to his post. And again
over the case of a man sent from Iseyin to be emasculated for
the usual offence for which that was the form of punishment.
This resulted in what was known as " the bombardment of Ọyọ,"
during which a ricochet shot hit the ALÂFIN on the knee. This
was however admitted to be a blunder, and the matter was
speedily adjusted by the Governor on his return from furlough.
After a short time the people and the energetic Resident got to
know each other better, and there was not only harmony, but
even friendship between them, especially at Ọyọ : for it was
subsequently found out that the mistakes and misunderstandings
were all due to imperfect information in which the part played
by the interpreter was not only dishonourable but highly repre-
hensible, and he was condignly dealt with.

But Ibadan never really settled down till after about eighteen
months, when the Government of Lagos enlisted two battalions
of men for military service in Northern Nigeria. This opening
afforded relief to all those ardent spirits whose profession was arms,
and with a wonderful celerity they imbibed and assimilated the
new method of drill and discipline, by which they were led to a
successful campaign. Again, the railway undertaking absorbed
the energies of many. Since then, Ibadan has had varied
experience under various Residents.

§ 3. Ijesa

It was hardly recognised that the Ijesas under Ogedemgbe were given to warfare as much as the Ibadans, only that the scene of their operations was distant from Lagos but nearer Benin. Chief Ogedemgbe's war boys were known as Ipayes, and much mischief was done by them to the country people during the war. This habit they found hard to give up now that wars were over. All warlike spirits, including princes who thought they could do anything with impunity were among the number of his war-boys. Molestations of their country people, robberies, brigandage, and violence of every kind were of frequent occurrence, and he of course always shared the booty or plunder with them.

Matters were from time to time reported to the Resident at Ibadan. Capt. Bower wrote twice to warn Ogedemgbe to keep his men in check ; the old chief regarded this warning as a huge joke. That the soldiery should be given to violence was a matter of course to him, he simply laughed over the matter. The offence was repeated and that in an aggravated form on the men of Ara, and was duly reported. Capt. Bower, after due notice, went over to Ilesa,. and according to arrangement, summoned at the King's palace a meeting of all the chiefs. Ogedemgbe, after a delay of about forty minutes, met him there, and the Captain after relating the cases and the warnings he had given their chief, there arrested him in the presence of them all. Ogedemgbe had the good sense to warn his boys to refrain from any violent act in order to rescue him, and thus he prevented bloodshed— but by forced marches ere the news became generally known he was far distant. He was interned at Iwo instead of being brought to Ibadan the headquarters, " lest his old enemies might exalt over him." This, however was a mistake, for Ogedemgbe would simply have come back to his old home. The actual perpetrators of the crime were also seized and cast into prison at Ibadan. Capt. Bower also seized those rifles now in Ogedemgbe's possession which were used against the Ibadans at Kiriji. They were said to be an alarming number of perfect weapons of precision.

Ogedemgbe remained at Iwo for a little over a year. When in 1896 Mr. Haastrup (generally known as Daddy Kumoku) was elected the Qwa of Ilesa, he pleaded for him with the Governor and Ogedemgbe was released and restored to Ilesa. He was given the title of Oba'la, the next in rank to the Qwa himself. The war-boys have since been suppressed and dispersed.

§ 4. The Ekitis

The Ekitis are mostly farmers and traders ; there was only one chief amongst them who was devoted to wars. This was Fabūmi of Imesi Ọloja Oke. He also had war-boys given to violence as those of Ogedemgbe. Reports had from time to time to be made of him to the officer stationed at the River Ọtin of violence to peaceful traders, capturing and selling them as slaves to Benin, and other acts of brigandage. The captain usually sent to warn the King of Oke Mẹsi, till on one occasion even the King himself sent his son to complain of Fabūmi : then it was that the situation dawned upon Captain Tucker. Then he knew that Fabūmi was the culprit and not the King, who was powerless, being a man of about 120 years of age ! Next he found a list drawn up by Captain Bower in which the name of Fabūmi appeared as one of the troublesome spirits of the country, next after Ogedemgbe, and one to be arrested. He consequently went up with about twenty Hausa soldiers and arrested him, and brought him bound to the River Ọtin camp, and the next day he sent him on to the Resident, Captain Hawtayne, at Ibadan. The Captain gave him a good warning and set him at liberty. He was henceforth quiet, and subsequently became King of Mesi Ipole. It will be remembered that it was he who effected the capture of Ilọri the Osi, by simulating Akintọla's war cry ; it was he who decoyed the Ibadan army to the clefts of Mesi Ipole ; but he failed to take Modakẹkẹ. He was an honourable warrior.

§ 5. IFẸ AND MODAKẸKẸ

According to the Treaty of 1886, Modakẹkẹ was to be removed from Ifẹ soil, and rebuilt in a place between the Rivers Ọsun and Ọba, and the Ibadans were to see that this was carried out.

That portion of the Treaty was galling to the Ibadans, the Modakẹkẹs simply would not hear of it, but the Ifẹs were jubilant, and were determined to see it carried out.

Modakẹkẹ was a large town, and the immediate removal was simply impracticable. In vain did they ask that a reconciliation be made between themselves and the Ifẹs so that they might remain on the spot dear to them, containing as it did the ashes of their fathers ; the present generation knew no other home. But the Lagos authorities would not stultify themselves by going behind the Treaty, as it were, although they took no steps to enforce it, nor would the Ifẹs yield to anything except removal. Thus they remained together for years.

Subsequent Governors, who actually knew the towns, had their hands tied by the Treaty, much though they would have liked to see things effected differently. In course of time, however, the Ifẹs were practically indifferent about it, as intermarriages between them had all but made them one people, and the hope was being entertained that the matter would die away, and that Modakeke would remain. But Adelekan, the newly-created Owoni of Ife, a man as austere as he was uncompromising, was unremitting in his efforts to see Modakeke removed. He went so far as to conciliate Governor Carter in 1896 by giving him three of those national and ancestral works of art known as the " Ife Marbles." But since the general peace was kept, and the Modakekes were as industrious as they were loyal to the Ifes, and both populations seemed to live together in amity except for the Owoni, neither he nor his successors renewed the proposal to remove Modakeke.

Sir William MacGregor, during his regime as Governor, among other places visited Ile Ife. He granted the Owoni an annual subsidy on account of his position. Thinking he had secured his man in this Governor, the Owoni with plausible excuses, but chiefly for this purpose, undertook the unusual course of visiting Lagos in person. He did so but without effect, for Sir William had seen the towns himself. But still, Adelekan was unremitting in his hostilities towards the Modakekes, causing them repeated annoyance, fomenting disorders, and by false reports and unsubstantiated charges, got the two most powerful chiefs—the Balogun and the Otun—transported to Ibadan under charges of disturbing the peace. Then, later on, during the regime of Sir Walter Egerton (himself being on furlough at the time) the Owoni, armed with a copy of the old Treaty, got round the officer stationed at Ile Ife, and it would seem secured his connivance. The Ifes thereupon took it upon themselves to molest and annoy the Modakekes in every possible way, even to the extent of entering their houses and seizing anything they took a fancy to, doing violence to men and women in a way they dared not do without provoking a war, before the Pax Britannica was imposed. The Owoni knew what he was about when he got the Balogun and the Otun removed to Ibadan. The officer located at Ile Ife saw all this but said and did nothing, which was very significant. The Modakekes saw that a higher power was now behind the Ifes and that they would have no redress. Thus it came to pass that on the 27th day of March, 1909, twenty-three years after the imposition of the Treaty, the town was broken up. Those of them who were descended from the Owus removed to their ancestral homes to Owu Ipole, between Ife and Ijebu, others to Gbangan, some to Odûabon, others to Ede ; the bulk of the people, however, with the Ogunsua or Bale of Modakeke removed to a place called Odekomu somewhere midway between Ede, Ife and the Ijesas, about ten miles from Ifẹ, just beyond the river Saṣa which after the war was made the boundary of Ifẹ territory.

Adelẹkan seems to have been raised up for the purpose of breaking up Modakẹkẹ, for he commenced his hostilities against the town soon after he was raised to the stool of the Ọwọni, and he died the year after the breaking up of the town. " They drove **us** twice from our home," he used to say, " and we must see that they are driven permanently from theirs."

Want of sufficient land for farming prevented the people from concentrating in a spot as at Modakẹkẹ. Unfortunately Ọdẹ-komu is not on a caravan route, and that has restricted its population ; but it is a small, compact and flourishing town, the people happy, contented and progressive as usual.

Providence, who ordereth and controlleth all things, saw that it was time Modakẹkẹ should cease to exist after they had nobly done their part in shaping the history of the Yoruba country.

§ 6. ILỌRIN

The Ilọrins quickly showed themselves as the real disturbers of the peace of the country, and the real cause of the protracted war : for whereas the disturbances in the other provinces were more or less domestic and local, it was left for them to engage in political disturbances which under the old regime would have drawn forth the Ibadan army out of home.

No sooner had the Ibadans gone home from Ikirun, and Governor Carter and his party had left them, than they broke the agreement arrived at with them and placed Ajẹlẹs (political Residents) at Ikirun and Oṣogbo.

The boundary between the Ibadan and Ilọrin territory had been fixed at the Awẹrẹ stream, to the south of Ẹrin, leaving Ẹrin and Ọfa to the Ilọrins, but the towns and villages hitherto under Ibadan protection were definitely excluded from Ilọrin interference.

For this encroachment therefore Captain Bower had to go to Ilọrin to remonstrate with the Emir for disregarding the compact made with the Ilọrins by Sir Gilbert Carter. The Ilọrin chiefs took great exception to the manner Captain Bower was addressing their King, but partly from fear, and partly from the intervention of the Emir, they were restrained from laying violent hands on him. They called Captain Bower " Bawa " (pronounced Bah-wah) ; that in Hausa is the name of a slave. All their great men have each one a Bawa—their principal slave—and hence Captain Bower was taken for Sir Gilbert Carter's slave ! For a slave to be talking after that manner to, and threatening their King, was intolerable ; as it was, he was said to have been literally hustled out of Ilọrin.

Captain Bower, having driven the Ilọrin political Residents out of Ikirun and Ọṣọgbo, encamped with his handful of Hausa soldiers at the banks of the River Ọtin—a river of ill-omen to the Ilọrins since the Jalumi War—about five miles north of Ikirun. He sent to Lagos for re-inforcement, and he was granted a force of about 200 men with which he effectually protected the northern provinces of Yoruba from Ilọrin encroachments.

All was apparently well after this, the weekly caravans from Ilọrin and beyond went to and returned from the coast, the messengers of the Emir of Ilọrin frequently came to the camp and as the Hausa soldiers were all Gambaris, mostly from beyond Ilọrin, the intercourse between them and Hausas from Ilọrin was frequent and natural, not knowing they were all spies ! All of a sudden at the end of March, 1896,—Captain Bower being then at Ibadan—the Ilọrins came in force one morning, swooped down upon this small garrison and nearly overwhelmed it. With shell and shrapnel, and by the use of rockets, the noise of which they called Sango, the garrison succeeded in driving them back. The force was naturally strengthened, and wisely so, for within three months the same thing was repeated ; however, the Ilọrins then made but a poor show.

Towards the end of 1896 the Ilọrin army came out for a regular campaign. It was a very large army, and they carried all before them till they came within a few miles of the camp. The reception they had twice received on previous occasions ill-disposed them to make a third trial of a frontal attack. For the present they swept along their old haunts to the Northern Ekiti laying siege to Ọtun and Orimope, both within the Lagos protectorate, with the intention of getting round to Ikirun and Ọṣọgbo and taking the camp at Odo Ọtin in the rear.

From private information received of there being spies in the camp who would set fire to it immediately the Ilọrins came and the fight commenced, Captain Shaw, the officer then in command drew up the whole of the men on parade and then with a sergeant and two privates entered each tent and turned out about twenty-three men in all who had no business to be there ! They were " on a visit to their countrymen," they said. Strict precautions were then enforced about admitting strangers into the camp.

From messages received from the Owore of Ọtun, about twenty men of the Hausa force were sent under Asani, a sergeant, to observe the movements and intentions of the Ilọrin hosts ; and these reported an overwhelming force, and that Ọtun was sure to be

taken unless they received timely assistance.   For this reason
Sergeant-Major Dangana was sent with about eighty men with
some rockets.   The Sergeant-Major was a skilful and reliable
leader : he dared not expose his small force to the overwhelming
hosts of the Ilọrins, but he hid some in a bush commanding a by-
path to their rear, and the rest he posted on a rock in full view
of the Ilọrins.   At the sight of them the Ilọrins gave a shout and
made for them, led by their Balogun Adamu, son of the late
Karara and leader of the expedition.   But the horses could not go
on the craggy rocks, and the Lagos troops were therefore safe from
their lances.   Dangana then ordered volleys to be fired on them,
the rockets also rent the air about them and frightened many away.
Adamu was fatally hit on the neck, and in their presence he
divested himself of his war-dress, and entrusted it to one of his
men with orders not to stop till he reached home with it, for that
he himself might not reach home.   The dress was an heirloom
in the family, from his grandfather Ali.

Their leader wounded, the Ilọrins gave way and the Lagos
troops followed them cautiously till they came within striking
distance of the camp.   There they discharged two or three rockets
which set the camp on fire, and the host gave way ! A large
portion of them had gone a-pillaging in the morning, and these,
returning to find their leader dead and the camp fired and broken
up, made the best of their way home, being pursued only a little
way by the Ekitis of Ọtun and neighbourhood.   Here the Ilọrins
lost hundreds of riderless horses.

Thus the camp at the River Ọtin was again saved from the
determined attack of these intrepid horsemen.

By these repeated attacks on the Lagos troops and the disturbance of the peace, the hopes of the Ibadans were for a while raised
for an Ilọrin campaign.   But in February, 1897, the forces of
the Royal Niger Company having its headquarters at Lokoja,
with the two battalions raised at Ibadan, entered Ilọrin from the
north after a single pitched battle before the gate of that city.
Thus Ilọrin has been subjugated and a Resident placed there to
this day.

The disappointment of the Ibadans was shared by those who
had hopes of seeing the Yoruba country once more united under
the ALÂFIN of Ọyọ by the subjugation of Ilọrin by the Ibadan
forces backed by a force of British troops.   But it seemed this
was not to be.   The Ilọrin power has thus been thoroughly broken,
and the garrison was removed from the River Ọtin.

APPENDIX A

TREATIES

§ 1. Abeokuta

Treaty of friendship and commerce made at Abeokuta in the Egba country this 18th (eighteenth) day of January in the year 1893.

Between His Excellency Gilbert Thomas Carter, Esq., Companion of the Most Distinguished Order of Saint Michael and Saint George, Governor and Commander-in-Chief of the Colony of Lagos, for and on behalf of Her Majesty the Queen of Great Britain and Ireland, Empress of India, etc., her heirs and successors on the one part, and the undersigned king (Alake) and Authorities of Abeokuta representing the Egba Kingdom, for and on behalf of their heirs and successors on the other part. We the undersigned King and Authorities do, in the presence of the Elders, Headmen, and people assembled at this place hereby promise :—

1st. That there shall be peace and friendship between the subjects of the Queen and Egba subjects, and should any difference or dispute accidentally arise between us and the said subjects of the Queen, it shall be referred to the Governor of Lagos for settlement as may be deemed expedient.

2nd. That there shall be complete freedom of Trade between the Egba country and Lagos, and in view of the injury to Commerce arising from the arbitrary closing of roads, we the said King and Authorities hereby declare that no roads shall in future be closed without the consent and approval of the Governor of Lagos.

3rd. That we the said King and Authorities pledge ourselves to use every means in our power to foster and promote trade with the countries adjoining Egba and with Lagos.

4th. That we the said King and Authorities will, as heretofore, afford complete protection and every assistance and encouragement to all ministers of the Christian religion.

5th. It is further agreed and stipulated by the said Gilbert Thomas Carter, on behalf of Her Majesty the Queen of England, that so long as the provisions of this Treaty are strictly kept, no annexation of any portion of the Egba country shall be made by Her Majesty's Government without the consent of the lawful Authorities of the country, no aggressive action shall be taken

651

against the said country and its independence shall be fully recognised.

6th. The said King and Authorities having promised that the practice of offering human sacrifices shall be abolished in the one township where it at present exists, and having explained that British subjects have already freedom to occupy land, build houses, and carry on trade and manufacture in any part of the Ẹgba country, and likewise that there is no possibility of a cession of any portion of the Ẹgba country to a Foreign Power without the consent of Her Majesty's Government, it is desired that no special provision be made in regard to these subjects in this Treaty.

Done at Abẹokuta this eighteenth day of January, 1893.

OṢOKALU × (his mark) *King Alake.*
OṢUNDARE ONLADO × ⎫ *Representatives   of   King.*
SORUNKE JAGUNA   × ⎬ *Alake   and   Ẹgba   United*
OGUNDEYI MAGAJI   × ⎭ *Government.*

G. T. CARTER, *Governor and Commander in Chief, Colony Lagos.*

Witnessed at Abẹokuta this 18th day of January, 1893.

G. B. HADDON-SMITH, *Political Officer.*
R. L. BOWER, *Captain, Asst. Inspector, Lagos Constabulary.*
J. B. WOOD, *Missionary of the Church Missionary Society.*
A. L. HETHERSETT, *Clerk and Interpreter, Governor's Office.*
E. R. BICKERSTETH, *Trader.*
W. F. TINNEY SOMOYE, *Clerk to the Ẹgba Authorities.*

I, the undersigned, do swear that I have truly and honestly interpreted the terms of the foregoing Treaty to the contracting parties in the Yoruba language.

A L. HETHERSETT.

Witness to signature :

E. R. BICKERSTETH, *Trader.*

§ 2. OYỌ.

Treaty made at Oyọ in the Yoruba country, this 3rd day of February, in the year 1893, between His Excellency Gilbert Thomas Carter, Esq., Companion of the Most Distinguished Order of Saint Michael and Saint George, Governor and Commander-in-Chief of Lagos, for and on behalf of Her Majesty the Queen of Great Britain and Ireland, Empress of India, etc., Her Heirs and Successors on the one part, and the undersigned King ALÂFIN of Oyọ and Head of Yoruba-land, for and on behalf of his Heirs and Successors, on the other part.

I the undersigned ALÂFIN of Oyọ do hereby promise :—

1st. That there shall be peace between the subjects of the Queen of England and Yoruba subjects, and should any difference or dispute accidentally arise between us and the said subjects of the Queen, it shall be referred to the Governor of Lagos for the time being, whose decision shall be final and binding upon us all.

2nd. That British subjects shall have free access to all parts of Yoruba-land, and shall have the right to build houses and possess property according to the laws in force in this country. They shall further have full liberty to carry on such trade and manufacture as may be approved by the Governor of Lagos.

3rd. That I, the said ALÂFIN of ỌYỌ, agree to allow a right of way to Lagos to all persons wishing to go there.

4th. That I, the said ALÂFIN of ỌYỌ, pledge myself to use every means in my power to foster and promote trade with the countries adjoining Yoruba-land and with Lagos.

5th. That I, the said ALÂFIN of ỌYỌ, will afford complete protection and every assistance and encouragement to all ministers of the Christian religion.

6th. That I, the said ALÂFIN of ỌYỌ, solemnly promise to prohibit the practice of offering human sacrifices, and to prohibit it throughout the country under my control.

7th. That I, the said ALÂFIN of ỌYỌ, will not enter into any war, or commit any act of aggression, on any of the chiefs bordering on Lagos, by which the trade of the country with Lagos shall be interrupted, or the safety of the persons and property of the subjects of the Queen of England shall be lost, compromised, or endangered.

8th. That I, the said ALÂFIN of ỌYỌ, will at no time whatever cede any of my territory to any other power, or enter into any agreement, treaty, or arrangement with any foreign Government except through and with the consent of the Government of Her Majesty the Queen of England, etc.

9th. It is hereby agreed that all disputes that may arise between the parties to this Treaty shall be inquired into and adjusted by two arbitrators, the one appointed by the Governor of Lagos, the other by the ALÂFIN of ỌYỌ, and in any case, when the arbitrators so appointed shall not agree, the matter in dispute shall be referred to the Governor of Lagos, whose decision shall be final.

10th. In consideration of the faithful observance of all the foregoing articles of this Treaty, the Governor of Lagos will make from 1st January next ensuing unto the King of ỌYỌ a yearly present of one hundred pounds ; but such present may, upon breach of all or any one or more of the provisions of this agreement, and at the discretion of the Governor of Lagos for the time being, be altogether withdrawn or suspended.

Z

11th. I likewise pledge myself to obtain the consent and co-operation of all the subordinate kings and authorities of representative towns in Yoruba-land to the provisions of this Treaty.

ADEYẸMI, *Alâfin of Qyọ and Head of Yoruba-land* × (his mark).

G. T. CARTER, *Governor and Commander-in-Chief, Colony of Lagos.*

Done at Ọyọ this 3rd day of February, 1893.

Signed in the presence of,

G. B. HADDON-SMITH, *Political Officer.*

I, the undersigned, do swear that I have truly and honestly interpreted the terms of the foregoing agreement to the contracting party in the Yoruba language.

A. L. HETHERSETT.

Witness to signature,

G. B. HADDON-SMITH, *Political Officer.*

§ 3. IBADAN

AGREEMENT made at Ibadan this 15th day of August, 1893, between His Excellency George Chardin Denton, Esq., Companion of the Most Distinguished Order of Saint Michael and Saint George, Acting-Governor and Commander-in-Chief of the Colony of Lagos, for and on behalf of Her Majesty the Queen of Great Britain and Ireland, Empress of India, her heirs and successors of the one part, and the undersigned Balẹ and Authorities of Ibadan, for and on behalf of their heirs and of the people of Ibadan of the other part.

We, the undersigned Balẹ and Authorities of Ibadan on behalf of ourselves and of the people of Ibadan, do hereby agree and declare as follows :—

1. That the general administration of the internal affairs of the following Yoruba towns, *viz.* : Iwo, Ede, Oṣogbo, Ikirun, Ogbomọṣọ, Ejigbo and Isẹyin and in all countries in the so-called Ẹkun Ọtun, Ẹkun Osi, is vested in the general government of Ibadan and the local authorities of the said towns act in harmony with and are subject to Ibadan notwithstanding that the Alâfin is recognised as the King and Head of Yoruba-land.

2. That we fully recognise all the provisions of the Treaty dated the 3rd February, 1893, made at Ọyọ between His Excellency Sir Gilbert Thomas Carter, Knight Commander of the Most Distinguished Order of Saint Michael and Saint George, then Companion of the Most Distiguished Order, on behalf of Her Majesty the Queen of Great Britain and Ireland, and the Alâfin of Ọyọ as Head of Yoruba-land.

3. That we fully agree to carry out within the territory of Ibadan all the provisions of the said Treaty.

4. That we further agree in amplification of the said Treaty on our own behalf to the following terms and conditions :—

First. That we will use every effort to secure the free passage of all persons coming through Ibadan either from the interior to Lagos, or from Lagos to the interior, and we promise to afford protection to persons and property so passing.

Second. That for the purpose of better securing the performance of the said Treaty of the 3rd February, 1893, and of this agreement, we do hereby agree to receive at Ibadan such European officers and such a force of the Lagos constabulary as the Governor shall from time to time deem necessary for the said purpose and for securing to us the benefits of the said Treaty and Agreement ; and we also agree to provide land for the occupation of such officers and force.

Third. We further agree, upon the request of the Government of Lagos, to provide land for the construction and maintenance of a railway through our territory, should the construction of such a railway be determined upon, and to accept for such land such compensation, if any, as shall be agreed upon between the parties hereto or between the authorities of Ibadan and the persons undertaking the construction of such railway.

5. And we do finally agree that all disputes which may arise under or in reference to this Agreement shall be enquired into and adjusted by two arbitrators, the one to be appointed by the Governor of Lagos for the time being, the other by the Balẹ and authorities of Ibadan, and in any case where the arbitrators so appointed shall not agree the matter in dispute shall be referred to the Governor of Lagos whose decision shall be final.

Done at Ibadan this fifteenth day of August, one thousand eight hundred and ninety three.

GEORGE CHARDIN DENTON, C.M.G., *Acting Governor.*

FIJABI, *the Balẹ*	X
OSUNTOKI, *the Otun Balẹ*	X
FAJINMI, *the Osi Balẹ*	X
AKINTỌLA, *the Balogun, by his representative*, OYENIYI	X
BABALOLA, *the Otun Balogun*	X
KONGI, *the Osi Balogun*	X
SUMỌNU APAMPA, *the Aṣipa*	X
OGUNDIPO, *the Seriki*	X (their marks)

Signed in the presence of :

G. B. HADDON-SMITH, *Acting Inspector General, Lagos Constabulary*.
W. R. HENDERSON, *Acting Travelling Commissioner*.
D. W. STEWART, Capt., *Asst. Inspector, Lagos Constabulary*.

We, the undersigned, do swear that we have truly and honestly interpreted the terms of the foregoing Agreement to the contracting parties in the Yoruba language.

JOHN A. WILLIAMS, *Clerk to Travelling Commissioner*.
C. J. P. BOYLE, *Clerk and Interpreter*.

Participators in and witnesses to the Agreement :

LANLATU, *the Iyalode*	×	
MOSADERIN, *the Ekerin*	×	
OGUNGBESAN *the Ekarun*	×	
OBISESAN *the Agbakin*	×	
TANIPEYI *the Maye*	×	
AKINTUNDE, *the Ekefa*	×	
SALAKO, *the Are Alasa*	×	
BAMGBEGBIN, *the Areagoro*	×	
ENIMOWU, *the Abese*	×	
OLAIFA , *the Asaju*	×	
OMOSANYA, *the Otun Seriki*	×	
AINA FAGBEMI, *the Osi Seriki*	×	
EWEJE, *the Sarumi*, by his representative ALAWO	×	
DADA OJO, *the Ekerin Seriki*	×	(their marks).

Signed in our presence,
JOHN A. WILLIAMS, *Clerk to Travelling Commissioner*.
C. J. P. BOYLE, *Clerk and Interpreter*.

§ 4. EGBA (BOUNDARIES)

Agreement entered into at Abeokuta between His Excellency Sir Gilbert Thomas Carter, Knight Commander of the Most Distinguished Order of Saint Michael and Saint George, Governor and Commander-in-Chief of the Colony of Lagos, and the King and Authorities of the Egba nation.

Whereas it is expedient to define the boundaries between the Egba country and the territories bordering on, or under the British Protectorate of Lagos, we, the undersigned Governor of Lagos and the King and Authorities of the Egba Nation residing at Abeokuta, agree as follows, *viz.* :

1. The line of demarcation between the two countries shall commence on the eastward at the town of Orisi on the left bank

of the River Ogun, which shall be considered as falling within the Lagos sphere of influence ; the boundary line shall then cross the river at right-angles, and take the most direct established road to the town of Ọta, which as at present shall be considered as under Ẹgba jurisdiction. From Ọta the boundary line shall follow the main road leading through Ilogbo, Ilogboro and Epoto to Ilaro.

2. All towns which may be actually on the said main road leading from Ọta to the protected town of Ilaro shall be considered to be outside the sphere of Ẹgba influence, but any Ẹgbas who may have farms on the southern or lagoon side of the said road may continue in their occupation without molestation from the Lagos government, and similarly all Lagos subjects who may have farms on the north of the said boundary shall be accorded the same privilege by the Ẹgba Authorities. With this proviso all towns to the north of the said road shall be considered as belonging to Ẹgba territory, and all towns to the south shall be liable to be included in the British protectorate of Lagos.

3. The boundaries between the Ilaro kingdom and Ẹgba must be determined by the position of the towns and farms held under the king of Ilaro, which kingdom was formerly tributary to Ẹgba, but all Ẹgbas who may have farms in the territory now known as the Ilaro kingdom may continue to work them as heretofore, any complaints upon either side being made to the Travelling Commissioner for the District, through the officer in charge of Ilaro.

4. It is understood that this Agreement is subject to the strict fulfilment of the provisions of the Treaty signed at Abẹokuta on the 18th January, 1893, and may be subject to modification in the event of the position of any towns enumerated being wrongly placed in the Intelligence Map of 1888 by the aid of which this Agreement has been drawn up.

Signed at Abẹokuta this fifth day of January, 1894.

> G. T. CARTER, *Governor of Lagos.*
>
> OSHOKALU, *Alake of Abẹokuta* ✕ (his mark)
> OSUNDARE, *Onlado* ✕
> SORINKE, *Jaguna* ✕
> OGUNDEYI, *Magaji* ✕ (their marks)

Witnesses to Agreement :

ALEX. F. TARBET, Capt., *Private Secretary.*
E. R. BICKERSTETH, *Trader.*
WM. R. TINNEY SOMOYE, *Sec. to the Ẹgba Government.*

We, the undersigned, declare that we have truly and honestly. interpreted the terms of this Agreement to the contracting parties in the Yoruba language.

C. J. P. BOYLE, *Governor's Clerk and Interpreter.*
E. R. BICKERSTETH, *Trader.*
Witness to the signature :
WM. R. TINNEY SOMOYE, *Sec. to the Ẹgba Government.*

§ 5. ABẸOKUTA (RAILWAY)

Agreement made this 21st day of February, 1899, between His Excellency George Chardin Denton, Esq., Companion of the Most Distinguished Order of Saint ·Michael and Saint George, Acting-Governor and Commander-in-Chief of the. Colony of Lagos, for and on behalf of Her Majesty the Queen of Great Britain and Ireland, Empress of India, her heirs and successors, of the one part, and the Alake and Authorities of the Ẹgba nation for and on behalf of themselves, their heirs and successors, and the Ẹgba nation of the other part.

Whereas the Alake and Authorities of the Ẹgba nation, for and on behalf of themselves, their heirs and successors and the Ẹgba nation, have granted (as they hereby acknowledge) to Her Majesty the Queen of Great Britain and Ireland, Empress of India, her heirs and successors, the right to construct, establish and maintain a railway with the proper works and conveniences for the conveyance of passengers, animals and goods through and on the Ẹgba territories. And whereas it is deemed expedient to make provision for the protection of the said railway works and conveniences and for the purposes hereinafter appearing.

Now therefore the Alake and Authorities of the Ẹgba nation, for and on behalf of themselves, their heirs and successors and the Ẹgba nation, hereby grant to Her Majesty the Queen of Great Britain and Ireland, Empress of India, her heirs and successors, for a period of ninety-nine years from the date hereof the following rights :—

1. To enter upon and occupy land to a distance of 100 yards on both sides of the railway.

2. To exercise upon such land all the powers for making, maintaining, altering, repairing and using the railway conferred upon the Government of Lagos by the law for the time being of the Colony of Lagos relating to railways.

3. To apprehend in any part of the Ẹgba territories and to try and, if found guilty, to punish any person, whether a British subject or not, accused or suspected of having committed upon

the land aforesaid any offence of whatsoever nature against the Law for the time being of the Colony of Lagos relating to railways, or against any regulation or bye-law made in accordance with such law.

To apprehend in any part of the Egba territories and to try and, if found guilty, to punish :

(*a*) Any British subject and any officer or servant, whether British subject or not, employed by the Government of Lagos on or in connection with the railway, accused, or suspected of having committed upon the land aforesaid any offence of whatsoever nature against the person or property of any British subject or other person ; and

(*b*) Any person other than a British subject accused or suspected of having committed upon the land aforesaid any offence of whatsoever nature against the person or property of any British subject or any officer or servant aforesaid.

And the Alake and Authorities of the Egba nation for and on behalf of themselves, their heirs and successors and the Egba nation, hereby undertake—

To apprehend and to deliver up to the Government of Lagos, and to aid and assist in apprehending, any of the persons above specified accused or suspected of having committed any offence as aforesaid.

And His Excellency the said George Chardin Denton, for and on behalf of Her Majesty the Queen of Great Britain and Ireland, Empress of India, her heirs and successors, in consideration of the rights hereinbefore granted, and the undertaking hereinbefore given, hereby promise—

To pay to the Alake and Authorities of the Egba nation, their heirs and successors during the continuance of this Agreement, the annual sum of two hundred pounds by four quarterly payments, payable on the 25th day of March, the 24th day of June, the 29th day of September, and the 25th day of December in every year, the first of such payments to be made on the 25th March, 1899.

And it is hereby agreed that if, owing to unforeseen circumstances, it shall be considered by Her Majesty the Queen of Great Britain and Ireland, Empress of India, her heirs and successors, that the provisions of this Agreement or any of them, require alteration, amendment or revocation, Her Majesty, her heirs and successors shall be entitled by giving three months' previous notice in writing to the Alake and Authorities of the Egba nation, their heirs and successors, to determine the Agreement at any itme, and negotiations shall thereupon be entered into for the purpose of making a new Agreement in lieu thereof.

In witness whereof the said parties have set their hands and seals the day and year first above written.

(Signed) GEORGE C. DENTON, (L.S.), *Acting Governor*.
GBADEBQ, *Alake*   ×
ADEPAGBA, *Olowu*   ×
OLUBUMI, *Agura*   ×
SULE, *Mohammedan Chief*   ×
ALI DELOKUN, *Balogun*   ×
ALI IJEUN, *Seriki*   ×
IDOWU, *Apena Íporo*   ×
C SORUNTUN, *Head Parakoyi* × (their mark).

Signed and sealed at Abẹokuta by the said Alake and Authorities of the Ẹgba nation in the presence of :

(Sgd.) FRANK ROHRWEGER.
GEORGE ANDERSON.
D. O. WILLIAMS.

I do hereby certify that I have truly and honestly interpreted and explained in the Yoruba language the terms of the foregoing Agreement to the Alake and authorities of the Ẹgba nation.

(Signed) WM. ALFRED ALLEN.
Signed by the said W. A. Allen in the presence of
LADAPO ADEMOLA.

§ 6. IBADAN (RAILWAY)

This Indenture, made the 14th day of December, 1900, between His Excellency Sir George Chardin Denton, Knight Commander of the Most Distinguished Order of Saint Michael and Saint George, Lieutenant-Governor of the Colony of Lagos, for and on behalf of Her Majesty the Queen of Great Britain and Ireland, Empress of India, her heirs and successors of the one part, and the Baṣọrun and Authorities of Ibadan for and on behalf of themselves, their heirs and successors, and the people of Ibadan of the other part.

Whereas by an Agreement made at Ibadan on the 15th day of August, 1893, between His Excellency George Chardin Denton, Esq., Companion of the Most Distinguished Order of Saint Michael and Saint George, Acting-Governor and Commander-in-Chief of the Colony of Lagos, for and on behalf of Her Majesty the Queen of Great Britain and Ireland, Empress of India, her heirs and successors, of the one part, and the Balẹ and Authorities of Ibadan for and on behalf of themselves and the people of Ibadan on the other part, the said Balẹ and Authorities agreed among other things to provide land for the construction and maintenance of a railway through Ibadan territory. And whereas the said railway is in course of construction through the said territory, and it is deemed expedient to make provision for the protection of the said railway works and conveniences and for the purposes hereinafter mentioned.

And whereas the Baṣọrun and Authorities of Ibadan for and on behalf of themselves, their heirs and successors and the people of Ibadan, have agreed to grant, subject to the conditions hereinafter mentioned, to Her Majesty the Queen of Great Britain and Ireland, Empress of India, her heirs and successors, for a period of ninety-nine years, certain lands hereinafter described.

Now this INDENTURE WITNESSETH that, in consideration of the above premises, they, the said Baṣọrun and Authorities of Ibadan do hereby grant to Her Majesty the Queen of Great Britain and Ireland, Empress of India, her heirs and successors, all the land to a distance of 100 yards on both sides of the said railway and have also agreed to grant for a like period to Her Majesty the Queen of Great Britain and Ireland, Empress of India, her heirs and successors, all that piece of land near the Iddo Gate at Ibadan which, as to its position, dimensions, and boundaries, is particularly shown in the plan hereto attached, marked A, and coloured red thereon, and have also agreed to grant for a like period to Her Majesty the Queen of Great Britain and Ireland, Empress of India, her heirs and successors, all that piece of land on the right bank of the River Ogun at Olokemeji which, as to its position, dimensions, and boundaries, is particularly shown in the plan hereto attached, marked B, and thereon coloured red. To the use of the said Her Majesty the Queen of Great Britain and Ireland Empress of India, her heirs and successors, for a period of ninety-nine years from the date hereof, and the said Baṣọrun and Authorities of Ibadan do hereby agree that the said Her Majesty the Queen of Great Britain and Ireland, Empress of India, her heirs and successors, shall have and exercise the following rights :—

(1) To enter upon and occupy and use the said land in any manner and for any purpose that may seem desirable to the said Her Majesty the Queen of Great Britain and Ireland, Empress of India, her heirs and successors.

(2) To exercise upon such lands all the power for making, maintaining, altering, repairing, and using the railway conferred on the Government of Lagos by the law for the time being of the Colony of Lagos relating to Railways.

(3) To apprehend in any part of the Ibadan territories and to try and, if found guilty, to punish any person whether a British subject or not, accused or suspected of having committed upon

the land aforesaid any offence of whatsoever nature against the law for the time being of the Colony of Lagos relating to railways, or against any regulation or bye-law made in accordance with such law.

(4) To apprehend in any part of the Ibadan territories, and to try, and, if found guilty, to punish—

(a) Any British subject and any officer or servant, whether British subject or not, employed by the Government of Lagos, accused or suspected of having committed upon the land aforesaid any offence of whatsoever nature against the law for the time being of the Colony of Lagos ; and

(b) Any person other than a British subject accused or suspected of having committed upon the land aforesaid any offence of whatsoever nature against the person or property of any British subject, or subject of a civilised power, or any officer or servant aforesaid.

And the Baṣọrun and Authorities of Ibadan, for and on behalf of themselves, their heirs and successors and the Ibadan people hereby undertake—

To apprehend and to deliver up to the Government of Lagos, and to aid and assist in apprehending any of the persons above specified accused or suspected of having committed any offence as aforesaid.

And His Excellency the said George Chardin Denton, for and on behalf of Her Majesty the Queen of Great Britain and Ireland, Empress of India, her heirs and successors, in consideration of the rights hereinbefore granted and the undertaking hereinbefore given, hereby promise—

To pay to the Baṣọrun and Authorities of Ibadan, their heirs and successors, during the continuance of this Agreement, the annual sum of twenty pounds by four quarterly payments, payable on the 25th day of March, the 24th day of June, the 29th day of September, and the 25th day of December in every year, the first of such payments to be made on the 25th day of December, 1900.

And it is hereby agreed that if owing to unforeseen circumstances, it shall be considered by Her Majesty the Queen of Great Britain and Ireland, Empress of India, her heirs and successors, that the provisions of this Agreement or any of them require alteration, amendment, or revocation, Her Majesty, her heirs and successors shall be entitled, by giving three months' previous notice in writing to the Baṣọrun and Authorities of Ibadan, their heirs and successors, to determine the Agreement at any time, and negotiations shall thereupon be entered into for the purpose of making a new Agreement in lieu thereof.

In witness whereof the said parties have hereunto set their hands and seals the day and year first above written.

(Signed) GEORGE C. DENTON (L.S.), *Lieut.-Governor.*

FAJINMA, *Basọrun of Ibadan*	×
OGUNDBẸSAN, *Osi Basọrun*	×
DADA, *Ẹkẹrin Basọrun*	×
OLAIFA, *Mayẹ Basọrun*	×
SUMỌNU, *Otun Balogun*	×
BAMGBEGBIN, *Osi Balogun*	×
SHITU, *Asipa*	×
SUBERU, *Ẹkerin Balogun*	× (their marks).

Signed in the presence of

(Signed) F. C. FULLER, *President, Ibadan.*

C. E. JOHNSTONE, *Private Secretary.*

I, the undersigned, do swear that I have truly and honestly interpreted the terms of the foregoing Agreement to the contracting parties in the Yoruba language.

(Signed) HENRY LIBERT, *Clerk and Interpreter.*

C. A. SODIPẸ, *Clerk and Interpreter, Witness to signature.*

§ 7. IJẸSA
ENACTMENT FOR THE ABOLITION OF HUMAN SACRIFICES IN THE IJẸSA COUNTRIES

Whereas the practice of immolating human beings is cruel, barbarous, futile and unjust in the eyes of all civilised nations and right-minded persons ; and whereas the said practice has fallen into disuse amongst the Ijẹsas, and the present time appears opportune for its total abolition in the Ijẹsa country ; and whereas the Ijẹsas are under a deep and lasting obligation to His Excellency the Governor of Lagos for having established peace between them and their late enemies, the Ibadans, and for having thereby secured the independence of the Ijẹsa country ; and whereas His Excellency the Governor of Lagos desires no other proof of gratitude of the Ijẹsas for what he has done for them than that they should abolish the abominable practice ; and whereas the Ijẹsas have resolved to abolish the said practice accordingly : Now, therefore, we the undersigned, as representing the Ijẹsa nation, do hereby enact, ordain, and declare as follows, *viz.* :—

1. The practice of immolating human beings, whether at the festival of any deity or before, at, or after the funeral of any king or subject, or on any other public or private occasion, shall be and hereby is abolished for ever.

2. It shall be and is hereby constituted a criminal offence for any one in the kingdom of Ijẹṣa or for any subject of the Ijẹṣa king to perform or participate in, or to aid and abet others in performing or participating in any human sacrifice.

3. Every such criminal offence shall be punished by the infliction of a heavy fine, imprisonment, or forced labour.

4. No person condemned to death for a crime punishable with death under the laws of the Ijẹṣa country shall be utilised for the purpose of sacrifice.

Given under our hands and seals this 29th day of September, 1886.

> AGUNLOYE, *Ọwa of Ileṣa* ✕
> OGEDEMGBE, *Seriki of Ijẹṣa* ✕ (their marks).

Signed and sealed in our presence after the contents had been read and interpreted to the signatories by the Rev. Charles Phillips.

> H. HIGGINS
> OLIVER SMITH } *Special Commissioners.*

§ 8. EKITI

ENACTMENT FOR THE ABOLITION OF HUMAN SACRIFICES IN THE EKITI COUNTRIES

Whereas the practice of immolating human beings is cruel, barbarous, futile and unjust in the eyes of all civilised nations and right-minded persons, and whereas the said practice has fallen into disuse in the Ekiti countries, and the present time appears opportune for its total abolition in those countries ; and whereas the Ekitis are under a deep and lasting obligation to His Excellency the Governor of Lagos for having established peace between them and their late enemies the Ibadans, and for having thereby secured the independence of the said Ekiti countries ; and whereas His Excellency the Governor of Lagos desires no other proof of the gratitude of the Ekitis for what he has done for them than that they should abolish the said abominable practice ; and whereas the Ekitis have resolved to abolish the said practice accordingly : Now therefore we, the undersigned, representing all the Ekiti kings and countries, and being duly authorised to speak in their name, and on their behalf, do hereby enact, ordain, and declare as follows, *viz.* :—

1. The practice of immolating human beings, whether at the festival of any deity, or before, at, or after the funeral of any king or subject or on any other public or private occasion, shall be and hereby is abolished for ever.

2. It shall be and hereby is constituted a criminal offence for

anyone in any Ekiti country, or for any subject of any Ekiti king to perform or participate in or to aid or abet others in performing or participating in any human sacrifice.

3. Every such criminal offence shall be punished by the infliction of a heavy fine, imprisonment, or forced labour.

4. No person condemned to death for a crime shall be utilised for the purpose of human sacrifice.

Given under our hands and seals this 29th day of September, 1886.

OKINBALOYE, *Owore of Qtun* ✕
OYIYOSOJE, *Ajero of Ijero* ✕
QDUNDUN, *Olojudo of Ido* ✕ (their marks).

I guarantee the enactment of the above-written promise.

OGEDEMGBE, *Seriki of Ijęsa* ✕ (his mark).

Signed and sealed in our presence after the contents had been read and interpreted to the signatories by the Rev. Charles Phillips.

H. HIGGINS } *Special Commissioners.*
OLIVER SMITH

§9. IFĘ

ABOLITION OF THE CUSTOM OF HUMAN SACRIFICE BY THE COUNCIL OF IFĘ

Whereas the practice of immolating human beings is cruel, barbarous, futile and unjust ; and whereas His Excellency the Governor of Lagos, to whom the Ifę nation is greatly indebted for having magnanimously mediated between them and their enemies, will be pleased to hear that the Ifę nation has abolished the said detestable practice ; and whereas the Council of Ifę has already undertaken through its representatives at Kiriji to abolish the said abominable practice : Now therefore we, the undersigned members of the Council of Ifę, hereby declare and promise that the practice of immolating human beings is and henceforth for ever shall remain abolished in the Ifę country.

In witness whereof we have hereunto affixed our hands and seals on the date hereunder written opposite our names.

AWOTUNDE, *Olalufe of Ifę* ✕ Nov. 2nd, 1886.
ORAMUIYQN, *Obaji of Ifę* ✕ ,, ,,
AWONRILE, *Orisamile of Ifę* ✕ ,, ,,
TOJO, *Asoje of Ifę* ✕ ,, ,,

(their marks).

Signed and sealed in our presence, after the contents had been read and interpreted to the signatories by the Rev. Chas. Phillips.

H. HIGGINS } *Special Commissioners.*
OLIVER SMITH

§10. France

Arrangement concerning the delimitation of the English and French possessions on the West Coast of Africa. Signed at Paris, August 10th, 1889. (Annex B.)

The undersigned, selected by the Government of Her Majesty the Queen of Great Britain and Ireland and by the Government of the French Republic for the purpose of preparing a general understanding with a view to settle all the questions at issue, between England and France, with regard to their respective possessions on the West Coast of Africa, have agreed on the following provisions :—

*　　*　　*　　*　　*

Article IV

Sect. 1. On the slave coast the line of demarcation between the spheres of influence of the two powers shall be identical with the meridian which intersects the territory of Porto Novo at the Ajara Creek, leaving Ipokia to the English Colony of Lagos. It shall follow the above-mentioned meridian as far as the ninth degree of north latitude, where it shall stop. To the south it shall terminate on the seashore after having passed through the territory of Appah, the capital of which shall continue to belong to England.

The navigation of the Ajara and of the River Ado shall be free and open to the inhabitants and boats of both protectorates.

Sect. 2. French traders shall be guaranteed full liberty of trade with such districts as shall not be included in the French sphere of influence, and especially as regards the Egbas.

English traders shall likewise be guaranteed full liberty of trade with such districts as shall not be included in the English sphere of influence.

Sect. 3. Guarantees shall also be given in favour of the inhabitants of Ketonu and of the French portion of the territory of Appah. These inhabitants shall be free to leave the country should they so desire, and those who remain shall be protected by the French authorities against any act of aggression on their person, their position, or their property, on the part of the king of Porto Novo or of his people.

Similar guarantees shall be given in favour of the inhabitants of the territory of Ipokia.

Sect. 4. It is furthermore agreed that (i) the English Government shall have full liberty of political action to the east of the frontier line ; and that (ii) the French Government shall have full liberty of political action to the west of the frontier line.

Sect. 5. In consequence of the understanding defined as above, and with a view to obviate any conflict to which the daily relations of the inhabitants of the Porto Novo country with those of Ipokia might give rise if a Custom-house were to be established by one or other of the contracting parties on the Ajara Creek, the English and French Delegates agree in recommending to their respective Governments the neutralization, from a Customs point of view, of that portion of the territory of Ipokia, which is comprised between the Ajara Creek and the Ado until such time as a definitive Customs Agreement can be arrived at between the French establishments of Porto Novo and the Colony of Lagos

ARTICLE V

The two Governments reserve to themselves the right of nominating Special Commissioners of Delimitation to trace upon the spot, wherever they may consider it necessary, the line of demarcation between the English and French possessions in conformity with the general provisions which are set forth above.

In witness thereof the undersigned delegates have drawn up and signed the present Agreement, subject to the approval of their respective Governments.

Done at Paris in duplicate the 10th day of August, 1889.

(Signed) EDWIN H. EGERTON.
AUGUSTUS W. L. HEMMING.
A. NISARD.
JEAN BAYOL.

* * * * *

§ 11. PORTO NOVO

Sect. 1. " The meridian which intersects the territory of Porto Novo at the Ajara Creek " shall be taken to mean—

1. (To the north of the Porto Novo lagoon) the middle of the stream of the Ajara River to the point where the said riverceases to separate the kingdom of Porto Novo from that of Ipokia and from thence the meridian thereof as far as the ninth parallel of north latitude.

2. (To the south of the Porto Novo lagoon) the meridian of the middle of the Ajara River, where it flows into the Porto Novo lagoon.

3. The frontier line has been based in this Convention upon the

Sketch Survey of the Inland Water Communication in the Colony of Lagos by Harbour Master Speeding, 1886.

§ 12.   PROCLAMATION OF 13TH AUGUST, 1891

By His Excellency George Chardin Denton, Esq., C.M.G., Acting Governor of Lagos, etc., etc.

GEORGE C. DENTON, (L.S.), *Acting Governor.*

Whereas Her Majesty has been advised that it is for the best interests of the people of the Colony and protectorate of Lagos, and also of the people of the kingdom of Ilaro that the said kingdom should be transferred to the Government of Her Majesty and that Her Majesty should assume the Protectorate thereof :

And whereas the King, Chiefs, Elders, and people of the kingdom of Ilaro have expressed their desire that the said kingdom should be so transferred and that Her Majesty should assume the Protectorate thereof :

And whereas it is Her Majesty's pleasure that the kingdom of Ilaro be attached to the Colony of Lagos and form part of the protectorate thereof :

Now therefore I, George Chardin Denton, Esquire, Companion of the Most Distinguished Order of Saint Michael and Saint George, Acting Governor of the Colony of Lagos, do publish, make known and proclaim as follows :—

1. The kingdom of Ilaro is now under the Sovereignty and protection of Her Majesty.
2. The kingdom of Ilaro is attached to the Colony of Lagos and forms part of the Protectorate thereof.

Given under my hand and the Great Seal of the Colony of Lagos this thirteenth day of August in the year of our Lord one thousand eight hundred and ninety one.

A. F. TARBET, *Acting Asst. Colonial Secretary.*

APPENDIX B

§ 1. YORUBA KINGS, BAṢỌRUNS, AND NOTABLE EVENTS.

Kings.	Baṣọruns.	Events.
1. Oduduwa	Ọlorun-fun-mi	Capital—Ile Ifẹ
2. Ọrañyan	Ẹfufu ko-fẹ-ori	Ancient Ọyọ built
3. Ajaka	Ẹrindinlogun-Agbọu	
4. Sango	Salẹ ku odi	
5. Ajaka	,,	
6. Aganju	Banija	
Regent Iyayun	,,	
7. Kori	Ẹran-kò-gbina	Ẹdẹ and Oṣogbo built
8. Oluaṣo	Ẹṣugbiri-ẹlu	
9. Onigbogi	Aiyagbarò	
10. Ofiran	Sokia	Saki built by this King
11. Egũoju	Ọbalohun	Igboho built
12. Ọrọmpọtọ	Aṣamu	
13. Ajiboyede	Ibatẹ	The Bẹbẹ celebrated
14. Abipa	,,	Ọyọ rebuilt
15. Ọbalokun	Ibæ Magaji	Salt introduced
16. Ajagbo	Akidayin	
17. Odarawu	,,	
18. Kanran	Woruda	
19. Jayin	Iba-Biri	The first Awujalẹ of Ijẹbu appointed
Interregnum		
20. Ayibi	Olu aja and Yabi	
21. Ọsiyago	Apala	
22. Ojigi	Yamba	Circumnavigation of the Niger and the Lagoon
23. Gberu	Jambu	
24. Amuniwaiye	Kogbọu and Kokiki	
25. Onisile ⎫	Soyiki alias Eṣuogbo	
26. Labisi ⎪	Gahà	
27. Awọnbioju ⎬	,,	
28. Agboluaje ⎭	,,	The Bẹbẹ celebrated
29. Majẹogbe	Gáhà	
30. Abiodun	Gáhà and Kangidi	
31. Aolẹ ⎫	Aṣamu alias	
32 Adebọ ⎬	· Agbakolekàn	
33. Maku ⎭	,,	
Interregnum		

669

Kings	Basọruns.	Events.
34. Majotu	Ojo and Akioso	Seizure of Ilorin by the Fulanis
35. Amọdo	,, ,,	Ijaye and Modakẹkẹ
36. Oluewu	,, ,,	occupied. Ibadan and Abẹokuta founded.
Interregnum		Fall of Ancient Ọyọ
37. Atiba	Oluyọle and Gbenla	Agọ became Ọyọ of the present day. Bẹbẹ celebrated
38. Adelu	Gbenla and Ogunsoro	
39. Adeyẹmi	Ogunsoro,Iye,Layọde	

§ 2. IBADAN CHIEF RULERS AND THEIR BALOGUNS FROM ITS
OCCUPATION TO THE BEGINNING OF THE BRITISH
PROTECTORATE.

1. Ibadan as a Military Camp.

Mayẹ	Generalissimo
Labọsinde	Baba Isalẹ
Lakanlẹ	Leader of the Ọyọs

2. Transition Stage.

Oluyedun	Kakanfo (honorary)
Lakanlẹ	Ọtun Kakanfo
Oluyọle	Osi Kakanfo

3. As a Settlement.

Rulers.		Titles.	Baloguns.
	Oluyọle	Basọrun	Ọdẹrinlọ
	Ọpẹagbe	Balẹ	vacant
1855	Olugbode	,,	Ibikunle
1866	Ogunmọla	Basọrun	Akere
1870	Orowusi	Balẹ	Ajọbọ
1872	Latòsisa	Kakanfo	Ajayi Ogboriẹfọu
	vacant		Ọsungbẹkun
1892	Fijabi	Balẹ	Akintọla

§ 3. THE LEADING CHIEFS OF ABẸOKUTA FROM ITS FOUNDATION
TO THE BEGINNING OF THE BRITISH PROTECTORATE

Sodekẹ, Leader of the Ẹgbas to Abẹokuta

Apati[1], Balogun of Kemta   } His associates in the Govern-
Agbunrin, Balogun of Ilugun } ment.

---

[1] Apati bought the title of Basọrun from Oluyọle of Ibadan
but never lived to enjoy it. It passed on to Somoye.

Okukẹnu, alias Sagbua, King

Ogunbọna, Balogun of Ikija ⎫
Sokẹnu, Balogun of Ijeun ⎪ Associates who
Anọba, Balogun of Ika ⎬ helped to rule
Somoye, Balogun of Iporo, ⎪ the town.
   afterwards Basọrun ⎭

Ademọla, Alake or Primus ⎧Ogundipẹ, Balogun of Ikija
Oyekan,   ,,   ,, ⎨Onlado,   ,,   ,, Kemta
Oluwajin[1]   ,,   ,, ⎪Solankẹ, Jaguna of Igbein
            ⎩Ogundeyi, Balogun of Iporo
     The Quadrumvirate who actually ruled.

Oṣokalu, Alake or Primus Ogundeyi[2]

Other distinguished Baloguns more or less independent each in his own township.

Ẹgẹ of Oko   Obirinti of Ijaye Kukudi
Agbadu of Ijẹmọ   Ajagunjẹun of Itoko
Atambala of Ikereku   Ogunṣọla of Ijẹja
Anọba of Ika   Olumloye of Ilugun

§ 4. *The Emirs of Ilọrin.*

Alimi the Fulani priest of Afọnja who headed the mutiny of the Jâmâs and murdered their lord paved the way for his eldest son to become the first king or Emir of Ilọrin under the Sultan of Sokoto.

At his death he left four sons, the succession in the Emirate being confined to the descendants of the first two.

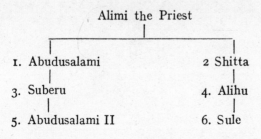

Alimi the Priest

1. Abudusalami   2 Shitta

3. Suberu   4. Alihu

5. Abudusalami II   6. Sule

---

[1] Oluwajin was a wealthy Itoku man who bought the title of Alake.

[2] Ogundeyi having out-lived his rivals assumed the title of Basọrun (being nephew to Somoye) and ruled the town singly, the Alake being only a figure head.

INDEX